Sturmgeschütze vor!

Assault Guns to the Front!

by

Franz Kurowski

J.J. Fedorowicz Publishing

Sturmgeschütz vor!

Assault Guns to the Front!

By Franz Kurowski

An English Translation by Robert Dohrenwend
With additional assistance by Robert J. Edwards, Jr. and Michael Olive

Published by
J.J. Fedorowicz Publishing, Inc.
104 browning Boulevard
Winnipeg, Manitoba
Canada R3K 0L7
Tel: (204) 837-6080
Fax: (204) 889-1960
e-mail: jjfpub@escape.ca
web: www.jjfpub.mb.ca

J.J. Fedorowicz Publishing wishes to thank the authors of "Die Truppenkennzeichen der Verbände und Einheiten der deutschen Wehrmacht und Waffen-SS und ihre Einsätze im Zweiten Weltkrieg," Peter Schmitz and Klaus-Jürgen Thies, for permission to use the unit and organizational insignia illustrated in their book to accompany the majority of the Sturmgeschütz formation histories presented here. The multi-volume series is available from Biblio Verlag (Osnabrück, Germany).

Printed in Canada
ISBN 0-921991-45-2

Printed by Friesens Printers, Altona , Manitoba, Canada

Publisher's Acknowledgements

Translation: Robert Dohrenwend and Robert J. Edwards, Jr.

Typesetting and layout: A special assist from Jake Fehr at Friesens Printers.

Sturmgeschutze Profiles: George Bradford

We also wish to thank you, the reader, for purchasing this book and all of you who have written us with kind words of praise and encouragement. It gives us the impetus to continue translating the best available German language books and produce original titles. Our catalog of books is listed below and can be viewed on our web site at www.jjfpub.mb.ca. We have also listed titles which are near production and can be expected in the near future. Many of these are due to your helpful suggestions.

John Fedorowicz, Mike Olive and Bob Edwards

Books published by J.J. Fedorowicz Publishing:

The Leibstandarte (1. SS-Panzer-Division): Volumes I, II, III, IV/1 and IV/2
European Volunteers (5. SS-Panzer-Division)
Das Reich (2. SS-Panzer-Division): Volumes I and II
The History of Panzer-Korps "Großdeutschland": Volumes I and II
Otto Weidinger
Otto Kumm
Manhay, The Ardennes: Christmas 1944
Armor Battles of the Waffen-SS, 1943-1945
Tiger: The History of a Legendary Weapon, 1942-1945
Hitler Moves east
Tigers in the Mud
Panzer Aces
Footsteps of the Hunter
History of the 12. SS-Panzer-Division "Hitlerjugend"
Grenadiers, the Autobiography of Kurt Meyer
Field Uniforms of German Army Panzer Forces in World War 2
Tigers in Combat, Volumes I and II
Infanterie Aces
Freineaux and Lamormenil—The Ardennes
The Caucasus and the Oil
East Front Drama—1944
The History of the Fallschirm-Panzer-Korps "Hermann Göring"
Michael Wittmann and the Tiger Commanders of the Leibstandarte
The Western front 1944: Memoirs of a Panzer Lehr Officer
Luftwaffe Aces
Quiet Flows the Rhine
Decision in the Ukraine: Summer 1943
Combat History of the schwere Panzer-Jäger-Abteilung 653
Brandenburgers: Global Mission
Field Uniforms of Germany's Panzer Elite
Soldiers of the Waffen-SS: Many Nations, One Motto
In the Firestorm of the Last Years of the War
The Meuse First and Then Antwerp
Jochen Peiper: Commander, Panzer-Regiment "Leibstandarte"
Sturmgeschütze vor! Assault Guns to the Front!

In preparation for publication:
Karl Baur: A Pilot's Pilot
Kharkov
The History of Panzer-Korps "Großdeutschland": Volume III
The History of Panzer-Regiment "Großdeutschland"

J.J. Fedorowicz Publishing

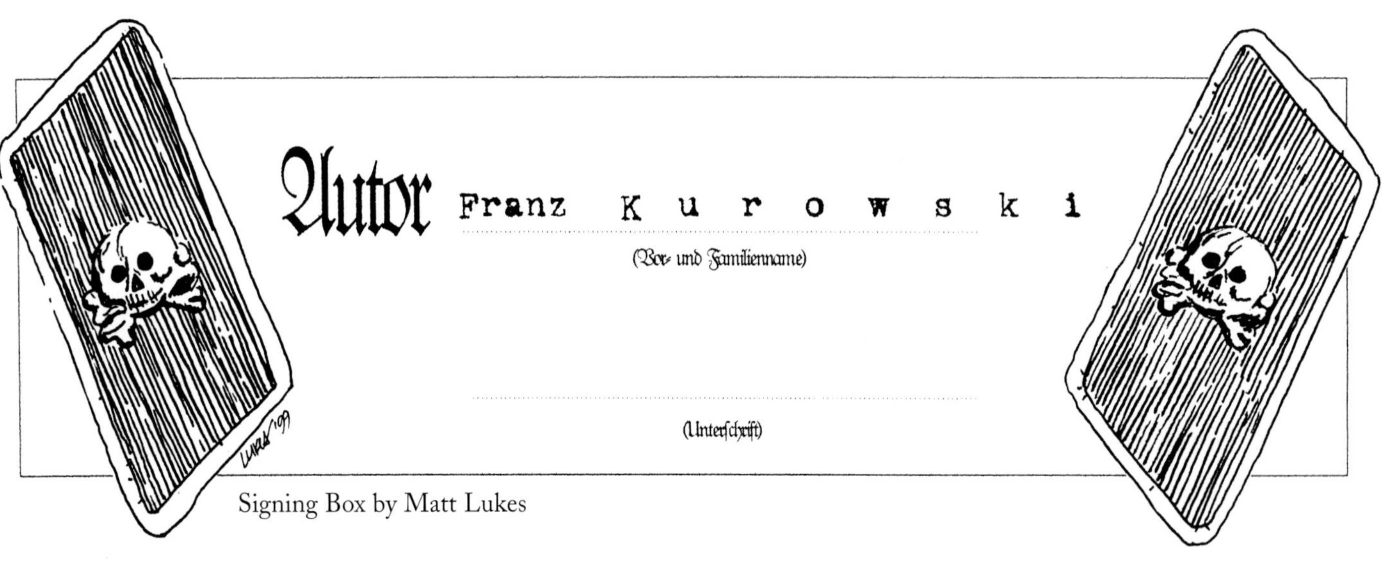

Signing Box by Matt Lukes

Table of Contents

Dedication

A Word of Greeting!

Every comrade who takes this volume in hand deserves my special friendly greeting.

I remember gratefully those who made the Sturmartillerie the finest support for the infantry in the last war, and respectfully those who sacrificed their lives. For me, I am proud to remember that the idea of creating the Sturmartillerie was granted to me, and that I was able to carry out that idea.

v. Manstein

Field Marshall

Introduction

"Sturmgeschütze vor!" "Assault Guns to the Front!"

Is there anyone who did not hear this order, when enemy tanks suddenly appeared and the situation became critical for the infantry?

"Sturmgeschütze vor!" was the cry when the enemy had broken in and the front was threatened with collapse. This outstanding weapon and its courageous crews always lived up to their reputation.

The spirit of these men in their old field gray uniforms is still alive today. This book is dedicated to the memory of those who volunteered to put their lives on the line with the Sturmartillerie and to the memory of their deeds.

May it bring back memories of both the hard times and of the good times together with their comrades to every former member of the Sturmartillerie.

May every young Panzer man today be spurred on by these accounts to equal these men, so that - as then - the enemy will say that combat on equal terms with this powerful weapon is to be avoided.

All this can be a real contribution to peace.

Oskar Munzel

Generalmajor (ret.)

Bundeswehr Inspector of

Armored Troops

1957-1962

Generalfeldmarschall Erich von Manstein—Creator of the German Sturmartillerie

Erich von Manstein, born von Lewinski, was born on 24 November 1887 in Berlin as the son of Edward von Lewinski who would become General of Artillery and Commanding General of the VI. Armee-Korps. Through his adoption by General Georg von Manstein, whose wife was a sister of the child's mother, the newborn child received the name of von Manstein.

Both his paternal and maternal families had at one time carried the name of von Sperling. General von Sperling was Chief of Staff for the 1. Armee under General von Steinmetz during the war of 1870/71. Two of his three daughters married the officers Edward von Lewinski and Georg von Manstein. (General von Sperling's third daughter later married Generalfeldmarschall Paul von Hindenburg.)

From 1900 to 1906 Erich von Manstein was a member of the Prussian cadet corps and, in the spring of 1906, he entered the 3. Garderegiment zu Fuß (3rd Guards Regiment of Foot) as a Fähnrich (officer candidate). A number of his comrades at that time would later reach prominent positions, as for example, Freiherr von Hammerstein-Equord who would become Chief of the Army High Command (Heeresleitung), Schleicher who would become chancellor of Germany, and many others.

Von Manstein attended the War College from 1913-1914 where he became thoroughly familiar with the scientific basis for military strategy. This training was interrupted by the outbreak of war in August 1914. First Lieutenant von Manstein became the regimental adjutant for the 2. Garde-Reserve-Regiment (2nd Guards Reserve Regiment) and fought in Belgium, East Prussia, and southern Poland. He especially distinguished himself during the Masurian Lakes Battle. He was wounded at Katowice on 17 November 1914 when he was hit by two rifle bullets during close combat as part of an assault battalion.

After his recovery, von Manstein was assigned to the staff of General von Gallwitz' Army Group.

He was promoted to Captain in the summer of 1916. He gained experience with the headquarters of the 1. Armee in Serbia and again at Verdun. These experiences would later prepare him for his great defensive successes, allowing him to hold out against massive enemy superiority and permit him to rescue an entire army group from annihilation.

He was on the staff of 1. Armee during the defensive battles on the Somme and in Champagne in 1917. Starting in May 1918 he was the operations officer with the 213. Infanterie-Division where he fought in the last German offensive at Reims and the defensive fighting at Sedan.

In the beginning of 1919 von Manstein was assigned to Southern Border Guard Headquarters (Oberkommando des Grenzschutzes Süd) in Breslau as a staff officer. Following that, he was accepted into the Reichswehr. He was company commander in the 5. Infanterie-Regiment and commanded a Jäger-Bataillon in the 4. Infanterie-Regiment.

In February 1938 Erich von Manstein, who had been a colonel since 1 December 1933, became Chief of Staff for Wehrkreis III (Berlin).

On 1 July 1935 von Manstein was given the assignment of Chief of the Operations Section of the Army General Staff. On 1 October 1936 he was promoted to Generalmajor and became Quartermaster General I and thus a Deputy Chief of Staff under Generaloberst Beck, who was Chief of Staff at that time.

The Panzer arm was built up during this period and it was tirelessly promoted by the later Generaloberst Guderian. This new arm opened up an entirely new field of strategy , and von Manstein did everything in his power to promote it. In addition, however, von Manstein saw more than anything else a possibility for infantry to gain greater operational freedom of mobility in any future conflict.

In pursuit of this new goal, after his appointment as Chief of the Operations Section, he involved himself in the development of a new weapon: the Sturmartillerie (Assault Artillery).

From his varied experience during the First World War, and especially from his service as operations officer for the 213. Infanterie-Division, von Manstein knew that after breaking through an enemy defensive position into open country, the infantry was often unable to make further progress, because isolated pockets of enemy resistance, MG positions, and even bunkers halted its attack. Too much time was lost until guns were finally brought forward, and the artillery, in its covered positions, was unable to detect these small, covered and often camouflaged targets rapidly enough and put them out of action.

What was needed was a weapon which could accompany the infantry into the combat zone during the attack and breakthrough, and which would be in a position to immediately and effectively engage new targets as they appeared and put them out of action. That meant providing the infantry with an all-terrain, armored weapon with heavy firepower.

In a memo to the Chief of Staff and to the Commander in Chief of the Army in 1935, Oberst von Manstein made a proposition to reconsider some ideas with their roots in the use of an escort weapon for World War I infantry. Taking advantage of possibilities offered by recent technical advances, he wanted to develop armored cannon on self-propelled carriages for the direct support of the infantry.

Erich von Manstein coined the name for the new weapon in this memo, which he called Sturmartillerie.

Von Manstein encouraged the separation of this new weapon from conventional artillery, in order to make it a truly offensive weapon. Each infantry division was to have a battalion with three batteries of 6 guns each.

Not without initial resistance from certain positions within the German High Command (Oberkommando des Heeres—OKH), this proposal finally gained the approval of the General Staff and the Commander-in-Chief of the Army, Generaloberst von Fritsch.

That fall, after the weapon had been developed in a very short time by the Waffenamt, Generaloberst von Fritsch signed a program, which would provide every active division with an Sturmartillerie-Abteilung by the fall of 1939. By the fall of 1940, every reserve division would also have a Sturmartillerie-Abteilung. Initially, however, each battery would only have four guns.

This program was considerably delayed after Generaloberst von Fritsch's resignation. Erich von Manstein was transferred at about the same time from the position of Quartermaster General 1 to Liegnitz to command the 18. Infanterie-Division. He was thus no longer in a position to push for a more rapid formation of combat-ready Sturmgeschütz organizations.

This delay was as unnecessary as it was disadvantageous. It arose first of all from a change in the plans by the successor to the position of Army Commander-in-Chief, Generaloberst von Brauchitsch. At that time—even after the tests of the first Sturmgeschütze (Sturmgeschütze) had given such positive results at the beginning of 1938 in Döberitz—there was only to be a much reduced number of Sturmgeschütz-Abteilungen raised, and they were to be general headquarters units. Ultimately this created the situation that only a few independent batteries went into action in the French Campaign during the summer of 1940.

Thus, the Sturmgeschütz arm had already been developed before the outbreak of the Second World War and, when war broke out, it could have been available to an extent that unfortunately it was never to achieve. Its development had been held back and delayed, because those persons who had suggested and accepted it, above all Generals von Manstein, von Fritsch and Beck, had been removed from the German High Command.

Naturally, planning in 1935 went in the direction of essentially offensive employment with the goal of providing the infantry with a supporting weapon that could move with them and which had to be able to crush any kind of stubborn enemy resistance, to clear the way for further attacks, penetrations, and breakthroughs. So, according to von Manstein's directive, the main task of the Sturmartillerie was to fill the frequently critical gap which arises in fire support when the infantry penetrates enemy lines. And this moment was exactly the moment when the infantry really needed such a weapon. It was particularly then, during the hardest and most decisive phase of the fighting, that the infantry was without the protection and support of artillery, since at this point every additional round fired into the area of the penetration was also a hazard to friendly troops.

Moreover, since Sturmgeschütze could also be used on the defensive in cooperation with infantry, they could be used to break the back of enemy tank attacks preceding an infantry attack.

The Development of the Sturmgeschütz and its Branch of Service

The development of this new infantry support weapon was carried out by the newly formed 8th (Technical) Section of the Army General Staff. Generalmajor von Manstein put together a team consisting of General Staff Colonel Walter Model and General Staff Major Röttiger, who put themselves 100 percent behind the realization of this weapon.

During the period of its development this weapon was, so to speak, the stepchild of the German Army High Command, which wasn't really interested in seeing it grow up. This impression grew even stronger when several attempts were made during the war by the infantry and by armor to remove the Sturmgeschütze from artillery command for direct assignment. Fortunately, these attempts were unsuccessful.

It was understandable that at the beginning of the development of Sturmgeschütze as an infantry support weapon, the idea was always present of making this arm an organic part of infantry organization. The Infantry Inspectorate at that time had always been the first and most far-seeing in its recognition of the value of this weapon. But it was also reasonable enough to recognize the insuperable difficulties concerning supply of ammunition and fuel, as well as the difficulties of technical maintenance and repair. This led to the Infantry Inspectorate abandoning the idea of taking over further development of the Sturmartillerie.

The armored branch (Panzerwaffe) repeatedly and adamantly opposed this new branch of service. Its opposition was based on considerations of its effect on production capacity. It too was in the midst of its development of a tank program and any switch of production from tank chassis to Sturmgeschütze would have weakened its own situation.

In this case it was Guderian, later to become Generaloberst, who single-mindedly pushed for the use of total productive capacity for the construction of battle tanks. Although it was pointed out that the production of Sturmgeschütze was essentially cheaper, and even when it was admitted that this would increase the total number of armored weapons, it made no difference. Battle tank construction was not to be "diverted".

Even the argument that the elimination of the tank turret allowed the Sturmgeschütz to be armed with a heavier caliber cannon was not accepted, although this point was of immense importance in the light of the later developments in enemy tanks.

The promoters of the Sturmartillerie, with Erich von Manstein at their head, were even called "the grave diggers of the tank force." Even so, since the day it went into action, the Sturmartillerie proved itself to be extraordinarily effective. It became the decisive support weapon for the infantry.

Even the Artillery Inspectorate initially resisted General von Manstein's ideas, and this resistance was reinforced by arguments from its own ranks. The artillery resisted motorization to a degree which virtually reached pathological heights. The lack of appreciation, even detestation, of modern technology, and the advantages which it offered, initially went so far as to lead to serious proposals by the Artillery Inspectorate that the new support weapon be horse drawn.

This time Erich von Manstein exploded. He explained to the "horse nuts" that even during the First World War, victory had been achieved by the enemy's motorized troops, that mobile weapons would be decisive in any future war, and that horse-drawn weapons would in no way be equal to the task.

With all the force of his personality, the subsequent Field Marshall finally managed to convince the Artillery Inspectorate of the value of the concepts of the "Sturmgeschütz" and the "Sturmartillerie" and of the overriding significance of their planned development.

So much for the squabble concerning the necessity for the Sturmgeschütz and for controlling authority over it. The ice was broken, and it was time for action.

In the initial development period, there were still some different ideas. These were rapidly harmonized, as everyone was united on the three main requirements which the Sturmgeschütze would have to meet:

For firepower, a cannon of 7.5 cm caliber with one-piece ammunition was required.

The weapon and sufficient ammunition had to be mounted in or on an all-terrain, fully tracked chassis.

The crew had to be protected by armor against shrapnel and at least 2 cm weapons.

Finally, as a fourth requirement, the weapon had to present as low a profile as possible.

At the beginning of development, the idea was for a self-propelled chassis with armor only in front and on the sides, open both on top and to the rear. This left out of consideration the fact that a Sturmgeschütz, when rolling forward in a position for decisive action at the point of the attack, could also be fired on from the rear and would be rapidly put out of action if the crew compartment were open. As a result, it was very quickly decided on complete armored protection from all sides.

The breakthrough came when there was finally success in diverting a few Panzer III chassis from Panzer production for use in the eventual development of Sturmgeschütze. Instead of the Panzer superstructure with its rotating turret, a fixed fighting compartment was built up. The ability to rapidly fire to all sides was soon discarded, since this requirement was thought unnecessary inasmuch as the Sturmgeschütze were not needed in the case of an independent operation which involved penetrations in the depths of an enemy-occupied area.

A 7.5 cm L/24 Sturmkanone (StuK) 37 was installed on the chassis of the Panzer III with full armor protection allowing a 12° traverse to both sides and a 30° elevation (-10° to +20°).

By eliminating the rotating turret, the Sturmgeschütz could be made quite a bit lower than a Panzer. Because of the reduction in weight, the front armor could be made thicker without the weapon becoming nose-heavy. (Sturmgeschütze only had a problem with nose-heaviness when cannon barrels became longer and longer during the course of the war, transferring weight to the front of the vehicle.)

From Development to Frontline Employment

The first Sturmgeschütz prototype was demonstrated on the artillery range at Kümmersdorf in 1937, where it was shown to a small, very critical circle from the German Army High Command, who were, however, convinced of its value.

This prototype was provided with the 7.5 cm KwK L 24. It carried 44 rounds of ammunition in internal bins, and it was driven by a 300 HP internal combustion engine. The otherwise unaltered Panzer III B chassis had already been given reinforced frontal armor at 50 mm. As planned, the weapon had full armor protection and the required traverse. The crew consisted of four men: the gun commander, the gunner, the driver and the loader. Access to the fighting compartment was provided by two hatches in the armor, which could be closed during combat.

The gun commander observed through a scissors periscope with exterior objective lenses and the ocular lenses within the vehicle. The gunner had the artillery panoramic sight, so that with the help of an additional piece he also had capability for indirect fire. Because of ammunition considerations, indirect fire was only used rarely during the Second World War.

The loader was also the radioman, while the driver, along with his main job, helped the commander with battlefield observation, especially at close range.

The introduction and testing of the prototype was a complete success for the supporters of this new weapon. Immediately following this test, the Artillerie-Lehr-Regiment in Jüterbog was assigned the duty of working up principles for its use and possibilities for its employment according to guidelines of the IN IV (Artillery Inspectorate at German Army High Command).

In the fall of 1937 the 7./Artillerie-Lehr-Regiment (mot.) was formed as an experimental battery for this purpose and trials had already begun by the winter of 1937/38. By 1938/39, unit exercises had already taken place with the Infanterie-Lehr-Regiment at Döberitz. All of these trial exercises were carried out with prototypes or just with Panzer III chassis on which dummy cannon had been built and which had been brought up to weight with iron ballast. For reasons of security, at that time they were referred to as 3.7 cm Panzerabwehrkanone (PaK) (Selbstfahrlafette—self-propelled).

Assault artillery firing instruction was carried out at the same time but initially had negligible influence on the Panzertruppe. The Sturmartilleristen—in this arena the soldiers of the Sturmartillerie could not deny their origins—used the artillery bracketing method right from the beginning and so were able to hit their target by the third shot virtually 100 percent of the time. The Panzertruppe "walked their rounds" on to the target, in the process using more ammunition and taking longer. Only later did it too adopt the bracketing method.

Although the technical firing tests came out positively and the extensive unit trials were carried out to everyone's complete satisfaction, there arose a delay in the production of the planned series, as discussed above. This delay was as substantial as it was unnecessary, and only a total of six batteries had been formed by the beginning of the campaign against France in the summer of 1940. Moreover, an unfortunate manufacturing defect had occurred in these "handmade" Sturmgeschütze, so that really only four (!) batteries (640, 659, 660 and 665), went into action. One of these was assigned to the reinforced Infanterie-Regiment (mot.) "Großdeutschland."

In any case, the success of these few Sturmgeschütze was so striking and made such a compelling case against those who still doubted the value of this weapon, that they were put into full production immediately after the end of the French Campaign and the formation of the first Sturmgeschütz-Abteilungen was begun.

Formation of the Battalions

The formation of these battalions initially took place exclusively under the IV./Artillerie-Lehr-Regiment and, after the regiment was reorganized into two regiments, under the III./Artillerie-Lehr-Regiment (mot.) in "Camp Adolf Hitler" and in the village of Zinna near Jüterbog.

Including an unavoidable shakedown period, two battalions could initially be made combat ready in three months and, later, this was accelerated to three battalions in two months.

Starting in 1941 the replacement battalions were available to help in the formation of additional battalions. Starting in 1943 the Sturmgeschütz-Schule (Assault Gun School) could also contribute to the formation of new units.

The time lost couldn't be entirely made up, but at least two additional battalions were able to participate in the Balkan Campaign against Yugoslavia and Greece in the spring of 1941. By the beginning of the Russian campaign, six fully combat-ready battalions were available, and two each were assigned to Army Groups North, Center and South.

After the beginning of the war in the east, additional battalions could be rapidly sent to the Eastern Front.

Any final doubts were completely swept away. The new weapon spoke convincingly on its own behalf. It literally took only a few months before the weapon enjoyed an especially fine reputation with the entire Army, and especially with the infantry.

The officers, noncommissioned officers and soldiers of the Sturmartillerie fought for, and earned, this reputation using the weapons and technical equipment entrusted to them. In their own way, the enthusiastic and willing men under the leadership of tough and technically qualified noncommissioned and officers repaid the creator and architect of this weapon, which had been so controversial at first. Grinning, the tale of the "horse-drawn Sturmartillerie" was sometimes told here and there in "selected circles." But the Sturmartillerie had been spared this fiasco.

The Weapons of the Sturmartillerie

Although the Sturmgeschütze of the battalions formed in 1941-43 underwent a few small but decisive technical improvements during the production of the series, they remained basically the same as the prototypes which appeared in 1937.

Their main weapon was changed only to the extent that instead of the 7.5 cm KwK L 24, a small proportion of the Sturmgeschütze were provided with the 10.5 cm howitzer L 28. The necessity of equipping a small percentage of the Sturmgeschütz production with howitzers instead of guns was and remained challenged during the first two years of the Russian Campaign.

Right from the start, knowledgeable people believed that the major advantage lay with guns rather than howitzers. Opinions to the contrary may perhaps have been justified objectively in so far as they were determined by missions, terrain and the enemy situation.

Guns were certainly more advantageous than howitzers during the later war years, as both sides believed that a decision on the battlefield was essentially the result of destroying enemy tanks.

In any event, arming Sturmgeschütze with howitzers was discontinued late in the war. This decision may have been the result of either an evaluation of the relative combat value of the two weapons, or the destruction of essential production capacity for the manufacture of German armor by enemy air forces.

From an organizational point of view in 1940-41 a battalion was composed of three batteries with six guns belonging to each battery. The batteries were in turn divided into three sections of two Sturmgeschütze each.

All battalion, company, and section commanders were provided with a so-called command vehicle, a thinly armored 3 ton Sd Kfz. 251 or 253 half-track. This vehicle was almost immediately used for different purposes in all of the battalions, and the officers took the gun commander's place in a Sturmgeschütz. Only in this way, could they command from in front, as demanded by their aggressiveness and élan. Otherwise they ran the risk of suicide in the "sardine cans," or had to either stay behind their Sturmgeschütze or try to relocate them after being forced to detour, because of the limited off-road capability of the half-tracked command vehicles.

It is only because production capacity, the pressing intent to activate additional units and the replacements required by the heavy losses of Sturmgeschütze, that it took an entire year before the Kriegsausrüstungs-Nachweisung (KNA) (table of organization and equipment) were changed and the number of Sturmgeschütze in the battalions could be increased.

In 1942, the three section leaders each received a Sturmgeschütz instead of the command vehicle. In 1942/43, each battery received a tenth Sturmgeschütz for its commander and, during 1943, each battalion commander was provided with his own Sturmgeschütz. Reserve vehicles, however, were unavailable, so that with the loss of a fighting vehicle, crews would have to transfer to another. The battalion thus consisted of 31 vehicles.

In most battalions equipped with howitzers, the howitzer vehicles were assigned to one section in the batteries or one battery in the battalion within the framework of its triangular organization. But in every case, these arrangements could be temporarily changed when the enemy, mission or terrain required it.

The first years the Sturmgeschütze were used in action was not easy for their commanders. Battalion, battery and section commanders and leaders frequently had to hold out against or convince uncomprehending or inexperienced superior officers who still misunderstood that the basic rule: Don't wade in, jump! was also valid for the Sturmgeschütze.

Very often they needed considerable courage of conviction and ample powers of persuasion to prevent the batteries from being divided among different divisions or even different regiments, and sections among different battalions, or even the individual guns among companies.

Even if these initial efforts by the commanders weren't successful in every case, the correct concept gradually trickled through later. In general the batteries at least, and the battalions in most cases as well, managed to go into action as integral units.

Although it was a great compliment that every infantry company was calling for Sturmgeschütze, decisive success could only be achieved by massing the guns at the point of greatest effort or in other sectors when they had to charge into the breach.

In most cases joint action with the infantry was established down to the smallest detail in a face-to-face meeting. Frequently, a battery would be placed under the operational control of an infantry battalion assigned to fight at the Schwerpunkt (point of main effort). Because the Sturmartillerie battalion and battery commanders had the greatest experience in working with the infantry while, on the other hand, most infantry officers only seldom had the advantage of Sturmgeschütz support, the suggestions of the Sturmgeschütz men were almost always taken under consideration. So it happened that in crisis situations, the decisions of young battery commanders or brigade commanders who had learned to think in terms of "combined arms combat" strongly influenced the actions of even large units. The fighting power of even a single Sturmgeschütz battery could often prove decisive, even within an infantry division.

Highly detailed, intensive terrain reconnaissance was a priority whenever time or technical means were at all available. The infantry battalion commanders and the Sturmartillerie battery commanders worked closely together throughout the battle. On occasion, the infantry commander rode along with the battery commander on his gun. Even the infantry company commanders kept very close contact with the Sturmgeschütze. Radio communications were unavailable; prearranged signals had to be used.

Sometimes when combat led unavoidably into open terrain with no natural cover, the infantry sought cover by "bunching up" immediately behind the Sturmgeschütze. Although understandable, this behavior often led to considerable losses among the infantry, for the enemy concentrated his fire on the far more dangerous Sturmgeschütze which could only be put out of action by a direct hit.

Radio Communications, Uniforms and Logistics

For communications, the Sturmgeschütze were provided with a 10-watt radio. However, only the battalion commanders, battery commanders and section leaders had both a transmitter and receiver. All other Sturmgeschütze were equipped only with a receiver. In addition, the battalion staff was also provided with a 100-watt transmitter, and very often the most rapid reporting of immediate events on the battlefield from the lead company to division headquarters was possible only over the radio net of the Sturmgeschütze.

Uniforms for the soldiers of the Sturmgeschütze were of the same style as those of the Panzer force, however, they were gray in color with red piping corresponding to branch color of the artillery. The Sturmgeschütz uniforms were not the same color as the Panzer uniforms since it was believed, and not without cause, that black uniforms would identify them as Panzer troops to the enemy if they were spotted while on reconnaissance while working with the infantry. The consequence would be a reinforcement of enemy anti-tank measures or movement of enemy tanks into the area in question. The black uniform was also unsuited for reconnaissance for concealment reasons.

In retrospect this was a good idea and certainly saved the troops even greater losses. For the sake of completeness, one must mention that when this branch was first being organized, the soldiers were still dressed in black. Even later the black uniform was still worn here and there in individual cases, because it "was so sharp, and good for morale!"

Up to 1943 ammunition and fuel was brought to supply points by truck. From there it was brought up to the Sturmgeschütze by both open and armored 1-ton half-tracks. This allowed refueling and taking on more ammunition on the battlefield when the situation permitted, and the Sturmgeschütze didn't have to go back to the rear. Unfortunately, this possibility no longer existed after 1943 due to lack of production of the half-tracked vehicles. From then on all of the supplies could only be carried by truck and "mules" (trucks converted to half-tracks), and these vehicles could not be brought directly up to the Sturmgeschütze in action.

New Weapons: From Battalion to Brigade

1943 brought a few significant changes. Late in 1942 Sturmgeschütze coming off the production line were equipped with a new gun , the 7.5 cm Sturmkanone 40 L 48, and the older Sturmgeschütze still in service were gradually converted. The barrels of these guns had to be lengthened another 24 caliber lengths in order to be able to successfully use the proper ammunition against massed formations of enemy T-34's, "Josef Stalin's" and enemy assault guns.

The amount of ammunition carried was reduced. There were bins for only 42 shells available within the Sturmgeschütze. However, these bins—just like those in the Sturmgeschütze still equipped with the L 24—were removed by their crews. It had earlier been possible to carry 120 rounds by stacking the ammunition in layers in the fighting compartment of the individual Sturmgeschütz, but now the amount of ammunition carried on board had to be reduced to between 90 and 100 rounds. It is obvious that this amount of ammunition meant that the crew had either to sit on the ammunition or be "packaged" in among the shells.

The length of the barrels of the new cannon made the Sturmgeschütz somewhat "top-heavy." Its maneuverability and mobility were somewhat reduced, in part by the addition of the armored "Schürzen" (side skirts) and the placement of additional armor on a few especially endangered areas which reduced the HP/ton ratio. The advantages, especially of the new cannon, far outweighed the relatively insignificant disadvantages however.

The hatch cover for the commander was replaced by a circular commander's cupola with a periscope, so that even when the hatch was closed the battlefield could be observed through the binocular optics, but also through the cupola vision ports. At first this cupola would rotate 360°, but after the destruction of the ball-bearing factory in the area of Schweinfurt it had to be produced without this capability. Eventually, this feature was reintroduced in August 1944 and kept until the end of the war.

Although this raised the height of the Sturmgeschütz a few centimeters, the significantly improved vision on all sides was of very considerable advantage since the fighting vehicles went into action with increasing frequency with closed hatches.

For reasons of deception, the Sturmgeschütz-Bataillone were renamed Sturmgeschütz-Brigaden. Of course this was a "poor man's" trick, which really didn't deceive the enemy concerning the real strength of the units. It certainly couldn't compensate for what was really needed and couldn't be achieved: reinforcement of the battalions and an increase in their number.

Moreover, the brigades remained army-level troops, and only a few divisions, for example, the divisions belonging to the Panzer-Korps "Großdeutschland," a few divisions of the Waffen-SS, e.g., the "Leibstandarte SS Adolf Hitler" and "Das Reich," the Fallschirm-Panzer-Division "Hermann Göring" and a few others, were provided with Sturmgeschütze on at least a temporary basis or as part of their organizational documents.

During 1944 and at the beginning of 1945, Sturmgeschütze in some brigades were equipped with a much improved cannon—the 7.5 cm L 70 mounted on the Jagdpanzer IV. Organizationally, a number of Sturmgeschütz brigades were expanded to become Sturmartillerie brigades. In addition to the staff headquarters battery and the three gun batteries, these new brigades had a Begleit-Grenadier-Batterie (escort grenadier battery) which was composed of three platoons of grenadiers equipped with the model 44 assault rifle (Sturmgewehr 44) and a platoon of combat engineers.

Moreover, the gun batteries were strengthened to 14 guns with three sections of four guns each, along with a gun for the company commander and an additional reserve vehicle. Three Sturmgeschütze were provided to the brigade staff. With these additional guns, the Sturmartillerie brigade had over 45 Sturmgeschütze available.

This organization proved itself particularly effective, since in the two last years of the war neither Sturmgeschütze nor Panzer could be used for the missions for which they were originally intended, but for those dictated by necessity, namely defense and counterattack. So, in general, the combat roles of these two weapons could no longer be really differentiated.

The Sturmgeschütze needed friendly infantry as cover because of the great danger from enemy infantry. The constantly changing infantry personnel with whom they had to work made this coordination difficult from a purely human perspective. In addition, this coordination was technically difficult inasmuch as there was no possibility of direct radio contact.

In the Sturmartillerie brigades, the Sturmartilleristen and their "infantry serfs" (as provided by the late-war organization) gradually became a blood brotherhood. Such a relationship has seldom been seen anywhere; it could not be expected after only several operations together with the same units. Unfortunately, there were only a few Sturmartillerie brigades organized in this way, but they were very successful.

Ersatz-Abteilungen and the Sturmgeschütz-Schule

Until 1943, the Sturmartillerie Instruction Staff in Jüterbog, which arose from the 7./Artillerie-Lehr-Regiment via the VI./Artillerie-Lehr-Regiment and, later, the III./Artillerie-Lehr-Regiment (mot.) 2, was the center of the Sturmartillerie branch. In

1943, the Sturmartillerie School at Burg near Magdeburg was occupied with its initial cadre and began to expand.

This school was established within the shortest possible time under Günther Hoffmann-Schoenborn (later to become a Generalmajor) who, as Major and Commander of Sturmgeschütz-Abteilung 191, became the 49th German soldier to receive the Oak Leaves to the Knight's Cross of the Iron Cross on 31 December 1941. He was one of the best known officers within this branch, and at the same time the officer with the most time in service with it. The school enjoyed an especially fine reputation well beyond the borders of Germany.

The school consisted of a command staff with an experimental group, a press section, a technical instruction staff and a tactical instruction staff, as well as an instruction battalion and a staff devoted to establishing new battalions and brigades. Its primary duties were to organize the entire Sturmartillerie branch in the field replacement army (Feldersatzheer) and to train and instruct personnel replacements for the branch. This included instruction for many delegations from allied powers such as Hungary, Finland, Rumania, Bulgaria and Spain.

Moreover, at Burg, as at all the other branch schools, after-action reports were evaluated, technical innovations developed, tradition carried on, recruits trained and the troops in the field cared for.

The replacement battalions (Ersatz-Abteilungen) raised during 1940-43 at Schweinfurt, Neiße, Hadersleben (Denmark), Posten (Warthegau) and Deutsch-Eylau, as well as the Aufstellungsstab West (Unit Activation Staff West) at Tours (France) were also placed directly under the school's command.

During the few years of its existence, the Sturmartillerie expanded very rapidly. It is largely thanks to the activity of all those soldiers in responsible positions, that no fewer than nearly 100 Sturmgeschütz/Sturmartillerie brigades and 15 independent batteries were raised along with the aforementioned school and replacement battalions. (This does not include divisional Panzerjäger or Panzer units and elements which were equipped with Sturmgeschütze.)

Insistent demands for Sturmgeschütze from all sides could not be met by a wide margin, which can be partly blamed on delay in the development of this weapon which occurred for reasons already mentioned. But there was also an undeniable scarcity of men and materiél.

The battalions, brigades and batteries bore their own insignia as approved by the high command , and they were displayed on all vehicles. Among these were the "flaming sword" ("Flammenschwert"), the "buffalo" ("Büffel"), the "Maltese Cross" ("Johanniterkreuz"), the "Knight of St. George" (Sankt Georgsritter"), the "griffin" ("Greifen"), and the "lion" ("Löwe") insignia, to mention only a few.

It is certainly a good sign that both during the war and afterwards many soldiers were more aware of their Sturmgeschütz unit's insignia than its number, and this is what they remember from the combat they experienced together.

Wartime Experiences and Successes

Assault guns were employed in every theater of war, in burning heat and icy cold. They fought in the high north on the Arctic Front as well as in the furnace of the North African desert. They helped the infantry in the west, in the Russian expanses and in the Balkans. In the final battle for Germany, they did their duty up to the last day of the war.

Experiences gained during the war years in many cases and in many respects corresponded to those of the Panzertruppe, inasmuch as both branches, under the pressure of necessity, were given tasks as time went on for which they were not originally designed.

During the last phase of the war the era of large-scale armored attacks was a thing of the past. Occasional opportunities otherwise did nothing to obscure that fact. The increasingly weak Panzertruppe, like the Sturmgeschütz forces, was employed to support the hard-pressed infantry in both the attack and the defense. On the other hand, Sturmgeschütze were sometimes used for regular armor attacks. This happened especially at the beginning of the war, although naturally on a smaller scale and in a smaller framework than the Panzer forces themselves. Such attacks took place especially when aggressive young commanders could no longer bear to maintain the slow tempo of a foot infantry attack. They charged ahead without regard for escort security and close protection, often making extremely successful attacks and breaking through to gain ground deep in enemy-held territory.

In any event we must look beyond the scope of those mission responsibilities which the Sturmartillerie originally had and which were influenced by the enemy, the time available and German production capabilities, if we are to adapt the lessons of the past to the needs of the present and future. In this respect, it is especially important to classify the various experiences and lessons learned and separate them clearly from each other if we are to use them for planning and development.

In hindsight it may be said without any false or unhealthy arrogance, but with justified and genuine pride, that the Sturmgeschütz with its Panzer III chassis and a battle cannon ranging from the L 24 to the L 70 in length (corresponding to the tactical requirements and technical possibilities of the period), delivered exceptional performance and proved to be one of most outstanding fighting vehicles in the west.

Other similar types, such as the "Hetzer" (Agitator)—constructed on the 38 T chassis with a Skoda engine—and the Sturmgeschütz on the Panzer IV chassis were produced in far smaller numbers and only in the last years of the war. For those reasons, they, along with the "Jagdpanther" and the "Jagdtiger," played only a subordinate role in the scope of the development of the Sturmgeschütz branch. Seen from the tactical-technical side, it is remarkable however that every Panzer model also had a Sturmgeschütz variant. That speaks for itself and is more convincing than any orator's slick tongue could ever be.

By the end of 1943 German Sturmgeschütze alone had destroyed 13,000 enemy tanks, and the figure of 20,000 had already been reached by the spring of 1944. Is it not an absolutely unique accomplishment for just one Sturmgeschütz brigade to destroy 1,000 tanks in the area of Rshew in just 15 months? The respect merited by such a shining example certainly increases when one considers that on the average the brigade was only able to put a maximum of 20 Sturmgeschütze into action at any one time

The enemy feared German Sturmgeschütze like the plague. Considering the Soviet military mentality, it was highly significant that Russian tank soldiers were instructed to avoid duels with Sturmgeschütze. Such an order would certainly never have been given without in-the-field experience and without an introduction written in the enemy's blood.

As a concrete expression of public recognition, numerous soldiers of the Sturmgeschütze received the Iron Cross, Second Class and First Class along with other high orders and decorations for their personal courage.

Here is a numerical summary of the award lists and the Army announcements for soldiers of the Sturmartillerie:

The German Cross in Gold: 361 soldiers

Army Honor Roll: 140 soldiers

Knights Cross of the Iron Cross: 150 soldiers

Oak Leaves to the Knight's Cross: 14 soldiers

Anton Wickelmaier

The Sturmartillerie Association

When the soldiers of the Sturmartillerie laid down their weapons as ordered on 8 May 1945, they promised each other that the friendships which developed in combat would be maintained in the future and that they would keep in touch with each other.

At that time, scarcely anyone had any idea of how to do this. Naked survival now dominated everyone's thoughts. In addition to that, there was the search for family, and then the problem of food and an attempt to maintain a roof over ones head.

Although many individuals and some groups were able to fight their way through to the west, the greatest part of the Sturmartillerie units went into an uncertain captivity from which only a fraction made it back home. Many lost their homes and their homeland and had to look for and find new ones.

So it was only natural that it was years before the veterans were able to fulfill their earlier promise. Many were no longer alive, others were severely disabled by wounds and disease.

It is all the more astonishing today that in 1951, due to the initiative of their senior officer, Generalmajor (retired) Günther Hoffmann-Schoenborn, who had found a new home at Detmold with his family, 270 addresses could already be collected by word of mouth. On 2 and 3 June 1951, for the first time, 87 former Sturmartillerie soldiers got together at Detmold and decided to form a Sturmartillerie association. The association would search for MIA's, offer any help necessary to families in need, and in general give support to the former soldiers of the Sturmartillerie. Volunteer representatives in the various major cities were to help broaden and strengthen existing support for these activities.

The initial results were successful and visible at the second meeting at Detmold in 1952. Even though aid to comrades was still a priority, considerable interest in political and military questions already existed. These questions were raised and presented for discussion in the newsletters which were occasionally printed.

The comrades of the Sturmartillerie went to Karlstadt am Main for the third meeting in 1953, where, with the exception of the 1954 meeting at Volksmarschen, they found a home and a sponsoring city and where they had received considerable support from the local population right from the beginning.

A registered association was created and registered under the name *Gemeinschaft der Sturmartillerie e.V.* in order to give a democratic basis to this association for former soldiers of the Sturmartillerie and their activities.

The formation of the Bundeswehr (Federal Armed Forces) in the Federal Republic of Germany had a great effect on the association, as 150 of the former Sturmartillerie soldiers were brought into its organization as officers and noncommissioned officers, especially in the Panzertruppe.

The high point of association activities, which continued to broaden and strengthen, was the erection of a monument to honor the killed and missing in the memorial park of the city of Karlstadt am Main in 1958. Then, in 1961, the association witnessed the creation of a traditions room in a tower on the city wall ceded by the city (known as the "Katzenturm"), which has now developed into a museum.

The tradition standards with their insignia were dedicated to the memory of the individual Sturmartillerie units. The association continued to hope that their sponsor city would become a Bundeswehr garrison city. When this hope was disappointed, they found an active partner in Panzer-Bataillon 354 at the nearby troop training center of Hammelburg. Since that time, this sponsorship has significantly influenced the activity of the association, and its most public expression can be seen in the joint museum in the Katzenturm.

Of greater significance are the meetings of the respective "brigades," the northern meeting at Munsterlager and the southern meeting at Radstadt (Tauern) in the province of Salzburg (Austria). Along with the yearly association meeting, they bring together a large number of comrades. At Radstadt the city has erected an additional monument to the memory of this branch.

During its existence from 1940 to 1945, the Sturmartillerie branch consisted of more than 80 independent units—batteries, battalions, and brigades. Right from the start, they found that they needed a history of the entire branch, as each soldier of the Sturmartillerie naturally had only a limited grasp of it. As the various unit war diaries had been destroyed, and as the archives of the Sturmartillerie School at Burg have also been irretrievably lost, an overall picture was slowly but steadily put together in two books by Tornau and Kurowski and by Wegmann and Thomas from the rescued sources and the memories of the comrades themselves.

But the knowledge of this branch gradually became more complete as additional pieces of the history continued to be found and collected.

After more than 50 years after the end of the war, the Gemeinschaft der Sturmartillerie e.V. stands united and financially strong in its own right, something that is seldom the case for other traditional groups of soldiers. It comprises some 12,000 former comrades, maintaining contact among them. About 2000 of them support the association with their names and contributions, and many of the sons and widows of the killed, missing, or of those comrades who have died since the end of the war are among them.

Young soldiers of the Bundeswehr and other interested men have also joined. Far exceeding its original goals and tasks, its members strive to set a good example for others in their appearance and behavior and, above all, in their dedication to country and nation, to defense and to the maintenance of military standards, and especially to future comradeship.

The words on the monument to the memory of the Sturmartillerie in the memorial park in Karlstadt am Main read:

TO THE MEMORY OF THE FALLEN AND A REMINDER TO THOSE LIVING

To the soldiers of the Sturmartillerie, these words, spoken every year, are not just empty rhetoric. They engage the emotions as well as ones reason:

Pride of accomplishment under severe difficulty?

Grieving for the dead?

Depression because of the many sacrificed?

When former soldiers of the Sturmartillerie link arms during their meetings, they feel something that they value highly: the certainty that they were decent men in the most difficult of times. Above and before all, however, the dead are also in their thoughts. They remember them; they talk about them; the dead seem to be present and living once again. Everything comes back. Even those words which once meant *everything* to them. That order which everyone obeyed when it arrived:

STURMGESCHÜTZE VOR!

ASSAULT GUNS TO THE FRONT !

A Sturmgeschütz III A of 16. Sturmbatterie/Infanterie-Regiment "Großdeutschland." This A model was one of the first eight in Jüterbog in the Winter of 1940. In this photograph it is serving with the "Großdeutschland" during the French campaign with five other type A models. The number 12 is clearly visible on the hull side.

Loading a Sturmgeschütz III C for transport to the East. Note the MG-34 at the ready.

Top: A Sturmgeschütz III A, christened "Seydlitz," of the 2. SS-Panzer-Division "Das Reich" on 1 July 1941.

Bottom: Sturmgeschütz III B during operation Barbarossa. Due to the success of the Sturmgeschütze in the French Campaign, Hitler decided to increase the number of batteries. Only four batteries fought in France, but eleven started the Russian Campaign.

Facing Page, Top: A Sturmgeschütz III E, possibly from Sturmgeschütz-Abteilung 177, during Barbarossa. The is the gun of a battery commander.

Facing Page, Bottom: A Sturmgeschütz III E of the 177. Batterie during Barbarossa. The symbol on the front hull is a Griffin (Greif). Note the Panzergrenadiere riding on the engine compartment.

Top: A Sturmgeschütz III B of Sturmgeschütz-Abteilung 226 during the first days of the attack on Russia.

Left: A Sturmgeschütz III B or C from the Sturmgeschütz-Abteilung 190 in Russia in 1941. The crew is enjoying a "Marschpause" (break) before beginning a new engagement.

Facing Page, Top: A Sturmgeschütz III B from Sturmgeschütz-Abteilung 192. This photograph looks posed but gives a good impression of combat. Note the wooden planks at the side to assist the vehicle in negotiating muddy terrain.

Facing Page, Bottom: A Sturmgeschütz III D of Sturmgeschütz-Abteilung 192 passing the remains of Russian fortifications during the opening phases of Operation Barbarossa.

Top: Forest bivouac of Sturmgeschütz-Brigade 197.

Bottom: A Sturmgeschütz III B of Sturmgeschütz-Abteilung 201, christened "Scharnhorst."

Top: This wooden bridge did not hold up under the weight of this Sturmgeschütz III B.

Bottom: Another Sturmgeschütz comes to grief.

Top: Sturmgeschütze B, C and D from Sturmgeschütz-Abteilung 192 during Barbarossa. Note the different placement of the gun numbers, sometimes on the front glacis and other times on the upper glacis.

Left: Russia 1941. A Sturm-geschütz III C of Sturmgeschütz-Batterie 243, which has just destroyed the KV I burning in the background. Note the knight insignia designed for this battery.

Facing Page, Top: Sturmgeschütz III C or D of the 3. SS-Panzer-grenadier-Division "Totenkopf," Russia 1941.

Facing Page, Bottom: A Sturmgeschütz III B of Sturmgeschütz-Batterie 3 "Totenkopf" in September /October 1941.

Left: A Sturmartillerist fastens the radio antenna mast into position. This task was very dangerous in a combat situation.

Bottom: A Sturmgeschütz III B with destroyed running gear due to a devastating hit on the side.

Top: Sturmgeschütz III B from Sturmgeschütz-Abteilung 192 in Russia in 1942.

Bottom: Sturmgeschütz III B during the Russian Campaign. It was the best track-mounted weapon against the heavy KV I, KV II and T34.

Top: This Sturmgeschütz III B hit a mine in the northern sector of the Eastern Front.

Left: Wachtmeister Grimmling of Sturmgeschütz-Brigade 226.

Independent Assault Gun Batteries
selbständige Sturmgeschütz-Batterien

Sturmgeschütz-Batterie 640

In the first half of 1940 6 Sturmgeschütz batteries were formed at the Artillerie-Lehr-Regiment in Jüterbog, after a few experimental Sturmgeschütze had been previously employed in the Polish campaign and had shown promise. The first of these independent batteries, and thus the oldest combat unit of the Sturmartillerie, was Sturmgeschütz-Batterie 640 formed in March 1940. Its commander was Oberleutnant Freiherr von und zu Egloffstein. The activation took place under conditions of tightest security. The battery officers were: Oberleutnant With, Leutnant Peter Frantz, Leutnant von Werlhoff, Leutnant Tiarks and Leutnant Küster. The three sections of the battery contained two Sturmgeschütze each with the short 7.5 cm guns, panoramic binoculars and sights facing forward. A 3-ton Schützenpanzerwagen (armored personnel carrier = SPW) with scissors binoculars—the so-called command vehicle—was provided to each section leader. There was radio communication from the section leader to both guns, as well as from the section command vehicle to the battery commander's vehicle, who also received a 3-ton SPW.

When the battery received its orders to move out, it still didn't have any Sturmgeschütze. It was also missing its radio equipment and submachine guns. The battery headed west in its wheeled vehicles, while an officer of the battery was to take delivery of 6 Sturmgeschütze at Marienborn.

At the same time, Leutnant Frantz drove to Breslau in a staff car followed by a truck to get the radio equipment and submachine guns. When he got back to Jüterbog three days later, instead of the battery he found a telegram telling him how he could rejoin his battery while in transit.

In the meantime, the battery had been attached to the 1. Gebirgs-Division in the Eifel Mountains. But Infantry Regiment "Großdeutschland" was also trying to get it. Originally, it was intended to attach the battery to Infantry Regiment "Großdeutschland". After a few days of "tug-of-war," its attachment to the 1. Gebirgs-Division was revoked and, in the middle of April, 1940, the battery was moved to Infantry-Regiment "Großdeutschland" at Zell on the Moselle River. The final live-fire exercise carried out at Baumholder Troop Training Area had convinced the regimental command of "GD" that the battery was a powerful, combat-ready unit.

Combat operations began for the battery on 10 May 1940. Put into action at the focal points of Infantry-Regiment "Großdeutschland," the Sturmartilleristen fought at Bastogne, Sedan, Stonne, Dunkirk and Amiens. The battery destroyed or captured numerous enemy weapons while in pursuit of the French Army as it withdrew to the south.

As commander of the advance guard during this pursuit, Leutnant Frantz pushed south into Lyon at the head of his section. His Sturmgeschütz reached a speed of nearly 50 kilometers an hour on the highway, so that it pulled ahead of the German troop-carrying vehicles. Lyon was captured.

During the fighting in France, the battery lost 1 officer and 15 noncommissioned officers and men.

Defects in the organization were revealed during this first Sturmgeschütz action. Most of all, the 3-ton SPW (command vehicles) were found to be unable to follow the Sturmgeschütze into combat because of their inadequate armor. Because of this, the section commanders usually had to bring their tactical orders to the guns on foot.

After the French Campaign was over, Sturmgeschütz-Batterie 640 was made an organic part of Infantry-Regiment "Großdeutschland." There it formed the 16th Company of the IV. (schweres) Bataillon.

In 1942, this battery made up the foundation for the newly-formed Sturmgeschütz-Brigade for Panzer-Grenadier-Division "Großdeutschland." (See also Sturmgeschütz-Abteilung 192 and Sturmgeschütz-Brigade "Großdeutschland" for additional information.)

Hauptmann von Egloffstein went to Jüterbog as chief instructor for a Sturmartillerie class. He was killed on the Eastern Front in 1944.

Sturmgeschütz-Batterie 659 (Sturmgeschütz-Batterie 287)

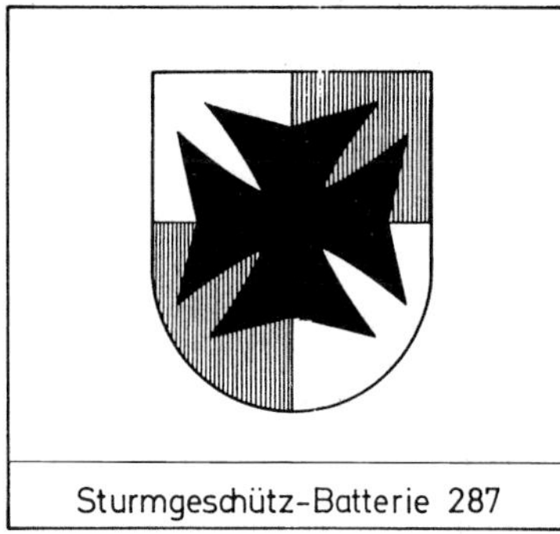

Sturmgeschütz-Batterie 287

The battery was formed at Jüterbog on 20 January 1940. The activation was completed on 19 April 1940, and the battery was moved to Aachen under the command of Oberleutnant Freiherr von und zu Frauenberg. The battery had an outstanding commander in Oberleutnant von Frauenberg.

The first fighting involving this battery took place on 10 and 11 May 1940, at the crossing of the Meuse at Fumei. The fighting at Laon during the advance followed, and the battery distinguished itself once again during the defensive fighting on the Oisne-Aisne Canal. The infantry was delighted with this new support weapon.

During the early morning hours of 1 June and under the personal command of Oberleutnant von Frauenberg, the battery attacked enemy positions at Chareau-Porcien for the crossing over the Aisne Canal. The attack was successful and was crowned by the capture of Juneville. This was the first time that the infantry, which had gotten into a difficult position at Chalons, called on the Sturmgeschütze for help:

"Sturmgeschütz vor!" ("Assault guns to the front!")

Once again the battery intervened in a struggle for a French city. It shot its way through enemy strong points and cleared the way into the city for the infantry, some of whom were riding on the guns.

Even while the infantry were mopping up in the city, the Sturmgeschütze continued their advance and reached the French Troop Training Area at Mourmelon. Once again a cry for help reached the battery, this time from another division that had bogged down at St. Dizier. There too, the new weapon broke down tough resistance and forced the enemy to run.

On 15 June 1940 the Sturmgeschütze captured the Langres Plateau. One day later they rolled into Besancon after hard fighting and, on 18 June, the Sturmgeschütze stormed ahead in the direction of Belfort. The infantry, involved in heavy street fighting, received support in breaking enemy resistance. Belfort fell, and Sturmgeschütz-Batterie 659 stormed through the Burgundian Gate as far as the Swiss border.

Oberleutnant von und zu Frauenberg drove his vehicle over a mine during this assault and was killed. He was buried with all military honors next to the church at Perth.

The battery remained in France until 26 February 1941. Only then was it sent back to Jüterbog. It was immediately given a refit. The new battery commander was Oberleutnant Schaupensteiner.

Sturmgeschütz-Batterie 659 was to take part in the advance to Russia, and ended up in East Prussia after a long, roundabout journey. On 22 June 1941, as soon as it was light enough to aim, it crossed the Lithuanian border and, fighting its way rapidly forward as an advance guard, reached the Njemen, one of the first German units to cross that river. Kowno fell four days later. The Düna was crossed and the advance began through East Lithuania and Latvia.

After considerable fighting from 8 July to 9 August 1941, the Sturmgeschütze rolled across the old Russian border south of Lake Ilmen.

On 10 August the battery was brought into the battle for Nowgorod in a night march. There it also fought the way it had many times in the past and deserved much of the credit for the victory. But by 25 August it was pulled out of the line so that it could provide fire support for the heavily pressed infantry on the Lowat and Polat.

During the following months the battery was involved in heavy fighting in that area. It suffered heavy casualties; despite that it was given no time to recover. On 8 January 1942, it was given orders to go into action at Staraja Russa during the fierce defensive fighting south of Lake Ilmen in the grim cold of a Russian winter. It threw the few combat ready Sturmgeschütze against the attacking enemy units and held them off.

The last operations carried out by the battery took place during the late fall and winter in the area of Demjansk. After that, the battery was completely burned out. On 13 January 1942 the remnants were transferred back home.

It wasn't until they got to Jüterbog that the men of Sturmgeschütz-Batterie 659 could go on a well-deserved group leave. Wounded comrades managed to rejoin the battery there. The new battery commander was Oberleutnant Ritzel.

New rumors kept the members of the battery in a constant state of tension until the final decision came down. Sturmgeschütz-Batterie 659 was deactivated and reconstituted as Sturmgeschütz-Batterie 287. It was attached to the Brandenburg Division as a special unit and received new Sturmgeschütze with the long-barreled cannon. The tropical equipment indicated action in the tropics, but after its formation the battery was unexpectedly marched to the east. On 14 October 1942 it went into action along with a grenadier battalion on the Terek and in the Kalmücken Steppes. Sturmgeschütz-Batterie 287 carried out real cavalry raids there. Always fighting far ahead of the main body, it smashed its way through the enemy. Enemy batteries, tanks and bunkers were destroyed. The battery reached the central Caucasus. It got stuck there, and the operational withdrawal began on 30 December 1942.

Nothing more was heard of the planned movement out of the Caucasus into Iraq and the Iraqi oil fields.

The continuous defensive fighting sapped the energy from every soldier. The Sturmgeschütze pulled back to the lower Don and the Manytsch, always hard pressed by the enemy, who constantly tried to destroy this special unit with fast-moving armor units.

On the Mius, the battery was thrown against one enemy penetration after another. As a "fire brigade," it mastered one critical situation after the other. At Taganrog and Stalino, the battery held out against a far superior enemy. The battery was pulled out only after the German main battle line on the Mius had been stabilized. Oberleutnant Ritzel was killed during this fighting. Hauptmann Stier took over command of the battery. He too won the hearts of his men. Any of them would have gone through Hell for him.

In a corps order of the day for 20 December 1942, General der Flieger Felmy, commander of the special element, devoted the following lines to recognition of the battery:

I wish to express my fullest thanks and appreciation to Sturmgeschütz-Batterie 287 for its courageous action on 19 December 1943. By its outstandingly aggressive conduct, it seized control of the extremely critical situation at Ssunshenkij. By its devotion to duty, it was a shining example to every other unit. Once again, I express my heartiest thanks to it.

Sturmgeschütz-Batterie 287 was transferred to Dennewitz near Jüterbog for rest and refitting, and it was rebuilt from the ground up. The battery was equipped with 15 Sturmgeschütze, and it got three additional guns "on the sly." When the battery was fully equipped and ready to move out, it was given a farewell address by Oberst Hoffmann-Schoenborn. His words remained unforgettable in the minds of the battery members.

This time it was going to Greece. The battery separated from the command of the Sturmartillerie. Its new replacement unit was Panzer-Ersatz-Regiment 8 at Böblingen.

The battery was attached to Panzer-Abteilung Rhodos (Oberstleutnant Graf Schulenburg)as its first company. The battery remained on Rhodes until the surrender. After the end of the war it went undefeated into captivity. The last soldiers of this battery didn't return home from Egypt until 1949.

Sturmgeschütz-Batterie 660

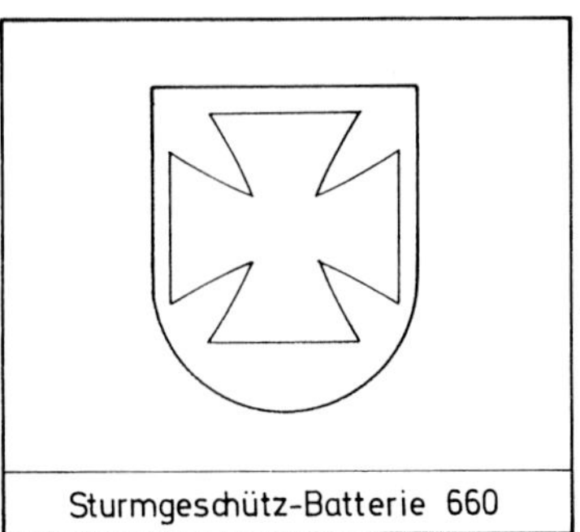

Sturmgeschütz-Batterie 660

At the beginning of April 1940 Sturmgeschütz-Batterie 660 was formed as the third independent Sturmgeschütz unit at Zinna near Jüterbog. Oberleutnant Ottheinrich Tolckmitt, who had been transferred to the 7./ Artillerie-Lehr-Regiment shortly before, was battery commander. The following officers joined the battery as section leaders and gun commanders: Leutnant Heins, Leutnant Böttcher. Leutnant Kaiser and Leutnant Perkuhn.

Because in 1940 there was still no activation cadre for newly forming units, the commander and officers had to overcome many difficulties and obstacles before the battery was ready with its 6 Sturmgeschütze, 3 armored command vehicles and the armored munitions carriers. But by 11 May 1940 the battery was loaded up at Jüterbog and set on the rail march to Luxembourg. Four days later the battery arrived in Nousonville, north of Sedan.

In the days that followed, the battery received its baptism of fire. It cleared the crossing of the Meuse for the 3. Infanterie-Division. Driving along the banks of the Meuse, the six Sturmgeschütze silenced the enemy positions on the other side of that river. To give the infantry even more support as they crossed, all guns used smoke shells to cover the crossing assault boats.

The infantrymen of this division experienced the fighting power of Sturmartillerie for the first time. They were wildly enthusiastic. The infantry battalion commander received the Knight's Cross for this successful crossing. He later said: "I don't believe that we would have managed to make the crossing and then silence the enemy defensive positions without the decisive support of the Sturmgeschütze."

In these initial operations, the officers commanding sections had already ignored doctrine by climbing into Sturmgeschütze themselves and then fighting to their objectives as both section leaders and gun commanders.

On 16 May the battery was attached to the 8. Panzer-Division. The first night operations were carried out without previous reconnaissance and without infantry support. After the fighting at Hirson and Bohain, the Sturmgeschütze were positioned among the lead elements of the 8. Panzer-Division. They were ordered to smash through towards the English Channel with the tanks. French tanks which challenged the Sturmgeschütze in the fighting were destroyed. The battery had still not suffered any losses.

The spearhead pushed through St. Quentin, closely passing Cambrai to advance to the La Basse Canal. There, the battery, attached to a division of the Waffen-SS, defended against the attacking English. It threw back the enemy forces fiercely defending the Bailleul Heights and reached Hazebrouck on 28 May, where it became involved in heavy fighting on the same day.

The English were defending themselves fiercely in a building complex. The infantry called not for the tanks of the 8. Panzer-Division, but rather for the Sturmgeschütze, which broke the enemy resistance after a short engagement.

A few days of quiet made it possible to repair the Sturmgeschütze and vehicles that had broken down. The armored munitions carriers configured out of the Panzer I were discarded as unusable. Then, after this brief period, the battery, whose commander had to arrange for supplies himself, was thrown into the Rethel area and there attached to the 6. Panzer-Division (Panzergruppe Guderian) for the attack on the Aisne.

The attack began on 9 June and a crossing was forced across the Aisne and the Ardennes Canal during the night of 10/11 June. The battery suffered its first casualties from the French 2.5 cm antitank guns whose shells penetrated the armor of the Sturmgeschütze. Leutnant Kaiser was fatally wounded while he was attempting to determine the firing position of just such a gun on foot so that he could silence it with his Sturmgeschütz.

The advance continued rapidly to the south. The battery was continuously in action from 14 to 19 June. Two Sturmgeschütze were put out of action by hits from antitank guns.

The Sturmgeschütze continued to advance to Epinal, crossing the Rhine-Marne Canal and the Marne at Dizier. They took Epinal on 19 June. The battery was then placed in reserve and remained in reserve until the armistice with France was announced by peals of church bells in the night of 22/23 June.

Sturmgeschütz -Batterie 660 was moved to Versailles. It was intended for it to participate in the parade in Paris celebrating the end of the war. But the war wasn't over yet, so the battery was moved back into the Lisieux-Deauville area. Leutnants Selle, Barklay and Koch and Offizieranwärter Bätke arrived at the battery to replace Leutnant Kaiser and Leutnant Bötcher, who was wounded.

The battery then prepared for "Operation Sea Lion," in which it was to cross the English Channel in the first wave. Loading exercises were held in Den Haag and Rotterdam. There it was discovered that loading Sturmgeschütze was an extremely difficult job.

Nothing more was heard of this operation and, by the end of 1940, the battery was transferred to Douai near Lille. There it was temporarily assigned to Abteilungsstab z.b.V. 600 (Special-Duty Detachment Staff 600) which had just been made operational. Sturmgeschütz-Batterien 659 and 666 were also assigned to this staff.

On Ash Wednesday of 1941 the battery was suddenly loaded up and transferred by rail through Hamburg to Mohrungen (East Prussia).

On the morning of 22 June it crossed the German eastern border at Ebenrode with Division Lancelle. After initial minor actions, it advanced via Kowno, Dünaburg and Pleskau to Luga. This Russian troop training area was fiercely defended by the Soviets. The enemy was dislodged by the Sturmgeschütze only after very heavy losses.

In the meantime, the Soviets had broken through at Staraja Russa in the course of their attempt to relieve Leningrad. The battery was committed there on the defense and immediately launched in a counterattack. The Russian breakthrough there could only be eliminated after long, heavy fighting.

Immediately thereafter the battery road marched toward Rshew. By the time the Sturmgeschütze had reached Kalinin, their supply vehicles were far back along the overcrowded roads. The Sturmgeschütze were employed individually in covering Kalinin. This action, contrary to all basic doctrine, was a case of necessity. The Russian tanks which had broken through were successfully countered. During this fighting, the Sturmgeschütz of Leutnant Tauschinski had a head-on collision at full speed with a Russian T-34 on the highway. The Leutnant ordered the crew to bail out.

After the attacking Soviet tanks had been destroyed, the hatch of a Russian tank was broken open. The crew sat closely huddled together inside, awaiting death at any moment. Death, however, would not greet them that day.

Oberleutnant Tolckmitt was relieved in December. Leutnant Barklay took over the battery, which suffered heavy losses in the subsequent severe fighting during the withdrawal in the icy winter.

This battery was never employed again.

In the spring of 1942 Sturmgeschütz-Batterie 660 joined with Sturmgeschütz-Batterien 665 and 666 to form leichte Sturmgeschütz-Abteilung 600 which later became Heeres-Sturmartillerie-Brigade 600. (See the entry for that formation for additional information.)

Sturmgeschütz-Batterie 665

Sturmgeschütz-Batterie 665, the fourth independent battery, was formed in the "Old Camp" at Jüterbog in April 1940. Oberleutnant Speyerer was the battery commander. Its section commanders were: Leutnant Vaerst, Leutnant Edelschmidt and Leutnant Bräuchle. Leutnant Stephani was the supply officer. Leutnant Schönborn also joined the battery later. The battery insignia was an ascending Prussian eagle holding a Sturmgeschütz in its talons.

This battery was still in the middle of it constitution at the beginning of the French Campaign. However, when the second phase of the campaign began on 10 June, the battery was moved to Saarbrücken, and from there rolled on into the Vosges Mountains. Launched against infantry objectives, the battery performed outstandingly. French tanks were not used in the trackless areas of the Vosges, so that there were no duels of tank against Sturmgeschütz. Sturmgeschütz-Batterie 665, the only heavy weapon in this sector of the front, demonstrated its power against bunkers, however. The French bunker line was penetrated. Leutnant Schönborn was killed on the Rhine-Marne Canal, when he was outside his Sturmgeschütz. On 17 June the fighting was over for the battery. It had been given its baptism of fire in the French Campaign.

Sturmgeschütz-Batterie 665 had also contributed proof of the combat effectiveness of Sturmgeschütze in this short period.

After the armistice went into effect on 22 June, the battery was first transferred to Zabern and then in July 1940 to Mons in southern Belgium. At Mons Leutnant Vaerst left the battery to go to the Artillerie-Lehr-Regiment at Jüterbog as an instructor to train more volunteers for the Sturmartillerie.

With the beginning of the Russian Campaign, the battery saw action on the northern sector of the Eastern Front. The battery commander, Oberleutnant Speyerer, was killed during the fighting at Lake Ilmen in the summer of 1941. At the end of 1941 the battery was pulled out of the front to join the other independent batteries (Sturmgeschütz-Batterien 660 and 666) to form Sturmgeschütz-Abteilung 600 which later became Heeres-Sturmartillerie-Brigade 600. (See the entry for that formation for additional information.)

Sturmgeschütz-Batterie 666

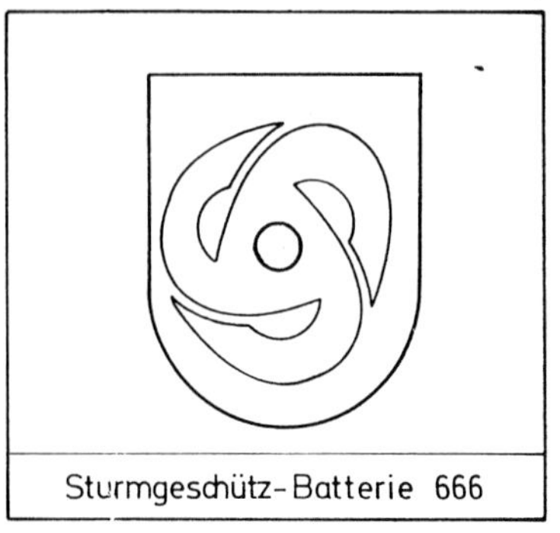
Sturmgeschütz-Batterie 666

In the middle of May 1940 Sturmgeschütz-Batterie 666 was raised at Zinna as the fifth independent Sturmgeschütz battery. During the formation it was attached to the VI./Artillerie-Lehr-Regiment whose commander was Major Steinkopf.

Three intertwined sixes were selected as the battery's insignia. Oberleutnant Alfred Müller was the battery commander. On 13 July 1940, he reported that the battery was ready to move out. A good three weeks later, the battery was transferred to Valenciennes from Zinna Forest by way of Magdeburg, Bentheim and Rotterdam. It left there a few hours later to be taken through Brussels to Ghent. It was unloaded in Ghent on 1 August.

In the area of Ghent, the battery was attached to the II./Artillerie-Regiment 7 (Major Dressler) of the 17. Infanterie-Division (Generalleutnant Loch). For the next few weeks, it carried out exercises with the division's infantry regiments. Then followed embarking and debarking exercises in Ostende and Dunkirk, clear indication that Sturmgeschütze-Batterie 666 was also being prepared for "Operation Sea Lion."

The battery was transferred to Douai at the beginning of winter training. There, it joined Sturmgeschütz-Batterien 659, 660, and. All of these batteries were temporarily consolidated and attached to the Special Duty Detachment Staff 600 (Abteilungsstab z.b.V. 600). At the end of winter training, Sturmgeschütz-Batterie 666 was loaded by rail in Arras on 27 February 1941 and transferred to Wirmditt in East Prussia by way of Roermond, Lübeck, Stettin and Elbing. Its new quarters were at Mohrungen. At Wirmditt it was attached to the 206. Infanterie-Division on 14 April 1941. Training exercises were conducted at the Arys Troop Training Area.

On 6 June 1941 the battery left the 206. Infanterie-Division and went to Brassen in two night marches, where it was allocated to II. Armee-Korps and attached to the 32. Infanterie-Division. On 18 June when the battery arrived at Eichkamp, only 6 kilometer from the Russian border, everyone was already at the highest state of readiness.

On the evening of 21 June Oberleutnant Müller read out the Führer Order for the soldiers in the east and briefed the order for the attack. The mood of the troops, which had been depressed by the long months of uncertainty, gave way to obvious enthusiasm.

At the beginning of the war with Russia, on 22 June at 0320 hours, the battery crossed the German/Lithuanian border just north of Vistitis with Infanterie-Regiment 94 (32 Infanterie-Division). With considerable effort it cleared a way through the rocks and swamp. More and more Sturmgeschütze stuck fast. Only the 18-ton prime movers were able to get them unstuck. Towards 1000 hours, the 2nd and 3rd Sections went into action for the first time. After a short firefight, the Sturmgeschütze broke the enemy resistance in field positions and farm houses and, towards 2200 hours, they reached the main highway between Vilkaviskis and Miriampol. When shortly before midnight the 2nd Section detected an enemy battery in the attack sector of the 12. Infanterie-Division's, it advanced on its own initiative without infantry protection and destroyed the Soviet 10.5 cm battery after overcoming a stubborn defense.

The Sasupe was crossed at noon on the following day. By evening, the battery had pushed forwards all the way across the Buburiaki. It was called back some 26 kilometers by the division, because the infantry was unable to follow it up rapidly enough.

The 1st Section managed to repulse a Soviet attack on the rear right flank on 24 June. One day later towards noon the Memel River was reached. The battery remained in a ready position there until the construction of a 20-ton bridge was completed. However, since the bridges finally built in the sector of the 32. Infanterie-Division's only had a maximum load of 16 tons, the battery had to cross on the 20-ton bridge at Kowno. This meant a detour of 80 kilometers for the battery, since the 32. Infanterie-Division crossed at Rusinske on its own bridge.

By 28 June the 3rd Section was assigned to the advance guard detachment and penetrated to a depth of about 3 kilometers, destroying 40 Soviet trucks, 4 guns, and an armored scout car. Through that action the section gave the advance guard detachment a little breathing space. Around noon on the same day, the 1st Section under Leutnant Holzmann pushed through Wislia. The enemy put up a stubborn defense. However, Holzmann led his section cleverly and was able to take Zosle. The 2nd and 3rd Sections followed immediately behind him.

Still on the same day, the Soviets launched a counterattack with strong forces. They managed to capture a German heavy field howitzer battery. In a counterattack Sturmgeschütz-Batterie 666 recaptured this battery from the enemy. This time it went into action without infantry support and functioning as tanks. The enemy suffered heavy casualties. Eighty trucks were captured and an enemy battery of four guns was destroyed. In a unified attack, Sturmgeschütz-Batterie 666 forced the remaining Soviets back into an area which was under fire by the rearward Russian batteries. The rest of the enemy force was destroyed there.

By 2 July 1941 the advance continued and reached Kasiskai. By this time, battery losses had become so great that it had to be reorganized into two sections. But, this freed up a command vehicle for the battery commander.

The battery passed through Mindunai, Widze and Zamosze to reach Kraslava on 6 July, where the Sturmgeschütze crossed the river on a ferry. In the early morning hours of 9 July, the battery took up a ready position in the forest west of Sarjenka. After preparatory artillery fire, it was to advance from there across the Sarjenka, a section of the Stalin Line. Friendly infantry had bogged down there in front of strong enemy positions 200-300 meters east of the river.

Under heavy enemy fire, Unteroffizier Panhans had determined that the water in the ford was 90 centimeters deep. In spite of heavy enemy fire, the uncertain ford was successfully crossed. The Sturmgeschütze attacked parallel to the infantry's assault front and destroyed every point of resistance they could find. Then the friendly infantry stormed the enemy positions and formed a bridgehead.

The battery went on through Zarbowje to Latikowo, where the enemy launched a surprise attack with about two companies from a woods. The 1st Section was able to halt the attack, inflicting bloody losses on the enemy. The battery then received orders on 11 July that, effective immediately, it was attached to the 121. Infanterie-Division. As part of the advance guard detachment of the 121. Infanterie-Division on 16 July, it was able to capture two bridges undamaged across the narrows at Sachodcy.

Enemy forces detected on the opposite side of the narrows were attacked by the battery without infantry support. Two antitank guns and one artillery piece were destroyed. There was heavy fighting the next day when the enemy tried to recapture the bridges with artillery support. The Soviets were well dug in among the houses and trees of Wydussowo. A Sturmgeschütz took a direct hit from a 7.62 cm gun. Fortunately, the shell remained stuck in the armor. The enemy was scattered.

On 19 July the battery was attached to Infanterie-Regiment 407 to take Krasnoje. The attack began at 1400 hours. The 1st and 2nd Sections under the command of Leutnant Schulte-Strathaus and Oberleutnant Gensicke overpowered the enemy's well constructed field positions. They destroyed a number of guns and antitank guns. As the battery continued to advance through thick, forested cover, it ran into heavy fire from artillery and antitank guns. The Soviets put up an incredibly stubborn defense and, in the evening, they launched a counterattack. But this too was smashed. Wachtmeister and Offizieranwärter Rosenbaum, the first member of the battery to die in action, was killed fighting as a gun commander in the front lines. On 20 July Gefreiter Kleinhans was killed in a new enemy attack and Obergefreiter van Freden severely wounded.

As the day progressed, Soviet snipers in the trees made themselves unpleasantly noticeable, especially in a small woods east of Hill 207.

Soviet field positions were rolled over, and the infantry broke the last enemy resistance.

On 24 July Sturmgeschütz-Batterie 666 was attached to the corps advance guard detachment (Cholm) and began moving toward Loknia.

After taking part in the fighting for Juchowa on 26 July, the battery was attached to Infanterie-Regiment 89 (12. Infanterie-Division) by order of the corps. It was attached to the advance guard detachment of this regiment and, on 27 July, went with it to a bridge across the Lowat that was still intact. It reached Tschernezkaja that same evening.

An enemy battalion was pursued and scattered in a breakneck assault on the following day. On 31 July the battery was ordered to block the Soviet withdrawal route from Cholm to the east. The battery ran into strong enemy field positions in front of the village of Soljzy. It attacked and threw back the enemy, who tried to destroy the Sturmgeschütze with Molotov cocktails and hand grenades. Finally, it advanced as far as Bobowna, just south of the eastern route from Cholm.

The enemy attacked Soljzy in the early morning hours of 1 August. In the total darkness the battery was unable to effectively intervene in the fighting and, for a while, the village was completely surrounded. Unteroffizier Dalbüdding was fatally wounded by a round. There was heavy artillery fire on the German positions on 2 and 3 August as well. The Sturmartillerie crews took cover under their guns and in trenches.

The senior army headquarters ordered the battery to shift to the west of Lake Ilmen on 5 August 1941. This meant a movement of 380 kilometers. Mechanical problems figured large during the road march. On 8 August, the battery had only 3 combat-ready Sturmgeschütze. A section of Sturmgeschütz-Batterie 659 under Leutnant Bielefeld was attached to the battery to bring the it back up to full strength. This section was designated as the 1st Section.

The battery advanced to the Mschaga River on 10 August and went into ready positions right on the river. There, on 10 August 1941, it witnessed the powerful air attack by the VIII. Flieger-Korps (Air Corps) on the Russian positions on the east bank of the Mschaga.

That same day, in the presence of the Commander-in-Chief 16. Army, the battery crossed the Mschaga on the very rapidly built 20-ton bridge and then went into ready positions in the German forward infantry positions. There was minor combat activity on the following day, when the battery continued the attack across the Korostym.

Obergefreiter Weber managed to shoot down a fighter with his machine gun when Russian fighters attacked the Sturmgeschütze. He was awarded the Iron Cross, First Class.

The battery was thrown forward to Schimsk and attached to Infanterie-Regiment 45. It supported this regiment's attack along the west bank of the Schelonj and along the main route toward Nowgorod. Unfortunately, it was not possible to directly support the attack on Nowgorod, as there was no adequate bridge available. At this point, the section of Leutnant Bielefeld was returned to Sturmgeschütz-Batterie 659.

Next came the attack on Tschudowo. There was very heavy fighting on 19 August. This operation lasted until the evening of 20 August; large numbers of enemy field positions and strong points were destroyed. Unteroffizier Helmchen was killed in this action. There was also heavy fighting on 21 August. Enemy forces which had broken through in the night were thrown back once again. Then enemy resistance slackened, and the battery was reorganized for new operations.

The 1st and 2nd Sections were attached to the 18. Infanterie-Division (mot.) for the attack along both sides of the road toward Leningrad; the 3rd Section was attached to the 21. Infanterie-Division for an attack toward Wolchow. On 25 August a Sturmgeschütz destroyed an enemy tank on the west edge of Pomeranje. The battery achieved further successes in the varied fighting during the next few days, before it was sent to II. Armee-Korps in Cholm on 28 August by order of the senior command.

As a result of the poor and sometimes catastrophic road conditions, the battery didn't reach Cholm until noon on 9 September 1941. It was attached to the 12. Infanterie-Division on the following day. On 6 September Obergefreiter Harloff shot down an enemy fighter with his machine gun.

The month of September passed in relative calm. It wasn't until 9 October 1941 that the 12. Infanterie-Division attacked to the southeast between Lake Seliger and Lake Stach. The battery, minus its 1st Section, supported the attack on the left wing of Infanterie-Regiment 48 while the 1st Section supported the spearhead of the attack by Infanterie-Regiment 27. Infanterie-Regiment 27 attacked out of the Kokowkino Bridgehead, from the west bank of Lake Stach, to the south. This attack pushed forward to a point just south of Gorodok.

Toward noon on the day of the attack the 2nd Section intervened in the forest fighting south of Swapuschtscha. Later it was joined by the command Sturmgeschütz of Oberleutnant Müller. A number of bunkers were put out of action. As the advance continued, the command Sturmgeschütz rolled onto a mine and was out of action with damaged running gear. Shortly thereafter, another Sturmgeschütz ran onto a demolition charge near a tree barricade and was a total loss. The section was pulled back to Swapuschtscha. On the following day, a third Sturmgeschütz ran onto a mine.

The battery fought its way forward with varying success. The attack on Krutiki began at 0715 hours on 17 October. The battery was ordered to support the attack of the III./ Infanterie-Regiment 27 to soften up the bunker positions around Krutiki and put enemy machine gun nests out of action. The 1st Section attacked, followed by the command Sturmgeschütz. The 1st Section's command vehicle ran onto a mine and was severely damaged. A little later, the command Sturmgeschütz ran onto a mine and was put out of action. The munitions carrier ran onto an antitank mine during the 2nd Section's attack and was a total loss. The attack lost impetus. The Sturmgeschütze had to limit themselves to firing on enemy positions. The enemy artillery placed massed fire on the Sturmgeschütze, forcing the commander to pull back his guns behind the village of Krutiki. The command Sturmgeschütz and the command vehicle were left in no-man's-land, as they were incapable of being driven. Since the infantry also had to move back, both vehicles fell into Soviet hands.

When yet another Sturmgeschütz ran onto an antitank mine on 18 October and was badly damaged, Oberleutnant Müller suggested to the divisional commander that the battery be pulled out of this mine-infested area before it was entirely destroyed. The battery was pulled back to Domaschi with 3 guns left. On 11 November, Oberleutnant Alfred Müller, who had been an exemplary leader for the battery, was transferred to Artillerie-Lehr-Regiment 2 (mot.) in Jüterbog. Oberleutnant Gensicke was named battery commander, effective 20 November 1941.

At the end of December 1941, the battery moved to Dno, about 80 kilometer to the west of Staraja Russa. Staraja Russa was the focal point for the combat elements. Operations took place in January and February on and south of Lake Ilmen. The temperature dropped to 50 degrees below zero (Celsius). The Sturmgeschütz engines wouldn't start. The breechblocks on the guns froze shut. When the March offensive began with the objective of opening up the Demjansk Pocket, the battery rolled along the frozen Polista River to 20 kilometers south of Staraja Russa and then swung left (to the east) toward the Staraja Russa-Cholm highway. It established a bridgehead there, from which the attack towards Staraja Russa-Demjansk could continue. The enemy put massed Stalin Organs into action. Snipers targeted the gun commanders. Leutnant Holzmann was severely wounded by a sniper.

The push through the 10-kilometer deep forested area took more than a week. The infantry suffered heavy casualties. A village at the edge of the woods was taken and a bridgehead established. The attack then continued from this bridgehead along both sides of the road to Demjansk.

On the 2nd day of Easter in 1942 the battery was put into action along with a Panzer-Abteilung. This attack bogged down in Russian defensive fire. Five of the battery's seven Sturmgeschütze were put out of action. Twenty two of the twenty eight men of the gun crews were killed or wounded. Oberleutnant Gensicke was also wounded. During the withdrawal in the darkness, the 1st gun missed a bridge which had only half a roadway and fell through. Two men of the crew were killed.

Oberleutnant Linke took over the battery in the area of Dno, and it was given a period for rest and refitting there. In May 1942 the battery went back into action from the bridgehead on the Staraja-Demjansk road to force a crossing of the Lowat and link up with II. Armee-Korps caught in the pocket. The Soviets had heavily mined this area as well. Two Sturmgeschütze hit mines. Oberleutnant Linke and Wachtmeister Schöller were put out of action by their wounds. Leutnant Nause, one of the section leaders, took over the battery.

The battery slipped into the pocket across the "underwater bridge" and along the almost 10-kilometer long "tunnel highway," a forced entry into the pocket.

Oberleutnant Feuerherd had taken over command of the battery. Once in the Demjansk Pocket, the battery was attached to Sturmgeschütz-Abteilung 184 as its 1st Battery. Sturmgeschütz-

Batterie 666 had lost its independent status.

Attached to various units, it then participated in the defensive fighting in the Waldai Heights. In June 1942 there was defensive fighting at the entrance to the "tunnel" at Hill 303. Some of the Sturmgeschütz crews were employed as infantry in the defensive line. Oberleutnant Feuerherd and Leutnant Nause were killed there. Oberleutnant Böhme took over the battery. He was severely wounded during an operation at the west side of the "tunnel." Unteroffizier Volle was killed.

A Leutnant (name unknown) took over the battery and also led it during the relief attacks carried out in August 1942 at Belli Bor toward Waldai. There two Sturmgeschütze managed to fight their way through to the surrounded German strong point and relieve it. One Sturmgeschütz sank into the swamp up to the top of its track guards. As the strong point could no longer be held, this gun had to be blown up. Along with the surrounded battalion, the crew fought its way back through to the German main battle line.

In September Oberleutnant Bischoff, the former battalion adjutant, took over the battery and led it during the hard defensive fighting east of Zemena. During a relief attack, the Sturmgeschütze ran into a swamp again and every Sturmgeschütz bogged down. It wasn't until night that the guns could be moved back to the main battle line thanks to the selfless activity of the recovery crews and covering infantry.

In November the battery fought west and east of Zemena in defensive actions and relief attacks. Snow drifts and snow-filled bomb craters hindered these operations. Unteroffiziere Volkmar and Nicolai were killed in these operations.

The Soviets attacked at Obschino shortly before Christmas. The 1st Battery, with one short-barreled gun, and the 2nd Battery, with one long-barreled gun, managed to halt a Russian tank attack there. Sturmgeschütz-Abteilung 184 had only these two operational Sturmgeschütze left. The short-barreled Sturmgeschütz from the former Sturmgeschütz-Batterie 666, destroyed eight tanks, some from only 20 meters away. At that point, a long-barreled gun of the 2nd Battery was put out of action. By 31 December the crew of the 1st Battery's famous gun had carried out 42 day and night operations. On 31 December, totally exhausted, the crew was relieved by a reserve crew. Twenty-four hours later the gun received a direct hit from a dug-in T-34 and exploded. None of the four men escaped alive.

At that point the 1st Battery was relieved and, at the beginning of February, Major Fischer, the commander of Sturmgeschütz-Abteilung 184, said farewell to this brave battery which headed back to Jüterbog in two freight trains. The battery was then deactivated. Most of the 80 surviving men were used as cadre for Sturmgeschütz-Abteilung 912, which was then being organized at Zinna. (See the entry for that formation for additional information.)

Sturmgeschütz-Batterie 667 (Sturmgeschütz-Abteilung 667; Sturmgeschütz-Brigade 667; and, Sturmartillerie-Brigade 667)

This battery was the last of the six independent batteries organized at Zinna during the summer of 1940. Oberleutnant Lützow was battery commander. Its establishment was completed in July. This battery was also intended to be employed in "Operation Sea Lion." Sea loading exercises took place in many of the French Atlantic ports. The training program was full of landing and attack exercises, and the battery members were disappointed when they were sent back home at the end of 1940.

Sturmgeschütz-Batterie 667

At the Döberitz Troop Training Area additional exercises became this battery's daily bread. "Working with the infantry" was the most important part of its training schedule.

Then in March 1941 it was transferred into the Heilsberg District in East Prussia. Leutnant Nové was killed in a training accident there. Right before the beginning of the Russian Campaign the battery was put into the area of the 30. Infanterie-Division (General von Tippelskirch).

The battery crossed the German border at Memelwalde in the early morning hours of 22 June 1941 as the spearhead for the 30. Infanterie-Division. In long, tiring marches, with exhaustion, thirst, and dust constant companions, the battery pursued the retreating enemy across the Niewiaza towards Kedaniai. The fighting pursuit in east Lithuania and then in Latvia lasted until 7 July 1941. The Düna River was crossed at Liewenhof, and the battery received its real baptism of fire on 8 July, when it supported two divisions of the Waffen-SS in their assault on Sebesh, which was defended by the "Stalin Guards."

With considerable verve, the battery rolled up the enemy positions and put the Soviet strongpoints out of action. This was its first real success and it reinforced the confidence of the men of the Sturmartillerie in their new weapon.

Once again with its old division, the battery fought its way through the Stalin Line at Opotschka and immediately afterwards reached Noworshef. The battery was again successful in a major operational offensive against two Russian Corps which took place shortly thereafter.

From the commander to the lowest ranking cannoneer, every man had given it his all with spectacular élan and, after a few tiring days on the march, the battery ran into the forward defense lines of Staraja Russa south of Borok. From that time on, every meter of ground had to be wrung from the enemy in bitter fighting.

The first member of the battery to be killed in action was Leutnant Iser, who fell at Rwy. The fighting at Jewanova and Murajewa required additional sacrifice. Oberleutnant Gröper, who had won the Iron Cross, First Class for an especially dashing action at Jewanova, was killed three days later at Murajewa.

However, the battery's fighting spirit was intact and, after the Lowata River had been reached, the battery fought its way forward toward Leningrad. The crossing of the Luga was forced in a grandiose attack. On that same day many bunkers and enemy positions were put out of action and a number of tanks and guns destroyed. Oberwachtmeister Kurt Kirchner distinguished himself exceptionally in the fighting to cross the lake narrows northwest of Luga. Those operations raged between 19 and 27 August. He was the cliff in the sea when the Soviets attacked in eight waves, one after the other. These eight attacks were brought to a halt.

The battery moved forward on muddy roads in the pouring rain. Movement was especially difficult on a 15-kilometer-long corduroy road. Despite these difficulties the battery was able to surmount them once again. The belt of fortifications around Leningrad came appreciably nearer.

The breakthrough through the Ishora position took place during the period from 12 to 15 September. The city of Sluzk fell into the battery's hands. Oberleutnant Lützow rolled through the enemy in a bold and sudden attack. Russian tanks opposing him were smashed and enemy positions rolled under. In this manner, the Oberleutnant, who rode at the head of his Sturmgeschütze, chewed his way through to the neighboring division and laid the groundwork for the Russian defeat.

For this selfless and decisive action, Oberleutnant Lützow received the Knight's Cross on 4 November 1941. The battery was placed in reserve for a few days in the Leningrad area. For the first time in months, the men had a roof over their heads. But on 26 September it was back again to hard, relentless combat.

The battle at the outskirts of Leningrad lasted until 8 December. Enemy forces, fighting with desperate courage in an attempt to break the German grip, had to be beaten off again and again. The battery was primarily engaged in duels with Russian T-34 tanks during this fighting. Oberwachtmeister Kirchner showed himself to be a world-class tank killer there, destroying more than 30 enemy tanks. On 9 March 1942 he was awarded the Knight's Cross.

At the end of November 1941, Oberleutnant Lützow was transferred to Jüterbog. His successor was Oberleutnant Bruno Lange, formerly a section leader.

On 9 December the battery was transferred to the north of Wolchow. There at Wolchow, in the pitiless cold of this terrible winter, the battery defended against Soviet forces attacking in greatly superior numbers. No member of the Einhornkopf-Batterie ("Unicorn" Battery) will ever forget the villages of Mga, Maluska, Sant Pogostiege and Schala. This battle for their very existence is indelibly burned into their memories.

The battery's trains were also employed as infantry. On 1 January 1942, as the mercury in the thermometers showed a low of 52 degrees below zero Celsius and with inadequate winter clothing, the battery suffered casualties from frostbite. But thanks to the tireless efforts of its officers, these losses were kept within bounds.

The battery was attached to the XXVII. Armee-Korps. Sturmgeschütz-Abteilung 185 under Hauptmann Krafft was temporarily in action near the battery. Both Sturmartillerie units were attached to Oberst Losch (later the defender of Breslau).

By the end of March this unforgettable, bloody operation was over. The battery, decimated but unbroken, was pulled out of action. Twenty of its soldiers had been killed in action, and fifty men had been wounded. Along with the two who had been decorated with the Knight's Cross, 11 soldiers of the battery had won the Iron Cross, First Class and 62 the Iron Cross, Second Class.

Sturmgeschütz-Batterie 667 returned to Zinna. At Zinna it became the 1st Battery of the newly formed Sturmgeschütz-Abteilung 667, which was on its way back to the Eastern Front in July of that same year. On 14 February 1944 Sturmgeschütz-Abteilung 667 was redesignated as Sturmgeschütz-Brigade 667. On 10 June of the same year it was renamed once again: Sturmartillerie-Brigade 667. No information is available concerning the activities of the battalion/brigade other than that it was employed in the area of operations of the 4. Armee in June 1944. In December 1944 it participated in the Ardennes Offensive and saw the end of the war in the vicinity of Landau.

Sturmgeschütz-Batterien 741 and 742

At the end of 1942 Generaloberst Dietl had expressed a desire to the German Army High Command for Sturmgeschütz units to strengthen his Lapland Army operating in the far north. The Generaloberst had been hearing more and more good things about the amazing success of Sturmgeschütze in Russia and wanted to get a few of these powerful combat weapons for his own army.

The German Army High Command respected the wishes of this great soldier, but stipulated the condition that the batteries provided had to be supplied exclusively by the Lapland Army.

So in January 1943, volunteers for the Sturmgeschütze were sought in the Lapland Army. Personnel organization was to begin on 30 January 1943. Volunteers were transferred to Jüterbog throughout the spring, where courses were held for everybody. Hauptmann Peter Nebel, an experienced officer, was the chief instructor there. He was a well-versed and experienced Sturmartillerie man and born for the job.

During the summer these men were organized into two Sturmgeschütz batteries, which were numbered 741 and 742. Oberleutnant Kleybold was commander of Sturmgeschütz-Batterie 742. The other officers in both batteries were entirely Austrian.

That same summer, both batteries were sent together by ship from Gotenhafen to northern Finland. The batteries were unloaded at Uleoborg. From there the batteries went by land march to Kuusamo, the staging area for the Lapland Army's southern sector.

Sturmgeschütz-Batterien 741 and 742 road marched nearly 500 kilometers in all to Kuusamo and Kokossalmi on the road to Kiestinki. Once there, the batteries were transferred to the rear area of the XVIII. Gebirgs-Korps, the Louhi sector, on the Murmansk-Leningrad railroad line.

Both batteries were inspected by Generaloberst Dietl on 17 July 1943. Very pleased to then have this rolling "artillery" also at his disposal, the Commander-in-Chief of the Far North even climbed into a Sturmgeschütz and had everything explained to him.

Aside from repelling a few Soviet commando operations and a few Soviet air attacks, the guns saw no other action. After a conference with Oberst Hoffmann-Schoenborn at the Sturmgeschütz-Schule, Hauptmann Bauer, commander of both batteries, managed to arrange for both batteries to be sent overland to Oulu from northern Finland, where they were, in Hauptmann Bauer's words, "as superfluous as a goiter." Loaded onto the train there, they reached Turku at the end of September. On 3 October they were loaded on a freighter at Turku and transported to Danzig, where they were unloaded on 7 October at the Neufahrwasser harbor.

The Sturmgeschütz men remained in Danzig until 11 October. At that time, Sturmgeschütz-Batterie 742 was sent to the Aufstellungsstab West at Tours in France. There its personnel were incorporated into the staff or served as personnel replacements in the formation of additional Sturmgeschütz units. Sturmgeschütz-Batterie 741, on the other hand, was rail loaded to Wirballen via Königsberg and then sent from there to Wilna. It was allocated to the recently raised 18. Artillerie-Division under General Toholte for special missions. The mission of the artillery division, the first of its kind in the German Army, was to stop operational-level attacks of the enemy by firing an overpowering, simultaneous barrage on command to smash a breach in the enemy front or to put a stop to an enemy tank attack in progress.

The divisional fire control officer sat in an armored vehicle resembling a tank with his radio and direction gear as a forward observer. Since he was exposed to enemy fires and could be in considerable danger—his vehicle carried only a dummy cannon—he was supposed to get a Sturmgeschütz section as a security escort. The section leader's Sturmgeschütz was to serve as an alternate forward observation post, and was provided with an additional built-in 30 watt medium wave radio transmitter, so that if the artillery observer was put out of action, the section leader himself could give fire missions and targeting instructions.

Exercises in the area of Wilna showed that this was possible. Despite that, the concept was never put into practice.

The 18. Artillery Division was ordered into action on 3 December 1943. The Sturmgeschütze were sent by rail via Wilna-Kowel and Berditschew to Kasatin in the Ukraine. On 7 December they unloaded in the icy cold and marched overland to Biala-Zerkow south of Kiev. Things were quiet there until 23 December.

There was an alert until the following day. A strong armored spearhead of the Red Army had broken through in the sector of the 25. Panzer-Division. It rolled over those elements of the 18. Artillery Division already committed. Terrible tragedies unfolded in the fighting between the untrained artillerymen and the enemy tanks.

Sturmgeschütz-Batterie 741 was cut off on 25 December. It had been given orders to engage the tanks. They stood against the Russian armored steam roller along with a battalion of Panzergrenadiere and an army Flak battalion. They destroyed a few T-34's in intensive fighting, but one Sturmgeschütz was lost. On 30 December Hauptmann Bauer was killed in another such duel. Leutnant Weckerlein then took over the battery. During the course of the fighting that day his Sturmgeschütz was also hit and Leutnant Weckerlein was wounded. His gunner was killed on the spot.

At that point Leutnant Dörfeld sprang into the breach and withdrew the Sturmgeschütze in the general direction of Pikowez. The guns established combat outposts on the north edge of the village. A Panzergrenadier battalion and a few "Wespen" ("Wasps": self-propelled 10.5 cm howitzers) and three "Hummel" ("Bumble Bees": self-propelled 15 cm howitzers) were there at their side.

On 30 December when mounted Russian troops, their saber-swinging officers in front, attacked across the completely bare ground, they fell in the rain of fire from these guns and a few additional infantry pieces.

Everything that could still move rolled back like a thunderously increasing avalanche. The attack was repelled before the enemy could even get within hand-grenade range.

When the battery was celebrating New Year's Eve, the festivities were suddenly interrupted by loud engine noise and the rattling tracks of Russian tanks. T-34's raced through the village in the dark night, firing from every barrel. Seconds later, the chaos was multiplied threefold by the fire from the Sturmgeschütze, Hummeln and Wespen.

Unteroffizier Krüger saw a T-34 directly in front of his gun, as big as a barn door and impossible to miss. One shot took its turret off. A little later the battalion command post of the Panzergrenadiere was in flames , but the enemy was repulsed after a few more vehicles were knocked out by the Sturmgeschütze. Only their burning tanks gave light to this ghostly picture from a nightmare.

The Sturmgeschütze saw action against enemy tanks at Tutscha as the fighting continued. On 24 January there was a major enemy tank attack along a broad front at Priluka-Staraya. Stukas and Luftwaffe fighters joined battle against these enemy forces and brought some relief.

Then there were more defensive operations, fighting withdrawals at Pogrebischtsche, and the retreat across the Bug at Petschara. A 24-ton Sturmgeschütz crashed through a 12-ton bridge built by the combat engineers. The crew was saved after a cold bath.

That was followed by the march through Bessarabia in March 1944. The battery crossed the Dnjestr at Mogilew-Podolsk. The retreat continued through northern Rumania to Cernowitz.

On 29 March the battery was instructed to punch their way through to the 1. Panzer-Armee at Kamenez-Podolsk. The Sturmgeschütze made it into the pocket which held the army. They found supply units—kilometers long—which had been shot to pieces by the Russian tanks.

The battery moved with the "wandernde Kessel" ("wandering pocket") which continued to pull back under General Walther K. Nehring. It weathered a snowstorm which lasted for three days. It was supplied by air by Ju-52's, and then also by landing Ju-52's which carried emergency resupply. The battery lost gun after gun. Then, on Easter Sunday 9 April 1944, just before breaking out of the pocket at the Strypa, the last two Sturmgeschütze were hit by rounds from Russian antitank rifles. They exploded because they were stuffed full of ammunition. There were three dead and five severely wounded. Leutnant Weckerlein was among the dead.

The remnants of the battery were used as a corps reserve in various cities from 11 April to 18 April 1944, before the remaining equipment had to be given up on 18 April.

The personnel of Sturmgeschütz-Batterie traveled through Sandomirz and Breslau right across Germany to Saarbrücken, where they were able to rest through Pentecost.

Sturmgeschütz-Batterie 741 was refitted in a perfunctory manner and was employed in Normandy when the fighting erupted on 6 June 1944. In Normandy it was attached to Sturmgeschütz-Brigade 394 in the area of Azay. Sturmgeschütz-Brigade 394 had just been formed and still didn't have any Sturmgeschütze. Sturmgeschütz-Batterie 741 was dissolved on 19 June 1944 and its personnel apparently incorporated into Sturmgeschütz-Brigade 394. (See also the history of Sturmgeschütz-Brigade 394.)

Sturmgeschütz-Lehr-Batterie 901

When the situation of the 6. Armee (Generaloberst Paulus) began to turn critical in Stalingrad, Artillerie-Lehr-Regiment (mot.) 2 at Jüterbog received orders to form a Sturmgeschütz battery immediately. Hauptmann Alfred Müller volunteered at once for this dangerous duty with his 8. Lehr-Batterie.

The battery was mobilized on 15 December 1942 and renamed Sturmgeschütz-Lehr-Batterie 901. It selected a wind mill as its insignia.

The battery was completely equipped with new weapons, equipment and vehicles within a very short time. The "Wind Mill" Battery was sent to Infanterie-Lehr-Reg-iment (mot.) 901 (Oberst Scholze) and moved by priority transport to the focal point of the fighting at Stalingrad in the great bend of the Don.

Sturmgeschütz-Lehr-Batterie 901

Sturmgeschütz-Lehr-Batterie 901, formed recently out of thin air, fought for weeks while attached to the 19. Panzer-Division and Infanterie-Lehr-Regiment (mot.) 901. It fought with exceptional bravery and scored heavily against the enemy.

The battery engaged the enemy in intensive rear guard actions during the retreat of the XXXXVIII. Armee-Korps. It was surrounded and fought its way out through the encircling enemy forces. The battery relieved surrounded Kampfgruppen, and fought with an aggressive spirit that was beyond all praise.

Other units and Kampfgruppen were continually attached to Hauptmann Müller. These units fought together with his Sturmgeschütze and provided a substantial addition to his fighting power.

Names such as Nowo-Strelzowka, Belowdsk, Starobjelsk (where Infanterie-Lehr-Regiment (mot.) 901 also fought shoulder to shoulder with the battery), Werchneje, Belaja-Gora and Rudnik-Solotoi will be forever connected with the operations and successes of this battery. Hauptmann Müller received the Knight's Cross on 20 February 1943.

At the end of March Hauptmann Müller turned over this battery, which he had welded into an outstanding combat unit, to his successor, Oberleutnant Reich. But by the end of April, the battery was ordered back to Jüterbog to become the 8. Lehr-Batterie again.

Independent Assault Gun Battalions and Brigades

selbständige Sturmgeschütz-Abteilungen und -Brigaden

Sturmgeschütz-Abteilung 177 (Sturmgeschütz-Brigade 177; Panzer-Jäger-Abteilung 69)

Sturmgeschütz-Brigade 177

Sturmgeschütz-Abteilung 177 was formed in the summer of 1941 at Zinna near Jüterbog. It adopted the griffin from the Pomeranian coat of arms as its battalion insignia. Activation was completed on 9 August 1941.

On 9 August 1941, the battalion staff and command was:

Commander : Hauptmann Freiherr von Fahrenheim

Adjutant: Leutnant Burgschat

Battery Commanders:

Headquarters Battery: Oberleutnant Wein

1st Battery: Oberleutnant Matzat

2nd Battery: Oberleutnant Rohde

3rd Battery: Oberleutnant Nebel

The battalion loaded up for transport to the east by rail on 6 September. Four days later it was unloaded at Smolensk. The 4. Armee-Oberkommando allocated the battalion which was a general headquarters unit to the XII. Armee-Korps. In turn, it was attached to the 34., 98. and 267. Infanterie-Divisionen and to the 19. Panzer-Division.

The Desna River was crossed in the course of these operations on 2 October. Following that, the advance began south of the Roslawl-Moscow highway. Way stations of this advance were the towns and villages of Roslawl, Spas Demskoje, Juchno and Tarutino. There was hard fighting at Tarutino and Nedel-Noje, where the entire battalion fought for its very life. The battalion then moved through Borowsk to reach Kosselskaja, right in front of the gates of Moscow. The enemy defended himself there with a stubbornness not yet encountered. The battalion losses were alarming. The terrible winter with temperatures down to 50° degrees below zero Celsius were a contributing factor.

Oberleutnant Nebel distinguished himself again and again with his battery before the gates of Moscow. He smashed into Soviet attacks with savage counterattacks. Hauptmann von Fahrenheim recommended him for the Knight's Cross, and he received this award on 2 April 1942.

After being wounded, Oberleutnant Nebel gave up his battery to Leutnant Korf, who was promoted to Oberleutnant on the same day. After a short employment as infantry at Spas Demskoje, the 3rd Battery was transferred to Witebsk for city security. Hauptmann von Fahrenheim left the battalion at Spas Demskoje. Major Käppler took command. Oberleutnant Matzat was killed at Spas Demskoje. Oberleutnant Koch took his place.

The entire battalion was transferred to Mogilew in March 1942. At Mogilew, the battalion turned in its short-barreled Sturmgeschütze for long-barreled ones. The battalion received a complete refitting at the same time.

In March 1942 the entire battalion was moved to Bjelgorod and, in the last days of June, a major operational offensive was launched through the Russian winter positions toward Woronesh. The battalion was attached to the 168. Infanterie-Division, which was attacking under General Kraiss as a part of the summer offensive. The attack was a great success. In his Order of the Day for 7 July 1942, General Kraiss stated, among other things, that:

All elements of the division can share the credit for the victorious conclusion of this destructive battle for Woronesh. It was our trusty comrades of Sturmgeschütz-Abteilung 177 which cleared the way—shoulder to shoulder—with Infanterie-Regiment 417...The decisive action was carried out by Aufklärungs-Abteilung 248 along with the attached elements from Panzer-Jäger-Abteilung 248, a battery from Sturmgeschütz-Abteilung 177 and a platoon of the 3./Pionier-Bataillon 175, all under the exemplary leadership of their commander, Rittmeister Heyrowski, who was killed in action.

The battalion was employed in the advance to the great bend of the Don in the course of the follow-on fighting and took part in the positional warfare there with considerable success. Oberleutnant Korf, who up to then had led the 3rd Battery, was killed at the end of July. A round from a Russian antitank rifle passed through his Sturmgeschütz from the side. The round killed him.

After rest and refitting, the battalion staff and command positions were filled as follows:

Commander: Hauptmann Hilgers

Adjutant: Oberleutnant Trispel

Orderly Officer: Leutnant Heinzle

Battery Commanders:

Headquarters Battery: Oberleutnant Fiegl

1st Battery: Hauptmann. Schmidt

2nd Battery: Hauptmann Zitzen

3rd Battery: Oberleutnant Kleinknecht

At the end of August, the battalion moved out once more. It played a considerable role in establishing a bridgehead across the Don north of Kalatsch. Fighting, it stormed all the way into the city of Stalingrad and, as the fighting in that city developed, it was placed in blocking positions to the north. Then, at the beginning of November, it was moved into winter rest positions at Jewlampiesky on the west bank of the Don.

Meanwhile, Oberleutnant Mai had been transferred to Sturmgeschütz-Abteilung 177 on 27 October 1942 in Schweinfurt. He arrived in Tschir on 4 November 1942, and then continued on through Karpowka to Gorodischtsche, the battalion command post, by truck. There he reported in to Major Bochum, who had relieved the severely ill Major Käppler a few days earlier.

On 8 November Oberleutnant Mai led the battery of 15 cm heavy self-propelled infantry guns sent from the German High Command against the enemy positions at Spartakowka. On 11 November the battalion was assigned directly to 6. Armee and was ordered to examine possibilities for operations with the Rumanian 1st Cavalry Division, the 376. Infanterie-Division and the 76. Infanterie-Division. The battalion staff, 2nd Battery and 3rd Battery moved to Jewlampiesky in the great bend of the Don. It was intended they would be used there in the upcoming defensive fighting.

Oberleutnant Mai was assigned to the operations officer of the 6. Armee as a liaison officer and went immediately to Golubinsky on the west bank of the Don. There, Oberstleutnant Echlepp, the operations officer of the 6. Armee, gave him orders for the battalion. The estimate of the situation given by the operations officer was extraordinarily favorable. Through 17 November the Soviets made their preparations at Kletschkaja and Beketowka south of Stalingrad. Sturmgeschütz-Abteilung 177 occupied its ready positions.

On 18 November, the battalion staff and command positions were filled as follows:

Headquarters:

Battalion Commander: Hauptmann Bochum

Special staff duties: Oberleutnant Mai

Adjutant: Leutnant Wibel

Supply Officer: Leutnant Stobernack

Unit Surgeon: Assistenz-Arst Dr. Rhomberg

Paymaster: Oberzahlmeister Rhode

Headquarters Battery: Oberleutnant Schubert

1st Battery: Oberleutnant Koch

Section Leaders: Leutnant Dittmann, Leutnant Siebenbürger, Leutnant Kirsch, Leutnant Eisel von Eislingen

2nd Battery: Hauptmann Rhode

Section Leaders: Leutnant Münchmeyer, Leutnant Baier, Wachtmeister (Offizieranwärter) Deibert

3rd Battery: Oberleutnant Niederprün

Section Leaders: Leutnant Sparn, Leutnant Frank, Leutnant Weinhold, Leutnant Vost

On 19 November the Russian operational attack began. Its goal: Cut off the 6. Armee. By evening the army had been surrounded. The Soviets were successful in breaking through the positions of the Rumanian 1st Cavalry Division south of Kletschkaja. Sturmgeschütz-Abteilung 177 was immediately attached to the 14. Panzer-Division and was put into action south of Kletschkaja. A Russian cavalry regiment which had overrun the German combat outpost line on 21 November was annihilated in a counterattack. The Sturmgeschütze totally crippled this enemy attack. On the next day they also managed to repulse a Russian infantry attack in a snowstorm.

The battalion shifted further to the east towards the Don crossings and was attached to the 24. Panzer-Division in the areas of Wertschtschj and Pesskowatka.

The desperate battle of the 6. Armee was in full progress and with it, that of Sturmgeschütz-Abteilung 177. After pulling back to the east bank of the Don, the bridges were blown up on 27 November. The day before the 3rd Battery, under Oberleutnant Niederprün, had destroyed 5 T-34's and damaged two others on the Don Heights road, when the Russians attacked the bridgehead with tanks.

On 28 November the battalion covered the withdrawal of the forces streaming out of the Don bend to the new defense lines. On the next day the new main battle line along the pocket's front was occupied. The battalion was attached to the 44. Infanterie-Division at Barbukin.

Up to the end of 1942 the battalion distinguished itself repeatedly by the number of tanks it destroyed in the fierce defensive fighting. The battle for Hill 124.5, which changed hands several times, was some of the bitterest fighting on this sector of the front, and the battalion lost most of its guns. On 31 December 1942, only 6 Sturmgeschütze were still operational.

By the time the Russian surrender terms were rejected by General Paulus on 5 January 1943, Sturmgeschütz-Abteilung 177, along with Infanterie-Regimenter 131, 132 and 134 of the 44. Infanterie-Division (Hoch- und Deutschmeister), had put some costly fighting behind them. On 9 January the last four Sturmgeschütze stood in desperate, bloody combat in the deep snow at the Kotluban railroad station. These last four guns were commanded by Oberleutnant Mai, Leutnant Kirsch, and two Wachtmeister. They inflicted heavy losses on the enemy.

Again on 10 January these four Sturmgeschütze destroyed numerous T-34's and armored personnel carriers. But two of the guns were lost to direct hits and their entire crews were killed. The Sturmgeschütz of Oberleutnant Mai was then put out of action by a hit on the drive sprocket. Oberleutnant Mai was badly wounded while fighting bravely with his crew as infantry.

Leutnant Kirsch was still fighting with the last gun on the collective farm at Saponwjewka. What this gun accomplished bordered on the incredible. This single gun repeatedly managed to bring the Russians to a halt. But then, it too fell prey to the Russian rounds. Oberleutnant Mai reached the main field hospital at Bolsche-Rossoschka. And then, on 21 January 1943, he was flown out of the pocket from Gumrak Air Field and transferred to the hospital at Swerewo near Rostow.

However, the battalion had been destroyed at Stalingrad. The surviving members of the batteries had set up in a cellar on Red Square. They were made prisoners on 31 January 1943. There were still about 40 men left who started off to the east.

The few surviving members of the battalion who had been flown wounded out of Stalingrad were assigned to Sturmgeschütz-Ersatz-Abteilung 300 at Neiße (Upper Silesia), and then transferred to the newly formed Sturmgeschütz-Abteilung 911 at Wildflecken. This battalion was then renamed as Sturmgeschütz-Abteilung 177. This was the third time that the battalion had been formed.

Right before Easter, it was dispatched to the bend in the Orel and fought at Smyjewka, Krasmy-Gorka and Glebowsky. It was involved in fierce fighting at Nikolskoje. Oberleutnant Zitzen led the battalion. He received the Knight's Cross on 7 August 1943 after costly fighting and operations, especially in the areas of Briansk and Kursk. Shortly thereafter, he was promoted to Hauptmann.

The battalion pulled back to the west through Drobruwka, Pistosch and Orel. Hauptmann Zitzen led the battalion through all the tribulations of the withdrawal. It reached the area around Wilna in the winter of 1943/44, where it again had a period of rest and refitting. As the defensive fighting continued, the battalion fought its way into the area west of Bialystock at Ostrolenka. Hauptmann Hillgers took over the battalion there. On 17 February 1944 the battalion was redesignated as a brigade and, on 9 August 1944, the battalion was reconstituted as Panzer-Jäger-Abteilung 69 and attached to the 3. Kavallerie-Brigade, which had asked for an armored unit.

Only a few days later, on 24 August 1944, the brigade commander, Oberstleutnant von Boeselager, was killed in action at Ostrolenka-Lomscha.

After more fighting in the areas of Augustow–Rominterheide-Goldap, the 3. Kavallerie-Brigade was transferred to Hungary at the beginning of December, 1944. Panzer-Jäger-Abteilung 69 was unloaded in Nagykaniza on 6 December 1944 and took part in the Budapest-Stuhlweißenburg offensive. The entire battalion was frequently in action with fewer than 10 Sturmgeschütze. At Many, on 4 February 1945, a Sturmgeschütz of the 2nd Battery Panzer-Jäger-Abteilung 69 under Gunner Unteroffizier Willi Dolle destroyed a T-34. This was the 750th tank destroyed by the battalion. Then there were the attacks on Hill 193 on 5 and 8 February 1945. The battalion pulled back continuously.

By the end of March, the battalion had reached Steiermark (Austria). For the men of Panzer-Jäger-Abteilung 69, the end of the war came at Wagna and at Leibnitz an der Murbrücke. Then they fled through the mountain ranges to Mauerkirchen. There were still some 70 men from Panzer-Jäger-Abteilung 69 and they were led by the commander of the 2nd Battery in an exemplary manner until they reached the POW camps.

Sturmgeschütz-Abteilung 184 (Sturmgeschütz-Brigade 184; Heeres-Sturmartillerie-Brigade 184)

Heeres-Sturmartillerie-Brigade 184

In the late summer of 1940, due to the considerable success achieved by the independent batteries employed during the French Campaign, Sturmgeschütz-Abteilung 184 was activated at the village of Zinna near Jüterbog as the first battalion in the Sturmartillerie and provided with six Sturmgeschütze with the short 7.5 cannon per battery.

Command and Staff Positions During the Existence of the Organization (incomplete):

Commander: Major Steinkopf (†), Oberstleutnant Will-Eugen Fischer (†), Major Ernst Schmidt (†)

Headquarters Battery Commander: Oberleutnant Adam (†), Oberleutnant Nebel

1st Battery Commander: Oberleutnant Buck (†), Oberleutnant Feuerherd (†), Oberleutnant Bischoff, Oberleutnant Ostheim (†)

2nd Battery Commander: Oberleutnant Steinau (†), Oberleutnant Hohenhausen, Oberleutnant Buchweiser

3rd Battery Commander: Oberleutnant von Barisani, Oberleutnant Schuster (†), Oberleutnant Hellmich, Oberleutnant Tornau, Oberleutnant Seth, Oberleutnant Pfaffendorf (†)

Battalion-Arzt: Stabsarzt von der Heyde

Administrator: Kriegsverwaltungsrat Wallishauser

Paymaster: Oberzahlmeister Koch

Shop Foreman: Werkmeister Koberstein

Other officers who were assigned to varying positions and sometimes at different ranks were:

Leutnant Hans-Gottfried Fischer, Leutnant Pfeiffer (†),Oberleutnant Fratt, Oberleutnant Phillip, Oberleutnant Gaschütz (†), Leutnant Pietschmann (†), Oberleutnant Granitza (†), Leutnant Pöll (†), Leutnant Haegele (†), Leutnant Rausch (†), Leutnant Kunad, Leutnant Schöne, Leutnant Lechens, Leutnant Schulze, Leutnant Malzan, Leutnant Stock (†), Leutnant Nagel (†), Leutnant Wagner (†), Leutnant Naumann, Leutnant Wirth, Leutnant Negele

Symbol: † = KIA

After activation was completed the battalion was transferred to France at the end of September 1940. At the beginning of January 1941 it was transferred to Kolmar in the Warthegau. Just a few weeks later, the battalion was moved to Austria on the Yugoslavian border because of changes in the general situation.

It went into action in Yugoslavia with Heeresgruppe Weichs. The battalion, whose insignia was a sword emerging from flames, crossed the Drau and Unna Rivers. Passing through Marburg and Agram, it reached Banja Luka and only saw minor action. The technical experience gathered, however, was of great importance for later use.

After a short rest period in Judenburg in Styria (Austria), the 184. Battalion was moved to Lötzen in a five-day train trip. Additional training was received at the Arys Training Camp.

The battalion passed through Chocki and Michakowska to reach its area of operations, the Suwalki District. From there, in the early morning hours of 22 June 1941, under its second commander, Will-Eugen Fischer, it joined the attack on the Soviet Union on the right wing of Heeresgruppe Nord.

There were some heavy fighting and remarkable distances covered on the march through Grodno, Welish, Lida, Witebsk, Smolensk and Toropez. The tank battle at Grodno can be cited here as an example; in only a few hours nearly 70 enemy tanks were destroyed, practically all by the 1st Battery.

Oberleutnant Pfeiffer was shot through the chest and upper arm and badly wounded while crossing the Wolkoschanka River. On 23 June the bunkers of the Soviet border line at Sopockinin were taken in cooperation with Infanterie-Regiment 49. Three days later, Unteroffizier Nowak, gun commander in the 3rd Battery, was killed by a round through the heart while reloading main gun ammunition.

On 28 June the battalion was attached to the 28. Infanterie-Division in Prawa-Mosty. Incorporated in the advance guard, it reached Orla on 30 June. On 6 July it was released from its attachment. A few days later it was attached to the 18. Infanterie-Division and, on 7 July, the battalion crossed the Düna with the division on a pontoon bridge.

When the enemy managed to penetrate into the position held by Infanterie-Regiment 51, the Sturmgeschütze sealed off this penetration in a counterattack. Wachtmeister Häussler, gun commander in the 1st Battery, was killed on 15 July at Antropowo. It reached Welish on 20 July. On this evening the 3rd Battery, advancing far ahead, managed to destroy a Russian battery, 7 tanks and 3 antitank guns. On the evening of 21 July the battalion, along with the II. Infanterie-Regiment 51 managed to take the village of Wassiwolicz and destroyed an ammunition dump at the Lomonossowo Railroad Station.

On 30 July Oberleutnant Steinau received the Iron Cross, First Class.

A Sturmgeschütz ran onto a mine on the Smolensk battlefield and was rendered immobile. It was blown up by Russian artillery. Cholm was reached on 9 August. Oberleutnant Nebel left the battalion at Cholm to take command of a newly-formed battery in Germany. He had been the replacement for Oberleutnant Adam, the former commander of the Headquarters Battery, who had also been transferred.

The Sturmgeschütze with the flaming sword insignia passed through Ussenyj by way of Demidowo, Welish and Teterewny. Then they were given a few days of rest. The new attack was launched from the assembly area at Glamasdy on 22 August 1941. At 1000 hours, Kotoba, the attack objective, was reached. The Sturmgeschütze advanced to Pynjki along with the advance guard of the 102. Infanterie-Division The units dug in there, in an all-round defensive position.

In spite of continuous Soviet air attacks, lead elements reached the railroad line from Welikije Luki to Toropez in the vicinity of the village of Bubnowa on 23 August. The combat engineers blew up the line in two places. Oberleutnant Steinau, who was driving in a command vehicle ahead of his battery, was killed at Trubizy, shot through the head by a sniper.

On 25 August the enemy attempted to break out of the pocket at Welikije Luki. The Sturmgeschütze of Sturmgeschütz-Abteilung 184 broke up the breakout attempt. Thirty-nine enemy trucks were destroyed. One gun received a direct hit when 5 Russian Martin bombers (Translator: US-built A-20 "Havoc" twin-engine medium bombers) attacked the Sturmgeschütze as they withdrew to Bubnowa on 26 August. Unteroffizier Hoffmann was killed.

The Sturmgeschütze advanced to Toropez as advance guard under the 102. Infanterie-Division There the guns were overhauled, to the extent possible in Russia. On 12 September a Sturmgeschütz was put out of action there by a direct hit in a Russian surprise artillery barrage. Leutnant Rausch and Gefreiter Artmann, Gefreiter Leiß, Gefreiter Stracke and Gefreiter Stabenow were wounded.

An order was issued on 10 October 1941 for the transfer of the battalion to Treuenbrietzen near Jüterbog for refitting. It was worn out, especially its materiél. Only the 1st Battery remained behind.

On 16 January 1942 the battalion received new orders to go back into action. The following day it started by rail from Jüterbog to Porchow, which it reached six days later.

A Sturmgeschütz fell from a bridge on the march from Porchow to the front. Unteroffizier Thiemau was killed. The battalion moved back to Cholm along the highway. Cholm was to be relieved. Kampfgruppe Scherer was completely surrounded by the Soviets.

The battalion reached Bor Grjada in varied fighting and pushed its attack on Cholm along both sides of the highway. The Sturmgeschütz of Leutnant Schöne received a direct hit during the attack on 9 March 1942. Leutnant Schöne, Unteroffizier Prischnegg and Unteroffizier Höhne were killed; Gefreiter Hausmann, the driver, was severely wounded. On the following day the Sturmgeschütz of Oberleutnant Schuster was destroyed. The Oberleutnant and two of his crew were killed. This left the 3rd Battery without a commander. The Sturmgeschütz of Leutnant Tornau was also knocked out on the same day, during the continuing attack to relieve Cholm. Within three days there were four direct hits. The fourth direct hit was a 17.2 cm dud, which smashed through the front armor like glass but, luckily for the crew, remained unexploded inside.

The badly battered 3rd Battery was relieved by the 2nd Battery. The attack on Cholm had to be delayed. The recovery section managed to recover the Sturmgeschütze of Tornau and Schöne. Schuster's gun which was located further forward, however, had to be given up, as the Soviets had already reached that point.

On 27 March Leutnant Granitza smashed a Russian battalion in its assembly area north of the Savina-Szopki road with two Sturmgeschütze.

Enemy pressure from the south increased. The woods on the right bank of the Lowat at point 56.3 and the "Pumpkin" and "Bear" Woods were full of Russians. Sturmgeschütz-Abteilung 184 placed these woods under fire. In reply, the Soviet artillery units fired at the German assembly areas.

On 1 April the Soviets attacked. In this phase of the fighting, the Sturmgeschütze were also used for indirect fire on the "Bear" Woods to prepare for the friendly planned attack. At 1400 hours the German infantry reached its attack objective. On 9 April the woods at Point 56.3 had to be given up once again. Along with Infanterie-Regiment 41 (Oberst Trumm) the Sturmgeschütze immediately regained the woods in a counterattack. On 20 April 1942 Oberwachtmeister Bock was killed in Szopki by a sniper's bullet. A thaw set in and with it, the mud season.

On 2 May Oberleutnant Buchweiser carried out an attack with two Sturmgeschütze on the "Herald's Clearing" north of Dubrowo. It was taken. The Soviets tried everything to capture Cholm and defeat the German defenders. In the meantime, 8,000 shells for the Sturmgeschütze had arrived in Dubrowo. Enough fuel had been brought up as well. The beginning of the attack for the relief of Cholm was set for 3 May 1942.

The clock showed exactly 1100 hours on 3 May 1942 when 5 Sturmgeschütze of the 2nd and 2 Sturmgeschütze of the 3rd Battery left Savina. It was raining in buckets when these guns reached the Pronino Woods and every gun fired into them. Oberleutnant Buchweiser fought two enemy tanks, which were destroyed. The Sturmgeschütze of Oberleutnant Granitza, Leutnant Negele and Oberwachtmeister Meyer remained in the belt of Russian mines between the bank of the Lowat and the highway, but they were brought back into action. The fighting for the

Pronino Woods lasted two hours. As a result, the stretch of land between the Lowat and the highway was firmly in German hands.

The attack was continued on the following day. Leutnant Pietschmann set a T-34 on fire in the "Panzer" Woods, and the remaining enemy tanks pulled back. Unteroffizier Welslau was killed by a round through the heart while trying to rescue a wounded comrade.

Oberleutnant Hohenhausen fired signal rounds when the Soviets were putting down smoke at the same time as German He 111's and Ju 88's were joining the battle. However, while in the process of doing that the trigger of the flare pistol caught on the scissors binoculars. The flare shot out and burned Hohenhausen's left hand, and set fire to the gun's camouflage. Obergefreiter Hambauer, who belonged to the gun crew, dismounted and put out the fires. Hohenhausen gave command of the gun to Oberwachtmeister Hönike but remained with his battery.

At 1200 hours the Kusemkino defile was cleared. The infantry worked its way forward under the protective fire of the Sturmgeschütze. As the bridge over the defile had been destroyed, the Sturmgeschütze worked their way 300 meters further north to the shallower edge of the defile. There Unteroffizier Hildebrandt was badly wounded by a splinter from a German bomb which fell into the defile.

The attack on Cholm was resumed at 0500 hours on 5 May 1942. One and a half hours later, the Sturmgeschütze reached the edge of the city of Cholm. After being under siege for 105 days, the city was once again free. Oberleutnant Hohenhausen, as commander of the Sturmgeschütze employed there, received the Knight's Cross of the Iron Cross.

On 6 May Leutnant Pietschmann was killed by a direct hit of a Ratschbum on the lens of his panoramic sight.

From January to May 1942 Sturmgeschütz-Abteilung 184 had covered only 84 kilometers in bitter fighting. The graves of fallen Sturmartilleristen were scattered across this sector of the Eastern Front.

In the early summer of 1942 the battalion was transferred to the Demjansk area. The Sturmgeschütze set up at the edge of the woods at Sdorowetz. In his first action Leutnant Stock had already destroyed two T-34's by 17 July 17. By 18 July the battalion had destroyed a total of 8 enemy tanks there.

On 3 August Oberstleutnant Fischer had to leave the battalion. He was transferred to Berlin. Every member of the battalion shook his hand in farewell. With Oberstleutnant Fischer, the battalion lost a commander who was honored and respected by all; but the battalion was pleased that he had been selected for service at a higher level. Major Schmidt took over command.

On 10 August there was heavy fighting in the area of Wassiljewschtschina. Two Sturmgeschütze received direct hits. Leutnant Rausch, who in the spring of 1942 had been the first soldier of the battalion to receive the German Cross in Gold, was killed while conducting reconnaissance for an operation when he drove into the middle of a Russian assembly area. The death of this lively and always good humored young officer affected everyone.

Leutnant Kunad destroyed three enemy tanks. On 24 August Oberleutnant Granitza also left the battalion.

The battalion had been attached to no fewer than 11 divisions in the course of that fighting. It fought successfully at every focal point of the Demjansk Fortress. During the attack on Rossino on 26 October, a new long barreled gun in the 2nd Battery received a direct hit from a 17.2 cm shell. Oberwachtmeister Meyer had just left the gun. Gefreiter Jost was immediately killed. Obergefreiter Grunwald was severely wounded. Unteroffizier Ehme was lightly wounded. The gun was torn apart by exploding ammunition. One day later, the battalion commander, Major Schmidt, was also wounded. Oberleutnant Ostheim, commander of the 1st Battery, was killed by an artillery round. Leutnant Nagel was killed on 4 November 1942.

Heavy Russian attacks began on 25 December. The Soviets had infiltrated the main line of battle at several points. The enemy attempted a breakthrough with tanks and flamethrowers. In the area of Sofronkowo on the morning of 1 January 1943, Unteroffizier Riss, with his long barreled Sturmgeschütz, and Unteroffizier Naumann, with his short-barreled Sturmgeschütz, were given a covering mission against enemy tanks in a blocking position 800 meters east of Sofronkowo. The after-action report of Unteroffizier Naumann follows here:

By order of the battalion commander, we took up our positions with the long-barreled gun to the right of the road, pointing east, and my short-barreled gun to the left of the road pointing north. The space between the two guns was about 100 meters. There was a rise between us, the forward-most point of our blocking position.

Up to 0930 hours there was comparative quiet, which was only broken by Russian mortar fire. In general, the Russians always attacked punctually at 1000 hours; and so it was now. Shortly after 0930 hours, all hell broke loose. Stalin organs, artillery, mortars, and white phosphorus rounds spread their devastation between us."

"Hatches shut!" ordered Unteroffizier Naumann.

Unteroffizier Riss was giving the same order at the same moment in his long-barreled Sturmgeschütz. The crews of the Sturmgeschütze sat for a full hour in their steel cans. Shells rained down, now closer, then farther away. Steel splinters splashed against the steel colossus. They all thought, "just don't lose your cool. It has to stop sometime."

Then it was quieter. Unteroffizier Naumann opened his hatch and looked out. At first he was unable to make anything out; everything was covered with thick smoke. He knew that from his position it was 400 meters to the edge of the woods. The enemy had to be somewhere in the swampy forest. He, Horst Naumann, the 21-year-old irrepressible Berliner, waited. He felt the same tension as during his first operation when, on 22 June, a loader, he rammed the first shell into the chamber. Up to this 1 January 1943 he had destroyed 15 enemy tanks. Would today see an addition to that list? Or would it be his turn today?

The commander let his gaze move back to the small knoll to the right of his position, which was 80 meters away. The enemy tanks would most likely appear there first. Suddenly he felt a warning. Wasn't that a...?

Yes, that was a tank turret that was rising up above the knoll. Then the hull appeared and the tank rolled rapidly closer.

"Turn to the right! Tanks coming!" Nauman yelled.

The first T-34 had climbed the knoll. The gunner had him in his sights. He adjusted his aim. The shot cracked out from the short barrel. Then a hard impact.

"Target!" reported the gun commander.

Then the gunner and loader worked as if possessed. The cannon spewed streaks of flame. The Russian crew tried to bail out of the first T-34. The hatches flew open. The T-34 was only 5 meters in front of the infantry lying on the reverse slope. Hand grenades and machine gun fire dropped the members of the escaping crew to the ground.

Now a second T-34 emerged. Four shots rang out from the short barrel. Then this T-34 was also destroyed. And then two 16 ton tanks emerged at the same time.

Rounds rained against the German Sturmgeschütz. Then two rounds apiece left the smaller tanks on fire as well.

For a few minutes it was quiet. The continuous closure of the breechblock, the harsh gasping for breath died out. The loader wiped his sweating brow and held the next round ready to load. The muzzle flashes from the enemy cannon had disappeared. But it certainly wasn't over yet...

Four enemy tanks lay burning in front of the Sturmgeschütz. This destruction had taken place in less than a minute.

"Man, Horst, we've never gotten rounds out like that so quickly before!" cried the gunner.

"Like a machine gun," seconded the driver.

"We're advancing up onto the knoll!" Naumann decided.

The driver stepped on the gas. The gun rumbled forward. The gun rose slowly and wasn't yet all the way on top of the knoll when Unteroffizier Naumann spied yet another approaching T-34 through the binocular periscope about 200 meters in front of them.

"There's another one!—Fire!" He ordered.

Again the precise, deadly interaction of men and machine began. Six rounds left the gun one after the other. The tank was hit several times. The flames shot out of the opening hatch. Its ready ammunition exploded in repeated flashes. The first Russian round howled towards the knoll.

"The enemy wants to fire artillery at us!"

"Go back, Horst?"

Just as Naumann was about to give this order to the driver, he spied a sixth enemy tank rolling towards the destroyed tank.

"There's another one!—Fire!"

Speed was the difference between life or death. The Sturmgeschütz was faster and a sixth enemy tank received its death blow and smoldered 40 meters in front of the Sturmgeschütz.

Naumann had his machine roll back up the knoll. When he recognized a movement near the first destroyed tank, he looked through the command periscope.

"There's one of them waving with a white rag", he said. Then he heard the calls of the German infantry and saw that the Russian was climbing down. However, he hadn't gotten completely out of the hatch when a shot rang out from the Russian positions, which cut him down.

"We're going to have to hit that tank again!" Naumann called. More shots rang out. The T-34 was hit again and began to burn.

This was the start of the New Year for Naumann's crew. On 4 January 1943, Horst Naumann, only 21 years old, received the Knight's Cross for this action. He and his gun crew had come through this hour of trial and tribulation with uncompromising toughness.

Sturmgeschütz-Abteilung 184 was mentioned three times in the Wehrmacht Report during the fighting on the Demjansk battlefield. That was the external recognition for combat in Fortress Demjansk.

On 3 March 1943 Sturmgeschütz-Abteilung 184 was pulled out of the fortress after taking heavy losses in the fighting. Demjansk was evacuated. The battalion was given a rest in the Cholm area until 30 March, before being sent back to Haanja near Werro in Estonia for refitting.

Oberleutnant Tornau, commander of the 3rd Battery, was sent to the Sturmgeschütz-Schule (Assault Gun School) at Burg as instructor in tactics. Oberleutnant Tornau and Oberleutnant Buchweiser, who in the meantime had become commander of the 2nd Battery, had both received the German Cross in Gold. (Oberleutnant Tornau was able to celebrate a reunion with his old battery a half year later while with Sturmgeschütz-Abteilung 322, for whose activation the 3./Sturmgeschütz-Abteilung 184 provided the cadre in the late fall of 1943.) The battalion remained in Estonia until 25 June 1943. That day it was moved back to the Eastern Front and attached to the II. Armee-Korps. The battalion took up billets in Borodino. A tragic accident occurred there. During a course on close-quarter tank fighting, Unteroffizier Roßner was explaining the long-barreled gun to some infantrymen, while at the same time loading was being explained to an infantry Oberleutnant inside the gun. One of the men inside the gun accidentally hit the emergency firing switch. The gun went off and tore apart Unteroffizier Roßner and nine infantrymen.

The 1st and 3rd Batteries were engaged in heavy defensive fighting at Staraja Russa. The 2nd Battery, which had still been assigned to training exercises, was then also put into action. On 22 August its 9 Sturmgeschütze moved towards Staraja Russa through Grigorowo and Shilina into its assembly area at Camp Erdmannsdorf.

It destroyed tanks in duels at Staraja Russa, in the Kosanka Woods and in the "Beam" Woods. The guns remained in their assembly area at Staraja Russa until 15 September. Then the battalion embarked for Borodino. On 7 October the 2nd Battery was alerted and moved into the threatened area of Newel, where the Soviets had made a surprise penetration and taken Newel.

The Sturmgeschütze of Rotenhäusler and Pinkl destroyed two T-34's in Saworuy and Selenaya. On 13 November Pinkl destroyed another five T-34's. While the headquarters battery was in Werbilowo, preparations were being made for an attack on Lugi. On 25 November Lugi fell. Since the beginning of the Newell operation the 2nd Battery had destroyed 36 enemy tanks. Wachtmeister Pinkl was wounded on 5 December. On 16 December the Soviets began a new series of strong attacks. Because the main battle line was in the form of a sack in this sector, the corps decided to pull the front back. The withdrawal began through Smolnicki-Begunowa to Lyly on 29 December. Kopatilowo was the battalion's rest area until 11 January. Then there was the fighting at Rybki-Wischnaja on Hill 166.4. Oberleutnant Pfaffendorf, commander of the 3rd Battery, and Unteroffizier Miosga were killed there on 18 January 1944. Wachtmeister Schmidt was killed two days later and Leutnant Schulze was wounded. On 14 February 1944 Sturmgeschütz-Abteilung 184 was redesignated as Sturmgeschütz-Brigade 184.

Starting 31 March 1944 greatly superior Soviet infantry and tank forces had made continuous attempts to break through south of Pleskau, and units under the command of Generalleutnant Matzky (21. Infanterie-Division) were thrown against them. Sturmgeschütz-Brigade 184, coming from the area of Newel, was also employed in this defensive fighting. The breakthrough attempts were broken up. A total of 306 enemy tanks were destroyed. Major Ernst Schmidt, the brigade commander, was mentioned by name along with the brigade in the Wehrmacht Report of 11 April 1944.

A little later Major Schmidt was killed. His adjutant, Leutnant Pöll, was killed with him.

On 3 April the brigade was involved in defensive fighting in the area north of Ostrow. It pulled back to southern Latvia. On 12 July, it reached Dünaburg. After varied levels of fighting the brigade was given a rest in Friedrichstadt on 31 July 1944. However, a few days later on 6 August it was put back into action in the Stockmannshof-Odzienas area. The brigade was in costly action in southern Latvia until 10 September. On 10 September it was shifted north from the area east of Madliena by rail and, on 12 September, it arrived at Walk, on the southern Estonian border, for use against the Russian summer offensive.

From 16 to 30 September 1944 the brigade received the mission to cover the withdrawal of Gruppe Narwa and the 16. Armee from Lake Peipus to Riga. The stations of that dramatic operation were Omuli, Rujen, Renceni and Burtnieki. Incukalns was reached via Lamsal-Umurga and Rapazi. On 16 October 1944 the brigade was renamed as Heeres-Sturmartillerie-Brigade 184 although it was probably never reorganized as such.

In Riga Sturmgeschütz-Brigade 184 received the order to move to Tilsit. In the meantime, however, the Red Army had employed strong forces in the direction of Mitau.

As a result, the brigade was forced to turn in the direction of Memel. Of its 200 soldiers, 100 were forced to remain in Memel. With it cadre personnel, Heeres-Sturmartillerie-Brigade 184 crossed the Kurische Nehrung from Memel. Crantz was reached. From there, Heeres-Sturmartillerie-Brigade 184 marched to the area of Braunsberg via Königsberg. It arrived at Böhmenhöfen in Braunsberg on 19 November 1944. On the next day it was moved from Böhmenhöfen to Möckern in the vicinity of the Sturmartillerie School at Burg. A few of the soldiers were transferred to the school and, after a short period of leave, the brigade rolled back to the northern sector of the Eastern Front after having received minimal refitting. It was transferred to Kurland. It arrived at Libau via Zoppot on 17 December 1944.

From 17 December 1944 to 28 January 1945 Heeres-Sturmartillerie-Brigade 184 operated with the 18. Armee in the Kurland Bridgehead in the area of Preekuln. Leutnant Sengel of the 2./Heeres-Sturmartillerie-Brigade 184, a nephew of Generalfeldmarschall Schörner, was knocked out at Preekuln. The crew was able to save itself.

Heeres-Sturmartillerie-Brigade 184 was transferred to the operational area of the 16. Armee on 29 January 1945. It was employed in the area around Kandava–Kandau and Schrunden. It also fought at Frauenburg.

When Heeresgruppe "Kurland" was directed by the High Command of the German Army to release two of its six Sturmgeschütz-Brigaden, Heeres-Sturmartillerie-Brigade 184 had to transfer its guns to Heeres-Sturmartillerie-Brigade 600. It was loaded on board ships at Libau with its personnel and transported to Stettin. From Stettin it moved to Fahrenwalde, southeast of Pasewalk, under the command of Hauptmann Hans Dratwa, the former commander of the 2./Heeres-Sturmartillerie-Brigade 184. From there it was employed on the Oder Bridgehead at Zehden. The bridgehead had to be abandoned. Heeres-Sturmartillerie-Brigade 184 moved into the area of Angermünde, where it was alerted on 1 April 1945 and marched into the operational area of the 1. Ostsee-Division ("Baltic" Division) at Neuendorf-Hohenstaaten. The new commander, Hauptmann Cornelius, arrived on 7 April 1945.

When the last Russian operational offensive began on 16 April, the Red Army was successful in crossing the Oder at that location. On 18 April Russian forces were already advancing in the direction of Bad Freienwalde. Heeres-Sturmartillerie-Brigade 184 was thrown into the area around Eberswalde and received the mission to cover to the east. Russian artillery was already firing into Eberswalde. German infantry was streaming back and, among them, streams of refugees were attempting to flee to the west.

On 18 April Hauptmann Cornelius drove through the devastated city to the commander of the 2./Sturmgeschütz-Brigade 184, Hauptmann Dratwa. Combat engineers were already in the process of preparing the bridges over the Finow Canal for demolition, even though the Sturmgeschütze were still east of the canal. Hauptmann Cornelius was able to bring the Sturmgeschütze back.

Finow was reached. During that period, Heeres-Sturmartillerie-Brigade 184 had a number of gun-barrel explosions which could be traced back to faulty ammunition. Hauptmann Cornelius conducted reconnaissance from Finow in the direction of Bernau. He already started to receive fire from the east at Lanke. When he encountered Russian advance guard elements, he returned. Heeres-Sturmartillerie-Brigade 184 succeeded in getting to Lychen via Liebenwalde and Zehdenick.

The Red Army had broken through north and south of Heeres-Sturmartillerie-Brigade 184 and was streaming west. There was no communications with the neighboring units any more. Hauptmann Cornelius understood his mission to be to get his brigade back as intact as possible. In the process, the Sturmgeschütze covered the withdrawal of the infantry.

The 2./Heeres-Sturmartillerie-Brigade 184 was employed at Neubrandenburg to cover the northern part of the city. When someone suggested to Hauptmann Cornelius to move back towards Holstein with the main body of the brigade and to leave three Sturmgeschütze forward under a Leutnant, he declined. The job of the commander and the battery commanders was to remain up front until the mission was completed.

The brigade succeeded in covering the withdrawal of the infantry. Not only the forward most infantry regiment of the 181. Infanterie-Division but also the Sturmgeschütze was able to be pulled out. The brigade withdrew via Güstrow and Sternberg. The remaining Sturmgeschütze had to be blown up between these two villages. There were neither replacement parts nor ammunition available.

On 1 May 1945 Hauptmann Cornelius released the vehicles of the trains for transporting the wounded to the rear. Two days later the remaining combat elements of the brigade reached Hohen–Viecheln. There they were taken prisoner.

Sturmgeschütz-Abteilung 185 (Sturmgeschütz-Brigade 185; Heeres-Sturmgeschütz-Brigade 185)

In September 1940 Sturmgeschütz-Abteilung 185 was formed at Zinna near Jüterbog. The first commander of the battalion was Major Lickfeld, who chose a lighthouse as the battalion's insignia. Coming from Hamburg, this was a very significant symbol for him. Oberleutnant Krafft, who would take over the battalion in the fall of 1942, was commander of 2nd Battery. Oberleutnant Gottfried Geißler, later commander of the battalion named after him,

Heeres-Sturmgeschütz-Brigade 185

Sturmgeschütz-Brigade 232 "Geißel" ("Scourge"), was commander of the 3rd Battery.

At the beginning of November 1940 the battalion was moved to East Prussia and was quartered at Braunsberg and Heiligenbeil. The combat effectiveness of the battalion was increased by training at the Stablack Troop Training Area and, during May 1941, it moved east towards the Russian border.

The battalion went into action on 22 June in the vicinity of Heidekrug, at Jurgo-Kantscheid. The advance progressed through Skirzene and Senojas to Schaulen and from there through Bausk towards Riga without encountering any significant resistance.

On 28 June the battalion was part of "Kampfgruppe Lasch" ahead of the forward elements of the 18. Armee in the Joniski area, when it received orders to thrust into the rear of the withdrawing Soviet 8th Army and take possession of the important Düna bridges.

When strong enemy forces attacked the flank guards of the Kampfgruppe toward noon on 28 June, the Sturmgeschütze moved forward, destroyed a Russian battery and brought the attack to a halt.

Oberst Lasch continued his advance toward Riga. The 3rd Battery, led by Oberleutnant Geißler, advanced as the lead element in the Kampfgruppe. At 1020 hours it reached the western edge of Riga. The Kampfgruppe cleaned out the houses in close combat, while Oberleutnant Geißler resumed his advance. Firing, the Sturmgeschütze cleared a way through the city. Four Sturmgeschütze reached the pontoon bridge over the Düna. The others stayed back, some destroyed, some still engaging enemy anti-aircraft and antitank guns which were firing from the east bank of the Düna.

"Move out! We're going across!" Oberleutnant Geißler ordered.

The Sturmgeschütze rolled across the bridge. Whistling ricochets and loudly bursting shells accompanied the Sturmgeschütze on their way. A pair of flamethrower teams joined the Sturmgeschütze. The enemy was even firing from the nearby railroad bridge. The Sturmgeschütze didn't dare stop to return the fire. They had to try to reach the east bank as rapidly as they could. They made it. The Sturmgeschütze reached the opposite bank, and then opened fire. During these first few minutes of hard fighting, two powerful explosions could be heard over the noise of the fighting. Startled, Oberleutnant Geißler turned his head. He saw a thick plume of smoke rise over the pontoon bridge. And then he saw flames from an explosion on the railroad bridge as well. Steel screeched downwards, and pieces of the bridges flew through the air.

"The enemy has blown both bridges over the Düna."

"Then we're cut off, Herr Oberleutnant!"

"Yes, I know! But we're going to keep fighting!"

No one knew what the Oberleutnant was thinking. No one but he himself. There they were, alone on the east bank. No Sturmgeschütz could make it across the river to help them out. They had to fight this battle on their own. On the other side of the Düna, Major Lickfeld clenched his fists.

"Fire! Fire on anything that shows itself!"

The Sturmgeschütze dispersed and tried to support their comrades on the other side of the river. A couple of men raced to examine the bridge. But there was no possible way to get the Sturmgeschütze across.

"Listen up, men! All round defense!" Oberleutnant Geißler's order brought the Sturmgeschütze closer in together.

"Demo parties!" cried the gunner in the commander's Sturmgeschütz hoarsely, as he identified the attacking enemy.

They fired with everything they had. The machine guns were mounted and began to fire. The flamethrower crews defended themselves desperately. Their streams of flame kept the enemy away, but then the Russian machine guns rattled, their rifles cracked, and their small machine guns sprayed lead.

The first flamethrower crew was knocked out and then the second. A demolition crew reached the first Sturmgeschütz. Three explosions ripped the gun and its crew into pieces. The enemy attacked in increasing strength, but the three remaining Sturmgeschütze continued to fire. Then the second Sturmgeschütz was silenced. Finally the third was also destroyed by the Russians. The surviving crew members bailed out and defended themselves bitterly.

"We're leaving the gun!" ordered Oberleutnant Geißler, when he recognized that the steel box would only become their tomb. The crew, already wounded—Oberleutnant Geißler twice—left the gun, taking cover behind the rubble. Bullets whipped past them. One of the men was killed. Two comrades from the third gun ran over to join them. They also fell in the fire of a Russian machine gun. The Sturmgeschütze fired from the other bank to give what support they could.

The decision to leave the Sturmgeschütze was the right one, as was proven shortly after when it was blown up by a round from an enemy antitank gun.

"We've got to get back, men!"

Under the cover of a clump of bushes, they raced to the railroad bridge and clambered across the remaining structure. They were joined by three infantry soldiers. The group was knocked off the bridge by the fire of their pursuers. Oberleutnant Geißler was wounded for a third time. But he made it. He and three of his men reached the west bank of the Düna in the darkness. All of the other German soldiers, the Sturmgeschütze and the flame-throwers remained behind on the east bank.

Sturmgeschütz-Abteilung 185 crossed the Düna on the pontoon bridge at Friedrichstadt and, repeatedly attached to different divisions and advance guards by the 18. Armee, fought at Koknese, Madona and Irboska, where it advanced across the Welikaja over a pontoon bridge to Todelkowa. Oberleutnant Gottfried Geißler was awarded the Knight's Cross of the Iron Cross on 21 August 1941.

The actual Russian border was crossed, and the Sturmgeschütze destroyed the Russian bunkers there. Dorpat was reached. Once again, the Sturmgeschütze had to sweep the Russian defenders out of the city.

After the capture of Dorpat, the 1st Battery advanced as "Vorausabteilung Krafft" ("Advance Guard Detachment Krafft") toward Mustvee on Lake Peipus. The battery was brought to a halt by a heavy Russian antiaircraft battery 20 kilometer in front of Mustvee. The enemy battery was destroyed after the loss of one Sturmgeschütz. The battalion passed through Rakke, Taps and Wesenburg to reach Johvi.

Oberleutnant Krafft received the Knight's Cross on 29 September 1941.

At Johvi the 3rd Battery was detached for the capture of Reval. During this same period the two remaining batteries advanced toward Narva. The Narva was crossed at Hermannsburg; the Russians defended Kingisepp and Kothly with all their strength, but the Sturmgeschütze were victorious there as well. Krasnoje Selo was reached in fighting varying in intensity but always in close contact with the enemy. Peterhof, Tossuo-Laskowo, and Schum-Moressowo witnessed successful fighting by the Sturmgeschütze of the battalion. Then the advance toward Leningrad came to an end.

The battalion moved back through Babino and Kransnowardeisk to the area of Wolgowo. It was the end of December. Both guns and crews found it hard to operate in the icy cold.

Hauptmann Horst Krafft, who took over command of the battalion in the fall of 1942, led the battalion into battle in the Leningrad area.

The battalion was still in a rest area at Wolossowo in October 1942. In the previous months it had defended against Soviet attacks. In October, the 3rd Battery received the new 10.5 Sturmhaubitzen. It transferred its 7.5 cm Sturmgeschütze to reinforce the 1st and 2nd Batteries.

The battalion was taken from Wolossowo and thrown into the Welikije Luki area. It was engaged in heavy defensive fighting from 22 November 1942 on. It was cut off by the enemy numerous times, but always mastered the situation and was able to break out. During this fighting the 3rd Battery lost all its officers and Sturmgeschütze.

In February 1943 the battalion was transferred to the Newel area. The 1st and 2nd Batteries were used against partisans at Witebsk. Shortly thereafter, Hauptmann Krafft was transferred to a different unit. Major Griffel took over command of the battalion.

The battalion went to Mogilew for rest and refitting. It received some new Sturmgeschütze and vehicles, and personnel replacements from the reserve unit. It wasn't until May when the battalion, combat-ready once again, was moved into the area of Smijewka-Borisoglebskoje. The German operational offensive for the elimination of the Kursk salient began in July 1943. The battalion went into action from its ready position at Glasunowka at the northwestern bend of the Kursk salient, moving toward Malo-Archangelsk.

After good initial progress, the entire German offensive bogged down. The Soviets, who had also prepared a major operational offensive, launched strong forces in counterattacks. They managed to tear open the German front in the Orel area. The battalion was thrown in at the threatened position. It took part in bitter defensive fighting there and suffered considerable losses.

Three Sturmgeschütze of the 1./Sturmgeschütz-Abteilung 185 moved into a gap ripped in the front by the enemy and closed it off, supported by some Panzergrenadiere. When the grenadiers pulled back during the night, the three Sturmgeschütze had to oppose a Russian tank attack on their own the next morning.

All three Sturmgeschütze destroyed a number of enemy tanks, before they were themselves destroyed. Two Sturmgeschütze received direct hits. Their entire crews were killed. The third Sturmgeschütz was disabled, but the wounded crew managed to get back to the battalion command post. Sturmgeschütz-Abteilung 185 suffered its heaviest losses in the Orel bend, but it was also able to accomplish its greatest deeds. A frontline newspaper reported:

Special Success of Sturmgeschütz-Abteilung 185

A Sturmgeschütz battalion, which can celebrate its third year of existence shortly, was again victorious. So far, 102 Russian tanks have fallen prey to it in the Orel Bend, 59 on just one day. Since its formation, the battalion has destroyed or captured 549 enemy tanks, 20 antitank guns, 244 guns, 260 vehicles, an armored train and a fuel train.

Major Griffel was transferred at Orel in the summer of 1943, and Hauptmann Fritz Glossner took over the battalion after him.

The battalion went back into action on the Smolensk-Wjasma Highway at Jarzewo-Duchowtschina. It was at the focal points of the heavy defensive fighting at Majekojo and Jelnja and again destroyed a large number of enemy tanks. The battalion was continuously used as a rear guard for the withdrawal to the Orscha-Gorki area, repeatedly freeing cut-off elements. The battalion passed a relatively peaceful winter in the Rogatschew Bridgehead, east of Bobruisk. On Christmas Eve it repelled the only major Russian attack, inflicting heavy enemy losses.

During the first two months of 1944 the brigade was involved in the defensive fighting at Shlobin-Tschirkowitschi-Paritschi. On 14 February 1944 it was redesignated a brigade. During March and April it fought at Kowel, Minsk and in the Rokitno Swamps and was then again transferred into the Mogilew area. From there it withdrew to Beresino, fighting fiercely and taking heavy casualties. Then the brigade went on to Wilna and Grodno and the heavy defensive fighting at Lomza and on the Narew River. Fighting in the area of Ostenburg-Serok, south of Nowgorod and at Kolno followed. On 10 July 1944 the brigade was renames as Heeres-Sturmgeschütz-Brigade 185.

In late fall of 1944 Major Glossner was transferred to Sturmgeschütz-Ersatz-Abteilung 200 at Schieratz. Hauptmann Ernst-August Twietmeyer took over the brigade. He was to command it to the bitter end.

In the fighting for East Prussia, the brigade fought furiously at Friedrichshof, Sensburg, Schippenbeil, Bartenstein, Mehlsack and Heiligenbeil. Taking heavy casualties in this bloody fighting, the brigade lost all but two Sturmgeschütze. Hauptmann Twietmeyer was awarded the German Cross in Gold.

After the loss of their guns it was intended to send the gun crews by sea to receive new Sturmgeschütze in the still unoccupied area of Germany. The men crossed the Frische Haff at Rosenberg and, together with members of Sturmgeschütz-Brigade 904, who had suffered the same fate, were used for security against enemy landings on the Haff coast at Kahlberg and then at Stutthof. The two brigades were not pulled out until the night of 7 May 1945. On 8 May they laid down their arms at the mouth of the Vistula. The survivors fell into Russian hands. However, this was not the end of these two consolidated brigades. They were still to take part in a truly unique operation.

The two brigades had to march through Danzig as prisoners for propaganda purposes, on their way to Dirschau. However, during the night, the two brigades separated from the column of prisoners and vanished into a broad marshy stretch of shore which was heavily overgrown with bushes. They went back again to Danzig. Continuously marching to the west they passed through Butow and Rummelsburg as far as Bublitz. The Soviets provided the rations. Both brigades thus reached the demobilization camp at Hammerstein in Pomerania. It was there that the history of Heeres-Sturmgeschütz-Brigade 185 ended on 10 June 1945.

Sturmgeschütz-Abteilung 189 (Sturmgeschütz-Brigade 189; Panzer-Jäger-Abteilung 178)

Sturmgeschütz-Brigade 189

The battalion was constituted by Oberleutnant Ernst Heß on 9 July 1941 and, by the beginning of August, it was already on its way to East Prussia, unloading in Reuß on 5 August. It reached the Witebsk area after a 950 kilometer road march through Kowno, Minsk and Borissow. Shortly before arriving, a bridge in front of Witebsk had collapsed under the weight of a Sturmgeschütz. The gun tipped over and sank with its running gear upward. The entire crew was killed.

Attached to the IX. Armee-Korps, the commander, battery commanders and reconnaissance group went to Ustwjati. There they were attached to the IX. Armee-Korps artillery commander, General Weidling.

The batteries were brought up the next day under the command of the Headquarters Battery commander and, on 18 August, along Nebelwerfer-Regiment 1, the battalion road marched north to Nimwy, where it was attached to the 110. Infanterie-Division At Nimwy, the staff and Headquarters Battery were attached to the 110. Infanterie-Division command post, while the 1./Sturmgeschütz-Abteilung 189 was attached to Infanterie-Regiment 254, the 2./Sturmgeschütz-Abteilung 189 Infanterie-Regiment 255 and the 3./Sturmgeschütz-Abteilung 189 to Infanterie-Regiment 252. The assembly areas were reached on 19 August. The Sturmgeschütze were intended to form a steel spearhead on the following day. It was unfortunate that in this case, as in others, the elementary principle: "Don't divide your forces!" was so grossly neglected. When the combat elements advanced out of their assembly areas on that morning, the attack had been called off. Rain and poor visibility had made it impossible for the Luftwaffe to provide the necessary air support.

On 21 August new orders arrived for an attack on 22 August at 0430 hours. The objective of this attack was to thrust through the Kunja Sector and the woods to its north, then wheel to the west to cut off Welikije Luki and take it from the east.

After the spearhead had broken through the Russian main battle line, it was intended for the 19. and 20. Panzer-Divisionen deployed further to the rear to smash through the hole and wheel to the east to Toropetz.

Leutnant Möller was severely wounded on "Bee Hive" Hill while he was carrying out a reconnaissance in the area of the encirclement.

The Sturmgeschütze moved forward at the beginning of the attack. They shot up the Russian tree obstacles and rolled on over them. By noon, the Sturmgeschütze had carried the attack far forward, even though the swampy terrain, mines and tank traps made the going difficult for them.

One section of the 3rd Battery was stuck fast in the swamp. It was pulled out by the prime movers of the Nebelwerfer-Regiment 1.

One of the antitank ditches ran all the way to the lake and couldn't be crossed by the Sturmgeschütze. It was bypassed by a Sturmgeschütz section which drove around it through the shallow lake. By evening on the day of the attack, the 110. Infanterie-Division had made it all the way to Krimozowa. At the same time, Wiedmann, the armorer, was killed. He had driven back in a truck to get ammunition and bring it forward. He got out of the truck at a road block, stepped on a mine and was torn apart.

Leutnant Kreimel, who was sent forward on reconnaissance, drove his vehicle onto a mine. Luckily, only the front wheel was torn off. The same thing happened to the commander of the 2./Sturmgeschütz-Abteilung 189, Oberleutnant von Malachowski, who was slightly wounded by a mine explosion.

The attack continued on 23 August. Once again, it gained ground. The battalion also made rapid progress on 24 August and reached its objective on 26 August.

The battalion had contributed a great deal to the victory at the capture of Welikije Luki. General Stumm, the corps commander, and General Seifert, commander of the 110. Infanterie-Division, gave full recognition to the battalion. Four men of the battalion were killed, 9 wounded.

The battalion fought with the same determination at the double battle of Wjasma-Briansk and at Kalinin as well as in the winter battle for Rshew. It was in heavy fighting with the enemy right up to the establishment of the bridgehead at Rshew-North. Oberleutnant Wilhelm von Malachowski received the Knight's Cross on 9 February 1942. On 26 February 1942 Oberleutnant Heß was transferred. As Hauptmann and commander of Sturmgeschütz-Abteilung 189, von Malachowski then received the Oak Leaves to the Knight's Cross on 6 March 1942. He was the fourth man of the Sturmartillerie to receive this decoration.

By 30 December 1942, the battalion had already been incorporated into the 78. Sturm-Division. It fought as part of this division until the summer of 1944. In June 1944, it was employed in the desperate defensive fighting between Orscha and Minsk. It was almost completely wiped out on the Beresina by the violently pursuing Soviets. It was officially redesignated as Sturmgeschütz-Brigade 189 on 10 June 1944.

The remnants who managed to save themselves and cross the Beresina to reach the newly established German main battle line to the west were assigned to the recently formed Panzer-Jäger-Abteilung 178. With the reconstitution as a Panzer-Jäger-Abteilung the history of Sturmgeschütz-Brigade 189 ended.

Sturmgeschütz-Abteilung 190 (leichte Sturmgeschütz-Abteilung 190; leichte Sturmgeschütz-Brigade 190)

On 1 October 1940 Major Haupt, commander of schwere Artillerie-Abteilung (mot.) 601 received orders to activate a Sturmgeschütz-Abteilung at Jüterbog by the end of the month. On 15 November 1940 he reported that the newly formed Sturmgeschütz-Abteilung 190 was ready for action.

A few days later, on 26 November 1940, the battalion moved out for an unknown objective. On 11 November the headquarters and the 2nd and 3rd Batteries arrived at Montbéliard and the 1st Battery at Lure in the west of France. On the following day, the battalion was attached to the 72. Infanterie-Division and was billeted in the area of Lure. On the same day, Major Haupt was promoted to Oberstleutnant.

Training with the new weapons continued in the billeting area.

All of the duties, which consisted mainly of exercises under combat conditions, were carried out with great military enthusiasm. The first deaths in the battalion were suffered on 1 December when a truck from the 1st Battery turned over. Two cannoneers were fatally injured in the accident.

The battalion's days in France were numbered. By 7 January 1941 it was in transport from Belfort by rail, reaching Munich around midnight on 9 January. Passing through Vienna and the Hungarian/Rumanian border railroad station of Lölöshza, the battalion arrived at Balaci (Rumania) on 15 January. From there, Oberstleutnant Haupt immediately sent details back to Germany to arrange for spare parts. The battalion was billeted as follows:

Headquarters: Raca

Headquarters Battery: Bucovu

1st Battery: Silestea-Gumesti

2nd Battery: Strambeni

3rd Battery: Caldararu

During a commanders' conference with the Commanding General of the XXX. Armee-Korps in Rosiorii de Vede, Oberstleutnant Haupt suggested possibilities for the employment of his unit in action. He was designated the commander of March Group H, but the battalion was pulled out of this March Group on 22 February. Now, it was expected to move independently to the assembly area at Giurgiu two hours after receiving orders to move out. On 28 February the battalion assembled at Giurgiu along the route from Bucharest to the Danube.

On D-Day—3 March 1941—Panzergruppe Kleist crossed the Danube. On the following day, Sturmgeschütz-Abteilung 190 also received orders to move out and was incorporated in the march group of Oberst Mühl. The battalion crossed the Danube in the early morning of March 3 and reached Novoselo on 5 March. The battalion was unable to get through the heavily obstructed Sipka Pass and reach Haskovo until 8 March. In the days that followed, Oberstleutnant Haupt carried out repeated reconnaissance. Oberleutnant Stein also carried out reconnaissance in the neighboring sector of the 164. Infanterie-Division.

Sturmgeschütz-Ersatz-Abteilung 200 in Schweinfurt was assigned to the battalion as a source of replacements.

On 5 April Oberstleutnant Haupt was informed by top-secret teletype that the operation against Greece would begin on the following day. H-Hour was 0520 hours. The battalion was integrated into the advance guard of Oberst Geyso at Tschorbadshisko. Their mission: Seize the passes out of the mountains and advance to Komotini.

All of the battalion guns moved out on the day of the attack. They ran into a fortified position laid out in 5 belts at Hill 510, four and a half kilometers after crossing into Greek territory. The advance was brought to a halt. Light and heavy antiaircraft guns fired on the bunkers but were ineffective.

Oberstleutnant Haupt sent in the 1st Section of the 3rd Battery under Oberleutnant Bender. It did the job with direct fire. But the infantry was unable to move under heavy enemy fire. In the late afternoon, the entire 3rd Battery was moved forward under the command of Oberleutnant Naether. During this phase of the fighting, the enemy blew up the narrow road through the pass at three places, making it impassable. The next morning, the entire battalion fired on Hill 510. The bunker positions were softened up and taken by the assault troops of Pionier-Bataillon 85. Not until the following afternoon did the advance guard move through Komotini and Xanthi and meet heavy enemy resistance at Taxote on the Nestos River. The enemy had established a defense on the west bank of the river. Every bridge across the river had been blown up. The attackers ran into enemy fire from MG nests and enemy field fortifications which, in some cases , were blasted into the rock. Oberstleutnant Haupt sent out the reconnaissance section to find fords across the Nestos. Leutnant Roever swam across the river at night to determine its depth to see if the combat elements of the battalion could cross. He was detected on the near bank while swimming back and shot at.

The next day, 9 April, the battalion moved through Pimni into attack positions and placed the enemy positions under fire. However, it was not possible to determine the location of two enemy heavy machine guns which shot up the attacking German infantry and the combat engineers of the mountain troops. The first attempted assault was shattered by the enemy. Leutnant Schwalb was wounded by a bullet in the thigh.

Generalmajor Hollidt, the commander of the 50. Infanterie-Division, to which the battalion was attached, decided on a new attack. The main burden again fell on the Strumgeschütze, especially in the preliminary fighting. At 0130 hours on 10 April they opened fire on the enemy bunkers from a distance of 1000 meters. One bunker after the other was silenced by a direct hit. A half hour later the infantry and engineers crossed the Nestos and immediately gained ground. The Strumgeschütze could take most of the credit for the success of this attack.

Effective 12 April the battalion was attached to the 2. Panzer-Division. One day later, the command staff reached Salonika. By 14 April the entire battalion had been brought as far forward as Langadas. From there, on 15 April, it moved on through Kavalki and Nea Chalkidon to Ida. In spite of special orders from the XVIII. Armee-Korps, neither the 2. Panzer-Division nor the 6. Gebirgsjäger-Division would allow the Strumgeschütze to pass them. Not until 16 April did the battalion arrive at the 2. Panzer-Division Command Post at Katerini at the foot of Mt. Olympus. The 2. Panzer-Division had run into heavy resistance at Dimitros, 20 kilometers south of Katerini. New Zealand troops kept the approach routes under fire to cover the withdrawal of the British army. The Sturmgeschütze were attached to Kampfgruppe I (Oberst von Kölitz) and on 17 April were pushed forward to within 1 kilometer of Dimitros. On 18 April, after taking a ridge line which could control Elason, they took it at 1400 hours. Around 1830 on the same day, the Sturmgeschütze, together with tanks and the I./Schützen-Regiment 2, advanced in the direction of the Menekses Hills. The riflemen were mounted.

The attackers were greeted by heavy artillery fire. One gun in the 2nd Battery took three hits but was still able to continue the advance. Enemy 4.7 cm antitank guns blocked the Sturmgeschütze from the way across the Serpentine Pass to the Menekses Hills. These antitank guns were destroyed at very close range by direct hits. Again and again, ammunition explosions sent columns of flame into the air. Then the Sturmgeschütze ran into obstacles in a narrow position and had to turn back to clear the way for the following combat engineers. During these difficult turning maneuvers, the Sturmgeschütz of Leutnant Pilkat (2nd Battery) came too close to the edge. The edge collapsed and the gun went over the side. There was one dead and four injured. The enemy were so demoralized by this action that they gave up the heights during the night and pulled back to occupy their next defensive positions at Larissa.

Sturmgeschütz-Abteilung 190 was allowed some rest. However, on 24 April, they were brought back to the front to push out enemy forces which had dug in south of Lamia on Thermopylae. This mission was aborted however at 0920 hours on the same day, when a special message was received informing them that point elements of the 5. Panzer-Division had reached Athens. The battalion was pulled back to the area of Thebes. By order of the 2. Panzer-Division, the battalion was represented by the 3./Sturmgeschütz-Abteilung 190 under Oberleutnant Naether in Athens, where the victory parade was reviewed by Generalfeldmarschall List on 3 May. The Balkan campaign was over. Oberleutnant von Stein and Oberleutnant Wersig, along with Hauptwachtmeister Middelhuß, received the Iron Cross, First Class, and 43 members of the battalion were decorated with the Iron Cross, Second Class. Wachtmeister Steinwachs, a "dirt old" veteran of World War I, received a clasp to his Iron Cross, First Class.

Sturmgeschütz-Abteilung 190 withdrew from Athens on 15 May. It crossed seven passes to get to Salonika and, on 14 June, the Sturmgeschütze arrived in Bucharest to receive a general overhaul at the Malaxa Works. However, this general overhaul did not take place. The war against the Soviet Union began on 22 June.

The battalion was transferred to the area of the 11. Armee in the last three days of June. By order of the 11. Armee, the 1st Battery under Oberleutnant Wersig was attached to the XXX. Armee-Korps. The 2nd Battery (Oberleutnant Nottebrock) and 3rd Battery (Oberleutnant Naether) were sent to the XI. Armee-Korps which attached them to the 76. and 22. Infanterie-Divisionen respectively.

The Sturmgeschütze first went into action in Russia on 20 July when the Soviets launched an encircling attack on Sokol where the staff of the 22. Infanterie-Division was located. Elements of the 3./Sturmgeschütz-Abteilung, attached the previous day to the reconnaissance battalion of the 22. Infanterie-Division, overpowered the penetrating enemy forces. Gefreiter Hertlein, driver of an command Schützenpanzerwagen, drove right into the middle of the attacking enemy with a few infantrymen mounted on his vehicle. These brave men drove back the enemy with machine gun and rifle fire plus grenades and explosive charges. Hertlein was given the Iron Cross, First Class on the field of battle by the Adjutant of the 22. Infanterie-Division.

By order of the IX. Armee-Korps, the battalion staff with two batteries were then attached to Vorausabteilung (Advance Guard Battalion) Lindemann. They rolled on with the Vorausabteilung up to Werbka, which was reached on 24 July. They moved forward again on the next day, then turned to the east towards Woloshtchino. They fought against individual Russian riflemen at Jassinowo. At 1930 hours, Oberstleutnant Haupt resumed his advance with the Sturmgeschütze. They rolled at the point of the advance guard. The Sturmgeschütze encountered enemy forces on the eastern edge of the city. Antonowka was reached two hours later. The Sturmgeschütze encountered the enemy on the eastern edge of town. Heavy machine gun fire whipped through the evening. The commander of the 2nd Battery, Oberleutnant Schilling, was killed, and Leutnant Wagner and three men were severely wounded.

In the same night, 26 July, the Vorausabteilung received orders to turn to the west towards Ploskoje to provide flank security on the heights there for the 239. Infanterie-Division. The battalion set up positions on the hills on both sides of Ploskoje. From there, Oberstleutnant Haupt had elements of the 2nd Battery advance on Posnanka-Perwaja. At about 1700 hours, these guns reported that the enemy was attacking in a strength of 2 companies. At the same time, a message arrived from the Vorausabteilung that an enemy company was also attacking southwest of Kajetanowka. Oberstleutnant Haupt placed the 3rd Battery on the right flank. He sent Oberleutnant Hartmann to the left flank with the 2nd Battery.

The Russian attack was completely smashed. Oberleutnant Hartmann destroyed a mine launcher which had advanced with his gun. This was the first tank battle: 3 Sturmgeschütze against 4 enemy tanks.

On 28 July the Vorausabteilung received orders to continue its advance through Pestchano-Bondurowo to Chaschtschewato. The 2nd Battery silenced an enemy battery at Bondurowo on 29 July. Two freight trains were halted by direct hits just north of Chaschtschewato. By order of Oberst Lindemann, a Kampfgruppe under Oberstleutnant Haupt advanced through Ssolomija to the Bug on 30 July. At 0500 hours there was heavy fighting with the Sturmgeschütze against enemy antitank guns and artillery on the heights just northwest of Ssolomija. It was only possible to discover the enemy positions by a flank attack. The Sturmgeschütze silenced one gun after the other. Two 15 cm howitzers, four 7.5 cm cannons and a number of antitank cannon were destroyed in this five-hour duel. At 10:10 hours, Oberstleutnant Haupt ordered an advance through Ssolomija. The Sturmgeschütze rolled right through the highest point in front of Gaiworon. The battalion took more than 200 prisoners, and captured the following materiél:

84 field wagons, 203 horses, 6 field kitchens.

10 heavy machine guns, 5 8 cm antitank cannon, 4 10.5 cm cannon, 2 howitzers.

One Sturmgeschütz was seriously damaged by a direct hit from a 15 cm howitzer, another received minor damage.

The Vorausabteilung was dissolved on the following day. Sturmgeschütz-Abteilung 190 was given 5 days of rest and, on 4 August, the staff and 2nd and 3rd Batteries were attached to a newly formed Vorausabteilung, once again commanded by Oberst Lindemann. The battalion (less the 1st Battery) arrived at the Vorausabteilung at Woloschtschino on the following day. While the 3rd Battery with 4 Sturmgeschütze was assigned to the lead element of the advance guard (Oberstleutnant von Boddien), the 2nd Battery, also with 4 guns, was assigned to the Kampfgruppe of Oberstleutnant Gerhard. The two remaining guns stayed with the main body. On the same day, both Kampfgruppen attacked Wradijewka. While crossing Hill 174 one gun from 3rd Battery took a direct hit from a 15 cm shell. The gun was torn apart when its ammunition exploded. The driver was killed and the other crewmen badly wounded.

The enemy pulled back in flight from the Sturmgeschütze. A severe cloudburst stopped the advance. The advance could not be resumed until 8 August, and one day later the battalion commander , with two attached companies, was ordered to move southeast to

Kolossowka south of Stara Ssirotskoje, reach Hills 112 and 117 on the Worms-Wiktorowka road, clear the enemy out of Winogradowka and take Worms.

Around 1800 hours, the battalion reached the fork in the road just north of Hill 112 after hard fighting and ran into Kampfgruppe von Boddien there. A radio message from the advance detachment ordered both groups back to Winogradowka.

On 11 August the battalion began its advance to Rasnopolje from Winogradowka. It ran into hard fighting at Krinitschki. The enemy fired from a sunflower field with mortars, heavy machine guns and a medium battery. Oberleutnant Naether took a section from his battery and launched an attack against the left flank of the enemy battery. All the enemy guns were destroyed in a fierce duel. While the battalion was still involved in this kind of fighting, it received orders to withdraw south and take over security duties west of Petrowka.

On the following night the enemy attempted to push tractors, antitank cannon and six trucks through Petrowka. The 3./Sturmgeschütz-Abteilung 190 destroyed this combat group entirely. The remaining eight guns of the battalion went into action when two enemy companies with heavy weapons attacked once again on 13 August. The attack was crushed.

On 13 August the battalion parted from Vorausabteilung Lindemann and marched via Goljowka and Waterloo to Munich. The 1st Battery, which had been attached to the XXX. Armee-Korps, was relieved of that assignment on 18 August and rejoined the battalion.

The battalion was attached to LIV. Armee-Korps Headquarters on 21 August. On 23 August it marched through Wasilinowo-Landau to Nikolajew and on the following day moved up to the 73. Infanterie-Division which was at Schirokoje on the bank of the Dnjepr. It was to support the planned crossing of the Dnjepr by the division. However, five days later, it was reattached to the XXX. Armee-Korps and entered Nowo Nikolskaja on 28 August, where Oberstleutnant Haupt reported in at the XXX. Armee-Korps command post.

After crossing the Ingul on 31 August the battalion fought along with the 22. Infanterie-Division in the street fighting for Malaya-Kachowka. The city was taken after two days of heavy street and house-to-house fighting.

The 3rd Battery was attached to Infanterie-Regiment 47 and put a cleverly constructed Russian field position out of action in a firefight. The 3rd Battery intervened in the fighting three times on the following day to break Russian counterattacks. A command vehicle was destroyed by a direct hit. On the night of 3 September, when the enemy took Infanterie-Regiment 47 completely by surprise and overran its position, the battery shot the enemy to pieces, often at very close range, and threw him back. On 4 September it rolled out against an enemy tank attack and destroyed 5 of the 12 attacking enemy tanks. The armor-piercing shells of the Sturmgeschütze were ineffective against one of the enemy heavy tanks.

On the afternoon of the same day, the battalion, led by Oberstleutnant Haupt, carried out an attack to the south with the 2nd and 3rd Batteries. Each battery shot an enemy 7.62 cm battery to pieces. In addition, the 3rd Battery destroyed its 6th tank that day. Just as the fighting reached its high point, the battalion commander's Sturmgeschütz received two direct hits from the rapidly firing Russian artillery. Oberstleutnant Haupt, his driver, his radio operator, and a Wachtmeister were killed.

The 1st Battery, still with Infanterie-Regiment 72, successfully supported this attack. Leutnant Lepper was killed during the attack by a shot to the head. Oberleutnant Naether, commander of the 3rd Battery, took command of the battalion on the battlefield.

Russian bombers attacked during the funeral for the commander and the three other soldiers killed in action. A gun from the 1st Battery was destroyed by a direct hit. Six members of the battalion, including 5 noncommissioned officers who had been decorated with the Iron Cross, First Class, were killed.

All of the batteries fought under the direct command of XXX. Armee-Korps headquarters up until 20 September. On 22 September the battalion was attached to the LIV. Armee-Korps with orders to support the breakthrough at the Crimean isthmus at Perekop. Up to this point the battalion had destroyed the following in the Eastern Campaign:

173 guns, 39 mortars, 122 antitank guns

45 tanks, 1 armored emplacement, 1 armored cupola, 11 bunkers

2 aircraft, 265 prime movers, trucks, cars, and tank trucks

It had expended 15,716 shells.

The following figures show the losses:

32 Officers, noncommissioned officers, and men were killed in this fighting.

8 Sturmgeschütze and 5 armored command and ammunition vehicles were lost.

The actual strength of the battalion was: 454 Officers, noncommissioned officers and men.

The 1st Battery received a letter of commendation from the Commander-in-Chief of the Army for distinguished conduct in the fighting from 3 to 6 July. The 3./Sturmgeschütz-Abteilung 190 received a letter of commendation from Generalleutnant Graf von Sponeck, the commander of the 22. Infanterie-Division.

The attack on the Perekop Isthmus began on 24 September 1941. Sturmgeschütz-Abteilung 190 moved out at daybreak. The Tartar Trench was taken on the second day of the attack. However, the Sturmgeschütze were then withdrawn and sent to Mariopol as fast as possible, where the Soviets had made a breakthrough at the beginning of October. The Sturmgeschütze were able to seal off this penetration. Then they were brought back again to the isthmus at Juschun, 15 kilometers south of Perekop, where the attack had bogged down.

On 15 October Oberleutnant Wersig was awarded the newly-created German Cross in Gold for gallantry in action. He was one of the first German soldiers to receive the decoration, and the first member of the Sturmartillerie to do so. On the same day he had to leave the battalion. He was transferred to one of the Artillerie-Lehr-Regimenter as adjutant.

Oberleutnant Hartmann was killed in the subsequent fighting for Juschun, where the 2nd Battery saw most of the action. Oberleutnant Bender took over command of the battery. The 1st and 3rd Batteries remained quiet while attached to the 22. Infanterie-Division Effective 29 September Major Vogt was the new battalion commander. He was designated as the commander of the lead elements of the Vorausabteilung, which was once more led by Oberstleutnant von Boddien.

On 15 October, after a few hours, the Vorausabteilung opened up the way into the Crimea and advanced at a daily rate of 60 to 80 kilometers. Always the lead element, it took fully occupied air fields, smashed into the rear of fleeing enemy columns and, 10 days later, reached the Fortress of Sevastopol. The attempt to take the fortress by a surprise attack failed. The enemy used his heaviest artillery pieces (38 cm) to fire on the Sturmgeschütze. Major Vogt was severely wounded during this attempted surprise attack. The battalion was pulled back and took up quarters in Bachtschissaraj.

The attack on Sevastopol began just before Christmas. It bogged down after several days. Those guns which were still serviceable were attached to the 24. Infanterie-Division (General von Tettau). However, they could not be used effectively in the forested terrain.

Hauptmann Peitz took over command of the battalion at the end of December. A few days earlier, Oberleutnant Cardeneo had taken over the 1st Battery and Oberleutnant Caesar had taken over the 2nd Battery. Leutnant von Harnier was the battalion's new orderly officer.

The members of the battalion celebrated New Years, 1942 in "Garden Valley" (Bachtschissaraj). There were minor operations against partisans there. On January 15, a section of three Sturmgeschütze under Oberleutnant Cardeneo supported the attack of the Infanterie-Regiment 72 on Nowo Petrowka. They had a fight with 2 T 26 B's only 300 meters outside of the village. While the Sturmgeschütze were destroying these two tanks, they came under direct fire from a 7.62 cm battery. The first Sturmgeschütz, commanded by Leutnant von Harnier, received a direct hit from a "Ratschbum." Leutnant von Harnier and his gunner were killed. The remaining Sturmgeschütze destroyed the battery but had to withdraw.

As orderly officer, Leutnant von Harnier was allowed along on this attack only after making repeated requests to do so. He was buried at Islam-Terek along with his gunner.

The same section, this time led by Leutnant Damman, ran right into the middle of a Russian tank assembly area on the heights southwest of Wladislawowka and destroyed 16 T 26 B's, 1 antitank cannon and several mortars and machine guns.

One day earlier, Oberleutnant Naether received the German Cross in Gold. Everyone was pleased with the decoration of their "hussar."

More partisan operations took place and on 1 March 1942 Oberleutnants Caesar and Cardeneo were promoted to Hauptmann. On 8 March one of the old warriors, Oberwachtmeister Schädlich of the 3rd Battery, became the first noncommissioned officer of the battalion and, at the same time, the first noncommissioned officer in all of the Sturmartillerie to receive the German Cross in Gold.

The battalion was then brought up to full strength by arriving equipment transports and on 1 April Hauptmann Peitz was able to report that the battalion was fully combat ready. Beginning on 23 March the battalion was moved to Feodosia.

On 9 April the Soviets attacked at Feodosia. The operations officer of the XXX. Armee-Korps, to whom the battalion had been attached for the major attack towards Kertsch, used the Sturmgeschütze as a buffer to catch the reported Soviet tank attack. However, the tank attack did not take place. On the same day Oberleutnant Naether was promoted to Hauptmann. (Eleven days later he was married via short-wave radio.)

On 10 April Leutnant Wagner's section destroyed 3 tanks, one of which was 44 tons.

Announcement was made for Operation "Bustard Hunt" (the attack on Kertsch). There was bitter bureaucratic in-fighting over the 6 new long-barreled L-48 Sturmgeschütze which had just arrived in Simferopol. Here too, Sturmgeschütz-Abteilung 190 was the victor and traded off 6 of its short-barreled guns to Sturmgeschütz-Abteilung 197.

The attack began on the morning of 8 May. The battalion, assigned to the 28. Infanterie-Division (mot.), rolled out with the first barrage at 0337 hours. The 3rd Battery was in the lead. Because the attack went smoothly, Hauptmann Peitz also ordered an immediate attack by the 2nd Battery. By 07:00 hours both batteries had broken into the Parpatsch position. In order to expand this penetration into a breakthrough, the 1st Battery, which had been kept in reserve, was launched into the attack. The enemy attempted to halt the forward thrust of the German Sturmgeschütze by counterattacks with strong tank forces. Duels flared up between Sturmgeschütze and tanks. The battlefield turned into a two-sided storm front and 24 enemy tanks lay destroyed by the thunderbolts of the cannon fire. Only the Sturmgeschütz of Oberwachtmeister Brückner was lost in this fighting.

The employment and offensive use of the Sturmgeschütze on this day were a model of how an entire Sturmgeschütz battalion should be used as the decisive weapon at the point of main effort—going into action as a unit under its own commander. The Silesian Jäger of Infanterie-Regiment 49 converted this breakthrough into a victory.

In the following days the Sturmgeschütze fought at every focal point of the battle. Leutnant Hennings of the 1st Battery was severely wounded on the evening of 11 May by a mortar round during the attack on Abigel. Three days later Leutnant Fürnschuß, with four Sturmgeschütze, supported the attack of Infanterie-Regiment 391 on the edge of the city of Kertsch. These guns were surrounded by Soviet forces of greatly superior strength at the edge of the city and attacked by machine guns, hand grenades, pistols and explosive charges. The men around Leutnant Fürnschuß fought in a desperate struggle. The lieutenant and Gefreiter Röstel were killed, and all the rest of the men were wounded. Even so, they brought their gun back. Shortly before, Wachtmeister Wüstner had been evacuated from one of the guns, severely wounded.

The next day, which saw the taking of Kertsch, also demanded heavy sacrifice. Around noon on 15 May Hauptmann Cardeneo was severely wounded by a shot from an antitank rifle. Oberleutnant Dr. Roever took command of the 1st Battery. Leutnant Fürnschuß and Gefreiter Röstel were buried in the military cemetery at Stary Krim.

The fighting to clear the steel works and suburbs of Kertsch lasted until 20 May. This concluded the fighting for the Kertsch Peninsula. In this fighting, the battalion could report the following accomplishments. It destroyed:

80 tanks, 4 Stalin-Organs, 2 automatic guns

102 field pieces, 14 antiaircraft guns, and 42 antitank guns

7 bunkers and 13 antitank rifles

On 23 May Wachtmeister Wüstner was promoted to Oberwachtmeister for bravery in the face of the enemy. Leutnants Fürnschuß, Hennings and Damman received the Iron Cross, First Class.

A few days of quiet followed, until notification was given of Operation "Störfang" (Disruption) (Attack on Sevastopol).

Sturmgeschütz-Abteilung 190 left its assembly area in the early morning hours of 7 June 1942. At 04:00 hours the 1st Battery reached Buse Hill which was heavily mined. As no engineers were available, the artillerymen cleared these mines themselves. While doing so, Oberleutnant Dr. Roever was killed by a head shot. Oberleutnant Ebinger took over command of the 1st Battery.

The 2nd Battery was also stuck in front of a minefield about half way up the Buse Hill. After hard fighting, the 3rd Battery broke through the positions north of Balbek. The withdrawal along the telegraph line became a fiasco. All three guns were lost.

The death of Oberleutnant Dr. Roever was a heavy blow for the battalion. "Uncle Luitpold" with his humor and his effervescence managed to put everyone else in a good mood. He was buried in the military cemetery at Bachtschissaraj. In the absence of Hauptmann Peitz, Leutnant Dr. Probst delivered the eulogy.

On 11 June Oberleutnant Ebinger was also killed along with his gunner Gefreiter Knöß. Leutnant Töpfer took over the battery. A few hours later, the Sturmgeschütz of Leutnant Töpfer also received a direct hit, just after it had successfully engaged an enemy battery. The entire crew was wounded. Leutnant Töpfer received the Iron Cross, First Class directly from Hauptmann Peitz. Five days later he died of his wounds. The 1st Battery had been orphaned once again.

13 June became the high-water day for the 2nd Battery. It rolled out of the Melzer Ravine to the assault line at 0100 hours on this day and, with mounted assault engineers, attacked the "Stalin" Fort. This fort, a dominating bulwark and the key position for the northern part of Severnaja Bay, was in the hands of the Sturmartillerie soldiers by 05:30 hours. Hauptmann Caesar received the Iron Cross, First Class on the battlefield directly from General Wolff (Commander of the 22. Infanterie-Division). One day later, the 2nd Battery and Hauptmann Caesar were mentioned in the Wehrmacht Report.

On 17 June the 2nd Battery, attached to Infanterie-Regiment 65, attacked Fort "Siberia". The battery was used primarily to eliminate flanking efforts by GPU units. When the infantry bogged down, the Sturmgeschütze were withdrawn. In the afternoon, Hauptmann Peitz personally attempted a new attack with the battery. But this time too, it bogged down in enemy fire.

The 3rd Battery, attached to the Infanterie-Regiment 97, attacked the enemy at points 614, 615, 616 and 617. It was able to push its attack to point 621, before massed artillery fire intervened and also stopped this attack. Afterwards, the commander of the Infanterie-Regiment 97 praised Hauptmann Naether highly.

On 20 June the Sturmgeschütze managed to penetrate the "Lenin" Fort. Assault troops occupied the fortification system, and the coastal fort at point 652 was captured. The armored towers of this fort were smashed by the armored piercing rounds from the Sturmgeschütze. The north fort was also taken. Hauptmann Caesar took over the battalion in the place of the battalion commander, who was sick with dysentery.

On 30 June the Sturmgeschütze managed to penetrate into Sevastopol. At 13:00 hours, the first guns reached the "Panorama" and raised the German flag here. At 14:00 hours the batteries were at Severnaja Bay and were relieved.

On the same day Oberleutnant Dr. Roever received a posthumous award of the German Cross in Gold. Oberleutnant Roettgermann was decorated with the Iron Cross, First Class. Hauptmann Naether and Oberleutnant Ebinger received the Honor Roll Clasp and were named to the Honor Roll of the German Army.

After this hard fighting with so many casualties, the battalion withdrew to its old billeting area on 2 July. The exhausted men recovered at Yalta, Alutscha, Gursuff and Alupka on the "Russian Riviera" with its white castles of the czars and pine groves. The great victory celebration of the Crimean army took place in Liwadia on 5 July. Oberleutnant Buff received the German Cross in Gold the day before and was allowed to take part in the celebration.

Hauptmann Naether was the first man in the battalion to go on leave, and when he left, he was in such a hurry that he even forgot his belt. On 15 July Oberwachtmeister Tadje was also awarded the German Cross in Gold. Beginning on 22 July the battalion was transferred to the area of the 2. Armee east of Kursk. 14 long-barreled guns arrived at the battalion on 5 August, commanded by Oberleutnant Hoheisel. One day later, the battalion received attack orders for Unternehmen Eingemeindung (Operation Annexation). For this operation, the battalion was attached to the commander of Sturmgeschütz-Abteilung 201.

The 1st Battery shot up 8 enemy tanks on the first day of the attack, 8 August 1942. Two of the Sturmgeschütze were put out of action by direct hits and a third one damaged. Heavy fighting took place in Heart Woods and in Battery Grove. On 12 August the 2nd Battery was able to stop a Soviet attack to the south of Artillery Grove. Leutnant Damman, who had only 3 Sturmgeschütze, detected a breakthrough by a pack of Russian tanks and moved against this greatly superior enemy force.

Flame spewed forth from the muzzles of the guns. All three Sturmgeschütze each destroyed an enemy tank with their first shot. At breakneck speed, Leutnant Damman charged in amidst the enemy tanks. The gunner set his sights on the next tank. Once again a shell from the long barreled cannon smashed into a tank and left it a burning wreck.

Over hill and dale, first stopping, then once again avoiding an enemy shell while moving at full speed, constantly engaging and destroying one enemy tank after the other, the lieutenant's Sturmgeschütz put 6 enemy tanks out of action. In the meantime, rounds from both accompanying Sturmgeschütze were hammering enemy tanks—steel whirled through the air, flames towered up and explosions ruptured the armor of the enemy tanks.

The Artillery Grove area resembled a scene from one of Breughel's paintings of hell. Muzzle flashes lit up the plain. But then two enemy tanks fired together at the commander's Sturmgeschütz. The deadly shells hit Leutnant Damman and his crew. His laurels were torn from him at the end of the battle as the price of military victory, and he was unable to savor the height of his personal success.

This critical situation, which was saved at the last second by the 2nd Battery's incredible decisiveness and firm courage, retained the bridgehead and denied the enemy his goal of smashing through to the Don bridges. A total of 22 enemy tanks were destroyed by the 2nd Battery in this action.

When Sturmgeschütz-Abteilung 201 was withdrawn on 18 August, Sturmgeschütz-Abteilung 190 once again set up its own command post. On 19 August, Hauptmann Braun and Leutnant Mulfinger received the Iron Cross, First Class.

Hard fighting continued in the Woronesh Bridgehead. On 28 August Leutnant Tadje took over command of the 1st Battery from Oberleutnant Roth, who was ill. The commander of 3rd Battery was also seriously ill and had to be sent to hospital on 31 August. Leutnant Ammon took the battery for him. Hauptmann Peitz was promoted to Major on 3 September. On the same day, Oberwachtmeister Brückner, who was severely wounded at Sevastopol, was awarded the German Cross in Gold.

With the 12 new Sturmgeschütze (L 48) which arrived at the battalion on 11 September, the unit now had 27 combat-ready guns. In the days that followed, the battalion was used in a counterattack on the Russian bridgehead at Kasino. In this action, the 3rd Battery, which had taken over antitank duties on 17 September, managed to break up a strong Soviet tank attack against Zieglei and Kasino and destroyed 17 T-34's. The battery was relieved by the 1st Battery after it had expended all its ammunition. The 1st Battery destroyed an additional 18 T-34's by 1430 hours. Finally, both batteries were sent to support the infantry in its attack on the "Red House," the brickworks and Kasino. The attack bogged down in the heavy Russian defensive fire.

The next day, the Soviets continued their movements around and out of Kasino. Their strong tank attack was broken up 300 m northeast of the brickworks by the 1st Battery. Leutnant Mulfinger was killed in this action by a direct hit from a shell. Hauptmann Caesar was killed by bomb shrapnel. The man who had stormed Fort "Stalin" was dead. Leutnant Mulfinger, an extremely gifted but modest scholar, was buried next to Hauptmann Caesar. Leutnant Tadje took over command of the 2nd Battery and Oberleutnant Hoheisel took command of the 1st Battery. The next four days brought additional victories to the battalion. The date of 22 September is recorded in a page of honor in the battalion history.

The battalion went into action with Infanterie-Regiment 532 to clean out the Russian salient at the brickworks. This attack bogged down. The second attack began at 1400 hours. In this engagement two enemy tanks held off the German infantry. Then Leutnant Tadje moved his Sturmgeschütz out in front of the lines by itself and began a firefight with the enemy. In a fierce duel, which was followed by those left behind with almost unbearable tension, Leutnant Tadje destroyed both tanks even though he had been under fire from antitank guns and howitzers ever since leaving his attack position at Kasino. Shell explosions mushroomed up all around the rocking Sturmgeschütz. Again and again the spectators were afraid that Leutnant Tadje had been hit. But he emerged again and again from the smoke and dirt. At the very moment when he destroyed the second tank, he received a direct hit. Leutnant Tadje was severely wounded and his entire crew was killed. After destroying 39 tanks, fate finally caught up with the Sturmgeschütz of Leutnant Tadje.

On 24 October Leutnant Tadje was awarded the Knight's Cross of the Iron Cross in the hospital. The third attack took place at 1700 hours on that eventful day. This attack had also bogged down by the fall of darkness. Eight enemy tanks were left burning on the plain. The battalion had become deeply worried about ammunition shortages. The battalion fought in the Trumpeter Grove until 26 September. Leutnants Ammon, Urban, Adam, Lenk and Bischof were decorated with the Iron Cross, First Class. Major Peitz received the German Cross in Gold for his exemplary personal conduct as well as for his well planned and successful leadership of the battalion in the Crimea and in the Woronesh Bridgehead.

During the period from 1 January 1942 to 1 October 1942, the battalion had a total of eight soldiers who received the German Cross in Gold. Forty-six were decorated with the Iron Cross, First Class and one hundred eight with the Iron Cross, Second Class. One-hundred forty eight Assault Badges were awarded. Two gold, fourteen silver, and eighty seven black wound badges bore witness to the extraordinary dedication of every individual soldier.

In November the situation in the Woronesh Bridgehead grew critical. The battalion was placed on defense. Just as every battery was celebrating New Year's Eve, an alert was given. The Sturmgeschütze were needed in the 2nd Hungarian Army's sector.

The entire front held by the Hungarians collapsed when the Soviets attacked on 17 January 1943. Two German divisions were rushed in, but they arrived too late to be able to prevent the disaster.

All of the Sturmgeschütze were in action day and night. The mission: Bring men and materiél back West out of the continuously reforming pocket. As the Soviets, reinforced by partisans, took the only bridge over the Don at Ostrogoschk—the only way across for the battalion—Oberleutnant Ammon once again fought the way clear using combat elements of the 3rd Battery. The other two batteries also smashed their way through. Leutnant Prieber was wounded during this fighting. He died in spite of everything the doctors could do to save him.

Just back from leave, Major Peitz rode back to his battalion in an armored prime mover to assume leadership at the critical points. On 22 October he was severely wounded and fell into Russian hands. Oberleutnant Ammon attacked once more with the 3rd Battery and freed his badly wounded commander. The battalion surgeon, Oberarzt Dr. von Kügelchen, was killed on the same day.

In February the Sturmgeschütze, together with the two German divisions, managed to stabilize the front at Oskol. The assault batteries were in action in the bitter cold at Stary Oskol, when suddenly the following teletype was received and there was tremendous joy:

"The entire Sturmgeschütz-Abteilung 190 is to depart for Jüterbog."

By 20 February, the lead elements were already in Treuenbrietzen. This was the first major reconstitution period in two years of combat. At the beginning of March, the entire battalion went on leave. Immediately afterwards, Hauptmann Wersig took over the battalion. For the first time, each battery received a heavy section with 10.5 cm howitzers. On 1 April 1943 the battalin was redesignated as leichte Sturmgeschütz-Abteilung 190.

On 23 June 1943 the battalion began its march back to the East. It reached Gomel on 27 June. It stayed there for three weeks and arrived at Karatschew on 14 July, where it was attached to the 4. Armee for immediate use by the 211. Infanterie-Division and the 5. Panzer-Division. Both divisions were defending against the Soviets, who were attacking ceaselessly to relieve their threatened forces at Shisdra in the Kursk area. Immediately after the 1st Battery went into action at Susseja, the Sturmgeschütz of Oberleutnant Hoheisel was reported missing in action.

As the fire brigade of the army, the battalion was then put into action at every hot spot on the front. It managed to keep the Soviets from penetrating the front. The 1st Battery destroyed 16 more T-34's at Granki. Fighting on the highway from Karatschew to the north and on the highway from Jarzewo to Duchowtschina and Kulagino followed. Oberleutnant Haebler was severely wounded at Kulagino on 26 August 1943. Assistant Surgeon Dr. Tiedje was killed in a Russian bombing attack on 13 September. Following that, all of the Sturmgeschütze were moved to Duchowtschina. Hauptmann Wersig and the entire crew of his command Sturmgeschütz were severely wounded while defending against a Russian tank attack north of Duchowtschina. Hauptmann Bender took over command of the battalion, orphaned once again.

The Sturmgeschütze broke up several Soviet tank attacks on the Smolensk—Orscha highway.

In the middle of November the battalion was transferred to the 3. Panzer-Armee, which was involved in extremely heavy defensive fighting in the Witebsk—Newel area. When the Russians managed to make a penetration, the Sturmgeschütze sealed it off and destroyed their 200th enemy tank since going into action in July of that year. For exemplary conduct in the face of the enemy, Leutnant Nävie, Oberleutnant Truxa, Leutnant Kanitz and Wachtmeister Windmüller received the German Cross in Gold.

The battalion was transferred to the VI. Armee-Korps. Hauptmann Kröhne took over command. He was to keep command of the battalion/brigade until the end of the war and led the brigade through the inferno of its last two years.

During the counterattack on 8 November 1943, which was executed with the objective of retaking the city of Newel, the battalion gave support to the infantry in the north and south groups. The Russians had taken Newel in a surprise attack. The 2nd Battery under Oberleutnant Truxa fought its way to the dominating heights and destroyed the defenses there. Unfortunately, one of those misfortunes occurred there which seem to be unavoidable in war. German Tigers, which had also been assigned these heights as an attack objective, took the Sturmgeschütze under fire and forced them off the heights.

Oberleutnant Truxa received the Knight's Cross for his initiative in destroying the enemy on the dominant heights and the aggressive way in which the attack was carried out. Hauptmann Bender, the commander of the 3rd Battery, was killed during the same attack in the isthmus between the lakes.

On 13 December 1943 no fewer than 12 Soviet rifle divisions went into action south of Lake Jeseritschie in the sector of the 129. Infanterie-Division. This initiated the first winter battle for Witebsk. Leichte Sturmgeschütz-Abteilung 190 threw itself against the attackers—functioning once again as a fire brigade—and destroyed a total of 40 enemy tanks. Witebsk remained in German hands. On 14 January 1944, the battalion was redesignated as leichte Sturmgeschütz-Brigade 190.

On 3 February 1944 6 Soviet armies began the second winter battle for Witebsk. Leichte Sturmgeschütz-Brigade 190 was at the Nowiki Bridgehead on the Lutschessa River at the center of the battle. Oberleutnant Urban, commander of the 2nd Battery, was killed by a direct hit. Fifteen enemy tanks were destroyed and on 25 February the brigade was pulled out and, by order of the Führer, transferred to Kowel for employment. The brigade rolled 600 kilometers to the southwest by rapid rail transport. At Cholm it received new guns. Kowel, cut-off by the Soviets, was to be relieved.

The Soviet occupied railroad line to Kowel was cleared. Leutnant Klapperstück and his section of the 1st Battery fought there with iron determination. Every tank the enemy could throw against his small number of guns was destroyed. This action was described in the Wehrmacht Report for 28 March 1944 as follows:

"Our Divisions gained ground through offensive actions north of Kowel and broke up enemy counterattacks. During the fighting in the Kowel area, Leutnant Klapperstück, Section Leader in an Sturmgeschütz-Brigade, especially distinguished himself by his outstanding bravery."

On 4 April 1944 leichte Sturmgeschütz-Brigade 190 destroyed 37 antitank guns during an attack on a Russian Pakriegel (antitank defensive belt). Six friendly guns were knocked out by hits. Once again, the Wehrmacht Report mentioned leichte Sturmgeschütz-Brigade 190:

"In spite of tenacious enemy resistance, our offensive actions in the area of Kowel made further advances and gained several dominating terrain features and villages. In this fighting, a Sturmgeschütz-Brigade destroyed 37 antitank guns by itself."

The Turia River was reached after more bitter fighting. This allowed the surrounded town of Kowel to be relieved. The exhausted brigade was pulled back to the area of Cholm for rest and refitting. However, on 26 May, it was already on its way to the area east of Mogilew in rapid rail transport. Just one month later the Soviet summer offensive was initiated there. Simultaneously, an estimated 50,000 strong partisan army attacked as well. Strong armored Soviet spearheads thrust deep into the German rear area and cut off the retreat of the desperately fighting German Kampfgruppen.

The individual batteries of the brigade fought at every critical point and destroyed numerous enemy tanks. Bands of partisans blew up roads and bridges. A disaster loomed.

The entire central front collapsed. The brigade fought on its own without orders from higher headquarters. In desperate, confused fighting for the very existence of not only the brigade, 25 enemy tanks were destroyed east of the Dnjepr on 24 and 25 June. Hauptmann Schwalb and his 1st Battery contributed substantially to this success. He received the Knight's Cross for this action.

The brigade pulled back to Beresina only after receiving express orders from the Commanding General of the XXXIX. Armee-Korps, General Martinek. One section of the 2nd Battery remained behind as rear guard for Division "Feldherrnhalle" under the command of the battery commander, Oberleutnant Nävie. The brigade was completely surrounded by the Soviets no fewer than five times before it reached the bridges which were already under Soviet fire. On 2 July the six Sturmgeschütze of the 2nd Battery also reached the Beresina Bridge. Commanding these six guns were:

Oberleutnant Nävie, Oberwachtmeister Greib, Stabswachtmeister Dörfel, Wachtmeister Schättler, Oberwachtmeister Genz and Wachtmeister Lensing.

In addition they were joined by two more guns from the 3rd Battery commanded by Wachtmeister Bader and Oberwachtmeister Windmeier.

An infantry colonel, who had taken command of the bridge on his own initiative, summoned Oberleutnant Nävie and ordered him to take his guns back into action to save what could still be saved. Oberleutnant Nävie went back to the assembly area for his Sturmgeschütze. "Everybody over here!" he ordered. The men grouped around their commander. The eyes of the Oberleutnant traveled over the faces of his loyal men. "We're going back into action", Oberleutnant Nävie continued. "I need four guns. The others will wait here on the Beresina and guard against any Soviet surprise attack." All six gun commanders volunteered. Oberleutnant Nävie selected the following crews:

Wachtmeister Schättler with Unteroffizier Tränkel, Obergefreiter Dieg and Obergefreiter Schmitt

Unteroffizier Zamar with Unteroffizier Nee, Unteroffizier Tjarks and an unknown crewman

Obergefreiter Krönchen, Gefreiter Märzhäuser, and two unknown crewmen

The crew of the command Sturmgeschütz consisted of: Oberleutnant Nävie, Oberwachtmeister Genz, Oberwachtmeister Windmeier and Wachtmeister Bader.

The four guns moved out. Just a short distance away, they ran into a pack of Russian tanks. The fighting began. Oberleutnant Nävie with his four Sturmgeschütze managed to destroy a large number of tanks and forced the others to pull back. Only by late evening did all four Sturmgeschütze return intact to the bridge.

Only after the last element of the combat-support trains had crossed the bridge, did the four Sturmgeschütze roll over the bridge after them. The bridge was then blown up. Through this self-sacrificing act, the bridge crossing was able to remain open one more full day.

On 6 July Oberleutnant Nävie destroyed 5 heavy tanks and 3 enemy antitank guns during a Russian attack. During the fighting his Sturmgeschütz also received three direct hits. Oberleutnant Nävie was wounded in the head. Oberleutnant Nävie, Oberwachtmeister Windmeier and the loader had to dismount. Just as they had left the gun, a fourth round blew it up and the driver was killed.

On 7 July this Kampfgruppe broke through a Russian blocking position. The Kampfgruppe got separated in a night attack by partisans. The rest of this Kampfgruppe didn't reach the German lines at the position held by Polizei-Regiment 31 until 27 July. Twenty six members of the brigade were missing. The remaining elements of the brigade moved through the trackless area under partisan control to reach the main highway east of Minsk, where the remains of three armies were streaming back under a constant hail of Russian bombs.

During a night march across a heavily damaged bridge, the lead Sturmgeschütz careened off. The crew drowned. The remaining guns did not cross the bridge until daybreak. Sixteen of them reached the west bank. The horrible odyssey ended for these elements of the brigade on 7 July. The Sturmgeschütze had put over 900 kilometers behind them. Written off by the high command, they still made it.

The elements of the brigade were assembled in the area of Lyck in East Prussia. There was only a short pause for rest and refitting, as they were already on their way back to Brest-Litowsk on 18 July 1944. There was no long any contiguous German line in the area of Bialystok-Brest-Litowsk. The batteries were thrown into combat as they arrived and mostly found themselves in heavy fighting against greatly superior forces of enemy tanks, which unceasingly thrust into the German rear area. The brigade was thrown into one critical spot after the other. Several enemy attempts to cross the Bug were blocked. Every day was a fight to gain time.

At Narew bloody duels flared up between individual Sturmgeschütze and Soviet tanks which had already made it across. The brigade prevented the Russians from expanding this bridgehead. On 9 November the exhausted Soviets suspended fighting. The "Löwe"-Brigade ("Lion" Brigade) was pulled back and went into a quieter position for refitting.

The beginning of the Russian winter offensive on 14 January 1945 found the brigade once again fighting out in front. On the evening of January 15 it went into an assembly area north of Nasielsk. During the night the men heard the ceaseless growl of Russian tank engines. German soldiers, who had escaped Russian capture, reported major Russian tank assembly areas in the immediate vicinity.

During the night Major Kröhne placed all the Sturmgeschütze in widely dispersed positions facing the east. As soon as there was enough light to shoot, the enemy tanks moved forward from their assembly areas only 500 meters away. They were greeted by simultaneous fire from every Sturmgeschütz. The shells flashed like lightning from a powerful storm. Fires flared up; explosions tore the morning air; and streamers of smoke rose into the sky like banners of destruction.

For five minutes the cannons thundered. For five minutes every man of the brigade did his utmost. Then 20 enemy tanks lay in front of the German position, and the rest fled in panic-stricken terror.

Major Kröhne moved his guns back behind the nearest crest. He waited for the next enemy attack, but the units of the 1st Russian Guards Tank Corps would not attack again that day. In the subsequent heavy tank fighting at Plöhnen from 17 to 18 January, 20 more tanks were destroyed under Major Kröhne's personal command. The Germans had regained control of the gap in the front. Major Rudolf Kröhne received the Knight's Cross for these actions. They moved back through Plöhnen, Sichelberg and Gollupp into the Drewens Position, reaching Graudenz on 26 January. The crossings over the Vistula had to be held. The brigade fought in continuous counterattacks to gain time. Major Kröhne led this strong brigade in masterly fashion from engagement to engagement and on 26 February 1945 the Wehrmacht Report mentioned Sturmgeschütz-Brigade 190 once again:

"Sturmgeschütz-Brigade 190 under the command of Major Kröhne has especially distinguished itself in uninterrupted offensive and defensive action in West Prussia and Pomerania. The brigade has played a decisive role in defending against enemy tank forces and in one month has destroyed 104 enemy tanks at a cost of only four friendly guns."

However, the brigade owed its successes at least as much to the outstanding performance of the repair and maintenance crews. In this regard Oberwerkmeister (Head Foreman) Hahnel and Kriegsverwaltungsrat (Military Administrator) Zeman were often able to accomplish the seemingly impossible.

The final battle for Danzig began. Leutnant Förster and Oberwachtmeister Seidel destroyed 26 Stalin tanks with their sections west of Danzig, in the area of Schäferei. There were more tank engagements at Oliva and at the Langfuhr Airfield. There, Wachtmeister Moj presented an example of the highest courage and devotion to duty. With his Sturmgeschütz in an hour-long battle—one Sturmgeschütz against a tank pack—he individually destroyed 12 enemy tanks before his own time came and his gun was blown up.

On 6 March the brigade was again mentioned in the Wehrmacht Report with respect to its 1000th enemy tank destroyed.

On 26 March Danzig had to be abandoned, and the brigade moved to Hela on 7 May. On the next day they received orders leave by sea. This last official radio contact ran: "2300 hours: Call it quits. Embark immediately on ships for Flensburg, passing the south coast of Sweden. Do not put in at Bornholm."

One hundred and twenty Sturmartilleristen went to sea on the river barge "Emma." An additional 120 members of the brigade were embarked on boats of Landungs-Brigade "Paul." Thirty men were taken on Navy landing craft in the Vistula Marsh. The two latter groups reached Kiel and were interned by the English at Gut Gaarz and soon released to go home. A fourth group remained in the Vistula Marsh. Of these men, Leutnant Hernekamp and Wachtmeister Kellermann fled to Gotenhafen in a rubber boat and from there back home. By 1 June 1945 Leutnant Hernekamp was standing in front of his parents' destroyed home in Dortmund.

However, the crew of the "Emma" reached Sweden. There the 120 Sturmartilleristen were interned. Although the war was at an end, the real horror then began for these last men of leichte Sturmgeschütz-Brigade 190. In November 1945—contrary to all international law—Sweden handed them over to the Soviet Union. The Sturmartilleristen were taken to Russia on the steamer "Kuban." The German soldiers in the Swedish camp at Ränneslätt who protested against this contravention of international law were beaten down with clubs.

Suicides and self mutilation followed for those despairing souls. Those who had been sold to the Russians in this unprecedented, lawless affair, disappeared into the east. A few returned home, sick after years of wandering and martyrdom. Most, however, vanished in the expanses of Russia.

Thus ended the history of leichte Sturmgeschütz-Brigade 190, a brigade which did great honor to its insignia, the lion, in more than four years of combat.

Command and Staff Positions in Sturmgeschütz-Abteilung 190

(from 1 October 1940 to 28 December 1941)

Commander: Oberstleutnant Haupt (†), Major Vogt (o)

Adjutant: Oberleutnant Nottebrock, Oberleutnant Bender, Leutnant Eyrich

Staff: Hauptmann Merl (x), Oberleutnant von Jena (x), Leutnant Roever, Leutnant Thesmacher, Leutnant Bischof, Assistenz-Arzt Dr. Körnig (x), Oberarzt Dr. Lang, Kriegsverwaltungsrat Zeman, Inspekteur Kohl, Werkmeister Hanel, KVI Claus.

1st Battery: Oberleutnant Wersig (x), Oberleutnant Noe (x), Leutnant Schwalb (o), Leutnant Lepper (†), Leutnant Bayer (†), Leutnant Tenner, Oberleutnant Cardeneo, Leutnant Nottebrock (o).

2nd Battery: Oberleutnant von Stein (†), Oberleutnant von Kittlitz (x), Oberleutnant Wein (x), Leutnant Plikat (x), Ober-leutnant Nottebrock (†), Oberleutnant Schilling (†), Oberleutnant Hartmann (†), Leutnant Wagner (o), Leutnant Roever, Oberleutnant Bender (o), Oberleutnant Caesar.

3rd Battery: Oberleutnant Naether, Oberleutnant Bender, Leutnant Ebinger (o), Leutnant Thesmacher (o), Leutnant Eyrich, Leutnant Buff, Leutnant Fürnschuß.

Symbols: † = KIA; o = WIA; x = transferred

Command and Staff Positions in leichte Sturmgeschütz-Brigade 190

(from 15 October1943 to 8 May 1945)

Commander: Major Kröhne

Adjutant: Oberleutnant Urban, Oberleutnant Bruns (o), Oberleutnant Sühring, Oberleutnant Ludwig (o), Oberleutnant Claus.

Staff: Oberleutnant Urban, Oberleutnant Bruns, Oberleutnant Mildenberger, Oberleutnant Kanitz (x), Oberleutnant Zülch, Leutnant Havenstein (x), Leutnant Heyer, Leutnant Klapperstück, Oberarzt Dr. Rister (x), Oberarzt Dr. Standacher (o), Oberarzt Dr. Orlowski, Kriegsverwaltungsrat Zeman (o), Oberinspekteur Kohl (x), Oberwachtmeister Hand, Oberzahlmeister Claus (†), Stabsint. Borchers (x), Oberzahlmeister Trabandt.

1st Battery: Hauptmann Schwalb (x), Hauptmann Zülch (o), Oberleutnant Urban (†), Hauptmann Adamowitzsch (x), Leutnant Mildenberger, Leutnant Hallmeier, Leutnant Köhler, Leutnant Dietrich (o).

2nd Battery: Hauptmann Truxa (x), Oberleutnant Nävie (v), Hauptmann Bruns, Leutnant Caesar (o), Leutnant Lewark (†), Leutnant Burmester (†), Leutnant Hernekamp.

3rd Battery: Oberleutnant Bender (†), Oberleutnant Giese (x), Oberleutnant Mildenberger, Leutnant Truxa (o), Leutnant Köhler, Leutnant Helmut (†), Leutnant Voß, Leutnant Förster (o), Leutnant Collbrunn (o).

Symbols: † = KIA; o = WIA; x = transferred, v = MIA

Sturmgeschütz-Abteilung 191 (Sturmgeschütz-Brigade 191)

Sturmgeschütz-Brigade 191

One of the four Sturmgeschütz battalions which had been formed on 1 October 1940 in the Artillerie-Lehr-Regiment at Jüterbog after the campaign in France was the "Büffel"-Abteilung ("Buffalo" Battalion). It was made up from personnel taking the Sturmartillerie course which started at the New Camp in August 1940. The first battalion commander was Hauptmann Günther Hoffmann-Schoenborn.

The commander, a professional soldier, came from an old military family in Posen. In 1924 he entered the Artillerie-Regiment 3 as an officer candidate. During the campaign in France he was decorated with both classes of the Iron Cross. Hoffmann-Schoenborn was promoted to the rank of Major in December 1940.

By the time the battalion rolled southeast on New Year's Day 1941 on several railroad trains, Major Hoffmann-Schoenborn had welded it into a powerful weapon. It traveled via Vienna, Budapest and Bucharest to the snow-covered oil fields at Ploesti. Major Hoffmann-Schoenborn continued his training there.

At the beginning of March 1941, the battalion road marched across the bridge at Giurgiu into Bulgaria. Passing through Stara Zagora (Valley of the Roses) and Sofia, the battalion reached the region of the Greek-Bulgarian border at the beginning of April and went into position facing south.

The Greeks occupied bunkers opposite the battalion which had been blasted into the bizarre rock formations. This was the Metaxas Line. Where in this broken, impassable mountain terrain were the Sturmgeschütze to be employed? Major Hoffmann-Schoenborn scouted these positions. He found the best places himself. Everywhere the Sturmgeschütze ran into trouble, their commander appeared and helped out.

Attack orders were issued to the battalion on 5 April. Final preparations were made, and the combat elements rolled into their ready positions in the black of night on 5/6 April 1941.

The artillery began its bombardment of the Greek fortifications on the next morning at 0530 hours. The war against Greece had begun. The Sturmgeschütze rolled forward from their ready positions. Following them, ammunition carriers and command vehicles reached the Bistriza, which was in flood stage, but which had already been crossed by the infantry on rapidly constructed wooden foot bridges. One Sturmgeschütz slid out of the ford into a hole. Immediately, Major Hoffmann-Schoenborn ordered a prime mover forward which pulled the gun out of the water. The crew bailed the water out of its gun with steel helmets.

"Support the assault battalion of Infanterie-Regiment 125!" the battalion commander ordered.

And then the 1st section rolled off towards Hill 350. The Sturmgeschütze fired on the bunkers which were recognizable by the muzzle flashes emanating from them. Hill 350 fell into German hands after a short assault, but then Greek resistance stiffened.

Under the personal command of Major Hoffmann-Schoenborn, the 1st Battery screened the assault by Infantry Regiment 125. The Sturmgeschütz muzzles swung to cover every fighting position detected. Rounds howled through the morning and smashed the points of resistance.

However, the attack bogged down in front of the bunkers in the Rupel Pass. The rock walls were steeper there, and a deep gorge kept the Sturmgeschütze from pushing forward.

Oberleutnant Wolfgang Kapp looked for a passable route for his battery in order to hook up with the infantry groups up front. His report is repeated here:

Nowhere did there appear to be any possibility for crossing the gorge. We moved deeper into the trackless badlands. Perhaps we could cross the gorge on the other side of the mountain. A sharp, splintering crack put a stop to our efforts. Antitank rounds had smashed through my command vehicle. It was on fire in a flash. With difficulty I managed to save myself, my radio operator and my driver, who later died of his wounds.

In the meantime, my Sturmgeschütze fired on the bunker on the other side of the gorge, where the antitank cannon was still shooting from its embrasure. I detected six, seven other bunkers next to it. They were silenced with a few well-aimed rounds. But scarcely did the guns from one grow silent, when another one came to life. There were fighting positions sprinkled all around these highlands.

Rapid orders to the section commanders. I climbed down the slope and then up the other side of the gorge. Pieces torn from my uniform were left hanging on the thorn bushes. The sun shone down with scorching rays from a steel-blue sky. Gasping and dripping sweat, I climbed a path on which our infantry battalion was bunched up. Fresh troops were coming up from the bottom of the gorge. They were stuck up there, just under the saddle, the key stone of the Rupel Position. Further advance onto the saddle was impossible. Anyone who let himself be seen there was riddled with bullets. Who would have thought that the few, so pitiful looking battle positions that we could see from the Bulgarian side of the border would be able to offer such hard and energetic resistance against us?

This wasn't helping! If I wanted to support the infantry with my Sturmgeschütze, I had to bring them up this path. In this murderous fire, only Sturmgeschütze could dare to move onto the saddle plateau to silence the enemy's heavy weapons and destroy his bunkers. On foot, I started to search for a place were we could cross the gorge. It took hours, but I managed to get four of my guns moving forward on the path which was just wide enough for such giants.

The new attack was set at 1730 hours. Stukas bombed the enemy positions. Massed artillery fire rained down and burst on them.

We breathed easier. Our enemy had never before been able to resist such a bombardment. Scarcely had the last bomb fallen and the last shell exploded, when the Sturmgeschütze moved up over the edge of the plateau. Pressed closely together, all four moved onto the tiny platform.

Firing rapidly, they sprayed rounds against the Greek bunkers. Then the infantry, which had been in ready positions just under the rim of the plateau, launched its attack.

Suddenly the air was filled with a whistling and howling. A roaring, cracking and booming wants to break our eardrums. The earth trembled. Steel shrieked. Stone and mud, tree stumps and chunks of rock whirled through the air and rained down on us. The Greeks had directed every weapon in these hills on us. Shells of every caliber smashed down around us. The infantry raced back into the shelter of its ready position.

For long minutes all of the Sturmgeschütze were veiled with dust and dirt. Rounds hammered with deafening noise on the armor plate. It seemed as if I should never see my men again. It was impossible to pull back. The drivers had no vision to the rear. To leave the path would have meant an immediate plunge into the gorge. But they did it! I breathed easier when I saw the guns back on the path. The loader in the first gun was killed. All the other men were still alive. But what did the guns look like! All of the sheet ,metal on the track guards and the superstructure were filled with holes, torn up and partly torn off. The armor plate was dented everywhere. But they made it.

A thin rain began to fall on the second day of the attack. Gradually it became heavier. Greek artillery and mortars fired into the German positions. Major Hoffmann-Schoenborn had still heard nothing from Major Ens, the commander of the II./ Infanterie-Regiment 125, who had taken a combat patrol composed of volunteers through the enemy lines during the night of 6 April to capture the southern route out of the Struma Pass and take the bridge there in a surprise attack.

The Sturmgeschütze were repaired as well as possible under the conditions. Isolated duels with bunkers took place. Then this second unsuccessful day ended.

On 8 April Major Hoffmann-Schoenborn ordered an infiltration attack against the bunkers on the ridge. The forward-most Sturmgeschütz rolled onto the saddle and opened fire. If the Greeks didn't answer the fire, the infiltrators were to attack immediately. Perhaps the Greeks had been softened up?

Hardly half a minute went by after the gun opened fire when every heavy weapon in these mountain fortifications hammered down on the Sturmgeschütz. Oberleutnant Kapp, who observed this fire, summoned the gun back. Once again it managed to get back under cover unharmed. The battery commander shook the hand of Oberwachtmeister Bauer, the gun commander.

"Now, our artillery will hit them again." he said to Oberwachtmeister Bauer. "It'll try to silence the enemy batteries. In half an hour we'll try again."

The Oberwachtmeister looked at Oberleutnant Kapp.

"That's alright by me, Herr Oberleutnant!" was all he said.

But the second attempt failed as well.

The Sturmgeschütze attacked once more on 9 April. Major Hoffmann-Schoenborn put in all of the guns and on the following day, the garrison of the Rupel Fortifications laid down its arms.

Major Hoffmann-Schoenborn received the Knight's Cross on 14 May 1941 for this tenacious action.

The battalion received orders to return to Saloniki at Lamia after it had advanced past Mount Olympus and through Larissa. The battalion was sent back from Saloniki to Olmütz, where it was given a complete refit.

Transferred to the Lublin area after its refit, Sturmgeschütz-Abteilung 191 joined the 6. Armee (General von Reichenau), attacking to the east on 22 June 1941. The commander accompanied the battalion's attack in an open-topped, speedy staff car.

The battalion crossed the Bug at Uscilug. It was in action continuously, with one clash following another. There was especially hard fighting at Wlodzimiers, Dubno, Kremenez, and Radomyschl. Servings as the backbone of different advance guard battalions, the battalion took part in the bitter fighting west of the Dnjepr at Malin. During those engagements, it was attached to the 98. Infanterie-Division.

On 20 July 1941 Major Hoffmann-Schoenborn received a mission which sent him and his battalion into an enemy-held area far beyond the front lines. The Sturmgeschütze were told to advance to Korosten along with the advance guard battalion of the 98. Infanterie-Division. Korosten was taken. By the end of the month the battalion had cleared the way to the Dnjepr for the LI. and XVII. Armee-Korps.

The battalion commander was always forward with his Sturmgeschütze. In difficult situations he pulled the Sturmgeschütze and their accompanying infantry forward by the force of his personal example. By the end of July 49 enemy cannon had been captured.

The battalion fought its most successful engagement at the end of August 1941. Attached to an advance guard detachment, the Sturmgeschütze of the "Büffel"-Abteilung advanced through a gap in the enemy lines for a distance of 100 kilometers all the way to the Dnjepr. Mounted grenadiers and combat engineers as well as antiaircraft and antitank elements accompanied this spearhead. The forward Soviet defense lines collapsed under the assault of this battalion. The enemy's rear guard was out distanced. The dust rose into the sky in thick clouds. An intoxicating aroma drifted towards the advancing Sturmgeschütze from the hops fields of Gornostaipol. At the same time they were engaged by Soviet fire from these fields. Soviet antitank cannon, artillery, machine guns and rifles all opened fire.

This enemy was defeated. They started to run, and then streamed back in wild flight. Leutnant Bingler, who led the lead elements, went in pursuit with his section of three guns. The direction of advance was to the east, wherever the Dnjepr was. The objective of the attack was the Dnjepr bridge which crossed that river. Leutnant Bingler didn't bother with anything behind him. The rest of the battalion would take care of that.

The Sturmgeschütz of Leutnant Bingler reached a fork in the road at the entry to a village. Unteroffizier Heinz Pfeiffer halted the gun with a jerk. Leutnant Bingler saw his two other guns about 200 meters behind him. The village looked like a ghost town.

Together with the Leutnant, the gunner, Unteroffizier Sablattnig, examined the village through his panoramic sights. Suddenly a truck emerged from behind the houses.

"Two hundred and fifty!" ordered the Leutnant. Sablattnig took aim.

"Fire!" The round was over, but the truck stopped and a group of Russians dismounted and took cover. Then the truck started up again. The second shot tore it apart. The combat engineers riding on the back deck of the Sturmgeschütz took a few prisoners. Leutnant Bingler turned to these prisoners. He pointed at the road running off at an angle to the right.

"Dnjepr?" he asked. And once again, "Dnjepr?"

"Da, da, Dnjepr; tri kilometr" declared the Russians, nodding their heads vigorously.

"Move out!" ordered Leutnant Bingler.

The engines raced, and off they moved at high speed. Leutnant Bingler drove through the village. He reached the exit from the village and approached a small bridge behind it. Russian columns streamed across the bridge, coming from the left.

"Demolition crew!" yelled one of the engineers riding the gun. Through his panoramic sights, Unteroffizier Sablattnig saw a Russian racing across the bridge with a cord in his hand.

"Herr Leutnant, they're going to blow the bridge!"

A shot rang out from the Sturmgeschütz; the Russian fell. One of the engineers sprang from the Sturmgeschütz and cut the fuse. Then the Sturmgeschütz rumbled across the planks of the bridge.

The paved road came to an end on the other side of the bridge. The tracks rattled onto the cobbled pavement. Bingler's Sturmgeschütz rolled forward at nearly 50 kilometers an hour. His two other guns had remained behind. After a curve, the shining ribbon of a river appeared in front of him. There was a barricade of thick bricks in front. The gun passed the barricade. There was a bridge ahead.

"Is that our bridge?" cried Pfeiffer.

"The Tetereff," Leutnant Bingler yelled back.

This was a tributary of the Dnjepr, which emptied into it at Gornostaipol. At top speed, the gun thundered over the planks of the wooden bridge. Just after crossing this bridge, they were greeted by muzzle flashes from the left.

"Antitank or antiaircraft weapons, Herr Leutnant!"

"Keep going! Labusch will take care of them!"

The road curved ahead. Suddenly a giant steel structure appeared in front of the Sturmgeschütz. Vehicles were moving towards the bridge ahead of the Sturmgeschütz. In front of them was a Panje wagon. They passed the Panje wagon. A passenger car moved faster. The gun quickly reached the ramp to the bridge. Glances to the left and right showed Leutnant Bingler sandbag barricades and Soviet soldiers. But no one fired. Shots rang out behind them from the second Sturmgeschütz commanded by Wachtmeister Labusch.

"Labusch is engaging the flak!" called the Leutnant.

Then the gun rolled onto the bridge's wooden roadway. Many Panje wagons clogged the road. A stream of refugees moved along on the right. The first Panje wagon was crushed beneath the tracks of the Sturmgeschütz. A few horsemen were thrown in a high arc from their saddles over the railings of the bridge after colliding with the Sturmgeschütz. The engineers on the lead Sturmgeschütz fired with their and pistols and machine pistols.

The iron arch of the bridge was quickly crossed. But the wooden roadway still stretched on to the east. It seemed endless to the driver. Their nerves were stretched to the breaking point. When would the bridge be blown up?

The passenger car kept moving ahead of the Sturmgeschütz. Suddenly it stopped. It was soon caught by the tracks, which crushed the car and rattled on over it. Then Unteroffizier Pfeiffer spied an approaching truck. The truck stopped and tried to turn. Pfeiffer hit the brakes. A shock went through the gun, then it slipped over to the right side of the bridge. The side railings cracked. With great presence of mind, Heinz Pfeiffer pulled on the emergency brakes. The gun stopped.

"I'm wounded!" cried Karl Postler, the radio operator and loader.

"Everyone out!" ordered Leutnant Bingler. "The slightest shock will push the gun over."

They scrambled out. Only Postler remained behind in the gun. He began to transmit.

"Bingler to all, Bingler to all!" he called six times one after the other, and then continued in the clear: "Every Buffalo forward! Bingler is stuck! Bingler has crashed! We are out of action! Every Buffalo forward!"

Again and again, he repeated this call, "Every Buffalo forward!" while the right track of the gun hung over the abyss.

"God damn it! Only another 150 meters and we would have been across!"

The rest of the crew and the engineers had taken cover behind the gun and the truck. Leutnant Bingler saw the bunker at the end of the bridge. But no one opened fire. There, where they were, was already past the river. There was swamp, dunes and then more enemy bunkers 10 to 15 meters beneath the Sturmgeschütz. Once more Karl Postler called: "Every Buffalo forward! Bingler is defenseless!"

"I'm going to bandage Karl" said Sablattnig and climbed back onto the gun. He bandaged the bullet hole through his upper arm. At this moment, the radio operator cried out triumphantly: "I have the battalion. It acknowledged the message!"

"Good, Postler, now get out of the can, or you'll fall into the swamp when it goes."

Suddenly a powerful explosion went off behind them. Shaken, the eight men who were far ahead of all the others there on the Dnjepr bridge, looked at one another. A half hour went by. What would happen if the Russians attacked? Suddenly they heard engine noise. Leutnant Bingler grabbed his field glasses.

"It's Labusch!" he cried, relieved.

The second gun of the section now also rolled onto the bridge and was greeted by the bellow of guns. The Russian bridge security, heavy antiaircraft and antitank cannon suddenly placed direct fire on the advancing Sturmgeschütz. The shells tore holes in the wooden bridge around the gun as it pushed its way forward. Now the shells were landing close by the stationary gun. Planks shattered deafeningly into splinters.

"Herr Leutnant, the road has been blown up!' yelled Labusch as he drove past. "Our third gun is stuck in a hole back there!"

So that had been the explosion behind them they had heard earlier.

"Keep going. Form a bridgehead on that side!" cried the Leutnant.

Labusch rolled forward. He then stopped at the end of the bridge and replied to the fire from the enemy antiaircraft guns. The Sturmgeschütz fired rapidly and precisely. More and more enemy guns fell silent. Stockpiles of ammunition flared up. Labusch was soon only firing antitank rounds.

"He's used up his high explosive rounds, Herr Leutnant."

"Yeah, he's in trouble."

But Labusch didn't quit. He turned his gun and fired on the enemy antiaircraft guns to the right of the end of the bridge. And he silenced these four guns. Not until then did he turn and roll back. He stopped when he reached the command gun.

"Herr Leutnant, the Ivans intend to blow it up!"

"Everyone back" ordered the Leutnant.

The wounded were lifted onto the gun. The combat engineers dismounted and Leutnant Bingler crawled through the loader's hatch to the gun commander. Machine gun and rifle bullets swarmed around the gun. It quickly reached the 700-meter-long steel stretch of the bridge. The men saw Russians loaded with explosives climbing into the girders. The German engineers fired with everything available at the enemy who intended to blow up the bridge. The Russian engineers dropped. Infantry weapons sounded from the right behind the bridge. The 10 cm cannon of the friendly advance guard detachment were already roaring out.

The bridge was crossed. A gigantic hole yawned in front of the gun. This was the site of the explosion.

"Take cover to the left. Quickly!" someone yelled at them. They raced to the left and dove into a trench.

"Bring up ammunition!"

The Sturmgeschütz of Labusch was quickly resupplied with ammunition. Leutnant Bingler ran over to where he saw his battery commander, Oberleutnant Haarberg, who had come up to pull out the stuck Sturmgeschütz. Major Hoffmann-Schoenborn came over, calm as always. The Knight's Cross was shining at his collar.

"Wachtmeister Labusch was wounded in the eye when he bailed out, Herr Major. I'll take over his gun and go back across."

"Good, Bingler!" The commander shook his hand. "Break a leg!"

Leutnant Bingler hurried back to the Sturmgeschütz of Labusch. The gun rolled back onto the bridge. Russian fighters appeared, fired at the bridge and then disappeared once again. Leutnant Bingler reached the far side of the bridge. A few guns were still firing, but they were silenced, one after another. Then the Dnjepr bridge was firmly in German hands. When another Russian fuel truck approached, Leutnant Bingler aimed at it. The first shell hit with a powerful shock. The fuel truck illuminated the falling night like a flaming torch. After an advance of 120 kilometers, the 2.5 kilometer long bridge over the Dnjepr at Gornostaipol fell undamaged into the hands of Sturmgeschütz-Abteilung 191.

On the next morning at 0900 hours, the lead elements, once again commanded by Leutnant Bingler, reached the Desna. Leutnant Bingler was killed during the assault across this river. A round from a Russian antitank rifle shot through his steel helmet and hit him in the head.

But after the entire advance guard detachment and most of the 11. Panzer-Division had crossed the Dnjepr, the Dnjepr bridge was set on fire during that same afternoon by a major Russian attack from the air and by river gun boats. The Sturmgeschütz of Leutnant Bingler fell into the swamp with the collapsing wooden structure.

The advance guard was cut off for four days. But the bridgehead held out. The German troops who crossed the Dnjepr there closed the ring around the trapped Russians and began the battle for Kiev from the north.

Leutnant Bingler received the Knight's Cross. In addition he was awarded the Honor Roll Clasp and was recorded in the Honor Roll of the German Army. Major Hoffmann-Schoenborn was recommended for the Oak Leaves.

Sturmgeschütz-Abteilung 191 fought together with Sturmgeschütz-Abteilung 244 in the battle of encirclement around Kiev.

Shifted to the north at the end of September, the battalion passed through Gomel, Rosslawl and Malojaroslawez to reach the area of operation of the 4. Armee (Generalfeldmarschall von Kluge). It was to participate in the attack on Moscow. The subsequent fighting along the highway in the unimaginable mud of late fall made great demands on the battalion. The attack bogged down. The Sturmgeschütze rolled forward again only after frost set in, in the middle of November. Without winter clothes, at 30° Celsius below zero, the battalion was still able to take Borowsk. The crossing of the Nara near Narofominsk was the last success of 1941. Major Hoffmann-Schoenborn was wounded in the fighting at the end of 1941.

On 31 December 1941 he became the 49th soldier of the German Wehrmacht to receive the Oak Leaves to the Knight's Cross. He was the first Sturmartillerist to receive that award.

In December 1941 Hauptmann Haarberg took over command of the battalion, which was shifted to Spass Demenskoje. It stayed there until the beginning of March 1942, to be used to break open the highway to Moscow. At the end of March it was pulled back to Mogilew for refit.

New operations for the "Büffel"-Abteilung began on 1 June 1942 with a 700-kilometer road march to the area of Kursk. Its new commander was Hauptmann Führ, who was killed a little later in the fighting in the area of Kursk-Woronesh.

In July 1942 Hauptmann Kapp took over command of the battalion which had been moved to the south into an area 200 kilometers northeast of Rostow. After crossing the Don while attached to the 1. Panzer-Armee, the "Büffel"-Abteilung fought its way through the Kalmücken Steppes.

The advance continued through fields of maize and sunflowers. At Mosdok the battalion forced the Terek crossing for the 111. Infanterie-Division (General Röpke). The battalion held this position. On 30 December 1942 it received a surprising order to withdraw after the relief attempt at Stalingrad had failed. At the beginning of January 1943 it moved to the west through Woroschilowsk up to the Kuban Delta. There, the "Büffel" were attached to the 17. Armee in the Kuban Bridgehead.

Hauptmann Alfred Müller took over command of the battalion in the spring of 1943. After heavy losses, the remaining Sturmgeschütze were consolidated into one combat battery. In April the battalion was refitted in Kertsch.

It fought in all the heavy fighting on the Kuban as the fire brigade for the 17. Armee. Hauptmann Müller, who had already been awarded the Knight's Cross on 20 February 1943 as commander of Sturmgeschütz-Lehr-Batterie 901 during the fighting between the Don and the Donez, became a legend along with his "Büffel" in the Kuban Bridgehead. Wherever he and his battalion were positioned as a breakwater against heavy Russian tank attacks the front held.

In the daily report of the Headquarters of the 17. Armee for 6 October 1943, these feats were acknowledged in the following words:

"Sturmgeschütz-Abteilung 191, under the command of Hauptmann Müller, has played a decisive role in the successful defense of the last few days against overwhelming enemy odds. It intervened with enormous energy on both the defense and in counterattacks. In particular, it has destroyed 95 enemy tanks and also several 12 cm assault howitzers in the Kuban Bridgehead. We request recognition in the Wehrmacht Report."

After the Kertsch Peninsula was encircled in November 1943, the "Büffel"-Abteilung broke up the enemy bridgehead at Bulganak and, in the beginning of December, the Soviet bridgehead at Eltingen as well.

During the evacuation of the Kuban Bridgehead, Sturmgeschütz-Abteilung 191 provided cover for the withdrawal at Noworossijsk and, within a few days destroyed, 150 enemy tanks. Together with the last infantry, the last Sturmgeschütz moved out on the road out of Kertsch.

In both attack and defense, Hauptmann Alfred Müller led his Sturmgeschütze from the front. On 13 December 1943 he became the 354th soldier of the Wehrmacht to receive the Oak Leaves to the Knight's Cross.

At the beginning of 1944 the brigade found itself in heavy defensive fighting north of Kertsch and in the isthmus at Perekop at the northern exit from the Crimea. The battalion was renamed Sturmgeschütz-Brigade 191 on 28 February 1944.

During Easter 1944 the Soviets managed to break through into the Crimea. The fighting withdrawal began. Consolidated with elements of Sturmgeschütz-Brigade 279 and reinforced by Jagdpanzer of Czech design, the brigade screened the area north of Stary Krim and covered the withdrawal of the 17. Armee through Yalta to the Black Sea coast. The last troops were carried across from the furthest point of the Crimean Peninsula to Konstanza in small boats and naval landing craft. They had fought with the eight remaining Sturmgeschütze of the "Büffel"-Brigade around the ruins of "Fort Maxim Gorki." Some of the combat elements went into Russian captivity there.

A teletype labeled "urgent" on 23 May 1944 from the headquarters of the 17. Armee to Heeresgruppe Südukraine ("Southern Ukraine") reported:

In the fighting in the Crimea from 10 April to 15 May 1944, Sturmgeschütz-Brigade 191, under the exceptional leadership of its commander, Oak Leaves winner Major Müller, has destroyed a total of 137 tanks, 48 antitank and antiaircraft guns, and a great number of other weapons and vehicles. The brigade, which has consistently distinguished itself starting with the defensive fighting in the Kuban Bridgehead, destroyed its 445th tank on 12 May 1944 and once again gave proof of its outstanding bravery and aggressiveness. We request that recognition be given to it in the press and on the radio.

After a few weeks of rest in Konstanza, the brigade received orders on 6 June 1944 for a refit and for transfer via Vienna to the Schieratz Training Area in Warthegau. There, the unit was taken over in the middle of June by Hauptmann Kollböck, an old member of the brigade. In August the brigade was then put into action in Serbia south of Nisch. The brigade fought south of Belgrade and yet again in the area of Semlin during the withdrawal of von Weichs' Army. After heavy fighting the 2nd Battery loaded up for Altengrabow and remained separated from the rest of the brigade for the rest of the war. It was transferred to Lehr-Brigade II ("Instruction Brigade II") under Oberleutnant Egelhaaf.

The rest of the brigade withdrew with the Army of von Weichs back to Esseg and Novi-Sad. Hauptmann Kollböck was killed during this fighting. Hauptmann Karl-Erich Berg, who had been awarded the Knight's Cross on 6 April 1944 as Oberleutnant and commander of the 2./Sturmgeschütz-Brigade 191, became the new commander of the brigade.

The brigade was employed in the fighting in Hungary at Groß-Betscherek, on the Theiß River and at Lake Balaton. The 1st Battery was moved to Esseg-Apatin and did not return to the brigade. It was captured virtually in its entirety by the Yugoslavians. In the winter of 1944 the remainder of the brigade was involved in the defensive fighting at Nagy and in the area of Kansza-Kaposvar. Losses rapidly rose to a new high when the Soviets attacked there in the spring of 1945 with the super-heavy Josef Stalin tanks. But the remnants of the brigade were still able to free the encircled Kavallerie-Korps Boeselager and hold out along with this unit for a few more weeks.

The Headquarters Battery was ambushed at night by partisans at Marburg an der Drau. Hauptwachtmeister Fröhlich was killed during this ambush. On the day of the surrender, 8 May 1945, the brigade was still covering the withdrawal of German units across the Mur River. It was taken prisoner at Mauerkirchen and Tamsweg.

This brigade had been in continuous combat on the Eastern Front for four and a half years.

The first commander of the "Büffel"-Brigade, Oberstleutnant Hoffmann-Schoenborn, became commander of the Sturmgeschütz-Schule at Burg after giving up the brigade to his successor. In that position he was promoted to Oberst. This officer had the longest service record in the Sturmartillerie and ended the war as a Generalmajor and division commander.

Sturmgeschütz-Abteilung 192 (Sturmgeschütz-Abteilung "Großdeutschland")

Sturmgeschütz-Abteilung 192

On 11 November 1940 Sturmgeschütz-Abteilung 192 was formed at Jüterbog (New Camp). The skull and cross bones was chosen and approved as its tactical insignia. The battalion was formed of volunteers, mostly from the artillery and the Panzertruppe. Hauptmann Erich Hammon, who came to the Sturmartillerie from Artillerie-Regiment 10, was the battalion commander.

After activation, the battalion was moved to Huta-Dambrova in Poland. It conducted its training exercises as a support weapon for the infantry there. After a final three-day major exercise, the battalion was combat ready only half a year after its formation. It moved into a forested position 30 kilometers north of Terespol. At Terespol the 3./Sturmgeschütz-Abteilung 192 received orders to prepare its vehicles for operation under water. This task was accomplished to everyone's satisfaction within a short time. Leutnant Gräfing, called the "Rühmann" of the battalion because of his resemblance to the noted German film actor, organized Russian languages courses. In the meantime, welding was performed on the hulls of the vehicles to prepare them for the under-water operations of the "Unterwasser-Batterie."

On the morning of 28 May 1941 the battalion marched out of its winter quarters behind the Bug River and moved to a forest camp in the area of Janow Podlaski. There it was attached to the 31. Infanterie-Division and was given reconnaissance missions. The results of these daily reconnaissance patrols were evaluated and formed the basis for the attack plans.

A lack of good observation positions as well as dominating positions for heavy infantry weapons on the German side required special measures for the attack. On "D" Day, the infantry had to attack from its ready positions without any fire preparation. The creation of gaps through heavy machine gun fire wasn't possible either, as the terrain was tortuous and overgrown with underbrush.

As a result, Sturmgeschütz-Abteilung 192 had as its mission the following: It had to bring its guns rapidly across the Bug, support the infantry through this difficult stretch of the attack and make it possible to fight through the zone in depth by engaging the enemy at minimal range. If it succeeded, it would win the trust of the infantry on the very first day of the battle and strengthen the fighting spirit of the troops.

As the construction of a 16-ton ferry would take four hours (there was no cover for a construction area right on the banks of the Bug), and the large railroad bridge on the Terespol-Brest-Litowsk line would certainly have been blown up, there was only one way left: "Swim" across the Bug with the Sturmgeschütze. For several nights at the end of May, battalion officers carefully examined the depths of the Bug. They found two crossing points of one and a half meters of water, but for the last twenty meters, the river bed fell to a depth of two to three meters.

Oberleutnant von Jena, commander of the 3rd Battery, had worked on experiments for operation under water and, after many failed attempts, finally succeeded in operating a Sturmgeschütz entirely under water in a training pond. The exhaust and air intake pipes were extended and raised to a height of 3 meters. An air intake was installed over the commander's hatch, through which fresh air could be taken in. A motor was installed within the gun itself to pump out any water that leaked in. Every hole in the armor was sealed with caulking material. In this way the 3. "Unterwasser-Batterie" was formed. It was intended to drive through the Bug on the first day of the offensive.

At the beginning of the attack in the early morning hours of 22 June 1941, 6 Sturmgeschütze of the 1st Battery, under the personal command of Hauptmann Hammon, moved up to the large railroad bridge. Under fire from enemy infantry, whose bullets ricocheted off the armor of the Sturmgeschütze, they forced their way across the bridge, expecting an explosion at any moment that would have destroyed both the bridge and them with it. However, the enemy's surprise was too great. The Soviet Casemate "B' on the other side of the Bug to the right of the bridge was rushed by all the Sturmgeschütze at the same time. Bullets sprayed the six Sturmgeschütze. Rounds flashed out their six short barrels into the enemy positions. Three bunkers were silenced. Three Sturmgeschütze were put out of action, damaged. Then Hauptmann Hammon ordered that the Russian garrison be put out of action.

The bunkers were cleaned out with submachine guns and hand

grenades. The first prisoners taken by the battalion were sent back to the rear. The following half hour was a critical period for the battery, as the infantry was not following up very rapidly and the three Sturmgeschütze still functioning suddenly found themselves confronted by a powerful old fort with meter-thick walls.

Even so, the Sturmgeschütze held until the infantry arrived. A breakout attempt by the fort's garrison was foiled. The 2000 men of Casement "B", who occupied the fort, were taken prisoner by the Germans. In a surprise leap forward, the battalion had cleared the way for the following infantry and made it possible for the infantry to fight past the fort and reach the day's objective.

The battalion rolled on to the east. It gave outstanding support during the major attack by the 131. Infanterie-Division (Generalleutnant Meier-Buerdorf) by its unstinting aggressiveness. Generalleutnant Meier-Buerdorf gave it his particular thanks and recognition.

Only a few days later, on 19 August 1941, Sturmgeschütz-Abteilung 192 with staff and all three batteries was once again attached to the 131. Infanterie-Division Its objective was to take Gomel. Infanterie-Regiment 431 had the mission of reaching the Ssosh east of Gomel with three battalions in the forward-most line. Since this mission was already accomplished by noon of 19 August, Sturmgeschütz-Abteilung 192 was assembled at Kalinowka for other duties.

When the neighboring regiment (Infanterie-Regiment 434) bogged down during this phase of the attack in heavy Russian flanking fire from the Jeremino-Prudok railroad embankment, Hauptmann Hammon asked permission from the 131. Infanterie-Division to carry out a surprise flank attack, using the Sturmgeschütze of the battalion as tanks. The Soviets had dug in forward of Prudok in strong field positions and were fighting stubbornly.

The recommendation was accepted. Hauptmann Hammon led the attack at the head of his Sturmgeschütze. Although the Sturmgeschütze had to pass through a thick minefield, they succeeded in penetrating the enemy position. Only one Sturmgeschütz was lost. Several hundred Soviets surrendered to the battalion and were left to the following infantry. Prudok fell into the hands of the battalion and Hauptmann Hammon decided to exploit this success and carry out a reconnaissance in force up to the north edge of Gomel.

The Sturmgeschütze rolled on. Wherever the enemy was still defending, he was silenced by rapid fire. One kilometer north of the Gomel airfield, the lead elements of the battalion met elements of the I./ Infanterie-Regiment 95 of the 17. Infanterie-Division who were lying behind a street barricade and firing at the enemy forces defending the airfield area. Hauptmann Hammon voluntarily attached his remaining 15 Sturmgeschütze to the infantry battalion. The Sturmgeschütze were enthusiastically welcomed by the infantry. The plan of attack was decided on in a short orders conference; then they stormed the enemy's defensive positions.

The attack on Gomel began at 1705 hours. The Sturmgeschütze rolled ahead at full speed on both sides of the barricade and both sides of the road. They reached the Russian field positions on the south edge of the airfield, wheeled to the left and overran them. This silenced effective enemy fire on the German infantry, who were also advancing in the ditches on both sides of the road.

Hauptmann Hammon and most of the battalion officers participated in the operation as gun commanders. The enemy was targeted and engaged at close range and put out of action, mostly dying in his positions. The infantry, attacking behind the Sturmgeschütze, reached the first houses in Gomel almost without casualties. Oberstleutnant Rotter, the infantry commander, rode in the forward Sturmgeschütz along with the battalion commander. He took the place of the loader. From there, he brought in the following company to mop up the airfield and provide for its security. The 7 Sturmgeschütze of the 1st Battery were detached for the same purpose. They then entered the city in short advances of perhaps 100 meters. A short but heavy firefight broke out in the market place, which the enemy had built into a strongpoint. A few Soviet cannon and quad-machine guns put up a stubborn defense there. Two enemy cannon and an advancing enemy tank were destroyed by the Sturmgeschütze. After this enemy resistance had been broken, the 1st Company mounted the Sturmgeschütze as darkness fell and rode with them at full speed deeper into the city. In several rushes, the three Sturmgeschütze in the lead destroyed 3 additional enemy cannon, 4 antitank guns and 4 trucks loaded with Soviet soldiers.

It was fully dark when the Sturmgeschütze reached the road bridge over the Ssosh, but unfortunately it had been blown up. Two burning Russian ammunition trucks illuminated this scene of desolation. A firefight broke out at the bridge between the Sturmgeschütze and Soviet cannon firing from open positions on the far side of the Ssosh. The Sturmgeschütze took several heavy caliber direct hits. Despite the fire received from the Soviet artillery pieces, the Sturmgeschütze were still successful in engaging the enemy columns fleeing over the Ssosh on a ferry. The day's objective was secured in conjunction with the infantry.

That night, Hauptmann Hammon requested by way of the 17. Infanterie-Division that XIII. Armee-Korps approve the battalion's attachment to that division, as the battalion itself had suggested.

On one of the advancing Sturmgeschütze, Oberfeldwebel Hans Postner of the 1./ Infanterie-Regiment 95 had supported the fire of the Sturmgeschütze with effective sweeping fire from his machine gun. Unflinching, he stayed in position in spite of enemy fire. On that same day, he was decorated with the Iron Cross, First Class.

The 2nd Battery was attached to Infanterie-Regiment 55 to expand the bridgehead. It supported the regiment in various crisis situations during the heavy forest fighting from 26 to 28 August and, in the words of Oberst Specht, provided "valuable service in the fighting and in bringing about the decision." Oberst Specht continued, "Leutnant Feiler particularly distinguished himself. I recommend him for the Iron Cross, First Class."

Leutnant Feiler became one of the first men in the battalion to receive this decoration.

The battalion was attached to the 124. Infanterie-Division from 29 August to 5 September and fought at Tschernigoff with it. Generalleutnant von Kochenhausen praised this operation in a letter to the battalion where, among other things, he wrote: "With its outstanding élan, Sturmgeschütz-Abteilung 192 pulled the infantry along with it and played an essential role in the successes of the last few days."

The 1st Battery was also present in the fighting north of Tschernigoff. It was attached to Infanterie-Regiment 510. The battery laid the groundwork for victory in the attack on Schestowiczi. The Sturmgeschütze showed up wherever the enemy was to be found during that period of aggressive advance.

In the advance guard of Oberstleutnant von Pannwitz, the 1st Battery—under its battery commander—again performed magnificently in the fighting of 17 September, at the capture of Pirjatin on 18 September and in the destruction of a Russian cavalry squadron. During this period the advance guard was able to capture 80 guns, take more than 5000 POW's, and break up the remnants of several Soviet divisions. The 1st Battery played a major role in all this.

This initiative was given special recognition in the 1 October 1941 Army Order of the Day for the 2. Armee-Oberkommando. Generaloberst Freiherr von Weichs, the Commander-in-Chief of the 2nd Army, wrote in his order of the day:

Sturmgeschütz-Abteilung 192, under the command of Hauptmann Hammon, has repeatedly distinguished itself by its outstanding bravery during the period it was attached to the 2. Armee. It fought in the forward-most positions at the penetration of the bridgehead at Mogilew, while surrounding enemy units at Rogatschew and during the attack on Gomel. It supported the infantry assaults everywhere in the most exemplary way by the reckless intervention of its guns.

I wish to express my special appreciation to every officer, noncommissioned officer and man of the battalion.

Sturmgeschütz-Abteilung 192, under the command of Hauptmann Hammon, has repeatedly distinguished itself by its outstanding bravery during the period it was attached to the 2. Armee. It fought in the forward-most positions at the penetration of the bridgehead at Mogilew, while surrounding enemy units at Rogatschew and during the attack on Gomel. It supported the infantry assaults everywhere in the most exemplary way by the reckless intervention of its guns.

I wish to express my special appreciation to every officer, noncommissioned officer and man of the battalion.

The battalion has been in continuous combat with the enemy since 22 June 1941. Serving with eight different army corps, it has forged its friendship with the infantry in heavy fighting. Our gun crews have driven 6000 kilometers in heat, dust, morass and in rain and cold. And our supply column drivers have driven a great deal further in tireless devotion to duty.

The crossing of the Bug, Orscha, Mogilew, Rogatschew, Gomel, Tschernigoff and Kaluga are so far the milestones in our unit history. The name "192" has become a legend for every simple infantry soldier with whom we go into combat.

The successes, upon which the battalion can look back, have been great, but the price which we have had to pay for them has been high.

We bow our heads in sorrow, respect and pride for those of our comrades who rest on Russia's battlefields.

The fighting during the "Ice Winter" made great demands on the crews of the Sturmgeschütze. But every crew gave its best. The commander's Sturmgeschütz destroyed four Soviet tanks during an attack in March 1942. The battalion repeatedly supported the defensive fighting of the infantry. On 21 March 1942 Hauptmann Hammon received the German Cross in Gold for repeated acts of gallantry in the face of the enemy.

Hauptmann Hammon owed the fact that he was still alive to receive the decoration to a package of tobacco. At the end of February 1942 he able to trade it to the enemy in exchange for his life. The following report describes this unusual occurrence:

When on 26 February one of his Sturmgeschütze became stuck fast in a deeply frozen hole in the ground, Hauptmann Hammon went back himself to get a prime mover from the division to which they were attached. The gun had to be recovered during that same night, so that Soviets couldn't destroy it with artillery fire on the following day.

When Hauptmann Hammon arrived in the village and entered the house where the divisional command post was supposed to be, he found himself suddenly confronted by 25 Soviet soldiers. The Russians jumped up at the appearance of a German officer. With two steps, Hauptmann Hammon reached the corner where the stove was and where the rifles and two machine guns were located. The enemies regarded each other critically.

At a gesture by Hauptmann Hammon, the Soviets sat back down. Hauptmann Hammon pulled a chair up to the table and sat so that his back covered the corner where the weapons were standing. He reached into his coat pocket and laid his pistol, still loaded with four rounds, and an almost flat packet of tobacco on the table. When he caught the longing looks of the Russians which were directed at the packet of tobacco, he knew that only two things could rescue him from this delicate situation: his iron nerves—and the packet of tobacco.

So in complete calm (outwardly only, naturally), he stuffed his pipe and then offered the tobacco around among the Russians, who happily took some. It was deathly quiet in the room. No one said a word. The tension was almost unendurable. Hour after hour went by. Pipe after pipe was lit up. Some Russians finally lay down in the straw to sleep. The tobacco packet was nearing its end. One hundred grams of tobacco doesn't last forever. If his nerves held out, he would see the morning. All at once the door was pushed open. Two Soviet soldiers with rifles slung on their shoulders stood in the doorway. Was this the end?

Without batting an eyelash, Hauptmann Hammon handed them the packet of tobacco. The unimaginable happened. The two men stacked their weapons and helped themselves.

Finally, the morning dawned. The Russians became impatient. Once again tension soared to a peak as the first men wished to leave the room. The packet of tobacco was empty. Hauptmann Hammon picked up his pistol, coolly holstered it and left the room with a firm, unhurried stride. No one tried to stop him. Outside, he walked with long strides for the nearby woods.

Immediately the Soviets' passivity vanished. They fired wildly after Hauptmann Hammon, but it was already too late. He had reached the woods. His nerve—and the tobacco—had won. Great was the joy of his comrades when the missing man returned and told of his odyssey.

After that night, Hauptmann Hammon was never without a packet of tobacco in his coat pocket.

In the 16 months of its existence, Sturmgeschütz-Abteilung 192 had destroyed 378 cannon of all calibers, 205 antitank guns, 2,209 trucks and 62 tanks. Six officers and 15 noncommissioned officers were killed in action. Twelve officers and 52 noncommissioned officers and men were wounded.

The men of this battalion, which had been in existence just over a year and had been in combat for nine months on the Eastern Front, received the following decorations:

One Knights Cross; one German Cross in Gold; 29 Iron Crosses, First Class; 212 Iron Crosses, Second Class; 219 Assault Badges; 1 War Merit Cross (Kriegsverdienstkreuz),First Class with Swords; 43 War Merit Crosses, Second Class with swords; 91 Wound Badges in black; 3 Wound Badges in silver; and, and 2 Wound Badges in gold.

In March 1942 Sturmgeschütz-Abteilung 192 was withdrawn from the front and deactivated in Germany on 4 April 1942 not far from its formation point at Treuenbrietzen. It was consolidated with

Sturmgeschütz-Batterie 640 to form Sturmgeschütz-Abteilung "Großdeutschland," which was organized as an organic component of Panzergrenadier-Division "Großdeutschland." (See the entry under Sturmgeschütz-Abteilung "Großdeutschland" for additional information.) The battalion had its own song which is presented here to close the history of the battalion:

> Unser das Land und unser die Straßen,
> die wir in stählernen Kasten durchrasen.
> Zu jagen den Feind, zu schlagen den Feind
> in blitzgleicher Schnelle.
> Wir tragen den Totenkopf am Geschütz
> und mit uns fährt die Hölle.
>
> Ours is the land and ours are the roads
> over which we race in steel boxes.
> To chase the enemy, to strike the enemy
> with the speed of lightning.
> We carry the death's head on our guns,
> and Hell travels with us.

As a footnote to the history of Sturmgeschütz-Abteilung 192, on 2 February 1945, Oberstleutnant Erich Hammon received the Knights Cross of the Iron Cross as commander of Panzer-Artillerie-Regiment 119. At the end of the war he managed to escape from Hela to Flensburg on 9 May 1945. On 29 May he was sentenced to death by a court of the military government in Flensburg for unauthorized use of weapons and for killing a member of an allied force. He had stopped a Russian looter who was robbing an 80-year-old woman, and shot him when he tried to escape. On 30 June 1945 he was shot at Rendsburg after an appeal for clemency by Naval Judge Advocate Franke was rejected by Field Marshall Montgomery.

schwere Sturmgeschütz-Abteilung 197 (schwere Panzer-Jäger-Abteilung 653)

schwere Sturmgeschütz-Abteilung 197/s.Pz.Jg.Abt. 653

Orders had already been issued for the formation of this battalion in October 1940, and it was constituted in the winter 1940/41 at Jüterbog. The battalion bore an eagle with a cannon barrel as its insignia. Major Christ was the first commander. Up until that time he had been commander of schwere Artillerie-Abteilung 506 (mot.) at Lötzen. Hauptmann Schepers, at the time commander of the VI./Artillerie-Lehr-Regiment 2 (mot.), provided the cadre personnel. In November, these first elements occupied quarters in the New Camp at Jüterbog, where Sturmgeschütz-Abteilung 192 (Hauptmann Hammon) was being formed at the same time.

Command and Staff Positions: Sturmgeschütz-Abteilung 197 (November 1940)

Commander: Major Christ

Adjutant: Oberleutnant Liedkte

Orderly Officer: Oberleutnant Gärtner

Battalion Surgeon: Assistant Surgeon Dr. Bauermeister

Paymaster: Oberzahlmeister Koch

Engineer: Technical Service Officer Schaffranek

Headquarters Battery:

Commander :Oberleutnant de la Renotière, Leutnant Preusser, Leutnant Seitz

1st Battery:

Commander: Oberleutnant Brinke (†)

Section Leaders: Leutnant Spielmann, Leutnant Ulbricht, Leutnant Wagner

2nd Battery:

Commander: Oberleutnant Führ (†)

Section Leaders: Leutnant Haager (†), Leutnant Kuntze, Leutnant Zemann, Leutnant Wegelin

3rd Battery:

Commander: Oberleutnant Goebe (†)

Section leaders: Leutnant Rüdiger, Leutnant Salomon, Leutnant Bobisch, Leutnant Rehbein, Leutnant Becker

Every member of the battalion received Christmas leave and, in January, it was moved by road march to Brieg in Silesia, where its training continued.

In the middle of March 1941, the battalion was moved to Ehringhausen on the Yugoslavian border. With the beginning of the war in the Balkans, the battalion rolled to Marburg, but was stuck at the Drau River, as the bridge over the river had been blown up. It was rerouted and passed through Agram-Karlstadt to reach Banjaluka. The repair units fell further behind every day of the march, for the flatbed trucks could only progress slowly on the twisting, narrow roads. There was no enemy activity. The 14. Panzer-Division had already sent the enemy running.

There wasn't an alert until Banjaluka. Yugoslavian partisan units were making themselves felt. They were sniping at individual soldiers from ambush positions. The battalion received orders to push forward to Banjaluka as rapidly as possible and break enemy resistance there. However, the partisans pulled back, and Banjaluka was reached without firing a shot. Yugoslavia surrendered and after a three-day pause for a rest, Sturmgeschütz-Abteilung 197 marched back through Karlstadt-Laibach and Klagenfurt to Villach. A 14-day rest period was granted in the hotels along Lake Wörther, which was used to put the vehicles back into good shape. Following that, the battalion was transferred by rail to Glatz in Silesia.

In May, after a number of training exercises, the battalion moved on into Poland and went into position in the forest at Tomaszow. On 15 June it moved as far as the heights of the village of Sokol. It was then attached to Heeresgruppe Kleist (K).

During the night of 21 June, all batteries of the battalion prepared to attack across the Bug. At 0430 hours on 22 June, the battalion advanced toward Sokol and the Styr. The enemy put up a defense at Sokol in well-constructed bunkers, but the Sturmgeschütze rolled on past them to the river. The battalion fought its way through Kremjenz and Konstantinowo into the Dubno area. The battalion was fully engaged in the tank battle at Dubno. It was victorious but suffered heavy losses. It went on through Berditschew to the area of Kiev. Put into action northwest and south of the city, the battalion was opposed by enemy forces fighting desperately for their freedom. Once more, the battalion lost many officers and men, Sturmgeschütze and ammo carriers in the fighting.

After pulling out and wheeling toward Krementschug, it crossed the Dnjepr on pontoons. The enemy also put up a stubborn defense on the east bank of the Dnjepr. The Sturmgeschütze were thrown into the battle as they arrived from across the river and did an outstanding job. They led the attack at Krementschug as its armored spearhead, and they did the same at Poltawa and Kharkov.

The battalion commander, Major Christ, was wounded in the right hip by a shell fragment at Poltawa on 9 September 1941. He was unable to move and had to give up his battalion. Hauptmann von Barisani took over temporary command. Hauptmann Steinwachs took over the battalion on 1 November. On 3 November 1941 the German High Command transferred the battalion from the 6. to the 11. Armee and ordered it to move to the Crimea. It marched through Krasnograd, Dnepropetrowsk, Saprosje and Melitopol to the Perekop Isthmus. The battalion had been weakened by four months of combat, and this road march for a distance of 900 kilometers on excessively poor roads and under very unfavorable weather conditions caused a number of mechanical losses. The Sturmgeschütze themselves held up to the road march best of all, but 70% of the wheeled vehicles fell out. The repair section had to get all the broken down vehicles back in operation, and the unit didn't reach the Crimea until January 1942.

Even so, Hauptmann Steinwachs reported in to the Commander-in-Chief of 11. Armee, General von Manstein, on 13 November 1941. The battalion was directed to a billeting area in the Ukrainka area north of Simferopol. The maintenance section of Sturmgeschütz-Abteilung 190 gave valuable assistance to their comrades in Sturmgeschütz-Abteilung 197.

When the first attack was launched on Sevastopol on 17 December 1941, the battalion was attached to the LIV. Armee-Korps. Hauptmann Steinwachs had suggested that his battalion go into action as a complete unit with the 22. Infanterie-Division, because terrain conditions there were ideal for his Sturmgeschütze. Most unfortunately, his proposals were not accepted.

The battalion was split among three divisions, which weakened it. The 1st Battery, which advanced on the right wing of the attack, had to move over completely open terrain and was rapidly smashed by Russian heavy artillery. The 2nd and 3rd Batteries, supported by infantry and combat engineers, had to chew their way through mine fields, fortifications with retracting armored cupolas, and well dug-in artillery. Sturmgeschütze from Sturmgeschütz-Abteilung 190 were attached to each battery. But the attack gained only little ground, and the attack on Sevastopol was canceled on 31 December 1941 when the Russians landed at a number of places on the Crimea. The German lines had to be pulled back. General Wolff, the commander of the 22. Infanterie-Division, thanked Hauptmann Steinwachs very heartily for the support given by the Sturmgeschütze. In the meantime, Major Christ had returned to the battalion for a short period, but had to be transferred out again because of health.

The battalion was given a period for rest and refitting in January and February of 1942. It was largely due to the efforts of the maintenance section under Kriegsverwaltungsrat (Technical Service Officer) Schaffranek, that it regained full combat readiness. The 1./Sturmgeschütz-Abteilung 197 received 6 new Sturmgeschütze.

By January 1942 the 3rd Battery had already been successfully employed in a counterattack on Feodosia, which had been taken by the Russians.

In the morning hours of 27 February 1942 the Soviets opened their expected "Stalin Offensive" with considerable numerical superiority on the Parpatsch Front and on the Kertsch Isthmus with the objective of retaking the Crimea. Sturmgeschütz-Abteilung 197, with 11 operational Sturmgeschütze of the 1st and 2nd Batteries, was attached first to the 46. Infanterie-Division, then to the 170. Infanterie-Division and finally to Infanterie-Regiment 213.

The massed Soviet tank attack lasted until 25 March 1942. With 80 tanks destroyed, Sturmgeschütz-Abteilung 197 played a large part in the successful defense. Above all, it was due to the section leader, Leutnant Spielmann, who attacked again and again with his few Sturmgeschütze. This young officer was the true embodiment of the fighting spirit of the Sturmartillerie. Leutnant Spielmann threw himself against enemy forces wherever they pushed into the main battle line. The Sturmgeschütze of Leutnant Spielmann—with the Leutnant himself at their head—destroyed 14 T-34's during the main Soviet attack on 13 and 14 March. The Wehrmacht Report for 15 March 1942 stated: "During the fighting on the Kertsch Peninsula, a section of Sturmgeschütze under the command of Leutnant Spielmann destroyed fourteen enemy tanks on 13 and 14 March."

On 11 April Johann Spielmann, who had already been promoted to Oberleutnant, received the Knight's Cross of the Iron Cross.

Oberwachtmeister Schrödel, one of the most successful gun commanders, also set an example for the rest of the battalion. He too destroyed numerous tanks on 13 March. With his Sturmgeschütz he engaged a swarm of tanks that had broken through, including three heavy tanks. He destroyed the three heavy tanks in a bold series of attacks and maneuvers. Five additional tanks were blown apart or burned out by hits from his gun. On 16 March the Wehrmacht Report stated: "During the fighting on 13 March, Oberwachtmeister Schrödel, gun commander in a Sturmgeschütz battalion, destroyed eight enemy tanks including three heavy tanks."

Oberwachtmeister Schrödel was awarded the German Cross in Gold.

After the end of this bitter fighting, which was a glorious page in the history of Sturmgeschütz-Abteilung 197, the battalion itself was also mentioned in the Wehrmacht Report. On 4 April 1942, it said: "Sturmgeschütz-Abteilung 197 has destroyed 200 enemy tanks since the beginning of the Eastern Campaign."

A difficult, costly, but brilliantly successful operation had come to an end. The battalion was pulled back to the Ukrainka billeting area for rest and refitting, and brought back to full operational strength. Preparations for Unternehmen Trappenjagd ("Operation Bustard Hunt")—the recapture of the Crimea—were in full swing.

On 8 May 1942, at the beginning of the breakthrough attack, the battalion (less the 3rd Battery which had been attached to the 170. Infanterie-Division) stormed forward with the 50. Infanterie-Division Immediately after the start of the attack, the commander of 1st Battery, Oberleutnant Liedkte, was severely wounded. Oberleutnant Spielmann took over the battery. The attack moved forward on mud-covered roads in the heavy rain.

The 3rd Battery was completely stuck by the second day of the attack. An improvement in the weather and a bold advance by the 22. Panzer-Division bought them a bit of a breathing space. At different periods, the battalion supported the advance of the 28. leichte Division and the attack of Infanterie-Regiment 213. By 20 May enemy resistance in the eastern section of Kertsch had been broken.

The commander of 2nd Battery, Oberleutnant Haager, was killed during this fighting. Oberleutnant Kuntze took over command on the battlefield. Once again, the battalion had performed outstandingly. And, once again, soldiers of the battalion were decorated highly.

But now the battalion had to face an operation that would be the most difficult that it had had to endure up to that point in the war—the battle for Sevastopol. When the attack on Sevastopol began on 7 June, the battalion, which had earlier been equipped with 6 of the new long-barreled Sturmgeschütze, supported the assault of the 50. Infanterie-Division assault in the northeastern sector. The terrain difficulties and the unheard-of heat on that day were hard on the men of the Sturmartillerie. The battalion fought its way forward over forested and scrub-covered land, with infantry and combat engineers mounted on the guns. On 13 June the Wehrmacht Report again reported: "Knight's Cross winner Oberleutnant Spielmann, battery commander in a Sturmgeschütz battalion, and Oberleutnant Frank, company commander in an infantry regiment, have especially distinguished themselves during the fighting for Sevastopol."

In the next few days the battalion was used to support the 24. Infanterie-Division and played a major part in the capture of the forts "GPU," "Molotov" and "Dnjepr." The Sturmgeschütze rolled up to the embrasures and silenced them with their accurate fire, smoothing the way for the infantry in this way. The heights of Gajtani were captured with the 50. Infanterie-Division and a bridgehead was fought clear across the Tschornaja. No member of Sturmgeschütz-Abteilung 197 will ever forget the day when the "Inkermann" cliff position was blown up by the Russians right before their eyes, along with its garrison and the hospital. It was a horrible experience.

The last operational Sturmgeschütze of the battalion carried the attack of the 50. Infanterie-Division across the antitank ditches to Sevastopol and, on 1 July, the hardest fought victory was won. The campaign for Sevastopol was over. Sturmgeschütz-Abteilung 197 had fought in this sector with admirable determination. Hauptmann Steinwachs, the battalion commander, received the German Cross in Gold.

After a short rest period, the battalion was transferred to the Woronesh area on 30 July 1942 and attached to the VII. Armee-Korps. In this sector Sturmgeschütz-Abteilung 197 pushed back a number of strong Soviet attacks with the 340., 377. and 387. Infanterie-Divisionen. A large number of enemy tanks were destroyed. Oberleutnant Gerald de la Renotière was decorated with the German Cross in Gold. Shortly after that, on 14 August 1942, he was severely wounded. The Soviets halted their costly attack on 17 August.

Orders were received to move back on 23 August. The battalion was allocated to the 2. Panzer-Armee-Oberkommando in the Orel area and attached to the LIII. Armee-Korps (General Clösser). It was given "open season" with the mission of neutralizing surprise attacks by Russian tanks on the German main battle line and providing additional protection to the infantry.

Hauptmann Steinwachs immediately sent out reconnaissance. Within three days, Leutnant Loeck and his section destroyed seven KV I's in surprise actions. This accomplished the battalion's mission, as the Russian tank attacks ceased.

At the beginning of October the battalion was moved to the 4. Armee at Spas Demensk. The battalion was employed in the LVI. Armee-Korps sector as a Army reserve. This was one of the few rest periods enjoyed by the battalion. On 23 December 1942 the chief of staff for the 4. Armee-Oberkommando, General Röttinger, issued the following order to the battalion commander: "The unit personnel of Sturmgeschütz-Abteilung 197 will be transferred to Jüterbog as rapidly as possible and rearmed with heavy Sturmgeschütze."

This was just the right Christmas surprise for the battalion, which hadn't had a single day of leave in the past year.

In January Sturmgeschütz-Abteilung 197 was relieved by Sturmgeschütz-Abteilung 270 and transferred to Jüterbog. As the "Ferdinands" designated for the battalion were not yet available, there was leave for everyone. Following the leave, officers, gun commanders and drivers were ordered to the St. Valentin factory at St. Pölten for instruction.

Effective 1 April 1943, the entire battalion was transferred from the Sturmartillerie to the Panzertruppe and renamed schwere Panzer-Jäger-Abteilung 653. Oberst Günther Hoffmann-Schoenborn bid farewell to these worthy men of the Sturmartillerie in a festive formation on 14 April 1943.

The battalion was moved to Neusiedl am See and there equipped with 45 "Ferdinands." On 24 and 25 March 1943, Generaloberst Guderian observed the battalion at live-fire exercises. At the end he had special words of praise for the 1st Battery, under Hauptmann Spielmann, which had demonstrated outstanding accuracy.

After that, the battalion became a part of schweres Panzer-Regiment 656 with an additional Ferdinand battalion and a Sturm-Haubitzen-Abteilung (assault howitzer battalion), in order to make up the leading steel spearhead for "Operation Citadel."

As part of this operation, on 5 July 1943, the battalion attacked across the "tank heights" with the 86. Infanterie-Division in the attack sector of the XXXXI. Armee-Korps. In spite of heavy enemy fire, 12 Ferdinands reached the attack objective at 1700 hours on the same day. Hauptmann Spielmann was severely wounded in this action.

During the following days, several Soviet tank attacks were beaten back. The long-barreled tank cannon in 8.8 cm caliber performed magnificently. Despite that, the battalion was no longer operational by 8 July. It was given 3 days rest for repairs.

During this period, the entire Russian 13th Tank Army and major infantry units began a large-scale offensive against the XXXV. Armee-Korps (General Rendulic) south of Orel. The battalion was immediately thrown into the threatened area, becoming involved in very heavy defensive fighting. It fought with all its strength while attached to the 36. Infanterie-Division, the 78. Sturm-Division, the 262. Infanterie-Division and the 299. I.D. It played a major role in pushing back the massed enemy forces attempting the breakthrough.

With 24 dead and missing and 13 vehicles totally unserviceable along with 126 wounded, the famous Sturmgeschütz-Abteilung 197 with its new name and weapons had destroyed 320 Russian tanks and a large number of guns, antitank guns and trucks in this defensive fighting. No member of the battalion will ever forget the names of Podmasslowo, Kasinka, Telegino or Tichnowka.

Leutnant Heinrich Terriete won the Knight's Cross there on 7 August 1943. General Rendulic mentioned this Sturmgeschütz battalion with high praise in an Order of the Day. In the middle of July, Major Steinwachs, who had led the battalion throughout all this fighting, was ordered to a regimental commander course in Berlin by teletype. However, he stayed with his battalion, and (covered by General Rendulic who promised him his fullest support) led his men of the Sturmartillerie to the end of this hard fighting. On 1 August he passed his command over to Hauptmann Baumungk at Briansk.

The history of Sturmgeschütz-Abteilung 197 will end here, as it continued to fight on in a different capacity as Panzer-Jäger-Abteilung 653.

Sturmgeschütz-Ersatz-Abteilung 200

The first, and thus the oldest, replacement and training battalion in the Sturmartillerie was organized as Sturmgeschütz-Ersatz-Abteilung 200 in January 1941 in Schweinfurt and stationed there. Major Keppler was the first commander of this battalion. He was followed by Oberstleutnant Christ and, finally, by Hauptmann Brinke.

Volunteers, who had requested service with the Sturmgeschütze, were trained in the replacement battalion, and then from there the replacements were sent to the front.

By the spring of 1944, the number of personnel in this battalion reached its high point. By that time some 5,000 members of the Sturmartillerie, including 150 officers, had been trained to replace the losses.

At the beginning of April 1944, Sturmgeschütz-Ersatz-Abteilung 200 was moved to Schieratz in the Warthegau and taken over by Major Gruber as the new commander. An "alert" battery was formed at Schieratz out of the entire replacement battalion in the summer of 1944. This alert battery was first used in Warsaw during the uprising at the end of July 1944, but played only a minor role in the fighting. Fortunately, there were few casualties.

As the Russian assault on the eastern German border continued, a convalescent battery and a Kampfgruppe were also formed in addition to the alert battery.

When the Soviets launched their great winter operational offensive on 12 January 1945, Oberleutnant Erker was called to see his commander in the late evening of the same day. Major Gruber, a Knight's Cross winner, told the Oberleutnant that the Soviets had broken out of the Baranow Bridgehead and were advancing rapidly toward the Tschenstochau area. He gave Erker immediate command of the alert battery and told him to move it toward Welun on the next day.

Early the next morning the six short-barreled Sturmgeschütze and a small supply train moved out.

At Welun Oberleutnant Erker reported to the local commander. The alert battery was attached to a training regiment east of the city.

In the morning hours of 16 January 1945, the battery had its first taste of action with the Russian spearhead which was cautiously feeling its way forward in the area of Warthbrück. During this fighting two Sturmgeschütze were knocked out while covering the infantry as "heavy weapons." However, the Soviets were unable to cross the Warthe at Warthbrück. Five more short-barreled Sturmgeschütze under Oberleutnant Mehrwald arrived at Warthbrück in the late evening hours of 17 January. There was heavy fighting when superior Soviet tank forces attacked again in the early morning hours of 18 January. The alert battery lost all its guns except two. The Soviets were held, but at great cost.

In the evening of that bloody day, Oberleutnant Erker went to Generalmajor Schrock to inquire about the whereabouts of the railhead where the long-barreled Sturmgeschütze which had been promised could be unloaded so they could be led back to the battery. While he was returning to Welun that evening, Russian tank forces broke into the town from all sides. The Russians took possession of virtually the entire city. The alert battery's motor pool fell into their hands. Oberleutnant Erker assembled all the survivors in a school. He was given permission from the high command to withdraw toward Kempen. Oberleutnant Mehrwald and many members of the battery who were still fighting as infantry were missing. At Kempen, Oberleutnant Erker and his remnants ran into the commander of Sturmgeschütz-Brigade 236, Major Kranz, and he asked the major to take charge of them. Major Kranz took these men on and they fought with Sturmgeschütz-Brigade 236 right to the war's end.

Sturmgeschütz-Ersatz-Abteilung 200 itself was placed on alert at Schieratz by the XXI. Armee-Korps headquarters in Posen because of the Russian breakthrough at the bend of the Vistula. An additional alert battery was organized the next day and thrown into action at Radomsko.

Oberleutnant Mehrwald (as already mentioned above) was sent to Welun by Major Gruber. Only Kanonier Hübsch and an attached Stabsfeldwebel came back to the battalion from the inferno of Welun. They reported to Major Gruber that both groups had been destroyed in action there.

Because of the critical situation immediately outside of Schieratz (about 40 kilometer from Welun), the battalion commander—on his own initiative—moved the "convalescent battery" and the youngest replacements through Kalisch to the west under the command of his adjutant, Hauptmann Groppel. When Hauptmann Groppel went out to reconnoiter the east edge of Kalisch, he did not return to the battery. He has been missing ever since.

Most of the members of the group that had been sent back, however, managed to fight their way through to Germany and assembled at the Sturmgeschütz-Schule at Burg. At Burg, they were organized into Sturmgeschütz-Ersatz-Abteilung 700 under Hauptmann Wende.

The remnants of Sturmgeschütz-Ersatz-Abteilung 200 were reorganized into companies as ordered. Those companies were placed in defensive positions east of Schieratz and used as infantry.

On 18 January 1945 Major Gruber, together with the 17 new Sturmgeschütze which he had "liberated" from a stranded freight train, received orders to form a new Kampfgruppe which was named "Kampfgruppe Gruber." To get him operational, the trains of Sturmgeschütz-Lehr-Brigade I were attached to him.

Sturmgeschütz-Brigade 920, which was completely destroyed and falling back, took the rest of the staff personnel of Sturmgeschütz-Ersatz-Abteilung 200 with it, including some 60 female communications personnel.

"Kampfgruppe Gruber" had a strength of 5 officers and 80 men. It went into action on 19 January 1945. Five of the unit's 17 Sturmgeschütze went into action at Niechmer. They never returned to the Kampfgruppe. Their fate remains obscure. The remaining 12 guns of the Kampfgruppe were attached to the 19. Panzer-Division at Schieratz on 21 January. The unit fought bravely in the heavy fighting in the area of Kalisch and Lissa, which took everything it had. At Oderbeltsch the Kampfgruppe went back across the Oder to the west, and again paid a high price in blood in the fighting for Queißen. Oberwachtmeister Heß, a brave gun commander, was killed there and Leutnant Schlesinger was wounded.

The Kampfgruppe then consisted of only 2 officers and 30 men. It was rail loaded at Moldau and transported to Kanth. The remnants reached Frauenhayn by way of Weicherau, Plaeswitz and Bockau. There the last surviving officer, Leutnant Schuster turned over his 15 men and the last Sturmgeschütze to Sturmgeschütz-Brigade 300. Major Gruber was given command of this brigade. Thus ended the history of Sturmgeschütz-Ersatz-Abteilung 200.

Sturmgeschütz-Abteilung (Feld) 200 (Sturmgeschütz-Brigade (Feld) 200; schwere Panzer-Jäger-Abteilung 673)

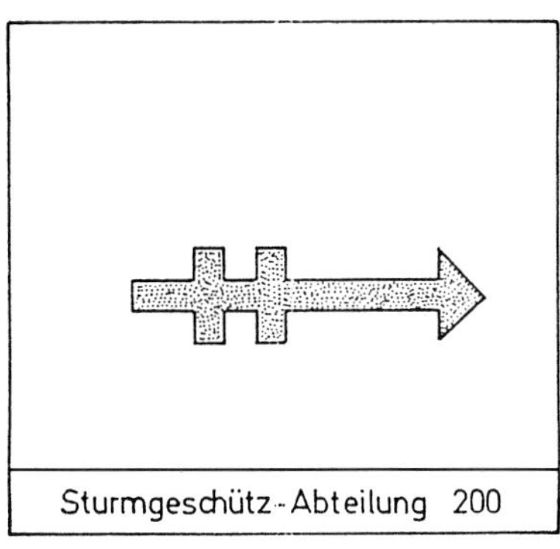
Sturmgeschütz-Abteilung 200

In 1943, Artillerie-Abteilung West was formed in Paris. This battalion consisted of Sturmgeschütze and, for this reason, it was renamed at the beginning of 1944 as Sturmgeschütz-Brigade (Feld) 2000. When the Führer-Begleit-Brigade "Großdeutschland" was formed from the "Führer-Begleit-Bataillon" in the fall of 1944, Sturmgeschütz-Brigade (Feld) 200 was attached to this unit. When the Führer-Begleit-Brigade was built up to a division Sturmgeschütz-Brigade (Feld) 200 became an organic part of the division. After that, in December 1944/ January 1945, the brigade was designated as: Sturmgeschütz-Brigade Führer-Begleit-Division "Großdeutschland."

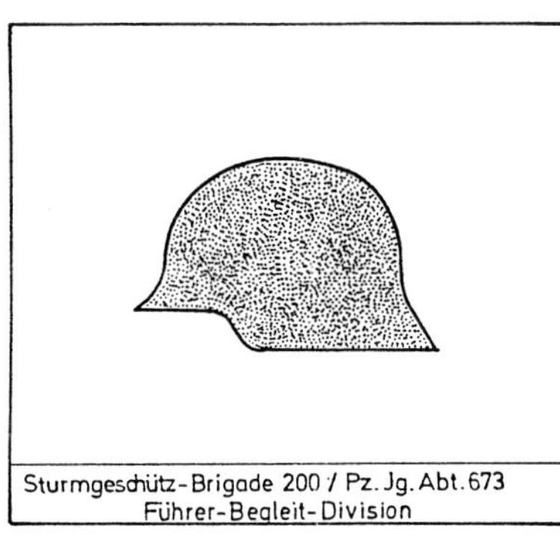
Sturmgeschütz-Brigade 200 / Pz. Jg. Abt. 673 Führer-Begleit-Division

The brigade fought under the command of this division and participated in the Ardennes Offensive. It was also present at the capture of Lauban in Silesia in March 1945. Effective 1 February 1945, following a divisional reorganization, it was renamed as the 5./ Panzer-Jäger-Abteilung 673.

The battle for Berlin was the last action fought by this brigade, which found its fate along with the Führer-Begleit-Division "Großdeutschland" at the end of the war.

Sturmgeschütz-Abteilung 201 (Sturmgeschütz-Brigade 201)

In March 1941 Sturmgeschütz-Abteilung 201 was constituted at Jüterbog and took part in every major battle on the Eastern Front from the beginning of the Russian Campaign until its destruction in 1943.

First it went by rail to its jump-off point at Terespol. From there, it pushed through Brest-Litowsk, Minsk, Borissow-Orscha and Mogilew to Smolensk. Then, it went on to Briansk and Wjasma, finally reaching the Nara Position east of Gshatsk, just 30 kilometers from Moscow.

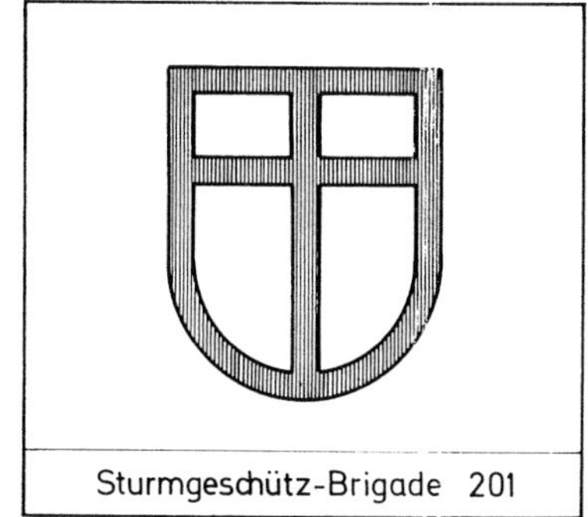
Sturmgeschütz-Brigade 201

After the winter battle, the battalion went to the Borissow area for rest and refitting and in June moved to a new jump-off point in the Kursk area.

At the end of June, it took part in "Operation Blue" while attached to the 23. Panzer-Division. It also fought in support of the 78. Sturm-Division. In this operation, the goal was to reach Woronesch as quickly as possible, conducting rapid operations and armor raids from there to the Caucasus and then to Stalingrad, taking the enemy by surprise.

It appeared, however, that in spite of all its reverses during the summer of 1941, the Red Army had grown stronger during the winter campaign and didn't seem ready to let the German Army gain another foot of ground without fighting for it. Sturmgeschütz-Abteilung 201 crossed the Don at Latnaja and reached Woronesch, its objective. Although the city was taken, fighting continued there during the following weeks and Sturmgeschütz-Abteilung 201 was involved in it during July and August 1942. The men of the Sturmgeschütze destroyed 189 enemy tanks in the Woronesch Bridgehead, at a cost of two of its guns destroyed.

Pulled out on 18 August, it received its first decorations and four men of the Sturmartillerie were especially honored. Hauptmann Hoffmann, commander of the 3./Sturmgeschütz-Abteilung 201, was the first soldier of the battalion to receive the Knight's Cross for his outstanding actions. (Otto Hoffmann was killed as a Hauptmann on 5 March 1944 at Novo Archangelsk, where he commanded Sturmgeschütz-Brigade 911.)

Personnel replacements arrived from Sturmgeschütz-Ersatz-Abteilung 200 in Schweinfurt. New Sturmgeschütze arrived. Vehicles, weapons and other equipment followed and turned the combat-weary battalion back into a strong fighting unit.

The next section of text requires a short introduction in order to make clear to the reader which units were employed and which missions were given. In August 1942 the 2. Armee, which had captured Woronesch, was engaged in heavy defensive fighting against the furiously fighting Red Army. The War Diary of the 2. Armee recorded on 14 August 1942:

The very heavy defensive fighting continues. New attacks from all sides are to be expected. In the VII. Armee-Korps sector, an enemy force of 100 tanks has managed to make a penetration 5 kilometers wide and 3 kilometers deep into the main battle area of the 387. Infanterie-Division. The Soviet Air Force is continuously increasing its activity. Constant heavy air attacks. Fighter cover by the Luftwaffe is absolutely necessary for the continuation of our defense. The Sturmgeschütze in the bridgehead will fire their last rounds of antitank ammunition tomorrow.

The War Diary of the Wehrmacht High Command also reported for that same 14 August: "Fourteen out of 25 attacking tanks were destroyed during the fighting at the north edge of Woronesch."

This was certainly so, but they say nothing about the conduct of the battle itself.

The Hungarian 2nd Army and the Italian 8th Army adjoined the sector of the 2. Armee in the employment area of Woronesch to the south along the Don River.

More than once, the commander of Sturmgeschütz-Abteilung 201, Major Heinz Huffmann, had to answer a cry for help from these armies and take his Sturmgeschütze into the threatened areas. However, this was only the beginning of an Odyssey which would demand everything they had from the Sturmgeschütz soldiers.

The Red Army established bridgeheads on the west bank of the Don further to the south throughout the summer of 1942 right up into the battles that fall. These were to serve as jump-off points for a new Soviet offensive. These were the Uryw, Storosh, Woje and Korotojak bridgeheads in the Hungarian Army's sector. The Italian 8th Army had the Werche Mamon bridgehead.

During the period that followed, Sturmgeschütz-Abteilung 201 would go into action in those areas.

After the battalion had a few days rest at the end of August 1942, days which were used for refitting and recovery, the young new replacements were distributed among the Sturmgeschütze. There was even a movie theater for the soldiers in Woronesch and often the roar of the cannon in the German newsreels couldn't really be separated from that coming from the nearby front lines.

On 23 August the battalion road marched 130 kilometers further south and took up billets in the areas of Ukolowo, Lessnoje and Ostrogoshk.

In spite of weeks of fighting, the Hungarians had not managed to eliminate the strong Russian bridgehead at Korotojak and push the enemy back across the Don. At that point, it was intended for the XXIV. Panzer-Korps to clean out that bridgehead with the 336. Infanterie-Division. All elements of Sturmgeschütz-Abteilung 201 were attached to the 336. Infanterie-Division.

The fighting units rolled into their jump-off positions in the evening of 31 August. During the night it rained in buckets. In the early morning they advanced with the assaulting infantry. The mission of the 336. Infanterie-Division was as follows: "The 336. Infanterie-Division will launch its attack at 0530 hours on 1 September 1942 to capture the Korotojak Bridgehead from the enemy and annihilate the enemy forces defending it. Sturmgeschütz-Abteilung 201 is to be assigned to the Infanterie-Regiment of von Bülow."

The attack began according to plan, but only made slow progress. Two Sturmgeschütze were out of action right at the start. At 1115 hours another one was lost and by 1730 hours four more were out of action. Although the battalion had some success, the breakthrough for the annihilation of the Red Army elements holding the bridgehead had not been made.

At 2015 hours Major Huffmann requested that the Sturmgeschütze be left with Kampfgruppe Mainka, as the southern sector where they were to be employed had been heavily mined. The division agreed.

The second day of the attack opened with heavy blows striking the Sturmgeschütze. The Russians had remained in their foxholes and fired with antitank rifles and snipers. A gun commander was shot through the head and killed. Although two lanes had been cleared through the minefields during the night, two additional Sturmgeschütze still ran onto mines and had to be left behind.

Sturmgeschütz "301" of Seemann's Section of the 3rd Battery was firing over another gun just a few meters in front of it. Their field of fire was completely clear, as the guns were on a steeply sloping road. With the crack of their gun, the gun in front of them exploded. A cold chill ran through the crew of the Section Leader's Sturmgeschütz, but a glance at the gun's elevation showed that they had a clear field of fire. Then they also saw that the gun had been torn apart on its left flank and that the roof had been blown several meters to one side. The direct hit had occurred simultaneously as the section commander's gun fired, but had come from the left. The gun commander and the gunner were killed immediately. The driver, full of shrapnel, was able to climb out of the gun by himself. The radio operator was severely wounded in the head and neck.

The two wounded men were immediately taken back by Sturmgeschütz "301." It was only a few minutes until the concealed Russian antitank cannon on the left was destroyed . But, at 0730 hours, Major Huffmann reported three additional Sturmgeschütze as out of action.

Even so, the Major continued the advance. They cleared a way, firing, rolling over antitank guns and destroyed tanks, until they finally destroyed the Russians' main point of resistance, the "Red House," and silenced this enemy strongpoint.

By 1625 hours, the attacking 336. Infanterie-Division had lost 1,700 men. The army headquarters issued the following order for the following day: "The division has to be tougher than the Russians."

That was easy to say, but ordering Kampfgruppe Mainka and Sturmgeschütz-Abteilung 201 to continue the assault didn't do much against these closely packed enemy forces. The assault troops finally requested Stuka support.

The Korotojak Bridgehead wasn't finally taken until 9 September, after the battalion had been attached to the 168. Infanterie-Division The battalion veterans called it "the most costly action since the crossing of the Bug on 22 June 1941."

Still attached to the 168. Infanterie-Division, the Sturmgeschütze next went into action in the bridgehead sector at Uryw-Stotoschewoje. The 1st and 2nd Batteries participated in that operation on 9 September. The Russians had heavily garrisoned this place, which was enormously strong with dug-in antitank and anti-aircraft cannon and had a double trench system, mine fields and trip wires. It was to be taken in the first assault. The two batteries rolled forward in a shallow semi-circle and fired on every target offered by the enemy. After their first rounds, a few enemy antitank guns waiting in ambush were detected and destroyed. Still, the enemy succeeded in destroying four Sturmgeschütze.

Despite that, by evening, half the village had been cleared of the enemy.

On the next morning, Hungarian troops, following the assault sections of the 168. Infanterie-Division, pushed into the village and cleared out the remaining enemy occupied sections.

However, the enemy was able to hold out in the woods to the south. His back was to the Don. Soviet assault groups broke out in a major operational offensive here on 13 and 14 January 1943, forming the northern arm of the great pocket around the Hungarian 2nd and Italian 8th Armies and the German 2. Armee. However, more about that later.

The combat elements of Sturmgeschütz-Abteilung 201 pulled back to Nowo Ukolowo on 18 September. It was supposed to be a rest area, but only a few days later it had to make a 100-kilometer road march into the sector of the 2. Armee northwest of Woronesch and take up quarters in Perlewka.

Initially it was employed in a forested area near Olchowatka to relieve a surrounded infantry battalion which belonged to the 377. Infanterie-Division. The 8 guns of the 1st Battery were supposed to clear up this precarious situation on 23 September and were sent to the I./Infanterie-Regiment 168 for that purpose.

The 1st Battery were able to free Kampfgruppe Auinger and prevent its destruction. The attack ran into an iron-hard enemy who had dug himself into strong positions in a sunflower field. The Sturmgeschütze and their escorting infantry made good progress up until noon, when the enemy opened fire with Stalin Organs, artillery, heavy mortars, ground attack aircraft and then even with tanks. The fighting lasted eleven hours before the first Sturmgeschütz broke through to Kampfgruppe Auinger.

The eight Sturmgeschütze proved their worth in this fighting. In a series of duels, they destroyed no fewer than 24 enemy tanks. They took up a hedgehog position in a small woods, which the men of the Sturmartillerie called "Bird Woods." They took cover there in trees and brush, completely out of ammunition and so condemned to doing nothing, and had to let the enemy fire pass over them without being able to respond.

Oberstleutnant Auinger reported by radio at 0730 hours on 9 September that contact with the Bird Woods, which meant with the Sturmgeschütze and their infantry, had been lost once again.

The attack launched at 1400 hours by Infanterie-Regiment 543 to clear up this situation collapsed in the fire of the enemy defense.

Oberstleutnant Huffmann sent six of his Sturmgeschütze to the Bird Woods to supply the others with ammunition and rations. They were to bring back the wounded. The thrust failed, and three Sturmgeschütze were knocked out.

At the end of the day, the corps commander had to make the decision to give up the Bird Woods. The Sturmgeschütze holding out there were called back: "To all units: Everyone fall back, everyone fall back!"

For the members of the Sturmartillerie, this order was something entirely new, as up to now it had always been: "Sturmgeschütze vor!"

A few of the Sturmgeschütze ran onto mines while pulling back. For example, Sturmgeschütz "306" ran onto a German mine. The crew bailed out and had to fight its way back with pistols and submachine guns. The other crews whose guns were put out of action had to do the same.

A few wounded comrades had been left behind—unnoticed at the time—so a patrol made up of officers went back into no-mans-land. Among other soldiers, it brought back two wounded from the last Sturmgeschütz which had been shot up and left behind, burning.

The encircled Kampfgruppe Auinger arrived back at the German main battle line at Olchowatka after freeing itself by moving through barrage fire from every available weapon. Twelve more enemy tanks were destroyed, but the battalion was only conditionally operational. Then, on the following morning, there were additional losses, especially among personnel when surprise fire from Russian artillery smashed down among the Sturmgeschütze.

During the next few days, the repair section worked feverishly to get the damaged Sturmgeschütze back into action. The guns had to take over security duties, before they were pulled out on 6 October and moved to Latnaja in the Woronesch area. They hoped that they would finally get a complete rest and refitting and be able to settle themselves in the surrounding villages for winter quarters.

On 4 November the battalion was attached to the 27. Panzer-Division along with Panzer-Verband 700 (Panzer-Späh-Kompanie 700). The commander reported to the commander of the 27. Panzer-Division on 15 November, but by 23 November the battalion had already been detached from that division. It was to be rail loaded, but nobody knew where it was going. A few rumors mentioned Africa. However, when the battalion was loaded onto the trains, it moved south where, on 19 November, the two great pincer movements of the Russian attack on Stalingrad had begun and had quickly gained ground.

Millerowo was reached after an uninterrupted 48-hour trip by rail. The battalion unloaded and then road marched in the direction of Stalingrad. It was halted in the middle of the march, directed back to Millerowo and then committed north to the city of Rossosch in the Italian 8th Army's sector, where things had heated up. The rear area services of the XXIV. Panzer-Korps were still in the city.

On 1 December some of the combat elements rolled through the deep snow into the Italian Tridentina Division's sector. Fortunately for the battalion a shipment of new Sturmgeschütze had arrived in Rossosch during this period.

The rest of the battalion, still attached to the 27. Panzer-Division, received orders from Heeresgruppe B on 8 December: "Early on 9 December 27. Panzer-Division is to move into the area of Bogutschar-Beliy and Kolodes-Pissarewka-Kusmenkoff. Three Kampfgruppen are to be formed...Sturmgeschütz-Abteilung 201 is assigned to Kampfgruppe I, Oberstleutnant Maempel."

On 12 December the 27. Panzer-Division was attached to the Italian 8th Army, to shore up the resolution of the Italians. The Italian 8th Army consisted of the Alpini Corps, the Italian II Corps and the Italian XXXV Corps. The 298. Infanterie-Division was also attached to the Italian 8th Army; it formed the southern boundary with the XXIX. Armee-Korps.

Kampfgruppe Maempel received orders to make contact with the 298. Infanterie-Division. Hans von Obstfelder had been commanding general of the XXIX. Armee-Korps since 1 June 1940 and had been very successful in the battle of encirclement at Kiev. He had received the Knight's Cross there on 27 July 1941. In this sector he was facing an extremely difficult test of his abilities.

The secondary Russian attack, beginning on 11 December in the sector of the Ravenna and Cosseria Divisions, lasted three days. The Italian positions were lost, and the Italian resistance in the II Corps area dissolved.

On 16 December the Red Army attacked with everything it had. Kampfgruppe Maempel and the attached Sturmgeschütz-Abteilung 201 were able to prevent a breakthrough in the Filonowo-Gatjutschje area. The Sturmgeschütze were successful in knocking out 20 enemy targets. Oberstleutnant Rolf Maempel led magnificently and knew that he could rely on the men of Sturmgeschütz-Abteilung 201.

When the defense collapsed at Botgutschar, the Sturmgeschütze were the last out of the city on 18 December, and a little later they were sucked into the gigantic confusion of the retreating Italian units. The Russian tank spearhead pushed into the fleeing mass from the south.

With thousands of Italians, the Sturmgeschütze reached Arbusow. Already encircled, they continued the attempt to breakout to the southwest on Christmas Eve and made it to the strongpoint at Tschertkowo. Thousands of Italian soldiers were left back on the banks of the Don: dead, frozen, wounded or missing. Some of them were already marching east into Russian captivity.

On 18 December command was transferred from the Italian II Corps to the XXIV. Panzer-Korps. Generalleutnant Martin Wandel (General der Artillerie effective 1 January 1943) set up his command post in Kantemirowka. Sturmgeschütz-Abteilung 201 wasn't able to pull itself out of the confusion of the defeat until January 1943. Its 3rd Battery had had an especially difficult time. This independent battery, under the command of Oberleutnant Anton Grünert, started off on 18 December as ordered by corps. It had eight Sturmgeschütze once again and the battery was in good shape. What follows is its Odyssey.

The objective of the eight Sturmgeschütze was the area of the Red Army breakthrough at Botgutschar. It was intended that it would break free the endangered Brigade Fegelein of the Waffen-SS. Rolling through the columns of fleeing Italians, the eight Sturmgeschütze reached an Italian unit that was moving against the flood toward the main battle line. It was the Alpini Division "Julia," which greeted the Sturmgeschütze with joy.

When the 3./Sturmgeschütz-Abteilung 201 reached its staging area, evening had fallen and it had just rolled into a village which stretched along the road. The Sturmartilleristen heard tank noise behind them. They immediately took up fighting positions, but this wasn't Russian armor. Instead, it was German tanks, Sturmgeschütze and antiaircraft and antitank cannon as well as a number of Schützenpanzerwagen from Eingreifgruppe (Assault Group) Pohlmann, with the main body of the Führer-Begleit-Bataillon of Panzer-Grenadier-Division "Großdeutschland".

Immediately afterwards, the German units encountered Brigade Fegelein of the Waffen-SS, which still had elements of the 387. Infanterie-Division in its ranks.

The XXIV. Panzer-Korps which commanded this area was ordered to establish a defensive line as a covering position behind the Italian Front between the Don and Nowaja Kalitwa (at the bend in the Don). The corps had the 27. Panzer-Division (in bad shape), Sturmgeschütz-Abteilung 201, the 385. Infanterie-Division (Generalleutnant Eibl) and the 387. Infanterie-Division (Generalleutnant Jahr). It also had the Brigade Fegelein, the Führer-Begleit-Bataillon "Großdeutschland," and the iron-hard Alpine Division "Julia".

The Sturmgeschütze under Oberleutnant Grünert were in action with all the units named above during the hard fighting up to Christmas. Penetrations were stopped, enemy tanks that had broken through were destroyed, and the front line was evened out. There was dramatic fighting between Kalitwa and Rossosch, which involved this subordinate element of the battalion. Along with Panzer-Abteilung 127, they formed Kampfgruppe Marx and fought as a part of this unit. During the night of 24/25 December, at Rossosch, Wachtmeister Schairer was called from his quarters and killed by several shots from an unknown assailant. This case has never been satisfactorily resolved.

A new Russian offensive began further south with the objective of surrounding and annihilating all German units and the Hungarian 2nd Army from Kantemirowka in the south to Woronesch in the north. This included the XXIV. Panzer-Korps and the entire 2. Armee, as well as the Alpine Corps.

The fighting against these massed Soviet forces lasted from 31 December 1942 until 15 January 1943.

The Russian operational offensive began on the morning of 14 January 1943. Numerous tanks advanced to the northwest out of the Kantemirowka area. Some defending elements were surrounded. General Wandel, the commanding general of the XXIV. Panzer-Korps, drove to the front to clear up the situation. He ran directly into the lead elements of the Russian tank forces, was taken prisoner, and shot on the spot by the Russians. His escort suffered the same fate.

At 1830 hours this Russian battle group reached the corps command post. The Chief of Staff, Oberst i.G. Heidkämper, was able to shoot his way through the Russians along with elements of the staff, fight his way through to the west across the Owtschinnaja and escape with his life. The survivors reached Rossosch on the morning of 15 January.

The commander of the 385. Infanterie-Division, General-leutnant Eibl, took over the XXIV. Panzer-Korps in General Wandel's place. It was a matter of saving what was left to save. Russian tanks had already reached Rossosch and taken it.

The last Sturmgeschütz of the 3./Sturmgeschütz-Abteilung 201 had repulsed yet another enemy attack on this decisive 14 January, before it had to pull back to Kalitwa. As the ice wouldn't support the Sturmgeschütz, it had to be blown up.

On the evening of 15 January a retreat began for all the Sturmgeschütz crews, a retreat that soon turned into unrestrained flight.

Fuel supplies were exhausted. The continued flight was ghastly with severe cold and snowed-over roads. But then the men encountered the division's trains fleeing from Rossosch and with them the last four Sturmgeschütze, which were immediately manned.

There was an immediate danger that all troops in this area would be cut off. A few T-34's had pushed all the way up to the repair shop and were destroyed. Afterwards, everyone was ordered to form up toward the airfield. Oberleutnant Grünert took the lead with the remaining Sturmgeschütze.

The front was moving back west along a width of 40 kilometers; it then angled toward the north. The first T-34's emerged in the rear of the Alpine Corps. The Tridentina, Cuneense and Vicenza Divisions rolled back smoothly until they ran into the thick mass of the retreating columns. This caused an unsolvable mess. Everything came to a complete halt within a few hours. March columns left the roads, which meant that they had to abandon their vehicles.

The commander of the Italian "Vicenza" Division opened fire on German march groups in order to shoot his way clear to the west. He thus killed those who had initially given him the possibility of escape. Feldwebel Ernst Hennersberger told the author: "The criminality and ferocity displayed by such a high-ranking officer of the Italian armed forces—merely to save his own skin—is simply indescribable."

As a result of the heavy snow drifts, every vehicle of the XXIV. Panzer-Korps had to drive on the only remaining negotiable road through Ssaprina-Ssergejewa to Podgornoje. They were cut off by Russian units attacking from Rossosch, and Sturmgeschütz-

Abteilung 201 was among these units.

The remaining four Sturmgeschütze continued their move on 19 January. The extra crews rode on top of them. These four Sturmgeschütze were the only mobile anti-armor defense left in the corps. They should have moved at the head of the column, but that wasn't the case.

In the early morning of 20 January Russian tanks advanced to within a kilometer of the XXIV. Panzer-Korps command post. They had broken through the line held by the Alpine Corps. When the first T-34's moved out on Opyt, the field trains and march columns broke and ran, panic-stricken. The individual columns fled to the west through the low-lying Gnilaja swamps, leaving the vehicles, sleds and equipment behind.

The Sturmgeschütze reached the Olchowatka sector toward noon. The worst was avoided only because Oberleutnant Grünert ordered these guns into action. The Tridentina Group, with the four Sturmgeschütze at their lead, crossed the Postojali-Rossosch road at Lessnitschanskij during the night of 20/21 January. They too bogged down shortly thereafter, and General Eibl arrived just before dawn sitting on the radiator of a prime mover. He attempted to motivate the Italians with the cry of "Avanti, Avanti!" and, just as he was overtaking this march column, an Italian threw a hand grenade which exploded right next to the general.

General Karl Eibl, the twenty-first recipient of the Swords to the Oak Leaves of the Knight's Cross (awarded 19 December 1942), would later die as a result of this treacherous murder attempt. Feldwebel Ernst Hennersberger: "It was more than any man of our battalion could bear. Any one of us would have done anything to help our Italian comrades. And to be repaid for that by this almost bestial act was something that we simply couldn't understand."

Krawozowka was reached in the afternoon of 21 January. Generalleutnant Eibl was operated on under the most primitive conditions while fully conscious in an attempt to save his life, which was hanging by a thread. He died at 1845 hours on that horrible day.

On 22 January the lead elements, with the four Sturmgeschütze of Sturmgeschütz-Abteilung 201 at the head, continued the retreat. Russian tanks halted the column at the Scheljakino Ridge. The field trains ran into the combat units, and a total of some 25,000 troops of widely different units found themselves thrown into a unique series of events.

It was only thanks to the four Sturmgeschütze that the enemy tanks were destroyed and the mass of the retreating men were able to cross this ridge. On two separate occasions, three T-34's were destroyed.

It was simply unimaginable. These four Sturmgeschütze continued to hold off the charging enemy tanks, destroyed others which opposed the march columns, and also moved out to the flanks to free cut-off units. Oberleutnant Grünert and his crew didn't do all this alone, but the other guns did the same thing. It is a shame that only one of the other crews is known to us by name: the gun commander, Unteroffizier Helmut Kremer; the gunner, Jorda; the loader, Kassel; and, the driver, Sepp Denner. They and the two other crews earned the reputation of continually doing the impossible to rescue lives while smashing open the way to freedom.

At Nikolajewka they ran into a Russian artillery column and destroyed it. They got food from a destroyed Russian field kitchen and from the bread bags of dead Russians, which they always carried suspended from their necks. Once they found apples preserved in vinegar; these too were devoured.

The units were inextricably mixed. It was impossible to separate them, and so they were allowed to fall back in the manner they had gotten themselves into by accident. When the German Army High Command asked for the combat strength and organization of the march groups, the XXIV. Panzer-Korps answered:

"Remnants of the 385. Infanterie-Division and attached units scattered by constant combat and without the means of command and control. Field trains with stragglers within the Tridentina. 385. Infanterie-Division without artillery; 387. Infanterie-Division a few guns; both without vehicles or antitank cannon. Four Sturmgeschütze at the head of the Alpine Corps.

For the Commander: Heidkämper, Oberst i.G. and Operations Officer of the XXIV. Panzer-Korps."

From then on, Oberst Heidkämper led the march groups. Although this should have been General Nasci's job, the latter had no means of command and control. It turned out that the commander of the Tridentina, General Reverberi, was one of the most courageous of the Italian officers. Disregarding his own safety, he always cared for his troops.

The first of the totally exhausted soldiers threw their weapons away and shortly after dropped where they were. Within a few minutes, there were only mounds of snow left in the blizzard. An enormous tragedy was taking place, comparable in scale only to that of Stalingrad.

At Malakajewka the Sturmgeschütze ran head on into massed Russian artillery in thich snowfall. In the first exchange of shots, two guns received direct hits from the flank and were put out of action. However, they were able to be repaired and put back into operation. The remaining two guns destroyed the massed Russian artillery. This was the first time the U.S. Studebaker prime movers that had been made available to the Russians were seen.

During the following night the entire march column of approximately 20,000 remaining soldiers took shelter in the 120-house village of Romachowo. Orders arrived there from Italian 8th Army Headquarters to change the direction of the breakout and march more to the northwest to reach the crossroads 16 kilometers southeast of Nowy Oskol.

In the early morning the march was resumed out of Romachowo. There was great joy when three Ju-52's showed up during the morning with fighter escort and dropped fuel, Sturmgeschütz ammunition and rations. Unfortunately, three fuel containers were opened by the Italians and drained. Some of the groups forcibly took some of the rations. Even so, a glimmer of hope!

In Nikitowka all of the Italian units were separated from the German units, so that both elements could go into action as Kampfgruppen and fight their way free separately. Unfortunately, the exchange of information between the Italians and Germans was sadly lacking. In the evening the troops rested in Arnautowa and Nikolajewka. At least 20,000 soldiers were assembled in these villages.

The retreat was entering its last desperate phase. The battleground was Nikolajewka on the Walui River and the railroad line from Waluki to Ostrogoshk. The latter city will never be forgotten by any of those who were there in the winter of 1943.

A high embankment ran along this railroad line perpendicular to the direction of the attack. It provided first-rate cover for the oncoming Russian troops and a major obstacle to the attacking Germans. Behind the embankment in the winter sun of 26 January 1943, a surprising picture was laid out to anyone coming from above: There were a few villages in the snow-covered countryside. There was a widespread town in the middle with a church with shining domes and a tower. Massively constructed houses and the large railroad station were located around the centrally-located church. That was Nikolajewka. The wide, snow-covered Ukraine stretched out behind it.

The troops of the 3rd Soviet Tank Army had set up in this strategically important area and lay in front of the starving and completely exhausted Italian and German formations.

The first German troops to appear on the ridge were greeted with artillery and mortar fire. The companies of the Tridentina Division assembled behind the ridge to wait for the arrival of additional battalions from Arnautowo. Oberleutnant Grünert was of the opinion, however, that an attack must be launched immediately, so as not to lose the moment of surprise.

The four Sturmgeschütze placed themselves in front of the Tridentina, and Grünert informed the Italians by radio that General Reverberi had ordered the attack.

Although that was not true, it got the Italians moving. They closed up on the Sturmgeschütze, which moved forward down the ridge toward the railroad station. They came under enemy fire immediately after crossing the ridge. They rapidly moved down the ridge toward the railroad line. The left wing reached the railroad embankment and then pushed on to the first houses. Nikolajewka was assaulted.

The first gun had its gun sights destroyed. Enemy fire increased and Oberleutnant Grünert had to order a withdrawal behind the ridge. While moving in reverse, the Sturmgeschütze continued to fire on the enemy as they climbed the ridge.

This meant the failure of the first, rapid attack. It revealed, however, that the town was full of Russians with dozens of antitank guns. The Alpine troops who had fought like lions in the town, also had to pull back.

In the meanwhile, the other troops had arrived and stared down on this hellish scene, where they too had to go if they wanted to capture Nikolajewka. General Nasci and General Reverberi were among these observers. The latter ordered a new attack by the rest of the Tridentina, Julia and Cuneense Divisions.

Once again the assault wave rolled down the ridge. Russian fire increased to an almost impenetrable wall of flame. Within a few minutes, the entire slope was covered with dead. Among them was General Martinat, Chief of Staff of the Alpine Corps, who charged at the head of his soldiers, rifle in hand.

The attack failed once again and, in the afternoon, the notorious "butchers," IL 2 ground-attack fighters, showed up. Flying low, they flitted over the ridge and shot at everything in sight.

During the afternoon, the third attack was ordered. General Reverberi climbed onto one of the Sturmgeschütze, moved forward with it and then, a little later, jumped off to run forward in the middle of his Alpine troops. The Sturmgeschütze rolled forward widely dispersed, but covering each other. They silenced antitank gun after antitank gun, rolled over the first Russian machine gun positions and then reached the eastern edge of Nikolajewka once again. The enemy fire lifted, giving courage to those to the rear to follow on and leave the protective cover of the ridge.

The Sturmgeschütze, Oberleutnant Grünert at the front, pushed through to the center of the city, closely followed by the soldiers. Approximately 10 antitank guns were destroyed at the edge of the city and on the way to the middle of the town.

A solid stream of limping and staggering field-train troops and stragglers on sleds, horseback, and horse-drawn vehicles poured into the town and, after defeating the Russians, found shelter against the deadly cold in the houses.

The Russians defending the town were simply pushed aside by this unstoppable flow and killed, sometimes with bare hands.

German and Italian casualties ran to about 5,000 men from this triple assault and the Russian defense.

Russian units were still dug in on the west edge of the town, and their heavy fire prevented the resumption of the retreat after a few hours rest. The Sturmgeschütze destroyed one gun after another by targeting their muzzle flashes. At 0500 hours the last resistance was broken, and the retreat could continue.

From that point on, it was a matter of breaking through to the German defense line in a single push.

At 0900 hours, a German transport glider landed right next to the march columns. The pilot, a young Gefreiter, delivered his load, grabbed his submachine gun and some hand grenades and, after blowing up his glider, joined the column marching toward almost certain death without a word, just as if it were the most natural thing in the world.

Hubertus Ohmann said to the author: "Those were our comrades in the transport gliders, all experienced glider pilots and all volunteers. They knew what they were signing up for and they did their duty, which took everything they had. We honor their memory."

When the march column encountered an enemy column of some 5,000 men and 100 vehicles—including a dozen T-34's—coming from the northeast, it became necessary to reach the security of the highway before them and to link up with the German armor force which was coming along this highway to meet them. The rendezvous point on the highway was Uspenka.

Uspenka was reached. Rescue was near. Although the forward elements of the Tridentina Division received instructions to rest at Uspenka, the German command under Oberstleutnant Heid-kämper ordered the Sturmgeschütze to resume their march immediately. The Tridentina were given the same orders. To remain there meant death.

The Sturmgeschütze rolled on and, after a 43-kilometer march, reached the crossroads at Nikolajewka. There, at 1715 hours, they linked up with the outposts of the Panzer-Späh-Kompanie 700, commanded by Oberleutnant Waldow. (Hermann Waldow received the Knight's Cross on 30 January 1943 for this and for the fighting immediately after.)

Oberleutnant Waldow had been ordered to make contact with Korpsgruppe Eibl and to haul it out at any cost. And that is exactly what this decisive Panzer officer did.

This small Kampfgruppe had been attached to Korpsgruppe Cramer, which had been stationed north of the Alpine Corps as a reserve for the Hungarian 2nd Army. It had then prepared a link-up position on the Oskol and held it until Korpsgruppe Eibl arrived.

Generalleutnant Hans Cramer had been in radio contact with Korpsgruppe Eibl since 24 January. (Hans Cramer, who already received the Knight's Cross in Africa on 27 June 1941 as Oberstleutnant and commander of Panzer-Regiment 8, returned to Africa after this action to take over command of Panzer Group Africa.)

The march columns, which had remained far behind the Sturmgeschütze, were brought out by a few tanks and Sturmgeschütze and reached Uspenka-Schenschinowka-Lwowka. This brought most of them to safety north of the highway. The Russians, who tried to get in front of them once again, arrived two hours too late.

Starting 27 January Oberleutnant Grünert and Oberleutnant Waldow maintained close contact with each other and exchanged reconnaissance results by runner. On 29 January the Wehrmacht High Command reported: "28 January: In the sector of the Italian 8th Army, where fighting is continuing, the Alpine Corps and Korpsgruppe Eibl have made contact with Korpsgruppe Cramer at Nikolajewka."

The remnants of the 385. Infanterie-Division and 387. Infanterie-Division, the army-level troops and Sturmgeschütz-Abteilung 201 reached Woltschansk by 1 February. In the days that followed the Sturmgeschütze rolled on to Kharkov. There, once again, they had to mount new short-barreled Sturmgeschütze and stop the pursuing Russians before they were finally relieved and sent with the main body of the battalion to Baruth.

On 15 March 1943 Oberleutnant Anton Grünert received the Knight's Cross which he had earned several times over. This outstanding soldier was killed on 8 August 1944 in action between the San and the Vistula. He was posthumously promoted to Hauptmann.

After a breakout march of 350 kilometers, they had managed to bring back 7,571 wounded and frostbitten soldiers.

None of the German generals of Korps Eibl survived this battle. All of them had expressly refused to be flown out of the various pockets. The last commanding general of the XXIV. Panzer-Korps, Generalleutnant Arno Jahr, winner of the German Cross in Gold and the Knight's Cross, was severely wounded and killed himself on 1 January 1943.

The survivors returned home after this superhuman accomplishment and, after a short convalescence leave, reported back to their branch of service, the Sturmartillerie, for further duty. The battalion was reestablished on 31 May 1943; it was renamed as Sturmgeschütz-Brigade 201 on 14 February 1944. The brigade was employed in the east with first the 2. Armee and then the 9. Armee. It last fought in the area around Stettin in 1945. No other details are known about its late-war employment.

Sturmgeschütz-Abteilung 202 (Sturmgeschütz-Brigade 202)

Sturmgeschütz-Abteilung 202, under the command of Hauptmann Dr. Marder, was raised at Jüterbog from former artillerymen at the beginning of September 1941. It took the marten as its heraldic animal, after the name of their commander (Marder = marten).

The battalion was loaded up by the middle of September and sent to the Eastern Front by rail. Smolensk was the disembarkation point. The only men in the battalion with combat experience in Sturmgeschütze were Leutnant Hans-Joachim Heise and a Wachtmeister.

Sturmgeschütz-Brigade 202

The battalion took up ready positions east of Berniki in the totally destroyed settlement of Nowo-Tischowo. In complete darkness the Sturmgeschütze moved forward to their jump-off point. It was deceptively quiet. They were employed in the sector of the 184. Infanterie-Division. The attack had been set for the early morning of 2 October 1941. It would initiate the great double battle of Briansk and Wjasma.

As soon as there was enough light to aim, the Sturmgeschütze rolled forward to shoot a way clear through the enemy lines for the infantry. One hour later the attack had already failed in the 1st Battery's sector. By this time 6 of the 7 Sturmgeschütze employed had already run onto mines and were put out of action. Luckily, they were not totally destroyed, but only suffered extensive damage to tracks and suspension.

When one of the section commanders, Leutnant Maurischat, ran back along the tracks left by his gun to get help in recovering the vehicle, he disappeared without a trace. In spite of an exhaustive search, he was never seen again.

Toward midday on 2 October only the Sturmgeschütz of Leutnant Heise was still in action, but it had expended all its ammunition during the course of the fighting. When the Sturmgeschütz moved back to get more rounds, it came under antitank fire from a wooded area on its flank. The gun swiveled and attempted to silence the antitank cannon with three rounds from the emergency reserve. However, it had no luck. Neither the gunner, Erwin Barth, nor Leutnant Heise could see the muzzle flash of the cannon or anything else.

The gun turned around but, at that very moment, it took a round in the flank. It impacted with a great deal of force, but at first the Sturmgeschütz kept going. Only when it had reached a depression, did it turn around on itself and get stuck. The antitank gun had not only hit a bogie wheel, it had damaged the track in such a fashion that it had then come apart. There was good luck with the bad, as the gun now lay safe in the depression.

Things didn't go much better with the 2nd and 3rd Batteries either. The 2nd Battery had lost its battery commander, who was killed along with his entire crew by a direct hit.

On 3 October 4 Sturmgeschütze were again operational. They were given to Leutnant Heise. Along with the Radfahr-Schwadron (bicycle squadron) of the 184. Division (Rittmeister Sachenbacher), the section commander was ordered to reconnoiter a gap which had arisen between them and the neighboring division. We will let Leutnant Heise tell us how he remembered this day:

We worked our way forward some hundred meters up onto a knoll that gave us a good view. We rapidly determined that this was no no-man's-land. The Russians lay well camouflaged in the surrounding grain fields. It was extremely difficult to detect their machine gun nests, let alone the dangerous mortars which we could never find. While we were engaged in clearing the area with our fire, I received a radio transmission from the Leutnant who was the leader of the second section. He reported that his second Sturmgeschütz had slipped a track sideways into a

Russian trench, and it was stuck with the hull resting on the edge of the trench. Since I knew how difficult the retrieval would be, I radioed back to wait until I could get there to help. As it happened, Rittmeister Sachenbacher had just called me to say that he considered his mission accomplished and that he was pulling back his people. I urgently requested him to stay and give us fire support until we could recover the stuck Sturmgeschütz. But apparently he was no longer able to contact his people, because when I took a look around a little later, I saw the last steel helmet of the infantry disappear far back behind us.

In the meanwhile, the Leutnant had tried to haul the Sturmgeschütz free himself, and had also hung up his vehicle about two meters behind the first one.

Neglecting our own defense, I first had to pull out the Sturmgeschütz of the Leutnant with my second Sturmgeschütz. The enemy fired on us with infantry weapons. We took casualties. Not until the Sturmgeschütz of the Leutnant was recovered could he give covering fire with his vehicle. The group returned from this operation with a sorry casualty list of several dead and, to top things off, my gun drove onto a mine.

The operation on 4 October was luckier. Combat engineers had cleared a lane in the minefields. Together with the infantry, Sturmgeschütz-Abteilung 202 reached the railroad line north of Jelnja. The Sturmgeschütze played a considerable role in silencing several Soviet batteries which had been making things difficult for both the infantry and the Sturmgeschütze.

The damage resulting from the three days of combat was so great that by 6 October only two Sturmgeschütze could be go into action with the advance guard detachment of the 184. Infanterie-Division at Dorogobusch, 30 kilometer to the east. These were the Sturmgeschütze of Leutnant Heise and Leutnant Pickert. The cyclists of Rittmeister Sachenbacher once again followed along behind the Sturmgeschütze. Rittmeister Sachenbacher commanded the advance guard detachment.

The Sturmgeschütze encountered very little enemy activity in the villages as the advance guard detachment passed through them. Contact consisted primarily of enemy supply columns which were fired on and destroyed.

Once, twenty aircraft approached a small hill near a village when both Sturmgeschütze were on it. Fortunately, they were Stukas. The aerial identification panels were immediately set out. The machines dropped down lower, circled the advance guard detachment once and then flew on to the east.

When the two Sturmgeschütze found themselves only 800 meters from Dorogobusch, the bicyclists of the squadron were still far behind them. Leutnant Heise saw a crowd of vehicles and men through his scissors scope. Enemy troop columns of considerable strength were moving toward the town.

We will let Leutnant Heise continue the story again:

My first thought was to charge forward at full speed to take at least the entrance to the village by surprise. Then my loader reported:

"Herr Leutnant, the ammo is low!"

I halted to discuss the situation with my friend Pickert, who had stayed close behind us. His ammo situation was no better. Together we still had about 20 rounds. To try it alone with only that amount would have been tantamount to taking an irresponsible risk.

In the meantime, we had been spotted by the Soviets. In all haste, the enemy deployed an antiaircraft battery at the entrance to the village, whose barrels were pointed at us. We had to expend a few of our precious rounds to deal with the battery while it was still unlimbering.

Then it became clear to me that we had to exploit the confusion that our rounds had caused among the Russians. We had to roll forward, otherwise they would be able to establish a defensive position and our advance detachment would be too weak to break it.

After a brief discussion with my fearless driver, Wachtmeister Frenzel, whom we called Timoshenko, we headed for the village at top speed; still chasing the enemy columns which were turning away to the right into the village. Indescribable confusion immediately arose. The village swarmed with Russians, crouching against house walls and hedges. I saw ash-gray faces, distorted with fear, but also fists clenching Molotov cocktails. It was clear to me that we dared not stop for an instant; If the Russians saw that we were alone, we would have had it.

With the few shells that we still had, we shot at point-blank range into the column in front of us. This must have been a monstrous shock to the Russians, as they didn't attempt to pick off either Leutnant Pickert or me, and we were both riding standing straight up in the open hatches.

Clanking and crashing, literally shooting our way clear, the two Sturmgeschütze drove through and over the rubble until the road was suddenly more open. At the same time I noticed a fork in the road which turned at a right angle to the left into a valley and then led directly across a large wooden bridge. That could only be the bridge across the Dnjepr, whose upper reaches led through Dorogobusch. I turned immediately, for we had to have that bridge, undamaged.

There was a guard posted in the middle of the 100-meter long bridge. Our round, reported by the loader to be the last one, swept him away. With butterflies in our stomachs, we rattled across the bridge.

But now we were alone on the opposite side of the Dnjepr, and we had to figure out what to do next. Into the bargain, Pickert hadn't noticed our turn and had continued to drive straight ahead.

At this point, we started to draw increasing enemy infantry fire. Then we noticed Russians approaching us from the brush on this side of the river.

"Grab the submachine guns. One to the loader and the second to me!" I ordered.

As we began to shoot, both of our guns jammed after the first rounds. Both submachine guns were full of sand. The same applied to my Luger, which wouldn't fire any more.

Now we had a dozen "pineapple" hand grenades to save ourselves. We used them in this way. We stuck our heads out of the hatches and pulled them back again immediately. This drew enemy fire which revealed their positions. We were then able to throw our grenades in that direction and quiet things down.

The whole thing lasted about ten minutes, but for us it seemed an eternity. We waited longingly for the arrival of the Radfahr-Schwadron. But before they arrived, a low vehicle popped up on the other side of the river and raced across the bridge toward us. We couldn't believe our eyes, but it really was our munitions carrier, which had followed us because the driver had calculated that we must be just about out of ammunition. They were alone. Fortunately they had also penetrated through the Russians and they had done it with their laughably weakly armored vehicle.

We took on ammunition and then heard the sounds of combat at the entrance to the village, a sure sign that the rest of the advance guard detachment had arrived. Then Leutnant Pickert finally found and joined us. He also replenished his ammunition. Then we established contact with Rittmeister Sachenbacher. We had Dorogobusch. But towards evening, the Russians attempted to take back Dorogobusch with artillery support from the north bank.

The fight for Dorogobusch continued until late in the night by the light of the burning houses. But even the longest night must end. When 7 October dawned, Dorogobusch was firmly in our hands. Rittmeister Sachenbacher received the Knight's Cross for the capture of Dorogobusch. The Sturmgeschütz crews were decorated with the Iron Cross.

As the fighting progressed, Roslawl, Briansk and Karatschew were reached. From there they advanced to Orel, and from Orel they moved south to Fatesch in the Kursk area.

Sturmgeschütz-Abteilung 202 advanced to just south of Tula. The battalion took the commander of a Cossack regiment prisoner and captured 11 guns in Nikitinskaja, a village east of Plawsk. This operation had an interesting prelude.

Leutnant Heise had been surrounded with two Sturmgeschütze and two companies of infantry in Toploje, south of Tula, from 8 to 10 November. Day and night, they fought bitterly for each house in the village. The Sturmgeschütze destroyed their first T-34's there. Finally, the Soviets abandoned the village during the night of 11 November 1941. After the driver of the second Sturmgeschütz had been killed, a Luftwaffe war correspondent (Kriegsberichter Kudicke), who had accompanied the Sturmgeschütze, joined Leutnant Heise as his loader. He did a splendid job.

On 11 November the two Sturmgeschütze moved back to the battalion, where they arrived at about noon. The men were hungry, but their hope for double rations from the field kitchen was disappointed by the battalion commander who informed Leutnant Heise that he was to join a Kampfgruppe which was already set to go. Luftwaffe pilots had seen a large Soviet troop concentration in a village called Nikitinskaja. This had to be destroyed.

The Kampfgruppe consisted of 12 Sturmgeschütze and several large artillery prime movers that were heavily loaded with infantry. Hauptmann Dr. Marder had also found a place on one of these machines.

Orders were orders, so, growling to himself, Leutnant Heise placed himself behind the Sturmgeschütz of his battery commander, who was leading the Kampfgruppe.

The fine powdered snow kicked up by the tracks of his commander's Sturmgeschütz iced up Leutnant Heise's glasses, so that he was soon unable to see. For this reason, he drove to the left of the commander's Sturmgeschütz and was able to see better. But, once again, we will let Leutnant Heise describe what happened next:

Once I could see, I soon noticed that about one kilometer in front of us, there was an enclosed village that had to be Nikitinskaja, if the maps were correct. I was puzzled that my commander didn't steer a course for it, but rather bypassed it so far to the left that we finally were out of sight of the village. A little later, I asked my commander, if we weren't heading in the wrong direction. We halted and were soon in agreement that we had rolled past Nikitinskaja.

This happened because I had cut to the left to escape the snow cloud. My battery commander had thought that because I knew the sector I had wanted to take over as guide. So he followed me to the left, and the more I edged to the left to keep the necessary distance, the more he and the entire column moved in the wrong direction.

So now we wheeled to the right and headed for Nikitinskaja at top speed, naturally from an entirely different direction than that which had been planned. In front of the village, we deployed in a crescent formation and launched our attack on positions which were in part completely unoccupied.

What happened was that we had surprised the Cossacks in this position at lunch. We were able to capture virtually the entire unit with its horses and heavy weapons without any casualties of our own. Only a few managed to escape on horseback.

It turned out that the minor misunderstanding between Hauptmann Marder and Leutnant Heise had saved the Kampfgruppe from heavy casualties. The Cossacks had at first gone on alert, but went back off alert when the column had rolled past the village.

The regimental commander of the Cossacks was taken prisoner.

It was not long before the winter battles at Bogorodizk, Stalinogorsk and Michailow. The withdrawal to the Oka Line began on Christmas 1941. On 30 December 1941 Hauptmann Dr. Marder was killed along with his driver when the Russians, who had broken through at Christmas, were beaten back in 30 to 40 degrees below zero Celsius. The two were only found two days later, sieved by machine gun fire. Hauptmann Marten Buhr took over the battalion.

During 1942, the battalion fought on the Bolchow front. Things were relatively quiet there. The deadly tank fighting didn't begin until autumn when the battalion was transferred to the front lines at Wjasma.

On 28 November 1942 the battalion was attached to the 78. Assault Division. By this time it had destroyed 500 enemy tanks. A period of the bitterest, hardest fighting began which demanded the most from every man. Wachtmeister Amling's star rose in this fighting. Amling and his gunner Bruno Guskowski destroyed 42 enemy tanks in 48 hours. On 5 December 1942, he became the first member of Sturmgeschütz-Abteilung 202 to receive the Knight's Cross. Only a few days later, on 12 December 1941, Oberwachtmeister Richard Schramm of the 1st Battery received the Knight's Cross. He too had destroyed more than 30 enemy tanks. Oberleutnant Sepp Brandner also distinguished himself in this fighting as a battery commander.

Transferred to the bend of the Orel, Sturmgeschütz-Abteilung 202 took part in the battle of Kharkov. Operating as a complete unit, it managed to prevent the Russians from breaking through to the Dnjepr. Because the battalion had suffered heavy casualties in this fighting, it was then given a rest at Sumy in the area south of Kharkov. The Sturmgeschütze still in operation were employed there for anti-partisan activities.

With the beginning of the major Soviet operational offensive at Kiev, the battalion, under Major Martin Buhr, was attached to the 7. Panzer-Division and was engaged in heavy defensive fighting until October. Major Buhr received the Knight's Cross on 17 September 1943. At the end of October, when Kiev was almost surrounded, orders were issued to withdraw. The battalion pulled back to Berditschew. It held the front there until Christmas. However, when the Soviets broke through in the 25. Panzer-Division's sector and tore that division completely apart, the battalion went into action to seal off the penetration. After incredible efforts, along with the remaining infantry, it managed to recapture the old main battle line and rebuild the front. However, a little later, the battalion had to pull back to Winniza. Major elements of the battalion were surrounded with other German units in the gigantic pocket at Tscherkassy. The entire 3rd Battery fought there.

The battalion was renamed as a brigade on 14 February 1944

and, on 24 February 1944, the 3./Sturmgeschütz-Brigade 202 under Oberleutnant Zollenkopf was given the mission of destroying a 8,000-man strong, heavily armed, enemy battle group. There was thick fog which limited visibility to 40 to 50 meters.

The enemy opened fire as the guns drew near a collective farm which had been converted into an enemy strongpoint. The Sturmgeschütze returned fire with high-explosive rounds. The enemy antitank guns also opened fire. However, a short time later, the collective farm was in flames and Oberleutnant Zollenkopf advanced into the enemy fortifications.

Unteroffizier Heimann took part in this attack with his Sturmgeschütz. This gun got stuck in a cleverly camouflaged Soviet field fortification and was unable to get out. Heimann ordered his crew to bail out.

Another Sturmgeschütz saw the Russian threat to the crew and reported the situation to the battery commander.

Oberleutnant Zollenkopf rolled up with his gun. He silenced the enemy position, squashed the Russian defenses and freed Heimann's crew. By the time darkness fell, the Russian battle group had been decimated. The Sturmgeschütz which had gotten stuck was recovered. But Unteroffizier Rinas, the gunner, and Hartz, the loader, were killed by Soviet fire. Unteroffizier Rinas jumped right onto a Russian's bayonet which pierced his heart. Cannoneer Hartz was killed by an explosive shell. Heimann was wounded by shrapnel from an antitank rifle. The 3./Sturmgeschütz-Brigade 202 lost one of its greatest gunners in Unteroffizier Rinas.

On 14 February 1944, after the preceding day and night attacks, the 3rd Battery was given the task of breaking open the pocket from the outside. The Sturmgeschütze bounded forward, supported by tanks, and smashed a small breech in the encircling lines which they held open against savage Russian attacks from both sides.

To all it was an unforgettable sight as the ragged figures of the encircled soldiers flowed out of the pocket in an unending stream.

After this difficult action, the brigade went to Uman for a refitting. Three Sturmgeschütze under the command of Leutnant Kuhn stayed some 70 kilometers northeast of Uman to provide security at the front.

When the Soviets attacked 10 days later with 2 divisions, the three Sturmgeschütze threw themselves against this attack on their own initiative. The Russians pulled back from the savagely attacking Sturmgeschütze. The Sturmgeschütz of Wachtmeister Krämer destroyed 6 T-34's. Krämer was awarded the German Cross in Gold. The other two guns destroyed an additional 7 T-34's.

In the following night, however, they had to withdraw across fields and along secondary roads. They were running out of both ammunition and fuel. Soviet tank units pushed through to the west parallel to these three Sturmgeschütze. When the three Sturmgeschütze reached a village toward morning they ran into a Russian attack which was aimed at a German artillery position. They held the Russians off, but then had to fall back again as they had no infantry support.

After receiving the alert, Oberleutnant Zollenkopf started those Sturmgeschütze of his battery which had been overhauled rolling out of Uman. He encountered the three Sturmgeschütze just at the moment when Wachtmeister Krämer was going to blow up his gun which had thrown a track.

With axe and spade, the commander of the 3./Sturmgeschütz-Brigade 202 joined in the repair work which was harassed by Russian machine-gun fire. Then the Sturmgeschütz was operational again. All the guns pulled back to a large village, which they reached about noon. All the roads there were blocked by retreating German units.

As the Russians pushed into the village with strong tank forces, Oberleutnant Zollenkopf opposed them with his battery. Seven T-34's and two antitank guns were destroyed before the Russians halted the attack. A German Oberst hurriedly collected what infantry he could find and counterattacked.

Oberleutnant Zollenkopf held the village until evening. In this way the 3./Sturmgeschütz-Brigade 202 made it possible for the beaten, retreating German units to reach Uman and assemble there. For this resolute action, Oberleutnant Martin Zollenkopf was named in the Honor Roll of the German Army and received the Honor Roll Clasp.

When he reached Uman with his Sturmgeschütze, everything had just been blown up by the German administration, including the fuel storage camp and the bridges. Oberleutnant Zollenkopf attempted to negotiate the river at a narrow place east of the bridge. However, he stuck fast, and when Wachtmeister Krämer attempted to pull out the command Sturmgeschütz, he landed in a swamp. A little later, three additional guns bogged down in the swamp. All of these guns had to be blown up.

The Sturmartilleristen reached the west bank and escaped the Russians by a hair. They had to continue their flight across open fields in the slush. The men of the battery lost their commander but found him again a few days later. Martin Zollenkopf had unloaded a new Sturmgeschütz from a freight car in an abandoned railroad station and drove back with a crew he had collected. Wachtmeister Krämer joined his commander as a driver. The Sturmgeschütz drove all the way back to the Bug. When they arrived there they were halted by an infantry Oberst with the words: "The Führer has ordered that the front is to be held here and a bridgehead established."

On the same day, Wachtmeister Sitzberger arrived. He was an experienced gun commander. Oberleutnant Zollenkopf gave him his Sturmgeschütz and that night went to the Gaiworon Railroad Station, where new Sturmgeschütze were supposed to be unloaded.

When Oberleutnant Zollenkopf and his men reached the next village, they took a small break to eat and to relax a little. The men had just eaten when Russian tanks rolled into the village. Machine gun fire broke the desperate German resistance, and Oberleutnant Zollenkopf and his three men had to run for their lives. They lost sight of one another. Wachtmeister Krämer ran toward the river. There he found Oberleutnant Zollenkopf again, who had also been able to get through. There was no trace of the other two men.

They were guided through the swamp to the next bridge across the Bug at Gaiworon by a Russian civilian. Complete chaos reigned there. Two German assault boats were engaged in bringing thousands of waiting German soldiers across. Oberleutnant Zollenkopf watched this confusion for a few minutes; he and Wachtmeister Krämer then went to an Organization Todt construction site located near the bridge. The men cobbled together a raft from the lumber lying around there and paddled across the Bug. Scarcely had they reached the west bank when Russian tanks appeared and fired into the soldiers waiting on the other side.

The southern front had completely collapsed. The remnants of the brigade reached Jassy. An attempt was again made there to stop the enemy. But there too, the brigade soon pulled back.

The brigade pushed back through Ploesti and Hermannstadt right through Hungary and all the way to Vienna. There, Oberleutnant Brandt, the commander of the 1./Sturmgeschütz-Brigade 202 said: "We have been ordered to move to Neiße for reorganization."

On Easter 1944 the members of this proud brigade spent an unforgettable leave in Ziegenhals and in June they went to Neufahrwasser near Danzig.

After a ten-week rest and refitting at Ziegenhals (Langendorf) Sturmgeschütz-Brigade 202 was loaded up at the railroad station at Deutsch-Welle in the first half of July 1944. Rumor had it that they were going to Finland. However, the train was halted in Danzig. The reason: A crisis situation had arisen in the Dünaburg-Wilna area and the brigade was to clear it up.

On the next day, when the train halted at a small railroad station outside of Dünaburg, it was already under Russian fire. There was bitter fighting around the town. As the Russians had blocked that stretch of line, the brigade unloaded in an open area. The three guns of the 1st Section of the 3rd Battery under the command of Leutnant Gebhard rolled into a firing position on the east side of the railroad station. Wachtmeister Scharf, who had already been very successful in tank fighting, commanded the second gun. Leo Heimann sat in the third Sturmgeschütz. While these three guns provided security in the direction of the woods, the unit continued to unload under the direction of Oberleutnant Zollenkopf.

When the first Russians emerged out of the woods, Gebhard's Section opened fire and drove them back in. The brigade reached the Latvian city of Zakischky, passing right through the middle of the partisan-held region.

In this way, a battle began which within a few days would reach an intensity which the brigade had never before experienced. The fighting spread into the Riga sector. When it flared up on the Bauske-Schaulen road, the brigade was committed there on 7 August 1944. By afternoon, it reached the command post of the regiment to which it had been attached. Once again, it was the 3rd Battery which was put into action at the focal point of events. The night of 7/8 August 1944 passed relatively quietly. In the morning of 8 August, the two guns of Leutnant Kühn's section remained behind when he took all the other guns of the brigade to the point of enemy penetration. In one, Wachtmeister Scharf commanded and Wachtmeister Krämer drove. Oberwachtmeister Schulz commanded the second gun. The crews loafed about in the August sun behind their guns, while the thunder of the fighting rolled toward them. But this quiet didn't last long. The battle would open soon there as well.

Wachtmeister Albert Krämer narrowed his eyes to small slits when he saw the infantry officer come running across toward them.

"Heinz, something's going on over there!" he said.

At the same moment he also heard the officer's voice.

"Tanks, tanks!" shouted the officer, out of breath. "Get ready quickly! Move out!"

The eight men jumped into the two guns as they were and rolled out of the yard to the battalion command post. They hadn't gone 500 meters when the first T-34 emerged which had already rolled over the German main battle line. The Russians were heading straight for the regimental command post with mounted infantry.

"Do you see the tanks, Albert?" Scharf cried.

"Where, Heinz?"

"To the left, left!" Scharf yelled again.

Albert Krämer responded immediately. The first three T-34's were visible and the gunner had them in his sights. The targeted T-34 flamed up when hit by the first round. The second and third rounds left the second T-34 without a turret and the third crippled and unable to move.

Oberwachtmeister Schulz also joined the battle. He too destroyed an enemy with his first round. This small tank pack was destroyed, but Wachtmeister Scharf had already detected the next tank.

"There are more coming from the right!"

These enemy tanks had moved into a barnyard. Suddenly, the first one charged out. Its turret turned toward Scharf's Sturmgeschütz. Wachtmeister Krämer saw that he had to move ahead to the right as quickly as possible. But suddenly his Sturmgeschütz wouldn't move forward.

"I'm locking the steering brakes!" he cried, shifted immediately into reverse and hit the left brake lever. The gun turned in position. At just the right moment, Wachtmeister Krämer stopped it. The gunner saw the enemy fill his sights. It was a matter of seconds as to which of these two steel giants would be destroyed.

"Herbert, fire! Fire!" cried Krämer to the gunner.

And then the first antitank round went off and the fourth enemy tank lay destroyed.

"Move up!" ordered Scharf.

"Heinz, there's a gun sticking out by the corner of the house!"

"Fire a round through the house, gunner!" ordered the Wachtmeister.

The round smashed into the house wall. Flames billowed up from the house, and the tank, which was lurking behind the corner, headed for the woods at full speed. It had turned its flank toward the Sturmgeschütz of Scharf. The cannon of the Sturmgeschütz cracked again and this tank also went up in flames.

"Follow Schulz. Advance into the enemy infantry! Load high explosive! Get the machine gun ready!"

But they hadn't yet started to move when a Feldwebel ran toward them waving his arms.

"Are you nuts! You're shooting at us!"

"How's that?" asked Scharf.

"Our battalion is still seven kilometers from here."

"And what do we have here?" asked Scharf and pointed at the destroyed enemy tanks.

"Oh...!" said the Feldwebel. "That's something else. We thought that you were going to chop us up."

He trotted off and Wachtmeister Scharf reported the Russian breakthrough and their defensive action to the regiment. The regimental commander talked to them himself. He ordered them to advance and break free the battalion seven kilometers out in front and bring it back to the trenches.

The two Sturmgeschütz commanders talked it over and then rolled out.

On the way forward, Scharf's Sturmgeschütz encountered two more T-34's. These too were destroyed. Oberwachtmeister Schulz destroyed four T-34's. When the Sturmgeschütz of Scharf had destroyed its seventh tank, the gunner, Wulf, was wounded.

"Pull yourself together, Herbert!" Krämer encouraged his comrade. In severe pain, Wulf then destroyed his eighth tank.

Wachtmeister Scharf pulled back. Wulf was immediately sent to the hospital. The three remaining men took on gas and ammunition. The loader, Othmar, took over the duties of the gunner. Wachtmeister Scharf performed the duties of both loader and gun commander. In this fashion, the gun rolled back to the front, defeated the Russians who had broken in and re-established the old battle line. The infantrymen reoccupied their old trenches.

As the gun moved back into cover behind some houses, Wachtmeister Krämer recognized the battalion command post.

"There's the command post, Heinz!" He pointed out to his comrade.

"I'll get out quick and report to the Major," Scharf said and left the gun.

He hadn't yet reached the bunker, when a heavy shell roared overhead and scored a direct hit on it.

"The command post is gone!" cried Othmar, horrified.

"Heinz! What's happened to Heinz!"

Then they saw him lying on the ground. Krämer left the gun. Othmar followed him and together they lifted their groaning comrade onto the hull.

In sixth gear, Krämer raced back across the field under murderous Russian fire. When he reached the brigade command post, a doctor immediately looked after Scharf. Krämer tried feverishly to make radio contact with his commander. Finally he reached Oberleutnant Zollenkopf on 2666 kHz. Briefly he reported what had happened. When he had finished, he heard the voice of the Oberleutnant.

"Go back along the road that we came up on yesterday. I'm coming back and I'll meet you. I have to talk to Scharf."

Krämer took off. After eight kilometers he encountered his commander. Oberleutnant Zollenkopf talked to Scharf. He found simple words which put a shine into the eyes of this brave man. At the end, he said:

"Scharf, with these eight tanks, you've destroyed 40 enemy tanks. You're getting the Knight's Cross!"

"That's OK, Herr Oberleutnant. The main thing is that we helped out the infantry."

Zollenkopf turned back to Krämer.

"Albert, take Scharf back. Go as far as you have to, and don't stop until you get Scharf to a hospital. Is that clear?"

"Clear, Herr Oberleutnant!"

On 9 August the Wehrmacht Report stated: "Wachtmeister Scharf in a Sturmgeschütz brigade has distinguished himself by outstanding gallantry in action against Soviet tanks."

On 5 September 1944, Wachtmeister Scharf received the Knight's Cross of the Iron Cross. A few days later, the following report appeared in an army field newspaper:

Four Recipients of the Knight's Cross in one Sturmgeschütz Brigade.

There are four recipients of the Knight's Cross and eight recipients of the German Cross in Gold in the Sturmgeschütz-Brigade of Major Essigke. The last Knight's Cross was awarded to Oberwachtmeister Heinz Scharf, who destroyed 8 enemy tanks in 5 minutes and who was severely wounded in that action himself. The Oberwachtmeister has destroyed a total of 40 enemy tanks in all. The brigade was constantly in action at the flash points of the front. Among its operations, only a few are mentioned here—19 August in the Bauske area: the brigade's counterattack drastically shrunk a Bolshevik bridgehead while destroying 21 enemy tanks and assault guns. After this engagement, the brigade immediately made a 100-kilometer-long night march into the area west of E., where a counterattack was in progress against an enemy penetration. Oberleutnant Zollenkopf's battery attacked there in a model of cooperation with the grenadiers. Twelve tanks and numerous trucks fell into the battery's hands in undamaged and operational condition. After E. was taken, 9 additional tanks were captured. This raised the total for the Sturmgeschütze in action there to 21 captured tanks and 2 destroyed. Shortly afterwards, the brigade destroyed an additional 16 enemy tanks further to the east.

Unteroffizier Wulf died of his wounds in a hospital at Riga. Heinz Scharf was promoted to Leutnant for bravery in the face of the enemy. Oberleutnant Zollenkopf was given the Honor Roll Clasp in September 1944 and was inscribed in the German Army's Roll of Honor.

The brigade was in position on the east bank of the Düna near the large Oger water power installation. When Oberleutnant Zollenkopf was ordered to brigade at the beginning of October to receive the golden Honor Roll Clasp, he came back to his 3rd Battery as a Hauptmann.

"Piepel" Krebs, driver of Leo Heimann's Sturmgeschütz, saw the commander first. Because he was wearing his motorcycle coat, no one could see his captain's shoulder boards. At this point we will let Leo Heimann continue the story:

We were sitting in front of our tent in the pines when the commander returned in his motorcycle jacket with a map board in it.

"This evening, you'll roast a decent fish for me. The commander is coming!" He said to me.

Piepel and I looked at each other.

"Something's not right here," Piepel said thoughtfully.

And then we saw the reason. With a charming, shy smile our commander took off his coat. Before us stood a freshly-baked Hauptmann with the Honor Roll Clasp glittering on his Iron Cross ribbon. As a result, we didn't let the old man go, but opened a bottle instead. The commander didn't care for alcohol, but this time, as the guest of honor, he had to have some.

When the second bottle was empty, the commander said: "Now, that's enough, go catch some fish! The commander will be here soon."

I don't know if it was the fault of the Schnapps or the weather, but we didn't catch a single fish. So we had to borrow a couple of fish from one of the other line batteries.

Hauptmann Martin Zollenkopf, one of those who learned his trade well and early, a brave and unassuming officer, wrote about this occasion: "I had never dared to dream that I would become a Hauptmann when I was only 22 years old."

The action continued. In October 1944 the brigade was at Tukkum in the Kurland Pocket, which was growing tighter and tighter. The brigade was attached to the 205. Infanterie-Division there. The first and second Kurland Battles raged. Then the third battle began. Once again the brigade was at every flash point of the action, and the 205. Infanterie-Division wrote in its war diary: "The I./Panzer-Grenadier-Regiment 25 and the 3./Sturmgeschütz-Brigade 202 also particularly distinguished themselves by their aggressiveness and élan."

The fighting increased in bitterness. The brigade spent

Christmas 1944 in the Frauenburg area. The 3rd Battery was billeted at Tukkum. The Russians beat against the German positions without stopping. The brigade fought for four days against the swarms of advancing enemy troops. Forty of the attached 60 assault infantry soldiers were killed. Eight new guns moved forward to replace those that had been destroyed. Hauptmann Hans Spielmann was now brigade commander. By the end of 1944, the brigade had destroyed its 1000th enemy tank. The following recognition of this combat unit appeared in the "Kurland Zeitung" (Kurland Newspaper):

During the third Kurland battle Sturmgeschütz-Brigade 202, led by Knight's Cross winner Hauptmann Spielmann, destroyed its 1000th enemy tank since its formation.

The victorious brigade, which bears a Marten insignia on its guns, has been engaged relatively infrequently in major tank battles. Its proud accomplishment is all the more worthwhile, as these tanks were destroyed almost as an after-thought. Most of the Marten's operations took place against infantry objectives.

On the Baltic battlefield, it destroyed more than 300 tanks in the last 5 months. A battery led by Oberleutnant Brandt, destroyed 54 tanks in nine days at Sworbe and had a major influence on the course of the fighting there.

The brigade, which has fought in every sector of the Eastern Front, has produced six wearers of the Knight's Cross and 12 holders of the German Cross in Gold. Members of the brigade have been inscribed in the Roll of Honor three times. Their commander, Hauptmann Spielmann, was mentioned three times in the High Command of the Wehrmacht Report and has received two certificates from the Führer.

Sturmgeschütz-Brigade 202 was once again at the flash points of the fighting in the third battle for Kurland. In addition to numerous infantry targets, it destroyed 44 tanks and 10 Soviet antitank guns in only three days of combat. The number of destroyed enemy tanks has risen to 1017 with these latest victories.

For his outstanding personal gallantry and the leadership of his battery in the fighting at Sworbe, Oberleutnant Gerhard Brandt was awarded the Knight's Cross of the Iron Cross on 12 December 1944. Over New Year's, the brigade was given a refitting at Tukkum.

There was hard fighting at Prekuln on 13 January 1945. Hauptmann Zollenkopf had temporarily taken over the brigade; Leutnant Kühn led the 3rd Battery. The brigade assembled together at Prekuln during the morning on 13 January. Hauptmann Zollenkopf summoned the battery commanders and gave out orders. The men of the 4. Panzer-Division, which was located there, advised against the operation.

"What are you going to do here with those cracker boxes of yours? They'll step on you like bugs."

The Sturmgeschütze soldiers were greeted with these words. The brigade rolled out despite them. It moved against the enemy with the command Sturmgeschütz in the lead. As the brigade rolled through a depression, the Sturmgeschütz of Unteroffizier Krämer was shot into flames. The driver was killed as the crew bailed out. The Sturmgeschütz of Unteroffizier Rau was also destroyed by a direct hit from a heavy antitank gun. Unteroffizier Rau and his entire crew were killed. Motivated by the example of the Sturmgeschütze, six Panthers of the 4. Panzer-Division also joined the fighting. The Russians were halted and scattered.

Once again, on 17 February 1945, Hauptmann Zollenkopf selflessly put his life on the line to rescue his comrades. The 3rd Battery was in position in meadowland north of Prekuln. Although the Soviets were beaten, a few units had managed to infiltrate into the woods. Hauptmann Zollenkopf held the middle of the German main battle line with 5 guns of the 3rd Battery. A sixth gun, commanded by Unteroffizier Heimann, had patrol duty, since the Soviets were already 2 kilometers behind the German front on the right. When Unteroffizier Heimann reached an temporary bridge across a 4-meter wide water-filled ditch, he saw a Sturmgeschütz of Sturmgeschütz-Brigade 912 just next to the bridge lying bottom up in the icy water. The hatches were underwater. Never before had Heimann gotten out of his Sturmgeschütz so fast as he did then. He raced to the overturned gun. Someone within answered his knocks. So, the crew was still alive. He had to work fast. Heimann ran back immediately to his radio, but the Hauptmann didn't answer. The gun raced forward madly toward the main battle line. While they were underway, Hauptmann Zollenkopf answered. Heimann requested help and turned back immediately. At the scene of the accident, there was already a Sturmgeschütz from Sturmgeschütz-Brigade 912 hard at work. Heimann helped out. But the slope was too steep. Every time, the gun rose half a meter and then the cable broke. Then Hauptmann Zollenkopf roared up in his gun. All three guns were then hooked up. Their engines howled, and slowly the sunken gun raised up. The hatches could be opened. Two of the men of the crew were saved. The other two had drowned.

During the last weeks of fighting in Kurland Hauptmann Spielmann functioned as the breakwater in a raging storm. He fought in every engagement of the Sturmgeschütze while at their lead. On 23 March 1945 he received the Knight's Cross.

Hauptmann Zollenkopf fought with the same determination. On 6 March 1945 this brave young officer was felled by a bullet.

Sturmgeschütz-Brigade 202 fought until the last day of the war in the Kurland Pocket.

Sturmgeschütz-Abteilung 203 (Sturmgeschütz-Brigade 203)

This Sturmgeschütz-Abteilung was formed in the camp at the village of Zinna in January 1941. The initial command and leader roster ran as follows:

Commander: Major Krokosius
Headquarters Battery: Oberleutnant Peetz
1st Battery: Oberleutnant Freiherr von Gleichenstein
2nd Battery: Oberleutnant Dostler
3rd Battery: Oberleutnant Wirth

The battalion was moved to Leslau-Brest-Kujawien in the middle of March and then marched at intervals through Warsaw into the Forest Camp at Malkinia near the Russian border.

On the evening of 21 June 1941 the Führer's orders for the attack on the USSR were read to the troops, and the Russian Campaign began in the early morning of 22 June 1941.

The battalion's batteries were divided among different regiments in the attack sectors. As a result, the 3rd Battery was attached to Infanterie-Regiment 19 of the 7. Infanterie-Division for this attack.

On the very first day of the attack, while advancing against Soviet field positions, the battery commander, Oberleutnant Wirth, was killed along with Leutnant Bausch.

Also attached to the 7. Infanterie-Division, the 1st Battery attacked the enemy bunkers which had been newly constructed in this sector.

The advance was continued after crossing the Narew over the bridge which was still intact. Grodno was reached and the battalion did its duty in several decisive assaults during the encirclement at Bialystok.

After a few days of rest, the battalion was attached to the 52. Infanterie-Division of the LIII. Armee-Korps and the advance proceeded. On 6 July more than 50 Russian light tanks were destroyed by the 2nd Battery in bold maneuvers and continuous assaults with only occasional halts for firing.

Borissow was reached by way of Brozki-Sluzk-Minsk. The battalion advanced along in continuous day and night marches. After reaching the Dnjepr on 11 July, and while attached to the 29. Infanterie-Division (mot.), the battalion crossed the river under cover provided by the first German Nebelwerfer in action. (These rocket launchers with six barrels were named after their inventor, an engineer named Nebel, and not after the type of round they fired.) The assault boats brought them rapidly to the other side. By 12 July the entire battalion had gotten across. The 1./Sturmgeschütz-Abteilung 203 was attached to the advance guard detachment of the 26. Infanterie-Division (mot.) to serve as a battering ram if this were to become necessary. However, the only actions were fought against Russian tanks lagging behind as the rear guard. These were destroyed for the most part or fell back.

The attack on Smolensk began on 16 July. The battalion advanced step-by-step in bitter street fighting, in spite of the Red Army's mastery of this form of combat. Wachtmeister Werner was severely wounded by a thrown hand grenade in this fighting. He was standing in an open hatch to yell out orders.

The fighting for the city lasted until 22 July. The enemy constantly tried to recapture this important city, but Stuka attacks against the spearheads of his tank forces always stopped him. The enemy employed the IL-2 Ground Attack Fighter for the first time there, but Smolensk remained in German hands. Quiet reigned from 28 to 30 July.

By 21 July the 2nd and 3rd Batteries, attached to the 197. Infanterie-Division (a division of the VII. Armee-Korps), advanced another 100 kilometers on to Choslawitzy. The 1st Battery remained in Smolensk until 14 August as an emergency reaction force.

The two other batteries marched on 1 and 2 August to Rosslawl. On 9 August Russian bombers attempted to attack the city. They were checked by German fighters, and turned back after four or five bombers were shot down. Three additional bombers were shot out of the skies after turning back.

The 1st Battery caught up with the battalion at Rosslawl on 14 August.

On occasion, a few bombers managed to make it through and dropped some bombs which caused no damage. The battalion continued its march on to Proletaria, where it waited for new orders. During this period Leutnant Kuhlenkampf of the 3rd Battery had a fatal accident.

Russian assault groups broke through the 23. Infanterie-Division during the night of 30 August. The battalion was alerted and went into action at Kostelje. Leutnant Metzger of the 1st Battery destroyed 23 enemy tanks in a magnificent charge. It was a great, well celebrated success, and it was rapidly rewarded. On 29 September Eugen Metzger became the first soldier of the battalion to receive the Knight's Cross.

Along with Infanterie-Regiment 497, the 3rd Battery attacked on 1 September and, on the same day, destroyed six enemy tanks. Sturmgeschütz "12," however, received a direct hit and was totally burned out. Every man in the crew was wounded.

The enemy was thrown back to the Desna in a series of rapid blows. The 3rd Battery combed out a woods there, where members of the Red Army had fallen back. Leutnant Schönemann was wounded by a sniper in a tree during this action.

Sturmgeschütz-Abteilung 203 was in a rest area from 7 September to 1 October. At this time the remaining delayed but essential Cholera inoculations were given. Sturmgeschütz "32," put out of action during a reconnaissance, was brought back by a scouting unit of the 3rd Battery.

The advance continued to the Desna on 2 October. During this movement a gun drove over a mine and Unteroffizier Weißhaupt was fatally wounded.

Serving as an advance guard detachment, the 3./Sturmgeschütz-Abteilung 203 advanced with an antitank section and bicycle squadron of the 9. Infanterie-Division This advance guard detachment was ambushed on 5 October by a Russian assault unit and two soldiers were wounded. The advance continued up until 10 October, when a defensive position on the Smolensk-Moska highway had to be occupied. The first snow fell there.

Leaving the 23. Infanterie-Division, the battalion pulled back to Wjasma. Then it moved forward again on 25 October to Moshaisk and reached Rusa on 26 October. There was a bomber attack on the battalion which cost six wounded.

The battalion remained at Rusa until 14 November. Some regrouping took place. The 1st Battery was attached to Infanterie-Regiment 187.

The battalion advanced again from 15 to 18 November and on the next day the battalion encountered enemy activity once more. A Sturmgeschütz from the 3./Sturmgeschütz-Abteilung 203 rolled onto a mine. In heavy fighting, in which partisans were also involved, Cannoneer Fischer was murdered by them. There were more wounded, and on 23 November four soldiers were killed and three wounded by the impacting rounds of a Stalin Organ. This was a heavy blow to the battalion. On 24 November Wachtmeister Frey, one of the best fighters, was killed.

The severe cold which had set in caused a series of mechanical losses. There was damage to clutches and connecting rods. The enemy laid down heavy fire from Stalin Organs. Friendly antiaircraft cannon managed to shoot down a few Ratas.

Leutnant Rudel of the 3rd Battery was killed in the forest fighting on 1 December and in the attack on Kosimo by a direct hit from an antitank cannon. The Sturmgeschütz could not be brought back into action and was blown up.

The combat trains were at Boroskowo at 32 degrees below zero Celsius. Since the 87. Infanterie-Division had to fall back, the bat-

talion also received orders to withdraw. A Sturmgeschütz which could not be driven had to be blown up. Thousands of Russians also fell back from the advancing Red Army along with the supply trains of the 87. Infanterie-Division and those of the Sturmgeschütze.

There was icy, blowing snow when the battalion had to fall back further in December. Russian ground attack fighters attacked the column. Then mounted troops, Cossacks, broke through. They went after the trains and medical vehicles first. They were smashed by the Sturmgeschütze in a counter blow and suffered heavy casualties.

The recaptured medical vehicles were a terrible sight. All of the wounded being taken back had been murdered by the Cossacks and some had been thrown out on the road.

The Sturmgeschütze were able to continue to fight until 16 December, using their last drop of gasoline to go into battle and cover the withdrawal. Then the last five Sturmgeschütze were ordered destroyed because of the lack of fuel. A lot of other material was also blown up so as not to leave it for the Russians.

On 18 December the battalion assembled in Borodino. After ten days of unbroken combat, the men of the Sturmgeschütze could wash for the first time. The battalion moved to Rusa. To everyone's great joy two missing Sturmgeschütze arrived back there. They had shot their way through the enemy to freedom.

After a short pause where Christmas could be celebrated, the withdrawal continued back to the area of Wjasma. From there, the battalion continued to fall back on 31 December, until it could rest in a village. There the New Year was greeted with gunfire, when a strong Russian assault unit with several tanks put on pressure, looking for a soft spot. All the enemy tanks were knocked out.

On 15 January another repaired Sturmgeschütz went back into action. Major Krokosius was transferred to the Sturmgeschütz-Schule at Burg, and Oberleutnant Behnke took over temporary command of the battalion. Leutnant Hagemann took command of Behnke's 3rd Battery.

Another Sturmgeschütz had to be blown up on 23 January. It was 42 degrees below zero Celsius and in the next few days the temperature dropped to 45 degrees below zero. The front had to be pulled back between Gshatsk and Moshaisk. All shelters and bridges were mined as the withdrawal continued. Using all of its strength, the German army kept the pursuing Russian units at a distance.

There was a sudden alert during the Führer's speech on the night of 31 January 1942. The Red Army had broken through at Wjasma. The Soviet division which had broken through was cut off and annihilated. Most of the battalion was fighting as infantry.

The defensive fighting in the next few weeks also saw action against partisans, who stole into the villages occupied by the battalion, stole food and horses, and once killed a Russian village policeman.

The retreat lasted until the beginning of April 1942. Following that, the remnants of the battalion collected at Kostriza near Borissow on the Beresina River. At Kostriza new Sturmgeschütze and replacements arrived from Germany. The battalion refitted and was able to attain complete combat readiness by June 1942. The battalion was ready to move out on 25 June 1942.

It moved out on the morning of 26 June towards the train station at Borissow in order to load up for a rail movement. Over the next few days it was transported via Minsk and Brobruisk to Shlobin. Bachmatsch and Romodan were reached on 28 June. A few of those in the know knew that the goal of the battalion was Rostow. Dnjepropetrowsk was reached on 30 June and all elements arrived in the area of Stalino on 4 July. It wasn't until it arrived in the assembly area at Katharinenhof that it received the Sturmgeschütze with the long-barreled cannon.

On 7 July the line batteries rolled into their first operation. The Headquarters Battery followed on 8 July. The advance went to Artemowsk from where it was intended to initiate the new summer offensive.

At the beginning of the attack several Sturmgeschütze ran onto mines. One them was a total loss. Leutnant Rudel was killed on the first day by a round through the head.

Sturmgeschütz-Abteilung 203 crossed the Donez River at Lissitschansk and Proletarsk on a pontoon bridge constructed by engineers in record time. In its advance there was little major fighting. It wasn't until the advance on Rostow began did it start to get serious.

The main body of the battalion crossed the Donez for a second time at Kamenskaya and reached the village of Aksaisskaja on 22 July. At the same time, the 1./Sturmgeschütz-Abteilung 203 was attached to the 1. Gebirgs-Division. The struggle for Aksaisskaja, an outlying village of Kharkov, was decided by the Sturmgeschütze in street fighting.

On 23 July Sturmgeschütz-Abteilung 203 advanced into Rostow. On the next day it moved as far as Nowotscherkassk where it stayed until 27 July. Major Ködel, the battalion commander, had his batteries well in hand and the battalion physician, Stabsarzt Dr. Altvater, cared for the wounded in an exemplary manner.

An advance on Radorskaya via Nowotscherkassk and Schachty to cross the Don River in the early morning of 28 July failed. The Russians had demolished the dams across the Manytsch. A crossing was out of the question. Sturmgeschütz-Abteilung 203 returned to Rostow.

The attempt to cross the Don near Rostow continued on 1 August in the area of Proletarskaja. At Proletarskaja the advance was continued in the direction of Armawir, to the south.

The battalion advanced as part of the spearhead of the III. Panzer-Korps, commanded by General der Kavallerie von Mackensen. It continued south through the heat-soaked steppes. Immense grain and corn fields lined the way. Sturmgeschütz-Abteilung 203 led the corps.

Armawir was reached by the end of 5 August. The battalion was involved in heavy fighting at Armawir. The Sturmgeschütz of the battery commander of the 3./Sturmgeschütz-Abteilung 203 reached a direct hit from close range. The battery commander, Oberleutnant Dostler, was killed. Leutnant Conradt took over command. Unteroffizier Henn also died and Gefreiter Stolz was lightly wounded.

The battalion was attached to an advance guard detachment on

6 August. Its mission was to take Maikop to the south through a rapid advance. Shortly before reaching its objective, the advance guard detachment encountered strong motorized forces of the enemy. A bitterly fought engagement ensued. Leutnant Conradt was killed by an antitank round in the ventilator tower. Assistenz-Arzt Gärtner was wounded by mortar shrapnel. That happened on 10 August after the first elements of the advance guard detachment had already penetrated into Maikop on the day before.

The battalion billeted on the grounds of an orphanage for the next four weeks. All disabled vehicles of the battalion were made combat-ready again. New equipment was brought forward. Some decorations could be awarded: Major Ködel, the battalion commander, received the Iron Cross, First Class. Leutnant Krämer and Stabsarzt Dr. Altvater received the Iron Cross, Second Class.

Major Ködel took gravely ill and had to leave the battalion. Hauptmann Behnke once again took over command. Leutnant Zojer became the adjutant. Oberleutnant Feurstein assumed command of the 2nd Battery.

On 16 September the battalion started out on its march into the Caucasus. By the next day the twin peaks of Mount Elbrus arose from the morning mist. Mount Elbrus would become a constant companion of the battalion because it could always be seen.

The battalion advanced close to the mountain range via Georgiewsk. Offensive action and security duties alternated. Hauptmann Behnke referred to them as "climbing outings." After Dr. Altvater was transferred to a Panzer regiment, Assistenz-Arzt Dr. Wille and Unterarzt Dr. Schwarzfischer became the "medicine men" of the battalion. Leutnants Zimmer-Vorhaus and Kühl took gravely ill and had to be admitted to the hospital. In their place, Oberleutnant Schmidt, Leutnant Koch and Leutnant Seth arrived.

The attack on Naltschik started on 25 October. The city was defended by elite Russian troops. The Sturmgeschütze approached Naltschik through the end of 26 October 1942. The 3rd Battery was attached to the Rumanian 2nd Mountain Division and the 1st Battery to the 1. Gebirgs-Division. The 2nd Battery found itself with the 13. Panzer-Division.

The defensive fire of the enemy hailed upon them from every house. Despite that, the Sturmgeschütze pressed on and continued the attack on 27 October. They advanced past shot-up houses into the center of the city and a large intersection. At that point, the Sturmgeschütze swung towards the railroad tracks and advanced along them to the train station. The bunkers established there were knocked out. The Rumanian and German mountain troops advanced behind the Sturmgeschütze. The train station was reached and cleared. On the next day all of Naltschik was in German hands and the Sturmgeschütze established contact with the 13. Panzer-Division which was northwest of the city.

During the next few days the 2nd Battery advanced with the 13. Panzer-Division as far as Ordschonikidse. While encircled with the 13. Panzer-Division, it knocked out 20 T-34's in a struggle which stretched over several days. The ordered withdrawal to the west with the 13. Panzer-Division succeeded.

There were considerable casualties during these days. Leutnant Döhler was killed by a bullet through the heart on 5 November. On 9 November Unteroffizier Haase of the 2nd Battery was killed. He had been covering the withdrawal of his comrades with his Sturmgeschütz. It was thanks to the efforts of the 5. SS-Panzer-Grenadier-Division "Wiking" that the breakout was successful. It had attacked to relieve the formations breaking out.

The battalion withdrew in the direction of Ardon. Oberleutnant Ostertag was killed by an antitank round in his chest. Oberleutnant Angelmaier, who had led the 3rd Battery during the difficult fighting at Naltschik in an exemplary manner, was wounded by the shrapnel of a round penetrating his Sturmgeschütz. He had to go to the hospital. Leutnant Krämer was wounded by the shrapnel of an antitank gun round hit in Naltschik. Oberleutnant Fürchtenicht and Leutnant Koch were lightly wounded but remained with the unit.

On 22 November Oberleutnant Metzger had to leave to go to the Artillerie-Schule at Jüterbog. With his transfer, the only remaining original officers of the battalion were Hauptmann Behnke and Oberleutnant Peetz.

Oberleutnant Lembke arrived from Jüterbog in Oberleutnant Metzger's place a few days later. Oberleutnant Feurstein was awarded the Iron Cross, First Class; Oberleutnant Rossbach was awarded the Iron Cross, Second Class.

The battalion was in the Caucasus until the middle of December. The initial elements were loaded by rail on 13 December at Prochlady. The battalion moved north towards Remontnaja via Ssalsk. The battalion was given makeshift quarters there. Everyone got ready to celebrate Christmas. But that didn't come to pass, because there was an alert on the evening of 24 December. The battalion was employed to defend against Russian attacks at Pimen-Tscherny in the Aksaj area. It was in action there, at the southern edge of the Stalingrad pocket, for several weeks. It had become ice cold and the fighting there from 25 December to 10 January demanded everything from the gun crews. During the defensive fighting of seventeen days Sturmgeschütz-Abteilung 203 knocked out 44 heavy and 9 light tanks, 14 artillery pieces, 11 heavy and 46 light antitank cannon, 32 heavy and 16 light machine guns, 6 mortars, 39 antitank rifles and 25 vehicles of all types.

This difficult fighting also demanded heavy sacrifices from the battalion. Among others, Leutnant Gassauer was wounded on 28 December by shrapnel from a mine. Oberleutnant Angelmaier had returned from the hospital on 25 December. He had barely recovered when he took over his old 3rd Battery. He was severely wounded on 11 January by a round which stuck in his throat.

Leutnant Koch assumed command of the 3rd Battery. But he would only command for a few days. On 14 January 1943 he was felled by a round to the head.

The fighting continued after 10 January. On 27 January Major Ködel returned to the battalion and reassumed command. Hauptmann Behnke was transferred to Jüterbog on 28 January. It was intended that he assume command of a new battalion which was being formed.

The battalion moved via Kotelnikowo and Ssalsk towards Rostow. The Sturmgeschütze were engaged in combat one week long against Russian forces exerting pressure there. After approximately 600 Russians had penetrated to the train station, they were wiped out completely in three days of fighting. Leutnant Zimmer-Vorhaus was killed by a round to the chest during this operation; he had received the Iron Cross, First Class on 13 January 1943.

On 8 February the news reached the battalion that Hauptmann Behnke had received the Knight's cross for his defensive success in the Caucasus.

Rostow, the center of mass for the southern front, had to be given up on 13 and 14 February 1943. In famous/infamous night marches the battalion reached the Mius Position on 17 February as ordered.

Russian assault troops broke thought the Mius Position the next night at two places. They wanted to encircle the German formations and seal off the front as far as the Sea of Asow. The breakthrough was contained with the help of the Sturmgeschütze. The fighting lasted for days. The Sturmgeschütze knocked out a number of enemy tanks; the enemy who had broken through was completely rubbed out.

On the morning of 23 February Major Ködel was seriously hurt in a tragic accident and died on the same day. Oberleutnant Feurstein assumed command of the battalion. The situation calmed down. Everyone was hoping for a few days of quiet in Taganrog.

The order to rail load with the destination of Kharkov shattered these hopes. The new destination was reached on 17 March 1943. Major Behnke met the battalion there. Instead of taking over a new battalion he assumed command of his old one again.

After a break of one week which was used to refit the unit, the battalion went into action again. It executed a battalion attack on two enemy bridgeheads on the Donez at Wollny and Gussarowka. On 24 March Major Behnke was wounded in the hand as a result of a round penetrating his Sturmgeschütz. Leutnant Zojer was wounded on 29 March. Oberleutnant Roßbach also got hit a few hours later. The Sturmgeschütz of Wachtmeister Daniel fell victim to an antitank round penetration; Wachtmeister Daniel was killed.

The fighting on the Donez continued. Leutnant Gießler, who had joined the battalion on 8 April, was killed on 10 April by a chest wound. Led by Oberleutnant Feurstein, the battalion fought in an exemplary manner as always. It remained in these positions until the end of July 1943. Oberleutnant Hammerschmidt and many other soldiers were killed; Leutnant von Stimpfl-Abele was wounded.

A Soviet attack at Deljenkawa was repulsed on 17 July and, on 25 July, the Sturmgeschütze were positioned in heavy vegetation at Slawjansk. On 27 July the news reached the battalion that the 2./ Sturmgeschütz-Abteilung 203 would be relieved by a personnel unit. The transfer of the Sturmgeschütze to the new personnel was done on 31 July. The soldiers of the 2./Sturmgeschütz-Abteilung 203 returned to Germany in order to form the cadre at Altengrabow for the newly formed Sturmgeschütz-Abteilung 278 and the refitting of the battalion. The battalion, like so many others, was renamed as Sturmgeschütz-Brigade 203 on 14 February 1944. It was employed exclusively on the Eastern Front with Heeresgruppe Süd until the end of the war. Unfortunately, nothing more is known of the formation after its refitting at Altengrabow.

Sturmgeschütz-Abteilung 209 (Sturmgeschütz-Brigade 209)

Sturmgeschütz-Abteilung 209 is first encountered as an operational unit when it was thrown into the Eastern Front as a stopgap formation in January 1942, in order to put a stop to a Soviet thrust far to the west. Hitler had issued the order to stand firm which required "holding out to the last man."

In hindsight, this turned out to have been the only correct thing to do to save the German Eastern Front, which led all the way up the gates of Moscow, from imminent collapse.

It is not certain just where this battalion received its baptism of fire. It has been determined however from the rare reports concerning it that it was in the center sector of the eastern Front.

Sturmgeschütz-Brigade 209

In the summer of 1942 it was fighting in the operational sector around Rshew, where a front sector extending close to Moscow was still being held. After consolidating the front, the German intention was to launch a new, decisive assault on the Russian metropolis from this point. (The history of the war reveals that nothing came of this idea, and that this gigantic salient finally had to be given up in the winter of 1942-43.)

This battalion, which had been in action against continuous Russian attacks, reached the end of its strength in September 1942. A large percentage of its armor had been destroyed or rendered inoperative by a variety of damage.

The battalion was pulled out of the front and reorganized in the area between Rouen and Le Havre in Yvetot. Hauptmann Rupert Gruber, former commander of the 1st Battery, was made battalion commander on 24 September 1942, right at the start of the reorganization. It was a position he held until 25 October 1943.

Two days later, Leutnant Konrad Sauer, section leader in the 2nd Battery, became the first soldier in Sturmgeschütz-Abteilung 209, the "Red Devil" Battalion, to receive the Knight's Cross. From the documents available we know that Sturmgeschütz-Abteilung 209 had been in Rshew, had participated in several sensational operations there and then, after reorganization, returned to Russia again at the end of October 1942.

Sauer received the Knight's Cross from his battery commander, Oberleutnant Frank, on 29 September 1942 at the Sytschewka Railroad Station during the trip home. (Konrad Sauer would continue to distinguish himself by his bold offensive and defensive actions and was awarded the Oak Leaves to the Knight's Cross on 30 September 1944 as the 603rd soldier to receive this honor. At the time of the Oak Leaves, he was section leader in the 1st Battery of Sturmgeschütz-Abteilung 393. He later became its commander.)

The Battalion went back into action in the Rshew sector with 31 new Sturmgeschütze, making up a very formidable fighting force.

In December 1942 it was transferred to the southern sector of the Eastern Front. It unloaded at Starobielsk and was attached to the 19. Panzer-Division.

It advanced to the east with that division. For a period of time, the battalion had to deal with Soviet camel troops which had been thrown in from Siberia in order to stop the German advance.

The advance didn't come to a halt until the battalion reached the Volga to the northeast of Stalingrad. The battalion could see the Red October Machinery Factory in Stalingrad through its scissors binoculars. The battalion was not surrounded there, but fought its way back foot by foot to the west after the Russian counteroffensive. It attacked Strelzowo, along with some hastily assembled elements from other units, at 20 degrees below zero Celsius and, in meter - high snow drifts, took the town which provided some shelter from the bitter cold.

After this, the battalion was divided into a number of smaller units and attached to various Kampfgruppen. Sturmgeschütz-Abteilung 209 was finally surrounded on 14 January 1943 in the Tschertkowo Pocket. But, along with all those cut off with them, it managed to fight its way free to the 298. Infanterie-Division, which was waiting to meet it just outside the pocket. It managed to hold a small lane open long enough for the last units and their wounded to escape from the pocket.

"It would never have crossed our minds to leave our comrades behind, even if it were to cost us our own lives." a survivor reported.

The continuing operations with the Kampfgruppen cost the battalion heavy casualties. The commander of the 3rd Battery, Oberleutnant Geppert, distinguished himself in particular during this fighting. Major Rupert Gruber, the battalion commander, recommended this magnificent soldier for the Knight's Cross, which he was awarded by radio from the Führer headquarters on 18 April.

On the Führer's birthday, 20 April, Erich Geppert received the Knight's Cross from the hands of his battalion commander at a battalion formation. At the end of the presentation, the entire battalion marched in review past its second recipient of the Knight's Cross.

The battalion spent the summer of 1943 between Stalino and the Dnjepr and also fought at Petroskoje. When a crisis arose at the 304. Infanterie-Division's position in this sector, and a divisional counterattack to eliminate a Russian penetration was unsuccessful, Major Gruber took command of the two infantry battalions in the attack. With the Sturmgeschütze at the front and on the flanks, a major Russian strong point was stormed and the sector was cleared again.

On 14 August Major Gruber was awarded the Knight's Cross for this action. Many soldiers of the battalion received the Iron Cross, First Class.

There was more heavy fighting in August, in which elements of Sturmgeschütz-Abteilung 210, under their commander Major Hubert Sichelschmidt, also took part. (Major Sichelschmidt received the Knight's Cross on 4 May 1944. He died of wounds received in this fighting on 7 July 1944 in the central hospital at Sogal.)

Kampfgruppe Gruber was given the mission to hold a front sector of 35 kilometers with some 800 soldiers against vastly superior enemy forces. It managed to hold back the enemy seven times, while taking very heavy casualties. On 1 September it was brought back up to strength with replacements. Major Gruber used his Sturmgeschütze and soldiers to cover the retreat of the army and the corps through Saporoshje to Nikopol.

On 10 October the soldiers around Rupert Gruber had a great success when they attacked and wiped out an advanced Soviet position with only six Sturmgeschütze and without infantry support. Three hundred dead Russians were left on the battlefield.

In Melitopol the battalion formed the kernel of the defense in the street fighting which raged for days.

Major Gruber was severely wounded at Melitopol on 25 October and had to leave the battalion, which was taken over by Hauptmann Frank. He was transferred out on 6 February and Major Schulte followed. The battalion was redesignated a brigade on 14 February 1944.

In the spring of 1944 the completely exhausted brigade was pulled out and transported to Ottmachau in Upper Silesia for rest and reorganization.

Ottmachau, a beautiful little city on the Glatzer Neiße with a castle on a hill above the river, was the background for a few weeks of rest and relaxation. The replacements and new Sturmgeschütze arrived from the Ersatz- und Ausbildungs-Abteilung at Neiße.

On 29 July the brigade said good-bye to Ottmachau. It was transported by rail to the Eastern Front. The central sector, where this unit had already been in action on several occasions, was once again the operational area for the "front's fire brigade" as the "Red Devils" were called. They fought a series of actions attached to the 28. Jäger Division and the 35., 292. and 541. Infanterie-Divisionen, one after another. Once more the unit had 31 new Sturmgeschütze.

The brigade lost 20 of its new guns on 9 July 1944 when it was sent into a Russian ambush, and only some of the crews were able to fight their way clear. This loss resulted from a major act of treachery, which has been the subject of considerable speculation, but which even now has not been completely cleared up. It was some time before new guns arrived from home.

In the defensive fighting that summer Oberleutnant Wolfram John, commander of 2nd Battery, was an inspiration, pulling the rest of his battery along with him in his charges against the enemy. He was always the last man to withdraw. On 18 November 1944 he received the Knight's Cross. (He was killed in action in the Samland on 27 April 1945.)

Hauptmann Helmut Gattermann, commander of the 1st Battery, received his Knight's Cross before Wolfram John—on 25 August—for his actions in the Nikopol Bridgehead in the spring of 1944.

In September Sturmgeschütz-Brigade 209 was again involved in heavy fighting which lasted until 27 September. The offensive and defensive fighting at the Narew took a heavy toll. The fighting lasted until 27 September. Then it was quiet until 11 October 1944, when the Russians launched their operational attack on the Narew. The fighting raged back and forth, with the Sturmgeschütze at every critical point.

Oberwachtmeister Herbert Schmidt, section leader of the 2nd Section in the 2nd Battery, earned the Knight's Cross on the Narew, which he received on 4 October.

Following that, the "Devil's Brigade" was employed in East Prussia.

When the Soviets began their operational attack across the Narew, the presence of the brigade in the Rozan Sector provided the necessary cover for the struggling infantry. Oberleutnant Wolfram John distinguished himself several times. But all the other members of the brigade also fought there with desperate courage.

In the evening of 16 October the guns of the 2nd and 3rd Batteries went to the brigade command post. The Sturmgeschütz of Oberwachtmeister Otto Maus was in a ready position in a patch of woods near Glasewo. As the Soviets were keeping heavy artillery fire on the German main battle line, the crew remained inside the gun. Then Maus also received orders to change position and return to the brigade command post.

There, on the next morning, Oberwachtmeister Maus was given orders to retake the village of Rupin, lying directly on the Narew northwest of Rozan, with his section and some infantry from the 292. Infanterie-Division riding on his guns.

It was a clear October morning. The operation was a success.

The Sturmgeschütze of the 1st Section of the 2nd Battery cleared the way for the infantry. However, during the fighting, a shell casing jammed in the breech of Oberwachtmeister Maus' gun. The loader, Jupp Schiermeyer, jumped out of the gun, in order to push the casing back out from the front with the cleaning rod. While the loader was outside, the Soviets fired like mad, but without hitting him.

Towards noon the section moved to the supply section to resupply itself with ammunition. The section was two kilometers to the rear. Just as the resupply action was completed, a Russian close air support aircraft appeared. Oberwachtmeister Maus, Waibel, the driver and Schiermeyer were already in the vehicle. They closed the hatches. Only Unteroffizier Großmann was still outside in order to fetch fuel cans from a truck. After the Russian aircraft had disappeared and Großmann had not returned, the others went out to search for their missing comrade. They found him lying half under the Sturmgeschütz with a bullet in his shoulder. He was dead.

Gefreiter Hans Raimann became the gunner. They went back to the main line where the Soviets had been thrown back as far as Hill 105.8. This hill had to be taken because the enemy could fire from it into the village of Rupin. After an artillery barrage, the 2nd Battery attacked the hill at 1700 hours. Seven Sturmgeschütze and 40 infantrymen charged. The Sturmgeschütz of the section leader had already fired 15 rounds and was only 200 meters from the hill when it received a direct hit. Fire shot into the fighting compartment.

"Bail out!" commanded the gun commander.

Gefreiter Schiermeyer wanted to climb out of a open hatch into the open but his legs didn't respond anymore. Once again the Sturmgeschütz was hit, followed by a third antitank round from a T-34 which again penetrated the vehicle.

Schiermeyer was tossed out of the Sturmgeschütz from the concussion of the last round. When he had gathered his wits about again, he was eight meters from the Sturmgeschütz. He screamed for his comrades. No one answered him. Only the crackle of the flames and the hammering of the weapons could be heard. Infantry hastened past Schiermeyer heading west. In these most pain-filled moments of his life, Schiermeyer was left all alone on the battlefield.

Not until it had begun to get dark was he found. Two infantrymen pulled him back. They were there with Oberwachtmeister Maus, who had also been wounded. He had fetched them so that they could save whoever was to be saved.

There was to be no salvation for comrades Waibel and Raimann. They had been burned to death in the Sturmgeschütz.

Schiermeyer was immediately transported to the field hospital. He remained in military and civilian hospitals until 16 November 1950—exactly six years to the day—before he had recovered enough from his wounds that he could be released.

The "Devil's brigade" was then employed in East Prussia. Oberleutnant Wolfram John received the Knight's cross on 15 December 1944. The commitment of this brave man thus found its public recognition. He was not able to see the end of the war, however; he was killed in action shortly before it ended.

On 8 May 1945 the rest of the brigade went into Russian captivity on the Hela Peninsula.

Sturmgeschütz-Abteilung 210 (Sturmgeschütz-Brigade 210)

Sturmgeschütz-Abteilung 210 was formed on 10 March 1941 in the Old Camp at Jüterbog. Its insignia was a tiger's head. By the first days of April it had already been transferred to the area of Luckenwalde. There it was issued its first Sturmgeschütze (with the short barrel) and other equipment. Hauptmann Schlawe was its first commander; the adjutant was Oberleutnant Wienz. The batteries were commanded by:

1st Battery: Oberleutnant Wiegels
2nd Battery: Oberleutnant Schlesinger
3rd Battery: Oberleutnant Pelikan

Sturmgeschütz-Brigade 210

Formation was completed by the middle of May. Immediately afterwards, the battalion was transferred to Straßburg in West Prussia. After a short stay, it went on to the Suwalki district.

There, the battalion was attached to the 256. Infanterie-Division, and it was one of the first German units to cross the border on 22 June 1941. It rapidly broke through the forward-most Soviet defense line.

Advancing through Lidya, Witebsk and Deminow, the battalion managed to close off the Brest pocket. The "Tiger's Head" Battalion was mentioned in the Wehrmacht Report for the first time. Oberleutnant Pelikan was also mentioned in the Wehrmacht Report for 5 July 1941.

Together with the 6. and 7. Panzer-Divisionen, the battalion continued its advance as the steel spearhead of the Panzer-Korps. The Smolensk pocket was the result of this lightning assault. The battle at Welikije Luki saw the battalion, once again with the 256. Infanterie-Division, in an attack crowned by a splendid victory.

Ordered back to the Panzer-Korps, the battalion contributed to the breakthrough and to the pocket battle for Wjasma and Briansk. Always fighting in the first wave of the attack, the battalion once again fought in a reliable manner. It closed off gaps torn open in the north of the pocket and kept the surrounding ring closed.

The advance continued to the east. The battalion made it up to the gates of Moscow. On 16 December 1941 it took part in the last thrust toward Moscow from the north. This attack only gained ground slowly. On Christmas Eve, 50 degrees below zero Celsius were measured. The advance bogged down 30 kilometers in front of Moscow. Out of the entire battalion, only 14 guns were still in action. The Königsberg Line north of the road was occupied, and the battalion was employed there for the most part as infantry.

From January to March 1942, the battalion found itself in an increasingly critical situation. It stood its ground, however, and prevented a Soviet breakthrough. It was in the heaviest fighting north of the road at the Nowo Dugino strongpoint. Completely cut off, the men of the Sturmartillerie defended their assigned positions against attacks from the east and then from the west, fighting for their very lives.

The battalion wasn't pulled out of the front until April. It was sent to Tscherwen near Minsk for rest and refitting. This was its first

day of rest since the beginning of the war.

Newly equipped and back at full strength at the beginning of July, the "Tiger's Head" Battalion marched to the southern sector of the Eastern Front. It was used to make a breakthrough towards Stalingrad north of Stalino. However, the right flank of this attacking force, and Sturmgeschütz-Abteilung 210 with it, made a surprise turn toward Rostow in the south. The objective was the Caucasus.

The battalion distinguished itself several times in combat and at the taking of Noworossijsk. It stood shoulder to shoulder with the 97. Jäger-Division and then the 1. Gebirgs-Division in very difficult mountain fighting.

There was positional warfare during the late fall and winter 1942/43. The retreat from the Caucasus began when the 6. Army had to surrender in Stalingrad. The battalion crossed over to the Crimea without equipment. It was finally put into action on the Mius front in the positional fighting raging there. Within only a few days, it suffered the heaviest manpower losses of the entire war there, when the Soviets pushed into its positions.

Strong Soviets forces attacked on a Sunday. The 3rd Battery threw itself against the enemy. It stopped the enemy in dramatic, bloody fighting, but it was completely cut to pieces. Not a single man of that line battery came back to the German positions. They fell where they had fought.

After Major Schlawe was transferred to the army procurement office, Hauptmann Sichelschmidt, who had commanded the 2nd Battery up until then, took over command of the battalion. He had done splendidly with his 2nd Battery, and more than once inflicted heavy casualties on the enemy. The battalion was entrusted to him, and there was no one better qualified to lead this combat unit. On 14 February 1944 the battalion was redesignated a brigade.

The withdrawal led through Stalino to Nikopol. And there too, the "Tiger's Head" soldiers were used in continuous defensive fighting. Major Sichelschmidt received the German Cross in Gold there.

Sturmgeschütz-Abteilung 210 drew back all the way to Stanislaus. At Stanislaus the Sturmartilleristen of the "Tiger's Head" Brigade roared again. The Sturmgeschütze attacked, their battalion commander in front. A large number of enemy tanks was destroyed. The attacking enemy infantry was defeated and thrown back. On 15 May 1944, Major Herbert Sichelschmidt received the Knight's Cross for this action and for the fighting determination of his battalion.

Major Sichelschmidt wouldn't wear this honor very long. It only inspired him to do even more and to push himself even harder. He was killed on 17 July 1944. Major Nebel took over command of the brigade in his place. Nebel had already received the Knight's Cross on 2 April 1942 as an Oberleutnant. The brigade fought at Ostrowitsche under his command. The commander of 2nd Battery, Oberleutnant Erwin Glander, was killed there on 2 August 1944, after gallantry in action which ensured him undying fame. Erwin Glander plunged into action, sweeping along not only his battery but the entire brigade in an irresistible manner. He must never be forgotten. On 5 October 1944, Oberleutnant Glander was posthumously awarded the Knight's Cross.

Major Nebel distinguished himself once again at the great bend of the Vistula. He led the brigade with enormous verve and soldierly passion. The Wehrmacht Report for 1 September 1944 reported: "Sturmgeschütz-Brigade 210 under the command of Hauptmann Nebel has done an outstanding job in the great bend of the Weichsel."

Inexorably, the Soviets attacked again in greatly superior numbers. Tirelessly, they pressed against the German defensive belts. The brigade fell back again. The Soviets stormed forward to the Baranow Bridgehead. Three Sturmgeschütz brigades went into action there, right next to each other. During the Russian operational offensive on 12 January 1945, Sturmgeschütz-Brigade 201 (Major Langél) and Sturmgeschütz-Brigade 322 (Hauptmann Baurmann) were employed with Sturmgeschütz-Brigade 210 at the decisive point of this winter offensive.

Sturmgeschütz-Brigade 201 was completely destroyed. Sturmgeschütz-Brigade 322 also suffered heavy losses in its action in the Kielce area. Although Sturmgeschütz-Brigade 210 destroyed a large number of enemy tanks, it too was quickly torn apart. Three days later it consisted only of remnants.

On 31 January 1945 all three brigades received orders to withdraw. Hauptmann Baurmann was transferred to the Führer Reserve of the German Army High Command. Major Langél was ordered to organize a new Sturmgeschütz-Brigade 210 from the remnants of these three brigades.

The command and staff positions in this brigade were held by:

Commander: Major Langél
Adjutant: Oberleutnant Althoff
Orderly Officer: Leutnant Apprich, Leutnant Ingendaay
Paymaster: Oberzahlmeister Schöbe
Unit Physician: Oberarzt Dr. Carl
Maintenance Officer: Oberleutnant Latzel
Terrain reconnaissance officer: Oberleutnant Wiloth
Battery Commanders:
Headquarters Battery: Oberleutnant Ahrendt
1st Battery: Oberleutnant Gedeck
Section Leaders: Oberleutnant Randzio,
Leutnant Hanstein
2nd Battery: Oberleutnant Schmeing-Engberding
Section Leaders: Leutnant Uhlig, Leutnant Knechtel
3rd Battery: Hauptmann Vincon
Section Leaders: Leutnant Köhler, Leutnant Naumann
5th Battery: Oberleutnant Lindemann
Section Leader: Oberleutnant Bachmann

The new brigade was instructed to report to II. Armee-Korps Headquarters in Stettin. It was loaded up by rail on 2 February 1945 and unloaded on 3 February at Angermünde. Thirty-one Sturmgeschütze arrived at Angermünde on the following day. On 6 February Major Langél reported that his brigade was ready for action and on 7 February it was pushed forward to Schwedt on the Oder. The operations orders read, in part: "Establish a bridgehead on the east bank of the Oder along with SS units."

This was the SS-Regiment z.b.V. (for special duties) under the command of Obersturmbannführer Otto Skorzeny.

However, as this bridgehead was too small to provide an assembly area for a larger attacking force, SS-Regiment z.b.V. with the attached Sturmgeschütz-Brigade 210 was ordered to attack.

In the morning hours of 8 February 1945, the antiaircraft guns of the Schwedt Fortress opened fire from Hohenkränich, providing artillery preparation for the attack. The Sturmgeschütze of the 3rd Battery under the command of Hauptmann Vincon formed the lead element of the attacking forces. The two section leaders, Leutnant Köhler and Knight's Cross winner Horst Naumann, risked everything on one toss of the coin. Grabow and Hausberg were torn from Soviet hands in a quick advance forward. The SS-Regiment z.b.V. fought magnificently, and 13 enemy tanks were left burning and destroyed on the battlefield.

Two days later, Obersturmbannführer Skorzeny ordered an attack on Johannisgrund. This attack also made rapid progress. However, a heavy Russian battery which had dug in and was sheltered by farm buildings held out until nightfall. At that point, the SS men attacked and stormed the farm.

On the following day the Soviets brought up strong forces in an attempt to turn the tables and push in the German bridgehead. The Sturmgeschütze and the SS-Regiment held off enemy forces on Hill 63, southwest of Grabow, and inflicted heavy casualties on them. The front was straightened out and expanded. However, a little later, the Sturmgeschütze were withdrawn in order to initiate a similar attack from the area of Kolbitzow-Greifenhagen and enlarge the small bridgehead there. There weren't enough forces there, however. The brigade was given a new job. It was to eliminate the Russian bridgehead at Küstrin west of the Oder.

The brigade launched its attack from Seelow. The attack bogged down in heavy Soviet artillery fire. The few Sturmgeschütze which made it through got stuck in the new Soviet steel-wire barricades and were immobilized.

In the early days of March the brigade was suddenly loaded up and moved to Stettin. There it was to reinforce the existing Stettin-Altdamm bridgehead in order to protect the refugees streaming out of Pomerania and fleeing to the west across the highway bridge south of Stettin.

Starting 8 March 1945, the brigade was involved in heavy defensive fighting. Taking heavy losses, it fought fiercely at Wittstock, Klebow and on Hill 42 north of Wintersfeld. The brigade was attached to the 1. Marine-Infanterie-Division in that fighting.

Leutnant Hanstein, a section leader in the 1st Battery, found himself opposed by a swarm of T-34 tanks. Within minutes, he destroyed 6 tanks. The Wehrmacht Report for 22 March reported: "In the heavy fighting southeast of Stettin, Leutnant Hanstein, section leader in a Sturmgeschütz brigade of the 1. Marine-Infanterie-Division destroyed 6 tanks out of an attacking swarm of 28 Soviet tanks in 16 minutes and, as a result, defeated the entire attack."

Leutnant Hanstein was recommended by the brigade commander for inclusion in the Honor Roll of the German Army. Leutnant Köhler, a section leader in 3rd Battery, held off three Russian attacks with his few Sturmgeschütze on Hill 42. He too, destroyed six enemy tanks.

Here is the report of the fighting for Hill 42:

The Russian attack began in the morning on 15 March, after heavy preparatory fire from Russian artillery and mortars. Leutnant Köhler with a few Sturmgeschütze of the 3rd Battery held the boundary between the 1. Marine-Infanterie-Division and Panzer-Division "Schlesien" ("Silesia"), when the Soviets attacked with 18 Sherman tanks. The Sturmgeschütze opened fire. Within a few minutes, eleven Sherman tanks were stopped in the open terrain. There were soon a total of 15 tanks which were in flames or destroyed. The rest turned and moved back. The Russian infantry was pinned down, its attack had also bogged down.

Leutnant Köhler formed up his Sturmgeschütze once again. He himself had credit for six destroyed tanks. That afternoon, Hauptmann Vincon joined this small Kampfgruppe. He took cover in a defile with a fruit tree covering him from view from the air.

The Russian artillery fire which rained down on the German main battle line gradually increased in strength. Suddenly a shell exploded in the branches of the fruit tree. Hauptmann Vincon was gravely wounded by shell shrapnel. Leutnant Köhler had him taken immediately to the main aid station. But, on 17 March 1945, the Commander of 3rd Battery died of his wounds in Stettin.

On 16 March the brigade held off the attackers on the highway at Ferdinandstein and Untermühle. The attacking Russian forces were exhausted when orders were given on the German side to abandon this bridgehead. Leutnant Köhler took the rearguard mission with the last 11 Sturmgeschütze of the brigade. He received orders to be at the middle of the long highway bridge at 0300 hours on 18 March 1945. When the rear guard reached this point, an armored unit had already been employed there to stop the pursuing Soviets at all costs. The bridge was then blown up in the gray light of dawn. It collapsed into the Oder.

The brigade occupied quarters in the villages west of Kolbitzow. Once again the Sturmgeschütz crews had distinguished themselves with their remarkable bravery in the preceding fighting, especially during the breakout from the bridgehead which was already half surrounded by Soviet infantry.

After this tough fighting, in which it had destroyed 75 enemy tanks, the brigade was mentioned once more in the Wehrmacht Report. Following that, it was renamed Sturmgeschütz-Lehr-Brigade 210.

At the end of March, the brigade moved into the Schwedt area. There it was attached to the 547. Volks-Grenadier-Division. Immediately before the beginning of the new Russian offensive with the objective of Berlin, the brigade was once more put into action in the Kolbitzow area, where the Soviets had managed to establish a large bridgehead on the west bank of the Oder.

As Major Langél had been transferred, Hauptmann Bock took over command of the brigade. He was severely wounded by a neck wound during the first attack at Kolbitzow. His adjutant, Oberleutnant Althoff, took over command of the brigade. Oberleutnant Schmeing-Engberding, who was next in line, had been killed next to Oberleutnant Althoff, just as he had asked him to take over command. A bomb fragment had put an end to his service and his life.

A little later Oberleutnant Randzio took command of the brigade.

On 25 April 1945 the Sturmgeschütz of Leutnant Köhler' was destroyed at Prenzlau. His driver was killed. Köhler continued on in another Sturmgeschütz. He was stopped by Obersturmbannführer Skorzeny, who ordered him to position himself under a railroad bridge to block the road.

A little later, Leutnant Köhler saw the first enemy tank roll up. It was a T-34 with the new 8.5 cm cannon. Köhler opened fire, but this time the enemy was luckier. His first round smashed the Sturmgeschütz. Luckily, despite enemy machine-gun fire, the entire crew was able to bail out and make its way back to the brigade on foot with only surface wounds.

Sturmgeschütz-Brigade 210 reached the area of Hagenow by way of Neustrelitz, Waren, Goldberg and Crivitz. At Hagenow the Sturmartilleristen were interned on the American air field.

The war was over.

Sturmgeschütz-Abteilung 226 (Sturmgeschütz-Brigade 226)

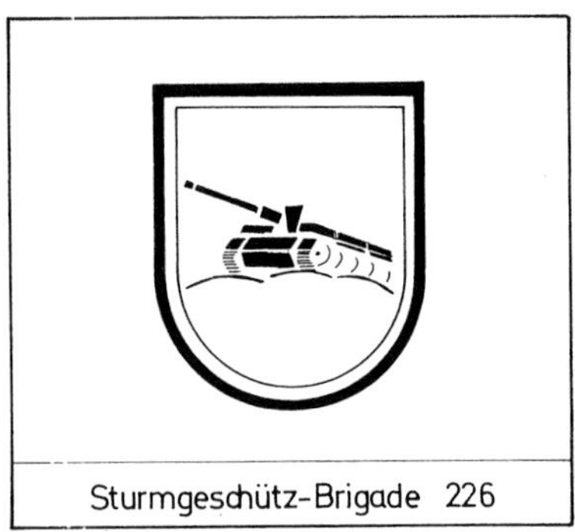

Sturmgeschütz-Brigade 226

Sturmgeschütz-Abteilung 226 was activated on 17 February 1941 at the Old Camp at Jüterbog. After its formation was complete it was rail loaded on 29 May 1941 and sent to Warsaw. Its commander was Hauptmann Pritzbuer. The four batteries were commanded by Oberleutnants Rünger (Headquarters Battery), Schmock (1st Battery), Bumm (2nd Battery) and Einbeck (3rd Battery).

The battalion was moved to an assembly area at Wegrow, 70 kilometers east of the Polish capital. When the battalion arrived at the Bug River, it was attached to the IX. Armee-Korps (General Geyer). The commanding general was not in agreement with the request of the battalion to be employed as a unit. Instead, he attached the 1st Battery to the 137. Infanterie-Division, the 2nd Battery to the 292. Infanterie-Division and the 3rd Battery to the 263. Infanterie-Division. In turn, the batteries were divided into sections among the regiments so that the opposite occurred of what should have with regard to the employment principles of the Sturmartillerie. Instead of using mass, the forces were dissipated.

The battalion was moved forward a few days before the start of the Russian campaign. The Headquarters Battery went to Wicomierz, the 1st Battery to Grodek, the 2nd Battery to Molozew and the 3rd Battery to the area north of Grodek.

The Sturmgeschütze of the battalion advanced with all three divisions on 22 June 1941 and were involved in penetrating the Russian border emplacements. The battalion knocked out its first tanks. The conduct of those first days of the offensive was recorded in the war diary of Hauptmann Pritzbuer:

The morning was beginning to dawn when I went forward with my adjutant, Oberleutnant von Werlhof, the commander of the Headquarters battery, Oberleutnant Rünger, and a few message runners. Leutnant Flemming had already departed during the night to occupy his position on the Bug for carrying out his reconnaissance mission.

We had just gotten into the recently dug-out position for the command post when the first rounds of the Russian Campaign flew over our heads and exploded on the far side of the river in the Russian bunker line. The first fires lit up the sky...

Now it was time for us to get to work. I saw Leutnant Flemming wade into the Bug in full gear. I noticed he was already struggling with the strong current. I was distracted for a moment by the motor noise of the approaching Sturmgeschütze of Oberleutnant Schmock, the commander of the 1st Battery. He stopped near us and fired the first round towards the enemy bunker which was approximately 600 meters away. A little later the bunkers were covered in thick smoke.

In the meantime, Leutnant Flemming who was supposed to recon for our Sturmgeschütze had waded further into the Bug. The water had already approached his chin. That meant it was too deep for our Sturmgeschütze. As a result there would be no ford there.

Leutnant Flemming reported to me and said that there was no ford here. He requested permission to try it again 400 meters further downstream. I told him to be careful and he took off.

In the meantime the infantry had brought up their pneumatic boats to the river at many places and had crossed. They approached the bunker system spread out.

We then hurried to the commander's vehicle and drove to the neighboring batteries. Not only the left battery, the 3rd, but also the right-hand one, the 2nd, reported that the results of their ford reconnaissance were negative. Leutnant Flemming appeared dripping wet and reported that the second attempt to find a ford had floundered. When Major Braunsberger, the commander of the Pionier-Bataillon, came to us and reported that the construction of the 16-ton ferry was impossible, our hopes began to sink as to whether we would be able to help the infantry with our Sturmgeschütze.

I then drove to the neighboring division on the right, the 292. Infanterie-Division, and was pleasantly surprised to find a way to a 16-ton ferry after a few kilometers while driving cross-country through a grain field.

Oberleutnant Bumm was already there. I greeted Bumm and got permission from the corps engineer to lead my remaining batteries over the river here. I then drove back to bring up the 1st Battery.

I encountered the commanding general, Geyer, at Molozew who asked me if I knew how I was going to get my Sturmgeschütze across the river: "Jawohl, Herr General! Over the 16-ton ferry of the 292. Infanterie-Division."

Now that radio communications were working again, I called Oberleutnant Einbeck and ordered him to cross over the river with his battery in the sector of the 292. Infanterie-Division.

I myself moved forward with the reconnaissance section to the ferry site of the 2nd Battery and crossed the Bug towards 0930 hours.

We made good progress initially and reached the improved road leading through Skrzeszew-Frankepol-Drohiczyn. We had driven a section of that road when we suddenly received fire from the right from bunkers which apparently hadn't been taken. I decided to drive back in order to turn on to one of the field paths which led to the north from Tonkiele and get to the sector of the 137. Infanterie-Division. This turned out to be a wise decision because we discovered later that the bunkers which controlled the main road defended themselves until 27 June.

We drove on past the burning villages of Cholkowice and Chakowice and reached Putcowice.

We continued along on the east bank of the Bug. Because our Headquarters Battery had not arrived yet, I ordered my driver to turn east and follow the 1st Battery which was committed along the avenue of advance of the 137. Infanterie-Division. We drove through the bunker system of the Soviets. We reached Mariyki via Rotki, Wilkowice and Skiwi. At Skiwi the infantry told us to be careful. Heavy fighting had just taken place. On the outskirts of the village I ran into Oberst Noack, the commander of Infanterie-Regiment 449. He showed me our forward-most Sturmgeschütze which were advancing in the direction of Skiwi. I reached the 1st Battery and departed from Skiwi with the section of Leutnant Henning. I saw the first Russian tanks on the side of the road. They had been penetrated by infantry antitank rounds.

I was mounting the vehicle of Leutnant Henning when he received orders from Oberleutnant Schmock to advance to his position. We moved a few hundred meters through the vegetation until we found the battery commander's vehicle.

Once there we discovered that our Sturmgeschütze were responsible for the advance of the infantry. Oberleutnant Schmock had knocked out two enemy tanks and, in the process, had received two hits which, however, did not put the vehicle out of commission.

On 23 June Leutnant Streng, a section leader in the 3rd Battery, came to us and reported that the battery had knocked out 20 enemy tanks. One of our Sturmgeschütze was out of action due to motor problems and two other ones due to enemy action.

Because the Headquarters Battery had not caught up, I drove to Oledy. At Oledy I saw Oberleutnant Einbeck, commander of the 3rd Battery, who reported to me that the battery had been involved in heavy fighting and had destroyed 39 tanks. Of these, 16 alone were by Leutnant Steinmann. Unteroffizier Maibohm knocked out 12; Oberleutnant Einbeck 7; and, two each by Leutnants Metzger and Moser. They had driven into a Russian armor attack from the right and had stopped it. A follow-on tank attack from the north was also stopped. The Sturmgeschütze had won a great victory during their first large operation. On the other hand, it was only light tanks which were knocked out there.

The advance continued. On 26 June the 3rd Battery blocked the retreat route of the Russians at Olekszyce. What had happened to the 1st Battery?

The river crossing at Grodek turned out to be difficult. The 1st Battery at Grodek was not able to cross the Bug until 1100 hours on 22 June. It succeeded in reaching the bridge at the Nurzrc River before the enemy blew it skyward. The river ran perpendicular to the axis of advance. On 24 June Bielsk was reached. The Woods of Bialowice were then in front of the 1st Battery. Two days later the battery had penetrated the woods which were crawling with the enemy. It was located on its northern edge along the retreat axis of the Russians. The Russians were moving back to Wolkowysk from the direction of Bialystok. The Sturmgeschütze of the 1st Battery encountered heavy Russian tanks for the first time there. A Sturmgeschütz commander reported:

A truck driver told us on 27 June about an attack of Russian superheavy tanks. We stormed ahead to a small elevation with our Sturmgeschütz. Once we got there we saw a large tank on the next hill. My gunner fired the first round in his flank. The second and third rounds also hit home. The enemy tank turned to the left and the crew bailed out.

To guard against a surprise attack on the left flank we rolled back a bit from the top of the hill. As we were doing that a second tank appeared on the hill rising to the left. He turned his turret in our direction and advanced up the hill. We advanced forward quickly and fired twice at him. Our rounds hit home, but he disappeared in a depression.

While I was taking a serious look around, the infantry called out to me: "Tanks to the left!"

"Turn left!" I called out to my driver. The motor screamed. The Sturmgeschütz turned to the left with a jolt and the first round left the barrel with a loud report.

"Target!" the gunner yelled. Despite that, the tank continued on. The next round burst in his turret. The armored colossus then turned away and attempted to reach the hill again. We followed and brought him to a halt with a few well-aimed rounds. A final round from really close destroyed his running gear. As a result, he couldn't move. None of the crew came out of the vehicle.

When I pulled my Sturmgeschütz back to a depression, I noticed a tank turret through my optics as we were rolling back. The turret was popping up from behind the hill. I opened fire and after several hits he disappeared in the direction of the enemy. His turret was still visible when an even heavier tank appeared over the slope, massive and powerful. We fired our rounds against it. Round after round left the barrel but the tank continued into the depression despite the numerous hits.

The loader then reported that the ammunition was just about out. We fired a few smoke rounds against the tank which was scooting away to the left. But they weren't capable of stopping him either. I then decided to ram him. We chased after him, faster and faster, and I was successful in reaching him and ramming him from the rear. From the violence of the impact two of my men were injured. The enemy rolled another 50 meters and then stopped.

I left the vehicle with hand grenades and a pistol and jumped behind the Sturmgeschütz. The crew of the Russian tank climbed out of the hull escape hatch and attempted to escape. I had the Sturmgeschütz approach the enemy slowly to within 10 meters and followed it on foot. Suddenly, I saw a Russian spying out from behind the left-hand running gear and cock his revolver at me. A hand grenade took care of him.

At that point it was quiet and I discovered six dead soldiers around the mighty steel crate. I reached the tank. All of the hatches with the exception of the access hatch to the engine compartment were closed. When I climbed onto the tank, a machine pistol suddenly fired from within the turret. I threw a couple of hand grenades into the engine compartment...

Some smoke rose from the tank; it was through. When we looked at this felled giant we noticed that the armor on the turret was 95 millimeters. The powerful cannon was 15.2 centimeters; several machine guns were on-board armament. We estimated its weight to be about 60 tons.

(Author: It was the KW II which is listed at 68 tons.)

During the attack on Wolkowysk the Sturmgeschütz section under Leutnant Schließmann was placed under the operational control of the advance guard detachment of Panzer-Jäger-Abteilung 137. It was intended for his section to clear a path for the infantry. When Russian tanks were sighted on the right Leutnant Schließmann opened fire at 1,500 meters. Leutnant Schließmann reported:

The antitank rounds bounced off. The distance was still too great. As a result we had to move forward. We opened fire a second time when we had closed to 400 meters. The first round from our Sturmgeschütz hit right in the side of the hull of the enemy about even with the engine compartment. The tank exploded with a powerful detonation. The next tank we hit pulled another 100 meters closer only to then explode. The third tank also suffered its fate. The fourth and last tank was knocked out. The crew climbed out and was killed in combat.

The advance continued. Three kilometers out of Wolkowysk the Sturmgeschütze turned north and reached Jagdwitz. With that move the Sturmgeschütze had pushed behind the retreating enemy. Combat engineers laid mines on the road. Soon the call was heard: "Enemy tanks coming from the west!"

Three heavy tanks approached. Two of them ran onto mines; the third one was destroyed by the Sturmgeschütz of Leutnant Schließmann. Long after evening twilight three additional T-34's were sighted which attempted to break out from the west. Following them were even more. Ten T-34's were definitely hit and, despite that, continued to move on. Leutnant Schließmann's section returned to its starting point.

The next morning an infantry Leutnant reported that approximately 200 meters east of the point where the Sturmgeschütz section had fired at the 10 enemy tanks, eight of them were found knocked out.

At the end of June there was an armor battle at Czyke. Several tanks were knocked out, however, the battalion suffered considerable losses.

By 3 July Sturmgeschütz-Abteilung 226 had knocked out 107 tanks. On that day the commanders of four Sturmgeschütz battalions met when they were attached to the Panzergruppe. Besides Sturmgeschütz-Abteilung 226 there was Sturmgeschütz-Abteilung 192 under Hauptmann Hammon, Sturmgeschütz-Abteilung 201 under Hauptmann Hoffmann and Sturmgeschütz-Abteilung 203, the "Elephant" battalion.

Hauptmann Pritzbuer wrote the following in his personal diary on 4 July 1943:

Yesterday I greeted the commander of Sturmgeschütz-Abteilung 201 who, along with Leutnant Diehl, Oberleutnant Zwicke and Oberleutnant Schmidt, came to the command post. Besides them were a Major Scheppers and a Major (Ing.) Stolberg from VI./Artillerie-Lehr-Regiment 2 at Jüterbog. Now that led to some war stories!

The battalion advanced to Minsk via Baranowitschi and Kojdano. The advance then continued towards Borissow on the Beresina River. At Borissow the battalion was allocated to Panzergruppe 2 of Generaloberst Guderian. It was then attached to the XXXXVII. Panzer-Korps under General Lemelsen.

Minsk was reached on 9 July. All three batteries were employed in the fighting between Orscha and Witebsk from 9 to 12 July. The Stalin Line was breached and the road east of Minsk was reached on 14 July. The advance along this improved road could be continued at a considerably faster pace. The area around Orscha was reached without enemy contact by 16 July. The battalion was attached to the Kampfgruppe of Oberst Usinger at Orscha. The battalion had the mission to break through the Russian positions and turn north at Obolay towards Konowtschino and establish contact with the 12. Panzer-Division at Podbariza. Sturmgeschütz-Abteilung 192 was also ordered to Podbariza in order to attack along the railroad embankment to Jelion together with Sturmgeschütz-Abteilung 226. That attack did not succeed in breaking through.

Leutnant Henning was killed outside of his vehicle in the left-hand portion of Borodino on 18 July. He was shot through the chest. His crew drove him back. Just before that happened Leutnant Hoffmann had been the first officer of the battalion killed. He, too, had been outside of his vehicle.

Borodino was conquered on 21 July.

On 25 July the maintenance section of the battalion was completely destroyed by a fire at Monastyrschina, where it had been established. That was a difficult blow. Oberleutnant von Werlhof immediately flew to Germany to get replacements.

In the following days the Sturmgeschütze succeeded in providing the necessary relief to the infantry again and again while employed with various divisions and other formations. When the Russians overran Infanterie-Regiment 463 (263. Infanterie-Division) on 30 July the last remaining reserves of Sturmgeschütz-Abteilung 226 were able to stop the enemy and throw him out of Michalowka.

The 1st and 2nd Batteries were in action at the end of July south of Smolensk on the Sosh River. After the Sosh had been forced and Jelnja conquered, Panzergruppe Guderian was collected for the decisive advance to Moscow.

At that phase of the fighting Panzergruppe Guderian was turned south by the German Army High Command. Sturmgeschütz-Abteilung 226 was placed under the operational control of the 292. Infanterie-Division which had been given the mission to attack Rosslawl as the lead division. The Sturmgeschütze were the lead elements. On that morning of 2 August 1941 Generaloberst Guderian advanced behind the Sturmgeschütze as an "infantryman" in order to convince himself of the difficulty of this advance.

The "Moscow Road" was reached on 3 August. When the enemy tried to break out at Kosaki on 5 August, Generaloberst Guderian moved there with the Sturmgeschütze, tanks and artillery and defeated the breakout attempt.

Sturmgeschütz-Abteilung 226 took part in all of the fighting for Rosslawl. Following that it stormed Weissejewko. After that it continued in the direction of Gomel. Nowo-Beliza was taken by the battalion on 8 August.

From Gomel the battalion advanced to the south, attached to the XXIV. Panzer-Korps under General von Geyr. Its objective was Kiev. There was an armored battle at Kritschew. The fighting lasted until 20 August. The enemy was thrown back and pursued in the direction of the Defena River. Marshall Timoschenko's troops were thrown back 80 kilometers. After some fighting at Gorrdnja and Njeshin Sturmgeschütz-Abteilung 226 was outside of Tschernigow at the beginning of September. The battle for that city lasted eight days, at which point the Sturmgeschütze with mounted infantry rolled into the city and conquered it.

The advance south continued. It was critical to link up quickly from the north with the soldiers of Panzergruppe Kleist. The pursuit against the retreating enemy in the direction of Kiev began on 9 September 1941. Sturmgeschütz-Abteilung 226 reached the edge of the city on 18 September and began the assault on the city on 19 September after regrouping its forces. The Soviets blew up all the bridges over the Dnjepr on that day. Kiev fell one day later after the Sturmgeschütze had fought at all of the focal points of the battle. It was the 71. Infanterie-Division which had advanced into Kiev on the afternoon of 19 September. The battle for Kiev was over on 24 September. This battle brought immeasurable success. In the largest encirclement in the history of warfare, the following losses were reported by the German High Command in its after-action report on 27 September 1942 (three Sturmgeschütz battalions had participated in the operation):

As has already been reported by a special announcement, the great battle at Kiev is over. In a two-side envelopment over a huge area we have succeeded in unhinging the defense of Dnjepr and destroying five armies. Only weak elements were able to escape the encirclement. In the course of this operation which witnessed singular cooperation between the army and the air force 665,000 prisoners were taken and 884 armored vehicles, 3718 field pieces and innumerable quantities of assorted war materiel were captured or destroyed.

Once again Panzergruppe 2 under Generaloberst Guderian turned north in order to participate in Unternehmen "Taifun" (Operation "Typhoon"), the attack on Moscow.

Sturmgeschütz-Abteilung 226 also turned around and headed north. It was employed in the breakthrough at the Desna Position from 2 –4 October. In the twin battles of Wjasma-Briansk it suffered casualties and continued its advance on Moscow on 14 October. The first defensive line out of Moscow (on the Protwa) was penetrated. It was then critical to cross large tracts of woods between this river and the next one, the Nara. The woods were infested with positions of all types. The woods were traversed and the second Moscow defensive line on the Nara was penetrated. Sturmgeschütz-Abteilung 226 was only 65 kilometers from Moscow at that point. The greatest enemy at that point, however, was not the enemy, but rather the powerful onset of the Russian winter. From 1–12 December the quicksilver of the thermometer fell to 45 degrees below zero Celsius. The advance came to a standstill; the Russian counterstrokes began.

The fighting withdrawal took the battalion to Kaluga by the end of December. At Kaluga the bitter defensive fighting began during which parts of the battalion were separated from the main body and reported missing. Fortunately they returned later.

At the beginning of 1942 Sturmgeschütz-Abteilung 226 was employed at Spass-Demenskoje. The fighting at Aleksin followed. The winter operations weren't over, however. On 16 and 17 January 1942 the battalion moved out from Schisdra with all of its remaining Sturmgeschütze to relieve the encircled 216. Infanterie-Division at Suchinitschi. It moved against Suchinitschi through snow more than a meter deep. The enemy was thrown back at temperatures 40 degrees below zero Celsius and the 216. Infanterie-Division was relieved. The encircled infantrymen greeted their liberators with tears in their eyes.

The battalion's next operation was at Juchnow. Hauptmann Pritzbuer had become a Major in the meantime. The battalion had made a name for itself as the sector's "fire brigade" in the decisive defensive fighting. When the commander took ill on 21 March 1942, Hauptmann Bergmann became his successor. The adjutant was Leutnant Jekosch.

Everything disappeared in the spring thaw and mud. As a result the operations of both sides came to a halt. Moscow was still in Russian hands and would remain so. But the Russian attempts to break through the German Eastern Front and destroy it had also failed.

Still led by Hauptmann Bergmann, Sturmgeschütz-Abteilung 226 moved towards Kursk in June 1942. It was intended for the battalion to participate in Unternehmen "Blau" (Operation "Blue") which was intended to take Stalingrad and the Caucasus.

At the start of the offensive Sturmgeschütz-Abteilung 226 rolled in the direction of Woronesch and helped in conquering this toughly defended city from the Soviets. Before this could be done, however, the bridge over the Don leading to Woronesch had to be taken. This formed the basis for assaulting into the city. On 18 June Kriegsverwaltungsrat Wallishauser and Hauptmann Bergmann traveled to Germany.

On 26 June the entire battalion conducted a thrust in the direction of Kamenka with the infantry of Grenadier-Regiment 1 "Großdeutschland." Kamenka was taken. After having returned to the bridgehead, the attack on the city of Woronesch commenced in the early morning of 5 July 1942. Infantry of Infanterie-Regiment "Großdeutschland" rode on the Sturmgeschütze into the city as far as the train station. At that point the attack bogged down and the Sturmgeschütze, together with the infantry, were ordered back.

Two days later the western part of the city was occupied.

Inspektor Jakob joined the battalion on 6 July. Three days later, 9 July 1942, the refitting order for the battalion arrived. Sturmgeschütz-Abteilung 226 left the front and moved to Spass-Demenskoje where it was loaded on trains on 13 July. The battalion went to Kowno via Wjasma Dorogobusch, Smolensk, Witebsk and Dünaburg.

It arrived at Treuenbrietzen on 19 July 1942. Everyone was sent on leave. The batteries were divided. One half of each battery was equipped with long-barreled Sturmgeschütze and formed the basis for the refitted Sturmgeschütz-Abteilung 226. The remaining halves of the batteries served as cadre for a Sturmgeschütz battalion which was forming.

On 11 August 1942 Sturmgeschütz-Abteilung 226 was loaded on trains at Treuenbrietzen and transferred to the channel coast. It moved via Wuppertal, Düsseldorf and Amiens to Motteville.

When Canadian commandos landed at Dieppe on 19 August, the battalion was ordered to march there. Because the attempted landings were smashed very quickly, Sturmgeschütz-Abteilung 226 was not employed.

The battalion was rail loaded on 9 September at Motteville and transported clear across Germany to the east. The battalion went to Jassnow in the northern sector of the front.

Sturmgeschütz-Abteilung 226 was first employed from Jassnow at Schapki Virsino on the southwestern edge of the Leningrad front. It suffered very high casualties during this operation. Sixteen Sturmgeschütze were out of action. For the most part they were total losses. Forty-two soldiers of the battalion were killed.

The battalion was ordered back to Siwerskaja which was also the headquarters of the 18. Armee. Generalfeldmarschall von Manstein had set up his Armee-Oberkommando 11 as well. He had been ordered there from the Crimea. The divisions of the 11. Armee had stormed Sevastopol and were now supposed to take Leningrad as well.

But there never was an attack on Leningrad since the Red Army had started the battles of Lake Ladoga.

Moved to the area of Mga, Sturmgeschütz-Abteilung 226 took up an assembly area 5 kilometers east of that city and received the mission to advance to the north with the 170. Infanterie-Division and the 5. Gebirgs-Division. That would cut off the retreat route for the Russian 2nd Shock Army and separate it from its logistical lines of communication.

The 2nd Shock Army had advanced over the Wolchow with the objective of Mga. In the northern area of the penetration, however, the troops under Oberst Wengler (Grenadier-Regiment 366) were holding the strongpoint of Gontowaja on the Tschernaja. Likewise, Tortolowo was being held in the southern part of the breakthrough area. When the pocket closed behind the 2nd Shock Army, Sturmgeschütz-Abteilung 226 was ordered back to Mga. It received the mission to clear out the pocket together with the 3. Gebirgs-Division.

Major Brauneisen led the battalion and moved it forward into the assembly area from where the attack was intended to be launched on 20 September 1942. At 0712 hours on the morning of 20 September Russian mortar rounds of 15 centimeter caliber suddenly began to impact. The friendly attack started at 0830 hours. The bunker line of the Soviets was penetrated by the mountain troops. The advance proceeded through a dense forest which had been uprooted by the preceding artillery barrage. Swamps and natural tree obstacles forced detours. The bunkers were destroyed by firing over open sights. The Sturmgeschütze swung to the northwest with the mountain troops following. The advance proceeded slowly along an old forest trail. Two guns rolled onto mines. The first enemy tanks then surfaced along a narrow clearing. The Sturmgeschütz christened "Caesar" knocked out 2 T-34's. Then it received a hit. The crew was able to bail out only slightly wounded. The gun was put back into action the following morning by the maintenance section.

The fighting in the pocket was over on 2 October 1942 at Gaitolowo.

Sturmgeschütz-Abteilung 226 then moved into the area of operations of the 170. Infanterie-Division at Gorodok on the Newa Front. On 10 October Oberleutnant Metzger, the commander of the 3./Sturmgeschütz-Abteilung 226, was killed at Proto on the "Bloody Bridge."

The fighting in that area lasted until December 1942. On 2 January 1943 Hauptmann Bergmann was transferred. Oberleutnant Schleburg took over temporary command of the battalion. On 4 January Oberleutnant Bausch took over the battalion for a short period of time.

On 12 January 1943 there was an ice-cold wind blowing across the frozen over Newa. It was 28 degrees below zero Celsius. At 0700 hours the Russians initiated a heavy artillery barrage south of Gorodok which lasted more than two hours. The banks of the Newa were 12 meters high there. Following the barrage the red Army attacked over the ice of the Newa. It succeeded in breaking through north of Gorodok. As a result of the penetration, five Sturmgeschütze were encircled at Posselok. The 61. Infanterie-Division (Generalmajor Hühner), together with the rest of the battalion, attacked in the direction of Schlüsselburg and penetrated the Russian front outside of it. The front closed again behind the troops. When Schlüsselburg could no longer be held the Kampfgruppe was directed to break out.

The breakout began on 18 January. The Sturmgeschütze cleared a path for the infantry. All the wounded and the dead were carried along. When the rear guard reach "Posselok 5" that strongpoint was also evacuated. As a rear guard, the surviving Sturmartilleristen finally reached the heights at Ssinjawino. The new commander of the battalion, Major Keysler, arrived at Ssinjawino in 18 January 1943. Up until the end of January 1943 the Sturmgeschütz-Abteilung 226 had knocked out 88 enemy tanks on the Leningrad front. With that amount the battalion raised its score from 22 June 1941 to the end of January 1943 to 309 tank kills.

In February and March 1943 Sturmgeschütz-Abteilung 226 was attached to the 227. Infanterie-Division and fought defensively under the command of Major Keysler east of Mga, at Gaitolowo and south of "Posselok 7." The battalion destroyed its 400th tank in the Wengler strongpoint at "Posselok 7." The strongpoint was defended by Infanterie-Regiment 366 under Oberst Maximilian Wengler. The battalion was named to the Honor Roll of the German Army on 26 March 1943 which stated: "Sturmgeschütz-Abteilung 226, currently south of Lake Ladoga, has destroyed 414 enemy tanks since going into action on the Eastern Front."

The subsequent fighting at Ssinjawino and north of Mga at the railroad triangle, as well as for Mga itself, was bitter. The Red Army attempted to take possession of this important transportation nodal point. If it succeeded it would also be back in control of the Kirow line to Leningrad. However, all its efforts were in vain. The Germans held at Mga and on the Ssinjawino Heights. The Sturmgeschütze of Sturmgeschütz-Abteilung 226 deserve much of the credit for this defense.

There were more and more losses, and the number of guns melted away. The replacements for a battery, sent from Sturmgeschütz-Ersatz-Abteilung 200 in Schweinfurt, were enthusiastically greeted on their arrival at Mga in June 1943. A that point the members of the 2nd Battery went back home while the new soldiers took over their old guns.

The new Sturmartillerie men were introduced to daily life at the front in a quiet sector outside of Oranienburg. When they moved up to the front at Mga, Sturmgeschütz-Abteilung 226 was loaded up by rail and sent to the Newel area, where the Red Army was preparing for a new operational-level offensive. The attack was launched on 6 October 1943.

The Sturmgeschütze defended there until the middle of December. Luckily they suffered only minor losses. Toward the end of the year, the battalion was shifted to the Pleskau area. When the retreat from Pleskau to the "Panther" Position was carried out in February 1944, the Sturmgeschütze participated. They moved to Petrowskoje between Pleskau and Ostrow. On 14 February 1944 the battalion was redesignated a brigade.

Sturmgeschütz-Brigade 226 shifted to Narwa in the middle of March to eliminate the Russian bridgehead there. It traveled through a knee-deep swamp. Although the brigade managed to gain some ground it was unable to force this bridgehead to collapse. The attack was called off on 24 April. In May 1944, the unit was transferred to the Polozk area on the Düna. Major Keysler was wounded there while personally leading an attack. Major Michael, the new commander, arrived with replacements from Sturmgeschütz-Ersatz- und Ausbildungs-Abteilung 200 which had been relocated to Schieratz. He would command Sturmgeschütz-Brigade 226 to its bitter end.

At this time the 1st Battery was commanded by Hauptmann Gierkens. After he was wounded, Oberleutnant Binz took over command, to be followed later by Hauptmann von Arnim, who was named to the German Army's Honor Roll and received the Honor Roll Clasp on 27 November 1944.

Hauptmann Schmidt commanded the 2nd Battery. He was relieved by Hauptmann Schleburg in the spring of 1944. The 3rd Battery was commanded by Oberleutnant Hamke. He too was named to the German Army's Honor Roll on 27 September 1944.

The Düna Position was expanded in the middle of June 1944. Sturmgeschütz-Brigade 226 was still located south of Polozk. When Russian tanks broke through there on 2 July 1944 at about 1000 hours, they were stopped cold by fire from the Sturmgeschütze. The counterattack with the 24. Infanterie-Division didn't break through and, in the early afternoon, Generaloberst Frießner, Commander-in-Chief of Heeresgruppe North, issued orders to evacuate Polozk. Because the bridge at Polozk had fallen prey to Russian bombers, Sturmgeschütz-Brigade 226 had to fall back south of the Düna to Dünaburg.

At the beginning of July, the II. Armee-Korps assembled west of Lake Dissna to launch another attack to the south to hit the Soviet 6th Guards Army in the flank and re-establish contact with the 3. Panzer-Armee. The attack began with an initial promise of success. But then it bogged down and the attackers pulled back to their jump-off positions.

On 19 July the Soviets launched an attack with 5 rifle divisions, one tank division and a mechanized brigade. Their objective was the city of Düna. Although the Soviets were able to get across the river on both sides of the city, the city itself held out. Sturmgeschütz-Brigade 226 deserved much of the credit for this defensive success. It made up the rear guard when Dünaburg was evacuated on 26 July, and the Sturmgeschütze were the last to pull back across the Düna Bridge. They had destroyed a large number of enemy tanks and assault guns, but had also suffered considerable losses themselves. The Düna Bridge was blown up behind them. On the same day, Generaloberst Schörner took over command of Heeresgruppe Nord.

Sturmgeschütz-Brigade 226 moved into the Pleskau area once again. At Pleskau it was necessary to withstand bitter defensive fighting. Two guns turned up missing there, apparently captured by the enemy. A third gun from 1st Battery was also missing. A gun commander reported that he had seen it burning on the battlefield. It had to be considered lost. A few days later, however, the crew arrived back at the battalion. The gun commander, Unteroffizier Bohling reported:

We were informed suddenly that Russian tanks had broken through the infantry on our right, and I immediately changed position to engage these tanks. When I got there, I saw that the Russian tanks had already rolled over the infantry. On my right I recognized two T-34's which were showing me their flanks. The next minute both were burning. Two other T-34's now rolled directly toward us. I gave the range. Gunner Öhlers aimed at the first and fired. Loader Tornof reloaded and, after the second round, this T-34 was on fire too. The fourth was knocked out immediately after that.

Then we placed their following infantry under fire with high-explosive rounds. The enemy attack came to a halt. The Red Army men fled back. Then they tried to attack our left side, from a small grove. We heard tank motors over there; our driver turned the gun in that direction. When the first T-34 rolled out of the woods, it was destroyed with a few rounds, then whenever another T-34 tried it, we fired. Suddenly, a shell jammed in the breech. We pulled back behind a shed. I bailed out and knocked the shell loose with the cleaning rod.

We then fired another round, but the casing jammed again. I bailed out again and knocked it loose. And we had to knock the casing loose after every round. Using this method we still managed to destroy another two T-34's. When we had to knock the round loose once again—Öhlers was outside this time—a T-34 approached us at high speed. We wanted to jump up on it, for I saw that his hatches were open, but he raced by us too fast.

We rolled back behind the shed, where we had taken cover each time we had to knock the casings out. Now the last round was really stuck. We had to blow up our gun and fight our way back.

We set the charge and moved out. Bullets whipped past our ears. The Russian infantry had gotten awfully close. But we made it back along with 6 grenadiers we picked up on the way. When we reached our old strongpoint, the guns had already gone. We didn't know that the German lines had been pulled back 30 kilometers that night.

We stalked through the woods that night in single file and reached a gun position; it was a position alright—a Russian one. At dawn we reached a village. Red Army men were ransacking the place. Soviet tanks and trucks were assembling in the vicinity.

Forty-eight hours later Unteroffizier Bohling and his comrades reached the "Modon" Position, 45 kilometers west of Pleskau; they were saved.

Sturmgeschütz-Brigade 226 repeatedly rolled out from this position to defend threatened sectors from enemy tank attacks or eliminate enemy penetrations. A number of T-34's, KV-1's and Josef Stalin tanks were destroyed. But the brigade also suffered heavy losses. Everyone breathed easier when new guns arrived in the middle of September. Each battery also received three 10.5 cm Sturmhaubitzen.

Always fighting as rear guard, the brigade pulled back through Werro, Walk and Wenden into the "Segewold" Position. On 10 October it received orders there for Unternehmen "Donner" (Operation "Thunder").

Under this code name the retreat was carried out back to the "East Riga" Position. On 11 October the Sturmgeschütze arrived in Riga which was already under Russian fire. It was immediately loaded up by rail and sent to Libau. The wheeled vehicles went there by road. The plan was for Sturmgeschütz-Brigade 226 along with another Sturmgeschütz brigade, the 14. Panzer-Division and the 126. Infanterie-Division to lead the breakout attempt of Heeresgruppe Nord. But nothing came of it.

The Red Army attacked earlier and Sturmgeschütz-Brigade 226 was involved in the First Kurland Battle. The brigade shifted into the Frauenburg area at the end of October. There it received new guns. It gave up the Sturmhaubitzen and in their place received the new Jagdpanzer IV with the KwK L70 cannon. At this time it was apparently renamed Heeres-Sturmartillerie-Brigade 226, although no official records of its redesignation exist, and it was given a 4th Battery, an infantry-support battery. The brigade then had its own infantry and could operate independently. It kept this position at Frauenburg, fighting enemy tanks, up until the end of the year.

In the middle of January 1945 the brigade was moved to Preekuln. It defended there with the 30. Infanterie-Division. Three crews which had been detailed to the division were left behind when the brigade was unexpectedly loaded by ship at Libau on 20 and 21 February 1945. Thirty-three Sturmgeschütze were loaded on the 5,000-ton freighter. Led by Major Michael, the Sturmgeschütze were unloaded as soon as they arrived at Danzig-Neufahrwasser and attached to the SS-Freiwilligen-Division "Langemarck." Together with the division, the brigade penetrated the Ihme Sector, moved far into the enemy-occupied area and relieved Arnswalde which had been encircled. The fighting ended there on 27 February. On the next morning the withdrawal began.

Defensive fighting was conducted with the 32. Infanterie-Division in the area around Schlawe and then Rügenwalde. The brigade moved back along the coastal road to Gotenhafen.

Heeres-Sturmartillerie-Brigade 226 defended Zoppot on 20 March. When the Red Army reached the coast at Zoppot on 23 March, Heeres-Sturmartillerie-Brigade 226 withdrew to Gotenhafen, where it defended until 30 March. The last fighting for the city occurred at the beach hotel, at which time the brigade moved back to Oxhöfter Kämpe. The brigade held there until after Easter when the last ground soldiers were transported to Hela. On 4 April the brigade also crossed over to Hela.

Oberleutnant von Arnim, the commander of the 1st Battery, witnessed the hard defensive fighting in the forward-most lines.

From Hela the brigade was supposed to return to Germany. Instead it took over the weapons of a Panzer unit which had been bogged down there for four weeks. Despite that the brigade would not use the tanks it received.

Hauptmann von Arnim was able to hold his ground at Neufahrwasser with only four Sturmgeschütze. He was able to conduct several counterattacks with them. He was decorated with the German Cross in Gold.

The soldiers of Heeres-Sturmartillerie-Brigade 226 went into captivity on 8 May 1945.

Sturmgeschütz-Abteilung 232 (Sturmgeschütz-Brigade 232)

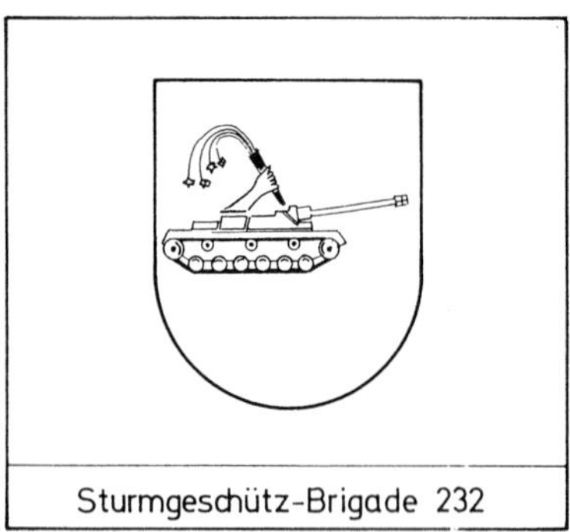
Sturmgeschütz-Brigade 232

Sturmgeschütz-Abteilung 232 was formed at Jüterbog within the Artillerie-Lehr-Regiment in October 1942 under Major Gottfried Geißler. In Major Geißler, the brigade received a commander who, as Oberleutnant and battery commander in Sturmgeschütz-Abteilung 185, had already been awarded the Knight's Cross on 21 August 1941. In his honor, the battalion bore the insignia of a brandished whip (geschwungene Geißel).

The battalion completed its formation in December. It was planned to send it to Africa, and it was outfitted with tropical uniforms. However, when it was alerted on Christmas Eve and rapidly transported to its first operational area, it rolled towards the Eastern Front. The objective was the Kalmücken Steppes.

The battalion was unloaded at Sailz and immediately went into action. This rapid operation had the objective of relieving the 6. Army, surrounded in Stalingrad, and to support its breakout attempt. This objective was not accomplished, however, as the 6. Army had been forbidden to break out. The battalion participated in the defensive fighting between the Don and the Donez.

When, during the night of 11 February 1943, a Soviet tank division managed to make a surprise push into the Grischino area, northwest of Stalino, civilian officials and Red Cross nurses, as well as 50 female communications specialists, fell into Soviet hands along with numerous German, Rumanian and Italian units. On 18 February the "Whip" Battalion along with a mounted infantry battalion received orders to attack and take back the Grassno–Armeskoje-Grischino area.

Every man in the battalion knew that everything depended on speed, with no concern for what might be going on to the right or left of the penetration. Oberleutnant Brockschmidt had only two Sturmgeschütze available from his 3rd Battery for this mission. Since he considered this to be too weak for the expected street and house-to-house fighting, he brought two more Sturmgeschütze forward on his own initiative in a forced march during the night.

Subsequent events confirmed that this was the correct decision. During the attack on the next morning, the Soviets defended themselves with a surprising number of antitank rifles. Even so, Oberleutnant Brockschmidt managed to reach Grischino in the first assault. His Sturmgeschütze reached the railroad station. The Soviets put up a really stubborn defense at the train station. Oberleutnant Brockschmidt concentrated his Sturmgeschütze at appropriate places which systematically broke the enemy resistance. The enemy fled, and the prisoners, soldiers, Red Cross nurses and the communications specialists were freed. The freed prisoners were almost hysterical with joy.

Then Oberleutnant Brockschmidt moved on further to the south. Enemy tanks rolled against the Sturmgeschütze. Three T-34's were destroyed within the space of a few minutes. Other tanks burst into flames. The Soviet points of resistance were torn apart with deliberately aimed fire.

The accompanying infantry battalion under Hauptmann Gotzschaan was carried along by this élan. The infantry followed the Sturmgeschütze and destroyed the enemy in house-to-house fighting. Bunkers, cellars and other Soviet resistance points were destroyed, some from as close as 10 meters away. Oberleutnant Brockschmidt achieved a magnificent victory. He was decorated with the German Cross in Gold.

Most of the Soviet tanks, which had broken through earlier, retreated and were destroyed.

When a cry for assistance came from a Waffen-SS unit that had bogged down in front of a line of bunkers, the battalion moved there and, after thirty minutes, the last enemy bunker was destroyed. The infantry took possession of that line.

During the following night a few more enemy tanks had pushed forward and were destroyed. In a counterattack, the Sturmgeschütze made a surprise attack on the village of Roog and captured it after a short battle.

In these two days of combat, the 3rd Battery alone destroyed 28 enemy tanks and a large number of antitank and antiaircraft guns, antitank rifles, bunkers and resistance points.

Toward noon on 19 February, an attack on Molodejkoje was ordered. The attack got stuck in the middle of the village because of the enemy's very heavy antitank weapons. The Sturmgeschütz of Oberleutnant Brockschmidt was put out of action by a direct hit, and the crew had to bail out. Oberleutnant Brockschmidt conferred with Hauptmann Gotzschaan before climbing into another Sturmgeschütz and, after two more hours of fighting, they took the entire village.

The village had to be cleared meter by meter in the face of savage Soviet antiaircraft fire.

On 20 February, when the Soviets undertook to break out with heavy tank forces, these were destroyed by the Sturmgeschütze. The number of tanks destroyed by the 3rd Battery climbed again. The Sturmgeschütz of Oberleutnant Brockschmidt alone destroyed 9 enemy tanks during the three days of fighting.

The battalion was in heavy defensive fighting in the Mius-Donez position for the entire month of March. It distinguished itself there by its remarkable steadiness. During the subsequent positional warfare on the central Don, it was used by Heeresgruppe Süd at the hot spots of the fighting. This fighting lasted until 20 July 20 1943. It was a question of stopping the wildly attacking Soviet forces and pushing them back in strong counterattacks.

A little later, the severely hit, almost decimated battalion was ordered back to Patschkau for reorganization. After reorganization, it was immediately employed back in the east, where it took part in the heavy defensive fighting and the retreats. It was redesignated a brigade on 14 February 1944.

It reached Heiligenbeil at the beginning of January 1945. For the entire time that it had been in action, from 1 November 1942 to

31 January 1945, the 3rd Battery had destroyed the following enemy weapons and equipment: 236 enemy tanks, 194 antitank guns, 30 artillery pieces, 39 mortars, 179 antitank rifles, 220 machine guns, 1 "Stalin Organ,", 12 armored cars, 52 trucks, 15 bunkers and 4 observation posts.

Sturmgeschütz-Brigade "Samland," as the "Geißel" Brigade was now called, was once again successful during the operational offensive moves to relieve the "Königsberg Fortress" on 7 January and 10 February 1945. It charged forward as far as Metgethen-Moditten to relieve the 5. Panzer-Division (which was under the command of Generalmajor Hoffmann-Schoenborn), and made it possible for the division to break out of the East Prussian capital.

Wischrodt was the brigade's new Command Post. Ammunition, fuel and rations were brought up from Pillau. More and more stragglers from other Sturmgeschütz units arrived there. By the middle of March 1945, the brigade's ration count had risen to 2,000 men. The brigade possessed 47 Sturmgeschütze, with four 15 cm howitzers among them. There was also a "Hummel" battery under Hauptmann Arnold.

In spite of the approaching end, the brigade continued to fight with exemplary loyalty and aggressiveness. On 7 April 1945, Oberwachtmeister Kurt Engelhardt received the Knight's Cross for outstanding bravery. It was awarded to him as he lay severely wounded in the Hospital at Neuhaus. Leutnants Trost and Vogel were killed.

The fighting rapidly grew in intensity in the Königsberg-Fischhausen sector. All of the elements of the brigade were concentrated in this sector. The Soviets tried everything to force a decision. They attacked every day with large groups of ground-attack fighters. The last fighting took place in the woods of Lochstadt. The last Sturmgeschütze and their crews met their fate there. The remnants of the brigade assembled at Pillau for the last time. From there they pulled back to Nickelswalde in the Danzig area.

In the early morning hours of 8 May 1945, the Geißel Brigade was brought to Hela by naval landing craft. They waited there for hours in the falling darkness for a ship. It was exactly 2300 hours when Torpedo Boat T-23 docked. Thanks to the remarkably fine men on guard duty, the brigade embarked within 15 minutes. And the boat was already at sea when, surprisingly, the loudspeaker on board began to blare. However, the words which came from the loud speaker to the listening Sturmartilleristen said: "Attention! Attention! Germany has surrendered unconditionally!"

The war was over. It was like a miracle that Sturmgeschütz-Brigade 232 made it to the west and was saved at the last second. From Copenhagen, they reached Mönckeberg near Kiel a few days later. Release from captivity took place a few weeks after that at Klaustorg near Heiligenhafen. We will let the closing words from the diary of a member of the brigade serve as the final words for the history of this brigade: "We fought firmly believing in the justice of our cause. We have shouldered burdens and loads past the limits of endurance, and we received no thanks. We want no thanks. The loyalty and comradeship, that today and for all time bind us together over the graves of our fallen comrades, are recognition enough that we always did our duty fairly and decently."

Sturmgeschütz-Abteilung 236 (Sturmgeschütz-Brigade 236 and Heeres-Sturmartillerie-Brigade 236)

Sturmgeschütz-Abteilung 236 was formed relatively late—on 17 March 1943—at Jüterbog. This battalion was formed from the 3rd Battery of Sturmgeschütz-Abteilung 189 and Sturmgeschütz-Ersatz-Abteilung 300 at Neiße. Hauptmann Rolf Brede was the first battalion commander. He selected a centaur as the battalion insignia.

Heeres-Sturmartillerie-Brigade 236

Immediately after its formation, the battalion set off to the east. The battalion received its baptism of fire in the Kuibyschew sector. When it struck this, its first blow, the battalion became a legend for the entire front, as it destroyed 139 tanks within a few days. On 7 July 1943 the battalion was mentioned in the Wehrmacht Report on the occasion it having destroyed 150 tanks.

It was employed on the Mius at the beginning of August. There the battalion was attached alternately to the 16. and 23rd Panzer-Divisionen, and also temporarily served as a spearhead for units in the SS-Divisionen "Totenkopf" and "Das Reich" and for the SS-Panzer-Grenadier-Regiment "Der Führer." The battalion suffered numerous losses of men and materiél. Above all, it was the officers who paid a tribute in blood.

In the middle of August, Sturmgeschütz-Abteilung 236 was transferred to the Salawjansk area. Once again, it took heavy casualties in the defensive fighting east of Dubrowna, but it was able to halt the attacking enemy forces. The high point of these operations, however, was the fighting at Isjum. Several Soviet tank brigades attacked at Isjum on 26 August 1943. The tank battle raged for an entire day. The Sturmgeschütz crews surpassed themselves. As evening fell on 26 August, 60 enemy tanks lay burning, shot up, and out of action on the battlefield. And on the following day, the Wehrmacht Report had this to say: "...Likewise, Sturmgeschütz-Abteilung 236 particularly distinguished itself in the fighting for Isjum."

In September, the costly action in the Saporoshje bridgehead took place. The battalion was employed at every threatened point in this bridgehead, and the Sturmgeschütze took heavy losses. By the evening of 14 October, the battalion had exactly 5 Sturmgeschütze which were still serviceable for combat.

The battalion fought in the bend of the Dnjepr in the major defensive battles of early winter. Places such as Kriwoi Rog, Guljai Polje, Nikolajewskaja, Nasorowka and Busuluk cost the battalion heavily in lives. On 14 December 1943, Hauptmann Scherer, commander of 3rd Battery, received the Knight's Cross. This award went to an Sturmartillerie man who knew how to get the very most from his new type of weapon.

When the Soviets began their major operational offensive in the bend of the Dnjepr on 1 February, the entire supply trains of the battalion was destroyed on 2 February 1944. One element of the trains had to be blown up at Michailowka. The battalion occupied a bridgehead on the east bank of the Junkuletz at Schirokoje in order to be able to give the infantry a chance to withdraw and get clear. It went into action there with only 11 Sturmgeschütze left. Despite that, it held off the enemy from this bridgehead until 14 February. Once again, numerous enemy tanks were destroyed. The battalion was redesignated a brigade on 14 February 1944.

But then the brigade—completely worn out and without any further combat value—had to be pulled out of the front and transferred back home for rest and refitting.

After an unbelievable odyssey, in which it traveled first by Panje wagon, then on foot, and finally by rail to Braila, the brigade moved through Rumania, Hungary and Austria to get to the Altengrabow area near Magdeburg, where its reorganization began.

There, Sturmgeschütz-Brigade 236 was given a 4th Battery, which was equipped as an escort battery. This changed Sturmgeschütz-Brigade 236 to a Heeres-Sturmartillerie-Brigade. This occurred on 10 June 1944.

Oberst Günther Hoffmann-Schoenborn, commandant of the Sturmartillerie-Schule said farewell to the brigade on 11 June 1944. All of his best wishes accompanied it. The Oberst was commander of one of the first battalions. He had shown the power of this weapon on both the attack and the defense and had achieved many great things with it. He wanted his Sturmartillerie men to have only the best. When they fought, they were to have the best possible weapons and equipment.

The brigade was transferred into the sector of Heeresgruppe Süd. It was unloaded in the area of Jassy. It went into action on the night of 20 August 1944, when the Soviets managed to make a penetration in the front at Jassy.

The weeks following this employment became a singular nightmare, full of unimaginable terror. The Rumanians withdrew from their alliance with Germany, and this left a completely open flank at Jassy. The Soviets stormed into this gap in the front with the attacking force of an entire army. There were no German troops available to block them. The brigade's tiny Kampfgruppen were committed wherever the battle raged most fiercely. There were always too few Sturmgeschütze and too few escorting infantry. The individual Kampfgruppen were severely mauled, fighting against vastly superior numbers of enemy forces. The combat strength of Heeres-Sturmartillerie-Brigade 236 gradually melted away. The crews fought as infantry wherever the Sturmgeschütze were put out of action.

Only through blind luck did the supply trains and the repair section escape into the Carpathian Mountains. From there, they had to fight their way through to Hungary, thereby avoiding the Soviet grasp.

The rest of the two German armies employed in Rumania found themselves in a gigantic pocket from which there seemed to be no escape. Individual Kampfgruppen under the command of determined officers attempted to break through to the west.

Even Hauptmann Brede, who had commanded the brigade since its formation, formed a Kampfgruppe from the remnants of the brigade and any infantry that it encountered. It was intended that the last combat-ready Sturmgeschütze were to force a breakout.

On 28 August 1944 they were ready. Once again the brigade moved out. It was a fight for survival. But the breakout failed, and the Soviets destroyed the last Sturmgeschütz. The enemy ring was too deeply echeloned for such weak forces to manage a breakout.

The chaos in the pocket took monstrous forms. On 2 September 1944, the fate of every German soldier still caught in the pocket was sealed, and Heeres-Sturmartillerie-Brigade 236 ceased to exist. Fighting bravely up to the last minute, the soldiers lost the battle and their lives and liberty.

In the meantime, the trains had reached the area of Sächsisch-Regen and were billeted there. A few more men of the brigade, who had managed to get out of the pocket alone under adventurous circumstances, showed up during the next few days.

When a continuous main battle line was set up south of the Carpathian Mountains on 12 September 1944, the brigade gave all its materiél to Sturmgeschütz-Brigade 239 which was supposed to be employed there.

The price for these few weeks of constant combat was devastating. Heeres-Sturmartillerie-Brigade 236 had lost 520 men and almost all of its Sturmgeschütze.

On 25 September the survivors were loaded up at Nagy-Karoly. They reached Posen on 6 October. There were 87 men left to form the nucleus for the third reorganization of the formation at the home base of Sturmgeschütz-Ersatz-Abteilung 500.

On 8 November 1944 Major Rudolf Kranz took over the brigade. He had received the Knight's Cross two days earlier. It had been awarded to him as commander of Sturmgeschütz-Brigade 249.

When the Russian Winter Offensive broke loose out of the Baranow Bridgehead on 12 January 1945, the brigade, which had been completely refitted in the meantime, was brought by rail to Rosenberg in east Silesia. The individual batteries went into action as they were unloaded. The brigade managed to build a new front east of the Oder with rapidly cobbled together infantry forces. However, the individual batteries had to pull back to the Oder under increasingly heavy Soviet pressure.

The brigade, once again badly mangled, moved via Welun, Kempen and Breslau to reach the area around Oppeln. It was given new Sturmgeschütze at Oppeln that would allow it to make its presence known in the battle for the Oder. The brigade carried out relief attacks at Brieg, Groß Strehlitz and Burgwasser and, more than once, it had no infantry support for its engagements. Villages and towns already captured by the Soviets were retaken by rapid counterattacks with annihilating assault power and the German soldiers taken prisoner were freed. Above all, however, the brigade managed to hold a corridor open for the masses of refugees streaming back.

On 27 March 1945 the brigade once more went into action as a complete formation at the beginning of the great Russian operational offensive on both sides of Ratibor.

Heavy casualties were inflicted on the enemy in fighting which lasted for days. Above all, the Soviets lost many tanks and guns. But then the brigade had to give way to overwhelming force. It pulled back proudly, in the knowledge that it had faced the enemy as long as humanly possible. So far, the brigade had destroyed no fewer than 499 tanks. All of the Sturmgeschütze in action at Ratibor were lost.

The remnants of the brigade had been transferred for another rest and refitting in Saxony, where it received new Sturmgeschütze. During the relief attacks on Bautzen and Weißenburg, all of the batteries once again gave proof of the unbroken fighting spirit of the Sturmartillerie, when they threw back a vastly superior enemy. The 3rd Battery was cut off in Niesky, but it was able to break free on its own.

It went into action for the last time north of Dresden. Then the brigade was loaded up and moved to Teplitz-Schönau in Czechoslovakia. The war ended there. It broke up into small detachments which were led across the Erz Mountains by their officers to Saxony. Most of the brigade went into American captivity there.

The brigade's victories during its existence were paid for by an incomparably high number of all ranks killed in action. An entire book would be inadequate to express the tragedy of the costly actions of just this one brigade which was completely destroyed several times. May this history ensure that these young German men and their sacrifice are not forgotten.

A Sturmgeschütz III A of Infanterie-Regiment (mot.) "Großdeutschland" during the French Campaign of 1940. Only eight of these vehicles were built. They are easily recognizable by the emergency exit hatch on both sides of the lower hull.

A Sturmgeschütz III B of the 1./Sturmgeschütz-Abteilung 197 during the Balkans Campaign. This unit was later trained on the Jagdpanzer "Ferdinand" and converted to schwere Panzerjäger-Abteilung 653.

A Sturmgeschütz III C of Sturmgeschütz-Batterie 201 during training in Germany. For Barbarossa this unit used a 3-digit numbering system on the superstructure sides.

A Sturmgeschütz III D of Sturmgeschütz-Batterie 184 during Barbarossa. The large white cross and the 2-digit identification number were characteristic of this unit. At the beginning of Barbarossa Sturmgeschütz-Batterie 184 fought on the right flank of Army Group North.

A Sturmgeschütz III C of 2./Sturmgeschütz-Abteilung 197. Note the logs attached to the side to aid in crossing difficult terrain.

A Sturmgeschütz III E of the 2./Sturmgeschütz-Abteilung 192 during the fighting for Gomel in Russia. Sturmgeschütz-Abteilung 192 advanced from the Bug River and fought from 22 June 1941 to the end of March 1942 on the Eastern Front.

Detail view of assault gun "13" from the 1. Batterie in 1942 (red insignia).

The Sturmgeschütz III E (with the 75 mm Sturmkanone 40 L43) equipped the 3./Sturmgeschütz-Abteilung 203. It had an elephant as a unit symbol. The color was different for the headquarters section and the line batteries. From mid-1942 on all assault guns were repainted in sand with areas of green camouflage.

The Sturmgeschütz III F/8 of Oberwachtmeister Kochanowski of the 2./Sturmgeschütz-Abteilung 201 during the fighting in the summer of 1942. The second and third batteries were attached to the 24. Panzer-Division and fought in the south during the second half of 1942. The first battery was attached to the 78. Sturm-Division. Note the impressive tally of 45 kill rings on the gun barrel.

This Sturmgeschütz III G (the early version of the final Sturmgeschütz III variant) was from the 2./Sturmgeschütz-Abteilung 226 and fought during the second battle of Lake Lagoda on the northern front near Leningrad. Sturmgeschütz-Abteilung 226 fought alongside schwere Panzer-Abteilung 502 (Tiger) with great success.

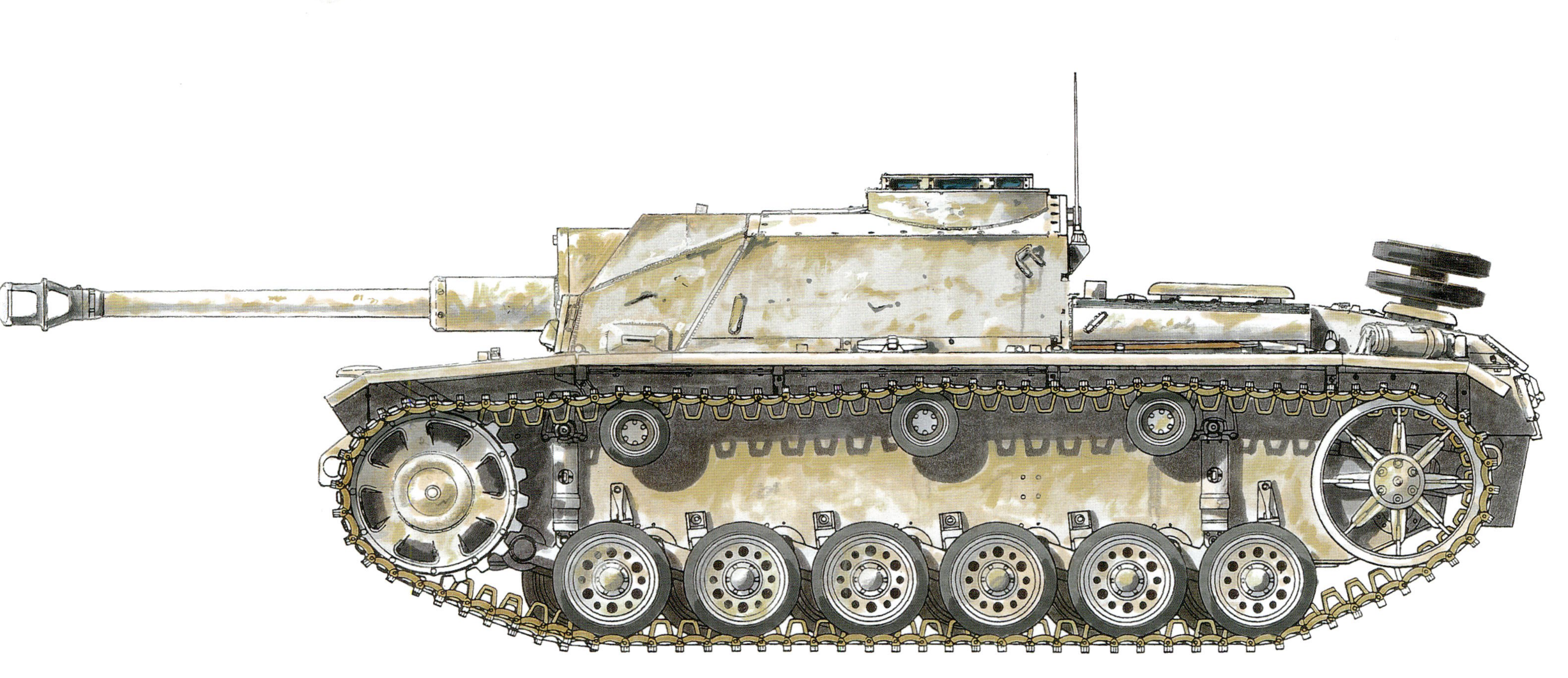

A Sturmgeschütz III G of Sturmgeschütz-Brigade 325 in Rumania. Some of this unit's vehicles did not use a numbering system. Instead, the vehicles were given individual animal names such as "Puma," "Löwe" (lion), "Panther" and "Luchs" (lynx).

A Sturmgeschütz III G of an unknown unit during the last winter of the war, 1944/45. Note that due to a hit on the side, a "Schürze" has been replaced under the Balkan cross. Note also the addition of the vehicle's number on the gun commander's cupola.

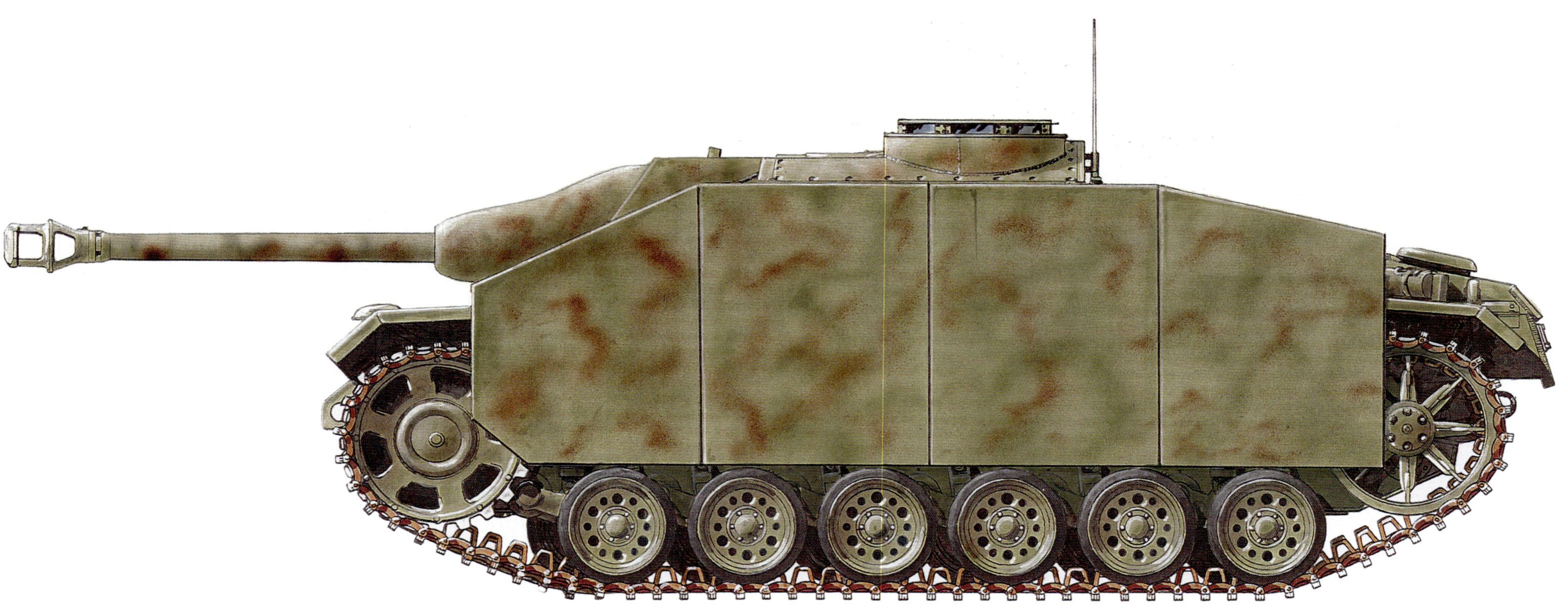

A Sturmgeschütz III G of Sturmgeschütz-Brigade 280 during the Arnhem battles. The vehicles of this unit are usually incorrectly identified as belonging to 10. SS-Panzer-Division "Frundsberg." Although no unit insignia were visible at Arnhem, the assault gun crews all wore army uniforms and insignia.

A Sturmgeschütz III G of Sturmgeschütz-Brigade 341 in Normandy. The unit fought for the first time on 31 July 1944 in the Avranches—Brecey sector, suffering considerable losses.

A Sturmhaubitze 42 with 10.5 cm howitzer belonging to the 2./Sturmgeschütz-Brigade 394 at the Normandy Front during the fighting for Vire.

A Jagdpanzer IV L48 from the 5. Panzer-Division on the Eastern Front (Army Group North) in August 1944. This vehicle was part of Panzerjäger-Abteilung 53 under the command of Hauptmann von Ramin. The unit was mentioned in the Wehrmacht daily report due to its excellent combat performance on 27 August 1944.

A Jagdpanzer IV L48, possibly of the 7. Panzer-Division, in February 1945 on the Eastern Front. Note the two steel roadwheels at the front (copied from Russian KV-series tanks), used to counteract the excessive nose heaviness due to the overhang of the long-barreled gun, which was same one used in the Panzerkampfwagen V "Panther."

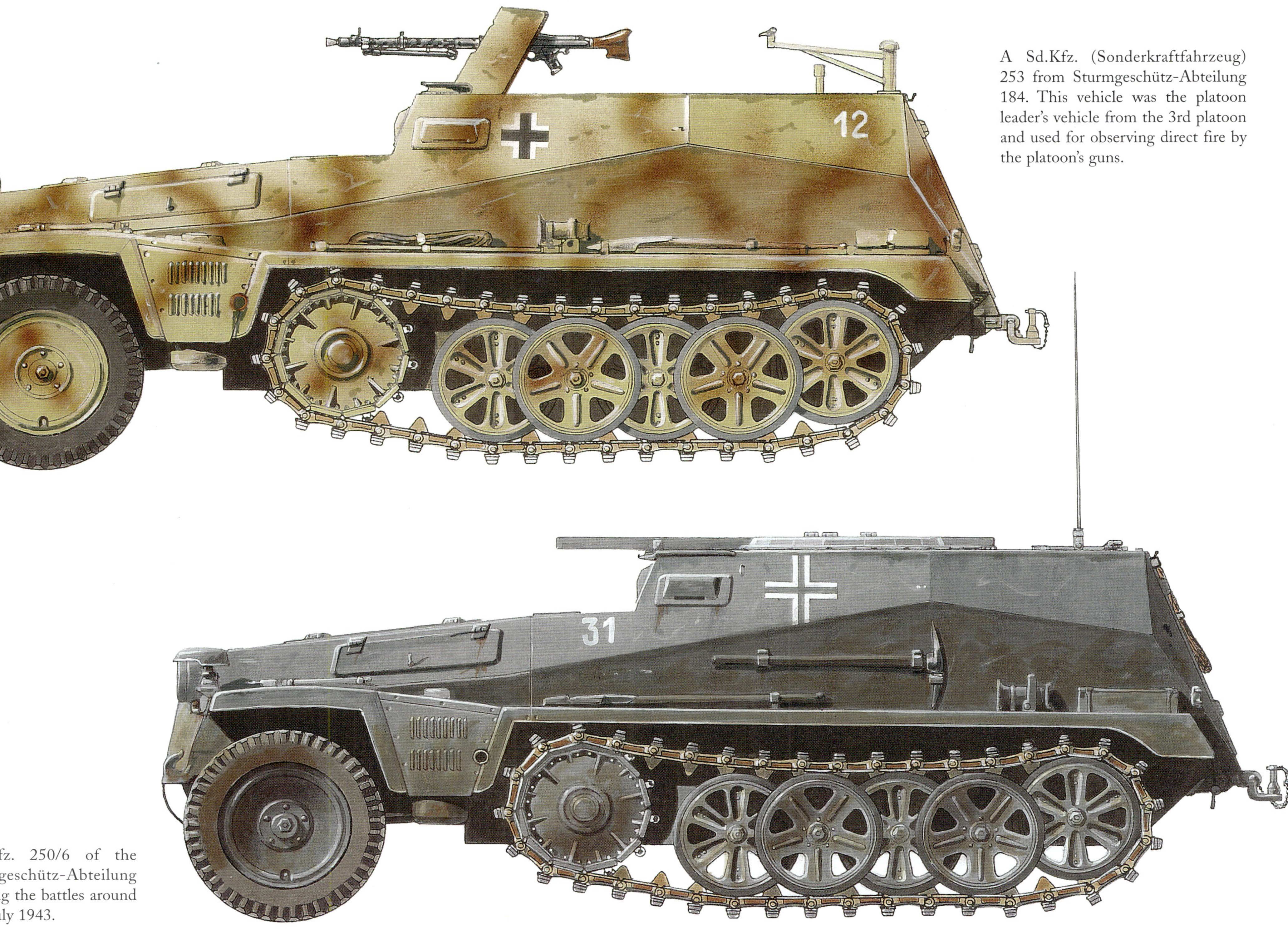

A Sd.Kfz. (Sonderkraftfahrzeug) 253 from Sturmgeschütz-Abteilung 184. This vehicle was the platoon leader's vehicle from the 3rd platoon and used for observing direct fire by the platoon's guns.

A Sd.Kfz. 250/6 of the 2./Sturmgeschütz-Abteilung 185 during the battles around Orel in July 1943.

A Sd.Kfz. 250/6 of the 1./Sturmgeschütz-Abteilung 191 during the initial phase of Operation Barbarossa.

Rear view of the Sd.Kfz. 253 seen in the previous plate. Although used as a command vehicle, the Sd.Kfz. 253 was not popular with commanders due to its more limited mobility and thin armor.

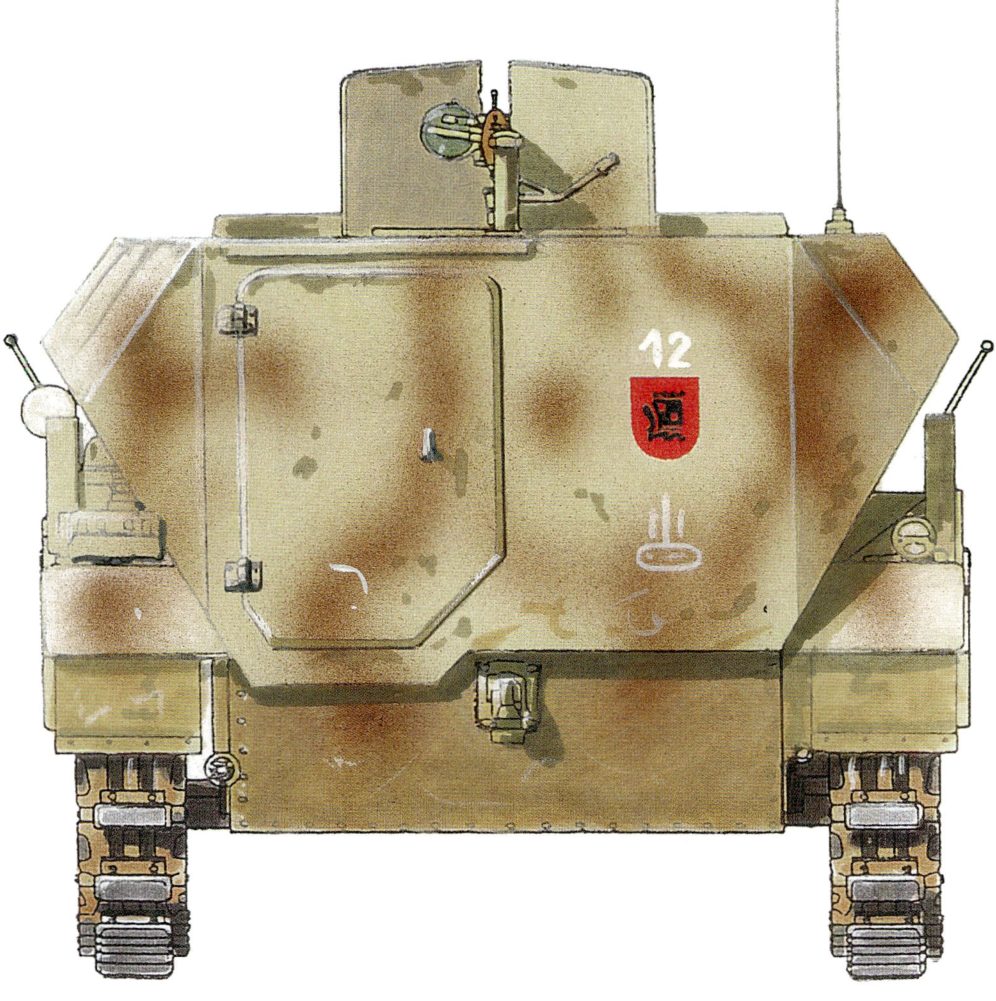

A Sd.Kfz. 250/6 of the 2./Sturmgeschütz-Abteilung 185 during the battle of Kursk in the Orel sector in July 1943.

Knight's Cross and Oakleaves recipient Hugo Primozic.

Right: A recruiting poster for volunteers for the assault artillery branch of the army. This poster features the new, long-barreled Sturmgeschütz III F. The heading: "Quite the fellow."

Left: German propaganda poster aimed at demoralized Russian troops featuring victorious German soldiers with an assault gun in the background.

Training movement at the Sturmgeschütz-Schule at Burg (near Magdeburg) using a Sturmgeschütz III F.

A nice view of a Sturmgeschütz III F at Burg.

Left: A Sturmgeschütz III F named "Ulla"—for a wife or girlfriend back in Germany. The camouflage is very interesting with small green or brown mottled patterns over a base coat of sand. The soldier with a white cloth around his hat is a "Schiedsrichter" (umpire) during maneuver exercises.

Below: A Sturmgeschütz III F, the first model with the long-barreled 75 mm L/48 cannon.

Sturmgeschütz III G's with single-baffle muzzle brakes.

Sturmgeschütz III F/8 in typical Russian open terrain. The gun barrel is near maximum elevation as this assault gun is being used in an indirect fire mode against a distant target.

After the action at the Koza Canal. The first platoon of Sturmgeschütz-Batterie 191 has destroyed 12 enemy tanks with its F model Sturmgeschütze.

A Sturmgeschütz III F belonging to the brigade surgeon of Sturmgeschütz-Brigade 191, Dr. Schröder, negotiates difficult terrain.

A Sturmgeschütz III F which probably belongs to either Sturmgeschütz-Brigade 191 or 237.

Bogged down Sturmgeschütz III F being recovered and brought back into action.

A Sturmgeschütz III F with "Ostketten" (literally: "East tracks"). The Ostketten were grousers which were fitted on to the normal tracks to reduce ground pressure and allow increased traction and mobility in difficult terrain, especially snow, mud and ice. This assault gun fought with the 19. Panzer-Division in the Ukraine during the winter of 1942.

A late model Sturmgeschütz III F of Sturmgeschütz-Brigade 197 in 1943.

The long-barreled G model assault guns arrive at Sturmgeschütz-Brigade 226.

The 2./Sturmgeschütz-Brigade 226 prepares for the attack at Ssinjawino.

Another view of the newly arrived Sturmgeschütz III G's at Sturmgeschütz-Brigade 226.

A Sturmgeschütz III G of Sturmgeschütz-Brigade 226 at Lake Lagoda.

Left: Details of the Sturmgeschütz III G: gun optics, scissors scope and observation slits.

Right: Another Sturmgeschütz III G of Sturmgeschütz-Brigade 226 after the second battle of Lake Lagoda.

Left: A bogged down T34 is being towed away by the battery commander's assault gun (2./Sturmgeschütz-Brigade 226) during the second battle for Lake Lagoda.

Right: A Sturmgeschütz III G of Sturmgeschütz-Brigade 226. Of interest here is the external stowage.

Top: A Sturmgeschütz III G of Sturmgeschütz-Brigade 226 during or just after heavy combat, as indicated by the spent shell casings next to the vehicle.

Facing page, top: Sturmgeschütz III G "311" of 3./ Sturmgeschütz-Brigade 226. The number is in black over sand paint while the rest of the vehicle has recently been painted dark green for the spring period. This photograph was taken after the second battle for Lake Lagoda in 1943.

Facing page, bottom: The signals center for Sturmgeschütz-Abteilung 234.

Right: A pack of Russian T34's attacks Sturmgeschütz-Brigade 226.

The Sturmartillerist and his gun (a Sturmgeschütz III F). The Iron Cross, First Class figures prominently on his distinctive gray Sturmartillerie uniform tunic.

An early model Sturmgeschütz III G without any camouflage scheme. The tactical insignia on the right-front hull indicates an assault gun unit; the "T" indicates a Panzerjäger-Kompanie. Note the "Notek" lamp for driving under blackout conditions.

The Sturmgeschütz III G of Hugo Primozic in 1943. It has 42 "kill rings" on the barrel.

With a bridge too weak to support the weight of an assault gun, this Sturmhaubitze G (mounting a 10.5 cm L/28 gun) fords the brook instead.

A Sturmgeschütz III G with "Ostketten" in support of the SS-Panzer-Korps at Kharkov in 1943.

An early-model Sturmgeschütz III G with "Ostketten," also at Kharkov in 1943.

Above: A Sturmgeschütz III F with the long-barreled 75 mm L/43 gun belonging to a Waffen-SS unit during the fighting for Kharkov in the winter of 1942.

Right: A Sturmgeschütz III G of SS-Sturmgeschütz-Abteilung 1 "Leibstandarte SS Adolf Hitler" at Kharkov.

Top: A Sturmgeschütz III G of SS-Sturmgeschütz-Abteilung 1 "Leibstandarte SS Adolf Hitler." Note the kill markings and the scissors periscope.

Facing page, top: A Sturmgeschütz III G of SS-Sturmgeschütz-Abteilung 1 "Leibstandarte SS Adolf Hitler" at Kharkov.

Facing page, bottom: Sturmgeschütz III G's of SS-Sturmgeschütz-Abteilung 1 "Leibstandarte SS Adolf Hitler" at Kharkov.

Above: A Sturmgeschütz III F mounting the "Ostketten." While a boon in added maneuverability, the grousers were knocked off relatively easily and proved to be a maintenance nightmare for gun crews.

Top: Loading a Sturmgeschütz III G of a SS unit (possibly "Totenkopf") with 75 mm rounds.

Facing page, top: A Sturmgeschütz III F named "Bismarck" of SS-Sturmgeschütz-Abteilung 2 "Das Reich" after the battle for Kharkov in the late summer or early fall of 1943.

Facing page, bottom: A Sturmgeschütz III G of SS-Sturmgeschütz-Abteilung 3 "Totenkopf."

Right: Dinner in the field. Members of an unidentified SS unit (possibly "Totenkopf") line up for rations. Note the interesting mixture of uniforms among the personnel. In the background are Sturmgeschütz III G's.

A column of Sturmgeschütz III G's from SS-Sturmgeschütz-Abteilung 3 "Totenkopf" at Kursk.

A Sturmgeschütz III G of SS-Sturmgeschütz-Abteilung 2 "Das Reich" during Operation Citadel. Note the spare tracks and stowage box.

A Sturmgeschütz III F/8 crosses an antitank ditch at Kursk.

A Sturmgeschütz III G, with concrete-reinforced armor, at the end of fighting for Orel.

Top: Stuck in the mud: A FAMO 18-ton half-track in recovery operations.

Above: The Soviet T34/76. Here: a very early model.

Left: The enemy: a T34/76 lying in ambush.

Sturmgeschütz-Abteilung 237 (Sturmgeschütz-Brigade 237; Sturm-Panzer-Abteilung 218; and, Sturm-Panzer-Abteilung 219)

Sturmgeschütz-Brigade 237

This battalion was formed in the summer of 1943 at the Sturmgeschütz-Ersatz-Abteilung at Posen. Its insignia was a leaping greyhound. In the fall of that year it was sent to the central sector of the Eastern Front, and it was in action there effective October 1943. It fought at Tschaussy, east of Mogilew, from 27 to 31 October 1943. It cleared the enemy out of the villages of Barischewka, Skwarsk and Prilepowka. In particular, Oberleutnant Plate distinguished himself during that fighting. On 31 October he was severely wounded and died of his wounds on the following day. He never knew that he was awarded the German Cross in Gold. He was buried in the military cemetery at Mogilew. Wachtmeister Rombach was also killed on the same day, after he had destroyed three T-34's in a fight with Soviet tanks.

After that fighting, the battalion went into new ready positions at Warwarino and Kamarnitzka. However, it was not employed there, because it was transferred by rail on 16 November via Mogilew-Slobin to Usa in the Gomel area. By 17 November the battalion was already employed. The fighting at Bartschenok and Tschernjatzka Polje lasted for four days. Unteroffizier Kuhlmann was killed there on 20 November.

After taking up ready positions again, the battalion pulled back through Rogin to the area of Slobin on 21 November. It had a few days of rest before going back into ready positions in the areas of Schdanowa-Mormal-Alexandroff. It was employed at Bor and in particular at the Jachtschitzky railroad station, in fighting which lasted until 6 December. The "Greyhounds" did honor to their name. The enemy pulled back wherever the battalion went into action, leaving burning and shot up tanks behind on the battleground.

But the battalion suffered high casualties as well. On 12 December it had to be pulled back from Bobruisk through Krasni Bereg-Rogatschew to Mogilew for repairs. But by 27 December it was back in new ready positions in the Nikonowitschi sector. The battalion held its own in the fighting at Pribor from 4 and 5 January 1944 and while protecting the withdrawal axis up to 17 January 1944. It was moved through Dubowoje to Mogilew and from there sent to the combat sectors at Blagowitschi and Schtschekotowo. On 14 February 1944 the battalion was redesignated a brigade. Gefreiter Hecktor was killed at Schtschekotowo on 13 February 1944.

From Schtschekotowo the brigade was transported by rail on 14 February to Witebsk, and from there on back to Star Byschoff, where it was finally unloaded.

The brigade then went into action at a number of places in rapid succession. From 22 to 25 February it fought at Wiljaschowka, Mogutschi and Taimanowo. Then it was given a covering force mission in the Komaritschi area. The brigade provided security there until 7 March 1944 before it returned once again to Mogilew for repairs on 14 March 1944.

The brigade went back to Mogilew for a third time after new, costly actions south of Tschaussy and at Ssutoki. It was moved out of there by rail and committed into action west of Kowel. The brigade fought on the Turja River at Turiczcany until 3 May 1944. After that it was employed in the Janowka, Smydin, Tarowiscze and Kruhel sectors until 4 July. Leutnant Werner Fiehler of 3rd Battery was killed during this fighting on 21 June in Smydin, west of Kowel. He was buried near the church in Smydin.

In the days that followed, serious enemy disruptions of the withdrawal made further heavy demands on the brigade and its commanders. The fighting at Maciejow demanded great sacrifices. The brigade passed through Rudnia and Stara Huta to reach the Gorniki area on the Pripet Marshes. The brigade provided cover for additional infantry withdrawals in its combat sector from Osawa and Adampol to Davidy. Then, with all the strength it had left, it smashed open a breakout route to Miedzyrzec and held it open until the last German soldier had made it through.

Completely shattered, the brigade was pulled out of the fighting and sent back through Warsaw to Möckern near Magdeburg for reorganization.

Sturmgeschütz-Brigade 237 was transferred to the Panzertruppe and redesignated a Sturm-Panzer-Abteilung. It was initially designated Sturm-Panzer-Abteilung 218 and sent to Camp Zwettl at the Döllersheim Troop Training Area for training. It was soon renamed Sturm-Panzer-Abteilung 219.

These Sturmpanzer were a new development conceptually based on the Sturmgeschütz and built on a Panzer IV chassis. They had a heavy infantry support gun of 15 cm caliber with separate cartridges and shells in place of the various Sturmartillerie cannons. The front of these Sturmpanzer had 120 mm thick vertical armor plating.

This heavy armor made the vehicle extremely nose-heavy, which caused difficulties with the steering brake and the traversing gear for the cross shaft. Long road marches were out of the question with this monster. Its speed was 16 kilometers per hour cross-country. From the tactical point of view, therefore, it could not be employed as a tank.

Its maximum effective range for accuracy and terminal effect, however, was around 3,500 meters with a number 6 charge. That meant that the Sturmpanzer would be very suitable for defense. On the offense, they were intended to be positioned at short intervals up to 500 meters behind the Panzer and Sturmgeschütze.

They were reorganized as three line companies and a supply company. The line companies consisted only of the gun crews, a communications section, a Spieß and a company clerk. The command and staff list for Sturm-Panzer-Abteilung 219 has survived. It reads:

Commander: Major Paul Friedrich Schaupensteiner
Adjutant: Leutnant Waldemar Preiss
Orderly Officer: Leutnant Warnfried, Leutnant Heynemann
Battalion Surgeon: Assistenz-Arzt Otto Vinke
Maintenance Officer: Oberleutnant Paul Vacque

Headquarters Company Commander: Oberleutnant Hans Otto Meyer
Terrain Reconnaissance Platoon Leader: Leutnant Friedrich Brucks, Leutnant Karlheinz Burmeister

Supply Company Commander: Oberleutnant Heinz Schütt
Orderly Officer: Leutnant Walter Affeld
Weapons Officer: Leutnant Walter Heinzelmann
Assistant Surgeon: Unterarzt Dr. Wilhelm Marasch
1st Company Commander: Hauptmann Ludwig Bertram
Platoon Leaders: Leutnant Hugo Block, Leutnant Heinrich Lücking, Leutnant Adolf Garthe
2nd Company Commander: Oberleutnant Rolf Meißner
Platoon Leaders: Leutnant Bernhard Sowada, Leutnant Heinrich Becker
3rd Company Commander: Oberleutnant Fritz Otto
Platoon Leaders: Leutnant Hans-Diether Hofmann, Leutnant Helfried Müller, Leutnant Anders Rathjen
Tracked Maintenance Section Officer: Leutnant Herbert Stöcker
Technical Inspector: Inspector Michael Guillot

After intensive training the battalion was placed on alert on 15 October 1944. Preparations for a coup by the Hungarian Regent, Admiral Horthy, had leaked out. The 1st Company took over all of the 10 Sturmpanzer, that had been delivered up to that point and moved through Vienna, Györ (Raab) and Komaron to Budapest, with the battalion commander at the head of the company.

Arriving in Budapest on 19 October, it found that the explosive situation had been resolved three days earlier. For this reason the battalion was not unloaded there, but was sent on to St. Martin in Slovakia where it was taken off the train in the morning of 23 October. The rest of the battalion remained at its home station. The formation and provisioning of the battalion with personnel, Sturmpanzer and vehicles continued.

The main body was rail loaded between 3 and 6 December and sent along the Waag River through Sillein and Komaron to Kisber. From there the battalion road marched to Stuhlweißenburg.

The Red Army had already reached the southern shore of Lake Balaton in the Stuhlweißenburg battle sector on 7 December. The battalion had been selected along with other units to break the momentum of the Soviet attack. Accordingly, it moved out in the direction of Budapest to Baracskar, where it was employed on 12 December.

As a part of the defense, it managed to stop a tank-supported Soviet attack at Baracskar and destroyed the first enemy tanks in this battle sector. Then the battalion went to support one of the friendly attacks southwest of Kismarton and was able to help eliminate a Red Army penetration there.

It moved on 17 December in the direction of Kapolnasnyek on the north shore of Lake Valence to participate in the counterattack to the south and southeast of Kapolnasnyek. A Sturmpanzer was put out of action there by a direct hit and the crew killed.

Another Sturmpanzer was disabled with a burst barrel, so that the commander of the 1st Company prohibited firing the cannon until the defect was found. The last combat-ready Sturmpanzer of 1st Company had to be turned over to the 2nd Company.

The operational units of the battalion moved to Csakvar when Russian tank forces broke through between Lowasbereny and Vereb and wheeled far behind the weak German line.

The objective of this Russian attack was to cut off Budapest, and they closed the ring around the Hungarian capital on 23 December.

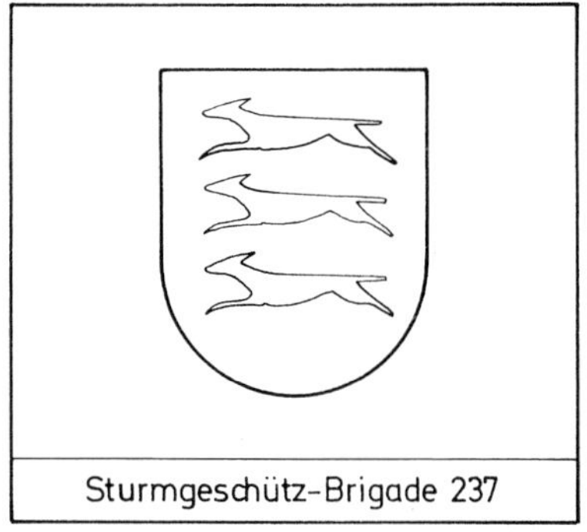
Sturmgeschütz-Brigade 237

Although the 1st Company could be pulled back to Bicske and then to Nagyigmand, elements of the 2nd Company and the entire 3rd Company under Oberleutnant Otto along with a few Panthers from another unit were encircled. They were able to fight their way out with the effective support of Major Rudel's Stukas, after these aircraft had bombed and strafed a hole in the surrounding ring of Russians.

On 24 December 1944 Leutnant Sowada was killed at Vertessomio. Bernhard Sowada had already received the Knight's Cross as a section leader in the 1./Sturmgeschütz-Abteilung 237 on 12 October 1943. He was posthumously promoted to Oberleutnant for bravery in the face of the enemy.

Leutnant Becker of the 2nd Company was in command of the third Sturmpanzer to blow up with a burst barrel. Four men of the crew were killed. (An investigation discovered that a series of cartridges had been filled with dynamite instead of the normal propellant. Many considered it sabotage, but the identity of the perpetrator was never discovered.)

The retreat then continued back through Raab and Komaron to Kisber. From there, the battalion was to take part in the attack planned for 4 January 1945 to relieve the besieged Budapest. It participated in the attack but had to turn back on 13 January 1945 when the attack was canceled just before reaching Budapest.

The battalion then moved on towards Stuhlweißenburg in the attack sector of the 23. Panzer-Division. A number of T-34's were destroyed, and the attack reached the Danube on 26 January 1945.

The Sturmpanzer of Leutnant Garthe was knocked out during the fighting south of Lake Balaton. The attempt to relieve Budapest from the south also had to be called off. The Sturmpanzer pulled back with the other units of the Wehrmacht to the prepared lines between Stuhlweißenburg and Komaron.

A Soviet assault wave hit there on 20 March 1945, which broke through this shaky line and forced the Sturmpanzer battalion to join the general retreat in the withdrawal to Steinamanger and Günz. On the way back, the Sturmpanzer of Wachtmeister Delbos was lost to a bomb. The entire crew was killed by this direct hit.

Bruck was reached after marching through Graz. The battalion was rail loaded there on 4 April. The transport by rail went through Leoben and Linz to Budweis and then on to Frauenburg.

Effective 15 February Major Schaupensteiner turned over command of the battalion to Hauptmann Trumpa.

The 2nd Company, which arrived at the Döllersheim Troop Training Area on 22 April 1945, was transferred to Oberndorf, to be retrained as Panzerjäger on the Skoda "Hetzer."

This conversion meant that this Sturmgeschütz unit had gone into action in nearly every type of assault and armored artillery. Its cadre was still made up of men from the old Sturmgeschütz-Abteilung 237. We give them just recognition here.

When it became known that the crews of the Sturmartillerie and the Sturmpanzer were to be used as infantry from then on, their last commander, Hauptmann Trumpa, managed to get the Heeresgruppe to which is was allocated to approve the formation of Panzerjagd-Brigade 123 "Trumpa" from the battalion (without its 3rd Company). The new organization was effective as of 25 April 1945. This brigade never saw action as a unit. The brigade pulled back to the west to reach the demarcation line at Freistadt. When it arrived there on 10 May, it was disarmed but not allowed to cross the demarcation line.

Everyone on that side of the line was handed over to the Russians. A few of the Sturmartillerie men managed to save themselves by sneaking across to the other side unnoticed. They broke through to freedom, in some cases crossing all of Germany. A few groups of civilians joined these veteran soldiers, and they too escaped to freedom.

Sturmgeschütz-Abteilung 239 (Sturmgeschütz-Brigade 239)

Heeres-Sturmartillerie-Brigade 239

Sturmgeschütz-Abteilung 239 was formed in Baruth, south of Berlin, in June 1943. Hauptmann Reppenhagen was its first commander, and the adjutant was Oberleutnant Erwin Patkze. Hauptmann Pohl commanded the 1st Battery. However, the battalion was really formed by Hauptmann Pohl as Hauptmann Reppenhagen received bomb damage leave for Hamburg on several occasions. The battalion insignia, a sun wheel, was selected because Robert Ley, the Reich-Arbeits-Dienst leader, had taken on sponsorship of the battalion.

In August 1943 the battalion was moved east. It reached Poltava after five days on the train, and it was unloaded on the east bank of the Dnjepr. There followed three days of rest, before the battalion moved to Achtyrka. It went into action for the first time at the beginning of September at Achtyrka.

In the following period, the battalion was involved in heavy fighting. Hauptmann Pohl was severely wounded in action east of Mirgorow on 11 September 1943 and had to leave the battalion.

The battalion continued to fight at the hot spots in its sector. Sometimes it had to put long intervals of marching behind it before it could come to grips with the enemy. The high point of this fighting was an engagement lasting 72 hours, which demanded the most in doggedness and courage from every single man in the battalion. High losses were the price of great success.

After this fighting, the battalion was pulled out of the line, rested and refitted and then sent to Rumania. Sturmgeschütz-Abteilung 239 became Sturmgeschütz-Brigade 239 on 14 February 1944. The brigade was committed in Rumania under a new commander, Hauptmann Bundesmann, in the summer of 1944. The brigade was officially redesignated as Heeres-Sturmartillerie-Brigade 239 on 10 June 1944, although it was frequently referred to by its old designation of Sturmgeschütz-Brigade 239 in official reports.

Its combat operations in Rumania began under an unlucky star. The brigade became immediately involved in heavy fighting while still unloading off the ramps in the railroad station. The 1st Battery was almost totally destroyed in the fighting.

The brigade was severely weakened once again in the subsequent summer fighting. In August 1944 Oberleutnant Kettl arrived at Heeres-Sturmartillerie-Brigade 239 from the completely destroyed Sturmgeschütz-Brigade 236 and formed a new 3rd Battery. The survivors of Sturmgeschütz-Brigaden 184, 189 and 236 were assembled in this battery along with the remnants of the 3./ Sturmgeschütz-Brigade 239. Leutnants Wahle, Heer, and Marx were the section leaders of this new battery and Franz Aßmann was the "Spieß".

At first, while being formed in the Transylvanian hinterland, this battery still didn't have any Sturmgeschütze. When the 4. Gebirgs-Division reported that there were six Sturmgeschütze in its sector, Oberleutnant Kettl hurried there and "snatched them up at the last minute." The battery then went into action as an independent battery with the 4. Gebirgs-Division. Under the command of Oberleutnant Kettl, it fought magnificently, especially in the frontlines of the infantry. The battery was given high praise in several orders of the day. On 29 October 1944 the Wehrmacht Report also mentioned it: "The 3rd Battery of Sturmgeschütz-Brigade 239 under the command of Oberleutnant Kettl has especially distinguished itself in the heavy fighting in southern Hungary."

The battery was in action with the 357. Infanterie-Division along the banks of the Gran from Christmas 1944 until 15 February 1945. It was attached to this threatened division directly by the Heeresgruppe.

Oberleutnant Kettl fought at the head of his battery with great personal élan and he provided outstanding tactical leadership. The battery was known as the "Proud 3rd" to every unit in this sector of operations.

At the end of February 1945, the battery returned to the brigade to whose history it had contributed so much. The end of the brigade lies shrouded in darkness. We only know that it remained loyal to the traditions of true soldiers.

Sturmgeschütz-Brigade 242 (and Selbständige Sturmgeschütz-Batterie "Afrika")

The staff and 1st and 2nd Batteries of this battalion were assembled on 1 November 1942 at the Jüterbog Troop Training Area, in the village of Zinna. The 3rd Battery was formed in the village of Grüna at the edge of the Troop Training Area. The personnel for this new battalion came mostly from Sturmgeschütz-Ersatz-Abteilung 300 at Neiße. The officer's command and staff position list is incomplete:

Commander: Hauptmann Basserer
Adjutant: Oberleutnant Dahlke
Commander 1st Battery: Hauptmann Benz
Commander 2nd Battery: Oberleutnant Schmidt
Commander 3rd Battery: Oberleutnant Firnhaber

This battalion was selected for employment in Africa. The Commander-in-Chief of Panzerarmee-Afrika, Generaloberst Erwin Rommel, was eager to have such an assault group to place at the head of his attacking units and, above all, later on, to have it for a defensive wedge during the retreat to the west. In any case, he didn't get his wish, for instead of Sturmgeschütz-Abteilung 242, only the 1st Battery arrived in Africa. At the end of October 1942, the 2nd and 3rd Batteries of this new battalion were diverted to the southeast, to Hungary. Let us first turn our attention to the 1st Battery, which was sent to Africa.

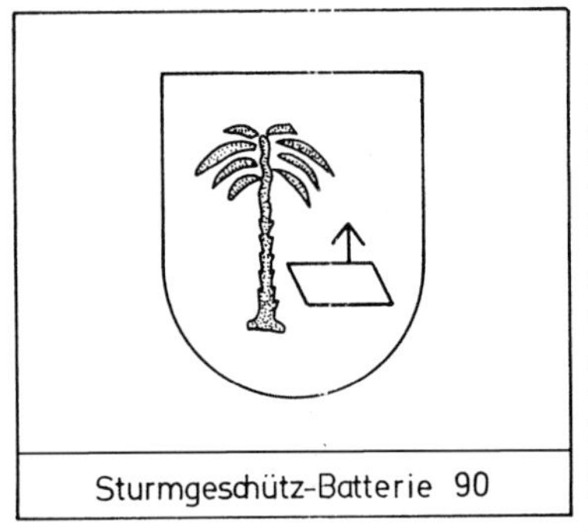

The 1st Battery was under the command of Hauptmann Benz. Oberleutnant Gilig and Leutnant Brendel were also in this battery. Hauptwachtmeister Grotzke became the "Spieß." The battery had six long-barreled 7.5 guns. The final teletype from the battalion staff read: "1st Battery detached from unit. Good Luck!" The 1st Battery traveled by rail over the Brenner Pass to Naples. In Naples is was transported to Sicily via Siebel ferries.

During the sea movement from Trapani the battery was attacked several times. Two Sturmgeschütze and a prime mover with trailer were sunk.

The battery arrived in Tunis. It was attached to Artillerie-Regiment 90 of the 90. leichte "Afrika"-Division. By the time the battery had arrived, Panzerarmee-Afrika had already withdrawn to Tunis. Shortly after that, the battery was placed under the operation control of Fallschirm-Brigade "Ramcke," which had saved itself through an adventurous withdrawal in captured English vehicles.

It was successfully used with Fallschirm-Regiment "Barenthin" in the northern sector of the Tunisian front and was always able to stop the enemy in the defensive fighting. It was also attached temporarily to the division commanded by von Manteuffel, where it was used splendidly by the small, wiry von Manteuffel, who understood armor so well and who was later to become a General der Panzertruppen. "If I had had the entire battalion there," said Hasso von Manteuffel, "I would have pushed the attackers back into the sea!"

When the final thrust for the capture of Tunisia began, and the US 1st Army and the British 8th Army swept the Tunisian mountains and roads clear to the sea with a steel broom, the battery, in action with the armored Kampfgruppe of Oberst Irkens, managed to score some successes and held the enemy back until the infantry units could be withdrawn. After initial good success, the battery was caught in the sweeping pincer movement by the British 8th Army and the American 1st Army. The battery was thrown back again and again to the north and the coast. Finally, the battery fought at Kap Bon Peninsula, where it was captured by the British on 11 May 1943.

The men of the 1./Sturmgeschütz-Abteilung 242 went into British captivity, and they were sent to the prisoner-of-war camp at Medjez el Bab. In Constantine, part of the battery was handed over to the French, who had requested "40 men or 20 horses" for forced labor.

At the end of July 1943, the men began their trip to captivity in America at Casablanca. From Norfolk, they were sent to the Huntsville Camp in Texas. There, Unteroffizier Oehm was sent to Alva in Oklahoma as punishment. He met with other members of the battery in the Alva Camp, including the "Spieß," Oberwachtmeister Grotzke.

They were released in February 1946. The way home ended in Le Havre where, in spite of valid papers releasing them as prisoners-of-war, the French took them from the ship and transported them to the lead mines in the Pyrenees. They finally returned home at the end of December 1948. They had spent five and a half years in captivity.

The majority of Sturmgeschütz-Battalion 242 was committed in Russia.

The staff, the Headquarters Battery and the 2nd and 3rd Batteries of Sturmgeschütz-Abteilung 242 were converted to "Winter-East" preparations and, beginning on 4 January 1943, were loaded up by rail at Jüterbog. The battalion went through Posen, Warsaw, Minsk, Kursk, Belgorod and Kupjansk to Ostrogoshsk, south of Woronesch by rail.

The 2nd and 3rd Batteries were committed as they were unloading on 12 January 1943. They were to intercept a Hungarian division retreating back from the Don area and to cover them in a temporary blocking position.

Oberleutnant Firnhaber, Section Leader in the 3rd Battery, was killed during this operation.

Both batteries destroyed seven Russian tanks in several duels during the fighting retreat between the Don and Ostrogoshsk. The battalion was attached to the 168. Infanterie-Division which had also just arrived there. There was heavy fighting against the Soviet troops which had surrounded this division in the struggle for Ostrogoshsk. The town had been declared a fortress.

All available Sturmgeschütze were used as a spearhead and to cover flanks. Shooting on the move, they pushed through and crushed the Russian infantry. Then they went back to fight enemy tanks, doing the seemingly impossible. The breakout and breakthrough succeeded.

Many of the members of the battalion were killed or wounded. The staff and the 3rd Battery reached the village of Gustomoj near Ljgow by way of Nowy Oskol. The rest of the 2nd Battery, which had lost some of its tanks and Sturmgeschütze, was used as infantry.

After a month of combat the battalion received orders by way of Heeres-Artillerie-Kommando 30 to return to Jüterbog by rail for a refitting. Between 22 and 27 February 1943, the surviving and unwounded soldiers returned to the village of Zinna near Jüterbog. Fifty percent of the men in the battalion had been killed or wounded or became missing in the recent fighting.

The reorganization of the battalion was not completed. Although it received all the necessary personnel replacements, the battalion did not receive adequate motorized equipment, especially with respect to Sturmgeschütze. It was intended to equip it anew in Italy, and then, like the 1st Battery, employ it in North Africa.

The Commander, Hauptmann Benz, had just returned from Africa. Oberleutnant Dahlke remained as adjutant. The three battery commanders were: 1st Battery, Oberleutnant Dreier; 2nd Battery, Oberleutnant Kutscher; and, 3rd Battery, Oberleutnant Pohl (Headquarters Battery).

Since Heeresgruppe Africa capitulated on 12 May 1943, and the battalion could no longer be employed in Africa, the battalion was moved to the area of Pisa-Livorno. It was moved to Sardinia in the middle of June—section by section—with the equipment on ferries. The personnel had been sent ahead in Ju-52's. The battalion took southeast of Oristano. The battalion made no contact with the enemy, but there were many casualties from the endemic malaria.

Attached to the 90. leichte "Afrika"-Division, it remained on Sardinia until the island was abandoned in the first week of September. It was used as rear guard but didn't fire a shot.

The unit was then shifted to Corsica. The battalion went to Bonifacio and to Porto Vecchio. Shortly thereafter it was transferred

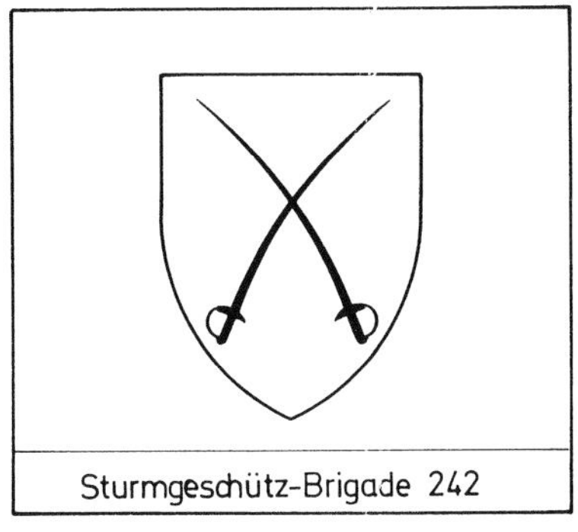
Sturmgeschütz-Brigade 242

to the area around Bastia. From there it covered the withdrawal of the German soldiers from Corsica to the Italian mainland.

The battalion went for a few weeks to Albano, with the 3rd Battery quartered in Cecchina, and covered additional sectors in the Piombino area and on Lake Trasimeni.

Attached to the 94. Infanterie-Division, the battalion was transferred to the southern Italian sector. At the beginning of 1944, it was committed to the defensive fighting south of Cassino. In the first fight, the 2nd Battery lost its commander, Oberleutnant Kohbruck. Oberleutnant Metzger took over command of the battery in his place. The battalion was redesignated a brigade on 14 February 1944.

Attached to the 71. Infanterie-Division, the 44. Infanterie-Division "Hoch und Deutschmeister," the "Hermann Göring" Division and the 1. Fallschirm-Jäger-Division, the brigade fought in every decisive battle in the area of Cassino, and accomplished its mission of "supporting the infantry" in a magnificent manner. In its first major operation, Oberleutnant Metzger, Wachtmeister Teppe and Wachtmeister Berneis, along with three other Sturmgeschütz men, took the crews of three Sherman tanks prisoner in a surprise move, and brought the three US tanks back through the German lines with the American drivers at the controls. A fourth Sherman that was not operational was blown up.

Wachtmeister Herbert Berneis received the German Cross in Gold on 15 April 1944 for this and for other gallant acts.

Oberleutnant Metzger was wounded during the fighting on 4 February 1944. Oberleutnant Pohl was his successor as battery commander.

The Sturmgeschütz crew of Oberwachtmeister Schumann crew made a name for itself during the fighting for Monte Cassino. His gun was located in the main hall of the destroyed Hotel Excelsior, and his well-aimed shots repulsed the attacking tanks.

The brigade's command post was detected and attacked by fighter-bombers in the area of Roccasecca on 15 March 1944, and it received several direct hits. Hauptmann Benz, his Orderly Officer Leutnant Schletter and some of their comrades lay dead among the ruins of the command post.

The orphaned brigade was led back into battle by Hauptmann Bussjäger.

Wachtmeister Riedmaier also distinguished himself at Monte Cassino. His last action against a swarm of US tanks ended with the destruction of four of them. When his gun was put out of action, the Wachtmeister was captured along with his crew, some wounded.

The fighting in Italy continued with the brigade attached to a variety of units, for example, the 114. Jäger-Division in the Tiber Valley at Umbertide. After a difficult road march across the Apennines it arrived at the Adriatic. There it next went into action between Ancona and Jesi with the 278. Infanterie-Division, under its old fire-eater Harry Hoppe, the successful conqueror of the north Russian city of Schüsselburg. In the area south of Fano, near the village of Monterado, the 3rd Battery destroyed 14 tanks under the personal leadership of its commander. The battery commander, who had destroyed three of these enemy tanks, received the German Cross in Gold. Many soldiers of the 3rd Battery were decorated with the Iron Cross, First Class. Oberfähnrich Wagner, who had destroyed six enemy tanks with his Sturmgeschütz, received a simultaneous award of the Iron Cross, First and Second Class.

Withdrawn from the front and sent to Modena for rest and refitting, the brigade was supplied with new vehicles in January 1945 and moved to Alfonsine on Lake Comacchio in the area of Ravenna. Once again, the brigade—the 2nd Battery in particular—fought especially well before it crossed the Po to Rovigo.

Further retreat brought it to Vicenca-Bassano, where its last Sturmgeschütz had to be blown up for lack of fuel. The rest of the brigade moved over the Rolle Pass to Bozen with one prime mover. It reached Brixen, and then Bruneck in the Puser Valley. It assembled at Niederwielenbach, where it was interned at the end of the war. The personnel of the brigade went to the large camp at Cesenatico. The soldiers were released from there to go home in January 1947.

Sturmgeschütz-Brigade 243

Sturmgeschütz-Abteilung 243

There were already a few Sturmgeschütz battalions ready for employment at the beginning of the Russian Campaign on 22 June 1941. Sturmgeschütz-Abteilung 243 belonged to this number. Its insignia was an armored knight.

This battalion was formed by Major Hesselbarth in the Old Camp at Jüterbog on 10 May 1941. The Command and Staff Positions were filled as follows:

Commander: Major Hesselbarth
Adjutant: Leutnant Günther Patzschke
Orderly Officer: Leutnant Schlenkert
Terrain Reconnaissance Officer: Leutnant Kühne
Medical Officer: Unterarzt Bergmann, (later) Stabsarzt Dr. Vogt
Technical Officer: Kriegsverwaltungsrat Kramer
Work Shop Foreman: Werkmeister Gerbsch
Headquarters Company Commander: Oberleutnant Keißhold
1st Company Commander: Oberleutnant Gruber
Technical Officer: Oberleutnant Loose
Section Leaders: Leutnant Knüppel, Leutnant Vollheim, Leutnant Maubach
2nd Company: Commander: Oberleutnant Höfer
Technical Officer: Leutnant Jesch
Section Leaders: Leutnant Causemann, Leutnant Malzan, Leutnant Gerlitz
3rd Company Commander: Oberleutnant Sekirka
Technical Officer: Leutnant Gröger
Section Leaders: Leutnant Saitner, Leutnant Nadolny, Leutnant Simon

The battalion moved into its ready positions northeast of Przemysl three days before the beginning of the Russian Campaign.

At Przemysl the 1st Battery was detached from the battalion and placed directly under the 1. Gebirgs-Division. The other batteries were employed 50 kilometers further to the northeast.

During the first two hours of the attack Leutnant Loose and Leutnant Maubach of the 1st Battery were killed in the castle grounds at the village of Oleszyce, where the members of a Russian noncommissioned officer school put up a stubborn re-sistance.

Oberleutnant Gruber, the 1st Battery commander, was wounded on the same day and was sent back to a main aid station. But they didn't keep him in hospital for very long. He popped up one week later back at his battery, still heavily bandaged, and took up command once again.

During the period from 22 June to 26 August the battalion cleared a way through the Galician border fortifications. They took part in the battle for Lemburg and advanced directly on Tarnopol. The fighting at Proskurow and Starikonstantinow are an integral part of the battalion's history. Sturmgeschütz-Abteilung 243 made up the steel spearhead which cleared the way for the infantry when it broke through the Stalin Line.

It also fought successfully in the encirclement battle at Uman and in the pursuit to the Dnjepr, destroying enemy batteries, bunkers and field positions. On 1 August 1941 Oberwachtmeister Ernst Alex, who fought with the 1st Battery under the 1. Gebirgs-Division, became the first member of the battalion to receive the Knight's Cross.

The 1st Battery advanced with the "Edelweiß" Division in the direction of Kirowograd until 18 August, where it received orders to return to the battalion. On 26 August Oberleutnant Gruber reported back to battalion at Gornostaipol with his battery after a 600-kilometer trip on its own. The 1st Battery had painted the "Edelweiß" on its guns.

On 27 August the battalion took part in the encirclement of Kiev which lasted for a month. It established a bridgehead east of Gornostaipol, fought its way across the Desna, and took part in the fighting pursuit southeast of Kiev.

All three batteries were in action at the pocket battle at Krupol-Baryschewka-Pjereslaw. They fought Russian armored trains there, which often carried rich loot. But there was also hand-to-hand fighting with Russian Guards units which fought with desperate courage under the leadership of high-ranking officers in an attempt to break through to the east.

The advance to Briansk began on 27 September. The "Iron Knights" reached the Briansk area on 6 October, in a forced march through Gomel. However, as German armor units had already thrust through the city, and had even pushed on to Orel, only the 1st Battery was committed. It captured the northern industrial quarter which was still occupied by the enemy.

The battalion stayed in Briansk for a short period for rest and refitting.

The advance to the east through Orel and Nowosil began on 20 November 1941. Objective: Moscow. However, this advance came to a stop with the beginning of the Russian operational offensive on 5 December. There was already hard defensive fighting on 16 December at Werchowije, at Wschod and in the Sossna Sector. At 44 degrees below zero Celsius, some of the Sturmgeschütze iced up and became unserviceable.

For the first time, the battalion experienced the harshness of a defensive battle, as it held off the enemy with all its strength. On 24 January 1942 the battalion was committed in the area northwest of Liwny, in order to stop enemy forces attacking there. Although the battalion staff and the remnants of the 2nd and 3rd Batteries reached this area, the 1st Battery remained behind, deeply snowed in at Lomowoje. It followed slowly in three groups. The battalion wasn't entirely assembled until 13 February 1942 in the area of Maloarchangelsk.

The battalion went into action with individual batteries at the critical points of the defense at Kolpna. But no battery had more than three operational Sturmgeschütze.

When the thaw and mud season set in on 23 March 1942, the battalion became an operational reserve for the LV. Armee-Korps. It managed to persuade the corps to position the complete unit, whose fighting strength had now risen to 21 Sturmgeschütze, in a central location where it could provide support to the entire corps. As a result, the battalion was pulled back to Maloarchangelsk and took up positions for the first time as an integral unit.

The battalion broke through the Russian positions at Tim at the beginning of the German Summer Offensive on 28 June 1942. The 2nd Battery took the brunt of the action. The numerically superior Russian tank forces destroyed four Sturmgeschütze, including the command Sturmgeschütz for the 3rd Battery. The commander, Oberleutnant Höfer, who had played a major role with his Sturmgeschütz in forcing the breakthrough, was killed.

The battalion then went into action in the defensive fighting northwest of Woronesch, attached to a variety of infantry divisions. Its mission was to halt and destroy the massed Soviet tank and infantry forces. The Soviets attempted a counterstroke there to push into the extended left flank of the developing German offensive.

The battalion suffered heavy casualties in this fighting. The 1st Battery's military cemetery at Murawskij Schljach grew larger day by day. However, the number of enemy tanks destroyed was even larger. On 9 July the battalion was pulled out of the fighting and moved to the south in a forced march with other units to reach the Caucasus.

It crossed the bend of the Don under continuous attack by low-level fighters in an unparalleled, exhausting, 800-kilometer road march across the steppe, which took place during the blazing heat of a Russian summer. Temperatures reached 40 degrees Celsius in the shade. On 30 July it crossed the lower Don at Zymlianskaja and pushed on to the Sal, which it reached on 2 August 1942 at Tschegow. There was heavy fighting in the steppe, which offered no cover at all, but this didn't slow the battalion's momentum.

The battalion was included with the 14. and 24. Panzer-Divisionen and the 29. Infanterie-Division (mot.) when this assault group was turned around to move along the railroad line Krasnodar–Proletarskaja-Kotelnikowo-Stalingrad.

The advance began with an armor attack on Kotelnikowo on 3 August, long before the main attack on Stalingrad which would be carried out from within the great bend of the Don. This

Kampfgruppe reached the outer defensive barriers of Stalingrad on 1 September 1942 against increasing Soviet resistance.

However, after a 1500-kilometer march across the steppes and fierce fighting, these three German divisions and the Sturmgeschütz battalion were no longer strong enough for the decisive thrust which still might have been able to take Stalingrad. So any real hope of taking Stalingrad by a quick attack from the south faded away. Thus began a bitter and bloody episode in the Russian Campaign.

Starting 6 August 1942 those members of the battalion who were sick with steppe fever were assembled in Schutow, an oasis on the edge of the Kalmücken Steppe. For a period of time more than half the battalion's troops were ill with this dysentery-like fever.

At that point the 1st Battery was in position in the steppe between Stalingrad and Schutow. The objective for the combat elements was Stalingrad. From there the battery turned north. The villages of Koschara, Klieschewskij, Plantator, Gawrilowka, Petschanka and Zybenko were captured by the battery. During this fighting it became obvious that the Sturmgeschütze with their short 7.5 cm guns were at a disadvantage in duels against the T-34.

At that very time the 2nd Battery was in the rear being trained with the long-barreled Sturmgeschütze.

The entire battalion spent the last fine days of autumn on the Volga Heights outside of Stalingrad. The enemy stayed surprisingly quiet.

Not until 19 November 1942 was the "Iron Knight" Battalion committed against Beketowka and Krasnoarmeisk. Major Soviet tank factories were located at Krasnoarmeisk. The entire Stalingrad Front was supplied with T-34's from there.

This attack was brought to a halt by fire from enemy heavy antiaircraft batteries crewed by women. The battalion pulled back to Zybenko.

During the night of 20/21 November the battalion attacked Hills 125 and 128.2 east of Jagotin with infantry support and took them. The next day it became obvious that the battalion had been cut off. The situation was dangerous as it had also been cut off from its trains.

Oberstleutnant Hesselbarth took command of a Kampfgruppe there cobbled together from elements of every battery. It was committed with the infantry Kampfgruppen of Oberstleutnants Mäder and Drepper. The battalion lost more and more Sturmgeschütze during this costly fighting, until finally there were only two left in action. The rest of the battalion members were fighting as infantry.

On 19 December the surrounded elements of the battalion were told that the rest of the battalion, including the newly equipped 2nd Battery, was launching a relief attack and had advanced to within 30 kilometers. Relief could be expected the next day.

However the next day was a black day for the relief force. They had to pull back to Kotelnikowo in the face of overwhelming enemy pressure. The morale of the men in the pocket sank. For rations, all that was left was hardtack and horsemeat.

The Soviet operational attack on Stalingrad and the pocket began on 10 January. During those days the remaining Sturmgeschütze carried out counterattacks on the "Three Knoll Trench" and on Hill 119.7. There was still one Sturmgeschütz—commanded by Wachtmeister Brunisch—in front of the battalion command post. It was immobile but could still fire. Four days later, the Soviets attacked the Zariza Valley, where the battalion was positioned with the remnants of an infantry division. This division had received orders to pull back closer to Stalingrad. To make this possible for them, Oberstleutnant Hesselbarth gave the Sturmgeschütz of Brunisch orders to hold off the Soviets as long as possible so that the infantry could pull back through Pitomnik and Gontschara to Gumrak. An 18-ton tractor stood ready to tow the gun to the repair section of Sturmgeschütz-Abteilung 245 after it had carried out this difficult mission. That battalion was also surrounded in Stalingrad.

Wachtmeister Brunisch opened fire when the Soviets came within two kilometers. For four long hours, this gun stood alone fighting defensively. As the Soviets had no heavy weapons in this fighting, Brunisch managed to complete his mission. This crew outdid itself by a wide margin during the four hours of this bitter battle. Many of the light Soviet tanks were destroyed; the survivors turned back.

When the division had fallen back far enough, the tractor towed the Sturmgeschütz to the repair section of Sturmgeschütz-Abteilung 245 which was located 1 kilometer to the east of the Pitomnik Airfield. However, even there it was unable to get the gun up and running again. So once again Brunisch took up a defensive position amid a number of destroyed Sturmgeschütze. On 14 January he was attached to an infantry battalion that had to defend a stretch two kilometers wide with a total of 14 surviving soldiers. On 14 January Oberstleutnant Hesselbarth became missing in action along with many other members of the battalion.

Four days later the Soviets took Karpowka and Pitomnik had to be abandoned. But this last Sturmgeschütz under Wachtmeister Brunisch didn't dare leave its position. Stabsgefreiter Otto Ackel sat next to Brunisch in the gun.

In the evening of 20 January Brunisch was badly wounded in the neck as he was leaving his gun. He suffered a second wound—this time to the knee— a few hours later in the early morning hours of 21 January. Brunisch can thank two men that he is still alive today. First, Major and Knight's Cross winner Riedel, who brought him to Sturmgeschütz-Abteilung 245 at Gumrak with a 170 V, and then his brave comrade, Otto Ackel.

Under heavy enemy fire on 22 January Brunisch was brought to the Central Stalingrad Airfield on an 18-ton prime mover. When one more He 111 landed that same afternoon, Stabsgefreiter Ackel carried his comrade on his shoulders onto the runway through enemy fire. He reached the aircraft in a storm of shell explosions and machine-gun fire. Wachtmeister Brunisch was flown out and thus saved from certain death, but the fate of Sturmgeschütz-Abteilung 243 was sealed.

The remnants of the brigade which had escaped the siege were used to reorganize the brigade in the early part of 1943. Immediately after reorganization, it was put back into action on the Eastern Front. Its new commander was Hauptmann Maier.

Starting in May the brigade took part in the fighting withdrawal on the southern front. It suffered high casualties during the fighting on the Mius, which lasted until September. The defensive battle in October at Saparoshje and the fighting in the Nogai Steppe also cost a heavy price. The Wehrmacht Report for 8 October 1943 mentions the brigade in this fighting: "Sturmgeschütz-Abteilung 243 particularly distinguished itself during the defensive fighting southeast of Saparoshje."

The battalion managed to pull back into the Nikopol

Bridgehead. Starting on 2 February 1944 the retreat continued. On 14 February 1944 the battalion was redesignated a brigade. Then followed the defensive battle at Kriwoi Rog, the defensive fighting on the Dnjepr and north of Nikolajew and the fighting retreat to the Bug. It reached the lower Dnjepr, where German resistance stiffened once again.

The brigade fought in the Tiraspol-Akkerman area and then south of Grigoripol from the middle of April until 10 May 1944. The fighting in the Dnjestr Loop, at the "Marmalade Factory" and Kpschnitza once more cost the brigade a high price, which was paid in blood.

The brigade was decimated in these defensive and withdrawing actions with Heeresgruppe Südukraine, which continued along the Dnjestr in the area of Jassy. At Kischinew it fought completely surrounded one again and, for the second time, it suffered the fate that it had already undergone at Stalingrad: It was completely wiped out.

The major part of the brigade went into captivity there in Kischinew pocket. We will let the spare, straightforward prose of a report describe those August days:

When the Russians attacked the Marmalade Factory on 20 August 1944, Sturmgeschütz-Brigade 243 was committed to support the defense. We managed to halt the Russian attack and contain two of the Soviet penetrations. On 22 August Soviet tank forces attacked.

While the 3rd Battery under Hauptmann Nöllenburg went into action in the southern sector, the other batteries fought in the central and northern sector of the attack. The first enemy tank attack in the center was repulsed, but the Sturmgeschütze had to be pulled back since the Soviets had broken through on both flanks and had made considerable progress. Leutnant Ehemann was badly wounded. Leutnant Else took over command of the remaining operational Sturmgeschütze of this Kampfgruppe from him and brought them back.

More Sturmgeschütze were lost in heavy fighting northwest of Causani on 24 and 25 August. By 26 August only Leutnant Else's Sturmgeschütz was still in action. When this gun—now all by itself and with infantry mounted on it—ran into the middle of a Russian position, it was destroyed as well. On 27 August the crew of this last Sturmgeschütz, which included the gunner, Unteroffizier Willi Rein, and the driver, Wolfgang Jung, were taken prisoner by the Soviets.

In a reception camp, where the officers were separated from the men, Wolfgang Jung was able to speak once more with Hauptmann Maier, the brigade commander, who later died of his wounds in a prisoner-of-war camp in Odessa.

The remnants of the brigade arrived at Tuchheim in the Altengrabow district. It was established for the third time there in the fall of 1944. Sometime during the winter of 1944/45 Sturmgeschütz-Brigade 243 was redesignated Heeres-Sturmartillerie-Brigade 243, although the redesignation of the unit was not universally observed. The newly formed Heeres-Sturmartillerie-Brigade 243 went into action in the west during the Ardennes Offensive. There, in the Ardennes, it met its fate for the third time. It fought at every hot spot in this battle sector. Oberwachtmeister Gerhard Krieg received the German Cross in Gold for outstanding bravery.

When the remnants of Heeresgruppe Model pulled back to the east in the middle of January 1945, the brigade had once more lost all its guns. The remnants of the brigade were sent to Potsdam for the defense of Berlin. It arrived there at the beginning of March 1945 under the command of Hauptmann Rübig. However, as there were no Sturmgeschütze available, it was employed as infantry.

It went into position on the Teltow Canal between Babelsberg and Nowawes. Oberleutnant Günther Gerlitz, commander of 3rd Battery, was assigned the house of Reichspostminister (Minister of Mail and Communications) Dr. Ohnesorge, as his command post. The brigade had occupied these positions for only two days as infantry, when 40 new Sturmgeschütze arrived. The "Iron Knights" were Sturmartilleristen once more.

When the Americans crossed the Elbe at Barby and Schönebeck during this final phase of the war, they were thrown back by the 1st Battery. During this period Oberleutnant Gerlitz was in Potsdam with the 2nd and 3rd Batteries. There he received instructions directly from the German Army High Command to take both batteries to Bukow-Straußberg and deflect the Soviet tank units which had broken through there. However, Oberleutnant Gerlitz asked them to task Sturmgeschütz-Brigade 245, since without a headquarters battery or a maintenance section, he was in no position to support his two batteries.

Hauptmann Herbert Jaschke then carried out this mission with Sturmgeschütz-Brigade 245.

On the next day, 14 April 1945, the 2. and 3./ Heeres-Sturmartillerie-Brigade 243 were put on trains for Wiesenburg and the Headquarters and 1st Batteries were ordered to join them there. The entire brigade was attached to the newly formed Armee Wenck and Hauptmann Rübig once again had all his batteries at his disposal. The brigade was employed against Treuenbrietzen, which had fallen into Soviet hands. There, where the brigade had been formed in May 1941, it attacked to relieve the city. It smashed through the Soviet march columns, and it was able to completely destroy a Soviet Sturmgeschütz unit in a flank attack from the area of the lung sanitarium.

At the end, the brigade was attached to Division "Theodor Körner" (General Frankewitsch) for the relief of Berlin. "Lehr Brigade Schill" fought along with Sturmgeschütz-Brigade 243 there under Oberstleutnant Müller. He was an experienced commander who had been in several brigades and had finally been commander of the Sturmartillerie-Schule at Burg. In his final operation, Oberstleutnant Müller had rushed to the front to be with his soldiers at the final hour.

The relief attempt collapsed in the area of Beelitz. Heeres-Sturmartillerie-Brigade 243 was pulled out of the line and was instructed to report to the XXXXVIII. Panzer-Korps at Genthin. However, this Panzer-Korps no longer existed. As a result, Hauptmann Rübig went to the relief of Rathenow on his own initiative.

On 7 and 8 May Sturmgeschütz-Brigade 243 crossed the Elbe at Tangermünde and Ferchland and was interned by the Americans.

Five officers and sixty men of the brigade were handed over to the Soviets by the Americans. The others were sent to the English prisoner-of-war camps at Calbe an der Milde and Gardelegen.

This brigade had moved from the Volga to the Don, from there to France and finally to Berlin. Death was its constant companion, and only a few men of this brigade survived the war's end.

Sturmgeschütz-Abteilung 244 (Sturmgeschütz-Brigade 244)

Sturmgeschütz-Abteilung 244 was formed at Zinna in June 1941. Hauptmann Dr. Paul Gloger was the battalion commander, and the adjutant was Leutnant Dr. Schrader-Rottmers. Leutnant Rade commanded the Headquarters Battery, and the three line batteries

were commanded by Oberleutnants Roestel, Dupont and Zenefels.

A the beginning of July 1941, the battalion was sent by rail to the southern sector of the Eastern Front, where it arrived on 8 July 1941 and was allocated to the 6. Armee.

It first went into action at Zwiahel and Shitomir. The breakthrough through the Stalin Line followed and the battalion advanced through Korosten as far as the Dnjepr.

In September 1941 it fought in the great encirclement of Kiev and for the crossing of the Desna. The battalion successfully fought in engagements at the villages of Ssemipolki, Ivankowo, Borispol and Baryschewka during September. In October the battalion was already fighting in a rapid pursuit up to the Donez. It took Belgorod, and it distinguished itself yet again in the fighting around Kharkov.

During the most severe Russian winter in 50 years, the battalion fought magnificently in the defensive battles in the Kharkov area and on the Donez. It managed to hold its positions in the face of superior enemy forces, counterattack in the spring of 1942 and fight at the battle for Kharkov.

Wachtmeister Banze of the 1st Battery distinguished himself in particular at the battle for Kharkov. He had already destroyed a large number of tanks, and fought there with breathtaking élan. All on his own he destroyed an entire pack of Soviet tanks with his Sturmgeschütz, his personal score reaching 24 enemy tanks. The entire battalion also fought successfully there. On 14 May no fewer than 36 enemy tanks were destroyed. The Wehrmacht Report for 15 May acknowledged this feat in the following words: "Sturmgeschütz-Abteilung 244 destroyed 36 enemy tanks in fighting in the east on 14 May 1942. Of this number, Oberwachtmeister Banze, destroyed 13 of them himself."

The battalion's 2nd Battery under Hauptmann Stier was attached to the 113. Infanterie-Division for the period from 13 May to 27 July 1942. During these ten weeks the battery gave continuous proof of extraordinary bravery. The 2./Sturmgeschütz-Abteilung 244 destroyed 66 enemy tanks of the types T-34 and KV 1 in the encirclement battle south of Kharkov, in capturing bridgeheads across the Donez and in the fighting in the great bend of the Don and the wounding of Hauptmann Stier.

On 13 May the battery was attached to Infanterie-Regiment 260. When the regiment was attacked by several Russian tanks south of Kharkov, Hauptmann Stier took them on. He moved 400 meters in front of the lines, personally destroyed 6 enemy tanks with his Sturmgeschütz and damaged two others.

Then he climbed a dominant hill between Infanterie-Regiment 260 and Infanterie-Regiment 261 and smashed a Soviet attack there which was just deploying. When the division withdrew, Hauptmann Stier and his battery took the rear guard, screening the retreat from the threat of attack by strong Soviet tank groups.

On 17 May the battery was attached to Infanterie-Regiment 261. Hauptmann Stier surpassed himself that day. He destroyed 16 Russian T-34's with only four Sturmgeschütze. He personally destroyed the Russian brigade commander's KV 1.

One Sturmgeschütz destroyed two more T-34's during the counterattack which was launched immediately afterwards.

The eighteenth of May was yet another great day of battle for Batterie Stier. It destroyed several enemy guns, including two of 17 cm and two of 12 cm caliber.

On 1 July Batterie Stier was attached to the III./Infanterie-Regiment 260. Major Rüdiger, the commander of this outstanding combat battalion, described the action:

Stier was attached to my battalion on 1 July 1942. We had to capture the enemy's line of resistance whose key point was the village of Stonowalow. Stier had added a captured T-34 to his battery. While I pushed into the Soviet positions from the right with most of my battalion, Stier had the mission of slamming into the enemy from the left with weak infantry forces. His forward momentum and his battery's success in knocking out the Soviet armor gave the battalion so much support, that it was able to push into the village and rip this key position from enemy hands.

On 27 July Infanterie-Regiment 260 went into action at Kussilew in the great bend of the Don. When strong Soviet forces attacked there, Hauptmann Stier charged against the enemy with his battery. He managed by his personal action to throw back the enemy. Hauptmann Stier was wounded by shrapnel there and had to be taken to the hospital. Oberleutnant Rade took over the battery and commanded it during the advance across the great bend of the Don. Rade was wounded at the crossing of the Don, but he was soon able to get back to his battalion once again.

The advance continued to the Volga. The battalion charged on to Stalingrad. There it suffered heavy losses. The attack on the tartar wall and on "Red October" were the most costly operations. Oberleutnant Rade, just back, was wounded once again and had to leave the battalion. On 18 September 1942 Oberwachtmeister Pfreundtner received the Knight's Cross. He had distinguished himself several times with his Sturmgeschütz during the summer fighting in the great bend of the Don and had destroyed more than 30 enemy tanks. There were only 2 officers left of the 21 who had been with the battalion at its beginning. Of these 19, 15 had been killed in action and the other four wounded.

Cut off in Stalingrad, the battalion fought to the very end. At the end of January the last survivors of this horrible battle were taken prisoner. On 26 January 1943 Wachtmeister Josef Galle received the Knight's Cross for his actions in the Stalingrad battleground. Oberwachtmeister Eduard Müller was also decorated with the Knight's Cross on 26 January 1943, and the third member of the group, Major Dr. Paul Gloger, was also awarded the Knight's Cross on the same day. Major Dr. Gloger was later killed in action. Throughout, the battalion maintained an outstanding reputation for its performance which was beyond all praise and more than once saved the infantry fighting in its sector from annihilation.

The battalion was then reorganized for the first time in March 1943. Major Großkreutz was the new commander. He had lost a forearm in September 1942 at Stalingrad, but still reported back for duty with his Sturmartillerie. His soldierly energy and remarkable courage were an example to his men. The battalion was allocated to the 9. Armee, fighting in the central sector of the front. It went into action for the first time after its reorganization southeast of Orel. Major Großkreutz gave the battalion a new image there. He led every attack in the commander's vehicle.

Oberleutnant Rade, who had recovered in the meanwhile, had taken over the 2nd Battery. On 5 July 1943 his Sturmgeschütz hit a mine. The Sturmgeschütz was blown apart. Rade was sent back to hospital with a head wound and concussion.

Not five weeks later, he appeared before Major Großkreutz and reported back in to the unit. He was still heavily bandaged. He saluted: "Oberleutnant Rade reports in to the battalion!"

The commander looked at him, standing at attention with a pale, hollowed-out face. With the rough affection of an old soldier, he said: "How dare you just show up like this? Besides you reported in incorrectly, you've been a Hauptmann for two days, Rade."

The young Hauptmann beamed, and the two comrades shook hands. Then Rade took his cap off. His head was still shaved bald. The scars shone red.

"First take some convalescent leave, Rade." said the Major, attempting to persuade his battery commander. But Hauptmann Rade knew that the battalion needed every officer. He stayed. On the next morning, he took over his old battery and went into ready positions with it.

A little later, Hauptmann Rade managed to destroy three tanks with his Sturmgeschütz. A fourth was damaged. His battery reported eight tanks destroyed on the afternoon of that day of fighting.

Oberwachtmeister Herbert Meissner received the Knight's Cross on 18 August 1943. A little later Oberwachtmeister Butzlaff was also awarded the Knight's Cross.

During the late summer fighting the battalion held a bridgehead on the Desna south of Briansk and made it possible for the heavily engaged infantry to pull back.

Hauptmann Rade's Sturmgeschütz was destroyed at Tschernikow. He got into another gun and continued to lead the assault. The battalion reached the Dnjepr at Lojew and crossed over. At the beginning of October 1943, Hauptmann Rade was shot through the arm in the Gomel Bridgehead. This time he was sent back home, where he was awarded the German Cross in Gold, which Major Großkreutz had recommended for him.

In the meantime, the battalion was engaged in very heavy defensive action. Major Großkreutz and his Sturmgeschütze had become the terror of Soviet tank formations. In the fighting at Besujew, Major Großkreutz, on his own initiative, wheeled against a strong enemy formation which was already in the rear of the German units. The Sturm-geschütze fought like fiends. The enemy was annihilated and the bridgehead held.

Then came the legendary 22 November 1943. The battalion had been engaged in heavy fighting with Soviet tank formations since daybreak, and the Sturmgeschütze destroyed 11 enemy tanks. When it bivouacked that evening in a village, it was attacked by 20 T-34's. A Sturmgeschütz on guard at the east edge of the village was rammed by an attacking T-34, and it was spun around 180 degrees. The gunner saw the enemy's shadow, fired and blew off the T-34's turret.

Firing wildly into the village, the T-34's attempted to annihilate the battalion. Soon the village was in flames. Major Großkreutz moved against the enemy in his command vehicle. He turned his Sturmgeschütze on the enemy tanks amid the flaming debris and the muzzle flashes. One after another, the attacking T-34's were destroyed from ranges as close as 20 meters. The Major personally guided each individual gun to its firing position. All 20 enemy tanks were destroyed. On this single day, the battalion had destroyed 38 Soviet tanks.

On 11 November 1943, Major Friedrich Großkreutz received the Knight's Cross.

Once again the Soviets had found out that the Sturmgeschütze were an enemy they were not equal to.

In December Hauptmann Rade returned to the battalion once again. Major Großkreutz, who was ordered to Germany a little later, gave him the battalion. Up to that point the battalion had destroyed 269 enemy tanks against 14 losses of its own.

Hauptmann Rade was always at the center of the defense in his command Sturmgeschütz in the heavy defensive fighting south of Shlobin. Three of the five Sturmgeschütze engaged during the fighting at Lessez were put out of action. Hauptmann Rade charged forward with the last two Sturmgeschütze and destroyed the enemy.

Sturmgeschütz-Abteilung 244 fought with desperate courage from 16 January to 16 February against greatly superior attacking enemy forces between the Pripet Marshes and the Beresina. One hundred three enemy tank attacks had to be repulsed, and Hauptmann Rade led his brigade in 56 counterattacks against the enemy. The following numbers illustrate the severity of the fighting. During this period, the brigade destroyed or put out of action: 54 tanks, 76 antitank guns, 161 antitank rifles, 186 machine guns and 9 mortars.

The Soviets halted their attacks. On 14 February 1944 the battalion was redesignated a brigade. On that same date, it was mentioned in the Wehrmacht Report:

The Bolsheviks have stopped their attack between Pripet and Beresina. By its resolution during the period of 16 January to 10 February, our troops, supported by Luftwaffe ground attack and pursuit fighters, have blocked continuous enemy breakthrough attempts by 30 rifle divisions and numerous tanks and inflicted heavy losses in both men and materiél on the enemy. Sturmgeschütz-Brigade 244 was especially effective during the recent fighting there.

Only two days later, the Wehrmacht Report again reported: "During the fighting in the central sector of the front, Hauptmann Rade has especially distinguished himself as commander of a Sturmgeschütz brigade."

Up to that point Hauptmann Rade himself had destroyed 23 enemy tanks with his command Sturmgeschütz. Wachtmeister Halbig, who destroyed 8 enemy tanks in a splendid duel on 15 February 1944, also had a large share in this defensive success. The war correspondent, Karl Otto Zottmann, was at the command post of Sturmgeschütz-Brigade 244 when Wachtmeister Halbig made his report on 16 February 1944:

A couple of hours after the counterattack, I met Hauptmann Rade in the brigade command post. The little room was full of men. There was a table with a bench behind it under the tiny window. The radio was playing, and we were eating chocolates and candied fruit out of a large ration package. Members of the command staff sat next to the Russian stove on a heap of straw piled along the long side of the room. On the plank wall hung submachine guns, rifles, helmets and coats.

Runners came in to make reports. A battery commander was greeted by Hauptmann Rade and then a large, broad-shouldered Wachtmeister entered.

"That's Halbig!" One of the Sturmartillerie men said softly to me. Wachtmeister Halbig had a bandaged head and a broad bandage of adhesive tape on his left cheek. He reported his actions and confirmed his battery commander's report.

The focal point of the report, however, was undoubtedly Hauptmann Rade. This tall, thin man with the well-shaped head and the yellow horn-rimmed glasses was the eye of the storm, the center of authority there. And every single one of these men around him had been shaped by his example.

You had to listen to these men when they talked about their commander to understand what made them able to do what they had done and where they got their strong faith in themselves and their weapons. All of this resulted from their respect for the courage which their commander displayed all the time.

Altogether Sturmgeschütz-Brigade 244 destroyed 355 enemy tanks during the period from 4 July 1943 to 10 February 1944. It disabled 9 others. Seven of its own Sturmgeschütze were totally destroyed. On 8, 9 and 10 February the brigade destroyed 34 heavy tanks and shot 9 others into flames or put them out of action.

The line batteries were virtually ripped apart in the fighting for Bobruisk in July 1944. The Headquarters Battery and the maintenance section remained with the 9. Armee under the command of Oberleutnant Reymann and feverishly repaired the Sturmgeschütze until the front had withdrawn to Warsaw.

Because the brigade had been completely destroyed, its second reorganization took place at Theesen near Burg in the fall of 1944. Its new commander was Hauptmann Jaschke. Oberleutnant Dr. Schrader-Rottmers, who had already been placed on the Honor Roll of the German Army and awarded the Honor Roll Clasp, was commander of the 1st Battery.

In October the brigade was employed in Holland. It distinguished itself in the western theater in the fighting at Rosendahl, Breda, the Moerdijk Bridgehead and Dordrecht.

The brigade was engaged in continuous bitter fighting with the beginning of the Ardennes Offensive. By 17 December Leutnant Haas had already received the German Cross in Gold. On 29 December 1944 this action was recognized by a mention in the Wehrmacht Report, which stated: "In ten days of continuous combat on the Western Front, Heeres-Sturmgeschütz-Brigade 244, under the command of Hauptmann Jaschke, supported the heavily fighting infantry with particular determination and has destroyed 54 heavy English and American tanks as well as 12 armored cars with only two losses of its own."

Hauptmann Jaschke was promoted to Major and received the German Cross in Gold.

The brigade continued in action during the fighting for Düren, Aachen and Cologne, in the fighting at the Sieg River and in the Oberbergen area. It ended up in the Ruhr pocket and disbanded itself on 14 April 1945 at Cronenberg near Wuppertal. Some of the men managed to break through to their families. The rest were taken prisoner.

Ten men of this formation were awarded the Knight's Cross. Eleven men received the German Cross in Gold and four were decorated with the Honor Roll Clasp. But the brigade had been destroyed three times, fighting in Stalingrad, at Bobruisk and in the Ruhr pocket.

Sturmgeschütz-Abteilung 249 (Sturmgeschütz-Brigade 249; Heeres-Sturmartillerie-Brigade 249)

When the 2./Sturmgeschütz-Abteilung 249 was formed on 10 January 1942 in the "Adolf Hitler Camp" at Jüterbog, there were already a few Sturmgeschütz battalions in the southern sector of the Eastern Front and on the Crimean Peninsula. The newly-formed battery, under the command of Oberleutnant Nottebrock, took up quarters in the village of Zinna. It was also destined for the southern sector of the Eastern Front where there were too few armored units.

Heeres-Sturmartillerie-Brigade 249

After driving and terrain exercises at Zinna, there was a temporary transfer to Treuenbrietzen. On 17 February 1942 the battery moved from there to Jüterbog and was loaded on trains within two hours.

The railroad trip lasted eight days before ending at Thigina. The brigade went from there overland to Odessa. It got to Cherson by way of Nikolajew, where it crossed over the ice of the Dnjepr on 2 March. Its objective was Tschaplinka, which came into view on the evening of that day.

After a few days of rest, which served to repair a few damaged Sturmgeschütze, it continued its march through Armjansk and Perekop to Dshanskoje. It reached the Dalny-Bajbuga area, which lay 8 kilometers west of Feodosia, by way of Simferopol.

The battery's first day of action was 14 March 1942. Oberleutnant Nottebrock led the battery in a defense against a Russian attack. There was bitter fighting at Seit Assan and Koj Assan. On 15 March 1942 the Sturmgeschütze were in action at Wladiswalowka, and Korpetsch became the focal point of the battle. Oberleutnant Nottebrock was killed in his Sturmgeschütz when a round hit it on 15 March. Oberleutnant Engelke took over command.

The costly fighting lasted until the end of April. Often stranded, shot-up Sturmgeschütze had to be pulled out of the crater fields of the "Parpatsch" Position at night under enemy fire. The maintenance section had a difficult job there, which it did in cooperation with the crews of the immobilized guns. The battery's trains stayed in Nayman from the beginning of the operation until the beginning of May.

The night of 2 May 1942 is full of painful memories for every survivor of the unit. A work detail of the battery which was employed for bunker construction on the Dalny-Kamyschi railroad overpass was bombed by a Russian nuisance raider and some of the bombs from this machine were right on target. Eleven of the battery's soldiers were killed.

On 8 May 1942 the campaign to capture the Kertsch Peninsula was begun for the second time. Its most important terrain had been retaken by the Soviets after their landing at the end of December 1941. The attack on Kertsch was opened by German bombers. Artillery and Nebelwerfer joined in with barrage fire, and then the assault on Kertsch began.

The Sturmgeschütze moved forward on the right flank of the attack axis. Enemy antitank guns were destroyed. The first Sturmgeschütz was taken out of action. The battery moved faster and faster in pursuit of the withdrawing enemy until it reached the city of Kertsch. Then it was a matter of helping the assaulting infantry and eliminating pockets of enemy resistance which directed heavy fire at the infantry. The Sturmgeschütze fought splendidly in the fighting for the fortress itself, in the house-to-house fighting and in the fighting for the heavily defended Wojkow Foundry. At that point every crevice in Kertsch had been cleared of the enemy.

On 23 May the 2./Sturmgeschütz-Abteilung 249 moved along with the rest of the battalion to Feodosia and bivouacked in a brick plant. The battalion had arrived at the front in the meantime. (Unfortunately, there is no information available for the rest of the battalion.) On the next morning, Sturmgeschütz-Abteilung 249 continued on through Karasubasar and Stary Krim to Simferopol. On Whit-Sunday the Sturmgeschütze rolled down the winding road to Yalta on the south coast of the Crimea, where they bivouacked in a woods to the east of the city. The trains were quartered at Nikitazum. A little later the line batteries were sent to Sevastopol to join the ranks of the attacking forces assembled there and join in the assault on the fortress.

The 2./Sturmgeschütz-Abteilung 249 had some major successes during the fighting which lasted for 35 days, but it also took heavy casualties. The Sturmgeschütze fought their way forward, meter by meter, into the heavily defended, fortified terrain. Supply vehicles were on the road day and night in order to bring rations, fuel, ammunition and replacements to the line batteries.

Oberleutnant Kreimel, who distinguished himself in the fighting for Sevastopol several times, was the first member of the battalion to receive the German Cross in Gold. He was severely wounded during this fighting.

The 2./Sturmgeschütz-Abteilung 249 was given a long rest period in a sanitarium near Yalta. On 20 July it moved to Simferopol, where it was loaded on trains on 23 July and transported to Uspenskaja by way of Stalino. It arrived there on 28 July. Its march to the south began there.

The 2./Sturmgeschütz-Abteilung 249 moved south during the hot days of August that summer of 1942. Rostow was its first objective. There the guns and vehicles were given a final overhaul before starting the approach march which the Sturmgeschütze were to make within an advance guard detachment.

Rolling on after the withdrawing enemy, the battery passed destroyed villages and collective farms. The dust drifted over the vast fields of sunflowers, and the advance guard detachment reached the city of Krasnodar on 9 August in sweltering heat and thick dust. The Sturmgeschütze were employed in the taking of this city. They continued on towards the Caucasus, whose highest peaks were already visible in the distance. They passed through the villages of Ssewerskaja, Cholmskaja, Achtyrskaja and Albinskaja. There was tough and stubborn enemy resistance at Krymskaja and the infantry called out once again: "Sturmgeschütze to the front!"

The pockets of enemy resistance were wiped out, the way was cleared, and so the battery finally reached Noworossisk. There was a battle there for this important Black Sea port. The Sturmgeschütze cleared the way by fire for their comrades in the infantry when they attacked the "Stalin" and "Cinema" complexes as well as the fortified heights further east lying at the southern edge of the city.

In August Oberleutnant Meissner commanded the battery. After he was wounded Oberleutnant Reinstädler took over acting command in September. Leutnant Lohmann was acting battery commander from 1 October to 31 December 1942.

At the end of October the battery took up quarters in well-maintained houses in Kijewskoje. There the vehicles and guns, which had been badly overtaxed during the long road marches, were overhauled once again. On 10 November new quarters were occupied in Adagum. The battery had a long rest period there which lasted until the beginning of December.

On 10 December the 2./Sturmgeschütz-Abteilung 249 received orders to take over an armored train. Half of the battery's personnel was sent to Kesslorowo to be trained as antiaircraft personnel for the armored train. But the armored train was given to another unit on 6 January 1943, and the soldiers returned to their unit. New Sturmgeschütze had arrived.

The 2./Sturmgeschütz-Abteilung 249 celebrated Christmas in the school at Kesslorowo, and it was also able to celebrate the New Year in this village. The year 1942 thus ended in relative quiet for the 2./Sturmgeschütz-Abteilung 249.

Little information is available concerning this unit from the beginning of 1943 to the beginning of 1945. It was renamed a brigade on 14 February 1944 and, at the beginning of 1945, further redesignated as Heeres-Sturmartillerie-Brigade 249. During that time it was employed exclusively in the southern sector of the Eastern Front, primarily with the 4. Panzer-Armee.

At the beginning of 1945 Heeres-Sturmartillerie-Brigade 249 was in West Prussia attempting to halt the Red Army. Heavy, costly fighting had decimated the brigade which, to make matters worse, had been employed in a piecemeal fashion. One battery under Hauptmann Hoffmann had been pushed to the north. The 2nd Battery, commanded by Hauptmann Jaschke, pulled back to the west, fighting along with most of the army.

Hauptmann Hoffmann, Leutnant Brill and 100 other Sturmartilleristen found themselves in the Heiligenbeil Pocket until 14 March 1945. After this battery had lost its last Sturmgeschütz, the rest of its equipment was turned over to Heeres-Sturmartillerie-Brigade 277 under Hauptmann Stier by order of the army headquarters. The personnel were taken to Danzig in one car and 3 trucks. From Danzig they were shipped back to Altengrabow for reorganization.

At the end of March 1945 the entire brigade was assembled at Krampnitz after the other remnants had also been sent back to Germany. The Headquarters Battery and the three line batteries were replenished with personnel. An Infanterie-Begleit-Batterie was also added to the organization. On 24 April 1945 the gun crews traveled to the manufacturer, Alkett, at Spandau in order to pick up new Sturmgeschütze. That night the crews worked with the factory workers to get the vehicles ready for combat. On 25 April the guns rolled directly from the factory into a small woods near Spandau. That evening they received the order to move back to Krampnitz. It was then intended for the refitted brigade to be employed against the Americans on the Elbe.

When the brigade arrived at Berlin, a counter-order was received. The brigade went back in the direction of Berlin. It rolled past the Brandenburger Gate when entering the capital of the Reich. It was 27 April 1945 and the Red Army had already advanced to the outskirts of the city. Hauptmann Jaschke led the formation to the bunker at Friedrichshain. Oberleutnant Hundt moved with the 1st Battery to be employed at Lake Weiß. Three of his Sturmgeschütze were lost in the following fighting. Oberwachtmeister Heinz Heisse, a veteran Sturmartillerist, was also killed there.

The Sturmgeschütze were employed in sections and even individually in the days that followed. They knocked out Russian tanks which had penetrated into Berlin. Within three days of fighting for the capital more than 180 tanks were knocked out. Hauptmann Jaschke received the Knight's cross on 28 April 1945.

On 27 April Leutnant Rupprecht was arrested by SS men at the trains vehicles of his battery. He was found that evening hanged in the vicinity of the Alexanderplatz. The brigade was incensed. The accusation of cowardice certainly couldn't be leveled against that young officer. He had been awarded the German Cross in Gold and wore the Honor Roll Clasp.

The rest of the brigade assembled in the villa district of Berlin on 29 April. Russian bombers attacked in the early afternoon and caused heavy casualties. One Sturmgeschütz was put out of action. The brigade had nine Sturmgeschütze at its disposal. These were employed as a Kampfgruppe under Hauptmann Lange. The nine guns fought on the Frankfurter Allee, the Landsberger Straße and the Alexanderplatz. A few of them were knocked out.

The remaining guns were employed in the vicinity of the Technical College on 29 April. The brigade's command post was in the basement of the college. Oberwachtmeister Müller and Unteroffizier Wagner knocked out several enemy tanks. The crews without guns were outfitted with Panzerfäuste.

Two Sturmgeschütze also fought on 30 April on the Berliner Straße against a group of Soviet armor. The Sturmgeschütz of Oberwachtmeister Müller was hit. The Oberwachtmeister was killed; the rest of the crew bailed out. The commander's hatch of Oberwachtmeister Rohrbacher was shot off at pointblank distance. He was wounded. Despite that he was able to knock out five enemy tanks. The tanks which moved against the Technical College a little later were also knocked out.

On 1 May 1945 Hitler's death was announced. On 2 May Hauptmann Jaschke assembled his officers and soldiers and talked to them about the situation. It was decided to break out of Berlin and move in the direction of the Elbe.

On 3 May 1945, shortly after midnight, Heeres-Sturmartillerie-Brigade 249 set out with a few Sturmgeschütze, some SPW and the remaining trains vehicles. Everything went well as far as Spandau. At Spandau one of the bridges occupied by the Russians had to be cleared. Fired at from all sides the brigade could only proceed slowly. At the edge of the city the breakout attempt was stopped. At the point the brigade had already been split into two elements.

The element under Hauptmann Jaschke was able to punch its way through to the Elbe. The breakout of the second element took a dramatic turn. Using 3 Sturmgeschütze, another armored vehicle and three SPW approximately 3,000 men attempted to storm their way to freedom. These 3,000 soldiers attached themselves to the last Sturmgeschütz group which consisted of the guns of Oberwachtmeister Josef Rohrbacher, Leutnant "K" (the last name could not be determined) and Oberwachtmeister Dormann. About 100 Sturmartilleristen were a part of that group.

While attempting the breakout Leutnant "K" was able to surprise 11 tanks located off the right flank in a village he was moving through. He was able to destroy all of them. The remnant of the brigade got as far as Tetzin. At Tetzin they were taken under fire by a heavy enemy antiaircraft gun which had occupied a hill. Leutnant "K" received a direct hit. Only the loader of the Sturmgeschütz escaped with his life. When the gun of Oberwachtmeister Dormann got stuck, the Sturmgeschütz of Oberwachtmeister Rohrbacher came to assist. A direct hit destroyed Dormann's gun; a different round damaged Rohrbacher's Sturmgeschütz. While the crew of Oberwachtmeister Dormann was killed, Oberwachtmeister Rohrbacher and his three men were able to bail out and get to safety.

That spelled the end of Heeres-Sturmartillerie-Brigade 249 which had fought until the very end against the soldiers of the Red Army who had penetrated into the capital of the Reich.

Sturmgeschütz-Abteilung 259 (Sturmgeschütz-Brigade 259)

Sturmgeschütz-Brigade 259

In June 1943 Sturmgeschütz-Abteilung 259 was formed at Niemegk near Jüterbog from one of the oldest field units in the Sturmartillerie, Sturmgeschütz-Batterie 660. It adopted the emblem of Sturmgeschütz-Batterie 660, a white iron cross, and an eagle's head was added which gave the unit its name. Major Ottheinrich Tolckmitt, who had previously commanded Sturmgeschütz-Batterie 660, took command of the battalion.

Major Tolckmitt carried out the first training exercises at Jüterbog even before the unit had been completely formed.

At the end of July the battalion was committed into an area of operations on the Mius front where the Soviets had managed to break through.

The battalion was unloaded south of Stalino and attached to the 13. Panzer-Division. The battalion was told to leave behind its slow-moving trains and fight its way through the Russian spearhead to the 13. Panzer-Division with only its combat elements. No infantry support could be given to it. The mission could not be accomplished, however, in the vast corn fields and the rolling terrain with its depressions. The battalion did its best, but the breakthrough failed.

The battalion wasn't reunited with its trains until the front was pulled back to the "Tortoise Shell" Position, and then, for the first time, it could fight under normal conditions.

As the retreat continued, the battalion had to be constantly committed at threatened points as a "fire brigade." Action against enemy units which had broken through was followed by fighting to free surrounded Kampfgruppen. During the next three months the battalion was attached to different corps and divisions no fewer than seventy times.

The battalion's three batteries were immediately thrown into battle when the Soviets attacked the "Tortoise Shell" Position, which was not yet fully completed. There was fierce fighting, Sturmgeschütz against tank. In three days of offensive and defensive fighting, more than 100 Russian tanks lay on the battlefield—shot up, burning and destroyed.

Unteroffizier Heinrich Engel experienced the peak of his military career during that fighting. Surrounded in the middle of a Soviet tank formation, he smashed one tank after the other. His crew shared his unimaginable determination. Engel destroyed 15 enemy tanks. On 7 November 1943 he was awarded the Knight's Cross.

Despite that, as the fighting continued, the Russians managed to make a deep penetration. More and more Sturmgeschütze were put out of action during this bitter defensive fighting. In the end, only 10 of the battalion's 31 Sturmgeschütze were still operational.

At that point the battalion went into action with no more than one battery. The Soviets crushed the "Tortoise Shell" Position and broke through to the Black Sea. The battalion was surrounded along with the XXIX. Armee-Korps and other units.

Set as an iron spearhead at the point of the corps, the battalion broke through the encircling Russian ring and opened a way west for the corps.

The retreat continued, halting only when the German Front occupied the position connecting the bend of the Dnjepr at Saporoshje to the Black Sea. The Russian attack bogged down. The Soviets had to pay heavily for literally every meter of ground gained in the Nogai Steppe, which was completely level terrain, broken only by grain fields and acacia hedges. The Sturmgeschütze defended every hedge and every field.

Despite that the Russian operational offensive finally managed to break through. The German troops pulled back to Cherson and Nikopol. The battalion covered the retreat of those elements withdrawing to Nikopol. There was a bridgehead established there.

Sturmgeschütz-Abteilung 259 was the cliff in the breakers, the backbone of the defense in the Nikopol Bridgehead. It beat back every Russian attack. After the beginning of the rainy season in the fall of 1943, the exhausted battalion was pulled back to Cherson as an army reserve. There it held a small bridgehead on the other side of the Dnjepr. Towards Christmas, it was pulled out of this bridgehead, where the Sturmgeschütze had not gone into position and could not be employed because of the difficult terrain. Winter had started and the Russians had almost completely halted their attacks.

The Russian Winter offensive began at the beginning of 1944. Breaking through north of Saporoshje, the Soviets wheeled to the south and attempted to push the German forces back against the Black Sea, and so cut them off from any retreat.

General Schörner took over this sector of the front. He managed to get the German troops out of this mousetrap, establish a front to the north and thwart a Soviet break through towards Nikolajew.

The battalion was continuously committed during this fighting. Thrown in at the hot spots in sections, it could take some share of the credit for the defensive success. In early February 1944 the battalion was redesignated a brigade.

A little later, the mud season began. How much this mud affected operations may be seen from the fact that the support elements were unable to supply fuel to the 3rd Battery which was in action with 5 Sturmgeschütze only 10 kilometers to the north. Tracked and wheeled prime movers stuck fast in the mud. The individual batteries were supplied from the air. Even Nikolajew had to be abandoned. Sturmgeschütz-Brigade 259 pulled back across the Bug and moved on toward Odessa.

Even during this period, the mud was the brigade's worst enemy. The Russians thrust into the middle of the German withdrawal and reached the Dnjestr along a broad front, where they attempted to keep the retreating German troops and Sturmgeschütz-Brigade 259 from crossing the river at Akkermann. They were not successful.

Odessa could no longer be held. Depots and dumps were blown up when it was found impossible to evacuate the stores there. During the night the city was on fire everywhere. The brigade attempted to reach the crossing point at Akkermann. Rumanian units were supposedly holding back the enemy to the north.

The Rumanians broke under the first Soviet attack, and the brigade was committed against the enemy as quickly as possible to prevent the worst.

In the middle of the night the 1st Battery, under Oberleutnant Skell, moved forward to counterattack along the river bank. Surprisingly, the German infantry ran back leaving the 1st Battery all alone to face the Russians, who then attacked each individual Sturmgeschütz with overwhelming strength. The 1st Battery was almost entirely wiped out. For the most part, the guns were set on fire in close combat in the dark. No trace either of Oberleutnant Skell nor of any members of his battery were ever found after that night.

In the early hours of the following day, the brigade managed to make it across the Dnjestr on the dam at Akkermann, but only with great difficulty. The position stabilized on the near side of the Dnjestr. The mud disappeared and the brigade was employed in many minor operations. The fighting at Tiraspol and at the Butor Bridgehead were among the hardest fighting in this area. At the last second, the brigade was able to pull the Sturmgeschütze back out of the Butor Bridgehead across the river. New orders reached them on the friendly side of the Dnjestr to load up on trains. That came as a real surprise.

The central sector of the Eastern Front had broken apart. The Soviets were continuously advancing to the west. All available troops had to be thrown against them.

Sturmgeschütz-Brigade 259 passed through Hungary to reach the Praga railroad station near Warsaw. It was unloaded in Bialystock and attached to the 28. Jäger Division. The brigade remained attached for several months. Sturmgeschütz-Brigade 259 supported the operations of this splendid division with an average of 20 operational guns. The brigade rolled in to counterattack with mounted infantry wherever Russian penetrations were reported. Even when Russian regimental combat teams managed to penetrate at the Narew, these were wiped out. On 22 September the Wehrmacht Report reported these events: "A Jäger regiment under the command of Oberstleutnant von Salisch and Sturmgeschütz-Brigade 259 under the command of Major Tolckmitt fought splendidly in both attack and defense on the lower Narew."

However, this brave action was unable to prevent the Russians from continuing their push forward. The brigade was pushed back to the west south of Lomscha and had to withdraw back over the Narew.

Once again the brigade was surprised to be pulled back out of the front and sent by rail by way of Johannisburg to Treuburg in East Prussia. It received the mission to participate in the retaking of Goldap. It succeeded in retaking the city, but Goldap had been set on fire by the Russians.

The brigade was once more in action when the Russian operational offensive began on 14 January 1945. Because Major Tolckmitt was sick, Major Dr. Bumm, who had already received the German Cross in Gold as an Oberleutnant, took over command of the brigade.

Committed to cover the German retreat to Gumbinnen, the

brigade lost more and more Sturmgeschütze. The trains were employed as infantry troops. Those who survived went into Soviet captivity on 8 May 1945.

The members of the line elements were taken across the Haff to the Frische Nehrung and loaded on a ship at Danzig to go to Denmark for reorganization. However, that did not take place. The capitulation occurred while the rest of the brigade was in Denmark, where it went into English captivity.

Sturmgeschütz-Abteilung 270 (Sturmgeschütz-Brigade 270)

The personnel for Sturmgeschütz-Abteilung 270 were assembled at Neiße by Hauptmann Bumm, the commander at that time. The 1./Sturmgeschütz-Abteilung 270 was formed up from October to November 1942 under Oberleutnant Hermann Wolz. At the end of November 1942 his unit was the first to leave Neiße by rail and was taken through Russia between Heeresgruppe Mitte and Heeresgruppe Süd. The battery was moved there possibly because of the catastrophe beginning at Stalingrad. It went from Kiev to Mogilew and then from Smolensk to Jelnja. At Jelnja Sturmgeschütz-Abteilung 197 under Major Steinwachs was waiting for it. At the end of 1942 the 1./Sturmgeschütz-Abteilung 270 took over the equipment of Sturmgeschütz-Abteilung 197. The battalion was sent back home for rest and refitting. In the meantime, the battalion's other two batteries had arrived in Alexandrowka. The batteries were commanded by Oberleutnant Hellmich and Oberleutnant Türmer. Later on Oberleutnant Graf Konstantin zu Dohna Slobitten took over the 3rd Battery.

Major Bergholz commanded the battalion at that point. For a while it was the only armored unit between Rshew and Orel during the winter of 1942/43. Through February 1943 the individual batteries scouted the routes to the different divisional command posts and to the other staffs belonging to Heeresgruppe Mitte.

In February strong Soviet forces were detected in the Shisdra area and it was realized that these were the units which had been released for use elsewhere when Stalingrad fell.

In the middle of February Sturmgeschütz-Abteilung 270 was sent marching by night into the Shisdra area, a road march was very difficult because of the icy and snow-drifted roads. Fighting started there on 22 February which lasted until 20 March 1943. The enemy was interdicted and the battalion destroyed a number of tanks.

When around Whit-Sunday the enemy attacked in the bend of the Oka east of Bolchow, attempting to establish some bridgeheads across the Oka and so cut off the forward German positions, this attack was repelled and the enemy suffered heavy losses.

Sturmgeschütz-Abteilung 270 provided security in the area south of the Orel in the early summer.

With the beginning of "Operation Citadel" Sturmgeschütz-Abteilung 270 was initially the Heeresgruppe reserve. The 1./Sturmgeschütz-Abteilung 270 under Oberleutnant Wolz went into action in July to relieve the surrounded corps command post of General Gollwitz. The battery freed it in heavy fighting.

On 27 August 1943 Leutnant Hans-Christian Stock received the Knight's Cross for his outstanding service in this area of operations.

During the retreat from Orel Sturmgeschütz-Abteilung 270 was located just to the northeast of the city. During August it was pushed back to the Rosslawl area. The battalion lost more and more guns during this period, so that in September and October, it was only able to put together a single battery. This battery was commanded by Oberleutnant Wolz. It fought between Gomel and Mogilew until December 1943.

At the same time the battalion's two other batteries had been transferred into the Minsk area. Oberleutnant Wolz also arrived there with his battery personnel in the middle of December, after he had given up the rest of his Sturmgeschütze to another battalion.

On 1 January 1944 Sturmgeschütz-Abteilung 270 was attached to the 1. Skijäger-Brigade under Oberst von Schleebrügge and was equipped with the newest weapons and equipment. It arrived in the area of the Pripet Marshes along with the 1. Skijäger-Brigade in the early part of 1944. Leutnant Herwig Bittner received the Knight's Cross there on 11 February 1944. On 12 February 1944 the battalion was most likely redesignated a brigade.

Hauptmann Günther Hellmich had already received this decoration on 17 December 1943. Oberleutnant Wolz, who had destroyed 26 enemy tanks with the two remaining guns of his battery in a single day while assigned to the 293. Infanterie-Division (Generalmajor Arndt), was also recommended for the Knight's Cross. He did not receive this decoration, although he had earned it.

Sturmgeschütz-Brigade 270 was employed with the 1. Skijäger-Brigade in the region of the Pripet Marshes in the spring. They were located southeast of Brest-Litowsk. The guns and vehicles of Sturmgeschütz-Brigade 270 were up to their axles in mud and water. They secured a sector 30 to 60 kilometers long facing south.

After that operation the brigade was sent to Brest-Litowsk for an overhaul. The rest of the history of the brigade is bound to that of the 1. Skijäger-Brigade. Its path led across the Carpathian Mountains and to the relief of Kowel. After Hauptmann Bumm and Major Bergholz, this brigade was commanded in turn by Hauptmann Kruse, Hauptmann von Buddenbrock and Hauptmann Dreyer. No further information concerning this brigade is available.

Sturmgeschütz-Abteilung 276 (Sturmgeschütz-Brigade 276)

Sturmgeschütz-Brigade 276

Sturmgeschütz-Abteilung 276 was formed in the summer of 1943 in Altengrabow at Jüterbog. The cadre consisted of the former 2./Sturmgeschütz-Abteilung 190. This battalion, which had a leaping black panther as its insignia, was quickly assembled under the command of Hauptmann Rünger. Experienced Sturmartillerie officers were sent to each battery.

In the late fall the battalion was sent to the east by rail from the Jüterbog station. It went to Heeresgruppe Mitte, going into action for the first time south of Briansk. Hauptmann Rünger and his adjutant were killed immediately after the first operation by a surprise barrage from a Stalin Organ. Hauptmann Schulte, commander of the 1st Battery, commanded the battalion until Major Norbert

Braun arrived as the new commander and Hauptmann Schulte was transferred to another unit. The command of the 1st Battery was taken by Hauptmann Axel Severa, who had also just joined the battalion.

During the initial operations in the winter of 1943, Oberleutnant Ertel (later decorated with the Knight's Cross) was wounded and Leutnant Nippes, section leader in the 1st Battery, was killed. Leutnant Nippes fell after a bitter fight with Russian tanks in which he destroyed a number of them. He was posthumously awarded the Knight's Cross on 15 February 1944. Hauptmann Tobler, commander of the 3rd Battery, was also killed in Nippes' Sturmgeschütz.

The defensive fighting that winter also took the battalion into the Korosten-Winniza area. The battalion went into action with every available gun at the recapture of Korosten, where it was always able to clear the way for the infantry in heavy street fighting and destroying pockets of Russian resistance.

Despite that the withdrawal continued and this defensive fighting ended with Sturmgeschütz-Abteilung 276 inside the large pocket at Kamenez-Podolsk. Almost all of the guns that were still operational were destroyed there. Ninety percent of the personnel and a few trucks, Schwimmwagen and communications trucks were saved, however.

The battalion was renamed a brigade on 14 February 1944. It regrouped south of Jaroslau in the spring of 1944. Leutnant Alfred Regeniter from the Sturmgeschütz-Schule at Burg joined the brigade there. Along with 200 other new Leutnants, he had been sent on his way with a personal farewell by Oberst Hoffmann-Schoenborn. The brigade then went to Deutsch-Eylau in East Prussia for rest and refitting.

By 8 May 1944 Sturmgeschütz-Brigade 276 had been rebuilt and re-equipped at Deutsch-Eylau under its new commander, Major Norbert Braun. On 1 August 1944 it was loaded up by rail and sent to the area northeast of Eydtkau to oppose the Russian attack on East Prussia. On the first day of the attack, the enemy, who had pushed 6 kilometers deep into German territory, was thrown back along a 16 kilometer front. On 3 August 1944 the 3./Sturmgeschütz-Brigade 276 was at Schapten, 4 kilometers north of Eydtkau as army-level reserve. From there it went 30 kilometers to Neustadt-Schirwindt to the 3. Panzer Army where it was attached to the 4. Panzer-Division.

That evening, it went into action against Russian infantry. Wachtmeister Kampmann destroyed a T-34/85 there. An hour after midnight the 3./Sturmgeschütz-Brigade 276 was transferred into the area of operations of the 6. Panzer-Division.

There was an attack northeast of Zwirgzdaiziai on 4 August. The attack made good progress initially, but then the Sturmgeschütze ran into massive fire from Russian antitank guns. The attack made no further progress.

When Leutnant Regeniter detected an enemy antitank gun in a farm house 300 meters to his front, he destroyed it. Then he sighted Russians observing the action with field glasses on a knoll about 1 kilometer away. We will let him describe the following action in his own words:

Suddenly a mortar round landed about 100 meters in front of the gun. The second round hit behind the Sturmgeschütz. I dropped down into the gun to give the order to move out and, at that moment, we received a mortar round right next to the cupola. The scissors binoculars were blown away. Gunner Strohbach, Driver Tischler, everyone was shouting. The 1.5 cm thick armored plate was ripped open.

Despite that we were still able to move. There were no more Russians at the destroyed antitank gun. We took back the infantry Hauptmann by the name of Merten. He had had both thighs torn off by a mortar round. Two other wounded soldiers went with us. Unfortunately Hauptmann Merten died the next day.

The big attack on 5 August with SPW, Panthers and Tigers didn't penetrate. The next day Wachtmeister Mehner destroyed three T-34's. The commander of the 3./Sturmgeschütz-Brigade 276, Oberleutnant Stück, destroyed two T-34's while Wachtmeister Kampmann knocked out one. That evening the Sturmgeschütze pulled anti-armor security along the run of a brook.

The attack to the east from Zwirgzdaiziai took place on 7 August. Leutnant Regeniter, together with his Sturmhaubitze (vehicle "331"), fired on a patch of woods where there were hidden Russians. Thirty prisoners were taken and seven antitank guns and a tank were destroyed. The tank was knocked out by Wachtmeister Mehner. When the attack continued, the Sturmgeschütz of Leutnant Regeniter took a hit from an antitank gun on its left. A road wheel flew into the air. The 3./Sturmgeschütz-Brigade 276 was in action for 7 hours. It went back into action towards 1800 hours, just after it had been refueled and resupplied with ammo. On 8 August the guns of Regeniter, Mehner and Oberwachtmeister Taschka provided security. The enemy did not attack.

The 3./Sturmgeschütz-Brigade 276 was alerted on 12 August. The Russians had broken through Bataillon Stady near Panzkabudis. Nine Sturmgeschütze and six SPW counterattacked at 0330 hours. By 0600 hours, in spite of heavy antitank fire, the situation had been cleaned up.

Sunday, 13 August, was quiet in this sector of the front. The guns could get maintenance. Not until 15 August did the Russian large-scale offensive from Versiai to Neustadt begin. The 3./Sturmgeschütz-Brigade 276 had to screen the withdrawal of Grenadier-Regiment 1097. On the following day, the Soviets, who had infiltrated on the highway north of Neustadt, advanced from the south and pushed Sturmgeschütz-Brigade 276 and the infantry back to the north. While Oberleutnant Stück, commander of the 3rd Battery, was driving to the infantry command post in his Schwimmwagen, his vehicle was hit. His driver, Gefreiter Naschenweng, was killed.

On that evening of 16 August all the guns of the 3rd Battery assembled at the Uzpjauniai wind mill. Oberleutnant Stück held on there until dark, before he pulled back to Tocorcinai.

Because the Soviets had approached to within 1 kilometer of the important bridge at Bramerhusen, Leutnant Regeniter went to the division and had the bridge protected by 5 guns from the 2nd Battery. He then took Kampfgruppe Werthern from the bridge, in order to place it in a position to attack south with him. Two T-34's were destroyed during this attack. Oberleutnant Stück was wounded at 1955 hours; Leutnant Sehrt took over command of the 3rd Battery.

All of the brigade's guns were constantly in action during the next few days. The large bridge at Bramerhusen had to be protected. The 1. Infanterie-Division had to move back across that bridge. Major Braun, the brigade commander, was killed by a hit from an antitank gun on 21 August. He was buried at Ebenrode. Hauptmann Sewera took over command. Because all of the guns had become inoperable in the meantime, there were a few days of quiet. Leutnant Regeniter received the Iron Cross, First Class on 2 September 1944.

The quiet period lasted until 11 October. The brigade was alerted that day. The dug-in guns were made ready to move. The brigade rolled forward, once again ready for action with new and repaired guns. The Sturmgeschütz of Leutnant Regeniter was at the spearhead of the 11 guns of the 3./Sturmgeschütz-Brigade 276. They crossed over the ridgelines under enemy observation at full speed. They came under heavy antitank fire as they reached the command post of Grenadier-Regiment 1099. The sections led by Regeniter, Sellbach and Taschka sections protected the individual companies as they got ready to advance into their old trenches.

They moved forward as the attack began. When they reached the old trenches they came under antitank fire from 20 meters further out. They rolled back onto the reverse slope. Their mission had been accomplished.

The long-expected Russian offensive began on 16 October at Saugoniskiai-Uzpjauniai on both sides of the railroad line from Wilkowischken. Nine Russian divisions advanced against a single German division. The farm in which elements of Sturmgeschütz-Brigade 276 were quartered received a heavy barrage. A personnel bunker took a direct hit as did two guns. They had to be towed away by two other Sturmgeschütze.

The Sturmgeschütz men were finally able to leave their bunkers at around 1200 hours. They raced to their guns and took off.

The Red Army had broken through on both sides of the railroad. Fifteen enemy tanks were reported. The Sturmgeschütze undertook a counterattack together with the assault company of Grenadier-Regimnet 1099. The attack got as far as Boblaukis.

A counterattack was launched when the 1. Infanterie-Division reported an enemy penetration along its boundary with the 549. Volks-Grenadier-Division. During this operation a Sturmhaubitze advanced into a farm house surrounded by vegetation. In the close combat at the house, the driver of gun "331," Kanonier Mescher, was killed. Kanoniere Saunus and Rollin were wounded. The Sturmgeschütz of Leutnant Regeniter moved back and restored the situation.

The advance continued across grain fields. An enemy machine gun, detected through the scissors binoculars, was destroyed. Far to the left of the Sturmgeschütze, 1000 Russians with 15 tanks pushed to the west.

The Sturmgeschütz of Wachtmeister Amberg had to be blown up at the brigade command post. The brigade shifted to Ostai. The main battle line then ran past the eastern edge of Wirballen. Gun "301" had engine trouble.

The 3rd Battery was then reorganized as follows:

1st Section: Gun "323" with Leutnant Regeniter, "312" with Wachtmeister Taschka, "331" with Kettner and "332" with Unteroffizier Frech.

2nd Section: Gun "404" with Wachtmeister Amberg; and guns "531" with Hartung and "520" with Frischmann.

In the attack on Sandau north of Bilderweiten, the combat strength of Sturmgeschütz-Brigade 276 was considerably increased by 5 Sturmkanonen from Panzer-Jäger-Abteilung 1131 under Oberleutnant Schaumburger. Sandau was freed. Ten antitank guns and 5 heavy machine guns were destroyed. Wachtmeister Taschka destroyed a Soviet assault gun. Leutnant Regeniter was able to knock out a T-34/85. When some guns from the 3rd Battery were providing antitank protection northeast of Sodargen, the Russians opened fire from their Stalin Organs. The German infantry pulled back. Once again, we will let Leutnant Regeniter report:

New orders: Commitment between Grenadier-Regiment 974 and the Leibstandarte "Adolf Hitler." We moved through Sommerkrug to Wabbeln and into the middle of an enemy ground-assault fighter attack. An infantry Hauptmann gave us directions from a dug-in position. He said there were tanks in front of them. I took up an ambush position and saw three large Russian tanks about 1500 meters in front of me on the horizon. It was like being on a firing range! I had to get them with just three rounds. The first round. The round shredded an apple tree 50 meters half left from me. My gun was completely out of adjustment. Almost certainly caused by a 15 cm shell burst right next to my gun in the previous operation.

All the hatches were closed. Despite that my loader got shrapnel in his arm. The Russians had detected me. There were crashes and explosions all around me. Amberg took a direct hit. His driver, Korscher, was dead.

The Sturmgeschütze assembled at 2130 hours at Sommerkrug. Guns "312," "332," "333," "337" and "311" stayed back at the front to provide security. Guns "301" and "331" which were no longer ready for combat also stayed up front. Gun "531" of Oberleutnant Stück also remained in the front lines in spite of a damaged cannon.

On 19 October the brigade command post was at Königseichen near Trakehnen. Eight new Sturmgeschütze arrived at Königseichen. Leutnant Regeniter received four for his 3rd Battery and scraped together crews for them. A little later, five Sturmgeschütze of the 3rd Battery were in action at Sommerkrug and Birkenwalde. On 20 October seven Sturmgeschütze, six Sturmkanonen and 1 Sturmhaubitze went into action at Steinkrug. Another gun joined in as this attack pushed forward to the east as far as Kleinschellendorf.

During that attack Leutnant Regeniter fired no fewer than eight armor-piercing shells at a JS 122 which did not penetrate it. The attack stalled.

Then, with the fall of darkness, a village which was partly on fire had to be attacked. Just before reaching it, Russian infantry ran back on the right. The Sturmgeschütze drove around the circle of light from a burning haystack. All of the 3rd Battery's guns followed the lead of Leutnant Regeniter.

They took up positions in the village. Leutnant Regeniter succeeded in destroying one T-34 and one JS 122 in the village. At that point the battery pulled back.

In the early morning of 22 October, still before daybreak, the Sturmgeschütz crews went back into action attacking again along with 150 infantrymen. When they reached a farm yard, which Leutnant Regeniter had already recognized as held by the enemy, he called a halt. He then aimed between two long, extended outbuildings and opened fire. The T-34 posted there blew up in spectacular fireworks. Once more we will let Leutnant Regeniter speak:

I continued to roll forward to about 100 meters left of the house on the hill. I halted there and shot off a flare which lit everything up bright as day and saw three Russian tanks in front of us. In the meantime, I had advanced to within 60 meters. The cannon fired and the first T-34 on the left exploded. The second one was destroyed. It blew up simultaneously with the third one which Unteroffizier Banaskewitz had hit. I clapped Unteroffizier Strohbach, my gunner, on the shoulder. Three blazing torches stood before us. They glowed, hissed and crackled as the ammuni-

tion exploded.

The enemy pulled back and we occupied the village in the early morning fog. Our infantry provided security in the direction of the enemy. We crushed three light antitank guns under our tracks and took a 7.62 cm Ratschbum in tow. Those were my first 5 tanks and all were knocked out within a period of 24 hours.

Seven Sturmgeschütze began the attack on Kleinschellendorf around 1000 hours on the morning of 10 October. The guns, led by Leutnant Regeniter, rolled forward with a large group of infantry. The attack ran into a Russian attack. Oberwachtmeister Seelbach destroyed two self-propelled guns. Suddenly, heavy artillery fire was placed on the German attackers. The forward observer, a young Leutnant, fell dead from the Sturmgeschütz of Leutnant Regeniter. The guns stopped and the infantry fell back 300 meters. Then the Sturmgeschütze also had to pull back to the edge of the woods. When enemy tanks showed up moving past them at long range, the Sturmgeschütz of Leutnant Regeniter gun moved off the main road which led to Hainau and onto a narrow trail in the woods. The gun of Banaskewitz followed closely. They ran into two T-34/85's which they destroyed at a range of 1600 meters. At that point both Sturmgeschütze came under heavy artillery fire. Moving backwards, both guns pulled back out of the woods.

After returning to the brigade command post, Leutnant Regeniter moved forward once again with the last operational gun in the brigade. He went as far as Kleinföhrenhorst. At Seidlershöhe he encountered Sturmgeschütz-Brigade 912 in a defensive position.

On the next day the recently-repaired Sturmgeschütz of Gerlach lost a track in a barrage on a crossroads southeast of Hainau. It was repaired and reinstalled. The gun of Leutnant Regeniter moved to the south along the east edge of the Hainau woods. It ran into enemy antitank guns and destroyed three of them. Regeniter destroyed yet another T-34/85 at the southeastern point of the enemy-held woods. When another T-34 rolled out of a gully it too was knocked out.

Three Hetzer arrived which had been sent forward by Gerlach on his way back. They scattered Russian infantry approaching Hainau with high explosive shells. Despite that the village was occupied by the enemy that afternoon. The Regeniter crew was finally relieved after 72 hours without sleep.

The next few days were turbulent ones. Again and again, the brigade had to try to get some of its damaged guns back into action. Leutnant Rudolf Sehrt of the 2nd Battery was killed in the early morning hours of 26 October . He was buried at Insterburg.

The battle for East Prussia continued. On 17 November the brigade's Sturmgeschütze were in ready positions at the Burgkampfen estate. The front had stabilized. It was quiet.

On 25 November the 3./Sturmgeschütz-Brigade 276 got ready to roll. It was to support an attack on a hill north of Schloßberg. It reached its assembly area north of Adlerswalde on 26 November. Then it attacked with 10 guns. Only 2 reached the objective. The others broke down or got stuck. Four had rolled onto mines. The Sturmgeschütz of Leutnant Regeniter also hit a mine and the crew bailed out. Unteroffizier Stohbach was wounded in the heavy artillery fire. Loader Nickert was hit in the thigh. The only gun to reach the hill was that of Oberleutnant Stück, but then he had to pull back as well. A little later the Oberleutnant received the German Cross in Gold and was promoted to Hauptmann.

The brigade celebrated Christmas in the Chorzele-Polozk area. On 28 December it marched to Grucin by way of Chorzele-Praschnitz-Zichenau. From there it went on to Grudush on 30 December.

The German front collapsed when the Russians started their offensive with 4 armies on 15 January 1945 and rolled to the northwest from the Ostenburg Bridgehead in the bend of the Narew. Sturmgeschütz-Brigade 276 was also forced to join the retreat to Zichenau. It was heavily bombed at Zichenau on 16 January. In the evening, it changed position to Glinozeck and Galacing and reached Bielsk the following evening. On 18 January it moved to Gilino in the deep snow and biting cold.

Still without guns, Hauptmann Sewera attempted to get some from the army. He came back to Hermannsdorf on 22 January where the brigade had arrived in the meantime. On 26 January it arrived in Danzig. The promised Sturmgeschütze finally arrived at Danzig. Leutnant Regeniter took over the 3rd Battery which was equipped with 8 guns. The 3rd Battery rolled into action for the first time with its new guns on the Vistula dikes.

Leutnant Adalbert Müller, with some guns from the 2nd Battery, repelled a Russian attempt to cross south of Mewe. He shot the pontoons and ferries of the Russians to pieces.

On 29 January Sturmgeschütz-Brigade 276 received orders to go to the area of operations for the 251. Infanterie-Division. It was launched in an counterattack on Bucowiec by Generalmajor Heuke, commander of the division, two days later. Its objective was to protect the withdrawal of his troops.

Oberwachtmeister Glaumann, recipient of the German Cross in Gold, participated in this attack. He moved at an insane speed, reaching the village with the German name of Buchenau. It was swarming with Russians. A T-34 rolled around the corner of a house and was destroyed. Five minutes later, 5 more T-34's were on fire. At around 2300 hours this Kampfgruppe pulled back again to Dretz.

The 2nd Battery, which had been in action elsewhere, lost a total of 6 guns that day.

On 1 February 1945 enemy tanks which had overrun a Jäger battalion, were repelled 2 kilometers west of Dretz. The counterattack on Bellno and Katsau on 3 February was carried out as a surprise raid against the Russian assault guns, tanks and antitank guns located there. While Glaumann's section of the 3./Sturmgeschütz-Brigade 276 with its four guns climbed a slope until his guns could fire over it at Bellno, the section led by Leutnant Regeniter rolled at top speed into the middle of a 300 meter-wide field. It stopped to shoot at that point and, covered by its fire, Glaumann's section rolled into the village at top speed and destroyed the enemy antitank guns and tanks at very close range. Regeniter's section pushed in behind them and Bellno was captured.

The entire battery rolled forward in a wedge formation to Katsau where it continued its attack. At Katsau it used the same tactics as employed at Bellno. At Katsau, however, Regeniter's section was to be the first into the village. When Leutnant Regeniter pressed forward, he suddenly found himself alone about halfway into the village. Kampmann's gun had an engine failure and had dropped out.

The muzzle flash from a Russia assault gun whipped out at them. Two rounds passed over the Sturmgeschütz, missing it by a hair, before it could fire back. It moved forward at top speed and reached the village. The Russians raced back. German infantry moved in from the flank. Another Russia assault gun appeared. This too was destroyed by the Sturmgeschütz of Regeniter. Altogether five tanks and two antitank guns were destroyed at Bellno and Katsau.

The 3./Sturmgeschütz-Brigade 276 had no losses. But Katsau wasn't completely in German hands yet. The attack on this village was resumed and a little later the enemy was driven out.

On the evening of the same day the Sturmgeschütze pulled back to the railroad station at Lassewitz to refuel and replenish their ammunition. Forty-eight hours later Leutnant Bracksch destroyed two Russian tanks in close combat at the station. He did it firing through the window of one of the station buildings.

During the counterattack on Linne with seven of the brigade's Sturmgeschütze and six Sturmgeschütze from the Sturmgeschütz company of the 227. Infanterie-Division, which was joined by 40 paratroopers, Leutnant Regeniter's gun destroyed a JS Tank and an assault gun while still advancing. A third armored vehicle, a T-34 on a hill, was hit. At that point the Sturmgeschütze pushed into the village from the right. Altogether in this attack, 7 enemy tanks, including some of their heaviest, were destroyed. No friendly guns were lost.

The next two days passed without incident. On 10 February the Sturmgeschütze occupied ready positions in a patch of woods at Stenzlau. The enemy wanted to take this wooded area at the south edge of the Tucheler Heath. The Sturmgeschütze moved east along the south edge of the woods. There were some corduroy roads leading over the swampy ground at places. Leutnant Regeniter reported the following events:

We left the pines, moving about 10 meters out behind a flat hill. My driver, Gefreiter Tischler, shouted: "Herr Leutnant, we can be seen here, we have to get back!"

However, as I had seen an antitank gun being pulled by two horses in front of the houses in the small village, I thought that the Russians had no flank cover or that they were just starting to get it in place. I had barely got back into the gun and given my firing instructions for the antitank gun, when there was a terrific crash and everything went black.

I came back to myself from the darkest of nights and tried to get up from my seat. I couldn't. My left leg no longer obeyed me. My hand was stuck to the blood on my left thigh. My leather pants were ripped. My first thought: 'You're alive!—Get out, the next round will kill you!"

I grabbed my left leg with both hands. My foot was dangling to the rear. I raised myself out of the hatch with my right leg, continuing to pull my left leg along. Then I leaped backwards or sideways out of the gun and fell on the right side. I crawled on my back away from the gun, moving myself along with my elbows. My loader, Gefreiter Wenk, came for me and pulled me another 15 meters back. Then two comrades arrived from the second gun. They put me in a tarp and brought me back to their gun which was still in the shelter of the pines. They then took me to the brigade command post.

Leutnant Regeniter was put on a train in Heiderode. There he bid his comrades farewell, and Hauptmann Sewera told him that he had been recommended for the Knight's Cross. Regeniter didn't find out until 30 years later that he had in fact been awarded the Knight's Cross.

His driver, Gefreiter Tischler, and his gunner, Unteroffizier Stohbach, were both killed when the Sturmgeschütz was hit.

Sturmgeschütz-Brigade 276 was continuously pushed back across the Tucheler Heath. It made it back to Danzig where, at the end, it fought under the command of Oberleutnant Schäfer. It was employed in costly operations as infantry after its last gun had been destroyed.

Sturmgeschütz-Abteilung 277 (Sturmgeschütz-Brigade 277)

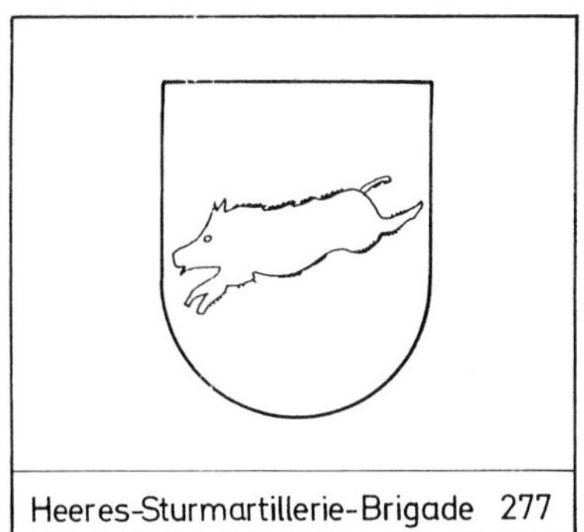
Heeres-Sturmartillerie-Brigade 277

Sturmgeschütz-Abteilung 277 was formed in the spring of 1943 from Sturmgeschütz-Ersatz-Abteilung 300 at Neiße. It bore a charging wild boar as its unit insignia. The battalion carried out its first training exercises at the Wischau Troop Training Area at Brünn, before it received its Sturmgeschütze in Altengrabow.

Hauptmann Bernhard Flachs, who had already been awarded the Knight's Cross as a Hauptmann on the staff of an artillery command, was the first commander of this battalion.

From Altengrabow the battalion was taken by rail to the southern sector of the Eastern Front. It went into action for the first time at Nikopol, east of the Dnjepr. It could be proud of its accomplishments during the weeks it was in action there. At Novo Mountal it destroyed 54 T-34 tanks in a single day during an engagement of tanks against Sturmgeschütze lasting several hours.

The young battalion paid a heavy price in blood during the subsequent defensive fighting in the area of Saporoshje and Kriwoi Rog. Wachtmeister Günther Carstens especially distinguished himself. On 17 November 1943 he became the first member of the battalion to receive the Knight's Cross.

Immediately after that fighting, the battalion had to be pulled out of action as it had suffered too many losses. The few guns and vehicles left after this long period of combat were given up and the personnel went to Odessa.

Major Bernhard Flachs became the 381st soldier of the Wehrmacht to receive the Oak Leaves to the Knight's Cross for his masterly command and for outstanding personal accomplishment in the heavy defensive fighting at Saporoshje and Kriwoi Rog. On 14 February 1944 the battalion was redesignated a brigade.

From Odessa the brigade marched to Braila on foot in March 1944. From there it was sent back to Altengrabow by rail.

It was rapidly re-equipped and the brigade was already back in action at Lepel in the Minsk area by July 1944. Oberleutnant Karl Buckel, commander of the 2nd Battery, pulled a proud victory out of a defensive action there against superior attacking Soviet forces. On 3 August 1944 he received the Knight's Cross for his unswerving devotion to duty.

The retreat back to East Prussia once again cost Sturmgeschütz-Brigade 277 heavily in men and materiél. In October it reached the new front line at Schloßberg in East Prussia. It fought hard and bitterly for ten days to establish the front there. Every individual man in the brigade far surpassed himself during those days. On 1 November 1944 the Wehrmacht Report had this to say about the fighting: "Sturmgeschütz-Brigade 277, under the command of Hauptmann Raeke, has destroyed 60 enemy tanks and 82 guns, as well as numerous mortars and other enemy weapons, in ten days of combat in decisive attacks in the East Prussian border area at a cost of only one gun. It especially distinguished itself as the backbone of the defense against enemy tank attack." Sometime during the winter of 1944/45 Sturmgeschütz-Brigade 277 was redesignated as Heeres-Sturmartillerie-Brigade 277 although its name change was not universally observed.

After that the brigade was once again brought back to fully operational condition. The Soviet storm was expected at any day and it was intended for the brigade to bring it to a halt at this line. Together with the infantry, a splendid system of defensive positions was constructed and the Sturmgeschütze were incorporated as its iron backbone.

There was bitter defensive fighting when the Soviets began their operational offensive there on 12 January 1945. The overwhelmingly superior enemy forces were halted for several days. Then, however, the defensive front broke apart and the retreat through Königsberg to Braunsberg began.

The Soviet thrust between Braunsberg and Elbing to the Haff closed the ring around Sturmgeschütz-Brigade 277. The brigade, which had only a few operational Sturmgeschütze left, filled the gaps in its structure with captured and repaired T-34's. It also had a few German Panthers.

At the end of February 1945 the brigade attempted to break out from Braunsberg to Elbing. The thrust was carried out along the Autobahn. The brigade trains were employed as infantry in this action. But only elements of the brigade succeeded in breaking out of the ring after a desperate struggle. Most of them remained in the pocket.

A Kampfgruppe was formed out of the remnants which had escaped the pocket. The last Sturmgeschütze of this Kampfgruppe were destroyed by the end of March. The survivors moved back through the Haff to the Kurische Nehrung, where they fought as infantry.

From there, Heeres-Sturmartillerie-Brigade 277 marched in formation into Soviet captivity on 9 May 1945.

Sturmgeschütz-Abteilung 278 (Sturmgeschütz-Brigade 278)

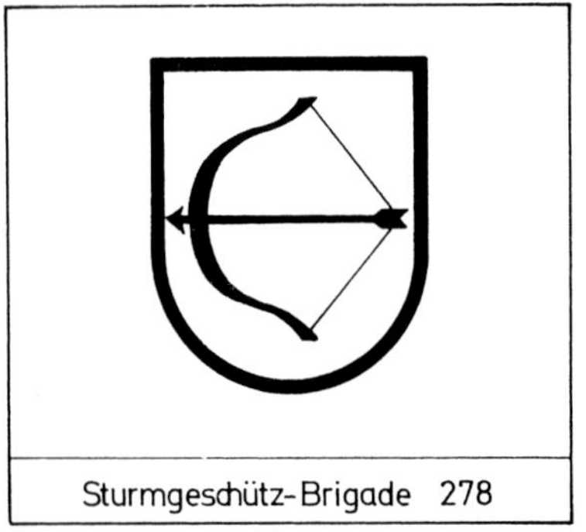
Sturmgeschütz-Brigade 278

The assembly of the personnel for Sturmgeschütz-Abteilung 278 began on 12 August 1943 under Hauptmann Johannes Stier at Sturmgeschütz-Ersatz-Abteilung 200 in Schweinfurt. Just one day later the battalion personnel were transferred to Aufstellungsstab (Organizational Staff) West at Tours in France. When it arrived there, it found out that Aufstellungsstab West didn't even exist yet. Not even the Commander-in-Chief West, Generalfeldmarschall von Rundstedt, knew anything about this staff. Only when Oberstleutnant Pritzbuer, the commander of Aufstellungsstab West, arrived in Tours could the chaotic conditions be normalized.

On 8 October 1943 Sturmgeschütz-Abteilung 278, still without Sturmgeschütze, was transferred to Altengrabow. On 15 October it was outfitted with guns and equipment at Altengrabow. As insignia, the battalion bore a bowed arrow directed to the left on its Sturmgeschütze and vehicles.

The training with guns and gear, however, could no longer be completed, as the battalion was loaded onto transports for the Eastern Front on 22 October 1943. At the time the battalion took to the field, command and staff positions were held as follows:

Commander: Hauptmann Johannes Stier
Adjutant: Leutnant Mader
Orderly Officer: Leutnant Tittus
Mess Officer: Leutnant Schindler
Unassigned: Leutnant Ruoff
Headquarters Battery Commander: Oberleutnant Otto
1st Company Commander: Hauptmann Reichert
Section Leaders: Oberleutnant Brause, Leutnant Loeffler
2nd Company Commander: Oberleutnant Feurstein
Section Leaders: Oberleutnant Bauer, Leutnant Hopf
3rd Company Commander: Oberleutnant Scheufler
Section Leaders: Oberleutnant Behne, Leutnant Bettinger
Unit Engineer: Kriegsverwaltungsrat Bohn
Paymaster: Oberzahlmeister Wiese
Technical Inspector: Inspector Knitze

On 28 October 1943 the transport reached the operational area of Kirowograd. The 1st and 2nd Battery were thrown into combat right off the ramp of the Koristowka railroad station where they were unloading. Strong Soviet mobile units had broken through and were advancing on Kriwoi Rog and Snamenka.

The battalion was attached to the 24. Panzer-Division in the XXXX. Panzer-Korps sector. It went into action on 28 October with Panzer-Grenadier-Regiment 21 at Nowaja Praga to cut off the overextended point of the enemy attack and, by breaking through, to bring relief to the hard-fighting infantry outside of Kriwoi Rog.

On its first day of combat, the battalion destroyed one KV 1 and two T-34's. But six Sturmgeschütze were disabled, mainly from engine and gear damage. The repair section, recovery section and maintenance section did excellent work, and soon all the guns could be reported as fully operational once again. Technical Officer Rudolf Bohn, Shop Foreman Dalichow and Wachtmeister Sall of the recovery section worked unceasingly to provide the crews with operational guns.

The 3rd Battery also arrived at Koristowka on 28 October and was immediately sent to the engaged battalion.

The advance was continued on 29 October. The battalion managed to overcome the strong Russian field positions at Dubowiy-Spassowo and destroy seven antitank guns. On the same day it made contact with German armor units attacking from the south and thus eliminated the threat to Kriwoi Rog.

The combat elements were pulled back to Dubowiy on 30 October. On 11 November the battalion command post was at Olympiadowka. On day later the battalion assembled in a ready position at Dubowiy. Together with the 24. Panzer-Division, it was moved into the Nikopol Bridgehead, where the IV. Armee-Korps and the XXIX. Armee-Korps were in position as "Gruppe Henrici" under General der Panzertruppen Henrici. By 11 November the battalion had already crossed the Dnjepr, marching into its new operational area. It moved on to Bolschaja-Snamenka and from there to Malaia-Lepaticha. It was ordered to push back the Russian penetration along the boundary between the IV. and XXIX. Armee-Korps in the highlands at Werchne Rogatschik.

The attack began at 0545 hours on 11 November. The 3rd Battery charged forward on the left flank of the spearhead. It rolled over strong antitank defenses, field guns and infantry positions. As a result of this momentum the attack rapidly pushed a few kilometers forward. The 2nd Battery made a frontal attack with mounted Panzergrenadiere, while the 1st Battery swung far to the south with Panzer-Grenadier-Regiment 26 in order to cut the enemy off from the rear.

Despite everything, the attack did not succeed entirely. Three Soviet divisional staffs managed to escape along with the greater part of their infantry. The old main battle line was re-established that evening. The enemy had suffered heavy casualties. The battalion's Sturmgeschütze went into ready positions just behind the main battle line. On 7 November the guns of Sturmgeschütz-Abteilung 278 occupied an antitank position behind Hill 61, west of Werchne Rogatschik. A Russian tank attack was expected. Although a few T-34's pushed into the village in the early morning hours of that day and rolled past the battalion command post undetected, the major tank attack didn't take place. German antitank cannon destroyed one of these T-34's as it moved through.

The battalion was then divided into two Kampfgruppen. While the 1st and 3rd Batteries were sent to Dnjeprowka and attached directly to the IV. Armee-Korps as a defensive reserve, the 2nd Battery marched to Perwomajewka on 9 November and was attached to Panzer-Grenadier-Regiment 26. On 11 November the Headquarters Battery, the maintenance section and the trains were sent to Nikopol. Through 20 November every attempt by the Soviets to split open the bridgehead had failed.

Three Soviet 7.62 antitank guns were destroyed in a diversionary attack on 21 November, which the 2nd Battery carried out with the II./Panzer-Grenadier-Regiment 26 in the area of Wessely. Oberleutnant Bauer's Sturmgeschütz took a direct hit from an antitank cannon.

The following day the 2nd Battery defended against strong enemy infantry and tank forces at Wessely-Nesamoshnik. Of the 16 attacking tanks, 7 were destroyed and 2 damaged.

The next day again saw the 2nd Battery engaged in hard fighting in a village. The battery commander, Oberleutnant Feurstein, was severely wounded. The Sturmgeschütz of Leutnant Hopf was knocked out.

Hauptmann Reichert, commander of 1st Battery, was the first officer of the battalion to be killed in action.. His battery destroyed 4 enemy tanks and damaged two others during the battle for Stachanow. Wachtmeister Fischer and Dentlen, experienced Sturmgeschütz commanders, were killed in this same fight. On 25 November Oberleutnant Scheufler was wounded with severe burns.

One day later the 1st and 3rd Batteries were sent to Dnjeprowka. They repulsed a Soviet tank attack on the village. Four T-34's and one KV 1 were left on the battlefield.

On 28 November the 2nd Battery marched to Konstantinowka. It managed to beat back a surprise attack by enemy tanks and destroy two T-34's and one KV 1 at a sheep farm 5 kilometers southwest of the village in the sector of Jäger-Regiment 106.

The enemy massed strong tank forces and 60 enemy tanks were counted just on 28 November. Despite that, the Soviets no longer attacked this bridgehead. As a result, the battalion staff and the 2nd Battery were pulled out of the bridgehead on 30 November. Up to that point, the battalion had the following score for only four losses of its own: 34 tanks, 73 antitank guns, 9 field guns, 6 mortars and 11 antitank rifles destroyed.

On 3 December the entire battalion was assembled at Gorodischtsche. From there the 2nd Battery was sent to the 46. Infanterie-Division at Lukijewka on 7 December. It was billeted at Krassindorf. On 8 December the 1st and 3rd Batteries were also relieved from the bridgehead and ordered to Krassindorf.

In the days that followed, the battalion continually regrouped and changed assignments. On 15 December three Sturmgeschütze eliminated a Soviet penetration at Hill 129.6 and re-established the old main battle line. Another enemy penetration on Hill 145 at Lubimowka was eliminated on 16 December. The Sturmgeschütze wiped out two Soviet infantry companies with machine-gun fire and high explosive shells in that action.

When 60 tanks of the Soviet 39th Tank Brigade attempted to break open the German front from the north, their tank spearhead was annihilated. Six T-34's and one KV 1 were destroyed and left on the battlefield. The attacking forces did not continue their deployment.

Together with Grenadier-Regiment 477, the battalion repulsed three rifle divisions and a tank brigade at Bishidar from 21 to 23 December. The Soviets, who were attempting to reach and cut the Dnjepropetrowsk-Nikopol road at Bishidar, were pushed back with bloody losses. Eight T-34's and a Soviet SU 152 were destroyed.

Sturmgeschütz-Abteilung 278 joined Sturmgeschütz-Abteilung 243 to form a strong reserve group in the Nikopol Bridgehead. Sturmgeschütz-Abteilung 278 still had 18 Sturmgeschütze, but there were never more than 12 guns fighting at any given time because of mechanical failures or combat damage. The battalion owed a debt of gratitude to the tireless efforts of the repair and recovery crews and the men of the other technical services for the fact that generally 12 guns could be kept in service continuously. The quiet devotion to duty of these men during uninterrupted, heavy labor—almost always under enemy fire—was what made success possible. They did as fine a job as German soldiers have ever done. These men, unknown and always unrecognized, always stood fast and held like iron in every desperate situation.

The front remained quiet up to the year's end. At the beginning of 1944, the Soviets shifted their attacks to the western section of the Nikopol Bridgehead. Their objective was to reach and block the bridge positions and the roads leading through the swamps of the Dnjepr lowlands. To reach this objective—controlling the bridges over the Dnjepr—the Soviets also took the heights to the south of Bolschaja-Lepaticha at the beginning of 1944. During the night of 2 January Sturmgeschütz-Abteilung 278 with elements of the 97. Jäger-Division launched a counterattack. The heights were regained and heavy losses inflicted on the enemy. Then, on 7 January, the battalion was moved to Nikopol.

Hauptmann Stier was appointed armor liaison officer to Heeresgruppe Schörner. Hauptmann Wilpricht, who had joined the battalion as commander of the 1st Battery, took over command of the battalion itself at Bolschaja-Lepaticha.

On 13 January 1944, the Russian New Year's Day, the Soviets attacked Bolschaja-Lepaticha once more after two and a half hours of intensive artillery and ground-attack fighter preparation. One hill was lost but was retaken in the evening hours of 14 January by Sturmgeschütz-Abteilung 278 along with the guns of Sturmgeschütz-Abteilung 243. At the end of this month Sturmgeschütz-Abteilung 278 received orders to move to Kriwoi Rog.

In Kriwoi Rog the battalion was attached to the LVII. Panzer-Korps. The line elements and trains, which had Dolginzewo as a march objective, were only able to make slow progress through the knee-deep mud in the early thaw. Integrated with the columns of the 24. Panzer-Division, the 3. Gebirgs-Division, the 16. Panzer-Grenadier-Division and several other formations, the vehicles bogged down in the morass. At the same time strong Soviet tank and infantry forces were able to expand their breakthrough to the west at Kamenka in the direction of Apostolowo and push forward all the way to Schirokoje.

On 4 February 1944, the road and the railroad line became the main battle line. The vehicles of the trains had to be blown up. The Headquarters Battery, under Oberleutnant Behne, which was two days behind the support troops, was ambushed by Soviet infantry southwest of Apostolowo. The Soviets captured the vehicles. Oberleutnant Behne was killed during his attempt to retake the vehicles in a counterattack. Hauptwachtmeister Behrens and four soldiers of the Headquarters Battery were also killed.

Further west, the Soviets wheeled to the northwest to surround Kriwoi Rog. Sturmgeschütz-Abteilung 278 had lost all of its logistical support, and it no longer had any maintenance services. Despite that, it continued to be committed to defend Kriwoi Rog.

Sturmgeschütz-Abteilung 278 was redesignated as Sturmgeschütz-Brigade 278 on 14 February 1944. On 16 February Sturmgeschütz-Abteilung 277, which was almost completely wiped out, was attached to the "Pfeil" ("Arrow") Brigade. However, this "addition" only amounted to one Sturmgeschütz. Just two days later the two brigades were separated again.

When the Soviets penetrated into the German positions for a distance of several kilometers, the "Pfeil" Brigade launched a counterattack on 17 February at Romanowka and Wolny Tabor on icy roads during a snow storm. By noon it had taken back the old main battle line. The final battle for Kriwoi Rog began. The Sturmgeschütze were the only heavy weapons in the hard fighting which raged day and night. They prevented any enemy breakthrough and gave the infantry assurance and confidence. During the defense of the village of Kriwoi Rog trains elements also fought as combat infantry under the command of Leutnant Ruoff.

During the night of 22 February the last four Sturmgeschütze, together with the commander and Leutnant Loeffler, forced their way back more than 15 kilometers through outer districts already occupied by the enemy. They crossed the Ingulez to occupy new defensive positions. This breakout took the enemy completely by surprise and several heavy antiaircraft cannon were overrun. The new brigade command post was set up in Gurowka.

At that point the brigade had only 3 or 4 operational Sturmgeschütze. Not until 23 February was it able to take over new guns and a maintenance platoon. When the Soviets reached Marinskij and dug in at this suburb of Kirwoi Rog, they converted it into an impregnable bulwark with heavy weapons. The brigade launched a counterattack the following night. With mounted assault troops, it broke through the raging Soviet antitank fire. The village was taken and the old battle line re-established. Leutnant Loeffler played an outstanding part in this attack. On the very same day the brigade and its last 5 Sturmgeschütze were attached to the 62. Infanterie-Division at Grigorjewka, northwest of Kriwoi Rog.

On 28 February it received 10 Sturmgeschütze from Sturmgeschütz-Brigaden 236 and 277, along with the maintenance section of Sturmgeschütz-Brigade 236. However, all of the Sturmgeschütze were damaged and first had to be repaired.

On 1 March 1944 the brigade joined Infanterie-Regiment 97 in ready positions in Bahndorf, but only three guns were still operational. On 3 March new Sturmhaubitzen arrived and, on the very same day, they eliminated an enemy penetration. On 3 March there was a major engagement when some thirty T-34's broke off from the enemy thrust to the west to wheel on Kasanka, where the brigade's maintenance section was positioned. Six Sturmgeschütze, which were only partially operational, were committed against these tanks. They destroyed seven T-34's. Despite that, the front had to be pulled back. Only two Sturmgeschütze were still operational: those of Hauptmann Stier and Leutnant Loeffler.

The brigade assembled in the Wosnessensk Bridgehead. It had been declared a "fortified area" by order of the Führer in order to keep the Bug crossing open for the German forces still located to the east of the river.

Hauptmann Stier managed to receive 14 Sturmgeschütze from Panzer-Jäger-Abteilung 1228 there, but they were only conditionally operational. In addition, nine new guns arrived. That gave the brigade 25 Sturmgeschütze. In three days of uninterrupted, intensive work, the maintenance section managed to get 18 of them operational. Once again, the men under Engineer Bohn, Foreman Dalichow and Wachtmeister Saal had outdone themselves.

The enemy had managed to establish a bridgehead across the Bug at Akmetschet as early as 23 March. The Sturmgeschütze and Grenadier-Regiment 106 attacked this Soviet bridgehead. Enemy antitank and antiaircraft guns and field positions were destroyed, and this kept him from expanding his bridgehead. However, the friendly forces were unable to eliminate the bridgehead entirely and throw the Soviets back across the Bug.

The withdrawal continued back in jumps of 15 kilometers. Again and again, the Sturmgeschütze had to wipe out enemy spearhead elements which had broken through in order to keep them from being surrounded. On 29 March the brigade was moved to Koschary and attached to the 348. Infanterie-Division. Sixty enemy heavy tanks advanced on Nowo Troizkoje on 30 March, in an attempt to reach the road to Jessajewo to control the only bridge across the Ingul and deny the river crossing to the entire corps. The 15 guns of the brigade attacked together with Grenadier-Regiment 535 and thrust into the enemy tank attack.

Twenty four T-34's were destroyed without a single loss in a fight which lasted for hours and which counted among the heaviest experienced by the brigade during the entire war. This outstanding action was mentioned in the Wehrmacht Report for 1 April 1944:

The defensive fighting in the south of the Eastern Front between the lower Ukrainian Bug and the Pruth continues in intensive, indecisive fighting. The Bolsheviks have again suffered heavy casualties and lost 38 tanks and 20 guns. The Silesian-Austrian 384. Infanterie-Division under the command of Generalleutnant de Salengre-Drabbe and Sturmgeschütz-Brigade 278 did a magnificent job in the fighting.

On 31 March 1944 the commander of the 384. Infanterie-Division wrote to Hauptmann Stier:

Sturmgeschütz-Brigade 278 was attached to the division from 28 to 31 March 1944. The brigade, under the outstanding leadership of its commander, Hauptmann Stier, supported the division magnificently during this period. It made an essential contribution to the success of the division's defense outside of Nowo Troizkoje on 3 March 1944.

I wish to express my appreciation and thanks to Sturmgeschütz-Brigade 278 and I wish it and its commander the best of luck in the future.

de Salengre-Drabbe, Generalleutnant

Following the complete destruction of their brigade, the officers and men, inspired by their unlimited will and unshakable belief in themselves and their weapons, brought their brigade back to a state of combat readiness by their own efforts, and it was again able to participate in a decisive battle and achieve a great victory.

The brigade moved to Nowosswetowka on 1 April 1944 in a rain and ice storm. The gun optics iced over on the following day when the temperature fell from 8° above zero to 25° minus zero Celsius. During the same period the enemy pushed into the German main battle line. Three guns broke down in the immediate counterattack. The 40 attacking enemy tanks were able to be stopped at 1430 hours when all of the Sturmgeschütze of the brigade could be employed. Seven enemy tanks remained behind, shot to pieces on the battlefield. In the evening the temperature rose again to zero. Snow showers raged and made the roads impassable.

The weather changed several times in the next few days. On 6 April the brigade's last four Sturmgeschütze were permanently put out of action. During the withdrawal it moved back through Nowo-Petrowka and Ploskoje to Tiraspol. On 7 April the trains and Headquarters Battery reached Causani Noui in Rumania. There it was possible to begin repairing the guns.

On 11 April 1944 the entire German main battle line in this area lay on the Dnjestr, beginning south of Gura Buculni dropping to the bend in the river south of Tighina. The Soviet penetration through the narrows at Plop-Stubai and the occupation of the important Hill 151.7 by the XX Russian Guards Corps, was pushed back during the following night. The hill was recovered in an infantry counterattack. Two Sturmgeschütze from the brigade supported this attack and wiped out pockets of enemy resistance.

The vehicles of Versorgungsstaffel (support section) Schindler were on the road day and night to bring fuel and munitions forward to the Sturmgeschütze. The situation on the Dnjestr Front stabilized. When 8 new Sturmgeschütze arrived on 21 April, the brigade once again had 19 operational guns.

The main battle line held along the line running Tokmadseja — southern edge of Buculni — See — Warnita — Borisowka — north edge of Tighina. From there it followed close to the Dnjestr south to Cioburciu. Every Soviet attack was repelled. The situation in the corps sector remained stable. On 28 May orders arrived from XXX. Armee-Korps, moving all 18 of the brigade's Sturmgeschütze to the XXIX. Armee-Korps, effective immediately. The XXIX. Armee-Korps intended to eliminate a Soviet bridgehead between Rascaeti and Purcari containing 3 infantry divisions. It had the brigade attached to it for this purpose. It was intended for the 9. Infanterie-Division to lead the infantry attack. The artillery was to support Unternehmen "Martha" with 200 guns and 4 super-heavy mortars.

In the meantime, the brigade had 21 operational Sturmgeschütze. The attack was to begin at 0315 hours on 8 June 1944. As the Sturmgeschütze rolled into their ready positions, Unternehmen "Martha" was canceled.

On 15 June 1944 Hauptmann Stier received the German Cross in Gold. This brave officer, who was greatly revered by his brigade, had more than earned this award.

During the night of 20 August 1944, very intense Soviet artillery fire began along a width of 10 kilometers. At 0600 hours, just as there was enough light to aim, there also began continuous Soviet air attacks. The Rumanian 4th Mountain Division and the Rumanian 21st Infantry Division, which were located in the sector of Sturmgeschütz-Brigade 278 next to the 304. Infanterie-Division, took to their heels. Only the Rumanian 3rd Mountain Division stayed with the brigade to face the enemy.

By 28 August the Rumanian 3rd Army was completely destroyed. Sturmgeschütz-Brigade 278 had been cut off. With desperate courage, it fought through three concentric lines of Russians surrounding it to the west.

Contrary to the Führer's orders at the beginning of the Soviet operational offensive, Hauptmann Stier sent his trains and rear elements back to the rear under the command of Baurat Bohn in order to save them this time from imminent annihilation. The line elements made it through individually. The last elements smashed through to the west under the command of their brigade commander and Hauptmann Scheufler, Leutnant Tittus and Leutnant Kirstein during the night of 30 August.

They moved with a Russian tank column for at least 15 kilometers undetected. In that manner the group got to within 30 kilometers of the Carpathian Mountains. The Sturmgeschütze were detected only when they separated from the Russian group, and they were destroyed by the superior Soviet forces. Hauptmann Stier assembled the survivors on foot. Leutnant Kirstein was killed at that point. Hauptmann Scheufler was taken prisoner. Leutnant Tittus and his men were got lost in a grain field while Hauptmann Stier was scouting out a breakout possibility.

The brigade commander marched 30 kilometers through the Carpathian Mountains by himself before he reached the rest of the brigade in Hungary.

Not until the middle of September 1944 did the brigade get transported back to Germany for refitting after having been employed in the Carpathian Mountains as infantry. It had suffered horribly and had taken heavy casualties. But it had also gone through an operation which had demanded the most of it in courage and toughness.

Sturmgeschütz-Brigade 278 was reorganized at Wörmlitz near Burg. On 9 October 1944 Major Karlheinz Schüssler took over command.

In December the brigade was transferred to East Prussia and went back into action for the first time at Memel. It's mission was to stop enemy preparations for an operational offensive and deny him any expansion of his main battle line as a preliminary to this offensive.

The Russian winter offensive began on 12 January 1945. The Soviets attacked with overwhelming numbers of infantry and tank units. Sturmgeschütz-Brigade 278 formed a solid bulwark against this flood of tanks. It destroyed tank after tank, but at the same time lost gun after gun. By the end of January the brigade was but a shadow of its former self, no longer fit for combat and at the end of its strength.

On 28 January 1945 it was merged with Sturmgeschütz-Brigade 232, which had also been decimated. The new commander was the commander of Sturmgeschütz-Brigade 232, Major Alfred Hinze.

With that Sturmgeschütz-Brigade 278 ceased to exist. The members of this brigade shared the fate of Sturmgeschütz-Brigade 232. A tragic event has to be reported at the conclusion of the brigade's history: Oberwachtmeister Ernst Spatzier, who as the clerk of the operations officer of Sturmgeschütz-Brigade 278 had coordinated and ensured the supply and care of the brigade from its beginning, was shot at Hela on 8 May 1945 by court martial order after an outrageous denunciation. And so this respectable, selfless and honorable soldier had to die unnecessarily on the last day of the war and add to the high number of the brigade's dead.

Sturmgeschütz-Abteilung 279 (Sturmgeschütz-Brigade 279)

Sturmgeschütz-Brigade 279

On 1 July 1943 500 soldiers assembled in front of the Dieskau Barracks at Neiße, the home station for Sturmgeschütz-Ersatz-Abteilung 300, to form the newly constituted Sturmgeschütz-Abteilung 279.

Hauptmann Hoppe was to be the battalion commander. But at that time he was still with his artillery unit on Sardinia. Oberleutnants Betjemann, Schulz and Heise commanded the three batteries.

One month later the brigade, still without weapons and guns, was transferred to Saumur in France. From Saumur it went back to Altengrabow, where it received its weapons, vehicles and equipment. Hauptmann Hoppe also arrived there and, quite unexpectedly, the battalion was loaded on trains and sent to the area of Nikopol by rail.

The battalion received an unpleasant surprise at Nikopol, when it had to give up its new Sturmgeschütze to a veteran brigade. It then had to wait for resupply before it could go into action.

After the equipment had finally arrived, the brigade went into action for the first time in the area west of Melitopol and south of Tschechowgrad. There were many settlements of German origin in its area of operations. This was evidenced by the fighting at Mariendorf and the night operation at Darmstadt. The brigade was surrounded for the first time.

The brigade broke through the Soviet ring along with a Panther Kampfgruppe. The trains which were located close to Wesseloje just managed to escape the enemy's grasp. The units were pulling back to the Dnjepr. However, they were engaged in heavy defensive fighting while still east of the river, and the brigade suffered heavy casualties.

Sturmgeschütz-Abteilung 279, which was to strengthen the German main battle line on the Dnjepr, fought its way back through the Nogai steppe to the Dnjepr. It crossed the Dnjepr at Berislaw. The 1st and 2nd Batteries worked on their Sturmgeschütze on the west bank. The 3rd Battery, on the other hand, was attached to the 4. Gebirgs-Division. It went back into action at the Cherson Bridgehead. It was unexpectedly relieved in the bridgehead. The battery had to give its guns to another battalion, march to Nikolajew and from there take naval landing craft across the Black Sea to Eupatoria. It was reunited with the two other batteries there.

The brigade waited at Simferopol for the arrival of new guns. Immediately thereafter it headed north where the 50. and 336. Infanterie-Divisionen defended both the isthmus at Perekop and the one on the Placid Sea against Soviet attacks from the north.

The Sturmgeschütze were then used as a fire brigade along the entire front. The brigade fought at Woinka and Dolinka, at Mamtshuk and Budanowka. Then winter set in, and the front became quiet.

Combat activity resumed in the spring, initially for the possession of the dominating heights. Hill 17.4 northeast of Maly Bem and the Tarchan Hill were retaken from the Soviets during nighttime counterattacks. The brigade managed this in spite of heavy fire from Stalin Organs.

Because the 17. Army was expecting a Soviet attack on the Siwasch Isthmus, Sturmgeschütz-Brigade 279 was divided up and put into widely separated ready positions at the critical points. The battalion had been redesignated as a brigade on 14 February 1944. The 1st and 2nd Batteries remained in the sectors of the 50. and 336. Infanterie-Divisionen. The 3rd Battery was moved to the northeast into the sector of the Rumanian 10th Infantry Division.

The Soviet operational attack on the Karanki Isthmus began on Good Friday, 7 April 1944. A section of the 3rd Battery under Leutnant Wollny was located there. The entire front was engaged in severe fighting for days. The Soviets first managed to make a penetration in the Rumanian sector. The Rumanian units abandoned their positions almost without fighting and fled to the rear. The 3rd Battery launched a counterattack along with a unit of Rumanian combat engineers who were fighting bravely. Then another night counterattack was ordered. It failed because the Rumanians lit up their positions all night long with white flares. Several Sturmgeschütze suffered direct hits and were lost as a result. The rest of the 3rd Battery had to be pulled out of the fighting.

The battery had to blow up its last guns when it became apparent early on Easter Sunday morning that the Soviets had already gotten past the Tomaschewka Isthmus into the rear of these units and the last Rumanian soldiers disappeared wading through the shallow water. The battery charged back to the mainland with the only two Sturmgeschütze which were still operational.

The entire Eastern Front had become fluid in the meantime. German troops were also moving back in the Armjansk area. The 1st and 2nd Batteries suffered heavy casualties there. The 11. Infanterie-Division and Sturmgeschütz-Brigade 191 were rapidly thrown in at the threatened point, but were in no position to stop the armored Russian thrust on Dshankoi.

The withdrawal of all units to Sevastopol began in the evening of 11 April 1944. They had to reach the fortress before the Soviets. There were 14 Sturmgeschütze and a battalion of light antiaircraft guns available to cover the flank for the German march column which moved on to Sevastopol. During the day the units positioned themselves for all-round defense. The Soviets would surround the German troops at night over and over again. There followed a nighttime breakout and a forced march until the next morning.

Things didn't look really bad until 13 April, on the last day of the march before reaching Sevastopol, when the Kampfgruppe fell into a cleverly established Soviet anti-armor trap at the Kontugan

Farm.

It was only possible to escape this trap by using every Sturmgeschütz to its utmost and with rapid fire from every barrel of the 2 cm antiaircraft guns. However, two Sturmgeschütze were set alight by the enemy.

When this Kampfgruppe reached the outer fortified perimeter of Sevastopol, the Sturmgeschütze were halted by General Six, the commander of the 50. Infanterie-Division, and incorporated into the forward-most defensive lines. Sturmgeschütz-Brigade 279 then defended the north side of Sevastopol along with the rest of Sturmgeschütz-Brigade 191. Following that, the remaining guns were turned over to another battalion, and Hauptmann Hoppe flew to Germany to take charge of the reorganization there.

Two Panzer-Zerstörer-Kompanien were formed from the remnants of the brigade which had remained behind. The first one was commanded by Oberleutnant Sticher, the second one by Oberleutnant Heise.

On 8 May 1944, with the beginning of the Russian operational attack on Sevastopol, these two companies, equipped with Panzerfaust and Panzerschreck, were at the focal point of the fighting on Nikolajewka Hill. However, the Soviets managed to overrun this position by 9 May with the help of heavy ground-attack fighter support. On 9 May Sturmgeschütz-Brigade 279 had 60 killed and missing to mourn. The rest were given permission for evacuation from the Crimea. More than anyone else, Major Müller, the commander of Sturmgeschütz-Brigade 191, played the greatest roll in saving these men from the Soviet clutches.

Despite that, many members of the brigade were killed on the Cherson Peninsula. Others died during the crossing to Konstanza when their transport ships were sunk by the Soviet Air Force. The rest of the brigade who left Cherson on 11 May 1944 on the Hungarian also experienced devastating Soviet air attacks. Only 48 men were left to report in with Oberleutnant Heise at Deutsch-Eylau after an interminable railroad trip from Konstanza through Bulgaria and Yugoslavia.

The reorganization took place at Sturmgeschütz-Ersatz-Abteilung 600 at Deutsch-Eylau. The men of the Sturmartillerie who had been released from hospital reassembled there. Two missing comrades even returned from Turkey. But, the brigade was re-equipped slowly.

They were loaded on trains during the night of 1 September 1944 and unloaded in Suwalki after a short trip by rail. The brigade then received its first operations order after its reorganization. It moved rapidly to the heights northeast of the city, where the 170. Infanterie-Division was already waiting for "its" Sturmgeschütze. There were unpleasant incidents during this operation. There were fist-sized rocks in the loose, sandy soil and so, when the Sturmgeschütze turned, these stones caused tracks to come off their sprockets. The tracks often had to be put back on while under enemy fire, which caused even more casualties.

The Soviets quit attacking at this point, however, and the brigade was sent further north to take up ready positions in the Rutka-Tartak Woods. From there, elements carried out terrain and route reconnaissance toward Wilkowischken.

But then, when the 170. Infanterie-Division ran into trouble on Hill 254 near Lake Lasczewo, the Sturmgeschütze went into action back there. Things quieted down only after 14 Russian observation posts on the hill had been destroyed, one after the other.

Strong Soviet forces attacked south of Wilkowischken in the morning hours of 16 October. Low level fighters attacked so often that the brigade couldn't go into action to relieve the hard-pressed division until afternoon. By evening, however, it had managed to establish a defensive position for the infantry after destroying several T-34's.

Strong Soviet tank forces attacked the next morning. Once more a considerable number of enemy tanks was destroyed, but this brought no relief and the brigade received orders by radio to pull back to the second East Prussian defense position. The infantry had already been sent marching back to that position earlier.

As the Sturmgeschütze rolled back, they ran into the middle of a swarm of Russian tanks which had already reached this position before them. For the first time, the brigade engaged in a firefight with the new Joseph Stalin tanks. One of these steel giants was destroyed. The others pulled back. While passing through a narrow lane in the mine field on the forward slope of the defense position, two Sturmgeschütze were lost to rounds fired from Soviet tanks lurking in hide positions.

Because of the unclear situation, Major Hoppe went back to division that evening. He never returned. As was later reported by one of the men accompanying the commander who survived, he ran into lead elements of the Russian tank forces. They were rolling forward unimpeded just to the north in the early morning while he was trying to get back to his brigade. He was killed after a brief fight.

In Major Gerhard Hoppe, the brigade lost a brave commander, who could take much of the credit for the brigade's many victories and for its success in the defensive battles. Not until 23 December 1944 did he finally receive the Knight's Cross posthumously, an award for which he had been recommended long before.

The situation of Sturmgeschütz-Brigade 279 became untenable when the infantry which was supposed to hold the position with it pulled back again. The Soviets to the north of the brigade were already far to the west in its rear. All that it could do was retreat to the first East Prussian Defense Position. When the Sturmgeschütze reached this position, the Soviets were already in it at that point, and had to be expelled in a bitter fight before it could be occupied.

Hauptmann Heise, who had already been awarded the German Cross in Gold, had taken over command of the brigade. He had to leave due to wounds suffered during the fighting on the north edge of the Rominter Heath.

Oberleutnant Stahlhacke, who until then had commanded a Kampfgruppe at battery strength, took over command of the brigade. Oberleutnant Stotz commanded the second Kampfgruppe in the brigade.

There was fighting during the following period when the individual Kampfgruppen were committed entirely on their own.

Then the new commander, Hauptmann Angelmaier, arrived. He had already been awarded the German Cross in Gold. Under his command the brigade played a considerable part in the retaking of Goldap.

The brigade was located in the Gumbinnen area during the winter of 1944/45. The bitterest chapter in the history of Sturmgeschütz-Brigade 279 began with the launching of the Soviet winter offensive on 12 January 1945. It was moved into the area of Gumbinnen, Insterburg and Georgenburg with 19 Sturmgeschütze. It was supposed to help eliminate the Russian penetration there.

However, it turned into a race with the Soviets, who were advancing on Königsberg north of the Pregel.

The brigade won another great victory in the Kreuzberg area. Leutnant Werner Scholz distinguished himself by his outstanding bravery during the fighting for Zinten, and he was awarded the Knight's Cross.

On 31 March 1945 Hauptmann Angelmaier also received a well-earned Knight's Cross for his tireless activity and his unparalleled resolution.

The remnants of the brigade fought a bitter action in the Heiligenbeil pocket, which again brought high casualties. There were only five Sturmgeschütze left. These were consolidated with the Panzer-Jäger-Abteilung of the 170. Infanterie-Division

Oberleutnant Stahlhacke was awarded the German Cross in Gold for his selfless leadership and for his decisive offensive and defensive victories.

When the Heiligenbeil pocket was abandoned, the brigade crossed over the already weak and fractured ice of the Haff to the Frische Nehrung. Because of the lack of guns, the brigade had to be converted into an infantry battalion. Hauptmann Heise, who had returned to the brigade after recovering from his wounds, led the brigade in infantry actions. He was once again severely wounded and had to go back to hospital. Hauptmann Seth took over command of the battalion. The battalion was attached to the 7. Infanterie-Division and fought in that division's sector.

The brigade was employed at Fischerbabke an der Elbinger Vistula in the Vistula lowlands for several weeks. It was pulled out at the end of April 1945 and shifted to a blocking position on the Nehrung.

The Soviets attacked once more there, just before the capitulation. The brigade put up extremely fierce resistance to the enemy and the Soviets were repelled in spite of overwhelming numerical superiority.

The German commanders capitulated there in the early morning of 9 May 1945, and the survivors of the proud Sturmgeschütz-Brigade 279 marched off into Russian captivity as a unit. Its pitilessly hard service had come to an end.

Sturmgeschütz-Abteilung 280 (Sturmgeschütz-Brigade 280): The "Sword" Brigade

This battalion was formed in Schweinfurt during the summer of 1943. The unit's further training, the final establishment and preparation for combat took place at Tours in France. There it was temporarily under the command of Hauptmann Heinzle. A number of experienced Sturmartillerie men joined the new "outfit" with Heinzle. They were mostly soldiers from Sturmgeschütz-Abteilung 191 who formed the cadre for the individual batteries.

Gradually, a number of additional officers showed up, so that the individual batteries and sections could be well furnished with leaders.

Oberleutnant Rossbach became adjutant. Dr. Hirtschiz was the unit physician. Oberinspektor Gerster was head inspector (shop supervisor). Oberzahlmeister Wachsmuth was the paymaster.

The designated commander of the battalion, Hauptmann Kühme, finally arrived on 14 October 1943 and, on 5 November, it was transported all the way across Germany from Tours to Berditschew.

The battalion was sent into action immediately upon leaving the unloading ramp to protect the road to Shitomir.

With great élan it advanced against a closed ring of Red Army units surrounding some 1,200 Waffen-SS trainees 1.5 kilometers south of Shitomir. These troops were freed.

"It was a really crazy feeling" Wachtmeister Haupt reported to the author. "We literally pulled them out of Hell."

Immediately thereafter the battalion rolled into the area of Gorodischtsche, followed by a battalion of Panzer-Grenadiere who had been attached to it. This new battalion was a significant reinforcement for the division which had been functioning as a "placeholder."

The men of Sturmgeschütz-Abteilung 280 carried out an attack in the area of Kiev with this division. Oberleutnant Meyer von Thenhausen, who had just joined the battalion, was fatally wounded during this action.

The division succeeded in pushing the Russians back to the Dnjepr, and the battalion was already hoping to be able to pass the winter there in secure quarters, when, during its Christmas celebration in Dorogun, it received orders to stand by. On New year's Eve Russian motorized units attacked the command post of the 2nd Battery and would have overrun it, if a sentry hadn't given the alarm in the nick of time.

It was a wild night fight. No one knew where the enemy was, and only the characteristic muzzle blasts from the cannons of the Soviet T-34's offered anything to aim at. The enemy was halted right in front of the command post and defeated there.

The battalion was engaged in constant defensive fighting in the area of Schepetowka from 12 January to 1 May 1944. It was redesignated a brigade on 14 February 1944. It was used in the Bogocar-Ljubar area, where the enemy continually tried to interrupt the flow of German supplies across the Dnjepr bridge.

By the end of January losses had become so serious that it was sent replacements from Sturmgeschütz-Ersatz-Abteilung 200 in Schweinfurt. The first Sturmgeschütze had already arrived by 9 January and, by Thursday, 10 January, available crews had been assigned to these guns.

The approach march for the attack began on 13 January and it took the brigade to Stary Konstantinow. The next morning at about 20 degrees below zero Celsius, it went into its assault positions against strongly held enemy positions on Hill 311. The attack wasn't launched until 13 February, after a few Russian tanks and vehicles had been destroyed in some minor skirmishes.

On the next morning the infantry advanced again in a howling snowstorm. Leutnant Meining took over the 2nd Battery on 28 February.

The brigade fought in additional skirmishes with varying luck. The Sturmgeschütz of Wachtmeister Paul was destroyed.

When the important traffic center of Tarnopol was surrounded on 25 March 1944, several German divisions, among them the 367. and 349. Infanterie-Divisionen, the 9. And 10. SS-Panzer-Divisionen and schwere Panzer-Jäger-Abteilung 653, were committed in this area.

Attached to the 9. SS-Panzer-Division, Sturmgeschütz-Brigade 280 moved forward on 8 April 1944 in the relief attack on Tarnopol. The formations fought their way forward through Uswje to Zlotniki, forced the crossing of the Strypa and expanded the bridgehead which had already been established there on 6 April by the 100. Jäger-Division.

Some of the Sturmgeschütze had to be blown up there because of lack of fuel. An infantry detail was formed under Oberwachtmeister Huse.

Although at the end of their strength, the committed units still managed to break open the ring of encirclement on 14 April. The remnants of Sturmgeschütz-Brigade 280 which had been surrounded at Pothajce smashed through with all the strength they had left and escaped the pocket.

The brigade pulled back and regrouped at Jaroslaw, west of Lemberg. News arrived there that the brigade was to be transferred to Denmark for reorganization.

First, however, the unit was sent to Sturmgeschütz-Abteilung 400 at Hadersleben. From there it was taken to Apenrade and new Sturmgeschütze and vehicles were received there during the following weeks. The first exercises took place and, at the beginning of July, the staff and the majority of the brigade were transferred to the North Sea coast at Öchsbyl. Shortly before departure, the newly reorganized brigade passed in review before Major Kühme in front of the Deutsches Haus at Apenrade.

After the landing of British paratroops at Arnhem in September 1944, Sturmgeschütz-Brigade 280 was transported directly to the Dutch border. It first went into action at Arnhem-Oosterbeek, where it took heavy casualties. Hauptmann Werner was killed in a duel with British tanks when his command gun was destroyed.

Allocated to the 15. Army-Oberkommando, the brigade was at Arnhem until the last day of the battle. It was attached to the LXIV. Armee-Korps, and it remained in an attached status to this organization until 9 February 1945.

It became apparent in the heavy fighting there that the inexperienced brigade was able to do an outstanding job in spite of its interrupted training. It also became apparent that the Sturmartillerie, composed almost entirely of volunteers, was in general the pick of the entire artillery branch.

The 7.5 cm L48 assault cannon performed well there. Later, the unit received the Jagdpanzer IV with the 7.5 cm L 70 assault cannon. It reached the unit at the turn of the year 1944-45. These were even better and proved to be an outstanding weapon in fighting with enemy tanks.

After the successful operation against the British 1st Airborne Division in the Arnhem-Oosterbeek area from 19 September to 29 September, the brigade was loaded back on trains at Apeldoorn on 29 September.

The defensive battle north of Antwerp had already begun on 30 September 1944, and this was followed by the retreat across the Moerdijk Deep. These operations were to last until 7 November and made up the second phase of this brigade's operations.

Its mission was to hold firm there with the rest of the 15. Armee in the face of the Canadian 1st Army which was supported by the British 2nd Army. Both of these armies were attacking to the north and northwest in an attempt to surround and destroy their German enemy.

The brigade was often in action with Fallschirm-Jäger-Regiment 6 under Oberstleutnant von der Heydte while this superior allied force pushed them back, step by step. The brigade was reorganized again and again. Experienced crews were killed and guns and transport vehicles were destroyed.

The brigade was committed in the Eschen area on 6 October along with Fallschirm-Jäger-Regiment 6. Two days later, Hauptmann Sebald, Oberleutnant Lange, Oberleutnant Feyl and Leutnant Acker joined the brigade to fill the vacant officer positions.

Divided into two Kampfgruppen under the command of Oberleutnants Roßbach and Stollmann, the brigade went into the fighting at Haarle which began on 23 October. Then the unit had to make preparations to pull out the bridgehead south of the Moerdijk Bridge. Oberleutnant Roßbach was killed on 26 October by a direct hit in a fight with an enemy tank.

On 1 November the brigade received five Sturmhaubitzen to compensate for its lost Sturmgeschütze.

The Moerdijk Bridgehead was abandoned on 6 November, and the combat elements were transferred to the area of operations of the 346. Infanterie-Division and attached to it. After moving to Barentrecht, the brigade was loaded by rail in Utrecht on 19 November 1944.

In the third phase of its operations in the west, it was intended for the brigade to fight in the Alsace Bridgehead, where the brigade arrived on 24 November. It would fight there until 9 February 1945.

The French 1st Army had broken through the positions of the 338. Volks-Grenadier-Division south of Belfort and had reached the banks of the Rhine at Rosenau near Basel.

Attached to Panzer-Brigade 106 "Feldherrnhalle" under Oberst Dr. Franz Bäke, an attempt was made to thrust into the flank of this movement and pinch off the enemy. After initial success, this plan went awry. Despite that, this operation succeeded in stabilizing the front south of Thann. The 198. And 159. Infanterie-Divisionen were committed there.

At the same time the French 1st Army was conducting this operation, additional French troops attached to the US 7th Army, smashed through the Zaberner Depression toward Straßburg. After a four-day siege, they took possession of the city on 27 November. Despite that, a thin security screen could be put in place south of Straßburg. In any event, a critical situation had arisen in this area under the command of the 19. Armee.

In the meantime, Sturmgeschütz-Brigade 280 had reached the area south of Baden by rail and, during the night of 24 November, was moved across the railroad bridge at Neubreisach which was still in German hands to the west bank of the Rhine.

The subsequent defensive operations in Alsace brought some victories but, above all, terrible losses, partly from enemy air activities.

Together with Panzer-Brigade 106, Sturmgeschütz-Brigade 280 was able to support an attack by the 198. Infanterie-Division on 7 January 1945 in the direction of Straßburg. It advanced as far as the outskirts of the city. It became apparent there that a small unified Kampfgruppe of some 50 tanks and Sturmgeschütze was capable of breaking through the front of the greatly superior, well-equipped enemy in the space of just a few hours.

The enemy forces broke and ran when faced with the tanks of Kampfgruppe Bäke and the Sturmgeschütze of Sturmgeschütz-Brigade 280.

The Alsace bridgehead was abandoned in mobile fighting during the period from the middle of January to 9 February.

On 14 December 1944 the brigade commander, Major Kurt Kühme, received the Knight's Cross which had been awarded to him on 9 December. On the same day Hauptmann Sebald was wounded.

During the night of 9/10 January the Sturmgeschütz of Leutnant Steier was destroyed in error by a round from a Panther, which was supposed to support the fighting of the brigade's combat elements. Oberleutnant Stollmann was killed by a head wound in urban fighting in Ensisheim, as he drove through this village standing in the open hatch of his Sturmgeschütz.

The brigade wasn't put back into action in the Saarpfalz until it had had a few days rest in the areas of Müllheim-Badenweiler and could be refitted there with men and materiél. Men on leave and those returning from the hospital hurried back to their units. When it received orders for rail transport in the area southwest of Trier, the unit was once again combat-ready, even if only conditionally.

The brigade was unloaded at Hermeskeil. Oberleutnant Feyl acted as Transport Officer for the brigade and was sent to the Railroad Directorate in Karlsruhe to ensure its rapid deployment. The brigade's rail transport was detected in the Wörth Railroad Station by a US observation plane, and the subsequent air attack inflicted heavy losses of soldiers and materiél.

The unit was strengthened by a few Jagdpanzer IV(A) 7.5 cm L 70 sent into the Hermeskeil area.

On 15 March US forces began their attack against the 1. Armee defending the area between Trier and Saarbrücken and the remnants of the 7. Armee forming a weak flank protection between Koblenz and Trier.

The elements of the brigade were separated by rapidly changing attachments and so it was unable to bring its full strength into play.

On 20 February Hauptmann Kühme bid farewell to the brigade. His successor was Hauptmann Lechens. At the beginning of March the line batteries were loaded on trains for Achern and the Headquarters Battery for Freiburg. The train with the headquarters Battery was disrupted by a heavy fighter-bomber attack which lasted 50 minutes. Despite that, it made it to St. Wendel by 7 March and was directed from there to Hermeskeil. There were additional attacks by fighter-bombers during a set of confusing operations which resembled road marches more than anything else. On 19 March one of these fighter-bomber attacks caused casualties.

On the following day there was a white phosphorous attack on the Headquarters Battery's forest position at Lindenberg. When enemy tanks pushed into this village, they were stopped by a few Sturmgeschütze. The enemy tanks pulled back after taking three losses.

The withdrawal of the Sturmgeschütze speeded up. They moved through Germersheim and Walldorf to Obergimpern and from there on to Massenbach on 25 March.

On 11 April the last guns of the brigade formed a tank destroyer unit under the command of Oberleutnant Feyl in the Schwäbisch Hall area. They were employed in two groups, which were led by Leutnant Preine and Leutnant Thöny. They were attached to the 198. Infanterie-Division. They were committed with this division east of Geildorf.

Kampfgruppe Lechens, which had been assembled on 20 April under Major Wilhelm Lechens, succeeded in stopping the enemy when it attacked an American tank penetration at Bopfingen. Four US tanks were left in flames on the battlefield. Lechens had received the German Cross in Gold on 7 October 1943 while with Sturmgeschütz-Abteilung 228.

Finally, on 26 April, the withdrawal was covered by the remaining Sturmgeschütze. On 27 April Chief Inspector Gerster took over command of the Headquarters Battery and those elements of the brigade still with it, after its commander had been wounded. South of Leipheim, Leutnant Preine was one of the last officers of Sturmgeschütz-Brigade 280 to be killed. That was the end of Sturmgeschütz-Brigade 280 and all the surviving members of this brigade who had continued to sacrifice themselves in the fighting in western Germany remember their fallen comrades with sorrow. As the last Wehrmacht Report from Grand Admiral Dönitz in the morning of 9 May 1945 said: "At this hour, the Wehrmacht remembers its comrades who fell facing the enemy. The dead bind us to unconditional loyalty, to obedience and discipline, in the eyes of our country, bleeding from countless wounds."

Sturmgeschütz-Abteilung 286 (Sturmgeschütz-Brigade 286)

Sturmgeschütz-Brigade 286

On 24 August 1943 the battalion was assembled under the command of Hauptmann Körner. On that day 21 noncommissioned officer's and 258 men arrived at Neiße from Sturmgeschütz-Ersatz- und Ausbildungs-Abteilung 300. On the same day, Hauptmann Körner was ordered temporarily to Berlin and Oberleutnant Schwinner took his place.

It was necessary to complete the training on various weapons over the next few weeks at Neiße. On 27 August Oberleutnant Reiss took command of the battalion's 4th Section.

The training continued under Hauptmann Körner, who had returned from Berlin, and only then did the activation orders (OKH/AHA/Ia (II) No. 17152/43) go into effect. According to this, it was officially designated Sturmgeschütz-Abteilung 286, and it was now brought together as a unit at Dieskau Barracks at Neiße (a temporary camp).

On 8 October the battalion received marching orders for France. On the next day, it marched in formation to music with its commander at its head to the Neiße railroad station. Four-hundred-ninety soldiers arrived at Pilsen after a two-day trip, and from there the battalion moved via Nuremberg and Kaiserslautern to reach the French border at Neuburg on 13 October. The battalion continued on through Paris, and after several intermediate stops, such as Orleans and Tours, it reached its goal, Azay le Rideau.

The training of the individual batteries began there starting 21 October.

On 26 October the commander of the Sturmartillerie-Schule at Burg at Magdeburg, Oberst Günther Hoffmann-Schoenborn, arrived there for a final inspection. The inspection met with the full approval of this experienced Sturmgeschütz veteran, who already wore the Knight's Cross with Oak Leaves. There was a noon meal following the inspection at the Grand Hotel in Tours for all the officers of the battalion to dine with their service's senior officer.

On 1 November a teletype arrived from the Sturmartillerie-Schule designating Hauptmann Dr. Albert Bausch as the new commander of the battalion. He arrived immediately afterwards at the battalion and took it to Altengrabow on 5 November, where the Sturmgeschütze and vehicles were to be issued to the battalion.

They took the first ten Sturmgeschütze, equipped with the assault cannon 42, and all vehicles to the Troop Training Area at Camp du Ruchard for training at unit level on 8 November 1943. On the next day, the battalion had a section live fire, which initiated a 10-day training program.

On 20 November, after completing unit training, the battalion occupied quarters in Tours, in the French Hillier Barracks.

After three additional transport trains had arrived, the battalion had a total of 41 operational Sturmgeschütze. It took these back to the Troop Training Area at Camp du Ruchard, where every Sturmgeschütz was allowed three rounds to calibrate and zero the guns. Any defect found in the guns was fixed, and a few improvements were made independently in a French work shop. At that point the commander reported that the battalion was ready for action.

A teletype on 28 November from the Transportation Commander Paris-South read as follows: " Sturmgeschütz-Abteilung 286 is to report itself as ready for field duty and will be loaded up in the next few days."

The embarkation railroad station was to be St. Comé at Tours.

As the battalion had not yet been provided with its basic load of ammunition, it could not report itself as ready for deployment. This delay gave the commander the opportunity to take the four Sturmgeschütze which had had defects back to the Troop Training Area to be zeroed once more.

On 5 December 1943 Sturmgeschütz-Abteilung 286 was loaded up in St. Comé. All three transport trains could be dispatched that day on a route which took them through Reims to Koblenz and from there by way of Limburg, Kassel, Göttingen, Breslau, Krakow and Lemburg to Winniza. From Winniza the battalion proceeded to the Monastyritsche to unload from the train.

The first stage of the journey was over when the battalion reached its final goal of Kirowograd on 13 December, and the last two transports arrived there on 14 December.

The battalion was sent to the XI. Armee-Korps where it was instructed to take up positions in the suburb of Kuschtschewka. It was to be used as an Heeresgruppe reserve according to the orders received by its commander from the corps.

The battalion was attached to the 11. Panzer-Division on 15 December by radio traffic from the XI. Armee-Korps. It road marched the 18 kilometers to Prokowskoje, southeast of Kirowograd. There it was placed under the operational control of the 2. Fallschirm-Jäger-Division, which was in assault positions at Klinzy. The paratroopers' objective was the Kamenka Valley and the southern part of the village of Nowgorodka, which was strongly held by the enemy. Fallschirm-Jäger-Regiment 7 was employed against these objectives and the 1st and 3rd Sturmgeschütz Batteries linked up with the I. and III./Fallschirm-Jäger-Regiment 7.

When the attack began in the morning of 18 December at 0630 hours, the Sturmgeschütze rolled ahead of the paratroops as their steel spearhead.

"Achtung, 1200 meters ahead, half right, enemy tank." Leutnant Kerner warned his comrades. He had taken the point of the 1st Battery.

Antitank rounds were loaded. The Sturmgeschütz men worked rapidly and efficiently and, when the first section halted to fire and four rounds left the muzzles of its Sturmgeschütze, two enemy tanks lay there in flames. Then the 3rd Battery also joined the fighting. Moving forward by bounds, halting and firing, they broke up the enemy tank attack. Of the fourteen T-34's which had been counted five remained behind destroyed and on fire.

They moved forward in a rush. Heavy Russian antitank guns laying in ambush were destroyed, forward machine-gun positions ground into the dirt, antitank rifles silenced with high explosive rounds, and the Red Army men who suddenly sprung out of their foxholes were shot down with high explosive rounds or machine gun fire.

The attack made it through. The paratroopers kept up with the Sturmgeschütze, but then they had to break off the attack, as they were running out of infantry ammunition. The paratroopers had to withdraw step-by-step back to the jump-off positions. The Sturmgeschütze covered this withdrawal against Russian attempts to push immediately after them and overrun the German main battle line. In the coming night all of the Sturmgeschütze had to go into position in the main battle line for security.

Even though the attack finally had to be broken off, this first full day of combat was a success for the new Sturmgeschütz-Abteilung 286, which had come through its great trial by fire with flying colors.

The attack was not resumed. A bridge was to be thrown across the Kamenka at another location. Combat engineers went to work. But then a ford across the Kamenka was detected by Unteroffizier Henke through which the Sturmgeschütze could reach the other side of the river.

On the other side of the river, they fought duels once again with tanks. Seven enemy tanks as well as six antitank guns and several trucks were destroyed by the Sturmgeschütze. Attacking Russian infantry was pushed back with machine gun fire.

On 18 December Hills 170.3 and 163.7 were supposed to be taken. The enemy was dug in there. The Sturmhaubitzen were instructed to take cover in hidden positions behind the forward-most lines and to destroy known enemy positions—above all machine gun nests and mortar positions—with aimed fire.

Despite these instructions, the Sturmhaubitzen advanced with the paratroopers. They rolled forward onto both flanks of Hill 170.3, then turned around and destroyed enemy positions. Oberleutnant Alban managed to destroy two T-34's which were rolling toward him with only four rounds.

After this hill had been cleared of the enemy, the attack continued onto Hill 163.7. The most important thing there was to get rid of the light and heavy antitank cannon. As soon as one was detected, they opened volley fire on it. Firing high-explosive rounds and killing the crews in the process, these positions were rolled over and crushed. In this fashion, the way up the hill was cleared for the paratroopers.

The Sturmgeschütze had to stay up front that night as well. Then, on 19 December, they had to clear the last enemy positions from the southeast edge of Hill 163.7 and the south edge of Nowgorodka.

The Sturmgeschütze managed to take this village by storm. Four tanks and seven antitank guns—all Ratschbumms (7.62 cm caliber flat trajectory guns)—as well as several other guns and mortars were destroyed.

An order from the paratroopers to send two Sturmgeschütze back up front for reconnaissance as the evening fell was fatal for those two guns. They were destroyed by two enemy antitank guns which were lurking, well camouflaged, behind low vegetation. Oberleutnant Alban was badly wounded, and a driver was killed.

The Sturmgeschütze were pulled back for rest and refitting during the night of 20 December, and the two battery commanders reported to the command post at Nowo-Federowka.

On 20 December a tank and 15 of the dangerous Russian antitank guns were destroyed in rapid raids to the front, and a number of enemy vehicles were shot into flames.

Nowgorodka, which had not yet been completely cleared, was attacked again on 21 December. The enemy occupied Hills 165.6, 187 and 159.9; these were attacked once again. The Sturmgeschütze were engaged in this fighting as the only available heavy weapons. They moved ahead of the infantry. Nowgorodka was driven through from all sides while firing and was taken by the following infantry. Following that, Hill 165.6 also fell to them after a short firefight with tanks and antitank guns. But then strong groups of Soviet tanks counterattacked. An enemy attack with 14 T-34 tanks was repelled by the battery commanded by Oberleutnant Dahms.

The Sturmgeschütz men managed to destroy six enemy tanks in this duel, but it was no longer possible to take Hill 187. There were too many antitank guns in the way. The battalion suffered four losses in these duels, but its score was impressive with 23 antitank guns destroyed.

The next night the Russians infiltrated back into the northern section of Nowgorodka from Hill 187. In spite of high losses, the paratroopers managed to take Hill 187. However, the northern section of Nowgorodka remained a no-mans-land, even after Hill 159.9 was taken by storm. Despite everything the German forces were too weak and, on 23 December, the 2. Fallschirm-Jäger-Division had to go over to the defense. Sturmgeschütz-Abteilung 286 shifted its command post to Nowgorodka.

The 2. Fallschirm-Jäger-Division, which had been brought in to Russia from positions in front of Monte Cassino in the Volturno Region in warm Italy, had fought with great dedication. Major Pietzonka, commander of Fallschirm-Jäger-Regiment 7, had lost half of his men there, but the Russian major attack had been repelled after 17 days of fierce action. Sturmgeschütz-Abteilung 286 along with the armor of the 11. Panzer-Division had played a big part.

The 11. Panzer-Division and the elements of the 13. Panzer-Division which were also committed were pulled out to be used elsewhere. At that point the two parachute regiments, Fallschirm-Jäger-Regimenter 2 and 7, had only the Sturmgeschütze left for use as heavy weapons. The Sturmgeschütze provided cover in the following days.

On 27 December three damaged Sturmgeschütze fell into Russian hands. When an attempt was made to save them, another gun was set alight and a second damaged by antitank fire.

On 3 January 1944 the battalion received orders to move to Dolinzkaja in order to rail load there. It went to Ingulo-Kamenka by rail where it was unloaded. The Sturmgeschütze had to move back by road march to their old area of operations.

Sturmgeschütz-Abteilung 286 stood ready to defend those areas known to be attack objectives when Russian artillery opened fire on the morning of 5 January 1944.

There was a wild firefight when strong enemy tank and infantry forces attacked. The well-positioned Sturmgeschütze were able to stop the first large armor group of some 25 tanks with rapid fire. Antitank and antiaircraft cannon joined in the defensive fire. This entire tank group was destroyed within a few minutes. Two Sturmgeschütze had been hit and damaged and were pulled out.

The second wave of tanks also moved directly towards the cleverly positioned Sturmgeschütze. In this duel of tank against Sturmgeschütz, the Sturmgeschütze showed their superiority in their rapid, well-aimed fire and the effectiveness of their hits. Thirty-six enemy tanks were destroyed by the Sturmgeschütz battalion during this day.

The Sturmgeschütze attached to the 9./Fallschirm-Jäger-Regiment 2, which had not been committed up that point, were launched against a Russian tank group rolling in out of the northeast. The Sturmgeschütz of the commander of the 2nd Battery charged forward into a depression where a Soviet tank group had taken up ready positions. In an incredibly hard and rapid fight this gun alone destroyed five T-34's. The regimental command post of the paratroopers was also protected by the commander's Sturmgeschütz. It entered the battle at 0930 hours on this day. It destroyed two T-34's that were heading straight for the command post. The Soviet infantry following the tanks was halted by high-explosive rounds and machine-gun fire.

When three more Sturmgeschütze came in from the 9./Fallschirm-Jäger-Regiment 2 area to provide cover to the north, an enemy armor attack was brought to a halt and four enemy T-34's knocked out.

After the three Sturmgeschütze ran out of ammunition, the command post had to be abandoned in the face of another approaching swarm of enemy tanks. With the support of the command gun, the Sturmgeschütze, by then four in number, took up a crescent shaped defensive position in the center of the village of Nowo Andrejewka. They held out there until 1400 hours. Enemy forces had pushed into the village from three sides. A cry for supporting infantry to help out went unheard. The four guns pulled back gradually. When two Sturmgeschütze from the 1st Battery arrived from Nowgorodka and took up firing positions on the western edge of a ravine, they destroyed three pursuing T-34's and effectively engaged the enemy infantry.

After the fall of darkness, the guns pulled back to refuel and load up ammunition. A few Sturmgeschütze managed to bring back the surrounded Bataillon Rollschwski along with its wounded. The last Sturmgeschütz had to be blown up at the site of the breakthrough because of an engine failure.

When the news arrived that evening that enemy tanks had broken through across the Nowgorodka-Kirowograd road in the area of Ryptschina, three Sturmgeschütze and a Sturmhaubitze with mounted paratroopers headed in that direction. They approached the enemy to within very close range. Fifteen T-34's and four trucks were seen. The Sturmgeschütze opened fire at a distance of 200 meters. In a wild melee, eight T-34's and all four trucks were destroyed. The latter were fully loaded with munitions and fuel and were blown sky high in columns of flame. The remnants of this enemy group fled to the northeast in panic. The lines of communication were again open.

Sturmgeschütz-Abteilung 286 did extraordinarily well in this battle. On this day a total of 60 T-34's were destroyed, along with six antitank guns, twelve machine guns, four mortars and an antitank rifle. Some ten trucks were destroyed and strong infantry forces were taken out of action.

The Sturmgeschütze occupied defensive positions between Kirowograd and Karlowka until 18 January 1944. One hundred forty prisoners were taken by the 1st Battery when it managed to surround an enemy battle group on 7 January. Four hundred Soviet soldiers lost their lives in this pocket. The battery captured an enormous amount of materiél, including important maps and radio codes.

Early in the afternoon the commander of 3rd Battery was killed during an attack on Fedorowka, recently occupied by enemy forces.

On 19 January 1944 the battalion received orders to conduct reconnaissance for firing positions in the sector of the 384. Infanterie-Division. The commander established contact with the division.

The 2nd Battery went into a ready position at Ingulo-Kamenka on order of the LII. Armee-Korps. That was on 29 January. One day later the commander was able to distribute the first well-earned Iron Crosses and assault badges to his soldiers.

The next few days and weeks passed without incident. The muddy season had already begun in this area by 5 February. On 11 February a teletype arrived at the battalion from the Commander-in-Chief of Heeresgruppe Süd, Generalfeldmarschall von Manstein:

To Hauptmann Dr. Bausch

Commander of Sturmgeschütz-Abteilung 286:

My heartiest congratulations on your award of the Knight's Cross.

/signed/ von Manstein

The command and staff list for the winter of 1943 (inasmuch as available) was:

Commander: Hauptmann Bausch
Headquarters Battery Commander: Hauptmann Roch
1st Battery Commander: Hauptmann Körner
2nd Battery Commander: Oberleutnant (Hauptmann) Dahms
Officers of the 1st Battery: Leutnant Horn, Leutnant Rothermund

On 14 February 1944, the battalion was redesignated a brigade. Sturmgeschütz-Brigade 286 fought in the Dnjestr Bridgehead east of Kischinew starting in January 1944 and, after the collapse of Rumania, fought from one desperate position to the next back to Transylvania. The new main battle line was established there.

This support enabled thousands of German soldiers to make their way back to their units. The brigade fought at Tokay Altsohl, Szeszeny and, above all, in the Gran Bridgehead where, once again, it was able to hold out against a vastly superior enemy. It moved back to Horn by way of Preßburg. With unswerving resolution, the brigade stood fast in the Gran Bridgehead at Preßburg and Horn in both defense and counterattack. The brigade was in action at Hills 236, 241, 333, 237 and 247. It fought as a unit to destroy enemy tanks massing at Kemend-puszta, and the Sturmgeschütze again showed that they were superior to the enemy tanks. Smoking, shot up wrecks remained behind on the battlefield, mostly enemy tanks. Three Sturmgeschütze were also destroyed

Innumerable attacks, counterattacks and relief actions transformed the young, inexperienced brigade into a band of dedicated fighters who went far beyond the call of duty. Never once during the short period that it was in action did this brigade ever get pushed back by the enemy. Most of those killed in action were shot in the head. And so they suffered the death of a Sturmartillerie man. Not one of the brigade's Sturmgeschütze ever fell into enemy hands. They always fought with everything they had.

The "voluntary demobilization" of the brigade, which was ordered "from on high," took place at Horn. Sturmgeschütze and vehicles were blown up, and the brigade members fought their way back home either alone or in small groups. The brigade had been sandwiched for 14 days between blocking lines of Americans and Russians, and the members of the brigade had to get through these lines.

While at first the Americans stood by without using their weapons, the men of the brigade had to defend themselves repeatedly from the firing Russians. It disbanded itself at noon on 8 May 1945.

The Americans, who had shaken hands with the German general and promised him that they and the civilian German refugees with them—women, the elderly, and children—would not be turned over to the Russians, did exactly the opposite. They handed over all "prisoners" to the Russians three days later.

A few soldiers of Sturmgeschütz-Brigade 286 managed to escape Russian captivity before the long trek to Russia began.

Sturmgeschütz-Abteilung 300 (Sturmgeschütz-Brigade 300) (Heeres-Sturmgeschütz-Brigade 300)

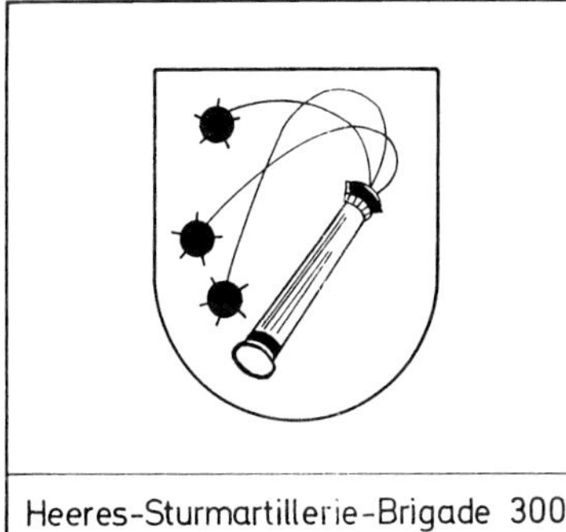

Heeres-Sturmartillerie-Brigade 300

Sturmgeschütz-Abteilung 300, which carried the designation "Feld" ("Field") to differentiate it from the Sturmgeschütz-Ersatz- und Ausbildings-Abteilung 300, was formed at Neiße on 18 October 1943.

Major H. Martin was the first commander, and the battery commanders were Oberleutnants Carls, Klute and Bluttner. The Headquarters Battery was commanded by Oberleutnant Saul. On the 15th day after activation, the personnel were transferred to Ausbildungsstab West at Tours. The battalion was issued its guns and vehicles there, as well as its equipment, which had been sent from the Sturmgeschütz-Schule at Burg.

On 25 December 1943 Sturmgeschütz-Abteilung 300 was rail loaded at Tours and sent to the Eastern Front, where it arrived on 31 December. It was unloaded near Witebsk. It immediately moved into its first operation. This lasted four days. Then it was loaded up again; this time the battalion's objective was the south Ukraine.

On 11 January 1944 the battalion was taken directly from the unloading ramps and thrown into the battle for Kiev. From then on it was engaged in defending continuously on the southern front. It paid a heavy price from 27 January to 3 March 1944 in the fighting at Shaschkow and Ilinzy and, later on, in the defensive fighting at Schepetowka and Jampol. It was redesignated a brigade on 14 February 1944.

The brigade fought from 4 March to 10 April 1944 at Winniza-Jampol-Taschernowitz and, starting 26 March, in the area of the breakthrough fighting at Kamenez-Podolsk. The defensive fighting on the upper Dnjepr and in the Carpathian Mountains saw the brigade in action there on 27 April.

During the final days of April 1944, the brigade was engaged in the positional fighting in the area of operations of Heeresgruppe Nordukraine and then covered the retreat as rear guard in the middle of July 1944.

The names of Tarnopol, Brody, Lemberg and Przemysl will forever be associated with the history of this brigade. Jaroslawl, the Dukla Pass, Tarnow, Sandomir and Krakow saw bitter fighting and exacted a heavy toll. Many members of the brigade were highly decorated. Major Martin received the German Cross in Gold. Hauptmann Klute and Hauptmann Bluttner also received the German Cross in Gold. Hauptmann Carls was included in the Honor Roll of the German Army and consequently received the Honor Roll Clasp.

The fighting on German soil saw the brigade in action at Neiße-Otmachau. On 19 February 1945 Major Rupert Gruber was given command of the brigade.

"Kampfgruppe Gruber," which he led and which had been formed from Sturmgeschütz-Ersatz- und Ausbildungs-Abteilung 300, was integrated into Sturmgeschütz-Brigade 300. There were only remnants left. The 3rd Battery of Sturmgeschütz-Brigade 184 under Hauptmann Kurt Negele was also attached to Sturmgeschütz-Brigade 300.

Between 19 February and 14 March 1945 this strong brigade fought at Würben, Saarau, Kallendorf, Seichau and Jägerndorf. On 15 March Major Gruber was transferred to the Sturmgeschütz-Schule at Burg.

Major Heinz Baurmann took over command of the brigade and, after the heavy fighting for Thomaswaldau, took it toward Dresden and across the Elbe at Pirna. Major Baurmann also received the Knight's Cross on 10 April 1945. During the month of April the brigade was renamed as Heeres-Sturmgeschütz-Brigade 300.

The brigade's last fighting was at Brüx and Komotau. Then, once again led by Hauptmann Martin, it went into captivity in the Sudetenland. Elements were taken prisoner at Karlsbad, with the majority interned at Treunitz near Cheb (Eger) on 10 and 11 May 1945.

Sturmgeschütz-Ersatz-Abteilung 300 (Sturmgeschütz-Ersatz- und Ausbildungs-Abteilung 300)

This second oldest of the Sturmartillerie replacement battalions was formed in 1941 at Neiße (Upper Silesia). Its commander was Hauptmann Bumm, one of the "old" combat veterans of the Sturmartillerie. The second commander was Major Krug.

New formations were created out of this replacement battalion. Convalescing men returning to their brigades from hospitals also returned there to be sent on to their old units. Many men of the Sturmartillerie who had received their initial training in this replacement battalion were extremely successful in their individual formations.

Sturmgesch. Ers. und Ausb. Abt. 300

As a result Sturmgeschütz-Ersatz-Abteilung 300 became a continuous source of strength for the Sturmartillerie. On 1 April 1953 the battalion was renamed as Sturmgeschütz-Ersatz- und Ausbildungs-Abteilung 300

We know no more concerning the fate of this unit and its combat activities than we have already reported at the end of the history of Sturmgeschütz-Brigade 300 above. Nor have any details survived concerning the last weeks in which the unit went under, fighting to the last. Even so, we will not forget Sturmgeschütz-Ersatz- und Ausbildungs-Abteilung 300 in this book. More than many other units, this was the departure point for new units which went into action in the east and which demonstrated the value of the Sturmartillerie through their victories. This replacement battalion, along with others still to be described, made it possible for them to do this with the necessary speed.

This Sturmgeschütz III G features an impressive shark-mouth design on its gun mantlet. For added protection spare track sections have been fastened to the lower hull and fighting compartment.

The driver of a Sturmgeschütz III G which has been coated in "Zimmerit." Note the wear of the captured Russian cap. Neither Sturmgeschütze or Panzer had heaters in them, resulting in temperatures on the inside being the same as the outside.

A Sturmgeschütz III G with light camouflage, a "Saukopf" (pig's head") gun mantlet and a MG 42. Note the light coating of "Zimmerit" on the front.

Two late-model Sturmgeschütz III G's with "Saukopf" gun mantlets. The vehicle on the left is covered with widely-spaced netting, presumably for attaching camouflage.

Above: A Sturmgeschütz III G moving back across the Lysa Gora in 1944.

Right: A heavily loaded Sturmgeschütz III G with an unusual side "Schürzen" (skirt) arrangement. The gun number —101—and rhomboid insignia are clearly visible. Note the protective shield for the MG 42.

A Sturmgeschütz III G at St. Raphael, a small village on the Mediterranean, which catered to "high society." The time is just prior to the invasion at Normandy.

Sturmgeschütze of SS-Panzer-Regiment 10 on the invasion front. Note the heavy camouflage, necessitated by Allied air supremacy.

A Sturmgeschütz III G during exercises in Holland. Note the "Saukopf" gun mantlet. The gun commander appears to be the battery "Spieß" (first sergeant), as indicated by the twin "Kolbenringe" (cylinder rings) on his tunic sleeves.

Another view of the vehicle seen above.

Late-model Sturmgeschütz III G's of Sturmgeschütz-Brigade 280 at Arnhem in September 1944. These assault guns have often been mistakenly identified as belonging to the 9. SS-Panzer-Division "Hohenstaufen," which did not have any assault guns at Arnhem.

A heavily camouflaged Sturmgeschütz III G of Panzerjäger-Abteilung 116 of the 116. Panzer-Division "Windhund" (Greyhound).

Italy, 1944: a Sturmgeschütz III G with a full set of "Schürzen" passes a M4 "Sherman" which has been disabled by mines. Defeating contemporary armor (particularly in the west) did not pose a problem for the long-barreled assault guns.

A Sturmgeschütz III G rolls through the bombed-out streets of Linnich on the Roer in December 1944.

A series of dramatic photographs showing assault guns of an unidentified unit in action in Russia in 1943 or 1944.

A Sturmgeschütz III G at the moment of firing.

Kirchenruine von Ssinjawino

The church ruins at Ssinjawino, as viewed from an assault gun.

A T34 knocked out on the steppes of Russia.

View through the gun optics on an assault gun.

Several enemy tanks on fire.

Sturmgeschütz-Abteilung 301 (Sturmgeschütz-Brigade 301)

Sturmgeschütz-Brigade 301

Sturmgeschütz-Abteilung 301 was formed by the Ausbildungsstab West at Tours (France) in the fall of 1943. The battalion was issued equipment by the Aufstellungsstab at Altengrabow. Under the command of Hauptmann Sekirka, who had been in action at Stalingrad until October 1942 as commander of the 3./Sturmgeschütz-Abteilung 243, as many soldiers as possible were brought to this new organization from that battalion. Sturmgeschütz-Abteilung 243 had been destroyed at Stalingrad.

Although the personnel were rapidly assembled, the unit initially lacked both equipment and guns. On the occasion of an inspection by Generaloberst von Blaskowitz, the battalion was informed that it was to become an army-level reserve , intended for operations against the Allied invasion that was expected somewhere on the French coast in the early part of 1944.

At the end of January 1944 the battalion was suddenly put on alert and sent to Sagan (Silesia) by rail. It was rapidly issued all the Sturmgeschütze, staff cars, trucks and radio equipment there that it still hadn't received. The battalion was redesignated as a brigade on 14 February 1944.

In the middle of February it was loaded on trains for an unknown destination and rolled to the southern sector of the Eastern Front, where the situation was critical everywhere. It had been intended to send the brigade to the 17. Armee in the Crimea. But that fell through after the 1st Ukrainian Front broke through the German lines, heading toward Tarnopol and Proskurow. The brigade was redirected. The staff, the Headquarters Battery and the 2nd and 3rd Batteries were unloaded in Proskurow and sent to the 1. Panzer-Armee.

The 1st Battery which had been loaded on the last train only got as far as Tarnopol. It was sent to the "Fortress," where it formed the backbone of the defense of this "Fortified Place." During the subsequent fighting, it was mentioned twice in the Wehrmacht Report, and Hauptmann Stiller and Leutnant Höpfl were given special notice. With the exception of the battery trains, which were located outside the ring of encircling Soviet troops around Tarnopol, the 1st Battery vanished without a trace. As far as is known, not one member of this battery survived this battle and the subsequent Russian captivity. The trains of the 1./Sturmgeschütz-Abteilung 301 did not rejoin the brigade until the beginning of May.

The 2. and 3./Sturmgeschütz-Brigade 301 were employed in the defensive fighting in the Proskurow area. They fought there against greatly superior Soviet numbers. The Soviets succeeded in pushing across the Dnjepr to the north and south of Czernowitz, however, and encircling the 1. Panzer-Armee at Kamenez-Podolsk.

The 1. Panzer-Armee under Generaloberst Hube received orders to break through the surrounding enemy lines to the west where it would then plug the gaps existing in the front.

Orders to break out were issued on 26 March. Two Soviet tank armies lay to the west in the path of the 1. Panzer-Armee. Moreover, no fewer than four rivers running from north to south had to be crossed: the Zbrucz, the Nicziawa, the Seret and the Duba. Heavy snowstorms made things harder for the troops breaking out.

Two corps groups were formed for the breakout. The northern group was under the command of General von der Chevallerie; the southern group was commanded by General der Panzertruppe Breith.

The Sturmgeschütze were at the lead elements and under the command of Hauptmann Sekirka. They cleared the way so that the following infantry could march through. Hauptmann Sekirka and Wachtmeister Fiebig distinguished themselves by their actions. The latter had already destroyed more than 50 tanks.

On 6 April 1944 the breakout groups made contact with the II. SS-Panzer-Korps coming to meet them from the west. The breakout had succeeded.

On 6 April Sturmgeschütz-Brigade 301 was attached to the 101. Jäger-Division and supported its Jäger regiments in repelling the enemy. The Sturmgeschütze fought against advancing tanks in the Stanislau area and destroyed them. On 1 May 1944 Hauptmann Sekirka was surprised by a bombardment from Russian rocket launchers and killed. He was buried at the military cemetery in Tlumacz near Stanislau. Oberleutnant Simon took over command of the orphaned brigade. A short time later Hauptmann Siebert arrived to take command. The Sturmgeschütze remained with the 101st Jäger-Division until May 5 and, during those 4 weeks, destroyed thirty T-34's, twenty-five heavy antitank guns and a large number of other weapons.

During the following weeks, the brigade was rested and received replacements of both men and materiél in the Monastrzyska-Buczacz area.

After the beginning of the Russian summer offensive in front of Heeresgruppe Mitte on 22 June 1944, the Soviet formations in the area around Lemberg also initiated their offensive. Sturmgeschütz-Brigade 301 was sent north to clean up the penetrations there. The brigade was able to score a large defensive success. Once again it was the Sturmgeschütz of Wachtmeister Fiebig which distinguished itself and knocked out a series of enemy tanks and antitank cannon. He received the German Cross in Gold.

Despite those successes Sturmgeschütz-Brigade 301 was encircled in the second half of June at Lemberg along with infantry elements. The breakout attempt to the southwest was only partially successful. A large number of Sturmgeschütze and support vehicles were lost in the process. The link-up with the front to the west was no longer possible, since the Red Army had advanced far to the southwest with strong forces.

The remnants of the brigade were forced back to the area around Sambor in the Carpathian Mountains. After a wild retreat over the Carpathians the rest of the brigade reached the area around Ungavar in northern Hungary in August 1944. It was attached to the 101. Jäger-Division once again from 19 July to 10 August. It had supported that division in difficult defensive fighting and prevented its destruction east of Lemberg and south of the Dnjestr south of Sambor. Oberst Aßmann, the acting commander of the 101. Jäger-Division, expressed his "thanks for the selfless determination and the model cooperation" of the brigade.

While the brigade was refitted in a perfunctory manner at

Sambor, a Kampfgruppe was moved to the Dukla Pass where it was to block the crossing into northern Hungary for the following Soviets. The fighting in this vast, wooded terrain—shoulder to shoulder with a Gebirgs-Jäger-Regiment—was difficult and costly in casualties. Despite that the mission was completed.

Sturmgeschütz-Brigade 301 was loaded by train in September 1944. It was intended to refit the brigade in the area around Krakow. While moving by train towards Krakow the brigade received the order to go instead to Slovakia, where an insurrection had broken out. The Sturmgeschütze were employed in the area of Presow-Kaschau. They crushed the insurrection and were employed in raids against identified partisan organizations.

The planned refitting in Krakow began in October 1944. At that time it was planned to convert it to an Heeres-Sturmartillerie-Brigade, but the necessary 4th Battery, the escort infantry, was never added to the organization. The brigade was transferred to the area around Tarnow in the middle of November 1944. It stayed there in relative quiet until the end of the year. The members of the brigade experienced a quiet Christmas.

The brigade was employed as a complete unit against enemy forces which had broken through at the beginning of the Russian winter offensive of 12 January 1945. The brigade was led by Major Siebert. It was employed with great success at Kasimirowka and a large number of enemy tanks were knocked out.

At that point the unit began to become overcome by events. Improvisations became necessary on a daily basis in order to keep pace with the requirements.

The brigade was committed at Krakow at the end of January to defend the city. But there were neither soldiers nor command and control staffs there. The withdrawal proceeded west via Ratibor Teschen and Schwarzwasser. Major Siebert was able to employ the entire brigade against Russian armored units. Leutnant Ehrenkrook was killed there. The Sturmgeschütze had only poor chances against the massed employment of the Stalin tanks. Despite that they were successful over and over again in knocking out these giants.

Sturmgeschütz-Brigade 301 was encircled with infantry units at the beginning of March 1945 at Oberglogau. The breakout in the direction of Hotzenplotz followed. It was led by Major Siebert who was killed in the process.

Sturmgeschütz-Brigade 301 was employed at Easter at Jägerndorf. It repulsed a strong armored attack on Easter Sunday. A large number of enemy tanks were left burning and shot up on the battlefield.

In the meantime enemy formations had penetrated from the south over the Carpathians into Czechoslovakia. In order to block these crossing points for the follow-on enemy infantry Sturmgeschütz-Brigade 301 was committed in the area around Hradschin (Hungary). Hauptmann Botschafter, the commander of the 3./ Sturmgeschütz-Brigade 301, was severely wounded there. He died in the middle of May at the military hospital at Bad Elster.

In spite of the increasingly critical ammunition situation the Sturmgeschütze always advanced into the threatened sectors, if only to help the infantry with their machine guns

The brigade reached the area around Olmütz at the beginning of May. Once again the brigade fought together with the 101. Jäger-Division, as it had done during the difficult fighting of 1944.

Elements of the brigade were attacked by Czech partisans on 8 May 1945. The partisans were dispersed with a few rounds of ammunition. Individual elements of the brigade succeeded in making it to the west. They advanced over the Moldau to the Americans. Other elements fell into Russian hands east of the Moldau. Those who had escaped to the west were delivered to the Russians at the end of May, however.

Sturmgeschütz-Abteilung 311 (Sturmgeschütz-Brigade 311)

Sturmgeschütz-Brigade 311

Sturmgeschütz-Abteilung 311 was formed on 9 November 1943 in Schweinfurt at Sturmgeschütz-Ersatz-Abteilung 200. Its insignia was a lion's head. Hauptmann Karl-Ludwig von Schönau was the first battalion commander. The battalion was sent to Tours for equipment and training. It was renamed a brigade on 14 February 1944.

When the brigade was put on alert on 5 March 1944, it had only 9 Sturmhaubitzen in its inventory. It had to be sent to the east by way of the Troop Training Area in Altengrabow in order to get the Sturmhaubitzen that it was still lacking.

Despite that detour, the brigade arrived at the village of Zloczow near Tarnopol on 14 March 1944, where it was unloaded. A few days later, the brigade went into action for the first time on the heights north of the Tarnopol-Shitomir road. Its mission: Take the highlands and clear the enemy occupied hills. The Soviets had dug in with numerous antitank weapons. The attack of Sturmgeschütz-Brigade 311—supported by both mounted and follow-on dismounted infantry—bogged down after modest initial success, gaining only a few hundred meters of ground. The two batteries employed suffered heavy losses from hits from the dominating enemy fire, but also losses from mechanical break-downs.

The brigade was almost completely worn down in the subsequent fierce fighting and, when the Soviets attacked to the south on a broad front in the early morning hours of 21 March 1944, the remaining combat elements were cut off from their contact with the rear.

The remaining German troops who had still been fighting east of Tarnopol and facing north were also cut off with the brigade. Under Oberst Freiherr von Künsberg the brigade's last Sturmgeschütze fought in "Kampfgruppe Künsberg." Oberleutnant Kaufmann commanded these last three guns. When "Kampfgruppe Künsberg" finally managed to establish radio communications with the 7. Panzer-Division, which was further to the east at Ssatanow, its commander, Oberst Mauss, sent a Tiger battalion to Grzymalow to wait there for the arrival of "Kampfgruppe Künsberg" and link up.

The Sturmgeschütze moved back with the Kampfgruppe. Two were left behind. Only one was still able to make it through the swamp. Oberleutnant Kaufmann managed to destroy a T-34 with his Sturmgeschütz at 50 meters. It had broken into the position of the Kampfgruppe.

The Tiger battalion attached to the 7. Panzer-Division was

unable to hold Grzymalow until "Kampfgruppe Künsberg" arrived. It pulled back to Tluste. The Kampfgruppe charged after them in a costly night march, but most of the soldiers were captured. Oberleutnant Kaufmann and seven other men of the Sturmartillerie managed to break through to Ssatanow after destroying the last Sturmgeschütz.

Only Oberleutnant Küchler, Oberleutnant Kaufmann, Leutnant Dürr and 12 men were left out of all the combat crews of Sturmgeschütz-Brigade 311. Hauptmann Hahn had been killed. Hauptmann Ammon, who had already been wounded in the recent fighting, had to be sent back and was in the hospital.

The brigade's few survivors waited south of Ssatanow for the arrival of the 1. Panzer-Armee (Generaloberst Hube) marching west from the Shitomir area. Together with this army, the brigade managed to reach the German main battle line in the Brzezany-Pomorzany area by way of Skalat, Buczacz and Podhajce. The completely surrounded army had managed to fight its way through several hundred kilometers to safety.

Sturmgeschütz-Brigade 311 was refitted in the Brzezany area. It received replacements of officers and men as well as new Sturmgeschütze.

It was back in action when the Soviet offensive began in July 1944. It fought stubbornly north of the Lemburg-Tarnopol road, and then south of it in the XXXXVIII. Panzer-Korps area. Once again the brigade took heavy losses.

The German troops south of the road pulled back through the Carpathian Mountains to Hungary when strong Soviet tank forces broke through at Brody and advanced to Lemberg. The remnants of Sturmgeschütz-Brigade 311 were taken by rail to Wielicza in the vicinity of Krakow. The brigade was refitted again.

On the way to Krakow, Hauptmann von Schönau was relieved by Hauptmann Hans Magold. The brigade fought under his command at Lysa Gora and in the Dukla Pass. Attached to the XIV. Panzer-Korps, it engaged in heavy defensive fighting and, on 14 September 1944, was given the mission of clearing the Zmigrod-Dukla axis.

The heights flanking this attack sector were already occupied by Soviet forces with heavy antitank weapons. The brigade had already experienced a terrible artillery barrage right in its assembly area in Zmigrod. Oberleutnant von Küchler was severely wounded.

On 15 September the brigade carried out the attack as ordered. When one of the Sturmgeschütze bogged down, the command Sturmgeschütz under Hauptmann Magold moved over to recover it. While attempting to do so, the command Sturmgeschütz received a direct hit. Hauptmann Magold was badly wounded. The commanders of the 2nd and 3rd Batteries, Hauptmann Ammon and Hauptmann Kaufmann, were also wounded in this operation.

On 25 September 1944 Hauptmann Wolfgang Tenner took over command of the brigade. A brief pause in the fighting was used for refitting; followed by additional heavy defensive fighting. The brigade smashed even more attacking Soviet units southwest of the Dukla Pass and in the area of Ungvar-Michalowce. By order of General Nehring, the commanding general of the XXIV. Panzer-Korps, all of the organic divisional Sturmgeschütze and a Sturmgeschütz battery from the 1. Ski-Jäger-Division were attached to Sturmgeschütz-Brigade 311 for these operations. This gave the brigade a total one-time fighting strength of 60 guns. It was placed only a few meters behind the main battle line and held off every enemy attack. These positions didn't have to be abandoned until after the beginning of the Soviet winter offensive on 12 January 1945. The brigade was taken to Upper Silesia by rail. There, its Sturmgeschütze were almost continually in combat. The fighting for Ratibor, on the Zobten, at Breslau and at Neiße became the touchstone of the brigade's quality. Hauptmann Laufmann, one of the best officers in the brigade, was killed at Neiße.

The brigade was once again in action against a far superior enemy at Ziegenhals and Bautzen. It was pushed back to Breslau when, together with one infantry division, it attempted to keep the last withdrawal route open against two Soviet tank corps. It remained engaged near Breslau in pitiless combat until the city's capitulation. Breslau was where Leutnant Leo Hartmann made his mark. This young officer fought like the lion on the brigade's insignia. On 1 May 1945 he received the Knight's Cross to the Iron Cross. There was no one who begrudged this sympathetic young soldier his high award. Everyone knew that he had earned it in bitter, hard fighting.

At the beginning of May Sturmgeschütz-Brigade 311, attached to Fallschirm-Panzer-Korps "Hermann Göring", was in action north of Dresden. Orders reached it there from Heeresgruppe Mitte to move to Ölmütz. The brigade moved by rail to Rengersdorf, 10 kilometers south of Glatz, where it was unloaded. Just as it was attempting to make contact with the XXXX. Panzer-Korps, it heard of the capitulation which was to go into effect on the following day.

The brigade attempted to march west on the clogged roads to escape the Soviet clutches. Despite its efforts it still went into Soviet captivity in Czechoslovakia.

Sturmgeschütz-Abteilung 322 (Sturmgeschütz-Brigade 322)

This battalion was formed at Tours at the end of 1943 under Hauptmann Zielke. Cadre personnel for this new formation were taken from the 3rd Battery of Sturmgeschütz-Abteilung 184. The command and staff positions of this new battalion were filled as follows:

Commander: Hauptmann Zielke
Adjutant: Oberleutnant Pietschmann
Orderly Officer: Leutnant Althoff (Leutnant Apprich)
Officer (special duties): Oberleutnant Vincon
Paymaster: Oberzahlmeister Schäfer
Unit Surgeon: Assistenzarzt Dr. Hoffmann
Technical Officer: Hauptmann Preuße
Headquarters Battery Commander: Oberleutnant Wieloth
1st Battery Commander: Hauptmann Rentzow (MIA)
Section Leaders: Oberleutnant Stündt (KIA), Leutnant Gast
2nd Battery Commander: Hauptmann Tornau
Section Leaders: Leutnant Ilgner, Leutnant Naumann
3rd Battery Commander: Oberleutnant Jesse (KIA)
Section Leaders: Leutnant Köhler, Leutnant Haug

The brigade received marching orders for Heeresgruppe Süd at Lemberg on 9 March 1944. It had been redesignated a brigade on 14 February 1944. The orderly officer, Leutnant Althoff, went ahead to Zlowczow as the advance party. A Kampfgruppe was formed at Zlowczow, to which Sturmgeschütz-Brigaden 311 and 322 along with reconnaissance units were to join.

Because the Sturmgeschütze of Sturmgeschütz-Brigade 322 hadn't been broken in yet, the commander had the 1st and 3rd Batteries unload at Lemberg and drive from there to Zlowczow in the Sturmgeschütze. The 3rd Battery arrived there on 16 March. On 17 March the brigade carried out its first attack in the area of Brody. Hauptmann Zielke was with the 3rd Battery. Because radio communications had broken down, contact could only be maintained through orderly officers. The brigade command post was set up in Beresteczko. A Soviet surprise attack then surrounded the brigade along with elements of an unidentified infantry division at Brody.

The encirclement was broken open to the south and all noncombat elements of the brigade were sent to the area of Olesko. The rear area command post was set up there, which was also to be the assembly point for the entire brigade. The fighting elements remained at Brody.

Oberleutnant Jesse, the commander of the 3rd Battery, fell in the heavy fighting east of Brody. Leutnant Haug, a section leader in this battery, was wounded. Oberleutnant Vincon took over the orphaned battery.

The brigade's final breakout through the enemy lines around Brody took place on 25 March 1944. The fighting at Brody had to be carried out by the 1st and 3rd Batteries without the 2nd Battery, because Hauptmann Tornau with the soldiers of his battery had been "lent" to Tarnopol before the Russian lines closed around Brody. Hauptmann Tornau, together with a thrown-together Kampfgruppe, was supposed to prevent the Russians from surrounding the Germans there.

Hauptmann Tornau was sent back to his brigade only after the fighting had died down in the Tarnopol area. He arrived back there after the fighting was over at Brody.

Contact between Brody and Olesko was re-established; following that the front stabilized.

In the next few days the Soviets attempted to place a new ring around Brody. They attacked from the area north of Brody in an attempt to surround the city from the west.

A Kampfgruppe led by the brigade commander spoiled this attempt. It was only with great difficulty that the Sturmgeschütze managed to make it back through the swamp to their attack positions. The command post was shifted to Olesko, and a few days later to Suchodoly. The brigade was then attached to the XIII. Armee-Korps (General der Infanterie Hauffe).

On 1 April Leutnant Althoff became the brigade adjutant, when Oberleutnant Pietschmann was transferred to the 1st Battery as a section leader. During these first few days of April, the brigade carried out successful relief attacks against Brody. Oberleutnant Stündt was killed during one of these attacks on 11 April 1944.

On 13 April the 1st Battery was launched against the forested area northwest of Brody. The following day was a black one for that battery. It had several losses from mines, artillery and mortar fire. Hauptmann Rentzow, who had led the battery magnificently, was wounded, as was Leutnant Gast. Oberleutnant Pietschmann took over this battery on 15 April. Hauptmann Rentzow was mentioned in the Honor of Roll for the German Army for the action in the Brody area during this period and received the Honor Roll Clasp.

The brigade was then shifted out of the Brody area into the Wladimir-Wolhynsk sector, where it was attached to the XXXXII. Armee-Korps (General der Infanterie Recknagel). On 1 June 1944 Hauptmann Rentzow again took command of the 1st Battery and Oberleutnant Pietschmann returned to staff duties.

During the following weeks, there were only local, limited operations. At the beginning of July Hauptmann Zielke went on leave to get married and, on 12 July, the major Soviet summer offensive began. The batteries were individually attached to the following divisions: 1st Battery to the 291st Infanterie-Division; 2nd Battery to the 88. Infanterie-Division; and, 3rd Battery to the 214. Infanterie-Division

The enemy's main thrust was expected against the 88. Infanterie-Division For that reason, the brigade's command post was set up in the vicinity of the divisional one. But against expectations, the Soviets attacked at the boundary between the XXXXII. Armee-Korps and the XIII. Armee-Korps. When that happened, all three batteries were shifted into the sector of the 291. Infanterie-Division. On 13 July, however, it was impossible for the brigade and the 291. Infanterie-Division to hold the positions which had been prepared to the rear. Since late in the morning on that day contact had been lost with their neighbor on the right, the XIII. Armee-Korps.

Hauptmann Rentzow was wounded again in the initial fighting at Horochow and since that day has been counted as missing in action. Oberleutnant Pietschmann once again took over the 1st Battery which suffered extraordinary losses during the following day.

Hauptmann Zielke had just returned from leave. When he tried to return to the brigade after a visit to the divisional command post on 14 July, he was killed by shell shrapnel near the command post, a particularly tragic occurrence in the case of this young, capable officer.

Hauptmann Gottfried Tornau took over command of the brigade on the field of battle and continued in command even during the subsequent difficult fighting retreat across the Bug and across the Vistula at Annapol. It was thanks to his leadership that the brigade was not lost.

The brigade assembled in the area southwest of Sondomiesz. The 72. and 88. Infanterie-Divisionen had established a bridgehead there. To halt the Soviet advance, a German Panzer-Korps attacked from the south with the objective of re-establishing contact with those two infantry divisions. The attacking spearheads were only 10 kilometers apart, when they received orders to pull back across the Vistula.

The Baranow Bridgehead was established by the Soviets. The eastern border of this hotly contested bridgehead, from which the Russians launched their assault on Germany in January 1945, was at Kielce. Under its new commander, Major Behnke, the brigade pushed back repeated Soviet attempts to further expand this bridgehead.

After Major Behnke arrived at the brigade, Hauptmann Tornau had to bid farewell to his soldiers. After completing a commander's course, he was assigned to command a new unit being activated at the Sturmgeschütz-Schule at Burg.

Sturmgeschütz-Brigade 322 destroyed 23 enemy tanks west of Baranow during the first days of August and was given credit for this in the Wehrmacht Report of 4 August. Despite that, this was not the high point of this defensive fighting. At Opatowka, the brigade was committed against the enemy as "Kampfgruppe

Behnke." It stood its ground, fighting against greatly superior attacking enemy tank forces from 8 to 17 August 1944.

When three enemy armored artillery brigades broke through on 8 August 1944 heading north toward Stodoly, Kampfgruppe Behnke with infantry riding on its Sturmgeschütze, was launched in a thrust to the south against the bridge positions at Opatowka. This thrust bogged down in the concentrated defensive fire of the Soviets.

When Major Behnke found out that "Gruppe Hansen" was preparing to attack along the line Gierczce-Stodoly-Janowicze, he joined that group on his own initiative. This decision was of far-reaching significance for the future progress of the fighting. Major Behnke advanced as far as Sadlowicze with his Sturmgeschütze (4 kilometers deep into the enemy). This thrust and the subsequent fighting delayed the enemy for a period of 11 days. During this period, the brigade destroyed 122 enemy tanks, 40 artillery pieces and 56 heavy antitank guns. Other materiél and light weapons were captured as well.

Major Behnke was the initiator of this attack. Whether in a Volkswagen, a Sturmgeschütz or on foot, he was always at the front of his brigade. He had just returned from a follow-up attack at Grochocicze on 16 August, when he immediately had to defend against an enemy surprise attack carried out on a broad front. We will follow the subsequent action in the recommendation for the Oak Leaves to the Knight's Cross which General der Infanterie Recknagel submitted:

With incredible élan he led his Sturmgeschütze in an unarmored vehicle. On this decisive day he succeeded in destroying 44 enemy tanks, stopped the enemy on the Opatow-Ozarow axis and thus permitted fresh forces to be employed.

His personal initiative and decisiveness and his total count of 92 destroyed tanks in 11 days—quite apart from the creation of operational possibilities—is so extraordinary that Major Behnke would seem to be deserving of the high decoration of the Oak Leaves to the Knights Cross of the Iron Cross.

On 27 August 1944 this action was described in the Wehrmacht Report: "In the defensive fighting northwest of Baranow, a Kampfgruppe of Sturmgeschütze under the command of Major Behnke has distinguished itself by its unshakable resolve."

Major Behnke was detached to attend a regimental commander's course in Germany. Oberleutnant Pietschmann was given command of the 1st Battery; Oberleutnant Seth had the 2nd. Battery; and, Oberleutnant Vincon commanded the 3rd Battery. Hauptmann Baurmann was the new brigade commander.

Things quieted down a bit. At the beginning of October the brigade had to give up 30 men to the replacement battalion at Posen. Up until the beginning of winter the brigade took part in several more engagements and carried out limited counterattacks. However, there were increasing signs of a forthcoming Soviet operational offensive. On 11 January 1945 the brigade moved to Milkow. On the next day, the Soviets moved out of the Baranow Bridgehead and rapidly gained ground.

The combat elements of Sturmgeschütz-Brigade 322 received orders on 14 January 1945 to go into ready positions in the Kielce area, and it immediately went into action there. On 15 January the 1st Battery was detached from the brigade and placed under the operational control of Pionier-Brigade 70, which was positioned in Kusniaki on the western edge of Lysa Gora.

In the days that followed the combat elements of the brigade were completely decimated in duels with strong enemy tank units. The 3./Sturmgeschütz-Brigade 322, which was given the mission to carry out a night attack on Barki and Granice on 15 January, accomplished its objective and held open the crossroads.

The rest of the brigade formed a hedgehog position on the Pilica, until a wooden bridge could be built over the river. Because the heavy 15 cm howitzers couldn't make it across the bridge, an attempt was made to move through the river. They became stuck in the middle of the river and had to be blown up. Only the exhaust pipes of the Panthers and Tigers were high enough so that they could wade through the river.

Only a few Sturmgeschütze could be brought across the river and saved. On 21 January they took part once more in a rear guard action, in which the last Sturmgeschütze were destroyed.

On 31 January 1945 Sturmgeschütz-Brigade 322 was dissolved. Hauptmann Baurmann was assigned to the officer reserve of the German Army High Command.

Elements of the brigade were transferred to Sturmgeschütz-Brigade 219. Other elements reached Sturmgeschütz-Brigade 911 (which, in the meantime, had been incorporated into the Führer-Begleit-Division "Großdeutschland" as its organic Sturmgeschütz brigade). Those elements reached Sturmgeschütz-Brigade 911 by way of the replacement system and met Hauptmann Tornau there, who had become its commander. Naturally, he was delighted to see "his old men" again.

Along with the two brigades mentioned above, the last remaining members of Sturmgeschütz-Brigade 322 suffered the fate of the conquered: captivity.

Sturmgeschütz-Abteilung 325 (Sturmgeschütz-Brigade 325)

Sturmgeschütz-Brigade 325

Sturmgeschütz-Abteilung 325 was formed at Neiße on 15 April 1943 at Sturmgeschütz-Ersatz-Abteilung 300. Hauptmann Vogler was its commander. Oberleutnant Schönmann commanded the 1st Battery. This was the old 1st Battery from Sturmgeschütz-Abteilung 912, which had been assigned to the new formation as cadre. Oberleutnant Hermes commanded the 2nd Battery and Hauptmann Preusser the 3rd Battery. Oberleutnant Wessel joined as adjutant. Hauptmann Weiland commanded the Headquarters Battery.

After several months of training at Neiße, the personnel were transferred to Altengrabow where they arrived in the middle of September 1943 and received new Sturmgeschütze. At the end of November it was loaded up and taken by rail to Tours to the Aufstellungsstab West. The soldiers were quartered in the old barracks at Tours until February 1944. The new guns were sighted in at the Camp du Ruchard Troop Training Area.

At the end of April the brigade was transferred to Jassy in Rumania. From its main base at a radio station the brigade was committed several times in the direction of the Bug River.

The operational offensive between Jassy and the Sereth by

strong forces of the Red Army had to be halted. In that area of operations Sturmgeschütz-Brigade 325 fought closely several times with the guns of Sturmgeschütz-Brigade "Großdeutschland." Sturmgeschütz-Brigade "Großdeutschland" was fighting there as part of its division. The support trains for Sturmgeschütz-Brigade 325 were in Targul Frumos. Sturmgeschütz-Brigade 325 had to repel Russian attacks again and again. The brigade continued to lose more and more guns.

The new Red Army offensive which began on 2 May 1944 with 20 divisions saw Sturmgeschütz-Brigade 325 in hard defensive fighting. The Russian attempt to reach the oil fields of Ploesti already cost the Red Army a total of 350 tanks on the first day. Sturmgeschütz-Brigade 325 contributed to this defensive success by destroying 20 tanks.

The subsequent fighting that summer moved all the way through Rumania into Hungary. Unfortunately, no reports have survived concerning that fighting. There is only one report concerning the Soviet offensive on 19 August 1944 by Fritz Ziedrich. It is quoted here:

On 19 August 1944 my battery commander, Oberleutnant Schönmann, showed up in Letcani, where our forward strongpoint was located. He told us that early the next morning we could expect a reinforced attack on Letcani. We were to pull back at an appropriate time.

In the early morning of 20 August I didn't wake up until the Russian bombardment had reached its peak. We were under fire from artillery and close-support fighters for four hours. At that point the Russians launched their attack.

Our Spieß, Oberwachtmeister Wirth, appeared and said to me: "Ziedrich, you have to come and drive for me. My driver is with the maintenance section."

We headed in the direction of the Russians. We tried to make contact with the section leader's vehicle, but in vain. So, on our own initiative, we headed for the sounds of the fighting. Suddenly we saw the Russians attacking in thick swarms. We fired at them with high explosive rounds.

When we had fired all our ammunition we tried to get back to our trains and get more ammunition. Our engine coolant grew hotter and hotter. Was the radiator leaking?

On our way, we ran into the section leader who was just coming back from the trains. We reported our damaged radiator to him, and the section leader told us that all our ammunition had been blown up by a Russian direct hit. We were going to have to try to reach the maintenance section with the damaged gun. We stopped at a well and filled up with water for the radiator. Then we moved on until we reached the maintenance section.

The Russian offensive broke through the German main battle line. The Red Army rolled forward with hundreds of tanks and assault guns. From then on Sturmgeschütz-Brigade 325 found itself constantly withdrawing. The Sturmgeschütz of Oberwachtmeister Wirth was knocked out at Barlad and Braila.

Sturmgeschütz-Brigade 325 fought against its complete destruction. The crews without guns attempted to escape on foot in small groups. Harry Prescher and three comrades managed to get through Ploesti and Sowata and across the Carpathians where they eventually linked up with the German front in Hungary. On 22 December 1944 Harry Prescher rejoined the remnants of the brigade in Baknybel (Hungary) and was assigned to the 1./Sturmgeschütz-Brigade 325. The fighting in Hungary and Slovenia started for Sturmgeschütz-Brigade 325. It fought stubbornly along the withdrawal routes against the fiercely pursuing enemy and destroyed a number of tanks. On 26 March 1945 the Sturmgeschütz of Harry Prescher gun was destroyed near Komoron and he was taken prisoner by the Russians.

The remnants of Sturmgeschütz-Brigade 325 fought on in Hungary and were pulled back to Austria where they were taken prisoner at the end of the war.

Sturmgeschütz-Abteilung 341 (Sturmgeschütz-Brigade 341)

In May 1943 the formation of Sturmgeschütz-Abteilung 341 began at Neiße under the designation "Kommando Greif" ("Condor Command"). Once again, most of the personnel for the new battalion were recruited from Sturmgeschütz-Ersatz-Abteilung 300. Hauptmann Bumm, the commander of Sturmgeschütz-Ersatz-Abteilung 300, took over command of the battalion. The formation was finally completed at the Dieskau Barracks in October 1943. The batteries were led by the following officers:

Headquarters Battery: Leutnant Kilger
1st Battery: Oberleutnant Pazur
2nd Battery: Oberleutnant Kolb
3rd Battery: Oberleutnant Ernst-Günther Diehl

In November this young battalion was transferred to Tours and attached to the Sturmgeschütz-Aufstellungsstab West (Oberstleutnant Pritzbuer). After a few training exercises the brigade received its Sturmgeschütze at the end of March 1944 and was completely equipped with vehicles. It had been redesignated a brigade on 14 February 1944.

Following that, it was moved to Narbonne and Carcassonne in southern France. This brigade was to be one of the few Sturmgeschütz units assigned to secure the rear area on the Mediterranean coast. At that time an invasion was still expected in this area. The brigade was left in peace except for one major anti-partisan operation. It was the calm before the storm; a storm that would demand everything that this brigade had to give.

With the beginning of the invasion the brigade expected to see action in Normandy. However, it wasn't committed into battle at Normandy until 27 July 1944, when it was employed against the furious advance of the American invasion troops.

The brigade received its baptism of fire in the areas of Brécy and Avranches. Hauptmann Pazur, the commander of the 1st Battery, was killed at Brécy. Oberwachtmeister Kurt Kirchner was also killed there. He was one of the most outstanding Sturmgeschütz commanders and had already received the Knight's Cross on 9 March 1942 as a Wachtmeister and gun commander.

The commander of 2nd Battery, Oberleutnant Kolb, was killed in the second operation on 1 August 1944. Leutnant Lermen was his successor. The 1st Battery, which was at the focal point of the fighting, was badly battered. It lost 12 of its 14 Sturmgeschütze, and the last two guns were also damaged. Despite that the battery had destroyed a succession of enemy tanks. The loss of its entire fighting strength was the price it paid for this success.

The 2nd and 3rd Batteries also lost almost all their Sturmgeschütze during this fighting. However, it was only a few days before new Sturmgeschütze arrived from Tours and Paris.

After a short pause, the fighting continued. It wasn't just the numerical superiority of the Anglo-American tank forces, the allied air forces also inflicted heavy losses on Sturmgeschütz-Brigade 341.

The brigade went selflessly into action in the area around Avranches, at Domfront, at Pontorson, at Dinant and at St. Malo. Oberleutnant Diehl, the commander of the 3rd Battery, was taken prisoner near St. Malo. Leutnant Schaller took over command of the battery and led it until the end of the war.

Hauptmann Bumm was wounded in the middle of August and had to leave the brigade. He had led the brigade splendidly. Hauptmann Drier took over, but he was to command the brigade for only a short time.

The enemy's incredible air superiority spelled the death of this brigade. For the second time, it lost all its Sturmgeschütze, as well as the greater part of its trains and supply vehicles, mainly to air attacks.

The brigade was re-equipped for the third time. It received new Sturmgeschütze and vehicles in the areas of Paris and St. Germaine.

Following that the "Condors" were in action day after day. Elements of this brigade held out in the Fontainbleau Bridgehead for several days, as was mentioned constantly in the Wehrmacht Report. After the fighting at the bridgehead it fought at Provins, Sézanne and Epernay.

Many fallen comrades lay along the route followed by the brigade while fighting in France. These fully trained Sturmgeschütz men could never be replaced.

The brigade was no longer fit for combat and was pulled back to the Aachen area by way of Reims and Lüttich. The Sturmgeschütze and vehicles were overhauled there. Personnel replacements also arrived. Hauptmann Barkley, who had already been a section leader in Sturmgeschütz-Batterie 660 ("The White-Cross Battery"), took over command of the brigade there in September 1944.

Under the command of this noble officer, the brigade carried out operations of incredible severity in the Hürtgen Forest. During the fighting in and around Aachen, elements of the brigade led by the commander of the 1st Battery, Oberleutnant Hermann Wolz, contributed significantly to the defense of this heavily contested city.

Starting in October 1944 the brigade was located in the Kaster area near Bedburg. On 8 December 1944 fate dealt the brigade a terrible blow. On that day the brigade command post was destroyed by a direct hit in a surprise artillery barrage.

Twelve officers, noncommissioned officers and men who were at the command post at that time were killed on the spot. Among them were their commander, Hauptmann Barkley, the commander of the 1st Battery, Oberleutnant Bender, who had been awarded the German Cross in Gold, and Major Bernhard Flachs, the commander of the technical training staff at the Sturmgeschütz-Schule at Burg, who by a twist of fate was there that day for a visit to the brigade. Bernhard Flachs, an example for all Sturmgeschütz men, had survived numerous battles in the front lines only to be killed while conducting a visit to a unit.

The brigade's dead were buried alongside Major Flachs. Hauptmann Reinhold Ertel became the brigade's new commander. He had been an outstanding battery commander in Sturmgeschütz-Brigade 276 and had worn the Knight's Cross since 15 February 1944. He led the brigade in the heavy fighting in the Düren-Jülich-Linnich area.

Hauptmann Ertel was killed in fighting there on 22 January 1945, when his Sturmgeschütz rolled over a mine and was blown up. Hauptmann Alfred Montag took over the brigade at the end of January. Previously, he had served as a battery commander in Sturmgeschütz-Brigade 909.

The brigade fought under this courageous commander until February in the areas of Holzweiler, Immerath and Otzerath. In March it was in action in the area of Siegerland, followed by Sauerland.

The brigade was divided in April 1945. The remnants of the combat elements went into action once more in the Harz, in the vicinity of Mägdesprung, where they were captured by the Americans at the end of April.

All of the other elements of the brigade were put into action as "Hunter/Killer Teams." A little later they arrived in Bad Tölz for a planned reorganization. Those who had not managed to make their way home were captured at Bad Tölz. It was the end of a brigade which had gone through the inferno of the invasion battles.

In 1946 the survivors of this brigade went to Kaster near Cologne, where the graves of 18 of their fallen comrades were to be found. Since that day, no year has passed when the men of the Sturmartillerie do not pay their respects to their fallen comrades there.

Sturmgeschütz-Brigade 393 (Heeres-Sturmartillerie-Brigade 393)

Heeres-Sturmartillerie-Brigade 393

This brigade, which had a charging rhinoceros as its insignia, was formed from personnel at the Sturmgeschütz-Ersatz-Ab-teilung 300 at Neiße before being sent to Tours. Haupt-mann Pelikan was the brigade commander. He had been wounded seven times and wore the Wound Badge in Gold. Hauptmann Karl-Ludwig Barths was commander of the 1st Battery, and Leutnant Konrad Sauer was a section leader in it. Oberleutnant Werner Junge was commander of the 3rd Battery, and his section leaders were Leutnants Georg Gedamke, Beigel and Leutnant Schröck-Opitz.

After formation was completed on 20 April 1944, the brigade was paraded through Tours. Then in May, it was transported to Oexböhl on Jütland Island, still without Sturmgeschütze. Assault guns were issued there, and the brigade was transported from Jütland to the Minsk area by way of Marienburg and Allenstein.

Because of the demolition of a railroad bridge, the brigade was detoured to Dünaburg. There it was put into action right off the unloading ramp. In addition to it being the first combat operation of the 3rd Battery, it was also committed at night. This attack bogged down 30 kilometers east of Dünaburg because of insufficient infantry support. There was a second attack the next morning, which was supported by the 1st Section of the 3rd Battery under Leutnant Schröck-Opitz.

Right at the beginning of the attack, the section leader's Sturmgeschütz received a direct hit from a Russian heavy antitank cannon and was put out of action. After two more Sturmgeschütze had been put out of action, the rest managed to locate the enemy antitank gun in a grain field. It was destroyed by a Sturmgeschütz which had pushed forward to within 500 meters on one side of the antitank gun. The crews of the knocked-out Sturmgeschütze were used as infantry to assault the village, which was taken in close combat.

A few days later the brigade launched an attack into the flank of the Russian divisions advancing toward East Prussia. Once more the 3rd Battery played the major role in this attack. Hauptmann Pelikan and his orderly officer, Leutnant Wecker, had joined them.

In the late afternoon three Sturmgeschütze with seven mounted infantry soldiers attacked a small village which was jammed full with Russian units. A quad-barreled Flak gave fire support to this tiny fighting force from a nearby hill. The three Sturmgeschütze tore into the enemy columns like a hurricane, firing as rapidly as possible. A large number of vehicles went up in flames. There were continuous explosions with columns of gasoline smoke reaching skyward. An enemy antitank unit was destroyed, even before it could go into action against these three savagely attacking Sturmgeschütze.

Hundreds of Soviets tried to flee. They were caught in the narrow village streets by high-explosive rounds and wiped out. The village fell into the hands of the Kampfgruppe. However, because its infantry support was too weak, the Kampfgruppe had to abandon the village as night fell and take up a defensive position on a height near the village.

By the next day strong enemy forces had come up and surrounded the three Sturmgeschütze. Their position was under heavy artillery fire and there were continuous enemy attacks from all sides. The Kampfgruppe pulled back slowly to the rest of the brigade.

Many times during the following retreat individual guns of the then reunified brigade found themselves stuck in the swamp. They helped each other to pull back out onto dry land. But many guns could not be recovered and had to be destroyed. Only a single Sturmgeschütz, fully loaded with wounded, finally reached a deep, water-filled ditch. It was destroyed by the Soviets at that spot.

Two-hundred-fifty infantry soldiers and Sturmartilleristen fought their way on foot from this ditch through the surrounding forest. Hauptmann Pelikan, Oberleutnant Junge and Leutnant Wecker, the orderly officer, were with the leading elements of this group together with the infantry regiment's commander. Leutnant Schröck-Opitz formed a rear guard with a handful of resolute men.

After only a few kilometers, the lead elements came under machine gun fire from German MG-42's which had evidently been captured by the enemy. The small Kampfgruppe suffered heavy casualties. Hauptmann Pelikan was killed. Oberleutnant Junge and Leutnant Wecker were captured by the Soviets. Leutnant Schröck-Opitz managed to break through into another stretch of woods with the rear guard and reached the German lines toward evening. Hauptmann Hoffmann, formerly commander of Sturmgeschütz-Brigade 912, took over command. A few days later Leutnant Schröck-Opitz received orders from Hauptmann Barths to recover two Sturmgeschütze left behind in no-mans-land during the night. The attempt, which had already failed on the previous night, succeeded with the help of a captured T 34.

The brigade was then transferred to the northern front of Heeresgruppe North. It participated in the defensive fighting from Dorpat through Riga and on into the Kurland Fortress.

After getting new Sturmgeschütze, Leutnant Schröck-Opitz' section attacked the edge of a Soviet-occupied wood across an open field during the fighting around Dorpat. He was supported by an infantry company. A "Tiger" provided fire support. The section commander's Sturmgeschütz again received a direct hit during this attack. The gunner was killed, and Leutnant Schröck-Opitz was wounded. The radio operator and the driver were unhurt.

Oberleutnant Sauer achieved special distinction west of Dorpat. He was leading the 1st Battery there and defeated a far superior enemy force. His personal initiative and his unshaken courage pulled the crews of the other Sturmgeschütze along with him. Oberleutnant Sauer was able to stop the Soviet attack and prevent a possible catastrophe. For his actions he became the 603rd soldier of the Wehrmacht to receive the Oak Leaves to the Knight's Cross.

Hauptmann Hoffmann was wounded in the defensive fighting at Törwa. Hauptmann Barths took over the brigade. Under his command, on 12 October 1944, the Sturmgeschütze were the last vehicles to cross over the Düna Bridge at Riga before it was blown up.

The brigade distinguished itself in the subsequent heavy defensive fighting in the Frauenburg area as part of the battles for Kurland. The brigade, giving all it had, managed to prevent a Russian breakthrough to Windau by way of Dzustke in the 3rd Kurland Battle around Christmas 1944. For his outstanding leadership of the brigade and his personal actions, Hauptmann Barth received the Knight's Cross there. Sometime during the winter of 1944/45 Sturmgeschütz-Brigade 393 was redesignated Heeres-Sturmartillerie-Brigade 393. This appears to have been a paper redesignation, since it does not appear the unit ever received a battery of escort infantry.

On the day of the capitulation Heeres-Sturmartillerie-Brigade 393 went into Soviet captivity along with Heeresgruppe Kurland, battered but unconquered. In the short period of its existence, this brigade had given proof of the courage, aggressiveness, and willingness to sacrifice itself that marked the men of the Sturmartillerie.

Sturmgeschütz-Abteilung 394 (Sturmgeschütz-Brigade 394)

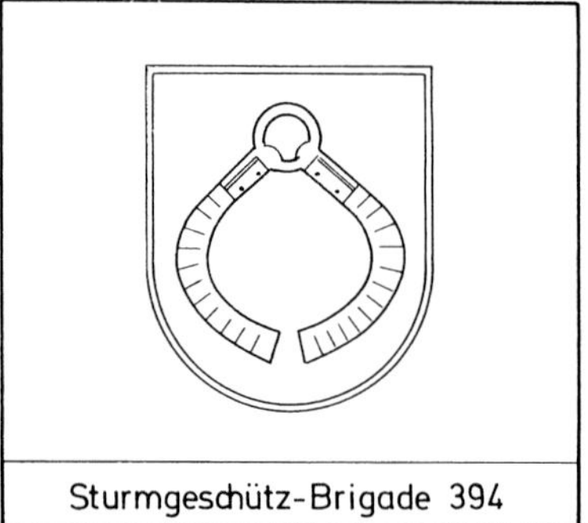
Sturmgeschütz-Brigade 394

The personnel for this battalion were assembled in April and May of 1944 at Deutsch Eylau. Sturmgeschütz-Ersatz-Abteilung 600, also under formation at that time, was to be its replacement depot.

In April the battalion was transferred to Tours in France, and was attached to Aufstellungsstab West (Major Pritzbuer). One week later the battalion was transferred by battery movement to the castles on the Cher. The battalion staff and the Headquarters Battery took up quarters in Beauvais. The 1st Battery was located in the vicinity of this castle, while the 2nd Battery under Leutnant Menzel was moved to Nitray. The 3rd Battery was located at Chesnay. The entire battalion was led by acting commanders. As a result, Oberleutnant Werther became acting battalion commander, Leutnant Hasper acting commander of the Headquarters Battery, Leutnant Anwander acting commander of the 1st Battery, Leutnant Menzel acting commander of the 2nd Battery and Leutnant Jäger acting commander of the 3rd Battery.

The battalion commander, Hauptmann von Jena, and the commanders of the 1st and 3rd Batteries, Hauptmann Tadje and Oberleutnant Thesmacher, were still at Altengrabow attempting to speed up the process of equipping the new battalion. The commander and the two other officers didn't arrive at the battalion until May. The battalion was then transferred to Azay le Rideau, where the batteries were quartered in the ancient castle of Islettes. At this time it was reinforced with the conditionally combat-ready Sturmgeschütz-Batterie 741. This battery was dissolved and became a part of the brigade on 19 June 1944. (See the section devoted to Sturmgeschütz-Batterien 741 and 742.)

With the beginning of the invasion on 6 June 1944, the batteries were put on alert and dug in around Azay le Rideau. The battalion moved into a nearby forest site in the middle of June. The only live-fire exercise prior to combat took place at Camp de Ruchard. On 10 June 1944 Sturmgeschütz-Abteilung 394 was redesignated Sturmgeschütz-Brigade 394. The guns moved to their area of operations along the roads in night marches to avoid fighter-bomber attack.

The final listing of command and staff positions ran as follows:

Commander: Hauptmann Freiherr von Jena
Adjutant: Leutnant Lenk
Orderly Officer: Leutnant Koch
Paymaster: Oberzahlmeister Franke
Brigade Physician: Oberarzt Dr. Schiffmacher
Maintenance Officer: Leutnant (Engr.) Jutz
Shop Chief: Werkmeister Knubben
Supply Officer: Leutnant Heinrichs
Unassigned: Oberleutnant Müller
Headquarters Battery Commander: Oberleutnant Quelle
1st Battery Commander: Hauptmann Tadje
Battery Officers: Leutnant Anwander, Leutnant Stolze
2nd Battery Commander: Oberleutnant Werther
Battery Officers: Leutnant Hasper, Leutnant Menzel
3rd Battery Commander: Oberleutnant Thesmacher
Battery Officers: Leutnant Heidrich, Leutnant Jägers

The brigade left Tours for Normandy at the end of July 1944. It suffered its first losses from air attack while on the march.

The attempt of the German Army High Command to cut off the US breakthrough at Avranches miscarried.

The brigade went into action at Vire while allocated to the 7. Armee, which was commanded by SS-Obergruppenführer Hausser. On 6 August 1944 the 3rd Battery destroyed 26 American tanks in a perfectly executed attack and one-hour fight. It freed an infantry battalion which had been taken prisoner by the Americans. The brigade commander, Hauptmann Freiherr von Jena, led the attack along with his 3rd Battery and, continuously dodging to avoid enemy shells, destroyed six Sherman tanks by himself in a wild charge, before he too was wounded. On 30 November 1944 he received the German Cross in Gold while in the hospital.

Oberleutnant Thesmacher was killed along with a number of the men of his 3rd Battery. Leutnants Jägers and Stolze and their crews were taken prisoner, as was the crew of the brigade commander's Sturmgeschütz. Oberwachtmeister Jahn of that crew was able to break back through to the brigade after 8 days with the Americans.

Hauptmann Tadje, commander of 1st Battery, took over command of the brigade and Oberleutnant Müller took over the 1st Battery.

The fighting in the Argentan-Falaise pocket became a battle of attrition and Sturmgeschütz-Brigade 394 emerged from it with just one operational Sturmgeschütz left. The fuel shortage became especially noticeable during the battle in the pocket.

Generaloberst Paul Hausser was referring to this when, during a commander's conference, he said: "Either they drop us fuel tonight, so we can keep going, or you're all going to have to try to get an English grammar book."

In spite of everything, most of the brigade personnel managed to get out of the pocket. With a loud cheer, it broke out at St. Germaine, where the ring of encirclement wasn't so densely held.

It retreated back through Clermont-Ferrand toward Aachen under its new commander, Hauptmann Schmock. The brigade was put on alert in the Lüttich area because of Maquis activity. It marched through the city at night so as not to endanger the inhabitants if it had to return fire in case of a Maquis attack.

But there was no attack and so the inhabitants of Lüttich had no losses to mourn.

After receiving new guns and wheeled vehicles, Sturmgeschütz-Brigade 394 was employed in the Aachen area. This was the first German city surrounded by enemy forces (in September). They were trying their hardest to capture it.

Some of the hardest fighting in a long time took place in the area around Würselen and during the battle in the Hürtgen Forest.

The brigade was used for flank protection in the Schnee Eifel during the Ardennes offensive. Many of the brigade's soldiers were killed or wounded. Replacements arrived and were immediately incorporated in the unit. Then the brigade was shifted into the area of Hagenau in Alsace from the middle to the end of January. A few days later it went to Koblenz and on into the Wesel area, where it ran into the landing zone of enemy glider troops who had crossed the Rhine during the night of 24 March. Hauptmann Tadje was captured while fighting this enemy, as were Hauptmann Schmock, the brigade commander, Oberleutnant Lenk, Leutnant Nissen and Stabsarzt Dr. Schiffmacher. One day later, Leutnant Hasper and Leutnant Menzel were also taken prisoner.

The rest of the brigade was then committed in its final operations until it became completely combat ineffective. It was transported to the Sturmgeschütz-Schule at Burg and again rebuilt in a perfunctory fashion.

It then headed for Berlin with the last available Sturmgeschütze to get through to the 12. Armee for the relief attack on the capital of the Reich. The brigade lost its guns in the fierce fighting and fought in Division "Schill" as infantry. It fell back across the Elbe with this division, after General der Panzertruppe von Edelsheim had made arrangements to surrender to the Americans.

In spite of the American promises, some of the Sturmgeschütz men were handed over to the Russians and had to endure almost ten years of captivity. Only a very few ever came back to Germany from Russia.

Sturmgeschütz-Ersatz-Abteilung 400

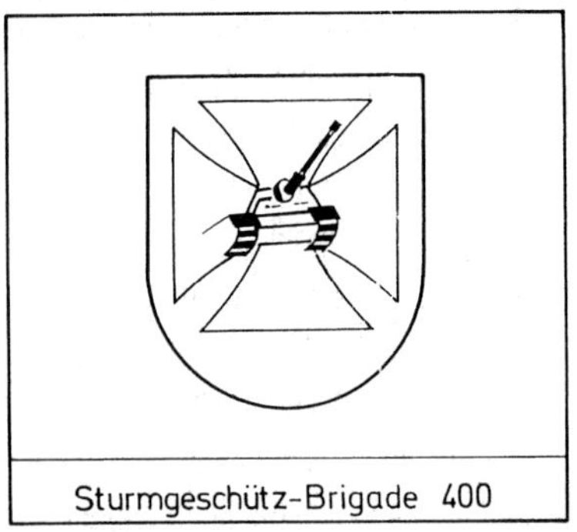
Sturmgeschütz-Brigade 400

Sturmgeschütz-Ersatz-Abteilung 400 like the other replacement battalions of the Sturmartillerie did its work behind the scenes. It was formed in 1942 at Demba (Poland) under the command of Major Bergmann. Oberleutnant Schlesinger was commander of the 2./Sturmgeschütz-Ersatz-Abteilung 400. After recovering from a wound, he was transferred from the hospital to Demba by way of Sturmgeschütz-Ersatz-Abteilung 200 in Schweinfurt.

The job of this replacement battalion at Demba was to rebuild and refit the battered Sturmgeschütz brigades and train and prepare both men and materiél. In the fall of 1943 Sturmgeschütz-Ersatz-Abteilung 400 was transferred to Denmark. It took up quarters in Fredrikshaven, at Aalborg and at Hadersleben. The staff was located at Hadersleben.

When Major Bergmann was transferred in August 1944, Major Kreishold took over command. The battalion provided trained personnel for numerous Sturmgeschütz brigades.

The instructors of all ranks are especially thanked for their tireless support in the rear area.

Sturmgeschütz-Ersatz-Abteilung 500

This replacement battalion was formed on 15 August 1943 at Burg at Magdeburg and given its oath on 24 September 1943 by Oberstleutnant Hoffmann-Schoenborn, the commander of the Sturmgeschütz-Schule at Burg. On 2 October Major Martin Buhr took over command of the brigade, which was transferred by rail through Berlin and Frankfurt/Oder to Posen on 15 November 1943.

The listing of command and staff positions ran as follows:

Commander: Major Buhr
Adjutant: Oberleutnant Westerhold
Orderly Officer: Oberleutnant Zschaege
Legal officer: Oberleutnant Heckmann
Special Duty Officer: Hauptmann Peters
Paymaster: Oberzahlmeister Römer
Administration: Kriegs-Verwaltungs-Ingenieur Loew
Engineer: Kriegs-Ingenieur Kronenberger
Technical Inspector: Technischer Inspektor Zahrnd
Headquarters Battery Commander: Oberleutnant Mai
Training Officers: Leutnant Dr. Drengenberg, Leutnant Körner, Oberleutnant Tamchina, Leutnant Zimmerlinka
1st Battery Commander: Oberleutnant Holzmann
Training Officers: Oberleutnant Römer, Leutnant Hesske
Small Group Leader: Oberleutnant Müller
Training Officers: Leutnant Gutwasser, Oberleutnant Holzer, Oberleutnant Riedel
2nd Battery Commander: Oberleutnant Hoffmann
Training Officers: Leutnant Hatzmann, Leutnant Neuerburg, Oberleutnant Schauer
Air Protection Officer: Oberleutnant Sievers
3rd Battery Commander: Oberleutnant Zander
Battery Officers: Oberleutnant Dr. Schaefer, Leutnant Rasch, Leutnant Braun
4th Battery Commander: Oberleutnant Hauber
Battery Officers: Oberleutnant Luft, Leutnant Poullain, Leutnant Oberthür

All of these soldiers came mainly from Sturmgeschütz units which had been in action and were experienced combat soldiers. This was one important qualification that they all had to have, as it was vital to train young and new Sturmartillerie men so that when they went into combat they would know what to do in any situation that might arise. This alone ensured survival in combat and dominance over an often untrained enemy.

The first unit to be raised from the "Five Hundred," as it was called, was Sturmgeschütz-Abteilung 914 on 24 January 1944 at Posen. This brigade had been assigned to operations in Italy, and advance elements were already on their way there by rail on 2 January 1944 (without Sturmgeschütze as were still none available for them).

A few more units were trained and made combat-ready by this replacement battalion before the end of the war. Many of the Sturmgeschütz men who went through this school and had often cursed it were later thankful for every tip that they received there, even when it had cost a damned lot of sweat at the time. But better to sweat in training than to bleed in combat.

leichte Sturmgeschütz-Abteilung (Feld) 600 (Sturmgeschütz-Brigade 600; Heeres-Sturmartillerie-Brigade 600)

Heeres-Sturmartillerie-Brigade 600

This Sturmgeschütz battalion, which is not to be confused with the Special Duty Detachment Staff 600 (Abteilungsstab z.b.V. 600) nor with Sturmgeschütz-Ersatz-Abteilung 600, was assembled from the consolidation of three independent Sturmgeschütz-Batterien (660, 665 and 666) in Russia in December 1941. Afterwards it went into action as leichte Sturmgeschütz-Abteilung (Feld) 600.

There is virtually nothing known concerning its combat activities, but it is certain that this battalion participated in the very front ranks in the fighting on the Eastern Front. It is believed to have been committed in the area of operations for the 2. Panzer-Armee in central Russia in 1942. In the spring of 1943 leichte Sturmgeschütz-Abteilung (Feld) 600—battered and without any guns—was pulled out of the front and sent to Jüterbog to be rebuilt and refitted. It was renamed as Sturmgeschütz-Brigade 600 on 14 February 1944 along with a number of other Sturmgeschütz formations. It was employed in around Cholm in June 1944 and was redesignated as Heeres-Sturmartillerie-Brigade 600 in the fall of that year. Whether the unit actually reorganized under that structure is unknown. Its last known area of operations was in the Kurland Pocket in 1945.

Abteilungsstab z.b.V. 600 (Special Duty Detachment Staff 600)

Abteilungsstab z.b.V. 600 was called into existence during the French Campaign to provide support for the first six independent Sturmgeschütz batteries. Major von Below was its commander. Leutnant Jahn was adjutant. In addition, approximately ten soldiers belonged to this staff. During the French Campaign the staff moved behind the rapidly advancing units, without ever catching sight of the batteries entrusted to its care.

The staff visited the individual batteries after the end of the campaign in the west. When Sturmgeschütz-Batterien 659, 660, 665 and 666 were moved to the Douai area at Lille, the battalion staff joined them.

The attachment of these batteries to the staff lasted until the beginning of 1941, when the batteries were sent to the east.

Major von Below, who was one of the very first staff officers to volunteer to command an independent battery, had no regrets at all for their detachment, but he did not succeed in converting the battalion staff into a Sturmgeschütz battery.

At the beginning of the Russian Campaign, Abteilungsstab z.b.V. 600 crossed the border at Vystitis with Sturmgeschütz-Batterie 659.

Major von Below was ordered by the corps headquarters to conduct a reconnaissance on the flank of the advance. On this occasion he ran into a group of Soviet stragglers—about 60 strong—some 10 kilometers outside of Mariampol. The unequal struggle lasted several hours, and Leutnant Jahn was killed during the fighting with Soviet defenders, who were being spurred on by a political officer. Eight men of the staff were killed in addition to Leutnant Jahn. Gefreiter Karmann was badly wounded. Major von Below was unhurt, but he too would have fallen in this massacre, if German infantry hadn't rescued him. Gefreiter Karmann who had been hit three times in the stomach, survived his wounds. He was promoted to Unteroffizier and decorated with the Iron Cross, Second Class.

At that point Abteilungsstab z.b.V. 600 ceased to exist.

Sturmgeschütz-Abteilung 667 (Sturmgeschütz-Brigade 667; Sturmartillerie-Brigade 667)

Sturmartillerie-Brigade 667

Sturmgeschütz-Abteilung 667 evolved from Sturmgeschütz-Batterie 667 in the summer of 1942. To differentiate it from the battery, it bore a rampant unicorn as its tactical symbol. Activation of the unit began on 28 June 1942 at Zinna.

Hauptmann Vagedes became the battalion commander. Oberleutnant Heinz Baurmann was battalion adjutant and later took over the 3rd Battery. Leutnant Messerschmidt took over the duties of orderly officer. Oberleutnant Bruno Lange, who had previously led Sturmgeschütz-Batterie 667 in exemplary fashion during the winter fighting in Russia, was commander of the 1st Battery. Hauptmann Zettler led the 2nd Battery and Oberleutnant Selle the 3rd Battery.

After the end of its establishment the battalion was loaded up by rail at Jüterbog at the end of July 1942 and taken through Dünaburg and Witebsk to the Wjasma area. It first went into action with the 5. Panzer-Division at the Chleppen Bridgehead.

When Russian tanks pushed forward along the Wasusa River and threatened to cut off the bridgehead from behind, the infantry panicked. Only rapid intervention by the 1st and 3rd Batteries managed to stop the Soviet spearhead. But this wasn't enough. The Sturmgeschütze then rolled forward with 20 infantrymen riding on them and stormed into the penetrating enemy forces in a mad assault to recapture this piece of blood-soaked ground.

The Sturmgeschütze kept winning duels against enemy tanks. The explosions of their hits continually resounded through the day. Enemy tanks repeatedly blew apart, with dark red flame and black spirals of smoke rising from the stricken T-34's. No fewer than 19 tanks were destroyed by the Sturmgeschütze. The battalion had passed its first test under fire with flying colors.

The Sturmgeschütze also distinguished themselves by their decisive action in the subsequent fighting at Gredjakino and Cholm. And there were more, serious, bitterly fought duels with strong Soviet tank forces during the heavy fighting in the Rshew-Sulzow area. On 29 and 30 August, Oberleutnant Klaus Wagner, commander of the 3rd Battery, destroyed 18 enemy tanks with his Sturmgeschütz alone. On 31 August 1942, the Wehrmacht Report noted:

"During the hard defensive fighting around Rshew, one Sturmgeschütz battalion destroyed 38 enemy tanks by itself on the preceding day."

On the same day the battalion destroyed 30 more enemy tanks. This success was also praised in the Wehrmacht Report of 1 September. Oberleutnant Klaus Wagner, commander of 3rd Battery, was severely wounded in these bitterly fought actions. He was recommended for the Knight's Cross. The battalion adjutant, Oberleutnant Baurmann took over the battery. So far, it had destroyed 83 enemy tanks in the Rshew area. The fighting with Russian tank units raged on, undiminished. On 9 September there was a duel of Sturmgeschütze against tanks. As the enemy attacked the 5 operational Sturmgeschütze of the 3rd Battery with a 10-fold superiority, this battle was as one-sided as a battle could be. But the enemy still didn't manage to knock out this steel wedge. The battle raged for two hours. Four of the five Sturmgeschütze were lost in this no-quarter struggle. Only the command Sturmgeschütz with Oberleutnant Baurmann was able to escape destruction. But along with the four Sturmgeschütze, 33 enemy tanks remained behind on the battlefield—burning, shot up, blown up.

Oberleutnant Baurmann led his guns into fighting in attacks which were unique in planning and execution. The Sturmgeschütze attacked repeatedly with unparalleled dash. Sturmgeschütze immobilized by hits continued to fight until they had fired off their last round or until a second hit silenced them forever.

Then, when the Russian infantry attacked in dense swarms, the command Sturmgeschütz opposed this attack by itself. Oberleutnant Baurmann fired into the middle of the attacking Soviets. The machine gun was mounted and rattled out bursts. And in spite of the monstrous superiority in enemy numbers, they managed to bring back the remaining elements of the battery. The 3rd Battery, virtually torn apart in this fighting, withdrew to the "Jägersruh" ("Hunter's Refuge") rest area. But the battle for Rshew wasn't over yet. Wachtmeister Hugo Primozic's star rose and shone there. His hour came on 15 September 1942.

"Here they come! Herr Wachtmeister!"

Swarms of Russian tanks emerged from the spruce forest in front of the German main battle line. They rolled through a field of grain, approached the German main battle line and ran into German antitank fire.

Wachtmeister Hugo Primozic hurried to his gun. Seconds later he gave the order to go into action:

"Section, move out of the ready position!"

The battlefield between the road embankment and the river was covered with wrecked tanks which had been destroyed there in the past few days. Russian artillery shells had plowed it up repeatedly, and the Soviets were trying to push through there once again in the hope of tipping the balance in the fighting for Rshew in their favor.

The three Sturmgeschütze rolled forward. The Wachtmeister heard the bark of the German antitank cannon and the unusual slurping noise made by Russian antitank rounds impacting the ground. The section, concealed by the low bush-covered knoll, rolled into its defensive position, undetected by the enemy.

Only when Hugo Primozic reached the last row of bushes did he give the order to halt. His two other guns stopped about 40 meters apart from one another.

"I'm going to find out what's going on from the infantry!"

Even before the crew could answer, the lanky Wachtmeister with the energetic lines in his face and the hooked nose had already left the gun and ran toward the infantry position. He disappeared in a cloud of smoke and cascading clumps of dirt from the shell explosions.

Breathless, Hugo Primozic kept going. With one glance around, he grasped the situation. Over there, more Russian tanks were on the way. He counted them. When he reached eight he had to take cover, as that was the moment they opened fire with everything they had.

Shells smashed into the German positions, tearing the antitank and machine gun positions apart. His vision was obscured by shattering explosions and erupting geysers of steel and dirt. And the Soviet artillery was still firing on the position. Then they lifted their fire all at once and moved it back 100 meters.

Suddenly they also began taking fire from tanks on their flank. Wachtmeister Primozic moved his head in that direction. Primozic spied tank turrets in that direction as well. He had to take out this enemy, or he would break through at that spot.

In long strides, he raced back to his section. He mounted his gun, put on his headset, grabbed the microphone and gave the order to advance.

The engines of the three Sturmgeschütze thundered from idling into full speed. Flames shot out of the exhaust pipes. They shot quickly forward and reached the open plain.

The gunner in Primozic's gun saw the first T-34, which was half hidden behind a haystack in disarray.

"Distance 800!" cried Primozic.

At the same moment a shell exploded right next to the gun. Shrapnel thundered deafeningly against the steel of the hull. Clumps of dirt rained down on the gun.

"Ready!" cried the gunner.

The shot rang out. Hugo Primozic, the binoculars in his hand, head raised over the edge of his hatch, saw a red flame flare out of the targeted T-34 followed by thick clouds of smoke. Then, after just one shot, a thunderous explosion ripped the enemy tank into pieces.

The gun commander detected another T-34 further to the right which had exposed its open flank. The turret with the cannon was turning. The gunner saw it too. He cranked the gun and pressed the firing button. Here too, a single shot was enough. The T-34 went up in flames.

"Good man!"

Primozic gave his gunner a smart slap on the shoulder. Down below, the driver growled something incomprehensible. The loader/radio operator laughed. His gray, dirt-smeared face virtually collapsed in this laugh, which revealed the tremendous excitement which had gripped them all.

The two other guns in the section were also firing. Their shots sounded muffled inside Primozic's Sturmgeschütz. He didn't have to tell them what to do. They knew their stuff as well as he did. The excitement of combat gripped them all. A German machine gun began to rattle next to them. It brought their attention to the brown-clad figures which appeared on the crest of the ridge in no-man's-land. Tanks were also emerging there. All were racing toward the German main battle line.

"High explosive!"

The first shells howled toward the attacking Soviets and ripped great holes in the assault waves. But after only a few rounds, antitank shells were loaded once again, for increasing numbers of enemy tanks were emerging over the low knoll and rolling toward the German main battle line.

Once again an enemy tank flared up. Another was disabled by a hit on its track. Then shells exploded in the ground to the left and right of Primozic's gun. Bushes shivered as if they were aware.

"Shift position to the left!" ordered the Wachtmeister.

The driver immediately put in the clutch. The gun turned and jumped forward with a jolt, rolling faster and faster to one side. The shells which would have hit the gun if it had stayed in position, missed. Speed, surprise, "a nose for things" and luck were what made a Sturmartillerie man.

The loader had loaded during the move, and the gunner was already looking for a target. The gun crashed its way through the thick bush. Once again, the driver advanced the Sturmgeschütz, and then turned it with a sudden jerk. They found themselves confronting an entire swarm of enemy tanks. Flame was spurting from the enemy guns. A 52 ton tank was firing straight ahead, barely 300 meters from the gun.

"Lay your sites on the turret!" cried Primozic.

That was the most vulnerable part of the colossus. The gunner aimed carefully. A shell hit the front armor of the Sturmgeschütz and screamed off to the side. The gunner fired. The round raced toward the enemy. It struck and—bounced off.

"Too low!"

"Dammit!" swore the gunner, while the loader rammed home the next shell.

"Calm down! Calm down!" came Primozic's deep voice.

The enemy's guns were flashing, but this time the shells weren't directed at them. They were directed at one of the other two guns. Covered by the bushes, it was obvious that the command Sturmgeschütz hadn't been detected yet. The second round left the long-barreled gun. The 52-ton tank shuddered under the impact. The hatch flew back and thin smoke rose into the air.

"Target!"

All at once, two T-34's rolled in from the flank. The two men serving the gun worked feverishly. Three rounds were fired as quickly as pos-

sible. The targeted T-34 stopped with a jammed turret and a torn-up chassis. The second swung away in a sharp curve and disappeared behind a knoll. But now the German Sturmgeschütz had been detected. The driver was dazzled by the muzzle blast directed at them from a tank in the grain field ahead.

"Target 400! In the middle of the grain field!" he reported to the commander.

But scarcely had the words left his mouth, when a hard blow shook the front end of the Sturmgeschütz. The gun shook. For a few seconds there was fire and thick smoke in the fighting compartment.

"Full speed! Let's go, fast!"

The driver stepped on the gas. The engine still worked, and the gun rolled forward. It became clear that the running gear was still intact. The gunner immediately sighted on the dark point in the grain field. The shot whipped from the cannon. Dirt sprayed up where he had aimed.

Primozic saw the hit through his optics. The Wachtmeister sat to the right of the gun, above the driver's seat.

"Get back under cover!"

Primozic did the best he could. The gun took evasive action, rolled back, and then broke out of the bushes at another place where no one expected them to be. Once again, Wachtmeister Primozic heard a shot from one of his Sturmgeschütze. The third gun was silent. It had taken a direct hit.

Just as the Sturmgeschütz burst out of the vegetation, a 52-ton tank halted 200 meters in front of it to open fire. Two rounds from the Sturmgeschütz had no apparent effect on this super-heavy enemy. The turret of the Russian tank turned towards the Sturmgeschütz, but it was a few seconds too late, for the third shot hit the 52-ton tank between turret and hull and jammed the turret.

But the Russian tank commander rolled on forward. The fourth round of the Sturmgeschütz hit him on the front slope. Pieces of steel flew across the ground. Smoke poured out of the giant's belly. It stopped and then the crew bailed out and raced back for its own lines.

Everything now moved at lightning speed. Hardly 80 meters away, a T-34 moved out from behind a straw stack. Even before the gunner had detected the tank, a shot rang out from it. The cracking detonation of the Russian tank round threw the Sturmgeschütz crew back against the wall of the fighting compartment. But the crew was lucky once again. The hit was ineffective, and the gunner was already acquiring this target.

He only saw a shadow in the thick smoke which surrounded the Sturmgeschütz. He stopped the sights in the middle of this shadow. The shot sped across to the enemy, and then a sharp explosion took place. Its pressure wave could be felt in the Sturmgeschütz. The enemy was destroyed.

This battle lasted one more hour. Hugo Primozic repeatedly brought the swarms of tanks to a halt. The victory would not have been possible without the other two Sturmgeschütze, however. The enemy drew back, and those enemy tanks which had not been left on the battlefield destroyed, burned out or inoperable also rolled back. The tank attack of 15 September had been repulsed.

By himself, Wachtmeister Hugo Primozic had destroyed 24 enemy tanks on 15 September 1942. He was awarded the Knight's Cross ten days later, and he was promoted to Oberwachtmeister for bravery in the face of the enemy.

Generaloberst Model expressed his appreciation to Sturmgeschütz-Abteilung 667 and especially to Oberwachtmeister Primozic in an Order of the Day. Rshew had become a page in the honor roll for this Sturmgeschütz battalion. The Soviets had paid for their tireless efforts to break through with the loss of many tanks.

The following appeared in the soldier's newspaper "Der Durchbruch" for 11 September 1942:

Rshew, which the Soviets hoped would tip the balance for them, was the tomb of the Soviet tank armies. Two thirds of the Soviet tank units known on the entire front went into action at the assault on Rshew. There were massed Soviet tank attacks against our infantry. In such a difficult position for the German defense, the appearance of the German heavy tank destroyers was like a deliverance. Even the news that Sturmgeschütze might be moving to the threatened points worked wonders.

One Sturmgeschütz battalion alone destroyed 38 tanks on one day and 30 on the next. The crews of individual Sturmgeschütze performed heroically, went into action unhesitatingly and gave outstanding help to the infantry hard pressed by the enemy tanks.

Along the entire front, there is only unstinted, unanimous praise for the Sturmgeschütze.

The commander of the division to which this victorious battalion was assigned, and who personally gave the Knight's Cross to an especially deserving wounded officer in a field hospital (this was Oberleutnant Wagner), said that this Sturmgeschütz battalion had resolved the tank problem at Rshew by its outstanding performance and by its beneficial and comprehensive cooperation with the infantry.

How proud a branch must be to receive such praise from those who are the toughest fighters, who have it the hardest—the infantry.

The 3rd Battery was completely refitted in the "Jägersruh" Rest Camp. During Russian breakthroughs in November, this combat battery often had to intervene against enemy swarms of tanks, consisting mainly of T-34's. Sometimes only a single gun was operational. So it happened that Oberleutnant Baurmann went out alone with just his Sturmgeschütz against a swarm of Russian tanks. Almost hopelessly outnumbered, this brave officer initiated the fighting. He fought against 16 enemy tanks. Luckily for him, Sturmgeschütz-Abteilung 202 was in the vicinity and joined the fighting. Oberleutnant Baurmann was decorated with the German Cross in Gold.

When the major Russian operational offensive began on 11 December 1942, and strong swarms of Soviet tanks broke through, the Sturmgeschütze threw themselves against this force, Hauptmann Vagedes in the lead. Hauptmann Vagedes was killed in this fighting which raged until 13 December. He was listed posthumously in the German Army's Roll of Honor, and he was awarded the Honor Roll Clasp.

Oberwachtmeister Primozic gave it his utmost once again. He destroyed seven enemy tanks in a single day. Tank after tank fell prey to his Sturmgeschütz. By the end of December, he had destroyed 60 enemy tanks. On 25 January 1943, as the 185th soldier of the German Wehrmacht, and as the first noncommissioned officer, he received the Oak Leaves to the Knight's Cross. His entire crew, which had a share in this great accomplishment, was awarded the German Cross in Gold. On 31 January on the occasion of his award of the Oak Leaves at Führer Headquarters, Primozic was promoted to Leutnant for bravery in the face of the enemy. That same day, he was Feldmarschall Model's guest at his headquarters.

In the four months it was in action, Sturmgeschütz-Abteilung 667 had had unique success. It had destroyed 468 enemy tanks with

21 Sturmgeschütze. Hauptmann Zettler led the battalion at this time, but it was taken over by Hauptmann Lützow a few days later. The first commander of Sturmgeschütz-Batterie 667 was back in command of the battalion. At Jüterbog, where he was an instructor with the Artillerie-Lehr-Regiment, he was given a farewell by Oberstleutnant Hoffmann-Schoenborn, commander of the Artillerie-Lehr-Regiment, and told: "Lützow, you are taking over the best and most successful Sturmgeschütz battalion that we have at the front!"

During the "Büffelbewegung" ("Buffalo Migration")—the great withdrawal from Rshew through Wjasma to the Dnjepr and from there to Dorogobusch—the battalion was again put in at the critical points in the fighting. The 3rd Battery was assigned to the XXXIX. Panzer-Korps during this period and participated in the storming of Sytschewka.

The battalion's mission then was to defend the highway southwest of Wjasma. There it was attached to the 98. Infanterie-Division and it had a great defensive victory at Djuki. Leutnant Walter Oberloskamp distinguished himself at Djuki, throwing his section against the enemy. In several days of fighting, he destroyed enemy after enemy with his gun.

In a legendary assault—an action without parallel—he defeated 40 enemy tanks. Forty times direct hits blew up the enemy. Forty times an enemy crew died, and one of the enemy's steel colossuses was destroyed. Walter Oberloskamp destroyed an entire Russian tank battalion. On 15 May 1943 he received the Knight's Cross for this unique accomplishment.

Generalleutnant Gareis, commander of the famous 98. Infanterie-Division, wrote in his Order of the Day for 25 March 1943: "Sturmgeschütz-Abteilung 667—considered the best after numerous battles—has plucked a new laurel for its wreath in the battle for Djuki. We owe the victory of Djuki to Hauptmann Lützow, the battalion's courageous commander, and the outstandingly trained and thoroughly aggressive crews as well as to the aggressiveness of the infantry."

In April 1943 Hauptmann Zettler took over the battalion once more. Oberleutnant Wagner, recovered from his wounds, was commander of the 2nd Battery. Oberleutnant Wölfle led the 3rd Battery.

The battalion employed in the areas of Jelnja, Roslawl and Kritschew. Then it was taken by rail from Mogilew and thrown into the line at Smolensk. On 14 February 1944 the battalion was redesignated a brigade.

Up until the summer of 1944, the brigade remained in action in the front sectors of Mogilew, Smolensk, Witebsk and Newel. It had already destroyed its 1000th enemy tank by 29 October 1943. The Wehrmacht Report stated on 11 November 1943: "Sturmgeschütz-Abteilung 667, under the command of Hauptmann Zettler and in action on the Eastern Front since August 1942, has destroyed its 1000th tank." When this report was published, a large number of additional tanks had already been destroyed. In December the number of enemy tanks which had fallen prey to this unit reached 1120.

It was regrouped once again, as wounded, transfers and death had torn holes in the battalion structure. Oberleutnant Oberloskamp took over the 2nd Battery, and Oberleutnant Messerschmidt took the 3rd Battery. The 1st Battery was taken over by Hauptmann Bünau and later by Oberleutnant Wandrey.

This brigade then became the strongest Sturmartillerie unit with 6 line batteries. The veteran frontline 3rd Battery was replaced by a battery from Germany when it was withdrawn from the front in July 1943. The brigade was further renamed on 10 June 1944 when it became Sturmartillerie-Brigade 667.

Sturmartillerie-Brigade 667 was almost completely wiped out during the powerful Russian summer offensive in 1944. The remnants reached the area of Posen for rest and refitting after a march of over 1000 kilometers and constant fighting with advancing Russian units. The brigade had been cut off more than once. Hauptmann Messerschmidt received the German Cross in Gold. Wachtmeister Gottwald Stier and Josef Trägner were decorated with the Knight's Cross in the summer fighting. Both had destroyed more than 30 enemy tanks.

In the Posen area, the brigade was consolidated with Sturmgeschütz-Brigade 254 which had also suffered heavy losses. It remained as Sturmartillerie-Brigade 667, however. Major Knüppling, the commander of Sturmgeschütz-Brigade 254, became its fourth commander. He led Sturmartillerie-Brigade 667 until the end of the war. It was employed in the west, in the heavy fighting for Aachen, and fought until the surrender.

Sturmgeschütz-Abteilung 904 (Sturmgeschütz-Brigade 904)

Sturmgeschütz-Abteilung 904 was formed in Treuenbrietzen at Jüterbog in the fall of 1942. Its insigna was a silver dragon's head with a red tongue. The command and staff positions were:

Commander: Hauptmann Wiegels
Adjutant: Oberleutnant Kampmann
Headquarters Battery Leutnant Kuhn
1st Battery: Oberleutnant Türke
2nd Battery: Leutnant Beise
3rd Battery: Oberleutnant Klövekorn

Hauptmann Wiegels was ill when the battalion was sent to the Eastern Front in a surprising hurry. He had just had a serious jaw operation. Hauptmann Sekirka led the brigade to Russia.

The battalion's first operation took place in the central sector of the Eastern Front, where the Soviets had managed to make a deep penetration into the German main battle line on each side of Ssewsk. The brigade was attached to the 4. Panzer-Division, which hardly had any tanks left.

Sturmgeschütz-Abteilung 904 fought there for the first time since it's formation, but it fought with a bravery which deserved the greatest respect. It moved into action wherever the cry of the hard pressed Panzergrenadiere was heard: "Sturmgeschütze vor!"

Within a few days the battalion had destroyed 70 enemy tanks. Hauptmann Türke received the German Cross in Gold. Many other members of the brigade also received high decorations.

The battalion put up a desperate defense during the fighting at Orel in the summer of 1943, when the Soviets counterattacked after the German offensive miscarried in the Kursk Salient. Major Wiegels, who had returned to the brigade after his illness and who had received the German Cross in Gold after fighting many brave actions, was killed in action there on 7 July 1943, his 27th birthday. The brigade mourned the death of this brave soldier and exemplary commander.

Hauptmann Türke took over the command of the orphaned battalion on the battlefield. Then he put his stamp on the "dragon" battalion. The battalion carried out relief attacks and counterattacks in the area of operations of the 2. Armee (Generaloberst Weiß). The combat operations of the 2. Armee are inextricably mixed with the operations conducted by Sturmgeschütz-Abteilung 904. This battalion's score of destroyed enemy tanks reached 500. In addition to that, 310 antitank cannon of all calibers and an innumerable quantity of vehicles were also destroyed.

In a supplementary report to the Wehrmacht Report, another operation is mentioned which took place from 15 January to 10 February 1944:

The assault of nearly 30 Soviet rifle divisions as well as numerous tank, artillery and ski units, repeated day after day, has been in vain.

During this battle Sturmgeschütz-Abteilung 904 defended against 103 Soviet attacks and participated in 56 friendly counterattacks. It destroyed numerous Bolshevik tanks and other heavy weapons. Thousands of the attackers were left lying in front of their positions.

The battalion was redesignated as Sturmgeschütz-Brigade 604 on 14 February 1944.

Major Türke was killed in action during the fighting in the late summer of 1944. As he lay dying, news reached him that, effective immediately, he had been promoted to Oberstleutnant for bravery in the face of the enemy. Hauptmann Kuhn took over command of the brigade. However, Oberstleutnant Türke was also given a permanent memorial in the Wehrmacht Report for 13 September 1944: "In defensive fighting on the lower Narew, the 7. bayerische (Bavarian) Infanterie-Division under Generalleutnant Ravpard and Sturmgeschütz-Brigade 904 under Major Türke gave solid proof of outstanding fighting spirit. Hauptmann Adamowitsch in particular excelled in the fighting against enemy armor."

Hauptmann Felix Adamowitsch, who had been assigned to the brigade and had taken over command of the 3rd Battery, repulsed six enemy tank attacks with his battery. His Sturmgeschütz, which destroyed more than 20 enemy tanks, was always at the flash point of the defensive fighting. Hauptmann Adamowitsch was decorated with the Knight's Cross on 20 October 1944. In part the citation read: "Up to 3 September Sturmgeschütz-Brigade 904 had destroyed 367 enemy tanks. Hauptmann Adamowitsch, assigned to this brigade, destroyed seven tanks and self-propelled guns in one day, and thereby raised his score to 23 tanks destroyed."

Once more the "dragons" were engaged in heavy fighting when they pulled out of the Bobruisk Pocket to the Narew. Together with the 1. Kavallerie-Korps (General der Kavallerie Gustav Harteneck) and the 129. Infanterie-Division (General Larisch), the brigade fought to cover the retreat of the German soldiers. Sturmgeschütz-Brigade 904 threw its guns against the Soviets wherever they managed to break in. And in doing so, it did the seemingly impossible.

On 1 November 1944, Hauptmann Knaup, a battery commander in Sturmgeschütz-Brigade 904, received the Knight's Cross.

Hauptmann Kuhn continued to command the brigade during the heavy fighting in southeast Prussia and then in east Prussia. Once again, the brigade was engaged in heavy defensive fighting. On 20 February 1945 it fought against an entire Soviet tank armada. The attacking Soviets suffered heavy losses, more than 40 tanks and other weapons. Once more, the brigade received praise in the Wehrmacht Report. That time it was on 21 February 1945. On that same day Oberleutnant Konrad Bretschneider received the Knight's Cross for his personal actions and the leadership he provided to his battery.

The remnants of the brigade went into captivity in East Prussia after the capitulation. During its existence it had destroyed 800 enemy tanks under the severest conditions at a cost of 70 of its own guns.

Sturmgeschütz-Abteilung 907 (Sturmgeschütz-Brigade 907)

Sturmgeschütz-Brigade 907

This battalion was formed in December 1943 at Sturmgeschütz-Ersatz-Abteilung 200 in Schweinfurt.

By January the battalion was already en route from Schweinfurt to Verona in Italy. At the end of January the battalion was issued its Sturmgeschütze at Ferentino near Alatri. Among them were a few from Fallschirm-Panzer-Division "Hermann Göring." The remaining vehicles were also received in Italy. On 14 February 1944 the battalion was redesignated a brigade.

In February the brigade was in the front lines facing the American bridgehead at Anzio-Nettuno. Following that it moved—for the first time as a full unit—to Pontecorvo in the Liri Valley and to the Via Casilina below Monte Cassino.

The first armor engagements took place there in May. After Cassino and the monastery had been voluntarily abandoned during the night of 18 May, American artillery put down extensive fire for the first time along the entire Cassino Front on 20 May. However, the subsequent US attack miscarried and Sturmgeschütz-Brigade 907 had a hand in this. On 26 May 1944 it had to pull back toward Frosinone under continuous attack by US fighter-bombers where it was strafed by rockets and machine-gun fire.

The heavily engaged brigade pulled back through Viterbo, Montefiascone and Orvieto into the Monteroni d'Arbia area. It was particularly plagued by fighter-bombers during these withdrawals. From Monteroni d'Arbia it had to withdraw under heavy enemy pressure through Castelina in the Chianti region to the area of San Donato.

On 16 July there was an armor battle at San Donato, which brought a number of victories, but also bitter losses. The trains and the maintenance section pulled back to the area south of Bologna.

For the time being, however, the Sturmgeschütze took up a hill position in the Fiesole area north of Florence, where the summer heat wasn't so fierce. Still, water became scarce, even in the city of Florence. Every day the men of the Sturmartillerie could see civilians leaving the city to go into the surrounding area in order to get their share of the water supplies which were still available there.

Generalfeldmarschall Albert Kesselring had allowed not only Rome but also Florence to be declared an open city, in order to protect the art and cultural treasures there. No German soldier was allowed into the city.

The Sturmgeschütze then also moved back, section by section, from the Arno defense lines to the "Green" positions. It set up south of Firenzuola. This retreat was successfully completed on 9 September, which meant that all the Sturmgeschütze came through without significant damage.

Sturmgeschütz-Brigade 907

This movement had not remained hidden from the enemy. Firenzuola had already been attacked by flights of heavy bombers on 12 September and completely destroyed in places. Antiaircraft fire shot down three of them. But this was only a pinprick against the apparently inexhaustible number of Allied air squadrons.

On 19 September the Sturmgeschütze joined the withdrawal to Pianoro. On 27 September the brigade then received orders to move into the Idice Valley, and halt the enemy forces spotted there. This time, they were British units.

Small groups of the Sturmgeschütze moved out to the endangered infantry positions and provided decisive help. A part of the brigade went into action with an infantry battalion under Kampfgruppe Böttcher. The trains had already shifted into the area south of Bologna by the end of October. Support elements and the supply center established quarters there.

On 18 December some of the brigade's Sturmgeschütze also moved into this area. They were overhauled and put back into operating condition to the extent possible with the limited means available.

January 1945 began with snow and a record cold for this area of 15 degrees below zero Celsius. The vehicles were provided with snow chains and the Sturmgeschütze were painted with white stripes to better merge with their surroundings.

The winter passed without major "difficulties." But the fighting had already begun again by 1 March 1945. The alerted brigade reached its operational area in the Cena Valley on 18 March. Enemy forces feeling their way forward there were pushed back and four tanks destroyed. In the weeks that followed the enemy forces felt their way forward only hesitantly.

On 15 April and continuing to 19 April, the enemy opened his offensive for the "final spurt" with waves of air attacks. The 1st Battery and Sturm-Panzer-Abteilung 216 which was next to it suffered heavy losses. There was a regular hail of bombs on the ring road circling Bologna. Artillery joined in this bombardment, whenever a German convoy was reported by the observation planes loitering over Bologna.

Division Pfeiffer occupied positions along with Sturmgeschütz-Brigade 907 on 21 April. The Sturmgeschütze were summoned when heavy enemy tanks attacked. But the Panzergrenadiere also engaged this enemy with Panzerfäuste and Teller mines. Some of the Sturmgeschütze took rounds from these tanks. General Pfeifer was often up at the front with his soldiers. Once he also paid a visit to the Sturmgeschütz men to thank them for their fine support.

The retreat continued, step by step, and 23 April saw the brigade in the area of Sermide. Everything that could move was on the road toward the Po during this period. Men and materiél were crowded together there. Burning vehicles lined the way to the river's edge, and there were no bridges left. Men and horses ran about. Soldiers attempted to swim the river with inner tubes. But the Po was at flood stage and the roar of its waters drowned the cries for help from the drowning soldiers.

Sturmgeschütz-Brigade 907

Enemy artillery fired on Borgo Franco, where the first white bed sheets started to appear. During the night of 24 April Sturmgeschütz-Brigade 907 managed to get across the river with most of its soldiers. The last three operational Sturmgeschütze fired against the enemy tanks which were trying to reach the Po dike in order to fire on the soldiers. Near the Po a row of enemy tanks stood in mute testimony to the prowess of the Sturmgeschütze.

The brigade, or more to the point, those who were still alive after crossing the Po, assembled at Schio.

Partisans fell on the groups of retreating soldiers, and they had a hard time ridding themselves of them. The withdrawal continued over the Pasubio Pass. On 2 May the Sturmartilleristen made it to Margreid in the Esch Valley with captured US semi-trailers. It was the brigade's last assembly area. Starting 8 May they were treated as internees. They didn't have to give up their weapons until 15 May, and ten days later they were taken by way of Vicenza and Mirandola to Modena, where a collection point had been established at the edge of the city. From there, elements of the Sturmgeschütz men went to Bellaria, before they arrived back in Germany in September-October 1945.

Sturmgeschütz-Abteilung 909 (Sturmgeschütz-Brigade 909)

Sturmgeschütz-Abteilung 909 was organized at Neiße at the beginning of 1943 under the command of Major Rossi. In the early spring the battalion was already on its way to Orel, where it was to relieve a worn-out Sturmgeschütz battalion that was still equipped with short-barreled Sturmgeschütze. In March 1943 Sturmgeschütz-Abteilung 909 received completely new guns. It received billets in the Glasunowka Armor Barracks as an army reserve. The battalion saw no action there.

The battalion didn't go into action for the first time until Easter, when it was transferred to Kromy near Kursk. The battalion fought against Soviet breakthrough forces there and destroyed them.

With the beginning of the German offensive for the elimination of the Kursk salient on 4 July 1943, the battalion went into action on this front, but it was not attached to either of the two attack groups, which were supposed to cut off this salient from the north and south.

The subsequent fighting withdrawal to Retschitza on the Dnjepr took a lot out of the battalion. Again and again it was launched against outflanking enemy forces and destroyed them. It was only through its actions that the enemy could be prevented from surrounding the German forces in this sector, and the battalion itself was surrounded three times. However, it was always able to break through the encirclement, thus saving itself and the surrounded infantry. Nothing is known concerning the exact details of that fighting.

On 12 January 1944 Hauptmann Pohl took over the battalion. Major Rossi had left the battalion around Christmas 1943. It was then allocated to the 9. Armee and committed in the Bobruisk-Paritschi area on the north edge of the Beresina Swamps. During this period the command positions were filled as follows:

Commander: Hauptmann Pohl
Battalion Surgeon: Stabsarzt Dr. Hess
Paymaster: Oberzahlmeister Griehl
Battalion Engineer: Ingenieur Sievers
Headquarters Battery: Oberleutnant Koch
1st Battery: Hauptmann Alfred Montag
2nd Battery: Oberleutnant Reuter
3rd Battery: Hauptmann Feiler

When Hauptmann Pohl arrived at the battalion, Hauptmann Montag was 40 kilometers east of Paritschi with the combat elements. Hauptmann Feiler was in command of the supporting troops and the trains. These were some 40 kilometers to the rear of Paritschi. The adjutant and the battalion command post were located at Paritschi itself. The 1st and 3rd Batteries still had 10 to 12 Sturmgeschütze in operation. The 2nd Battery was only complete in personnel. Hauptmann Pohl immediately requested materiél replacements. On 14 February 1944 the battalion was redesignated a brigade.

The brigade fought in this area attached to the 110. Infanterie-Division until 23 March 1944.

Hauptmann Montag distinguished himself again and again in the intense defensive fighting during this period. The brigade also had to engage in some night fighting. Night fighting placed enormous demands on the crews and their guns. Materiél replacements gradually trickled in, and once again the brigade had more guns available.

But when the thaw period set in, supply difficulties became continuously greater. There was a gap of 95 kilometers between the supply depot in Bobruisk and the brigade command post. These 95 kilometers were difficult to negotiate on the muddy roads. Even so, the brigade was once more at full strength by the end of March. Hauptmann Pohl had put together a considerable fighting force about him.

During this period Oberleutnant Bachmann was wounded. Leutnant Neuser replaced him as the new brigade adjutant.

Surprisingly, the brigade received orders to pull out of the line at the end of March. It was to go in for rest and refitting. Major Rossi had put in this request for a refitting back in December. Since then, however, all the deficiencies had been taken care of, and the brigade was a hundred percent combat-ready. It always had 30 to 34 Sturmgeschütze committed.

It had to give up all the equipment for which it had struggled for so long. The brigade went by rail from Bobruisk through Minsk to Polozk for refitting at I. Armee-Korps. It was partly billeted in the villages and partly billeted in Russian military facilities.

New equipment was received and made combat ready. Combat veterans gave additional training to the rest of the brigade. The small number of personnel replacements were absorbed by the brigade. On 5 May 1944 Hauptmann Montag received the Knight's Cross for his actions during March.

On 1 May 1944 the brigade had gone into action again for the first time since its refitting. It had been ordered to puncture a Soviet bulge in the front lines 30 kilometers east of Polozk.

Because of insufficient artillery preparation and extremely unfavorable terrain conditions, the brigade suffered heavy losses while moving up. Three guns were put out of action by direct hits. No one in their crews survived. The Sturmgeschütz commander in the first of these guns was the promising Leutnant Gottschalk.

The subsequent investigation by General Hilpert, the commanding general of I. Armee-Korps, fully cleared the brigade commander of any responsibility for this disaster.

Hauptmann Pohl then worked as if possessed, to re-establish calm and order and to bring the brigade back up to strength. He managed to bring back its old fighting strength, and the brigade went into action when the Soviet summer offensive hit I. Armee-Korps along both sides of the Düna from the Witebsk area on 22 June 1944.

The brigade helped I. Armee-Korps to hold its position for three days in an intensive and successful defense. But then, as more and more ground was lost to the Soviets on the south bank of the Düna on the left flank of Heeresgruppe Mitte, I. Armee-Korps had to pull back too, since otherwise it would have been completely isolated and surrounded. The brigade received instructions from the corps to cross the river from the north bank of the Düna (Heeresgruppe Nord) to the south bank of the Düna (Heeresgruppe Mitte) during the night. As a result, the brigade's entire rearward lines of communications had to change over from Königsberg to Warsaw.

Only Hauptmann Montag's 1st Battery received orders to remain with I. Armee-Korps for an additional day. As a result, the battery was separated from the brigade for a long period and was constantly engaged in heavy fighting, entirely on its own.

The Headquarters Battery and the maintenance section were marched overland through Dünaburg into the Swieciany area. This march was a masterpiece of organizational and technical ability on the part of Oberzahlmeister Griehl and Brigade Engineer Sievers.

During this period the 2nd and 3rd Batteries were engaged in bitter defensive fighting east of Lepel with divisions that had been moving since Witebsk and could barely be halted. The brigade pulled back toward Wilna-Kowno with these IX. Armee-Korps formations.

East of Kowno Hauptmann Pohl had to leave the brigade by reason of illness. He had taken over this brigade with great ability in a critical position during a difficult period and led it throughout the dangers of this retreat.

During this period, the 1st Battery under Hauptmann Montag held off the Soviets on their approach to Riga. This battery fought with unending courage. It had the effective support of the flying ace, Oberstleutnant Hans-Ulrich Rudel. More than once Rudel pulled the battery out of a tough spot and enabled it to go on fighting.

After pulling out of this area, the 1st Battery was once again back in action during the breakthrough on Tukkum in the direction of Memel. It was in the Frauenberg area until the end of November. On 1 December 1944 it was brought to Liebau, and from there sent to Gotenhafen by ship. A little later the unit was dissolved. It went back to Altengrabow, where it was converted to the 1st Battery in the newly formed Sturmgeschütz-Lehr-Brigade 111 at the end of January 1945.

Hauptmann Montag then commanded the rest of Sturmgeschütz-Brigade 909 in East Prussia. The brigade was engaged there, fighting to hold German ground until the end of the war. Hauptmann Montag was named to the German Army's Honor Roll and received the Honor Roll Clasp.

Sturmgeschütz-Brigade 909 didn't lay down its weapons until the day of the capitulation, and then it went into Soviet captivity.

Sturmgeschütz-Abteilung 911 (Sturmgeschütz-Brigade 911; Heeres-Sturmartillerie-Brigade 911)

Heeres-Sturmartillerie-Brigade 911
Führer-Grenadier-Division

Sturmgeschütz-Abteilung 911, which bore St. George fighting a dragon as its insignia, was formed in February 1943 from the Sturmgeschütz-Ersatz-Abteilung at Neiße. The personnel were then transferred to Niemegk at Jüterbog and equipped with guns and other gear. Oberstleutnant Wilhelm was the commander. Oberleutnant Pohle took over the Headquarters Battery, Oberleutnant Müller the 2nd Battery. Without warning, the 1st Battery was pulled out of the battalion and sent to the Mediterranean to the island of Corsica (some sources say Sardinia) as an independent battery. A new 1st Battery was raised in Niemegk, which was commanded by Oberleutnant Schulte-Strathaus.

By the middle of March the battalion was already en route by rail to the southern sector of the Eastern Front and was unloaded in the area of Kharkov-Poltawa. It was attached to the 11. Panzer-Division and was employed during the following period with this well-known division which was greatly feared by the enemy. In July the battalion fought in the Belgorod-Obojan area. The battalion commander distinguished himself particularly well there. He received the Honor Roll Clasp and was listed in the German Army's Honor Roll. A little later he was killed while defending against a Soviet attack that was ultimately repulsed. Oberleutnant Müller was killed in the same fighting. Together with the 11. Panzer-Division, the battalion was mentioned in the Wehrmacht Report for 21 July 1943.

The subsequent fighting during August in the area of Graiworon again cost the battalion heavily. The newly appointed battalion commander was killed there, as was the commander of the 2nd Battery, Oberleutnant Liedtke. His successor, Oberleutnant Hahn, was killed immediately after him. The 2nd Battery had three commanders killed in the space of a few weeks. Oberleutnant Lorek took over the battery.

The fighting at Achtyrka and Mirgorod came closely after the intensive, costly defensive fighting at Graiworon. In October 1943 the battalion crossed the Dnjepr at Tscherkassy. It went back into action a few days later at Tschigrin. The fighting at Alexandrija, Kriwoi Rog, Snamenka and Kirowograd took the last ounce of strength of Sturmgeschütz-Brigade 911. The battalion fought at these places on the front until January 1944. During that fighting it was attached to the 11. Panzer-Division and to the 2. Fallschirm-Jäger-Division (General der Fallschirmtruppe Ramcke). On 14 February 1944 the battalion was redesignated as Sturmgeschütz-Brigade 911.

The fighting in March 1944 at Swenigorodka and Talnoije, at Uman and Perwomaisk became new testing grounds for this severely tried brigade. The new commander, Hauptmann Hoffman, was badly wounded. Hauptmann Schulte-Strathaus took over command of the brigade, and Oberleutnant Hense took over his 1st Battery. Oberleutnant Jesse, who had been adjutant of the brigade at its formation, became commander of the 3rd Battery.

Sturmgeschütz-Brigade 911 crossed the Dnjestr at Dubossary in March. The brigade was committed in new operations in the areas of Orhai and Kischinew. In April 1944 the brigade left the 11. Panzer-Division, with which it had fought shoulder to shoulder since its first day of combat.

In the following period the brigade was attached to a number of divisions: the 168., 258. and 282. Infanterie-Divisionen; the 4. Gebirgs-Division; and, the 2. Fallschirm-Jäger-Division.

During the operations in Rumania the brigade was separated into two Kampfgruppen after the collapse of that country. Kampfgruppe I was formed from the 1st and 3rd Batteries. It was caught in a pocket by Soviet forces advancing with incredible speed and wiped out after a desperate defense.

Hauptmann Schulte-Strathaus, who had won the German Cross in Gold in the meantime, was on his way from Kampfgruppe I to Kampfgruppe II when the Soviets attacked. He was never seen again. He was either killed or taken prisoner.

Kampfgruppe II was formed from the 2nd Battery. This Kampfgruppe lost all of its Sturmgeschütze due to lack of fuel shortly after Kampfgruppe I had been wiped out.

As a result the combat elements of Sturmgeschütz-Brigade 911 were annihilated in Rumania. Only the trains escaped captivity. They managed to get back to Germany.

Sturmgeschütz-Brigade 911 was rebuilt at Lohburg near Lüneberg, under its new commander, Hauptmann Tornau. In December it was attached to Führer-Grenadier-Division "Großdeutschland." During this period it was officially redesignated as Heeres-Sturmartillerie-Brigade 911. Whether it was also reorganized as such is uncertain.

The brigade fought with Führer-Grenadier-Division "Großdeutschland" during the period from December 1944 to 9 May 1945. It was committed at every hot spot of the divisional fighting. It fought magnificently.

This brigade fought with everything it had during the Ardennes Offensive. In the middle of January the brigade was transported to the area of Stargard after this last effort of the Wehrmacht in the west and just before the beginning of the major Russian offensive out of the Baranow Bridgehead to the west. An intended operational-level attack toward Posen was unsuccessful. The division was pulled out and sent by priority transport to the area of Lauban in Silesia.

The Sturmgeschütz brigade played a large role in the recapture of Lauban.

The "Knights of Saint George" opposed the heaviest of enemy pressure in the Stettin-Altdamm Bridgehead. There too, it held on unwaveringly in spite of heavy losses. It served as the lead elements in the attempt to relieve Küstrin. The relief attack cost heavy losses and was unsuccessful in spite of the brigade's efforts.

Hauptmann Tornau was awarded the Knight's Cross on 28 March 1945.

The brigade's last operations, still as a part of Führer-Grenadier-Division "Großdeutschland," took place in the defensive fighting in and west of Vienna. After the capitulation it went into Russian captivity.

The exemplary divisional commander, Generalmajor Mäder, and Major Tornau returned home after almost ten and a half years as Russian prisoners. They were among the last ones to return. Many soldiers of this brigade did not survive captivity and never saw their homeland again. They should not be forgotten.

Sturmgeschütz-Abteilung 912 (912th Sturmgeschütz-Brigade; Heeres-Sturmartillerie-Brigade 912)

The personnel for this battalion were assembled as Sturmgeschütz-Abteilung 912 in the middle of February 1943 in the Panzer Barracks at Schweinfurt. The command positions were filled as follows:

Commander: Hauptmann Kruck
Adjutant: Oberleutnant Kicker
Battalion Surgeon: Oberarzt Dr. Rössler
Paymaster: Oberzahlmeister Kändig
Maintenance Officer: Technical Inspector Schättgen
Commanders
Headquarters Battery: Oberleutnant Preussner
1st Battery: Hauptmann Vogler
2nd Battery: Oberleutnant Schulz-Streek
3rd Battery: Oberleutnant Schönmann

On 1 March 1943 the unit personnel were transferred to Jüterbog in the area of Zinna, where they were equipped with guns, vehicles and the rest of their equipment.

When the 2nd Russian Assault Army broke through at Wolchow on 1 April 1943 and launched a relief attack towards Leningrad, the battalion was loaded up and sent by rail through East Prussia and Lithuania into the northern sector of the Eastern Front.

The battalion was unloaded in Chatschina near Krasnogwardeisk south of Leningrad and was immediately attached to the Corps there.

The 1st Battery was attached to the 21. Luftwaffe-Feld-Division, which was already equipped with Sturmgeschütze, at the Oranienbaum Pocket. The battery was employed in the Pulkowo-Kolpino. It was committed at Serlesi near Zarskoje Selo.

The 2nd Battery was placed at the boundary between the 16. and 18. Armeen and was positioned directly across the Leningrad-Moscow road. It executed a few attacks against infantry objectives there.

The 3rd Battery was committed to the northeast on the Wolchow, where it was heavily engaged in defensive action.

During this entire period, the Headquarters Battery remained at Tossno, where the battalion staff was also quartered.

The 2nd Battery was called back to the battalion after the fighting died down on the Wolchow. The entire unit was then within the area of operations of the 18. Armee. One after the other, 5 Sturmgeschütz batteries from the Luftwaffe-Feld-Divisionen were assigned to the battalion in order to be trained.

At the beginning of the 3rd Ladoga Battle all of Sturmgeschütz-Abteilung 912 was committed 9 kilometers south of Schüsselburg. The high points of the fighting were in the defensive battles at Mga and Zignri, on the Ssinjawino Heights and at the railroad triangle. Oberleutnant Engelmann destroyed the first three enemy tanks.

The 1st Battery fought west of Ssinjawino. The 2nd Battery, under Oberleutnant Hartl-Kusmanek, fought directly on the Ssinjawino Heights. It was undoubtedly the 3rd Battery, however, which had the heaviest fighting in the middle of the swamplands. A few of the Sturmgeschütze which got stuck in the swamp there had to be blown up so that they wouldn't fall into enemy hands.

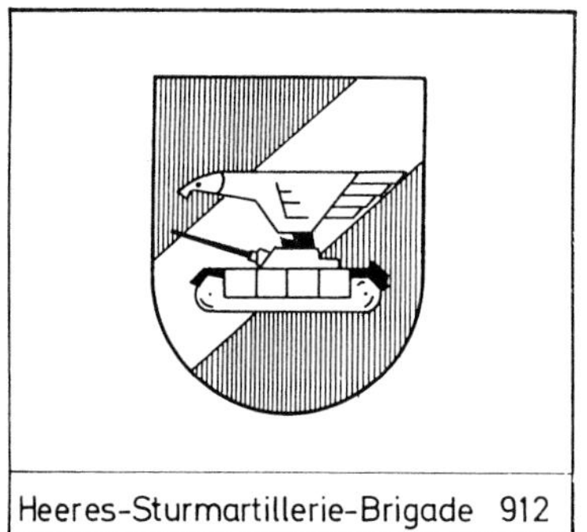
Heeres-Sturmartillerie-Brigade 912

Oberleutnant Schönmann gained special distinction there. He became the first member of Sturmgeschütz-Abteilung 912 to receive the Knight's Cross. He was promoted to Hauptmann for bravery in the face of the enemy.

The battalion was in action in the Ssinjawino area from 27 July to 10 September 1943. Then it was pulled out and sent into position in the southeast section of the Oranienbaum Pocket. The staff and the Headquarters Battery were then at Wolossowa.

Oberleutnant Kicker, the battalion adjutant, was killed in action on 15 November when he went along on an attack in the southern area of the Oranienbaum Pocket. Leutnant Strunz became battalion adjutant.

The battalion was employed against snipers and ground targets. The 3rd Battery, in particular, suffered heavy losses. Its commander, Hauptmann Schönmann, was also killed. Oberleutnant Preusser took over the battery temporarily until Hauptmann Schüßler arrived at the end of November.

During October the battalion repelled strong enemy tank attacks in the "Half Moon Position" at Gassilowo. On a single day Leutnant Egghart, a section leader in the 2nd Battery, destroyed 7 enemy tanks. Oberleutnant Engelmann was successful once again. The enemy was held off on 19 October 1943 when he attempted to collapse the "half moon position" with 5 rifle divisions and 1 tank brigade. Major Kruck launched a counterattack with the entire battalion. This attack ran into a German Stuka attack, in which the battalion's own Sturmgeschütze were bombed. Major Kruck was wounded and evacuated, and Hauptmann Morgener took over the battalion. However, he was transferred out to take command of another battalion a short while later.

The months of November and December were characterized by heavy defensive fighting. Sturmgeschütz-Abteilung 912 celebrated Christmas in the Sebijesh-Idriza area where its new commander, Hauptmann Karstens, arrived.

With the beginning of the Soviet operational-level offensive in February 1944 along the entire northern front, the batteries were once again spread out and went into combat individually. The 1st Battery pulled back slowly to Pustoschka. It was engaged in positional fighting in the Sebijesh-Idriza area until June 1944. Leutnant Schweizer was killed. The commander of the 2nd Battery, Hauptmann Hartl-Kusmanek, died in the arms of Leutnant Egghart. The front finally stabilized in the Polozk area. The 2nd Battery then put up a tough defense on Lake Schablino. Two Sturmgeschütze had to be blown up. Hauptmann Kleinschmied became the new commander of the 2nd Battery. On 14 February 1944 the battalion had been redesignated a brigade.

Sturmgeschütz-Brigade 912 stayed in the area of the Pustoschka-Opotschka road until the collapse of Heeresgruppe

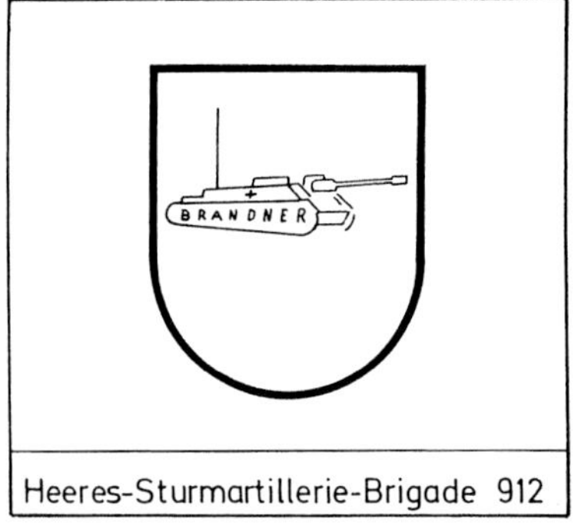

Heeres-Sturmartillerie-Brigade 912

Mitte. The three combat batteries were each provided with 2 to 3 additional Sturmhaubitzen. Even the headquarters section received three Sturmhaubitzen. Enemy penetrations were eliminated by the batteries. The brigade went into action to eliminate larger penetrations. Leutnant Egghart distinguished himself again and again by his remarkable bravery at Lake Schablino. He was decorated with the Honor Roll Clasp, the German Cross in Gold and 5 tank destruction badges.

Oberleutnant Engelmann also distinguished himself again by destroying several enemy tanks. He received the German Cross in Gold.

The operational-level offensive of the Russian 2nd Baltic Front began on 11 July 1944 between Pleskau and Opotschka. The German troops were battered and, in part, wiped out. They pulled back. Sturmgeschütz-Brigade 912 served as the rear guard and was engaged in very heavy fighting. When Hauptmann Vogler, commander of the 1st Battery, was severely wounded, Oberleutnant Engelmann took over the battery. A few days later he was promoted to Hauptmann. He covered the retreat and, at the end of July, with his gun alone, he destroyed an additional 17 enemy tanks on one day. By 4 August 1944 he had already received the Knight's Cross for this splendid aggressive behavior and tactical accomplishment. A few days later the Wehrmacht Report for 8 August 1944 gave recognition to the brigade's action: "During the fighting on the Düna Front in Latvia Sturmgeschütz-Brigade 912 destroyed 53 enemy tanks in the last few days. Of this number, Hauptmann Engelmann, Commander of the 1st Battery, destroyed 17 enemy tanks by himself."

In the next few days Hauptmann Engelmann repeated this splendid feat. Once again, he destroyed exactly 17 enemy tanks within a very few days. That raised his score to 54 enemy tanks knocked out. Hauptmann Engelmann received the Honor Roll Clasp and was named in the German Army's Roll of Honor.

Hauptmann Engelmann's loader, Gefreiter Diem, also distinguished himself on 4 August 1944 at the Jackony farmstead for his bravery in the face of the enemy. He too received the Honor Roll Clasp. This award decorated one of the bravest of the Sturmartillerie men. On 18 August 1944 the Wehrmacht Report once again mentioned Sturmgeschütz-Brigade 912: "Strong groups of attacking enemy forces—supported by armor—in the area north of Brisen were repulsed in heavy fighting by our defense. Sturmgeschütz-Brigade 912 under Hauptmann Karstens had a major share in the destruction of 108 tanks within 3 days."

Unteroffizier Schwarzenbacher also met his fate in this area of fighting. As a gun commander, he destroyed 7 enemy tanks within a few minutes and, entirely on his own, prevented the threat of an enemy penetration. On 5 September 1944 Unteroffizier Schwarzenbacher received the Knight's Cross. A few days later he was killed in heavy tank fighting after he had again destroyed a number of enemy tanks.

The commander of the 2nd Battery, Hauptmann Kleinschmied, was severely wounded in this fighting. Oberleutnant Strunz, the brigade adjutant, took over the orphaned battery and achieved considerable combat success with it. He had the old "vets" in his battery: Oberwachtmeister Fahlisch, Oberwachtmeister Störmer and Wachtmeister Pobanz. All three had received the German Cross in Gold after outstanding accomplishments. Oberleutnant Kratzel, a section leader in the 3rd Battery, also received the German Cross in Gold for his actions.

The brigade was back in action during Unternehmen "Donner" (Operation "Thunder"), an operation to pull the 18. Armee out of the Segewold Position and withdraw it behind the 16. Armee through Riga and Tukkum to Kurland. It was used to cover the positions of the 16. Armee in the Mietau–Doblen-Dzukste areas and had to put up a fierce defense there.

Mobile units of the Russian 51st Army reached the small port of Polangen north of Memel. This came as a great surprise and cut off Heeresgruppe Nord from land communications with Germany. The "Kurland Pocket" was formed and it included Sturmgeschütz-Brigade 912.

The First Battle for Kurland began on 13 October 1944. The 1./Sturmgeschütz-Brigade 912 stood on the defense in the Doblen area. Hauptmann Engelmann was killed there and was buried on 21 October 1944 in the church cemetery at Remote in Kurland. Oberleutnant Strunz took over the battery. The commander's Sturmgeschütz sank in a swamp and was lost.

The Second Battle for Kurland ran in two phases, from 27 October to 6 November and from 19 November to 27 November. The Sturmgeschütze fought at the focal points of the battle for the "Brunhilde Position" between Doblena and Autz and west of there on Lakes Zebres and Lielauce. The commanders of the 1st and 3rd Batteries, Oberleutnant Strunz and Hauptmann Schüßler, were wounded during this fighting. Major Karstens was also no longer fit for duty. On 17 December Hauptmann Sepp Brandner relieved the commander. Oberleutnant Schubert took over the 1st Battery and Oberleutnant Kratzel the 2nd Battery.

The Third Battle for Kurland flared up on 21 December 1944. For the third time, the Soviets prepared for a breakthrough. Sturmgeschütz-Brigade 912 was in position at the edge of the city of Frauenburg when the enemy fire began.

"Listen to that! Those are massed Stalin Organs. It looks like Ivan isn't just firing all his guns, he's tossing in the kitchen sink!"

"Good thing that I ordered the brigade into ready positions yesterday."

"You said it, Herr Hauptmann!" said Oberleutnant Opel, the orderly officer.

"What kind of radio traffic is there? Is there any news?"

"Nothing new, Herr Hauptmann," reported the signals noncommissioned officer Unteroffizier Kaiser.

"Heavy harassing fire!"

"That's harassing fire? I'd like to see a real barrage then."

One man in the command post of Sturmgeschütz-Brigade 912 laughed. But he stopped immediately when a salvo from a Stalin Organ hit nearby and the bunker shook. Sepp Brandner, the brigade commander, looked through the swirling clouds of cigarette smoke. Then he stood up from the cot.

"Get the Sturmgeschütze ready!"

Shortly afterwards, the powerful Maybach engines warmed up. Radios were switched to receive. It was 21 December 1944 and the

Soviets were preparing for a breakthrough in Kurland. The rolling barrage felt its way closer and closer to Frauenburg, where the brigade was positioned at the edge of the city. Up forward, on the main battle line, it had already started, and the Landser in their icy, snowed-in foxholes were being heavily battered. Then the barrage rolled on toward the rear. For Hauptmann Brander, the signs were unmistakable: the Third Battle of Kurland had begun.

"Herr Hauptmann, radio report from the line: heavy artillery fire on our ready positions."

"Tell them to keep their eyes open. One hundred per cent manning. Let me know immediately when the Russian attack begins!"

Ten minutes later, the attack began. The first T-34's felt their way forward. Their attack objective seemed clear enough from the previous fighting, the artillery barrage and the enemy tank concentrations. They were trying to reach the Tukkum-Frauenburg road. If the Soviets could reach it, they would then be in a position to split Heeresgruppe Kurland and destroy the German units north and south of Frauenburg piecemeal.

Here is Major Brandner's report for that critical morning of 21 December 1944.

It was 0720 hours. The Schwerpunkt for the attack had become obvious. I received orders to move the brigade there. Twenty minutes later the first Soviet attack and breakthrough at the point of main effort was reported to me. Heavy and super heavy enemy tanks were overrunning our infantry. I went to the front of the brigade and moved to the endangered position.

The enemy could recognize me by the brigade standard which fluttered on the right of the hatch cover. Maybe by the fifty white rings around the barrel as well. Let him have at it!

We moved well separated so as not to give the Soviets a compact target. In an armor battle you never know if the enemy's gun isn't already aimed at you, even before you see the enemy himself. A tank's muzzle blast flared ahead of us. Then the round burst just to the right of us. The driver grasped the situation; he pulled the stick to the right and then we were pointed toward our opponent. I talked the gunner in to the target. He got the range and our first round left the muzzle. A burst of flame on the enemy tank. The T-34 exploded.

Right up ahead a second T-34 broke through and reached the road.

"Fire at will!"

"Damn, a misfire!" the gunner swore. The loader swore too. Everything happened within a few seconds. Our nerves were stretched to the breaking point. The two following Sturmgeschütze were already engaged in action with other T-34's. Why hadn't our opponent shot at us yet? What was going on over there?

At that moment the shot rang out and then immediately afterwards burst in the crown of a tree right over us. I could almost hit the enemy with my binoculars, he had come so close to us. Then my gun recoiled from a fired round and I saw the fiery rosette of a hit on the hull of the T-34. Its crew bailed out and disappeared in the bushes.

Then the Soviet artillery began to fire and put down a curtain of steel, smoke, and flame on the road in front of us.

"They've recognized the brigade, Herr Hauptmann!"

Yes, the Soviets must have identified us, and they wanted to put us out of commission before we could really get into the fighting.

"Traffic from the 2nd Battery, Herr Hauptmann. Our infantry is leaving their positions to the right of us and falling back."

Shit! We can't give them support. There's a mess of tanks in front of us. Thirty T-34's with Joseph Stalin 2's.

The fighting began. Our comrades fired off everything they could stuff into their guns. Our gun also spewed forth steel and fire. We rolled in a wide sweep across the field. Burning T-34's and Joseph Stalin 2's were spread over the field. Black columns of smoke rose over the burning, wrecked tanks like over-sized exclamation points. Our driver dodged back and forth. Once we rocked really hard. The gunner and loader worked as if possessed. Rounds whistled over past us. Right and left. Another loud burst. Everything was still going well. Fire faster. In any case, faster than the enemy. That meant survival.

Tanks wherever you looked. Tanks, tanks, tanks. Fifteen shot up, hollowed out by the cannons on our fighting vehicles, exploded, ripped into pieces by detonating munitions.

"'Eagle' to the 'Wolf Tree' Group, east, northeast, farm house!"

One after the other, I directed my Sturmgeschütze. Just yesterday, I had scouted the land once again. Today, I had put my guns in just the right place. We moved in zigzags by fits and starts. The Russian barrage still lay on our sector.

"Floor it—Step on it!"

We made it through the barrage by the skin of our teeth. Shell bursts rose to the right and left of the gun, and behind and in front of us. The gun ran into a shell crater, tipped far over, righted itself, then pulled out with the engine howling. Where did my two other guns go? I could see nothing, so I had to call them.

"Brandner to Opel! Follow me, fast!"

He answered immediately.

"Opel to Brandner: We're on our way!"

We then moved toward our own infantry as they fell back. Our comrades stopped as soon as they saw us. They were no longer alone, no longer defenseless against the Russian tanks, which rolled over their trenches. Now they had the protection which they had to have during such a massed tank attack, if they didn't want to be wiped out.

"Brandner, this is Egghart...over on the right flank!" reported the commander of the second battery.

"What's going on there!"

"Fierce tank battle. More enemy tanks than you'd believe. Get over here!"

"We're coming, Egghart!"

Once again, we stormed ahead. We saw the flames shooting skyward from the burning enemy tanks. That's where we had to go. Maybe there were some of our guns burning there? My two Sturmgeschütze deployed behind me to the left and right. I called them:

"Brandner to Opel: Stop and give me covering fire. Cover the flanks. I'm going to try to reach the old lines."

"Understood! Remain here!"

Our command Sturmgeschütz rolled forward into the artillery fire which once again rose up to full intensity. Then I saw them breaking out of the billowing smoke, fumes, flames and noise. T-34's. There were a lot of them. This had to be the second wave. I called out:

"Halt! Tanks to left. Range 300—Fire!"

The first antitank round left the barrel. It hit the enemy right in the ammunition he was carrying. He blew apart in a bright splash of fire, but this didn't scare the rest of them. The enemy fired back. I saw their muz-

zle blasts shoot out from their barrels in long streams of flame without hearing the bursts around me in my excitement. Our driver dodged and turned, repeatedly coming back to firing position and, each time he did, the gunner fired.

The rounds flew toward the enemy tanks at very short range and smashed them. T-34's burned, others stopped, crippled. Smoke spiraled out of their hatches. The crews bailed out. And then our infantry came back up behind the two guns of my section. These two guns opened fire as well. The Landser reached the old lines, where the follow-on Russian infantry had already infiltrated. They threw the enemy back out in close combat. They fought decisively and with everything they had, now that they had support and were no longer helpless in front of the Soviet steel monstrosities.

"Russian heavy mortars!" came the voice of Oberleutnant Egghart over to me. Then the mortar rounds also impacted around us. But we didn't dare withdraw yet. If we were to withdraw now the enemy tanks would break through once again and the front would collapse.

It was a severe test of our nerves, but we all passed. The shell bursts came closer and closer. One of my guns was hit. But we had to stay, even if we had to pay with the final consequence. The Soviets were firing on us with heavy pieces. Then I came to a difficult decision. We had to take our guns on forward ahead of our lines and drive right into the middle of the Russian attack where the Russian mortar brigade wouldn't suspect we were. And during this effort, I had to keep my head out of the gun so that I could see what I needed to do.

Small arms fire zipped past again. Just like the time my throat was shot up. But what could I do? I had to lead my brigade properly. So, outside with my head!

Then we charged forward with every gun in the brigade. We fired with everything we had and reached the Russian trenches. The enemy fled back. The open field was covered with brown spots. We stayed out front; our other guns hammered down any pockets of resistance. We drove on right in among the Russians. A Russian hand grenade exploded on the hull. Luckily I had just pulled my head back inside the hatch. But I had to stick it back out again. I had to have a good view of the situation. And so I saw that our large "chow" box, which we always carried with us on the hull, had been completely ripped apart.

Behind me I saw a group of our Landser, who had closed up on me. I waved for them to close in. They came running up and climbed up on the back of the gun and we pushed on after the fleeing enemy. My other two guns followed along and kept my flanks clear.

Then the enemy artillery abruptly quit. They were changing position to the rear. They were probably afraid that we would overrun them. We had done it. It was already beginning to grow dark. We had been under fire for the entire day. It was time for this battle to end. There were only five antitank and three high-explosive rounds left in my Sturmgeschütz.

The casualty reports came in. Had I made any mistakes? Had I lost any men by my own inadequacies? It was a hard thing to be a commander. To be a commander meant to be responsible for every man in the brigade. To be responsible for them to the higher command, and to yourself.

Hauptmann Brandner received the Knight's Cross of the Iron Cross on 17 January 1945 for this operation. In his recommendation, General Feyerabend, commander of the 11. Infanterie-Division (to which the brigade was attached) wrote: "On the first day of the battle, Sturmgeschütz-Brigade 912 advanced into the Russian attack and wiped out the enemy armored spearhead. This first counterstroke was decisive. It smashed the enemy and denied him his objective of splitting Heeresgruppe Kurland."

The 1st Battery was in the area of operations of the 225. Infanterie-Division (Generalleutnant Risse) during Christmas 1944. It was employed on the Kalvas Heights east of Stedini. The main battle line was held in fierce forest fighting. The commander of the 1st Battery, Oberleutnant Schubert, was surrounded by the Russians at his command post over Christmas. But he held back the enemy and, the next morning, led the attack of the relief forces which Hauptmann Brandner had ordered by radio.

The 2nd Battery, under Oberleutnant Egghart, fought attached to the 290. Infanterie-Division in the Striki-Diki area. Oberleutnant Egghart destroyed his 6th tank in close combat and received an additional tank destruction badge.

Oberleutnant Kratzel, commander of the 3rd Battery, was killed in a counterattack in difficult broken terrain. Leutnant Siebenbürger took over command of the battery on the battlefield.

The Brandner Brigade, as Sturmgeschütz-Brigade 912 was then known throughout the Kurland Pocket, was also at the focal points of the fighting in the Fourth Battle of Kurland, which began on 25 January 1945 and lasted until 3 February 1945.

The I and II Baltic Fronts, under the commands of the Soviet Generals Bagramian and Jeremenkow, once again tried to push through the front at Frauenburg, but Sturmgeschütz-Brigade 912 stood firmly.

The 1st Battery, under Oberleutnant Schubert, smashed the main Russian attack. Schubert received the Knight's Cross for his efforts. In 6 to 7 counterattacks daily from the pivotal and critical points on the front, from the Mucikas estate to a height near Frauenburg, Oberleutnant Schubert pushed back constant attempts by enemy forces to force their way through.

In the first three days of the Fourth Battle of Kurland, the 1st Battery alone destroyed 57 enemy tanks in the Gobas Forest south of Kcklini. Eleven of these were destroyed by the battery commander himself. In the next 5 days the battery destroyed another 14 enemy tanks. The 3rd Battery, also attached to Oberleutnant Schubert, destroyed 6 enemy tanks. In all a total of 77 enemy tanks were destroyed in the Gobas Forest alone.

At the beginning of the Russian infantry attack, Sepp Brandner, who had since been promoted to Major, smashed into the enemy with his Sturmgeschütze. He fought at the head of his three headquarters Sturmgeschütze and destroyed his 57th tank.

Oberleutnant Egghart, still with his 2nd Battery, received the Knight's Cross when he destroyed his 7th tank in close combat with a Panzerfaust and knocked out several other tanks in the forest fighting. The way this young officer, with the constant smile and the youthful light in his eyes, always gave his utmost in the hell of combat, inspired his battery to ever greater efforts.

Personnel replacements arrived for the battered brigade during January 1945. The brigade also was given the Sturmgeschütze of a brigade which had previously occupied a position on the island of Ösel which was evacuated on 23 December 1944. Each battery was given 2 Sturmhaubitzen and 3 Sturmgeschütze. Sometime during the winter the brigade was officially redesignated Heeres-Sturmartillerie-Brigade 912.

Major Brandner, on his own initiative, formed "Sturmgeschütz-Begleit-Batterie 912," which consisted of three platoons that could be sent to any of the individual batteries in a crisis. With the new "battery" the Brandner Brigade went into the Fifth Kurland Battle which began on 20 February 1945 and didn't end until 11 March 1945.

The Russians made a surprise breakthrough on the Berzini corduroy road through a 2 kilometer gap in the front. Hauptmann Schubert threw himself and his battery against this enemy. Three T-34's were destroyed that night. On the next morning the Batterie Schubert destroyed another 37 enemy tanks. Hauptmann Schubert received the German Cross in Gold.

The next day the entire brigade went into action under the personal command of Major Brandner. Within 2 hours the brigade destroyed 45 tanks, and the gap in the front lines was closed by the 205. Infanterie-Division (Generalmajor Giese).

On the following night, Major Brandner, Hauptmann Schubert and the orderly officer, Oberleutnant Opel, led an attack into a wooded area. A German infantry command post had been surrounded by the Russians. During this attack the three guns destroyed 7 enemy tanks.

One day later Hauptmann Schubert ran into fire from Russian super-heavy 37.5 cm mortars. Both tracks were torn off. Suddenly he was attacked by 5 enemy tanks. The Hauptmann destroyed three of them, and the other two drove off.

Immediately afterwards, at almost the same spot, Major Brandner destroyed his 60th and 61st tank. While coming back, he was knocked out behind the 1st Battery's command post by a Russian antitank cannon, but he was unhurt. The Fifth Kurland Battle was a great victory for Sturmgeschütz-Brigade 912.

The Sixth and last Kurland Battle began on 18 March 1945. The attack was concentrated in the Frauenburg area and at Dangas and Skutini. The 1st Battery, under Hauptmann Schubert, fought south of Schrunden. The 2nd Battery, under Hauptmann Egghart, was committed in the Frauenburg area. When the Russians approached within 2 kilometers of the Frauenburg-Libau railroad on 18 March and took it under fire, Major Brandner caught up to the deploying 2nd Battery at the "Match Factory" and led it against the Russian tank spearhead. The 2nd Battery destroyed every tank. Hauptmann Egghart destroyed his 8th tank in close combat with a Panzerfaust.

On 1 April 1 the brigade received the first of the recently created Kurland cuff titles, and Major Brandner brought them personally to each of the batteries. The brigade had taken part in all of the Kurland battles.

On 30 April 1945 Major Sepp Brandner became the 847th soldier of the Wehrmacht to receive the Oak Leaves to the Knight's Cross.

The last Commander-in-Chief of Heeresgruppe Kurland, General Hilpert, together with his Operations Officer, General Foertsch, had negotiated on the capitulation of the Heeresgruppe for 8 May 1945 at 1400 hours. During the morning of 8 May 1945 at 1100 hours, Hauptmann Schubert passed these orders on to his men at his command post, the bitterest orders in his life as a soldier.

On 9 May 1945 the brigade went into captivity as a unit.

During the almost two years that it was in action, Heeres-Sturmartillerie-Brigade 912 had destroyed more than 600 enemy tanks and had lost 38 guns. Twelve of its officers were killed in action and twenty five were badly wounded.

Sturmgeschütz-Abteilung 914 (Sturmgeschütz-Brigade 914)

Sturmgeschütz-Brigade 914

Sturmgeschütz-Abteilung 914 was formed on 25 January 1944 at Posen. By 1 February it was already loaded on trains and sent by rail through Silesia and Moravia to Vienna. From there it went by way of Mürzzuschlag and Bruck an der Mur to Klagenfurt and then to Italy.

The brigade received its guns in Verona on 6 February 1944. From there it was sent to Pescara on the Adriatic. The brigade was attacked by an enemy bomber group at the Senigallia Railroad Station. Several soldiers were badly wounded. Vehicles were also damaged.

Sturmgeschütz-Abteilung 914 and the 305. Infanterie-Division blocked the Via Emilia south of Pescara. The English, in particular the Polish Army under General Anders, were in nearby Ortona.

Sturmgeschütz-Brigade 914 was alerted on 28 May and marched toward Rome-Frosinone by way of Popoli–Aquila-Rieti. In the meantime the enemy had managed to break through at Cassino and the southern front was pulled back. The guns reached the northern suburbs of Rome in the first days of June and, with their scissors binoculars, could watch the Americans from the Anzio-Nettuno Beachhead enter Rome.

On the way to Rome, the first guns had been lost to fighter-bomber attacks. The brigade lost its first dead in the fighting, and some of the guns were also lost in duels with tanks and artillery.

The necessary rest and refitting took place in the Forli area. The brigade commander, Major Domeyer, was badly injured in a car accident. Major Dr. Rabe took over command.

On 19 July 1944 the brigade went back into action. It moved through Riccione on the Via Emilia to the Ancona area.

The brigade occupied positions at Senegallia. There was heavy fighting there. On 23 July the commander of the 3./Sturmgeschütz-Brigade 914, Oberleutnant Fuchs, was killed by shell shrapnel. During this fighting the brigade was attached to the 278. Infanterie-Division, led by Generalleutnant Harry Hoppe.

After the enemy attacks dissipated, the brigade was shifted into the Parma area, where it finally received German Sturmgeschütze to replace the Italian assault guns it had been using.

Assigned anti-partisan duties in the Genua-Alessandria area, some sections from the brigade moved into the partisan area of Borgheto di Borbera and were used in the area of operations of the 232. Infanterie-Division.

On 23 November the brigade rolled into the Pavullo area in the Apennine Mountains south of Modena. There the positions were pulled back gradually, held as long as necessary to allow the infantry to make it back to the next fighting position. Castel d'Ayano-Montesse was the last of these positions. There was stubborn fighting there. The enemy air force and partisan ambushes also cost the unit casualties.

The southern front collapsed on 23 April 1945. Sturmgeschütz-Brigade 914 began a retreat in which many comrades lost their lives. The partial capitulation in Italy took place on 2 May 1945. That put an end to the short but rough period of combat in which this brigade found itself at the final stages of the war.

Sturmgeschütz-Abteilung 1170

Sturmgeschütz-Abteilung 1170

In January 1945 Sturmgeschütz-Brigade 322 was smashed in the Kielce-Lysa-Gora area. The survivors from this brigade were brought back together at Burg near Magdeburg. By order of the operations officer of the Sturmgeschütz-Schule, they were assembled by Hauptwachtmeister Anno Slawczynski at Lühe, some 8 kilometers south of Burg. The Hauptwachtmeister was to use these remnants to begin the formation of a Sturmgeschütz battery.

Oberleutnant Luft arrived at Lühe a little later as battery commander. Leutnants Kaunert and Putzig were assigned as section leaders. They too belonged to the former Sturmgeschütz-Brigade 322.

After assembling the personnel for the new battery, it was found to be over-strength and 40 men had to be transferred out.

On 19 March 1945 the new battery was transferred to Lostau, 10 kilometers west of Burg. It was given the mission of digging anti-tank ditches, but it received orders placing it on alert status on 31 March, ending this unpopular task. The battery was transferred to the Old Barracks at Burg. One day later they were moved to the New Barracks. There they were informed that they were to make up the 15th Company (Panzer-Zerstörer) in a newly forming infantry regiment.

This decision, however, was rescinded only a few days later, and the battery was moved once again, this time to the Pestalozzi School at Burg. Its new orders read: "The battery is to make up the cadre for a newly forming Sturmgeschütz battalion, which will be the 1170th. Effective immediately, it is the 1./Sturmgeschütz-Abteilung 1170."

The staff and the other two batteries arrived in the next few days. They too had been recruited from the remnants of battered field brigades. The remnants of Sturmgeschütz-Brigade 249 were among those who arrived at the new Sturmgeschütz-Abteilung 1170. An escort battery was formed as the 4th Battery. This fourth battery was made up exclusively of members of the Sturmartillerie. Because the line batteries had to be formed in compliance to an emergency table of organization and equipment, 24 more noncommissioned officers and men had to be given up. This reduction in personnel was mostly a result of a lack of ammunition and fuel vehicles. In this battalion, the individual batteries were to be supplied directly by the battalion.

Oberleutnant Poullain became the battalion adjutant. The battalion commander's name is unknown.

Battalion formation was completed by 8 April 1945. On 11 April 1945 it was transferred to the area of operations of the Division "Scharnhorst" in the Lindau area north of Zerbst. Regiment Langmeier was instructed to work with the battalion. The "Scharnhorst" Division belonged to the XX. Armee-Korps of the 12. Armee (General der Panzertruppe Wenck).

The battalion moved into action for the first time on 13 April between Dessau and Magdeburg. It was committed against the American bridgehead at Barby on the eastern bank of the Elbe. However, it was unable to eliminate the bridgehead. The enemy laid down massed fire from heavy and super-heavy weapons in the battalion's attack sector and destroyed some Sturmgeschütze. The allied air forces, who were operating constantly over the front and who enjoyed air supremacy, also joined in. The Sturmgeschütze fought together with Regiment Langmeier until 17 April, but they were denied any success.

Oberleutnant Luft was badly wounded in an air attack on the first day of the attack, 13 April 1945. He never returned to the battery. On 15 April Leutnant Putzig was wounded and also evacuated. The battery lost two guns to direct hits during the attack on 16 April. Leutnant Kaunert was killed there along with his entire crew. As the 1st Battery no longer had any officers left, the battalion assigned Leutnant Wobbe as battery commander.

Things quieted down a bit during the next few days. On their side, the Americans were no longer attacking from their bridgehead. Air activity died down, and the battalion had a chance to take a breath. On 23 April, however, orders were issued "to prepare to move east." Division "Scharnhorst" and Sturmgeschütz-Abteilung 1170 were transported to the east, arriving in the Belzig area on 25 April. Oberleutnant Schirnack took over the 1st Battery, and Leutnant Wobbe went back to the battalion staff.

The battalion participated in the attacks on 28 and 29 April 1945, which were launched to make contact with and relieve the surrounded 9. Armee. They broke open the Soviet grip and brought out a large part of the 9. Armee. The battalion fought there with everything it had.

By the evening of 29 April the battalion's combat strength had melted away to only a few guns. There could no longer be any question of a relief attack on Berlin for it.

After initially pulling covering force duties when the 12. Armee was pulled back to the Elbe, the battalion was then instructed to advance through Rathenow into the Genthin area and take part in a screening operation against the Soviet forces who had just pushed into Havelberg (Elbe). This mission was carried out with all the strength the battalion had left, and the enemy was brought to a halt.

Under fire from Soviet weapons, the remnants of the battalion—its last 80 soldiers—crossed the Elbe at Tangermünde. It was still attached to the 12. Armee. From there it went into captivity.

Lehr-Brigade Schill

The Sturmgeschütz-Schule at Burg was placed on alert on the Thursday before Easter in 1945. The last commander of the school, Oberstleutnant Alfred Müller, received orders to prepare to employ all elements of the school that were fit for combat. Those elements not fit for combat were to be transported to Austria, where they were to continue their instructional duties.

Oberstleutnant Müller led Kampfgruppe Burg to Magdeburg on the Elbe. The Kampfgruppe was initially positioned north of the city facing west toward the Americans. However, this mission didn't last long. The Kampfgruppe was moved from the Western Front to the Eastern Front, which at this time were only 80 kilometers apart.

Sturmgeschütz-Abteilung Burg

Other Kampfgruppen joined the brigade and Kampfgruppe Burg eventually became Division "Schill."

Alfred Müller, just promoted to Oberst, was assigned to command the division, which had been thrown together from elements of very different units. Sturmgeschütz-Lehr-Brigade III which had previously been at the Altengrabow Troop Training Area also joined Division "Schill."

Division "Schill" with Sturmgeschütz-Brigade "Schill" moved out of the Lehnin area with the XXII. Armee-Korps toward Berlin with the objective of breaking a gap through the Soviet forces surrounding the German capital. For this attack, the XXII. Armee-Korps and Division "Schill" were attached to the 12. Armee, led by its Commander-in-Chief, General der Panzertruppe Wenck.

The attack was unsuccessful, but it made it possible to receive the battered remnants of the 9. Armee falling back from the Frankfurt/Oder area through Jüterbog and Bezig. Otherwise these troops would have fallen into the hands of the Russians. As a result the Sturmgeschütz men could feel that their attack had had some real value.

Along with the soldiers of the 9. Armee, a large number of refugees were also picked up by Division "Schill" which would otherwise have been rolled over by the Russians and would have suffered a nasty fate.

In continuous combat and with the constant danger of being cut off themselves and surrounded, Division "Schill" and its Sturmgeschütz-Brigade "Schill" had fought back to the Elbe north of Magdeburg by 7 May 1945. Most of the division and the Sturmgeschütz brigade were taken prisoner by the Americans. Unfortunately, some of the prisoners were handed over to the Soviets by the Americans and were delivered into years of Soviet captivity.

Thus Sturmgeschütz-Brigade "Schill" met its end in the vicinity of the Sturmgeschütz-Schule at Burg where it was originally formed.

Panzerjäger-Sturmgeschütz-Kompanie 1269 (2./Jagd-Panzer-Abteilung I; 2./Panzer-Jagd-Abteilung I)

Panzerjäger-Sturmgeschütz-Kompanie 1269, which would later become the 2./Panzer-Jagd-Abteilung I, was formed in October 1944 in Herning in central Jütland. Reserve-Panzer-Jäger-Abteilung 3 provided the cadre for this independent Sturmgeschütz battery. Major Höhne was the commander. Hauptfeldwebel Nolden and Unteroffizier Stemmer were also part of the organizational staff.

After the personnel had been assembled, they began training to convert them from Panzerjäger crews to Sturmgeschütz crews. During this training Leutnant Guder showed up from Potsdam to command the company.

At the beginning of November, it was transferred to Germany for theoretical and practical training on Sturmgeschütze at Sturmgeschütz-Schule at Burg. The unit received its combat and unit training at the Altengrabow Troop Training Area. In the middle of January it was issued 12 Sturmgeschütze. All of them had the long-barreled 7.5 cm L 48 cannon. They were then equipped with vehicles for the combat and field trains and small arms. From 25 to 28 January 1945 the battery was in transport to the front in Pomerania by way of Küstrin and was unloaded in Kallies. There the battery commander reported in to General Oskar Munzel.

In the Stargard-Deutsch Krone area, the battery was given four additional independent Sturmgeschütz batteries, among them one from the Waffen-SS which was equipped with "Hetzer" assault guns. Panzerjäger-Sturmgeschütz-Kompanie 1269 was renamed Jagd-Panzer-Abteilung I after this expansion. Hauptmann Müller took over command of the battalion, which was attached to the 402. Infanterie-Division (General von Schleinitz).

Its first operation took place toward the end of January 1945. The battalion launched a counterattack from the Schloppe-Tütz-Deutsch Krone area at the head of an infantry regiment. It succeeded in throwing back the Soviets. The battalion destroyed its first tanks.

At the beginning of February, the battalion was fighting in a blocking position on the narrows east of Märkisch Friedland. It was intended to receive the garrison breaking out from the Schneidemühl Fortress, which it did.

In the middle of February there were continuous counterattacks and fierce defensive fighting in the areas of Kallies-Neuwedell, Falkenburg-Tempelburg and Dramburg-Schivelbein. When the 5. Jäger-Division was surrounded by the Soviets in the Dramburg-Falkenburg area, the entire battalion went into action to relieve the bravely fighting division. After bitter fighting and dramatic tank duels, it managed to break through the ring of surrounding Soviet troops and clear the way to freedom for the division.

At the end of February, the battalion was renamed Panzer-Jagd-Abteilung I. The battalion was surrounded with five German divisions and the French Freiwilligen-Division "Charlemagne" in the Belgard Pocket on the Persante. With these formations it formed a part of Korpsgruppe von Tettau. The Sturmgeschütze smashed a breech through the surrounding Soviet troops and, fighting fiercely, the entire Korpsgruppe was able to escape through it to Swinemünde by way of Dievenow.

During the month of March the Sturmgeschütz battalion relocated behind the Oder in assorted moves. Panzerjäger-Sturmgeschütz-Kompanie 1269 assembled at Löcknitz near Stettin. However, the courageous Leutnant Guder was still back in the pocket. Oberfähnrich Meisborn took over the company.

The company had lost most of its Sturmgeschütze in this operation. The Waffen-SS company separated from the battalion with the Hetzer that it had left. No new Sturmgeschütze were received. At that point only two companies with 10 guns each could be assembled. The superfluous technical personnel were sent back to the replacement battalion.

The former 1st and 3rd Companies then formed the 1st and 2nd Companies. Crews without guns were used to form two platoons of support infantry. Unteroffizier Stemmer led the 1st Platoon and Feldwebel Jaeger led the 2nd Platoon of these security troops.

On 18 April 1945 the 1st Company of the battalion went into position at Pölitz with the first escort platoon. It was placed on alert status on 20 April and committed to the Oder Front south of Stettin to help eliminate the Soviet bridgehead. This attack miscarried. The subsequent fighting retreat through Pomerania and Mecklenburg along the line Pasewalk-Neubrandenburg-Gustrow cost it a high price, since the Sturmgeschütze were constantly used as the rear guard and had to fend off unremitting Soviet tank attacks.

Several company commanders were killed, one after the other. The crews fought for their lives as individual guns and half sections, often entirely on their own.

On 3 May 1945 the survivors and the last Sturmgeschütze passed through the English-American lines at Bad Kleinen. They were interned and taken to Holstein, where they were released after the end of the war.

(Author's Note: The author cannot vouch for the unusual unit designations, which today seem doubtful, as they are only documented in a single source.)

Fallschirm-Sturmgeschütz-Brigade 1 (Fallschirm-Sturmgeschütz-Brigade XI or Sturmgeschütz-Brigade XI (LL = Luftlande))

In the middle of January 1944 officers, noncommissioned officers and men who had volunteered for parachute duty and already belonged to existing parachute units were detached for Sturmartillerie training.

Officers and tank drivers were sent to the Sturmgeschütz-Schule at Burg, and the gunners were sent to Altengrabow. Additional tank drivers were sent to Sturmgeschütz-Ersatz-Abteilung 300 at Neiße.

At these places the volunteers were trained as Sturmartillerie men in different courses until 24 March 1944. Then, at the end of March, two Fallschirm-Sturmgeschütz-Brigaden were formed. Initially they were designated as Fallschirm-Sturmgeschütz-Brigaden 1 and 2, but were redesignated as Fallschirm-Sturgeschütz-Brigaden XI and XII in June 1944. They were also referred to as the Green Devil Brigades.

Hauptmann Schäber was commander of Fallschirm-Sturmgeschütz-Brigade XI. This brigade was transferred to France. It continued its organization at Melun and was equipped with Sturmgeschütze. From there it went on to Donmarie and Dontilly.

The brigade first went into action after the allied breakthrough at Nancy. The brigade was committed against far superior forces and was completely wiped out in the subsequent bitter fighting even though it destroyed a number of tanks.

The few survivors who managed to escape this inferno formed a cadre under Oberleutnant Hollunder for rebuilding Fallschirm-Sturmgeschütz-Brigade XI. The brigade was placed under the operational control of the 5. Fallschirm-Jäger-Division (Generalmajor Heilmann) and, with that division, it was attached directly to Commander-in-Chief West for the Ardennes Offensive on 30 November 1944. Fighting with the 5. Fallschirm-Jäger-Division, the brigade was employed on the southern flank of the attacking spearhead in the Ardennes Offensive under the 7. Armee. It fought across the Clerf River and advanced on Wiltz. For a while the 5. Fallschirm-Jäger-Division was the unit which had advanced furthest to the west. On 22 December 1944, swept along by the Sturmgeschütze, it advanced through Vaux les Rosiéres to 15 kilometers south of Bastogne. The Sturmgeschütze also fought in the witches' caldron around Bastogne. The brigade suffered bloody losses in fighting with the US 4th Armored Division.

The remnants of the brigade made it back all the way across Germany. At the end of the war it was employed against the Soviets. The brigade went into Soviet captivity on 8 May 1945. (Author's Note: Some sources indicate the brigade also fought in Italy in 1944 and again in the west in 1945.)

Fallschirm-Sturmgeschütz-Abteilung 2 (Fallschirm-Sturmgeschütz-Brigade XII or Sturmgeschütz-Brigade XII (LL = Luftlande))

Fallschirm-Sturmgeschütz-Abteilung 2, which was composed of volunteer paratroopers from parachute units just Fallschirm-Sturmgeschütz-Brigade XI, was formed at Melun and Fontainebleau at the end of March 1944 under Haupt-mann Gersteuer. In June 1944 it was renamed as Fallschirm-Sturmgeschütz-Brigade XII. It was sometimes also referred to as Sturmgeschütz-Brigade XII (LL). Its command and staff positions were filled as follows:

Commander: Hauptmann Gersteuer
Adjutant: Leutnant Willibald Schulz
Orderly Officer: Leutnant Röltgen
Brigade Surgeon: Stabsarzt Dr. Saytz-Hermstein
Vehicle Inspectors: Inspector Werner Hilf, Inspector Knorr
Headquarters Battery Commander: Oberleutnant (later Hauptmann) Horn
1st Battery Commander: Hauptmann Heinrichs
Section Leaders: Leutnant Herzog, Leutnant Botzenhard
2nd Battery Commander: Oberleutnant Behne
Section Leaders: Hauptmann Raabe, Leutnant Winkler
3rd Battery Commander: Hauptmann Krall
Section Leaders: Oberleutnant Pohlmann, Leutnant Deutsch, Leutnant Köbel
Replacements: Oberleutnant Meyle, Leutnant Mappas

The brigade was moved into the area south of St. Lô on 6 June 1944 when the invasion of Normandy began. It was placed under the operational control of the 3. Parachute Division which was commanded by General Schimpf. The brigade was committed consecutively with the following formations: Fallschirm-Jäger-Regiment 9 (Major Becker), Infanterie-Regiment 8 (Oberst Liebach), and Infanterie-Regiment 9 (Major Stephani). The brigade was also committed at Bayeux, Torigny, Vive, Tinchebrai, and Condè.

The brigade took very heavy losses in the three pockets at Falaise. Despite that, about 60% of the combat troops and as much as 90% of the trains managed to reach the east bank of the Seine. There, the combat trains of the 3rd Battery under Oberfeldwebel Beyer and the Headquarters Battery did such an outstanding job in marking the route that within two days the survivors could begin their withdrawal through Rouen.

Even more members of the brigade rejoined the unit during the two-day rest stop at St. Quentin. The brigade moved back through Namur and Lüttich to Cologne-Wahn, where it was refitted.

The only Sturmgeschütz saved, a 10.5 cm Sturmhaubitze under Oberjäger Odya, had to suffice for training replacements. A little later, the brigade received four more guns which had been under repair in Germany.

After the allied parachute drops in the areas of Nymwegen and Arnhem in the middle of September 1944, Sturmgeschütz-Brigade XII was moved through Weeze and Wesel and committed in the Wyler area. However, its combat power was too low for them to be able to provide decisive support to the paratroopers of the newly formed 7. Fallschirm-Jäger-Division (Generalleutnant Erdmann).

On 4 January 1945 the brigade finally received its new guns and recovered its "fangs" once again. At this point, they were located at Amersfoort in Holland.

During the last months of the war, the "Green Devil" Brigade became the "tank killers" of the 7. Fallschirm-Jäger-Division. The Sturmgeschütze ran into enemy tanks for the first time since its refitting in the Reichswald west of Cleve. Leutnant Heinz Deutsch, together with two to three Sturmgeschütze, stayed fighting with the 7. Fallschirm-Jäger-Division from first to last.

Oberwachtmeister Grünwald, who had already received the Knight's Cross in November 1944 for exemplary conduct on the invasion front, again fought bitterly and hard. He destroyed a number of enemy tanks. Major Günter Gersteuer was also awarded the Knight's Cross. He was followed by Leutnant Stehle. The fighting became more and more intense.

On 8 February 1945 the expected allied operational offensive was launched in the Reichswald west of Cleve. General Schlemm, at that time Commander-in-Chief of the 1. Fallschirm-Jäger-Armee, put the 7. Fallschirm-Jäger-Division, located in the area east of Venlo as the army's reserve, on alert on the same day. It was loaded onto trucks and moved toward Goch-Gennep. The objective of this movement was to throw back the enemy in a counterattack. Sturmgeschütz-Brigade XII was committed with the 7. Fallschirm-Jäger-Division.

Leutnant Heinz Deutsch went back into action with sometimes two and sometimes three Sturmgeschütze and a group of Fallschimjäger as infantry support.

"What's it look like, Herr Leutnant?"

Oberfeldwebel Berndl, the gunner for Deutsch's gun greeted his commander with these words as he arrived back from the command post.

"Hunting season, Berndl! We'll be finding out where it's hot!"

Leutnant Deutsch gave his instructions to the commanders of the other two Sturmgeschütze. Then the wait began.

The sound of Allied heavy weapons grew louder from the direction of the main battle line, but only a few German guns replied. The Leutnant raised his head to listen when he heard a few tank gun rounds among the firing.

Minutes passed. The day which had begun with beautiful sunshine, seemed to be keeping the promise it had made at daybreak. The sun heated the ground. No wonder, on 25 March 1945, a few days before the beginning of spring.

A motorcycle shot around a hedge. Behind the hedge was the field road leading to Nienkampshof. The motorcycle messenger halted in front of Leutnant Deutsch's gun, where he had identified himself as the unit's commander by waving his hand.

"Herr Leutnant, enemy tanks have pushed into Nienkampshof. Our paratroopers are in trouble. They request support as fast as possible."

Feldwebel Stangassinger, who had overheard the report, engaged his idling engine. The gun rolled forward. Stangassinger turned sharply. The steel colossus rattled into a curve that shaved part of hedge away and turned onto the field road. Stangassinger increased his speed. The Leutnant called his two other guns, which followed him rapidly. They reached a patch of woods and headed in. The pounding of the enemy tank guns grew louder, more threatening.

Leutnant Deutsch halted on the far side of the woods. He looked over the open field first. Three, four, five Sherman tanks circled around over there, firing on German pockets of resistance. Flames rose to the sky from two low sheds.

"Eagle owl right, snowy owl left flank. Eagle takes center."

"Eagle" was the Sturmgeschütz of the Leutnant. He burst out of the woods at 15 kilometers per hour.

"Let's go, Beethoven. Step on it!"

With a jump, Feldwebel Ludwig Stangassinger, known to everyone by his nickname Beethoven, accelerated the gun forward. The speedometer showed twenty, thirty, thirty five. Finally "Eagle" reached 50 kilometers per hour. Once it dropped into a shallow depression. The gun creaked dangerously. The steel box leaned far over, and the men were thrown hard against the walls. The machine pistol of the Leutnant scraped hard against the metal of the Sturmgeschütz.

"Six hundred. Twelve o'clock, right against the big tree!"

"Identified!"

Berndl was already aiming at the enemy, whose gun had just spit fire. The roar of the discharge was hardly audible inside the Sturmgeschütz, only the jolt told the commander that the round had gone down range. Two seconds later, the round hit the enemy. It struck between the turret and the hull and knocked the Sherman's turret off its race, so that the tank's gun stuck straight up in the air. The crew bailed out. A group of charging infantry emerged behind them.

Oberjäger Lapp, both loader and machine gunner, fired at the group of attacking infantry which immediately took cover. At that point the two other guns joined the fight, and a duel began between the handful of Sturmgeschütze and the enemy tanks. When a round ripped past the bow of the commander's gun, Heinz Deutsch moved on rapidly. Through his scissors binoculars, he saw the paratroopers raising their arms in a cheer when they recognized the Sturmgeschütze. Another cannon discharge boomed. The round hit the gun's right skirt armor and exploded. It thundered inside the tank. A low building popped up in front of the Sturmgeschütz.

"Turn left , Beethoven!"

Feldwebel Ludwig Stangassinger let the Sturmgeschütz pivot sharply around. It rammed a side wall, which came down with a racket. After a short period, the Sturmgeschütz was able to move again. At that point, a Sherman tank emerged 200 meters in front of Stangassinger next to a turnip stack. The Sherman fired into the farm house. When it saw the Sturmgeschütz, it reversed to get behind the turnip stack.

The first round crippled it. When it turned on its one intact track and showed itself broadside to the Sturmgeschütz, the second round smashed into its hull. Seconds later two long tongues of flame shot out of the hull and turret hatch. The hatch dropped back with a clang. The enemy had been destroyed. The remaining Sherman tanks pulled back, firing.

Leutnant Deutsch pursued to try to get off one more shot. But only five minutes later he was fired on from a thicket. A hard blow shook the Sturmgeschütz. And then the driver reported:

"Gun's hit. Right track is shot off!"

"Eagle owl is coming up to give cover!" came the report from one of the section guns.

The gun rumbled forward, wiped out the enemy hiding in the trees and remained in front to cover the commander's gun until its damaged track could be repaired and Leutnant Deutsch could pull his gun back.

"Deutsch, you will cover the division's open flank with your two guns against enemy tank pursuit. The division is pulling back immediately. You will stay behind with your section and cover the withdrawal."

Leutnant Deutsch left the division's command post, which was already being torn down. He hurried back to his three Sturmgeschütze.

Arriving there, he grabbed his map, and tried to figure out probable enemy moves.

"Doesn't look too good, Herr Leutnant?" asked the commander of the second gun.

"We can't move out blind. Look there: difficult terrain with heavy cover in front of us. Woods with clearings. I'm going ahead on foot and scout out the enemy tank spearhead. You take your gun there along the north edge of the woods up to the end. Cover my open flank together with the third gun which will already be there so that the enemy doesn't catch me in a corner."

The one Sturmgeschütz moved out. But Heinz Deutsch worked his way forward through the middle of the woods. He stalked along its west edge in the shelter of a wild thorn hedge. At that same moment enemy tanks rolled out of the woods on the far side of the open field in front of Leutnant Deutsch. There were a few scout cars moving quickly far forward on the flanks. Behind them were the heavy and super-heavy tanks.

The Leutnant recognized upgunned and uparmored "Jumbo" Shermans and a mass of regular ones. They were still halted at the edge of the woods. Apparently they were going to wait for the results of the scout car reconnaissance before they chanced a further advance. Bent almost double, Heinz Deutsch ran back. He arrived at his gun out of breath. He mounted the vehicle, put on his earphones and throat mike and called the two other guns:

"Eagle Owl and Snowy Owl, watch out! Stop the enemy if he tries to go around us. I am attacking! The enemy's armored spearhead is in front, on the other side of the large clearing. I estimate 20 tanks."

"Well, that makes it hard to miss", said Oberjäger Lappe, smiling.

The gun moved forward, stopping for a moment when it reached the edge of the woods. Through his scissors binoculars, Leutnant Deutsch saw that the enemy had chanced a move out into the middle of the field. The scout cars had already disappeared into the woods to the right and left of them.

"Move along the hedge, Beethoven! It gives us great cover."

The Sturmgeschütz rolled slowly forward. An antitank round was already in the breech.

"Move out!" ordered the section leader when he saw that he had come to the end of the hedge.

The Sturmgeschütz rolled into the large clearing at top speed. The enemy tanks came closer at a frantic pace.

"Halt, Ludwig!—Fire at will!"

The Sturmgeschütz halted in the middle of the clearing. Range to the enemy was 1200 meters. The first round left the barrel. The detonation rang out across the field and one of the "Jumbos" burst into flames.

This was the overture to a fierce struggle against enormous odds. Leutnant Deutsch had his gun move back and forth across the field. Moving in rapid zigzags, it avoided the rounds fired at it. The shells which roared past the commander's gun burst back in the woods.

Oberjäger Lapp and Oberfeldwebel Berndl worked like machines. They rammed new rounds in the breech, aimed and then fired their steel projectiles against the enemy forces which were being fought by this single Sturmgeschütz.

Enemy tanks went up in flames. One of the scout cars emerged unexpectedly from the woods and rolled forward 200 meters in front of the Sturmgeschütz. It tried to escape but was blown into the air by a direct hit. Three, four, then five tanks stood burning, crippled on the battlefield. But the remaining tanks then attacked the Sturmgeschütz from three sides.

"Back in the woods!"

The gun turned. A glancing round hammered against the superstructure and ricocheted off to the side. The gun raced back at top speed. A pair of young birches were flattened into the forest floor. A couple of enemy rounds whipped through the crowns of the trees above the Sturmgeschütz.

After 300 meters, Leutnant Deutsch had the Sturmgeschütz turn. He moved four hundred meters to one side, turned back toward the enemy and there, where no one expected it, burst out of the woods again.

The appearance of the Sturmgeschütz took the enemy so much by surprise that the forward Sherman was unable to get off a shot. A direct hit caused it to explode. Another enemy tank was put out of action by the next round.

At that point tank cannon firing and explosions could also be heard from the place where the two section guns had remained.

All at once the enemy turned, rolled rapidly back to the west and disappeared into the extensive forest on the other side of the open field. A single Sturmgeschütz had stopped them cold at this spot. Three "Jumbos," three regular Shermans and 2 scout cars had been destroyed by Leutnant Deutsch's command vehicle. The enemy's armored point had shattered against the tiny but bold and effective shield for the 7. Fallschirm-Jäger-Division. In this way, Leutnant Deutsch delayed the enemy advance for two days, and so made it possible for the division to withdraw undisturbed.

On 15 April Deutsch was informed by radio that he had been awarded the Knight's Cross. Concerning this high decoration he said: "I was only one of the four men in our Sturmgeschütz."

Two days after receiving the Knight's Cross he defeated enemy forces just north of the Hunte-Ems canal at Edewecht.

The entire brigade was engaged in continuous hard fighting. Tank after enemy tank was destroyed. On 14 April the Wehrmacht Report had this to say: "Leutnant Heinz Deutsch, in Sturmgeschütz-Brigade XII, has destroyed 34 tanks and 2 armored scout cars with his Sturmgeschütz since 24 March and has displayed exemplary conduct and outstanding bravery."

On 24 April 1945 the Sturmgeschütz of Leutnant Deutsch destroyed a "Jumbo" at Edewecht. That was the 44th tank destroyed by Deutsch's crew. The three men of his crew—Oberjäger Lappe, Feldwebel Stangassinger and Oberfeldwebel Berndl—all received the German Cross in Gold.

A little later, when Leutnant Deutsch went into action for the last time, Oberjäger Lappe left the gun to carry out an order outside the vehicle. A stray round hit him.

Heinz Deutsch saw only a large cloud from the explosion. He feared the worst. He immediately left the gun and ran to the place under fire. When he reached it he saw that he was too late to be any help to his brave comrade. Oberjäger Lappe was dead.

The brigade moved on. Oberjäger Franz Meyer was awarded the German Cross in Gold.

In the last days of the war, the "Green Devil" Brigade was to be moved across the Elbe at Cuxhaven. It was intended for the forces to assemble on the other side of the river and execute a relief attack on the German capital. But by the morning of 8 May 1945, only two ships with wounded left the harbor at Cuxhaven.

The "Green Devil" Brigade was interned at Wilhelmshaven after the end of the war. During the short period that it was in action it had destroyed 260 enemy tanks. Of those, Leutnant Heinz Deutsch's score amounted to 44.

Every year on the anniversary of Oberjäger Lappe's death, the three surviving members of the Deutsch crew meet in remembrance at the grave of their fallen comrade.

Sturmgeschütz-Lehr-Brigade I (Sturmgeschütz-Lehr-Brigade 920; Panzer-Vernichtungs-Abteilung 303)

Sturmgeschütz-Lehr-Brigade 920

Sturmgeschütz-Lehr-Brigade I was formed at the Sturmgeschütz-Schule at Burg. The date of its activation is unknown. Nothing is also known of its functions or activities as an instructional brigade.

The 1st Battery of Sturmgeschütz-Lehr-Brigade I was sent to the Eastern Front when the central sector collapsed in the middle of July 1944 and the Soviets stormed rapidly to the west. In spite of all its efforts, the battery was unable to rejoin the brigade during the following period in southeastern Prussia.

On 24 July 1944 the remainder of the brigade was committed in the fighting on the Eastern Front. On 1 August it was committed against the Warka Bridgehead 50 kilometers south of Warsaw in the area east of Jedlinsk. The Soviets were trying to enlarge their bridgehead on the west bank of the Vistula there. The brigade fought in this area with all of its Sturmgeschütze in action, continuously counterattacking in different places and, in this way, preventing any additional expansion of the bridgehead. In September 1944 it was renamed as Sturmgeschütz-Lehr-Brigade 920.

When the Russian winter offensive began on 14 January 1945 in that sector of the front, the brigade, whose fighting strength had grown to four line batteries, was wiped out within a few days in the hail of bombs, in artillery fire and in duels with greatly superior Soviet tank forces. Only the Headquarters Battery and the trains managed to escape this hellish pocket.

Through military channels, Major Wolfgang Kapp, who commanded the brigade, found the rest of his unit south of Glogau and assembled it. By the beginning of February, his brigade had been rebuilt with three new line batteries. By the beginning of February it was already back in heavy fighting in the Zellien Bridgehead on the Oder, southeast of Wrietzen. It fought within the (303.) Infanterie-Division "Döberitz." Apparently while attached to this division it was temporarily renamed as Panzer-Vernichtungs-Abteilung 303 but soon returned to its original designation. On 3 March 1945 Major Kapp received the Knight's Cross for his leadership of the brigade and his personal actions.

In the middle of March Infanterie-Division "Döberitz," with the brigade still attached to it, was fighting at the bridgehead west of Küstrin. The brigade's operations on 14 April 1945 take an honorable page in its history. Under Major Kapp's personal command it broke up a strong Soviet attack at this point on the Oder front. The Wehrmacht Report for 18 April 1945 reported that engagement as follows: "Sturmgeschütz-Lehr Brigade 920 under the leadership of its commander, Major Kapp, destroyed 36 enemy tanks and 3 guns, and immobilized three additional tanks in one day on the Oder Front. The brigade itself lost only one gun."

The Soviet operational offensive on Berlin began on the morning of 16 April along the entire front. The brigade was wiped out to the last Sturmgeschütz in the ruthless fighting during the next few days. The remnants were finally surrounded on 27 April 1945 at Halbe and Märkisch-Buchholz with the remnants of the 9. Armee in a pocket in the area southwest of Fürstenwalde.

Only a few men of Sturmgeschütz-Lehr-Brigade 920 managed to break free from the Russian grasp south of Berlin and fight their way through to Beelitz south of Potsdam. These remnants of the brigade reached the Elbe with the units of the 12. Armee and were taken prisoner by the Americans at Tangermünde on 6 May 1945.

Sturmgeschütz-Lehr-Brigade II (Sturmartillerie-Lehr-Brigade 111)

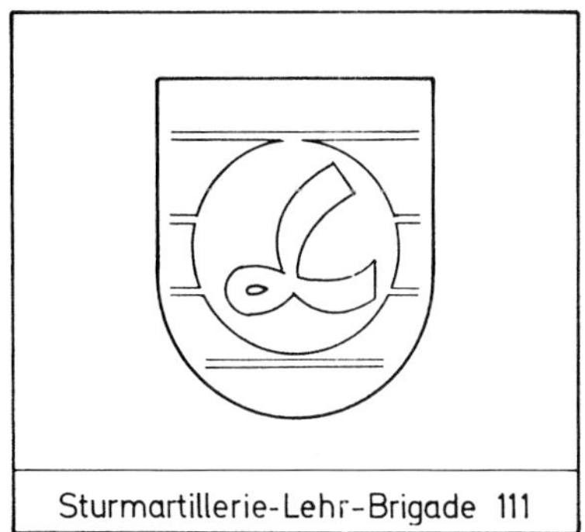

Sturmartillerie-Lehr-Brigade 111

This brigade was activated in October 1944 (some sources give February 1945) at the Sturmgeschütz-Schule at Burg, when Sturmgeschütz-Lehr-Brigade I (Sturmgeschütz-Lehr-Brigade 920) was pulled out to be used on the threatened Eastern Front.

This new instructional brigade remained at Burg until the middle of January 1945. It was not alerted until 22 January 1945 and then transported to the Eastern Front, where the Soviets were beating against the borders of Germany. This brigade bore an "L" as insignia. Its commander was Hauptmann Hans-Joachim Wagner, the adjutant Oberleutnant Liedtke.

It was given a headquarters battery and three line batteries for its upcoming operation. The Headquarters Battery was made up of the Burg School's officer personnel. The 1st Battery of Sturmgeschütz-Brigade 909, which was at Frauenberg after two years of combat in Russia, was converted to the 1st Battery in Sturmgeschütz-Lehr-Brigade II. The 2nd Battery consisted of the 2nd Battery of Sturmgeschütz-Brigade 191. Around Christmas 1944, Sturmgeschütz-Brigade 191 had been completely destroyed. The 2nd Battery was led by Oberleutnant Engelhaff. Kurt Ebert was the "Spieß." The 3rd Battery was made up of soldiers from the Sturmgeschütz-Schule at Burg. The commander was Oberleutnant Waitkuwait, the "Spieß" Bernd Kutzmann. In March 1945 a fourth battery was sent from Burg to the brigade, which was already engaged in combat. However, this battery was only equipped with field guns which had to be towed by truck.

Sturmgeschütz-Lehr-Brigade 111 was attached to a Kampfgruppe which was assigned to relieve Posen. Despite that, one of the brigade's batteries was loaded on the first transport trains and committed in the threatened Schneidemühl area. It was committed at once and immediately afterwards was surrounded by Soviet units. The battery was completely destroyed, and its survivors were taken prisoner by the Soviets.

The remaining batteries of Sturmgeschütz-Lehr-Brigade 111 reached the Meseritz-Tirschtiegel-Schwiebus area. After a few Sturmgeschütze had carried out a reconnaissance in force, the brigade was surrounded by the Soviets. Some of the guns had to be blown up in this pocket. The rest of the brigade attempted to fight its way through to Frankfurt/Oder. The advance guard under Hauptmann Wagner broke out successfully. After a five day march on foot, without guns and with only a few men left, the rear guard, led by Hauptmann Schmidt, also made it across the Oder near Guben.

Those survivors who had made it across the Oder with Hauptmann Wagner at Fürstenberg were employed in the Frankfurt/Oder Bridgehead. They were equipped with Sturmgeschütze at Landsberg and put into action at the Oderbruch. This element fought with invincible courage and aggressiveness. Again and again, it committed its Sturmgeschütze, individually and as a unit, against the Soviets. Sturmgeschütz-Lehr-Brigade 111 destroyed many tanks and guns. It held the Soviets off and made it possible for the infantry to withdraw to the new defense lines.

Hauptmann Wagner received the Knight's Cross on 21 February 1945. Much of the credit for his brigade's success belonged to him.

The brigade pulled back through Berlin, Friesack and Rathenow and, after a last-minute crossing of the Elbe at Sandau, these elements of the brigade were taken prisoner by the Americans.

The remaining elements of the brigade which had made it across the Oder at Guben with Hauptmann Schmidt reassembled and were later sent to the Sturmgeschütz-Schule at Burg. The brigade was rebuilt there. At the beginning of April 1945 it was transferred to the Freienwalde-Fürstenberg area. The Soviet offensive began there on 16 April 1945. The brigade made a fighting withdrawal past Berlin to the north.

At the beginning of May the 1st and 2nd Batteries crossed the Elbe at Wittenberge and were taken prisoner by the Americans. The 3rd Battery and the trains under the command of Hauptwachtmeister Lenzen crossed the Elbe at Gorlem on 6 May 1945 and were also taken prisoner by the Americans.

On the other hand, "Kampfgruppe Wagner," formed from the Sturmgeschütze of all the batteries and under the command of the brigade commander, ran into the main body of the attacking Soviets in the region of Lauenburg-Ludwigslust-Perleberg.

The Russian general who commanded the troops which contained this Kampfgruppe negotiated personally with Hauptmann Wagner. During these negotiations a Russian officer sent an order by radio for a heavy antitank gun to be brought up. When Hauptmann Wagner drove into the forested lane designated by the general as the surrender area, his Sturmgeschütz took a direct hit from the hidden antitank gun.

One after another, all the guns of the Kampfgruppe were knocked out. Almost all of these Sturmgeschütz crews were senselessly butchered by the Soviets after their surrender at the end of the war. Only a few survivors went into Soviet captivity. Even fewer of them returned home.

Sturmgeschütz-Lehr-Brigade III

After Sturmgeschütz-Lehr-Brigade II (Sturmgeschütz-Lehr-Brigade 111) was transported to the Eastern Front from Burg, Sturmgeschütz-Lehr-Brigade III was formed under Major Dr. Vaerst. Major Dr. Vaerst wasn't transferred to Burg until January and, at first, the brigade remained at the Altengrabow Troop Training Area, about 20 kilometers southeast of Burg. Sturmgeschütz-Lehr-Brigade III was placed on alert when the Americans approached the Elbe at Magdeburg in March 1945. It was sent west from the Altengrabow area to prevent the advancing Americans from crossing the Elbe.

The brigade first went into action on both sides of the highway to the northwest of the Elbe crossing and west of Magdeburg. It managed to keep the Americans from crossing the Elbe, halting them on the other side of the Elbe under the fire of the Sturmgeschütze.

At the beginning of May, as the Soviets approached from the east, the brigade was committed in the east. It then fought against the Soviets. The subsequent heavy fighting exacted a high cost in blood from this young brigade. Within a few days it was completely scattered and had lost a portion of its Sturmgeschütze.

The last operation of the brigade was the defense of the railroad bridge at Tangermünde against the advancing Soviets on 7 May 1945. Only Major Dr. Vaerst and a few members of the brigade were available to fight. This magnificent officer, holder of the German Cross in Gold, and his last loyal men fought virtually to the very end. On 8 May 1945 the survivors went into Soviet captivity and disappeared into Russia for years.

Sturmgeschütz-Abteilung "Großdeutschland" (II./Panzer-Regiment "Brandenburg")

Sturmgeschütz-Abteilung „Großdeutschland"

This battalion was born when Sturmgeschütz-Batterie 640 was made an organic part of Infanterie-Regiment (mot.) "Großdeutschland" after the end of the French Campaign. It became the 16th Company (belonging to the IV. Bataillon) of the regiment. It would be in action for long years on many fronts. The 16th Company took part in the Balkan campaign along with the Großdeutschland Regiment. In succession, its commanders were Oberleutnant Freiherr von und zu Egloffstein, Hauptmann Stückler and Oberleutnant Franz. Oberleutnant Frantz had been a section leader in the battery from its formation until he took command.

On 8 September 1941 Infanterie-Regiment (mot.) "Großdeutschland" received orders to send an advance guard detachment to the Sejm and establish a bridgehead at Putiwl. The Sejm was reached on the evening of 10 September and the regimental commander ordered an attack on Putiwl. The attack couldn't be launched until early on 11 September. When the 2. Bataillon ran into the enemy the Sturmgeschütz section under Oberleutnant Frantz attacked and broke the enemy resistance. The Sturmgeschütze destroyed two heavy machine guns, 1 antitank gun and 1 infantry gun. Oberleutnant Frantz and his Sturmgeschütze were also at the point of the attack on Sswetschkino on 17 September 1941 to clear the way for the infantry. Together with antitank guns, the Sturmgeschütze destroyed 8 enemy tanks and 9 antitank guns. The Sturmgeschütz company pursued the fleeing Russians. When the enemy trains showed up in front of the Sturmgeschütze they were wiped out with high-explosive rounds. Moving rapidly, the Oberleutnant and his guns thrust deep into the enemy forces. Vehicles went up in flames. Explosions ripped apart ammunition carriers. A great deal of booty fell into the regiment's hands, including some valuable military documents. The Sturmgeschütze advanced through Bankowa to Konotop. The infantry followed.

The fighting during the next few weeks required the Sturmgeschütze to be in action continuously. On 21 November 1941 Oberleutnant Adam received the Knight's Cross.

On 13 December 1941 there was heavy fighting on the west bank of the Upa at Upskaja Fati. The 16th Company achieved a great defensive victory there. It destroyed 15 enemy tanks within a few hours. This raised the unit's total score to 46 tanks destroyed.

The Sturmgeschütze moved out against the enemy once more when a report reached the regimental command post that the enemy was attacking the 14th Company (Panzer-Jäger-Kompanie). Within a few minutes Oberleutnant Frantz destroyed 5 enemy tanks with his Sturmgeschütz.

In this engagement the 1st Company pushed into an enemy-occupied village. But it had to pull back again when Russians poured out of all the houses. It was already in danger of being wiped out when Oberleutnant Frantz and his Sturmgeschütze showed up once again at the last second, annihilating the attacking Soviets, and thus avoided the worst. Oberleutnant Frantz was later decorated with the German Cross in Gold for this action.

In March 1942 Infanterie-Regiment (mot.) "Großdeutschland" was pulled out of its defensive position at Bolchow, in the northern part of the Orel Bend, and transferred to Germany for conversion to an Infanterie-Division (mot.). The 16th Company went to Treuenbrietzen to form the 1st Battery of Sturmgeschütz-Abteilung "Großdeutschland" which was being formed at that time. The majority of the battalion came from Sturmgeschütz-Abteilung 192. Major Schepers became the battalion's commander during its formation.

The battalion received 21 new Sturmgeschütze. For the first time, it was given the long-barrreled assault cannon. The commanders of the individual batteries were:

1st Battery: Oberleutnant Frantz
2nd Battery: Oberleutnant Adam
3rd Battery: Oberleutnant Lemme

The battalion rejoined the division after thorough training.

The new battalion first went into action in the summer offensive at Woronesh. After crossing the Tim, the 1st Battery was ordered to carry out a reconnaissance in force with the I./Infanterie-Regiment 2 "Großdeutschland" against a forested hill about 3 kilometers east of the Tim Bridge on the rail line. The battery advanced to scout out Suchoj Chutor to the southeast. When the I. Bataillon followed, it took enemy fire from the north and lost eight officers. Anything worse happening was prevented only when the Sturmgeschütze rapidly turned back.

Oberleutnant Frantz received the Knight's Cross on 13 June 1942. He had always acted according to the motto: "Success before safety."

The Sturmgeschütze were a great success again in the fighting against Soviet T-34's on 2 July 1942. Sturmgeschütz-Abteilung "Großdeutschland" reached the Don at Woronesh at the head of the division. During the night of 7 July Infanterie-Division "Großdeutschland" was then turned to the south. It was ordered to the lower Don at Rostow. It was intended for the Sturmgeschütze to remain behind for a day to support the 3. Infanterie-Division (mot.). On 7 July the Sturmgeschütze, with infantry from Infanterie-Regiment 28 mounted on them, pushed into Woronesh and occupied the city.

On 10 September 1942 at Tschermassowo the division was unable to take the village. It had to go over to the defensive for the night west of the village. The Sturmgeschütz battalion participated in the original attack, destroying 19 tanks, 13 antitank guns and 2 other guns. On the following day, headed by the Sturmgeschütze, the attack was resumed on Tschermassowo and "churchyard" hill. When the II./Infanterie-Regiment 1 "Großdeutschland" was engaged in an enemy armor counterattack, the Sturmgeschütze brought their surrounded comrades out. Again and again the individual batteries charged forward and, by evening, the battalion had destroyed another 15 enemy tanks.

The fighting in the Rshew area became ever more difficult and costly. On 30 September the division was to carry out an attack with limited objectives along with the 72. Infanterie-Division under the code name "Autumn Wind." The heavily battered division was no longer strong enough by itself for this attack.

Generalleutnant Hoernlein, the divisional commander, and Oberst Garski, commander of Infanterie-Regiment 2 "Groß deutschland," tried every way they knew to present this fact to the higher command. However, senior commanders insisted that the attack be carried out. Elements of the Sturmgeschütz battalion advanced with the infantry. The attack made good progress up to noon on 30 September, but then it collapsed under enemy fire.

During the fighting on 1 December 1942 for the Bogorodizkoje Bridge Sturmgeschütze were requested by the XXIII. Armee-Korps after a Soviet armored breakthrough. Hauptmann Adam, who had taken over the battalion in the meantime, took off immediately to scout out the situation. On the highway to Olenin, northeast of Bjeloy, his Kübelwagen was placed under fire by a single enemy tank which had broken through. This tank scored a direct hit at a range of 2000 m. Hauptmann Adam and his driver were killed immediately.

Hauptmann Lemme took over command of the orphaned battalion on the battlefield. With Hauptmann Adam the Sturmartillerie lost one of its bravest and most honorable soldiers.

Surprisingly, however, enemy pressure eased up, and the main danger was avoided for the next few hours. The first four guns of the 1st Battery arrived that night and provided the necessary reinforcements for the grenadiers. They could then look forward to the approach of 2 December with confidence.

All the Sturmgeschütze were committed in fighting on 2 and 3 December 1942. An enemy penetration with tank support into the village of Wereista against the grenadiers of the I. Bataillon was brought to a halt by the Sturmgeschütze. Thirteen of the fourteen attacking tanks were destroyed. Unteroffizier Nagel and Gefreiter Bösin were killed in this bitter fighting after they were able to destroy four tanks.

The Sturmgeschütze were attached to Kampfgruppe von Wietersheim which, in turn, was attached to the 1. Panzer-Division during the fighting to form the Dubrowka Pocket, southeast of Bjeloy. The Kampfgruppe closed off the pocket which contained a Russian tank corps.

A little later Hauptmann Frantz took over command of the battalion when Hauptmann Lemme was lost. Sturmgeschütz-Abteilung "Großdeutschland" was engaged in costly fighting during the subsequent fighting of the winter of 1942/43. The entire Panzer-Grenadier-Division "Großdeutschland" was stuck in heavy snow drifts on the Belgorod-Kharkov axis. The Sturmgeschütze pushed back Russian ski troops which tried to cut off the division by outflanking it. The individual batteries were attached to the various Kampfgruppen of the division. The individual batteries were only returned to battalion command after the bridge across the Ssewerniy-Donez had been reached.

The Sturmgeschütze of the 1st Battery were given security missions under Oberwachtmeister Wegener. During one of the following nights the battalion's forward command group was surrounded by the Soviets. However, it managed to smash through the encirclement and reach the German lines.

Panzer-Grenadier-Division "Großdeutschland" was then given orders to withdraw from Kharkov in the middle of February. On 15 and 16 February 1943 the Sturmgeschütze held the north edge of Kharkov against enemy tanks which might attempt to breakthrough. The decimated battalion then received 20 new Sturmgeschütze, which were unloaded at Walki. This brought its strength back up to 30 operational Sturmgeschütze. The division pulled back. It left the SPW Battalion under Remer to fight at the north edge of Kharkov and the Sturmgeschütze to provide cover in all directions on Red Square in the interior of the city. The Sturmgeschütze had the mission to receive Remer's battalion during the night, then follow the division to the southwest as a rear guard.

Everything went as planned. The division maintained its combat power. Finally, after successful offensive and defensive operations, it was in a position to take back Kharkov.

The Sturmgeschütze again played an outstanding role in both attack and defense. On 9 March 1943 a battery assisted in the capture of Kirassirskij, which was taken after a short firefight. At the same time, the 1st Battery under Hauptmann Magold attacked Woitenkoff with infantry and a section of 3.7 cm Flak. The city fell into its hands an hour later. Then the Kampfgruppen were reunited and Alexandrowka was taken on the very same evening after the Sturmgeschütze had destroyed the Soviet antitank front emplaced there. Seven enemy tanks, 4 12.2 cm caliber guns and 21 7.62 cm antitank guns were destroyed. Sixteen light antitank guns (4.5 cm) were also destroyed.

Hauptmann Magold had most of the credit for this success. Most of the destroyed enemy tanks were added to his personal score. The 1st and 2nd Batteries, with infantry riding on board, attacked Bol. Pissarewka on 12 March 1943. When the lead elements of the attack ran into the enemy outside of Iwanyi-Berdyni at 0645 hours and started taking antitank fire, the 2nd Battery under Oberleutnant Schenk made a frontal attack against the village. When his command Sturmgeschütz moved around a curve, he came under fire from an antitank cannon. The first round brought the gun to a stop, the second glanced off the top armor. This ricochet killed the battery commander who was standing in his hatch. Oberleutnant Schenk, who had won the German Cross in Gold, hung dead out of his hatch. At that moment the battalion commander's gun joined the fight. Hauptmann Frantz managed to knock out the enemy antitank gun, but for Oberleutnant Schenk, Unteroffizier Kempter, and Gefreiter Rausch, this help came too late. The infantry advanced towards the houses on foot. The village was taken and a little while later the divisional commander showed up in a Fieseler Storch, landed and joined the commanders. Haggard and listless, armed with a knobby cane, he came up to his officers and gave them the division's orders: "The division is to advance to Bol. Pissarewka!"

Strong Soviet tank forces were sighted on 14 March. At 0900 hours the three-day tank battle of Borissowka began, and it took everything that the Sturmgeschütze had to give.

During the attack on Stanowoje Hauptmann Magold destroyed 14 enemy tanks by himself. Magold fought back the enemy in a battle like few recorded in the history of the Sturmgeschütze. At 1145 hours, he reported: "Stanowoje is firmly in our hands!"

Then a pilot's report arrived which electrified everyone. It read as follows: "120 enemy tanks and 80 trucks are approaching Stanowoje."

Hauptmann Frantz formed up his battalion and threw it against the overwhelmingly superior enemy. The first pack of 18 T-34 tanks was attacked. The Sturmgeschütze took them under rapid fire. From all sides the steel of the antitank rounds hammered against the T-34's. Enemy tanks were blown sky high. Others burst into flames while still others were torn apart by the explosions of their own ammunition. Not one of these 18 T-34's escaped this bitter fate. This tank pack was totally wiped out. But that was no reason for the battalion to pull back.

"Forward, forward...Get the others!" And turning the words into action, the battalion continued to advance.

The next tank pack popped up. The Sturmgeschütze attacked again. This tank pack was also completely destroyed in rapid maneuvers, lightening-like advances and continuous fire. Not one of those tanks came back. The battlefield remained in German hands, and all the destroyed and inoperable enemy tanks could be counted. There were forty three T-34's left lying on the field, their remains bearing witness to the fierceness of this fight.

For this unique operation by his battalion, for his masterly tactical leadership and for his personal bravery, which at this place had been decisive and prevented a disaster, Hauptmann Peter Frantz became the 228th soldier of the Wehrmacht to receive the Oak Leaves to the Knight's Cross of the Iron Cross. Hauptmann Magold received the Knight's Cross. Oberwachtmeister Wegener, one of the "old hands" and a very successful Sturmartillerie man, was the third in the group to receive the Knight's Cross.

Every Sturmartillerist who was at this engagement merits the highest recognition. If only a few men are listed here, then it is to represent all of them, and all of them have deserved this praise to a quite unusual degree: Oberleutnant Wehmeyer (commander of 3rd Battery) and Oberwachtmeister "Mambo" Herbert Schmidt (1st Battery) both received the German Cross in Gold; Leutnant Reisenhofer (3rd Battery); Oberleutnant Verch (the battalion adjutant who had taken over the 2nd Battery after the death of Oberleutnant Schenk) also received the German Cross in Gold; and, finally, Sturmgeschütz commanders Oberwachtmeister Kliche and Wachtmeister Kaspar (who received the German Cross in Gold a little later as Oberwachtmeister).

On 19 March 1943 an attack was launched on Tomarowka. Because the terrain was impassable for wheeled vehicles, the attack was to be executed by the Panzer regiment along with the Sturmgeschütz battalion. When six Soviet tanks attacked from Kosytschew on the same morning, just before the start of the German attack, they were repulsed by the 3rd Battery. By 0940 hours 4 enemy tanks had been destroyed.

The 1st Battery, along with Aufklärungs-Abteilung "Großdeutschland", moved out at 0930 hours. Kosytschew fell 45 minutes later.

The 3rd Battery charged ahead after defeating the tanks. Oberleutnant Spaether led it to Tomarowka, where the enemy was also pushed back. Three days later the entire battalion was engaged in an attack in front of the main battle line. It had been given a reconnaissance mission. It cleared the area of scattered Russians and destroyed a number of guns.

Preparations began for "Operation Citadel." Panzer-Grenadier-Division "Großdeutschland" was attached to the XXXXVIII. Armee-Korps (General von Knobelsdorff) for this operation, which was devised to cut off and annihilate the enemy forces within the great salient at Kursk.

The attack began around 1500 hours on 4 July 1943. Once again it was the Sturmgeschütze which smashed through the first enemy positions and, by the evening of the first day of the attack, advanced as far as Tscherkasskoje, southwest of Alexejewka. On the third day of the attack, however, the division bogged down in the very swampy terrain along the banks of the Pena. The Soviets had constructed a strong defensive line there with earthen bunkers, dug-in antitank guns, flame-thrower positions, dug in T-34's and artillery.

In the early morning of the 4th day of the attack, the Soviets launched their first tank attack from the northwest. The attack was launched as the division assembled for an assault around both sides of Syrzewo as far as Hill 230.1 south of the village. More and more groups of enemy tanks appeared. They attacked in strengths of 20 to 40 tanks, and came in waves.

Peter Frantz, who had just been promoted to Major, threw himself at the attackers with his entire battalion. Frantz knew that he had to destroy these enemy tanks if the division was not to be halted.

For several hours all of the guns were in continuous combat. The Soviets brought antitank guns right up behind their armored forces in order to put the German Sturmgeschütze out of action. As a result, the enemy antitank guns had to be put out of action first.

This battle was stubbornly and bitterly fought. Again and again, flames from the explosions sprayed out when the tanks were hit. New explosions rang out constantly across the battlefield which was glutted with the burning wrecks of tanks and shot-up antitank guns. The battalion took its first casualties. Crews of damaged Sturmgeschütze advanced on the enemy's antitank gun positions with hand grenades and explosives. It was a struggle for victory and, more importantly, for survival. Three Sturmgeschütze were put out of action—one after the other—by one antitank cannon before Hauptmann Naether managed to destroy that gun.

At that point the Soviets' aggressive spirit melted away in the fire of the Sturmgeschütze. They pulled back. The Sturmgeschütze pushed after them. Rapidly taking infantry on board, the battalion took Hill 230.1. The Soviets pulled back to Gremutshy.

Thirty-five T-34's and eighteen heavy antitank guns lay behind on the battlefield, destroyed by the Sturmgeschütze. Once again, they were the victor and had pulled the fat out of the fire.

The right flank of the Panzer-Regiment "Großdeutschland" had been covered by the Sturmgeschütze and the reconnaissance battalion. When enemy tanks from Kalinowka and Kruglik were reported, Major Frantz engaged them with two batteries and elements of the 2nd (SPW) Squadron and chased the enemy away. In the early afternoon of that day the Sturmgeschütze and the 2nd (SPW) Squadron advanced through the Kubassowskij Ravine and took Point 285.5. As enemy flanking movements from the village of Kruglik were affecting the battalion's maneuvering, the Sturmgeschütze then rolled on towards Kruglik, covered by a rise in the ground. The 3rd Battery under Oberleutnant Wehmeyer stayed back on a hill outside of Kruglik and blocked enemy traffic on the road. In the twilight the 1st and 2nd Batteries under Oberleutnant Brehmer carried out an attack on Kruglik. The village was taken after strong Soviet resistance.

On 14 July the Sturmgeschütze formed a screen to the south in the areas of Nowosselowka and Werchopenje. When enemy tanks were sighted, the Sturmgeschütze attacked and destroyed 3 T-34's. In the afternoon of 14 July Distr. Tolstoje was taken. The Soviets continued their attack there for the next two days. Sturmgeschütz-Abteilung "Großdeutschland" played a large part in this successful defense as well.

On 11 August 1943 the Sturmgeschütze were on the eastern edge of Achtyrka. During the early morning hours of 12 August Soviet tanks attacked in the direction of Achtyrcha. While the battalion's wheeled elements rolled on into Achtyrcha, the Sturmgeschütze attacked this Soviet tank group and destroyed five T-34's before the Sturmgeschütz of Wachtmeister Brauner received a direct hit. Gefreiter Kilger, the gun's radio operator, was killed. The Sturmgeschütze then rolled on into Achtyrcha.

During 18 August the Sturmgeschütze took a Russian artillery position southeast of Osero in a surprise attack from the area of Achtyrcha.

In the months that followed Panzer-Grenadier-Division "Großdeutschland" and its Sturmgeschütz battalion were engaged in defensive fighting. The high point of this fighting was the Soviet tank attack from the Krassnyi-Orlik Ravine and the ruins of Businowataja.

With his command Sturmgeschütz and the escort gun commanded by Wachtmeister Brauner, Major Frantz drove into a Russian tank group which had broken into the sector of the 9. Panzer-Division. Both guns succeeded in integrating themselves into the Russian tank unit on a hill in a grain field. A little later they broke out of this group and opened fire on the Russians. Seven T-34's were destroyed by these two guns in that first surprising burst of fire before the Soviets could react.

Almost all of the 20 Russian tanks were destroyed as the battle progressed. Only a few got away.

On 16 November an attempt by Russian tanks to break in was beaten back and 11 enemy tanks were destroyed. A few days later, in a determined action, the brigade destroyed eighteen KV 1's and T-34's. Unteroffizier Bor was especially successful with his Sturmgeschütz in this fighting. He destroyed 8 enemy tanks all by himself and was awarded the German Cross in Gold for it.

On 5 February 1944 Major Frantz had to leave the battalion. Oberleutnant Steffani, commander of the 1st Battery, took over temporary command of the battalion. Sometime during this period the battalion was redesignated a brigade.

The Sturmgeschütze fought on in the Tscherkassy sector on the lower Dnjepr. Three Sturmgeschütze under Leutnant Döhn joined the battle along the main lines on the lower Dnjepr. Leutnant Döhn commanded these guns standing in his open hatch. The left Sturmgeschütz was hit by an antitank gun, however, the other two guns came out of the fighting undamaged.

The Sturmgeschütze moved through Parliti Sat to Ungheni Tagh in a snow storm during the evening of 1 April 1944. When Russian tanks attempted to push through, with their objective being Targul Frumos, the Sturmgeschütze held them off. They destroyed a large number of enemy tanks and provided decisive support to the infantry fighting there.

On 4 April 1944 six Sturmgeschütze were part of Kampfgruppe Heynitz. That Kampfgruppe launched a counterattack on Parliti Sat and Hill 154, which the enemy had taken on the previous day. The Sturmgeschütz of Leutnant der Reserve Hensinger was blown up by a round from an antitank gun. Oberleutnant Hans Sturm especially distinguished himself in this fighting. In a decisive maneuver, he destroyed nine enemy tanks with his 3rd Battery and was the first to push into Parliti Sat. He was recommended for the Knight's Cross by Generalleutnant Hasso von Manteuffel, the new divisional commander. This decoration was awarded to him on 15 July 1944.

The Sturmgeschütze fought along the Vascani road together with the division's Panzer regiment. Oberleutnant Rupert Reisenhofer and Obergefreiter Franz Viehweg were both killed there. Reisenhofer was one of the old experienced hands of the Sturmartillerie. Known for his cold-blooded courage, he was respected by everyone. His guiding principle was: "The life of an Sturmartillerie man is short, but powerful."

When the Soviets moved out north of Jassy on 23 April 1944, Oberleutnant Diddo Diddens committed his 1st Battery against the enemy and inflicted bloody losses on him. This action was mentioned in the Wehrmacht Report for 27 April 1944: "Strong Soviet forces launched an attack north of Jassy. It failed in the wake of the tough resistance offered by German and Rumanian troops. Local penetrations were sealed off. In this sector of the fighting, a Sturmgeschütz unit of Panzer-Grenadier-Division "Großdeutschland" under the command of Oberleutnant Diddens won special distinction."

On 15 June 1944, Oberleutnant Diddens became the 501st soldier of the German Wehrmacht to be awarded the Oak Leaves to the Knight's Cross.

With the transfer of Panzer-Grenadier-Division "Großdeutschland" to a screening mission to allow the establishment of the Memel Bridgehead, the Sturmgeschütz brigade received orders to clear the area southeast of Krottingen. The brigade, together with Panzer-Aufklärungs-Abteilung 7 of the 7. Panzer-Division, made a fighting withdrawal to Salantai towards noon on 9 October 1944. It crossed the border of the German Reich at Nimmersatt. This was where the East Prussian defensive line began.

Three Sturmgeschütze of the brigade won special distinction during the attempt to defend Memel against every enemy attack and hold it to the last as the corner post between East Prussia and Heeresgruppe Nord.

As the fighting progressed after the beginning of the Russian winter offensive on 12 January 1945, the newly named Panzer-Korps "Großdeutschland" then pushed through to the west along with Panzer-Grenadier-Division "Brandenburg," which was its other division. Sturmgeschütz-Brigade "Großdeutschland" was attached to this Kampfgruppe. At that point it was provisionally designated as the II./Panzer-Regiment "Brandenburg."

The breakthrough at Stören succeeded. The Kampfgruppe pushed through the enemy with the Sturmgeschütze in front as its spearhead. But Kalisch and Ostrowo were already in enemy hands. The Kampfgruppe had to penetrate between the two towns. The breakthrough succeeded at Krotoschin in the night of 23/24 January 1945.

The brigade forced a crossing over the Bartsch. During this crossing a Sturmgeschütz fell in and two of the crew were drowned. At Niesky the brigade went back on the defense. Hähnichen was held against strong Soviet pressure. The Soviets then attacked with strong tank forces. Whole swarms of tanks were moving west.

The Sturmgeschütze didn't have much left to stem this Soviet spring flood. German resistance collapsed between Bautzen and Neiße.

The last Sturmgeschütze of Sturmgeschütz-Brigade "Großdeutschland" led all the wounded and civilians out of the surrounded city of Niesky. During the evacuation the Sturmgeschütze towed damaged trucks. These last defenders left Niesky one hour after midnight on 21 April 1945. The Russians opposed them at the crossing of Reich Route 115 at Lake Kodersdorfer. The Sturmgeschütze swept them from the road.

With four Sturmgeschütze at the point, this group rolled on past the retreating Soviets, who seemed to think they were a column of prisoners, since they didn't fire on them. When German troops were found at Wilhelminental, the Kampfgruppe commander radioed: "To all SPW, to all Sturmgeschütze. Move out, move! German troops ahead of us!"

And they made it through. They reached the units of the 20. Panzer-Division and were safe.

After further fighting, Panzer-Korps "Großdeutschland" assembled west of Bautzen to join an attack on the city. However, this assault never took place.

The brigade's Sturmgeschütze fought in the defense at Ölmütz. At 1805 hours on 8 May 1945, however, they received the radio message concerning the armistice. Messengers were dispatched. The order was given to destroy the weapons. For the last time the engines of the Sturmgeschütze howled as they pulled into a deep ravine. Then explosions sounded through the night. The last Sturmgeschütze were destroyed, so as not to fall into enemy hands. The war was over.

Generalfeldmarschall Erich von Manstein: The originator of the Sturmartillerie concept.

Knight's Cross recipient Hauptmann Helmut Adam.

Knight's Cross winner Hauptmann Adamowitsch.

Knight's Cross winner Oberleutnant Ernst Alex.

Knight's Cross winner Hauptmann Herbert Amann.

Knight's Cross winner Oberwachtmeister Fritz Amling.

Knight's Cross winner Hauptmann Heinz Angelmaier.

Knight's Cross winner Hauptmann Friedrich Arnold.

Knight's Cross winner Hauptmann Dietrich Ascher.

Knight's Cross recipient Oberwachtmeister Karl-Heinrich Banze.

Knight's Cross recipient Hauptmann Karl-Ludwig Barthes.

Knight's Cross recipient Hauptmann Heinz Baurmann.

Knight's Cross recipient Major Dr. Albert Bausch.

Knight's Cross recipient Major Gerhard Behnke.

Knight's Cross recipient Hauptmann Karl-Erich Berg.

Knight's Cross recipient Hauptmann Ludwig Bertram.

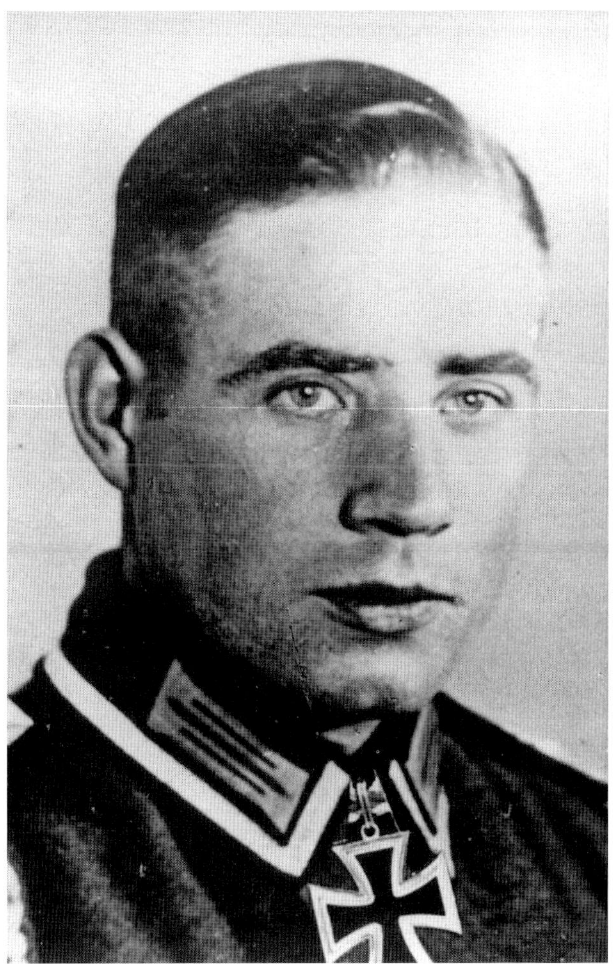
Knight's Cross recipient Oberwachtmeister Walter Beutler.

Knight's Cross recipient Leutnant Herwig Bittner.

Knight's Cross recipient Leutnant Georg Bose.

Knight's Cross and Oakleaves recipient Oberleutnant Wolfgang von Bostell.

Knight's Cross and Oakleaves recipient Major Josef Brandner.

Knight's cross recipient Oberleutnant Gerhard Brandt

Knight's Cross recipient Oberleutnant Konrad Brettschneider

Knight's Cross recipient Oberleutnant Karl Bucke.

Knight's Cross recipient Oberstleutnant Martin Buhr.

Knight's Cross recipient Oberwachtmeister Günter Carsten.

Knight's Cross recipient Hauptmann Paul Dahms

Knight's Cross recipient Oberwachtmeister Friedrich Daht.

Knight's Cross recipient SS-Sturmbannführer Ernst Dehmel.

Knight's Cross recipient Oberleutnant Heinz Deutsch.

Knight's Cross and Oakleaves recipient Hauptmann Diddo Diddens.

Knight's Cross recipient Hauptmann Hans Dratwa.

Knight's Cross recipient Oberleutnant Alfred Egghardt.

Knight's Cross recipient Wachtmeister Heinrich Engel.

Knight's Cross recipient Oberwachtmeister Kurt Engelhardt.

Knight's Cross recipient Hauptmann Richard Engelmann.

Knight's Cross recipient Hauptmann Reinhold Karl Ertel.

Knight's Cross recipient Oberwachtmeister Heinrich Feldkamp.

Knight's Cross and Oakleaves recipient Oberstleutnant Bernhard Flachs.

Knight's Cross and Oakleaves recipient Major Peter Frantz.

Knight's Cross recipient Oberwachtmeister Herbert Friedel.

Knight's Cross recipient Oberwachtmeister Josef Galle.

Knight's Cross recipient Hauptmann Helmut Gattermann.

Knight's Cross recipient Major Gottfried Geißler.

Knight's Cross recipient Hauptmann Erich Geppert.

Knight's Cross recipient Oberleutnant Erwin Glander.

Knight's Cross recipient Oberleutnant Dr. Paul Gloger.

Knight's Cross recipient Oberstleutnant Friedrich Großkreutz.

Knight's Cross recipient Hauptmann Anton Grünert.

Knight's Cross recipient Major Rupert Gruber.

Knight's Cross recipient SS-Hauptscharführer Anton Günther.

Knight's Cross recipient Leutnant Robert Haas.

Knight's Cross recipient Oberstleutnant Erich HammonHammon

Knight's Cross recipient Leutnant Leo Hartmann.

Knight's Cross recipient SS-Sturmbannführer HeinrichHeimann

Knight's Cross recipient Hauptmann Günther Hellmich.

Knight's Cross recipient SS-Untersturmführer Friedrich Henke.

Knight's Cross recipient Leutnant Ahrend Höper.

Knight's Cross recipient Hauptmann Johann Höring.

Above: Knight's Cross recipient Hauptmann Otto Hoffmann.

Right: Knight's Cross and Oakleaves recipient Generalmajor Günter Hoffmann-Schönborn.

Knight's Cross recipient Major Richard Hohenhausen.

Knight's Cross recipient Major Gerhard Hoppe.

Knight's Cross recipient Oberstleutnant Heinz Huffmann.

Knight's Cross recipient Hauptmann Herbert Jaschke.

Knight's Cross recipient Wolfgang Kapp.

Knight's Cross recipient Oberwachtmeister Kurt Kirchner.

Knight's Cross recipient Hauptmann d.R. Ludwig Knaup

Knight's Cross recipient SS-Sturmbannführer Walter Kniep

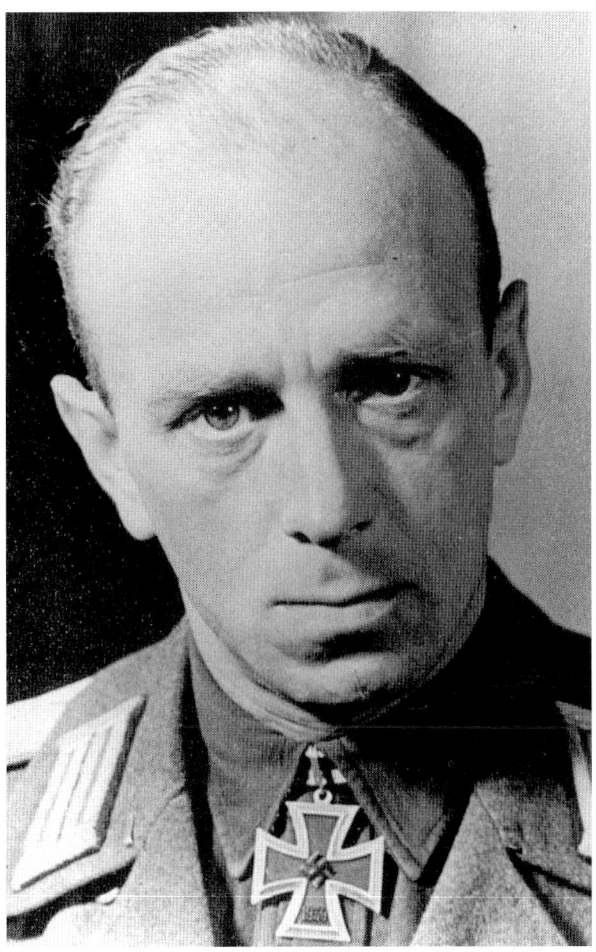

Knight's Cross recipient Leutnant Johannes Kochanowski.

Knight's Cross recipient Leutnant Heinrich Köhler.

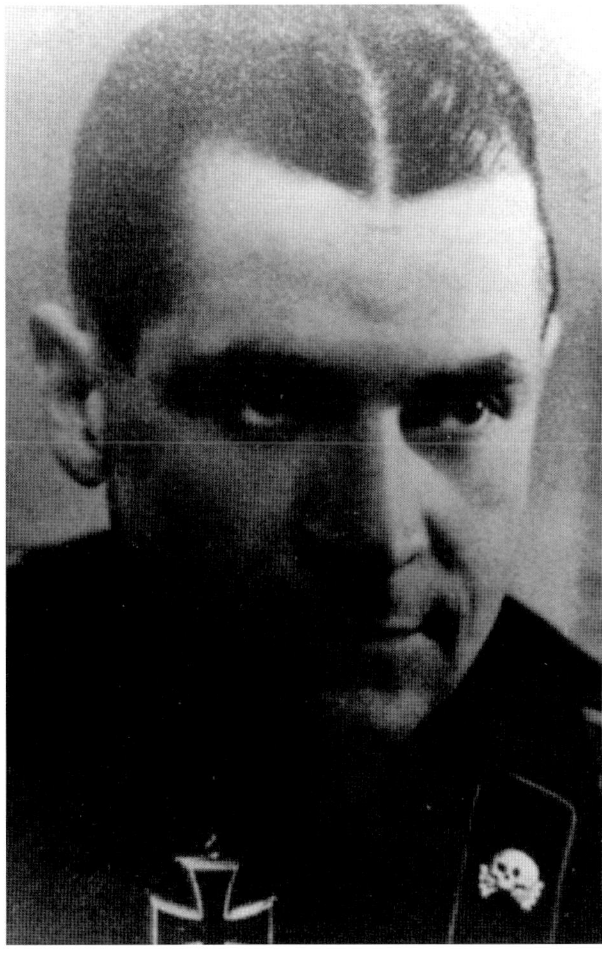

Knight's Cross recipient Oberleutnant Richard Krämer.

Knight's Cross recipient Major Horst Krafft.

Knight's Cross recipient Oberstleutnant Rudolf Kranz.

Knight's Cross recipient Leutnant Franz Kretschmer

Knight's Cross recipient Oberwachtmeister Gerhard Krieg

Knight's Cross recipient Major Wilhelm Kröhne

Knight's Cross recipient Major Kurt Kühme.

Knight's Cross recipient Hauptmann Ludwig Laubmayer.

Knight's Cross recipient Hauptmann Günter Liethmann.

Knight's Cross and Oakleaves recipient SS-Sturmbannführer Friedrich Lobmeyer.

Knight's Cross recipient Major Joachim Lützow.

Knight's Cross recipient Hauptmann Waldemar Lutz.

Knight's Cross recipient Hauptmann Johann Magold.

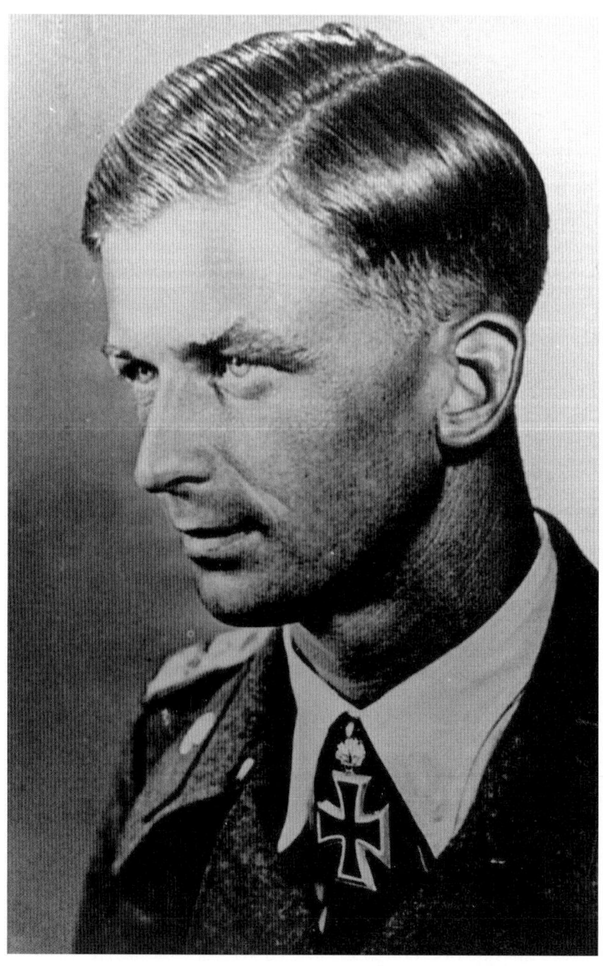

Knight's Cross recipient Major Wilhelm von Malachowski.

Knight's Cross recipient Oberwachtmeister Josef Mathes.

Knight's Cross recipient SS-Sturmbannführer Hubert Meierdress.

Knight's Cross recipient Oberwachtmeister Herbert Meißner.

Knight's Cross recipient Hauptmann d.R. Eugen Metzger

Knight's Cross recipient SS-Hauptsturmführer Bernd von Milovan.

Knight's Cross recipient Oberleutnant Günther Möller.

Knight's Cross recipient Hauptmann Alfred Montag.

Knight's Cross recipient Oberleutnant Edo von Müller

Knight's Cross recipient Oberstleutnant Alfred Müller.

Knight's Cross recipient Leutnant Horst Naumann.

Knight's Cross recipient Major Peter Nebel.

Knight's Cross recipient Oberleutnant d.R. Kurt Nippes

Knight's Cross recipient Oberleutnant d.R. Walter Oberloskamp

Knight's Cross recipient Hauptmann Armin Pfaffendorf

Knight's Cross recipient Oberwachtmeister Karl Pfreundtner.

Knight's Cross and Oakleaves recipient Leutnant Hubert-Georg Primozic.

Knight's Cross recipient SS-Unterscharführer Felix Przedwojewski.

Knight's Cross recipient Leutnant Alfred Regeniter.

Knight's Cross recipient SS-Sturmbannführer Karl Rettlinger.

Knight's Cross recipient SS-Hauptsturmführer Wilfried Richter

Knight's Cross recipient Dr. Wolfgang Röhder.

Knight's Cross recipient Oberwachtmeister Josef Rohrbacher

Knight's Cross recipient Hauptmann Konrad Sauer.

Knight's Cross recipient Oberwachtmeister Heinz Scharf.

Knight's Cross recipient Hauptmann Friedrich Scherer.

Knight's Cross recipient Hauptmann Kurt Schließmann.

Knight's Cross recipient Oberwachtmeister Hermann Schmidt.

Knight's Cross recipient Leutnant Johann Schmitt.

Knight's Cross recipient Oberleutnant Dr. Ing. Werner Scholz.

Knight's Cross recipient Oberwachtmeister Richard Schramm.

Knight's Cross recipient Hauptmann Helmut Schwalb.

Knight's Cross recipient Wachtmeister Josef Schwarzenbacher.

Knight's Cross recipient Oberwachtmeister d.R. Julius Serck

Knight's Cross and Oakleaves recipient Johann Spielmann.

Knight's Cross and Oakleaves recipient Bodo Spranz.

Knight's Cross recipient Wachtmeister d. R. Gottwald Stier

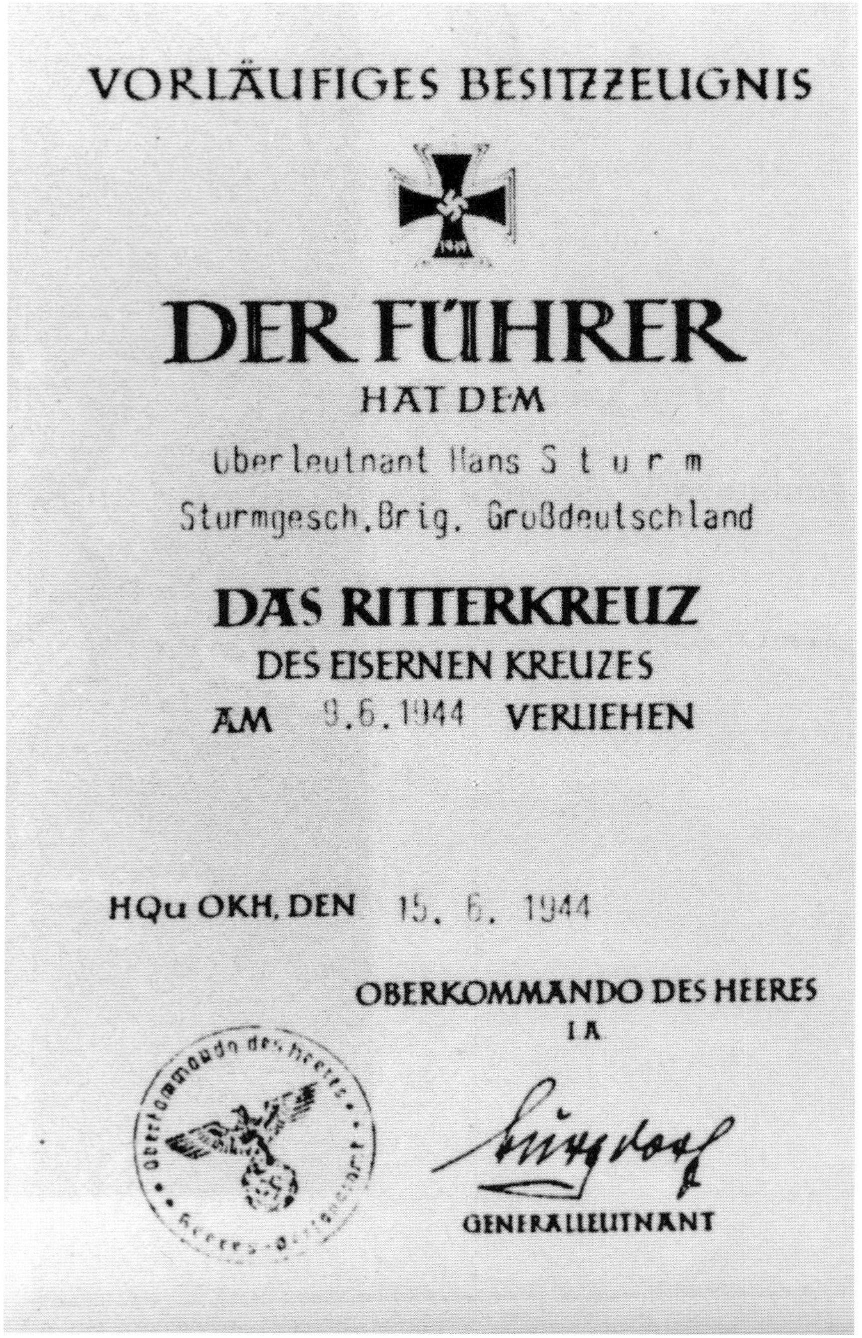

VORLÄUFIGES BESITZZEUGNIS

DER FÜHRER

HAT DEM

Oberleutnant Hans S t u r m

Sturmgesch.Brig. Großdeutschland

DAS RITTERKREUZ

DES EISERNEN KREUZES

AM 9.6.1944 VERLIEHEN

HQu OKH, DEN 15. 6. 1944

OBERKOMMANDO DES HEERES

IA

GENERALLEUTNANT

Sturm's preliminary notification of having been awarded the Knight's Cross.

Left: Knight's Cross recipient Hauptmann Hans-Hermann Sturm.

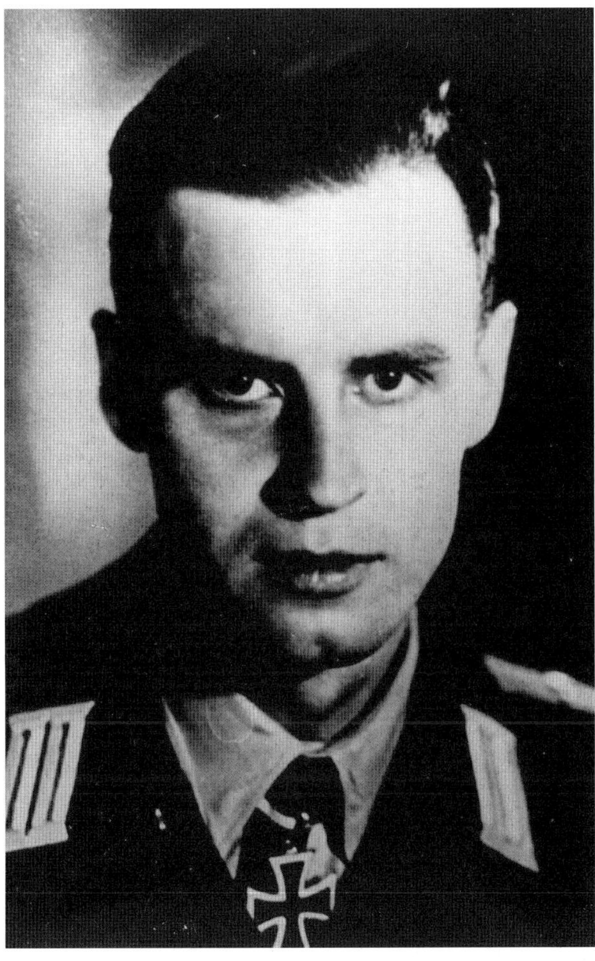

Knight's Cross recipient Hauptmann Hans Christian Stock

Knight's Cross recipient Hauptmann Friedrich Tadje.

Knight's Cross recipient Leutnant Heinrich Timpe.

Knight's Cross recipient Major Gottfried Tornau

Knight's Cross recipient Oberwachtmeister Josef Trägner

Knight's Cross recipient Hauptmann Rolf von Truxa.

Knight's Cross recipient Hauptmann Klaus Wagner.

Knight's Cross recipient Leutnant Wilhelm Wegner.

Knight's Cross recipient Oberwachtmeister Paul Wegener.

Knight's Cross recipient SS-Hauptsturmführer Emil Wiesemann

Knight's Cross recipient Oberleutnant Albert Witte.

Knight's Cross recipient Major Rudolf Zettler.

Knight's Cross recipient Hauptmann Günter Johannes Zieger

Knight Cross recipient Stabswachtmeister Erich Zillmann.

Knight's Cross recipient Hauptmann Kurt Zitzen.

Hitler presents newly awarded Oakleaves to the Knight's Cross at Berchtesgaden on the Obersalzberg. Major Bernhard Flachs is third from the right.

Camp du Richard, April 1944. Three outstanding officers of Sturmartillerie-Lehr-Brigade 902. From the left: Leutnant Feldner, Oberleutnant Wendel and Leutnant Ose. The three officers are posing with a Sturmgeschütz III G with "Saukopf" gun mantlet.

Major Buhr receives the Knight's Cross at Kiev.

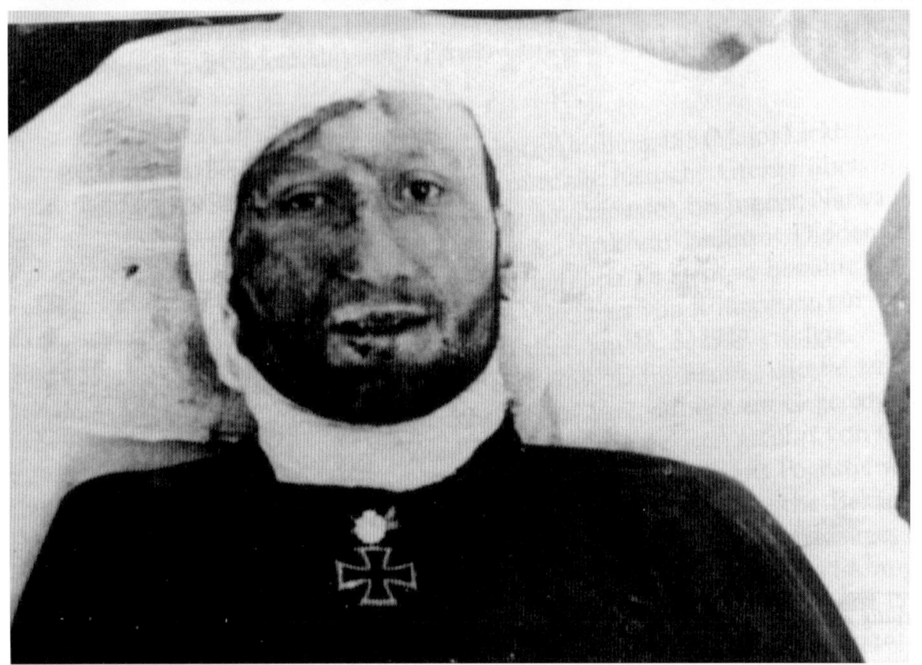

Diddo Diddens in the hospital after being severely wounded. He was awarded the Oakleaves to the Knight's cross there.

Oberwachtmeister Pfreundtner receives the Knight's cross from Major Gloger.

Oberwachtmeister Leo Hartmann with his Sturmgeschütz III F. He won the Knight's Cross at the Fortress at Breslau. Note his wearing of the black Panzer uniform but without the Totenkopf devices on the collar tabs. This was a common practice among Sturmartillerie crews.

Knight's Cross recipient Dr. Wolfgang Röhder.

Oberleutnant Schönmann and his wife at the wedding of his comrade, Oberleutnant Preusser.

Major Herbert Sichelschmidt, commander of Sturmgeschütz-Abteilung 210, with other officers of his command.

Oberleutnant Wolf Tanner, battery commander of the 3./Sturmgeschütz-Abteilung 191 in the Caucasus and in the Kuban Bridgehead.

Oberleutnant Wilhelm Heinzle, another fighter from the Kuban Bridgehead.

Oberleutnant Achim Hauber, a combat veteran of the assault artillery.

Knight's cross recipient Georg Sowada.

Knight Cross recipient Stabswachtmeister Erich Zillmann.

Two assault gun crewmen from the Sturmgeschütz-Batterie of Fallschirm-Panzer-Division "Hermann Göring." Note the folded camouflage net on the right.

Oberleutnant Anton Grünert on the way to Greece.

Fritz Amling on his assault gun after receiving the Knight's Cross.

Hauptmann Metzger, Oberst Hoffmann-Schönborn and Leutnant Primozic.

Leutnant Rolf Werner (left) and Leutnant Rudi Lenz, two battle-hardened battery officers of Sturmgeschütz-Brigade 191.

Knight's cross recipient Major Gottfried Tornau (left) and his orderly, Gefreiter Sepp Haitzmann.

Generalmajor Hoffmann-Schönborn, another "father" of the Sturmartillerie.

Staff Surgeon Dr. Willy Schröder saved 72 of his comrades from death on one day of heavy fighting.

Oberleutnant Franz Berndl (left) and Feldwebel Ludwig Stangassinger were crewmen on the famed Sturmgeschütz III christened "Deutsch."

The crew of Hugo Primozic's assault gun: the loader, Götte (left); Primozic; the driver, Bräun; and, the gunner, Sdimanek.

Highly decorated Sturmartillerie officers: Georg Rietscher, the 200th recipient of the Oakleaves (left); Hugo Primozic; and, Georg Gransee.

On the Dnieper River with Sturmgeschütz-Abteilung 243: Oberstleutnant Hesselbarth (left), the commander of the battalion; Leutnant Jaitner and Oberleutnant Sekirka are to his right. Oberleutnant Sekirka was the battery commander of the 3./Strumgeschütz-Abteilung 243.

Knight's Cross recipient Oberwachtmeister Bolte (third from the left) and his crew.

General der Panzertruppen Walter Model.

Sturmartillerie-Brigade 911 at Loburg with Gauleiter Jordan and Knight's Cross recipient Major Alfred Müller.

Oberstleutnant Müller (right) of the Assault Gun School at Burg in conversation with a Hungarian general and an unidentified German officer.

The officer corps of Sturmgeschütz-Abteilung 191. The commander, Major Hoffmann-Schönborn, is fourth form the left.

Officers of an unknown unit during its activation.

Officer corps of Sturmgeschütz-Brigade 236, March 1943. The brigade commander, Hauptmann Brede, is fourth from the left.

The officers of Sturmgeschütz-Brigade 600 prior to leaving for Russia in June 1943. The brigade commander, Major Ernst August von Harder (KIA on 7 January 1944 at Mogilow), is in the middle. He was later recommended for the Knight's Cross.

Im Namen des Führers und Obersten Befehlshabers der Wehrmacht

verleihe ich

dem

Leutnant Bodo S p r a n z

Stab Sturmgesch.Abt. 185

das

Eiserne Kreuz 1. Klasse.

K.H.Qu., den 2. Juli 1941.

Der Kommandierende General

General der Infanterie.

(Dienstgrad und Dienststellung)

Vorläufiges Besitzzeugnis

Im Namen des Führers und Obersten Befehlshabers der Wehrmacht

verleihe ich

dem

Leutnant S p r a n z

2./Sturmgesch.Abt.185

das

Deutsche Kreuz in Gold

HQu OKH, den 6.Mai 1942

Oberkommando des Heeres

Generalfeldmarschall

VORLÄUFIGES BESITZZEUGNIS

DER FÜHRER

HAT DEM

Oberleutnant S p r a n z ,

Chef 1./Sturmgesch.Abt.237

DAS RITTERKREUZ

DES EISERNEN KREUZES

AM 3.10.1943 VERLIEHEN

HQu OKH, DEN 4.Oktober 1943.

OBERKOMMANDO DES HEERES

I.A.

Generalleutnant

VORLÄUFIGES BESITZZEUGNIS

DER FÜHRER

HAT DEM

Oberleutnant S p r a n z ,

Chef 1./Sturmgesch.Abt.237

DAS EICHENLAUB

ZUM RITTERKREUZ DES EISERNEN KREUZES

AM 3.10.1943 VERLIEHEN

HQu OKH, DEN 8.Oktober 1943.

OBERKOMMANDO DES HEERES

I.A.

Generalleutnant

From the Iron Cross, First Class to the Oakleaves of the Knight's Cross—the award documents of Bodo Spranz.

Generaloberst Heinz Guderian while visiting the Assault Gun School at Burg.

France in the spring of 1944. Generalfeldmarschall Erwin Rommel (center) confers with Generalmajor Feuchtinger, the commander of the 21. Panzer-Division, and Major Alfred Becker, the commander of Sturmgeschütz-Brigade 200.

The gravesite of Hauptmann Helmut Adam who was killed in action on 1 December 1942.

Heinz Lappe, an assault gun driver, was killed on 25 April 1945 while defending against the enemy at Edewechter Dike.

The grave of Franz Lalowski, 3./Sturmgeschütz-Abteilung 234, who was killed in action on 2 August 1942.

Memorial to the Sturmartillerie at Radstadt (Tauern).

A reunion of former Sturmartillerie soldiers at Karlstadt am Main. Wearing the hat is Generalfeldmarschall Erich von Manstein. To the right is Generalmajor a.D. Günther Hoffmann-Schönborn.

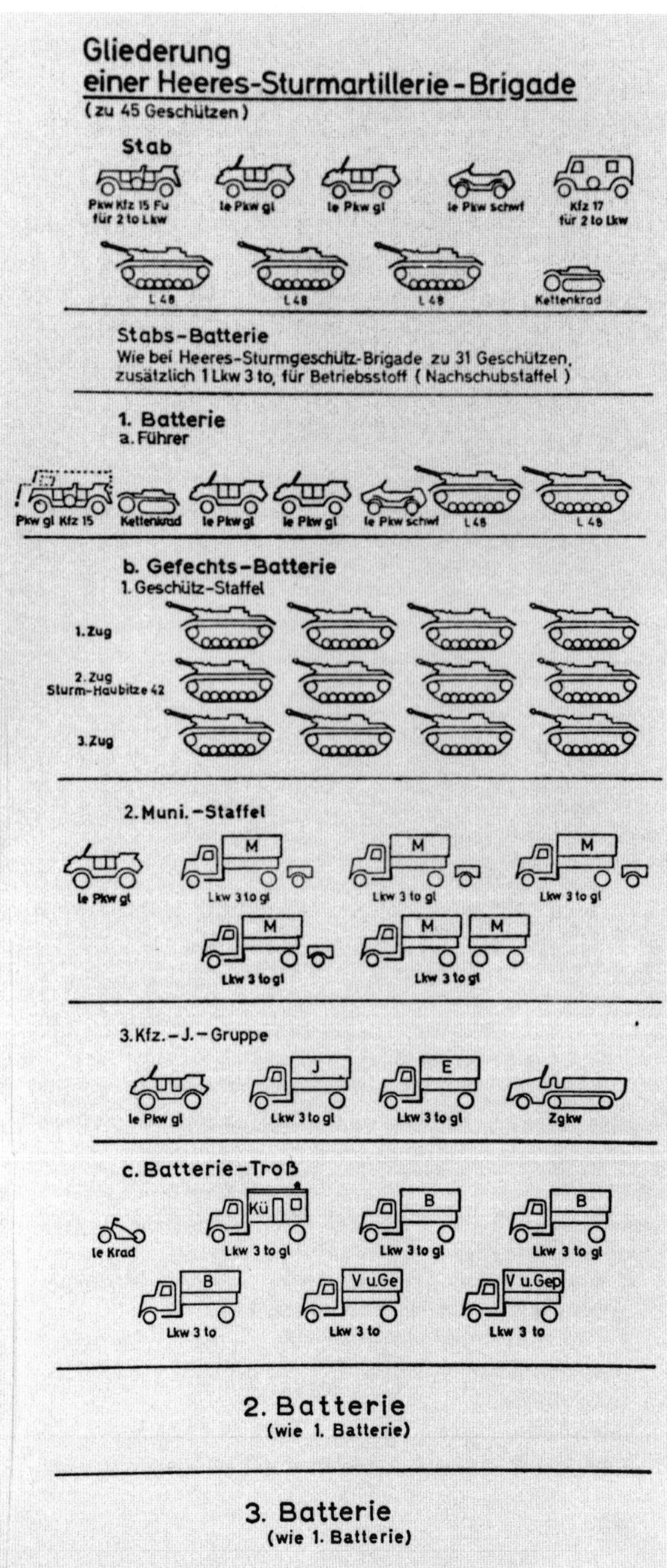

Table of organization and Equipment for a Heeres-Sturmartillerie-Brigade (without the Infanterie-Begleit-Batterie)

Appendices

Appendix A

Remaining Sturmartillerie Units

This section is devoted to Sturmartillerie units for which only minimal information is known.

Sturmgeschütz-Batterie 247

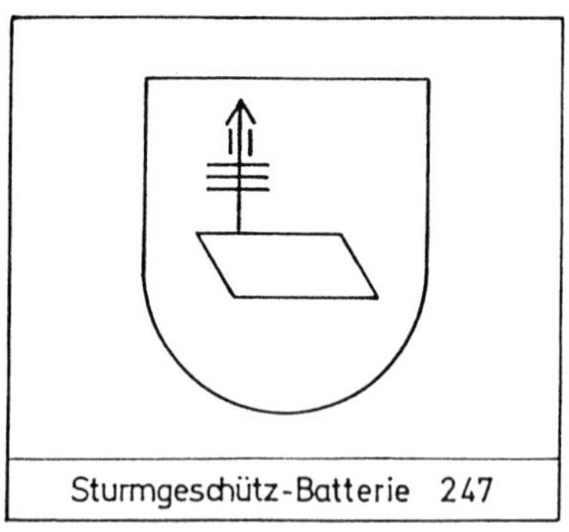
Sturmgeschütz-Batterie 247

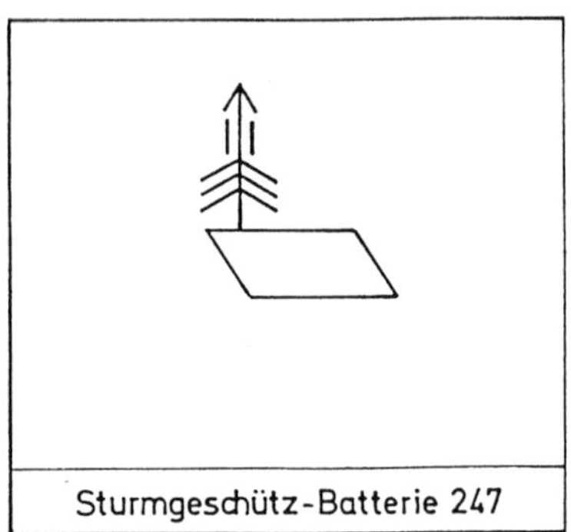
Sturmgeschütz-Batterie 247

Sturmgeschütz-Batterie 247 was established at Jüterbog in the early part of 1943 from elements which came from the 1./Sturmgeschütz-Abteilung 911. It was then immediately transported to Italy (Livorno) and then transferred to the island of Sardinia. Starting on 10 September 1943 the battery was transported to Corsica. It fought against partisans in the mountains of Corsica and outside of Bastia. It was transferred back to the Italian mainland on 4 October 1943 where it was sent back to Jüterbog at the end of October. From Jüterbog it went to Tours (France), where it was integrated into Sturmgeschütz-Brigade 902.

Sturmgeschütz-Batterie 393

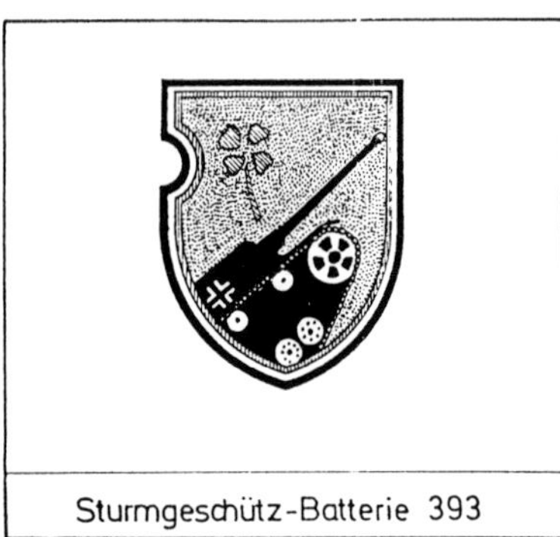
Sturmgeschütz-Batterie 393

No precise sources have been found concerning the activation of this unit. According to the statements of veterans, the unit was formed as Sturmgeschütz-Batterie 345 in the fall of 1942. It was soon attached to Sturm-Bataillon 343, however, and the battery assumed its number.

Sturm-Bataillon 393 was an army-level unit. It was employed in the sector of Heeresgruppe B (Italian 8th Army) in the Woronesch area at the end of November 1942. The battalion was destroyed in the Don Basin in February 1943. Nothing is known about Sturmgeschütz-Batterie 393 from that point on.

Sturmgeschütz-Batterie 900

Sturmgeschütz-Batterie 900 was formed in the middle of June 1941 and incorporated into Artillerie-Abteilung 900 as its 4th Battery on 17 June 1941. The battalion was employed with Heeresgruppe Mitte starting in July 1941 in the sector of the 9. Armee. It fought at Wilna, Minsk, Orscha, Witebsk, Smolensk and Gshatsk. It advanced into the area around Ssytschewka. The battery fought offensively and defensively on the Wop and on the Wotrja and then in the area around Welish. At the end of March 1942 the brigade was pulled out of the front and sent back to Germany. The elements which had been attached to the brigade were released to their originating units and schools. Sturmgeschütz-Batterie 900 was deactivated on 21 May 1942 at Jüterbog.

Sturmgeschütz-Batterie 900

Sturmgeschütz-Abteilung 228 (Sturmgeschütz-Brigade 228)

Sturmgeschütz-Brigade 228

Sturmgeschütz-Brigade 228

The battalion was established on 10 November 1942 at Treuenbrietzen (Wehrkreis III). As with many other Sturmgeschütz units, it was renamed as a brigade on 14 February 1944. The battalion was employed in the attempted relief of Stalingrad in late 1942. The year 1943 was marked by defensive fighting between the Don and the Donez in the area around Kharkov-Belgorod and on the Dnjepr around Krementschug. It continued to fight in the southern sector of the Eastern Front in 1944, where it was involved in the fighting withdrawal in the areas around Poltawa and Tscherkassa. It then fought in Rumania (Jassy) and Hungary (Gran Bridgehead at Szolnok). It finished the war fighting in Austria.

The unit had two insignia. The second insignia was introduced on 1 July 1944 when Hauptmann Kurt Teschke took over command of the brigade.

Sturmgeschütz-Abteilung 245 (Sturmgeschütz-Brigade 245)

The battalion was established on 13 June 1941. It was subsequently destroyed in January 1943 at Stalingrad. The unit was

Sturmgeschütz-Brigade 245

rebuilt on 10 April 1943 at Jüterbog and renamed a brigade on 14 February 1944. It was employed with the 17. and 6. Armeen. It was destroyed in June 1944 near Witebsk, when Heeresgruppe Mitte was effectively destroyed. The brigade was never rebuilt.

Sturmgeschütz-Abteilung 261 (Sturmgeschütz-Brigade 261; Heeres-Sturmartillerie-Brigade 261)

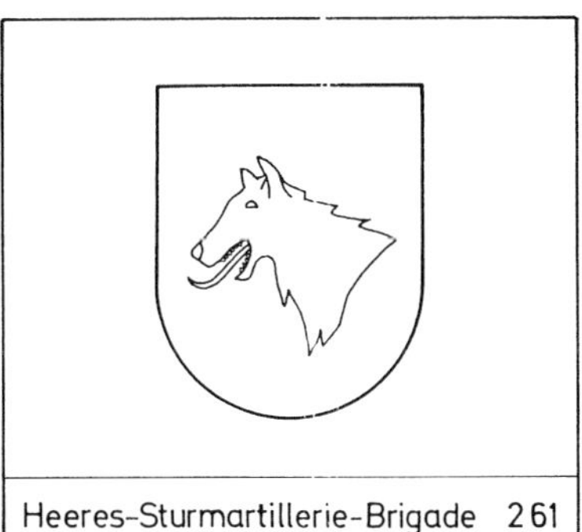
Heeres-Sturmartillerie-Brigade 261

This unit was formed as Sturmgeschütz-Abteilung 261 in Wehrkreis III on 1 July 1943. On 14 February 1944 it was renamed as Sturmgeschütz-Brigade 262. In the winter of 1944/45, it received its final redesignation, that of Heeres-Sturmartillerie-Brigade 261. The brigade was employed in Hungary in the final stages of the war. Nothing is known of its employment prior to that time.

Sturmgeschütz-Abteilung 303 (Sturmgeschütz-Brigade 303; Heeres-Sturmartillerie-Brigade 303)

Heeres-Sturmartillerie-Brigade 303

Sturmgeschütz-Abteilung 303 was formed at Burg on 24 October 1943. Nothing is known about this formation until its commitment in January 1944 with Heeresgruppe Nord. It is assumed that it was involved with its initial train-up and equipping from October 1943 to January 1944. On 14 February 1944 it was renamed as Sturmgeschütz-Brigade 303. Sometime in the summer of 1944 it was redesignated Heeres-Sturmartillerie-Brigade 303. Whether it was reorganized as such is unknown. In 1945 the brigade was employed in Hungary. Its final fate is unknown.

Sturmgeschütz-Brigade 396

Sturmgeschütz-Brigade 396

Sturmgeschütz-Brigade 396 was formed on 22 March 1944 in Denmark and moved to Tours (France) on 28 March 1944. The brigade was deactivated on 17 July 1944. Its individual batteries were used to form Sturmgeschütz-Abteilungen 1550-1553, 1558 and 1559, of which nothing is known.

Sturmgeschütz-Abteilung 905 (Sturmgeschütz-Brigade 905; Heeres-Sturmartillerie-Brigade 905)

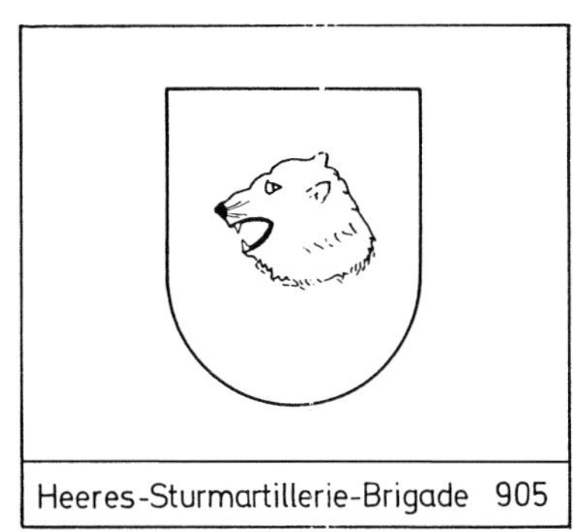
Heeres-Sturmartillerie-Brigade 905

Sturmgeschütz-Abteilung 905 was formed on 15 December 1942 at Jüterbog. It was renamed as a brigade on 14 February 1944 and then redesignated again as a Heeres-Sturmartillerie-Brigade in the fall of 1944. It was employed in June 1944 in the area of operations of Heeresgruppe Südukraine. It served in the west in 1945 in the Eifel and the Rhine.

Appendix B

Employment Principles for the Sturmartillerie

1.

The Sturmartillerie is a weapon best used at the decisive point of the battlefield.
The employment of the entire brigade ensures its greatest effectiveness.
Its shock and firepower—concentrated in a small area—will break any and all resistance.

2.

Long-range planning and proper resupply keep the brigade combat ready and functional.
Timely and sufficient supplies of munitions, fuel and replacement parts
is the highest commandment of superior leadership.

3.

Artillery and the Sturmartillerie complement one another and, therefore,
must work closely together and coordinate well.
The leaders of the Sturmartillerie—who must fight from the front—have the best opportunities
to observe and gain knowledge of the situation.
Radio links to the artillery ensure reliable fire control.

4.

Fighting with Sturmgeschütze demands knowledge of their properties and capabilities.
The Sturmartillerie has its own tactical fundamentals.
To neglect these principles in operation orders is to endanger their employment.

5.

The Sturmartillerie must be employed when the Schwerpunkt
of the enemy attack has been recognized.
The possibility of tactical surprise, enemy deception maneuvers and regrouping
makes it necessary to always hold a few Sturmgeschütze in reserve.

6.

The Sturmgeschütze attack with infantry deployed in depth.
Limited traverse of the gun, difficult close-in defense and weak side and rear armor
make continual protection by accompanying
grenadiers, infantry, or combat engineers an imperative.

7.

Too-hasty employment costs men and equipment.
The leader of Sturmgeschütze must conduct a reconnaissance of the terrain,
be familiar with the results of combat reconnaissance and
allow time for coordinating with all available weapons.

8.

The employment of Sturmgeschütze at night
against built-up positions and strong antitank defenses
promises success if it is conducted as a surprise,
if the terrain does not offer any special difficulties
and some visibility is available.
A limited objective and the closest coordination possible with the infantry is a prerequisite.

9.

After the operations order has been executed,
the Sturmgeschütze must be pulled out of the front lines
in order to restore their combat readiness.
Technical inspections, the continuous performance of maintenance and,
after several days of fighting, a basic overhaul of the vehicle
are the prerequisites for continued successful employment.

Appendix C

Sturmgeschütze in the Waffen-SS

Although this book deals primarily with the independent Sturmgeschütze units of the Heer many of the Waffen-SS divisions fielded Sturmgeschütz elements as an integral part of their organizational structure. As many of the photographs in this volume depict vehicles from SS formations a brief explanation of their employment within these formations follows:

Of the first thirty Sturmgeschütz III Ausführung A produced, the fifth battery of 6 guns formed was allocated to the "Leib-standarte SS Adolf Hitler." This independent battery, designated SS-Sturmgeschütz-Batterie 1 "LSSAH" was formed too late for action in the Western campaign.

In February 1941 the "Das Reich" also received an independent battery of 6 guns. These guns initiated the formation of SS-Sturmgeschütz-Batterie 2 "Das Reich."

Both of the above named batteries fought in the Balkans in April 1941. The battery for the "Totenkopf" was raised in early June 1941 but did not join the division until August of that year. The "Wiking" activated its seven-gun battery in September 1941. All four batteries fought on the Eastern Front in 1941/42.

In 1942 the 1., 2. and 3. SS-Panzer-Grenadier-Divisionen redesignated their Sturmgeschütz batteries as SS-Sturmgeschütz-Abteilungen 1, 2 and 3 respectively. The battalions consisted of 3 batteries composed of seven Sturmgeschütze each. This increase in establishment usually coincided with the upgrading of the formations to Panzer-Grenadier- and, in some cases later on, to Panzer-Division Status.

In 1942 the 7. SS-Gebirgs-Division "Prinz Eugen" and 8. SS-Kavallerie-Division "Florian Geyer" also activated seven-gun batteries.

In 1943 the 4. SS-Panzer-Grenadier-Division "Polizei," the 6. SS-Panzer-Grenadier-Division "Nord" and the 16. SS-Panzer-Grenadier-Division "Reichsführer-SS" received batteries consisting of 10 Sturmgeschütze. In July the 16. SS-Panzer-Grenadier-Division "Reichsführer-SS" activated Sturmgeschütz-Abteilung 16 consisting of 3 gun batteries of 10 Sturmgeschütze each. The 11. SS-Panzer-Grenadier-Division "Nordland" received a fourteen-gun battery as part of its Panzer-Abteilung 11 in December.

By 1944 many of the SS-Panzer- and Panzer-Genadier-Divisionen—in particular the 5. SS-Panzer-Division "Wiking," the 9. SS-Panzer-Division "Hohenstaufen," the 10. SS-Panzer-Division "Frundsberg," the 17. SS-Panzer-Grenadier-Division "Götz von Berlichingen" and the 18. SS-Panzer-Grenadier-Divison "Horst Wessel"—received a significant number of Sturmgeschütze, usually as part of their Panzer-Regimenter or -Abteilungen. In the case of the 17. SS-Panzer-Grenadier-Division "Götz von Berlichingen," its SS-Panzer-Abteilung 17 consisted solely of assault guns, as did SS-Panzer-Abteilung 18 of the 18. SS-Panzer-Grenadier-Divison "Horst Wessel." Many of the SS-Panzer-Divisionen found their main battle tanks, the Panzer IV's and V's, being replaced with the easier to manufacture Sturmgeschütze.

With the tide of war turning, and the Germans largely on the defensive, the assault guns were increasingly being used in the anti-tank role. Due to their relatively small size and the excellent anti-armor performance of their 75 mm L/48 cannon, this was a role to which Sturmgeschütze were ideally suited. By mid 1944 the SS-Sturmgeschütz-Abteilungen were being renamed as SS-Panzerjäger-Abteilungen, reflecting the increased anti-tank role. Due to the shortage of dedicated Panzerjäger, such as the Jagdpanzer IV and IV/70, the Panzerjäger-Abteilungen still contained significant numbers of both the Sturmgeschütz III and IV.

Finally, two independent SS Abteilungen were formed late in the war: SS-Sturmgeschütz-Abteilung 105 was created in September 1944 and SS-Jagd-Panzer-Abteilung 561 on 15 February 1945.

Appendix D

German Cross in Gold Recipients of the Sturmartillerie

Unlike the Knight's cross, this decoration was only awarded for exceptional combat performance. Adolf Hitler established the criteria concerning the award of the decoration as follows:

I establish the War Order of the German Cross to recognize repeated deeds of extraordinary bravery or leadership.

Article 1

The Order of the German Cross is a military award. The following orders are awarded: The German Cross in Silver and the German Cross in Gold.

Article 2

The Order consists of an eight-edged, dark-gray star edged in silver with a diameter of 65 millimeters which carries a black swastika edged in silver on a silver or golden oak wreath on a matte silver field. The oak wreath displays "1941" on the bottom. The German Cross is worn on the right side without a ribbon.

Article 3

The German Cross in Silver is awarded for repeated extraordinary services in military leadership. The German Cross in Gold is awarded for repeated, proven extraordinary bravery or for repeated excellent service in the leadership of soldiers. Prerequisite for the award of the German Cross in Silver or Gold is the possession of the Iron Cross, First Class of 1939 or the Clasp to the Iron Cross, First Class of the World War or the War Service Cross, First Class with Swords.

Article 4

The person awarded will receive an award certificate.

Article 5

The German Cross remains the property of survivors as a memento after the awardee is deceased.

Article 6

The Chief of the Oberkommando der Wehrmacht will establish the award procedures in coordination with the Staatsminister and the Chief of the Präsidialkanzlei.

Surname *Christian Name* *Date of Birth*	*Rank* *Iron Cross, Second Class* *Iron Cros, First Class*	*Date of Award* *Duty Position* *Unit*
Adam *Helmut* *3.11.1919*	*Oberleutnant* *EK II: 5. 10.1941* *EK I: 30. 9. 1942*	*23. 11.1944* *Battery Commander* *2./Stu.Gesch.Brig. „GD«*
Adamowitsch *Felix* *20. 11. 1919*	*Oberleutnant* *EK II: 29. 9. 1941* *EK I: 28. 8. 1943*	*29. 2. 1944* *Battery Commander* *3./Stu.Gesch.Abt. 904*
Alsleben *Dietrich* *6. 4. 1920*	*Leutnant der Reserve* *EK II: 26. 7. 1942* *EK I: 25. 7. 1944*	*15. 4. 1945* *Section Leader* *2./He.Stu.Gesch.Brig. 912*
Ammon *Lothar* *29. 9. 1917*	*Oberleutnant* *EK II: 30. 7. 1941* *EK I: 27. 9. 1942*	*9. 6. 1943* *Section Leader* *1./le.Stu. Gesch.Abt. 190*
Anacker *Friedrich* *17.9. 1916*	*Oberleutnant* *EK II: 9. 1. 1940* *EK I: 13. 6. 1941*	*15. 12.1941* *Battery Commander* *2./Stu. Gesch.Abt. 191*
Angelmaier *Heinz* *22. 7. 1918*	*Oberleutnant der Reserve* *EK II: 20. 7. 1941* *EK I: 24. 8. 1941*	*12. 10. 1943* *Battery Commander* *3. /Stu. Gesch. Abt. 203*

Arnold *Friedrich* *16. 5. 1919*	*Leutnant der Reserve* *EK II: 18. 8.1941* *EK I: 25. 8. 1941*	*9. 10. 1942* *Section Leader* *2./Stu.Gesch.Abt.201*
Barth *Erwin* *11. 4.1914*	*Oberwachtmeister* *EK II:: 14.10.1941* *EK I: 3. 12.1942*	*27. 11. 1944* *Section Leader* *3./Stu.Gesch.Brig. 279*
Bastian *Helmut* *17. 9. 1919*	*Oberwachtmeister* *EK II:: 8. 11. 1941* *EK I: 6. 8. 1943*	*4. 9.1944* *Section Leader* *2./Stu.Gesch.Brig. 232*
Baurmann *Heinz* *11.11.1919*	*Oberleutnant* *EK II:: 1. 7.1940* *EK I: 11. 9. 1941*	*16. 4. 1943* *Battery Commander* *3./Stu.Gesch.Abt. 667*
Bausch Dr. *Albert* *2. 7. 1904*	*Hauptmann der Reserve* *EK II: 13. 6. 1940* *EK I: 9. 10.1942*	*4. 7.1943* *Battery Commander* *1./Stu.Gesch.Abt.226*
Bauszus *Hans Dietrich* *16.9. 1918*	*Oberleutnant* *EK II: 13. 8. 1941* *EK I: 1. 9. 1941*	*24. 4. 1944* *Acting Commander* *2./Stu.Gesch.Brig.239*
Bayer *Rudolf* *21. 5. 1919*	*Oberleutnant* *EK II:: 23. 7.1941* *EK I: 11. 9. 1942*	*3. 10. 1944* *Battery Commander* *1./Stu.Gesch.Brig. 202*
Becker *Alfred* *20. 8. 1899*	*Oberleutnant* *EK II:: 18. 5. 1940 (Spange)* *EK I: 3. 6. 1940(Spange)*	*13. 5.1942* *Battery Commander* *15. (Stu.Gesch.)/Art.Regt.227*
Becker *Heinrich* *20. 4. 1913*	*Leutnant* *EK II: 21. 8. 1943* *EK I: 7. 3. 1944*	*8. 2. 1945* *Section Leader* *Sturm-Panzer-Abteilung 219*
Becker *Herbert* *19. 9. 1914*	*Hauptmann der Reserve* *EK II: 23. 9.1941* *EK I: 11. 10. 1941*	*8. 3. 1945* *Battery Commander* *1./He. Stu. Gesch. Brig. 244*
Becker *Willy* *2.8. 1914*	*Oberwachtmeister* *EK II: 17. 8.1941* *EK I: 16. 9. 1942*	*4.2. 1944* *Section Leader* *2./Stu.Gesch.Abt. „GD"*
Beise *Walter* *3. 8.1918*	*Leutnant der Reserve* *EK II: 13. 7. 1941* *EK I: 16. 9. 1941*	*25. 10. 1943* *Battery Commander* *2./Stu.Gesch.Abt. 904*
Bender *Dieter* *23. 6. 1917*	*Oberleutnant* *EK II: 14. 4. 1941* *EK I: 28. 8. 1941*	*1. 12. 1943* *Battery Commander* *3./Stu. Gesch. Abt. 190*
Beneckendorff *Wolf* *10. 7. 1915*	*Oberwachtmeister* *EK II: 12. 3. 1943* *EK I: 16. 10. 1943*	*4. 9. 1944* *Section Leader* *2./Stu. Gesch. Brig. 210*
Benz *Ernst* *3. 5. 1915*	*Hauptmann* *EK II: 18. 11. 1939* *EK I: 15. 6. 1941*	*17. 3. 1944* *Commander* *Stu.Gesch.Abt. 242*

Berg Alwin 5. 12. 1918	Unteroffizier EK II: 13. 10. 1942 EK I: 28. 1. 1943	14. 5. 1944 1./Stu. Gesch. Brig. 237
Berger Helmut 22. 11. 1915	Leutnant der Reserve EK II: 29.11.1939 EK I: 1. 7.1941	2. 4. 1942 Section Leader 3./Stu.Gesch.Abt. 210
Bergholz Karl 30. 9. 1903	Major EK II: 25. 5. 1940 EK I: 1. 6. 1940	19. 12. 1943 Commander Stu.Gesch.Abt. 270
Bergmann Fritz Gerhard 16. 8.1910	Unteroffizier der Reserve EK II: 26. 6.1940 EK I: 29.1. 1945	24. 4. 1945 Gun Commander 3./Führer-Pz.-Jäger-Abteilung 1
Berneis Herbert 19. 4.1915	Wachtmeister EK II: 15. 12. 1941 EK I: 17. 5. 1942	15. 4. 1944 Section Leader 2./Stu. Gesch. Brig. 242
Biberich Berthold 6. 5. 1914	Oberwachtmeister EK II: 17. 7. 1941 EK I: 20. 9. 1942	27.11.1944 Section Leader 1./Stu. Gesch. Brig. 201
Binder Erwin 21. 7.1913	Oberwachtmeister EK II: 16. 6. 1940 EK I: 8. 11. 1943	21. 10.1944 Section Leader 2./Stu. Gesch. Brig. 277
Bitsch Peter 12.10.1919	Leutnant der Reserve EK II: 5.11. 1943 EK I: 21. 11.1943	30. 11. 1944 Section Leader 1. /He. Stu. Gesch. Brig. 249
Bluttner Heinz 19.4. 1913	Oberleutnant der Reserve EK II: 1. 7.1941 EK I: 28. 7.1942	28. 5. 1944 Acting Commander 3./Stu. Gesch. Brig. 300
Börtitz Erich 6. 12.1915	Oberwachtmeister EK II: 1. 7. 1941 EK I: 19. 9. 1941	21.10.1943 1./Stu.Gesch.Abt. 203
Bohr Helmuth 16.5.1919	Wachtmeister EK II: 4.10. 1940 EK I: 20. 10. 1942	27. 1.1944 1./Stu.Gesch.Abt. „GD"
Bolte Hermann 28. 5.1922	SS-Obersturmführer EK II: 8. 3.1942 EK I: 17. 4.1942	2.6. 1944 Adjutant SS-Stu. Gesch. Abt. 2 „Das Reich"
Bonte Walter 17. 5.1918	Oberleutnant EK II: 30. 11. 1941 EK I: 7. 8. 1941	5. 11. 1942 Battery Commander 1./Stu. Gesch. Abt. 245
Brandner Josef („Brandner-Sepp")« 1. 9.1915	Hauptmann EK II: 14. 10. 1941 EK I: 26. 1. 1942	14. 9. 1943 Battery Commander 2./Stu.Gesch.Abt. 202
Braun Jobst Veit 19. 6. 1914	Major EK II: 2. 6. 1940 EK I: 19. 8. 1942	17. 3. 1944 Commander Stu.Gesch.Abt. 905

Braun *Josef Ludwig* *12.12.1919*	*Unteroffizier* *EK II: 24. 12.1941* *EK I: 15. 12.1942*	*4. 2. 1943* *Assault Gun Driver* *2. /Stu. Gesch. Abt. 667*
Brede *Rolf* *7.2.1915*	*Hauptmann* *EKII: 27. 6.1940* *EK I: 19. 9. 1941*	*14. 7.1944* *Commander* *Stu.Gesch.Abt. 236*
Brinke *Ulrich* *28.3. 1916*	*Oberleutnant* *EK II: 1939* *EK I: 13. 7. 1941*	*8. 1.1943* *Battery Commander* *1./Stu.Gesch.Abt. 197*
Bröcker *Bruno* *24. 5. 1921*	*SS-Obersturmführer* *EK II: 1941* *EK I: 30. 1. 1943*	*30. 12.1944* *Acting Commander* *3./SS-Stu. Gesch. Abt. 1 „LSSAH"*
Brockschmidt *Karl* *17. 8. 1914*	*Oberleutnant der Reserve* *EK II: 3. 8.1941* *EK I: 22. 8. 1941*	*20. 9. 1943* *Battery Commander* *3./Stu.Gesch.Abt. 232*
Brückner *Erich* *8.2. 1915*	*Oberwachtmeister* *EK II: 1. 5. 1941* *EK I: 13. 8.1941*	*12. 8. 1942* *Section Leader* *2./Stu. Gesch. Abt. 190*
Bruns *Hellmut* *27. 1.1915*	*Wachtmeister* *EK II: 25. 11. 1940* *EK I: 16.11. 1941*	*20.9. 1943* *2./Stu.Gesch.Abt. 236*
Buchwieser *Ludwig* *9. 7. 1915*	*Oberleutnant der Reserve* *EK II: 29. 6. 1941* *EK I: 8. 8. 1941*	*21. 4. 1943* *Battery Commander* *2./Stu. Gesch. Abt. 184*
Buckel *Karl* *20. 6.1920*	*Oberleutnant der Reserve* *EK II: 16.12. 1941* *EK I: 15. 10. 1942*	*2. 7. 1944* *Acting Commander* *3./Stu. Gesch. Brig. 277*
von Buddenbrock Freiherr *Wilhelm* *6.2. 1916*	*Oberleutnant* *EK II: 3. 7.1940* *EK I: 22. 7.1941*	*14. 1.1942* *Battery Commander* *2./Stu.Gesch.Abt. 185*
Buff *Walter* *9. 2.1917*	*Leutnant der Reserve* *EK II: 30. 4. 1941* *EK I: 27. 9. 1941*	*18. 6. 1942* *Section Leader* *3. /Stu. Gesch. Abt. 190*
Bumm *Karl Ernst* *26. 5.1915*	*Oberleutnant* *EK II: 30. 6. 1940* *EK I: 2. 7. 1941*	*19. 1. 1942* *Battery Commander* *2./Stu.Gesch.Abt.226*
Burckhardt *Walter* *8.2. 1919*	*Oberleutnant* *EK II: 20. 6. 1940* *EK I: 24. 6. 1940*	*15. 12.1943* *Acting Commander* *3./Stu.Gesch.Abt. 277*
Burk *Heinz* *14.2.1920*	*Leutnant* *EK II: 28. 6.1941* *EK I: 29. 1.1943*	*28. 4. 1944* *Acting Commander* *2. /Stu. Gesch. Abt. 236*
Butzlaff *Willy* *22.11.1912*	*Stabswachtmeister* *EK II: 9. 7. 1940* *EK I: 25. 8. 1942*	*20. 8.1943* *Section Leader* *1./Stu.Gesch.Abt. 244*

Cornelias Frank 11. 9. 1914	*Oberleutnant EK II: ? EK I: 9. 7. 1941*	*7. 2.1943 Battery Commander 1./Stu.Gesch.Abt. 201*
Cremer Herbert 28.3.1916	*Oberleutnant der Reserve EK II: 11. 8.1941 EK I: 18. 11. 1941*	*21. 12.1942 Section Leader 1./Stu.Gesch.Abt. 201*
Dahle Hermann 1. 4.1914	*Oberwachtmeister EK II: 26. 8. 1941 EK I: 5. 1. 1942*	*20. 11.1942 1./Stu.Gesch.Abt. 667*
Dahms Paul 28. 5.1913	*Oberleutnant EK II: 9. 6.1940 EK I: 24. 12. 1943*	*21. 7. 1944 Battery Commander 1./Stu.Gesch.Brig. 286*
Dee Walter 8. 12. 1920	*Wachtmeister der Reserve EK II: 20. 3. 1942 EK I: 9. 12. 1942*	*8. 2. 1945 Section Leader 3./Stu.Gesch.Brig. 184*
Diehl Gerhard 6. 2. 1917	*Oberwachtmeister EK II: 16. 8. 1942 EK I: 1.12. 1942*	*13. 12. 1944 2./He.Stu.Art.Brig. 667*
Diesinger Albert 29.1. 1920	*Oberleutnant der Reserve EK II: 13. 10. 1941 EK I: 14. 5. 1942*	*11. 4. 1944 Acting Commander 2. /Stu. Gesch. Abt. 244*
Graf zu Dohna Konstantin 13. 4.1912	*Hauptmann EK II: 29. 10. 1939 EK I: 18. 9. 1940*	*10.2. 1945 Battery Commander 3. /Stu. Art. Lehr. Brig. 111*
Drewes Klaus 5. 7. 1905	*Oberleutnant EK II: 4. 10. 1940 EK I: 10. 7. 1941*	*20. 7. 1942 Section Leader 16. (Stu.Gesch.)/Inf.Reg. „GD"*
Dreyer Günther 20. 9.1913	*Leutnant der Reserve EK II: 12. 6. 1940 EK I: 25. 6. 1940*	*29. 1. 1942 Section Leader 2./Stu.Gesch.Abt. 226*
Egghardt Alfred 17.2. 1920	*Leutnant derReserve EK II: 28. 7. 1941 EK I: 24. 12. 1943*	*4. 9.1944 Section Leader 2./Stu.Gesch.Brig. 912*
Engelhardt Kurt 25. 3. 1914	*Oberwachtmeister der Reserve EK II: 8. 2. 1943 EK I: 17. 12. 1943*	*30.12.1944 Section Leader 2./Stu.Gesch.Brig. 232*
Engelmann Richard 30.12.1919	*Oberleutnant EK II: 17. 6. 1940 EK I: 13.11. 1941*	*23.2. 1944 Battery Commander 1./le.Stu.Gesch.Abt. 912*
Erdweg Anton 8. 1. 1923	*Oberleutnant EK II: 7. 10. 1943 EK I: 22. 8.1944*	*22. 3. 1945 Battery Commander 2./Stu.Gesch.Brig. 276*
Essigke Gerhard 19. 8.1916	*Hauptmann EK II: 12. 9.1939 EK I: 24. 8. 1940*	*7. 8. 1944 Commander Stu.Gesch.Brig. 202*

Etz *Ernst* *16. 3.1914*	*Oberwachtmeister* *EK II: 7. 10.1941* *EK I: 16. 12. 1941*	*9.4. 1943* *Gun Commander* *2./Stu.Gesch.Abt. 189*
Evers Dr. *Helmuth* *15. 6. 1910*	*Oberleutnant* *EK II: 13. 10.1941* *EK I: 26. 12. 1941*	*11.4. 1944* *Adjutant* *Stu. Gesch. Abt. 189*
Fechtel *Walter* *11.2. 1913*	*Wachtmeister* *EK II: 17. 7. 1942* *EK I: 24. 8. 1942*	*(353/26) 9. 4. 1943* *3./Stu.Gesch.Abt. 189*
Feldkamp *Heinrich* *14. 8.1913*	*Feldwebel* *EK II: 30. 5.1940* *EK I: 7. 9. 1941*	*6. 1. 1942* *Section Leader* *11./Inf.-Regt. 453*
Feiler *Wolfgang* *15. 5. 1920*	*Oberleutnant* *EK II: 3. 7. 1941* *EK I: 2. 9. 1941*	*3. 8.1943* *Battery Commander* *3./Stu.Gesch.Abt. 909*
Feustel *Otto* *7. 6. 1921*	*Unteroffizier* *EK II: 26. 12. 1941* *EK I: 12. 10. 1942*	*1. 6.1944* *1./Stu.Gesch.Brig. „GD"*
Fiebig *Walter* *26. 1. 1913*	*Wachtmeister* *EK II: 4. 7.1941* *EK I: 18. 2. 1943*	*30. 9. 1944* *Section Leader* *1./He.Stu.Gesch.Brig. 301*
Fischer *Johann* *16. 1.1921*	*Obergefreiter* *EK II: 19. 2.1943* *EK I: 25. 2. 1944*	*18. 3. 1945* *Gun Commander* *3. /Stu. Gesch. Brig. 202*
Flachs *Bernhard* *2. 4. 1915*	*Hauptmann* *EK II: 5. 10. 1939* *EK I: 31. 5. 1940*	*24. 5. 1942* *Battery Commander* *6./Artillerie-Regiment (mot.) 14*
Focht *Walter* *18. 7.1920*	*Leutnant der Reserve* *EK II: 15. 7. 1943* *EK I: 31. 7. 1943*	*5.3. 1944* *Section Leader* *3./le.Stu.Gesch.Abt. 911*
Frank *Ernst* *11. 5. 1910*	*Hauptmann* *EK II: 24. 10. 1939* *EK I: 9. 9. 1942*	*13. 1. 1945* *Battery Commander* *3. /Stu. Gesch. Brig. 209*
Franke *Paul* *7.3. 1913*	*Hauptmann* *EK II: 14. 10. 1941* *EK I: 23. 7. 1942*	*14. 9. 1943* *Commander* *Stu.Gesch.Abt. 232*
Frantz *Peter* *24. 7. 1917*	*Oberleutnant* *EK II: 8. 11. 1939* *EK I: 3. 7. 1940*	*19. 1. 1942* *Gun Commander* *16. (Stu.Gesch.)/Inf.Reg. „GD"*
Frosch *Horst* *18. 12. 1919*	*Oberleutnant der Reserve* *EK II: 28. 7. 1941* *EK I: 29. 9. 1941*	*10. 1. 1944* *Battery Commander* *2./Stu.Gesch.Abt.244*
Gaa *Karl* *12. 5.1916*	*Leutnant der Reserve* *EK II: 12. 12. 1942* *EK I: 1. 8. 1944*	*22. 3. 1945* *Ordonnanz-Offizier* *Stu. Gesch. Brig. 279*

Gaschnitz	*SS-Obersturmführer*	*2. 10. 1943*
Ernst	*EK II: 2. 7. 1940*	*Acting Commander*
25.6. 1921	*EK I: 18. 2. 1942*	*1./Stu.Gesch.Abt. „LSSAH"*
Gedamke	*Leutnant*	*23. 11. 1944*
Georg	*EK II: 15. 9.1942*	*Section Leader*
26. 8.1919	*EK I: 12. 2. 1943*	*2./He.Stu.Gesch.Brig. 393*
Gemba	*Oberwachtmeister*	*16. 1.1944*
Albrecht	*EK II: 15. 3.1942*	*Section Leader*
23.2.1914	*EK I: 26. 2. 1943*	*3./Stu.Gesch.Abt. 191*
Gerlach	*SS-Untersturmführer*	*2. 7. 1944*
Karl	*EK II: 3. 6.1940*	*Section Leader*
9.12.1914	*EK I: 14. 7. 1940*	*SS-Stu. Gesch. Battr. „Das Reich"*
Gerlitz	*Leutnant der Reserve*	*1. 4. 1942*
Günter	*EK II: 4. 7.1941*	*Section Leader*
29.4.1914	*EK I: 25. 7. 1941*	*2. /Stu. Gesch. Abt. 243*
Giebel	*Fahnenjunker-Wachtmeister*	*22. 9.1943*
Heinz	*EK II: 23. 7.1941*	
15. 7. 1920	*EK I: 28. 8. 1942*	*1./Stu.Gesch.Abt. 249*
Giese	*Leutnant der Reserve*	*21.2. 1944*
Eberhard	*EK II: 12. 9.1941*	*Acting Commander*
11.6. 1921	*EK I: 28. 10.1943*	*3./Stu.Gesch.Abt. 190*
Glaumann	*Oberwachtmeister*	*30. 11. 1944*
Heinrich	*EK II: 8. 12. 1941*	*Section Leader*
2. 10. 1920	*EK I: 30. 4. 1942*	*1./Stu.Gesch.Brig. 276*
Gloger Dr.	*Major*	*26. 9. 1942*
Paul	*EK II: 23. 12. 1939 (Spange)*	*Commander*
2. 4. 1896	*EK I: 11. 8. 1941*	*Stu.Gesch.Abt. 244 (mot.)*
Glossner	*Major*	*7. 9.1944*
Friedrich	*EK II: 2. 10.1939*	*Commander*
17. 5. 1916	*EK I: 22. 1. 1942*	*Stu.Gesch.Brig. 185*
Göring	*Oberleutnant*	*19. 12. 1941*
Helmut	*EK II: 17. 6. 1940*	
3. 3. 1911	*EK I: 26. 6. 1941*	*Stu. Gesch.Abt. 191*
Götte	*Obergefreiter*	*4. 2. 1943*
Heinrich	*EK II: 23. 9.1942*	*Ladekanonier-Funker*
14. 10. 1921	*EK I: 15. 12. 1942*	*2./Stu.Gesch.Abt. 667*
Gogoll	*Oberwachtmeister*	*20. 6.1944*
Walter	*EK II: 16. 9. 1942*	*Section Leader*
22. 12. 1916	*EK I: 3. 10. 1943*	*2. /Stu. Gesch. Brig. „Großdeutschland"*
Graap	*Oberwachtmeister*	*24. 8.1943*
Herbert	*EK II: 8. 11.1941*	*Gun Commander*
2. 12. 1914	*EK I: 24. 9. 1942*	*2./Stu.Gesch.Abt. 244*
Graggo	*Wachtmeister*	*21. 10. 1944*
Roman	*EK II: 1. 8.1941*	*Gun Commander*
10. 7.1920	*EK I: 31. 7. 1943*	*3. /Stu. Gesch. Brig. 226*

Grau *Friedrich Wilhelm* *11. 3. 1916*	*SS-Obersturmführer* *EK II: 20. 10. 1941* *EK I: 10.1. 1942*	*16. 9. 1943* *Acting Commander* *1. /SS-Stu. Gesch. Abt. „Das Reich"*
Greib *Philipp* *13. 10. 1919*	*Oberwachtmeister* *EK II: 19. 8. 1941* *EK I: 10. 1. 1942*	*30. 9. 1944* *Gun Commander* *2. /He. Stu. Gesch. Brig. 190*
Großkreutz *Friedrich* *9. 7. 1901*	*Hauptmann* *EK II: 12. 6. 1940* *EK I: 15. 7. 1940*	*27. 10. 1941* *Commander* *I./Art.Regt. 196*
Grünert *Anton* *11. 10. 1917*	*Leutnant der Reserve* *EK II: 26. 6. 1941* *EK I: 24. 8. 1941*	*27. 8. 1942* *Section Leader* *3./Stu.Gesch.Abt.201*
Gudernatsch *Wilhelm* *15. 8.1919*	*Oberleutnant* *EK II: 13. 9.1941* *EK I: 9. 9. 1943*	*24. 4. 1944* *Battery Commander* *3./Stu.Gesch.Brig. 239*
Haaf *Anton* *31. 8. 1921*	*Unteroffizier der Reserve* *EK II: 16. 12.1941* *EK I: 24. 8. 1942*	*12. 3.1944* *2. /Stu. Gesch. Abt. 189*
Haar *Kurt* *26. 7. 1915*	*Oberwachtmeister der Reserve* *EK II: 24. 1. 1942* *EK I: 26. 1. 1944*	*22. 3. 1945* *Section Leader* *2. /He. Stu. Gesch. Brig.300*
Haarberg *Rudolf* *1. 7. 1899*	*Oberleutnant* *EK II: 5. 5. 1941 (Spange)* *EK I: 13. 5. 1941*	*6. 1. 1942* *Battery Commander* *3./Stu.Gesch.Abt. 191*
Haas *Robert* *25. 3. 1914*	*Oberwachtmeister* *EK II: 21. 7. 1941* *EK I: 24. 8. 1942*	*14. 3.1944* *Gun Commander* *1./Stu.Gesch.Abt. 244*
Haegele *Rudolf* *3. 5. 1920*	*Leutnant* *EK II: 25. 9. 1942* *EK I: 29. 11. 1942*	*(549/28) 29.3. 1944* *Gun Commander* *2./Stu.Gesch.Brig. 184*
Halbig *Alfons* *31. 1. 1918*	*Wachtmeister* *EK II: 28. 5. 1942* *EK I: 5. 10. 1942*	*14.3. 1944* *Gun Commander* *1./Stu.Gesch.Abt. 244*
Hammon *Erich* *18. 5. 1910*	*Hauptmann* *EK II: 21. 9. 1939* *EK I: 1. 10. 1939*	*26. 12. 1941* *Commander* *Stu.Gesch.Abt. 192*
Hanauer *Emil* *15.6. 1918*	*Unteroffizier* *EK II: 16. 2.1940* *EK I: 2. 9. 1942*	*21.10. 1943* *Stab* *Stu.Gesch.Abt. 189*
Handrik *Hans Eberhard* *8. 6. 1916*	*Hauptmann* *EK II: 12. 7. 1940* *EK I: 11. 10. 1941*	*11. 2. 1943* *Battery Commander* *3./Stu.Gesch.Abt. 202*
Handschuh *Heinz* *11. 2. 1918*	*Wachtmeister* *EK II: 2. 9. 1941* *EK I: 31. 12. 1941*	*28. 8.1943* *Gun Commander* *1./Stu.Gesch.Abt. „GD"*

Hanke *Wilhelm* *7. 8. 1912*	*Oberwachtmeister* *EK II: 14. 8. 1943* *EK I: 8. 9. 1943*	*28. 11.1944* *Section Leader* *3./He.Stu.Gesch.Brig. 904*
von Harder *Ernst* *4.1. 1910*	*Major* *EK II: 21. 9. 1939* *EK I: 19. 7. 1940*	*(552/5) 11. 4. 1944* *Commander* *Stu.Gesch.Abt. 600*
Hasdorf *Friedrich* *22. 11.1913*	*Leutnant der Reserve* *EK II: 16. 11.1939* *EK I: 21. 3. 1943*	*27. 4. 1945* *Gun Commander* *1./He.Stu.Gesch.Brig. 203*
Hecker *Gerhard* *18. 12.1918*	*SS-Hauptscharführer* *EK II: 1. 9.1941* *EK I: 15. 12. 1941*	*2. 7.1944* *Section Leader* *SS-Stu.Gesch. Battr./SS-Pz.* *Kampfgruppe „DR"*
Heederich *Hans* *22. 4. 1922*	*Leutnant der Reserve* *EK II: 30. 11.1941* *EK I: 14. 3. 1942*	*14. 3. 1944* *Adjutant* *Stu.Gesch.Abt. 185*
Heimann *Heinrich* *17.9.1915*	*SS-Hauptsturmführer* *EK II: 27. 5. 1941* *EK I: 14. 9. 1941*	*2. 9. 1943* *Commander* *SS-Stu. Gesch. Abt. „ LSSAH "*
Heimsath *Heinrich* *7. 10. 1912*	*Oberwachtmeister* *EK II: 17. 8.1941* *EK I: 6. 8. 1942*	*28. 8. 1943* *Section Leader* *2./Stu.Gesch.Abt. „GD"*
Heinzle *Hubert* *30. 9.1918*	*Oberleutnant* *EK II: 13. 5.1941* *EK I: 2. 8. 1941*	*14.2. 1943* *Battery Commander* *2. /Stu. Gesch. Abt. 191*
Heise *Hans Joachim* *28. 3. 1917*	*Hauptmann* *EK II: 26. 6. 1941* *EK I: 10. 10. 1941*	*15. 12. 1944* *Battery Commander* *2./Stu.Gesch.Brig.279*
Hensen *Rudolf* *17. 8. 1921*	*Leutnant der Reserve* *EK II: 15. 7. 1943* *EK I: 30. 7. 1943*	*14. 7.1944* *Acting Commander* *1./Stu.Gesch.Brig. 911*
Herbricht *Bernhard* *28.8.1913*	*Oberwachtmeister* *EK II: 1. 7.1941* *EK I: 30. 8. 1942*	*21. 10.1943* *Section Leader* *2. /Stu. Gesch. Abt. 667*
Herrmann *Kurt* *12.9. 1919*	*Oberwachtmeister* *EK II: 21. 5.1941* *EK I: 30. 7. 1943*	*28. 8.1944* *Section Leader* *2./Stu.Gesch.Brig. 280*
Hinske *Karl Heinz* *5. 9. 1915*	*Leutnant* *EK II: 24. 6. 1941* *EK I: 29. 6. 1941*	*5. 11. 1942* *Section Leader* *Stu. Gesch.Abt. 185*
Höller *Josef* *19. 5. 1915*	*Oberwachtmeister* *EK II: 19. 7. 1941* *EK I: 30. 3. 1943*	*28. 6.1944* *Section Leader* *2. /Stu. Gesch. Brig. „GD "*
Hoepfl *Helmut* *22. 1. 1920*	*Leutnant* *EK II: 17. 6. 1943* *EK I: 2. 9. 1943*	*5. 4. 1944* *Gun Commander* *1./Stu.Gesch.Brig. 301*

Höring *Hans* *1.4.1919*	*Oberleutnant* *EK II: 4. 7.1941* *EK I: 7. 12. 1942*	*15. 9. 1943* *Battery Commander* *3./Stu.Gesch.Abt. 245*
Holst *Otto* *24. 11.1921*	*SS-Obersturmführer* *EK II: 1. 9. 1941* *EK I: 30. 1. 1943*	*30. 12.1944* *Acting Commander* *1./SS-Stu.Gesch.Abt. 1 „LSSAH"*
Huber *Alfred* *19. 10. 1912*	*Leutnant* *EK II: 19. 9. 1941* *EK I: 15. 7. 1943*	*25. 3. 1944* *Acting Commander* *2./Stu.Gesch.Abt. 244*
Huffmann *Heinz* *29.12. 1905*	*Major* *EK II: 29. 6. 1940* *EK I: 29. 12. 1940*	*27. 8. 1942* *Commander* *Stu.Gesch.Abt. 201*
Hummel *Maximilian* *22. 4. 1919*	*Leutnant der Reserve* *EK II: 20. 12. 1941* *EK I: 22. 9. 1943*	*17. 9. 1944* *Section Leader* *3./Stu.Gesch.Brig.259*
Huse *Herbert* *30. 5.1914*	*Oberwachtmeister* *EK II: 5. 9. 1940* *EK I: 23. 10. 1940*	*29.2. 1944* *Section Leader* *2./Stu.Gesch.Abt. 280*
Idel *Alfred* *23. 8. 1919*	*SS-Unterscharführer* *EK II: 25. 7. 1940* *EK I: 28. 8. 1941*	*14.4. 1943* *Gun Commander* *2./SS-Stu.Gesch.Abt. 2 „DR"*
Isbrecht *Wilhelm* *27. 2.1915*	*Wachtmeister* *EK II: 2. 10. 1941* *EK I: 23.12. 1942*	*14. 2.1943* *Gun Commander* *2. /Stu. Gesch. Abt. 185*
Jacobi *Paul* *18. 12.1915*	*Oberwachtmeister* *EK II: 19. 12. 1942* *EK I: 16. 9. 1943*	*15.12.1944* *Acting Commander* *2./Stu.Gesch.Brig. 202*
Jahnke *Herbert* *31.8. 1917*	*Oberfähnrich der Reserve* *EK II: 15. 1.1942* *EK I: 7. 11. 1943*	*28.2. 1945* *Section Leader* *2. /Pz. -Jäger-Abteilung 69*
Jansen *Gerhard* *20.1.1920*	*Leutnant der Reserve* *EK II: 9. 7.1941* *EK I: 21. 8. 1943*	*23. 11. 1944* *Section Leader* *2./Stu.Gesch.Brig.202*
Janzon *Erich* *31. 7. 1914*	*Oberwachtmeister* *EK II: 23. 7. 1941* *EK I: 21. 10. 1941*	*29.10.1943* *Section Leader* *1./Stu.Gesch.Abt. 667*
von Jena Freiherr *Carl Friedrich* *1. 10. 1916*	*Hauptmann* *EK II: 21. 6.1940* *EK I: 19. 7. 1941*	*30. 11. 1944* *Commander* *Stu.Gesch.Brig. 394*
Joost *Heinrich* *10. 12.1910*	*Stabswachtmeister* *EK II: 14. 8.1941* *EK I: 9. 12. 1941*	*28. 6.1944* *Section Leader* *1./Stu.Gesch.Brig. 278*
Kaden *Gerhard* *17.3.1915*	*Oberleutnant* *EK II: ?* *EK I: 11. 9. 1941*	*7. 2. 1943* *Adjutant* *Stu.Gesch.Abt.201*

Käppler *Erich* *22. 1. 1906*	*Major* *EK II: 1. 10. 1939* *EK I: 24.11. 1940*	*1. 11. 1943* *Commander* *Stu. Gesch.Abt. 177*
Kanitz *Günter* *7. 7. 1918*	*Leutnant* *EK II: 4. 1. 1941* *EK I: 3. 3. 1943*	*29. 10. 1943* *Section Leader* *3./Stu.Gesch.Abt. 190*
Kaspar *Gustav* *20. 4. 1914*	*Oberwachtmeister* *EK II: 12. 7. 1940* *EK I: 21. 2; 1942*	*10. 2. 1944* *Section Leader* *1. /Stu. Gesch.Abt. „GD"*
Kaufmann *Ludwig* *26. 6. 1917*	*Oberleutnant* *EK II: 1. 10. 1939* *EK I: 28. 9. 1941*	*22. 9. 1944* *Battery Commander* *2. /He. Stu. Gesch. Brig. 311*
Kaulbars *Joachim* *1. 5. 1922*	*Leutnant* *EK II: 1. 7. 1941* *EK I: 30. 8. 1941*	*3. 8. 1943* *Section Leader* *1./Stu.Gesch.Abt. 270*
Keishold *Siegfried* *13.6. 1915*	*Hauptmann* *EK II: 7. 10. 1941* *EK I: 5. 11. 1942*	*17. 12. 1943* *Commander* *Stu.Gesch.Abt.243*
Keller *Hermann* *14. 4. 1914*	*Oberwachtmeister* *EK II: 1. 11. 1941* *EK I: 23. 7. 1943*	*30. 9. 1944* *Section Leader* *Pz.-Jäger-Abteilung 69*
Kessler *Gottfried* *13. 5. 1917*	*Leutnant der Reserve* *EK II: ?* *EK I: 3. 3. 1943*	*26. 11.1943* *Section Leader* *3./Stu.Gesch.Abt. 270*
Kicherer *Heinz* *23. 4. 1922*	*Leutnant* *EK II: 26. 5. 1942* *EK I: 15. 9. 1943*	*2. 8.1944* *Acting Commander* *3./Stu.Gesch.Brig. 245*
Kienle *Hans* *4. 12.1915*	*Oberwachtmeister* *EK II: 1. 7.1941* *EK I: 5. 12. 1943*	*21. 10.1944* *Section Leader* *3./Stu.Gesch.Brig.259*
Klapperstack *Herbert* *4. 5. 1921*	*Leutnant* *EK II: 18. 10. 1941* *EK I: 15. 12. 1943*	*23. 5. 1944* *Acting Commander* *1./Stu.Gesch.Brig. 190*
Klawes *Kuno* *26.9. 1916*	*Oberwachtmeister* *EK II: 7. 8.1941* *EK I: 26. 9. 1943*	*14. 5.1944* *Section Leader* *1./Stu.Gesch.Brig.191*
Kleinschmidt *Gerhard* *5.3.1916*	*Oberleutnant* *EK II: 2. 10. 1941* *EK I: 17. 8. 1942*	*2. 8. 1944* *Battery Commander* *2./Stu.Gesch.Brig. 912*
Kleis *Gerhard* *28.4.1915*	*Wachtmeister* *EK II: 15. 2. 1942* *EK I: 9. 12. 1942*	*20. 7. 1943* *Section Leader* *3. /Stu. Gesch. Abt. 184*
Klingler *Helmut* *15. 10.1920*	*Leutnant* *EK II: 20. 4. 1943* *EK I: 31. 7. 1943*	*25. 3. 1944* *Stu. Gesch. Abt. 904*

Klute *Axel* *20. 4.1919*	*Hauptmann* *EK II: 2. 7.1940* *EK I: 10. 6. 1943*	*28. 5. 1944* *Battery Commander* *2./Stu.Gesch.Brig. 300*
Kneißl *Franz* *14. 10.1912*	*SS-Untersturmführer* *EK II: 28. 5.1941* *EK I: 27. 6. 1941*	*2. 1. 1942* *Section Leader* *SS-Stu.Gesch.Battr. „Reich"*
Knief *Albert* *17.3. 1917*	*Leutnant* *EK II: 23. 10. 1941* *EK I: 7. 9. 1943*	*13.12. 1944* *Acting Commander* *3./He.Stu.Gesch.Brig. 907*
Knüppel *Rolf* *10. 12.1917*	*Oberleutnant* *EK II: 2. 7.1941* *EK I: 2. 7. 1941*	*11. 11. 1943* *Battery Commander* *2./Stu.Gesch.Abt.228*
Knapling *Ludwig* *He.Stu.Art.Brig. 667*	*Major*	*(/) 4. 5. 1945* *Commander*
Koch *Alfred* *21.2. 1920*	*Oberwachtmeister* *EK II: 30. 9. 1942* *EK I: 26. 9. 1943*	*12. 9. 1944* *Section Leader* *1./Stu.Gesch.Brig. 276*
Korf *Heinrich* *1. 4. 1915*	*Leutnant der Reserve* *EK II: 9. 11. 1941* *EK I: 20. 11. 1941*	*28. 2. 1942* *Acting Commander* *3./Stu.Gesch.Abt. 177*
Kornfeld *Wilhelm* *1.6. 1915*	*Leutnant* *EK II: 18. 6.1940* *EK I: 18. 10. 1941*	*3. 8. 1942* *Section Leader* *3./Stu.Gesch.Abt. 245*
Krag *Ernst* *20. 2.1915*	*SS-Obersturmführer* *EK II: 25. 7. 1940* *EK I: 6. 1942*	*9.4. 1943* *Acting Commander* *2./SS-Stu.Gesch.Abt. 2 „DR"*
Kranz *Rudolf* *27. 12. 1911*	*Hauptmann* *EK II: 14. 10. 1939* *EK I: 2. 8. 1941*	*28. 5. 1944* *Commander* *Stu.Gesch.Brig. 249*
Kreimel *Alois* *13.1.1915*	*Leutnant der Reserve* *EK II: 15. 10.1941* *EK I: 16. 1. 1942*	*21. 8. 1942* *Section Leader* *2./Stu.Gesch.Abt. 249 (mot)*
Kreutz *Gustav* *31.1. 1915*	*Oberwachtmeister* *EK II: 18. 3. 1943* *EK I: 3. 8. 1943*	*28. 6. 1944* *Section Leader* *2./Stu.Gesch.Brig. 243*
Krickser *Karl* *6. 10.1914*	*Feldwebel* *EK II: 13. 1.1941* *EK I: 13. 7. 1941*	*16. 6. 1944* *Stu.Gesch.Battr. 287*
Krieg *Gerhard* *24. 7.1915*	*Oberwachtmeister* *EK II: 2. 7. 1941* *EK I: 1. 9. 1941*	*6. 12.1943* *Section Leader* *1./Stu.Gesch.Abt. 243*
Kröhne *Wilhelm* *15. 8.1914*	*Hauptmann* *EK II: 19. 5. 1940* *EK I: 31. 8. 1940*	*1. 9. 1944* *Commander* *He.Stu.Gesch.Brig. 190*

Kroll *Paul* *29. 5. 1921*	*WachtmeisterderReserve* *EK II: 23. 9. 1941* *EK I: 28. 9. 1942*	*20. 1. 1945* *Gun Commander* *2./He. Stu. Gesch. Brig. 184*
Krupp *Arthur* *16. 12. 1917*	*Oberleutnant* *EK II: 1. 7. 1941* *EK I: 11. 9. 1941*	*20. 5. 1944* *Battery Commander* *3./Stu.Gesch.Brig. 210*
Kühn *Wolfgang* *27.2. 1917*	*Leutnant der Reserve* *EK II: 25. 2. 1944* *EK I: 25. 2. 1944*	*22.12. 1944* *Section Leader* *3. /Stu. Gesch. Brig. 202*
Kuhn *Leonard* *23.4.1919*	*Hauptmann der Reserve* *EK II: 1. 7.1940* *EK I: 17. 5. 1942*	*21.10. 1944* *Acting Commander* *He.Stu.Gesch.Brig. 904*
Kuntze *Eberhard* *31. 7. 1917*	*Hauptmann*	*21. 10. 1943* *Battery Commander* *2./Pz.-Jäger-Regiment656*
Kupczyk *Richard* *26.1.1917*	*Oberwachtmeister* *EK II: 6.12.1941* *EK I: 15. 11. 1942*	*23. 5. 1944* *Section Leader* *3./Stu.Gesch.Brig. 270*
Kutscher *Wilhelm* *13. 6.1920*	*Oberleutnant* *EK II: 21. 7. 1941* *EK I: 5. 2.1942*	*3. 10. 1944* *Battery Commander* *3. /He. Stu. Gesch. Brig. 242*
Lange *Bruno* *23. 10. 1911*	*Oberleutnant* *EK II: 23. 7. 1941* *EK I: 8. 8. 1941*	*13. 11. 1942* *Battery Commander* *1. /Stu. Gesch. Abt. 667*
Langèl *Dietrich* *18. 12. 1912*	*Major(a)* *EK II: 10. 11. 1939* *EK I: 30. 12. 1940*	*15. 4. 1945* *Commander* *He.Stu.Gesch.Brig. 210*
Lechens *Wilhelm* *16. 5.1914*	*Hauptmann* *EK II: 29. 6. 1941* *EK I: 13. 10. 1941*	*7. 10. 1943* *Battery Commander* *2./Stu.Gesch.Abt. 228*
Lembke *Wilhelm* *13. 4. 1915*	*Hauptmann* *EK II: 22. 6. 1940* *EK I: 16. 1. 1943*	*20.1. 1944* *Acting Commander* *Stu.Gesch.Abt. 203*
Leniger *Hermann* *28.11. 1912*	*Stabswachtmeister* *EK II: 3. 8. 1943* *EK I: 7. 11. 1943*	*29. 1. 1945* *Section Leader* *1. /He. Stu. Gesch. Brig. 236*
Liethmann *Günter* *10. 7. 1918*	*Oberleutnant* *EK II: 13. 10. 1941* *EK I: 14. 7.1942*	*31. 8.1943* *Battery Commander* *3./Stu.Gesch.Abt. 237*
Littmann *Ernst* *16. 11.1919*	*Oberleutnant der Reserve* *EK II: 14. 7.1941* *EK I: 21. 10. 1941*	*28. 8. 1943* *Section Leader* *1./Stu.Gesch.Abt. 667*
Maier *August* *12.9. 1914*	*Oberwachtmeister der Reserve* *EK II: 30. 6. 1941* *EK I: 4.10. 1941*	*20. 1.1945* *Section Leader* *2./Stu.Gesch.Brig. „GD"*

Maier *Walter* *16. 9.1919*	*Oberleutnant der Reserve* *EK II: 30. 6. 1941* *EK I: 9. 9. 1941*	*28. 5. 1944* *Acting Commander* *2./Stu.Gesch.Brig. „GD"*
Malzan *Friedrich* *13. 4.1920*	*Oberleutnant* *EK II: 4. 7. 1941* *EK I: 7.10. 1941*	*26. 9. 1942* *Acting Commander* *2./Stu.Gesch.Abt. 243*
Martin *Herbert* *21.11. 1909*	*Hauptmann* *EK II: 27. 6.1940* *EK I: 3. 12. 1942*	*26. 9. 1944* *Commander* *He.Stu.Gesch.Brig. 300*
Masurek *Karl Georg* *23. 1. 1920*	*Unteroffizier* *EK II: 21. 7. 1943* *EK I: 10. 2. 1944*	*10. 4. 1945* *3. /Stu. Gesch. Brig. 244*
Mathes *Josef* *4.2.1908*	*Oberwachtmeister* *EK II: 16. 6. 1941* *EK I: 14. 9.1942*	*25. 8. 1943* *Section Leader* *2./Stu.Gesch.Abt. 191*
Mathy *Otto* *3.4.1915*	*Oberleutnant* *EK II: 7. 10. 1941* *EK I: 16.12. 1941*	*21. 7.1944* *Battery Commander* *2./Stu.Gesch.Brig. 236*
Mayer *Franz* *15. 1.1920*	*Unteroffizier* *EK II: 26. 6. 1944* *EK I: 19. 3. 1945*	*8. 5. 1945* *Gun Commander* *3./Fallschirm-Stu.Gesch.Brig. 12*
Meigen *Friedrich Wilhelm* *16. 3. 1920*	*Oberfeldwebel* *EK II: 23. 9. 1941* *EK I: 18. 2. 1942*	*6. 9. 1943* *Section Leader* *2./schwerePz.Jg.Abtlg. 653*
Messerschmidt *Hans* *11.2. 1915*	*Oberleutnant* *EK II: 22. 6. 1941* *EK I: 20. 9. 1942*	*29. 8. 1944* *Battery Commander* *3./He.Stu.Gesch.Brig. 667*
Metzger *Karl* *28. 12. 1917*	*Leutnant der Reserve* *EK II: 29. 6. 1941* *EK I: 10. 8. 1941*	*18. 5. 1942* *Section Leader* *3./Stu.Gesch.Abt. 226*
Meyer Dr. *Georg* *6. 7. 1912*	*Oberleutnant der Reserve* *EK II: 29. 6. 1940* *EK I: 14. 10. 1941*	*12. 8. 1942* *Battery Commander* *Stu.Gesch.Abt.202*
Meyer *Gustav* *13.6.1913*	*Oberwachtmeister* *EK II: 29. 6. 1941* *EK I: 4. 2. 1942*	*11. 2. 1943* *Gun Commander* *2./Stu. Gesch.Abt. 184*
Michael *Brian* *8. 3.1916*	*Hauptmann* *EK II: 14. 6.1940* *EK I: 1941*	*16. 6. 1944* *Battery Commander* *1./Stu.Gesch.Brig. 184*
Michaelis *Wilhelm* *1.2. 1915*	*Oberwachtmeister(a)* *EK II: 5. 9. 1941* *EK I: 1. 7. 1942*	*28.4. 1945* *1./He.Stu.Gesch.Brig. 904*
Migge *Hans Joachim* *28.3. 1920*	*Leutnant* *EK II: 23. 12. 1940* *EK I: 2. 1. 1943*	*24. 4. 1943* *Section Leader* *Stu.Gesch.Abt. 228*

Mildenberger *Fritz* *25. 3. 1921*	*Oberleutnant* *EK II: 2. 7.1941* *EK I: 5. 11. 1941*	*7. 8.1944* *Battery Commander* *3./Stu.Gesch.Brig. 190*
Lubich von Milovan *Berndt* *7. 12. 1913*	*SS-Obersturmführer* *EK II: 9. 10. 1941* *EK I: 24. 1. 1942*	*9. 10. 1944* *Acting Commander* *3./SS-Pz.-Jg.-Abt. 3 „T"*
Mnich *Willi* *31. 7. 1918*	*Wachtmeister* *EK II: 18. 8.1941* *EK I: 30. 10. 1942*	*4. 10.1944* *Gun Commander* *1./Stu.Gesch.Brig. 277*
Mönch *Ernst* *23.9. 1915*	*Wachtmeister* *EK II: 14. 12.1941* *EK I: 29. 11. 1943*	*30. 9. 1944* *Section Leader* *3./Stu. Gesch.Abt. 177*
Moenig *Heinz* *21. 7. 1917*	*Hauptmann* *EK II: 21. 8. 1941* *EK I: 13. 11. 1941*	*4. 10.1944* *Battery Commander* *Stu.Gesch.Brig. 185*
Montag *Alfred* *15. 6. 1918*	*Oberleutnant* *EK II: 30. 7.1941* *EK I: 11. 2. 1942*	*3. 8. 1943* *Battery Commander* *2./Stu.Gesch.Abt. 909*
Mussack *Alfred* *25. 8. 1920*	*Wachtmeister der Reserve* *EK II: 11. 8.1941* *EK I: 25. 7.1943*	*16. 6. 1944* *Gun Commander* *1./Stu.Gesch.Brig. 210*
Muscheid *Rudolf* *10. 2.1917*	*SS-Oberscharführer* *EK II: 25. 7. 1940* *EK I: 15. 10. 1941*	*21. 5. 1943* *Section Leader* *Stu.Gesch.Battr./KGr. Fegelein*
Naether *Reinhard* *5. 1. 1914*	*Oberleutnant* *EK II: 27. 5. 1940* *EK I: 14. 4. 1941*	*16. 1.1942* *Battery Commander* *3./Stu. Gesch.Abt. 190*
Nävie *Alwin* *7. 7. 1920*	*Leutnant der Reserve* *EK II: 24. 9. 1941* *EK I: 1. 11. 1941*	*8.10. 1943* *Section Leader* *2./Stu. Gesch.Abt. 190*
Naßhan *Rupprecht* *19.12.1914*	*Wachtmeister* *EK II: 15. 10. 1941* *EK I: 4. 1. 1942*	*2. 9. 1943* *Gun Commander* *1./le.Stu.Gesch.Abt. 911*
Neusens *Albert* *22. 4. 1914*	*Oberwachtmeister* *EK II: 9. 10. 1941* *EK I: 16.10. 1941*	*27.11.1944* *Section Leader* *Stu.Gesch.Brig. 279*
Nicolai *Günther* *2. 2. 1914*	*Hauptmann* *EK II: 10. 7. 1941* *EK I: 9. 9. 1941*	*11. 4. 1944* *Battery Commander* *2./Stu.Gesch.Abt. 189*
Otto *Wolfgang* *28. 10. 1919*	*SS-Obersturmführer* *EK II: 27. 7. 1941* *EK I: 20. 8. 1941*	*12. 3.1944* *Acting Commander* *SS-Stu. Gesch. Battr. „DR"*
Pantel *Egon* *30. 12.1910*	*Oberleutnant* *EK II: 5. 10.1940* *EK I: 27. 6. 1941*	*2. 9. 1943* *Battery Commander* *1./Stu.Gesch.Abt. 191*

Paprotta *Gustav* *8. 12.1912*	*Fahnenjunker-Oberwachtmeister* *EK II: 12. 11.1942* *EK I: 20. 7. 1943*	*8.3. 1945* *Section Leader* *He.Stu.Gesch.Brig. 244*
Panl *Wilhelm* *26. 5. 1916*	*Wachtmeister* *EK II: 13. 3. 1942* *EK I: 4. 8.1943*	*9. 3.1945* *Gun Commander* *1./He.Stu.Gesch.Brig. 185*
Peitz *Gerhard* *8. 6. 1909*	*Major* *EK II: 3. 10. 1939* *EK I: 28. 8. 1941*	*12.11.1942* *Commander* *Stu. Gesch.Abt. 190*
Pelikan *Paul* *23. 10. 1918*	*Oberleutnant* *EK II: 2. 7. 1940* *EK I: 27. 6. 1941*	*2.1. 1942* *Battery Commander* *3./Stu.Gesch.Abt. 210*
Peterleitner *Ferdinand* *15.2. 1922*	*SS-Oberscharführer* *EK II: 8. 3. 1943* *EK I: 14. 7. 1943*	*30. 12. 1944* *Section Leader* *2./SS-Stu.Gesch.Abt. 1 „LSSAH"*
Plate *Helmut* *26. 6. 1915*	*Oberleutnant* *EK II: 2. 5. 1941* *EK I: 20. 7. 1942*	*22. 11.1943* *Acting Commander* *Stu.Gesch.Abt. 237*
Plath *Siegfried* *9. 11. 1914*	*Hauptmann der Reserve* *EK II: 27. 6.1942* *EK I: 12. 8. 1943*	*4. 9. 1944* *Battery Commander* *2./He.Stu.Gesch.Brig. 237*
Pötsch *Friedrich* *27. 7. 1907*	*Leutnant* *EK II: 12. 8. 1941* *EK I: 3. 8. 1943*	*29. 1.1945* *Acting Commander* *2./He.Sturm-Art.Brig. 236*
Pobanz *Hans* *10. 10.1922*	*Wachtmeister der Reserve* *EK II: 24. 12.1943* *EK I: 1. 8.1944*	*9. 5. 1945* *Gun Commander* *2./He.Stu.Gesch.Brig. 912*
Poorten *Heinrich* *8.6. 1921*	*Wachtmeister* *EK II: 20. 4. 1943* *EK I: 9. 2. 1944*	*28. 4.1945* *Gun Commander* *1./He.Stu.Gesch.Brig. 904*
Preis *Siegfried* *5.11.1912*	*Oberwachtmeister* *EK II: 20. 7. 1940* *EK I: 16.11. 1941*	*8. 12. 1942* *Gun Commander* *1./Stu.Gesch.Abt.202*
Prien *Hans* *2.9.1920*	*Unteroffizier* *EK II: 3. 8. 1942* *EK I: 10. 2. 1943*	*19. 8. 1944* *3./He.Stu.Gesch.Brig. 237*
Püttmann *Karl* *24. 4. 1916*	*Oberwachtmeister der Reserve* *EK II: 28. 7. 1941* *EK I: 13. 12. 1942*	*8. 3. 1945* *Section Leader* *1./He.Stu.Art.Brig. 667*
Puls *Erwin* *23.2. 1914*	*Oberwachtmeister*	*15. 4. 1945* *Section Leader* *3./Stu.Gesch.Brig. 277*
Pullich *Hans* *22. 8. 1917*	*SS-Hauptscharführer* *EK II: 1. 8. 1940* *EK I: 18. 2. 1942*	*2.9. 1943* *Section Leader* *2. /SS-Stu. Gesch. Abt. „ LSSAH"*

Rade *Hans Dietrich* *26. 6.1917*	*Hauptmann* *EK II: 11. 8. 1941* *EK I: 18. 5.1942*	*29. 10. 1943* *Battery Commander* *Stu.Gesch.Abt. 244*
Raich *Bruno* *14. 5.1916*	*Oberleutnant* *EK II: 9. 12. 1939* *EK I: 23. 9. 1941*	*14.1. 1942* *Battery Commander* *3./Stu. Gesch. Abt. 189*
Rasch *Walter* *14.10. 1918*	*Leutnant der Reserve* *EK II: 11. 2. 1942* *EK I: 22. 8. 1942*	*25. 10. 1943* *Section Leader* *3./Stu.Gesch.Abt. 232*
Raumer *Alfred* *23.2. 1921*	*Wachtmeister* *EK II: 4. 11. 1942* *EK I: 25. 7. 1943*	*16. 6. 1944* *Gun Commander* *1./Stu.Gesch.Brig. 210*
Rausch *Martin* *17.9. 1919*	*Leutnant* *EK II: 20. 6. 1940* *EK I: 22. 7. 1941*	*2. 4. 1942* *Section Leader* *2./Stu.Gesch.Abt. 184*
Reichmann *Walter* *17. 7.1920*	*Oberwachtmeister* *EK II: 3. 2. 1942* *EK I: 27. 7. 1943*	*28. 11.1944* *Section Leader* *1./He.Stu.Gesch.Brig. 249*
Reif *Anton* *11. 11.1914*	*Oberwachtmeister* *EK II: 5. 7. 1941* *EK I: 29. 7. 1942*	*27. 7. 1944* *Section Leader* *3./Stu.Gesch.Brig. „GD"*
Renotiere, de la *Gerald* *17.11.1917*	*Oberleutnant* *EK II: 6. 6.1940* *EK I: 2. 11. 1941*	*28. 7. 1942* *Battery Commander* *3. /Stu. Gesch. Abt. 197*
Rettlinger *Karl* *8.2. 1913*	*SS-Hauptsturmführer* *EK II: 12. 7. 1941* *EK I: 12. 7.1941*	*28. 3. 1943* *Battery Commander* *3. /SS-Stu. Gesch. Abt. „ LSSAH"*
Rieger *Franz* *21. 3.1914*	*Hauptmann* *EK II: 13. 6.1940* *EK I: 4. 2.1944*	*9. 10. 1944* *Battery Commander* *2./Stu.Gesch.Brig. 232*
Riehl *Wilhelm* *25. 5.1916*	*Oberwachtmeister* *EK II: 28. 2. 1943* *EK I: 9. - 7. 1943*	*15. 9. 1943* *Section Leader* *2./Stu.Gesch.Abt. 909*
Rieske *Kurt* *21. 10. 1912*	*Oberwachtmeister* *EK II: 1. 8. 1941* *EK I: 19. 5.1942*	*28. 6. 1944* *Section Leader* *3./Stu.Gesch.Brig. 325*
Robel *Heinz* *27. 6. 1923*	*Leutnant* *EK II: 25. 6.1941* *EK I: 27. 8. 1941*	*28. 5. 1944* *Section Leader* *2./Stu.Gesch.Brig. 243*
Roestel *Franz* *4. 5.1902*	*Hauptmann* *EK II: 15. 11. 1939* *EK I: 30. 7. 1941*	*26. 9. 1942* *Battery Commander* *1./Stu.Gesch.Abt. 244 (mot.)*
Roever Dr. *Liutpold* *12.3.1914*	*Oberleutnant der Reserve* *EK II: 14. 4.1941* *EK I: 28. 8. 1941*	*26. 6. 1942* *Acting Commander* *Stu. Gesch. Abt. 190*

Rohde *Ernst Dietrich* *23. 8.1916*	*Oberleutnant* *EK II: 11. 1.1941* *EK I: 9. 11. 1941*	*9. 10. 1942* *Battery Commander* *3./Stu.Gesch.Abt. 177(mot)*
Rowedder *Hans Kurt* *14. 9. 1919*	*Oberleutnant* *EK II: 4. 8. 1940* *EK I: 28. 2. 1942*	*22.3. 1945* *Battery Commander* *2. /He. Stu. Gesch. Brig. 244*
Rübig *Heinz* *16.5. 1915*	*Hauptmann der Reserve* *EK II: 7. 7.1940* *EK I: 3. 6.1942*	*28. 5. 1944* *Battery Commander* *1./Stu.Gesch.Brig. 243*
Ruf *Lorenz* *16. 4. 1917*	*Wachtmeister* *EK II: 25. 10. 1941* *EK I: 10. 3. 1944*	*7. 1. 1945* *Section Leader* *2./He.Stu.Gesch.Brig. 912*
Sajitz-Hermstein Dr. *Joseph Alfred* *15. 3.1912*	*Stabsarzt* *EK II: 8. 7.1940* *EK I: 25. 2.1942*	*8. 5. 1945* *Fallschirm-Stu.Gesch.Brig. 12*
Sausel *Adolf* *29. 7.1917*	*Oberwachtmeister* *EK II: 19. 8. 1941* *EK I: 13. 6. 1942*	*17. 12. 1943* *Section Leader* *2./Stu.Gesch.Abt. 276*
Schädlich *Werner* *4. 4. 1913*	*Oberwachtmeister* *EK II: 11. 5. 1940* *EK I: 17. 7. 1941*	*28. 2. 1942* *Section Leader* *3./Stu.Gesch.Abt. 190*
Schaelte *Otto* *9. 9.1920*	*SS-Oberscharführer* *EK II: 24. 9. 1941* *EK I: 1. 9. 1942*	*30. 12. 1944* *Section Leader* *3./SS-Stu.Gesch.Abt. 1 „LAH"*
Scharf *Heinz* *22. 4. 1920*	*Wachtmeister* *EK II: 13. 6. 1942* *EK I: 16. 2. 1943*	*28. 5.1944* *Section Leader* *3./Stu.Gesch.Brig. 202*
Schaufelberger *Ernst* *21.2.1921*	*Wachtmeister* *EK II: 17. 10. 1941* *EK I: 19. 8. 1942*	*12. 3. 1944* *Gun Commander* *2. /Stu. Gesch. Abt. 189*
von Schaumberg Freiherr *Heinrich* *18. 7.1913*	*Wachtmeister* *EK II: 15. 7.1941* *EK I: 23. 3. 1942*	*14. 5. 1944* *Gun Commander* *2./Stu.Gesch.Brig. 191*
Schaupensteiner *Paul Friedrich* *24. 12.1916*	*Major* *EK II: 3. 7.1941* *EK I: 20. 7. 1941*	*28. 6.1944* *Commander* *Stu.Gesch.Brig. 237*
Schenck *Heinz Walter* *5. 8. 1918*	*Oberleutnant* *EK II: 20. 9. 1939* *EK I: 6.10. 1939*	*13. 5. 1943* *Battery Commander* *2./Stu.Gesch.Abt. „GD"*
Scherer *Fritz* *26. 8. 1910*	*Oberleutnant* *EK II: 6. 12. 1941* *EK I: 30. 4. 1942*	*13. 11. 1942* *Battery Commander* *2./Stu.Gesch.Abt. 189*
Schimonek *Ernst* *22.10.1914*	*Wachtmeister* *EK II: 6. 8.1940* *EK I: 23. 9.1942*	*4. 2. 1943* *Gunner* *2./Stu.Gesch.Abt. 667*

Schlegl *Luitpold* *9.10.1921*	*Fahnenjunker-Wachtmeister* *EK II: 22. 3. 1943* *EK I: 16. 10. 1943*	*30. 8.1944* *Gun Commander* *2./Stu.Gesch.Brig. 210*
Schliessmann *Kurt* *6. 8. 1920*	*Leutnant der Reserve* *EK II: 29. 6. 1941* *EK I: 9. 8. 1941*	*5.4. 1943* *Section Leader* *Stab/Stu.Gesch.Abt. 226*
Schmähl *Günther* *21. 4. 1911*	*Oberleutnant der Reserve* *EK II: 4. 7. 1941* *EK I: 13. 11. 1941*	*19. 10. 1944* *Battery Commander* *3./Stu.Gesch.Brig.261*
Schmidhäuser *Erich* *31. 7.1916*	*Leutnant der Reserve* *EK II: 30. 7.1941* *EK I: 1. 1. 1942*	*24. 3.1945* *Section Leader* *3./Stu.Gesch.Brig. 259*
Schmidt *Ernst* *23. 10.1907*	*Major* *EK II: 2. 10. 1939* *EK I: 25. 8. 1940*	*10. 7.1943* *Commander* *Sturmgeschütz-Abteilung 184*
Schmidt *Fritz* *10. 2. 1914*	*Oberleutnant der Reserve* *EK II: 31. 10.1941* *EK I: 9. 11. 1941*	*8. 11. 1943* *Battery Commander* *2./Stu.Gesch.Abt. 177*
Schmidt *Fritz* *1. 5.1914*	*Oberleutnant der Reserve* *EK II: 31. 5.1940* *EK I: 27. 8. 1940*	*5. 5.1943* *Section Leader* *2./Stu.Gesch.Abt. 203*
Schmidt *Johann* *28. 12. 1922*	*Leutnant der Reserve* *EK II: 30. 8. 1943* *EK I: 27. 10. 1943*	*28. 9. 1944* *Section Leader* *3. /He. Stu. Gesch. Brig. 203*
Schmidt *Werner* *7. 4. 1924*	*Unteroffizier* *EK II: 7. 3. 1942* *EK I: 4. 4. 1943*	*20. 9. 1944* *Gun Commander* *1./Stu.Gesch.Brig. „GD"*
Schmidt *Wilhelm* *14. 2.1914*	*Oberwachtmeister* *EK II: 4. 10.1940* *EK I: 27. 9. 1941*	*29.11. 1942* *1/Stu.Gesch.Abt. „GD"*
Schmitt *Johann* *26. 4. 1915*	*Oberwachtmeister* *EK II: 11. S.1941* *EK I: 11. 10. 1942*	*26. 11. 1943* *Section Leader* *1. /Stu. Gesch. Abt. 210*
Schmock *Gert* *21. 6. 1913*	*Hauptmann* *EK II: 29. 6. 1941* *EK I: 27. 7. 1941*	*28. 4. 1945* *Commander* *He.Stu.Gesch.Brig. 394*
Schneider *Otto* *28. 9.1913*	*Oberwachtmeister* *EK II: 25. 6.1940* *EK I: 22. 7. 1943*	*26. 11. 1943* *Section Leader* *2. /Stu. Gesch. Abt. 600*
Schönberger *Georg* *21.2. 1911*	*SS-Sturmbannführer* *EK II: 1939* *EK I: 1939*	*26. 12. 1941* *Commander* *SS-Stu.Gesch.Abt. „LSSAH"*
Schönstedt *Ernst* *2. 10.1914*	*Wachtmeister* *EK II: 11. 7.1940* *EK I: 5. 1. 1943*	*11. 12. 1943* *Section Leader* *1./Stu.Gesch.Abt. „GD"*

Scholz Dr. Ing. *Werner* *9. 11. 1913*	*Leutnant* *EK II: 29. 6.1941* *EK I: 20. 5. 1942*	*26. 12. 1943* *Section Leader* *1./Stu.Gesch.Abt. 209(mot)*
Schammer *Jacob* *16. 9. 1913*	*Leutnant* *EK II: 21. 5. 1941* *EK I: 14. 10. 1941*	*9. 10. 1942* *Section Leader* *3./Stu.Gesch.Abt. 191*
Schrödel *Fritz* *29. 6. 1915*	*Oberwachtmeister* *EK II: 13. 7. 1941* *EK I: 26. 9. 1941*	*11. 4. 1942* *Section Leader* *1./Stu.Gesch.Abt. 197*
Schröder *Erich* *2.12. 1914*	*Major* *EK II: 26. 10. 1939* *EK I: 14. 9. 1941*	*13. 1. 1945* *Commander* *He.Stu.Gesch.Brig. 907*
Schröder *Ernst* *20.3. 1915*	*Oberwachtmeister* *EK II: 16. 5. 1943* *EK I: 3. 6. 1943*	*10. 8. 1944* *Section Leader* *3./St.Gesch.Brig. 232*
Schabert *Werner* *22.6.1920*	*Fahnenjunker-Oberwachtmeister* *EK II: 30. 9.1941* *EK I: 30. 6. 1942*	*30. 11.1944* *Section Leader* *1. /He. Stu. Gesch. Brig. 185*
Schatte *Friedrich* *11.9. 1915*	*Oberleutnant der Reserve* *EK II: 14. 6.-1940* *EK I: 28. 8. 1943*	*30. 8. 1944* *Battery Commander* *3./Stu.Gesch.Brig. 232*
Schulte-Strathaus *Hermann* *26. 4. 1917*	*Oberleutnant* *EK II: 4. 8. 1941* *EK I: 6. 8. 1941*	*9. 10.1942* *Battery Commander* *Stu.Gesch.Abt. 189*
Schulz *Alfons* *17. 3.1917*	*Oberleutnant der Reserve* *EK II: 18. 3.1941* *EK I: 19.8. 1943*	*8. 5. 1945* *Battery Commander* *Fallschirm-Stu.Gesch.Brig. 12*
Schwalb *Helmut* *17. 10. 1915*	*Oberleutnant* *EK II: 14. 4. 1941* *EK I: 21. 9.1943*	*20. 1. 1944* *Battery Commander* *1./Stu.Gesch.Abt. 190*
Seemann *Peter* *14. 4. 1917*	*Oberleutnant der Reserve* *EK II: 20. 7.1941* *EK I: 25. 11. 1941*	*14. 10. 1942* *Section Leader* *2./Stu.Gesch.Abt. 201*
Segieth *Bernhard* *9. 11. 1919*	*Wachtmeister* *EK II: 28. 9. 1939* *EK I: 6. 8. 1943*	*8. 11.1944* *Section Leader* *2./Stu.Gesch.Brig. „GD"*
Seidl *Josef* *6. 10. 1919*	*Unteroffizier* *EK II: 19. 8. 1942* *EK I: 29. 7. 1943*	*(575/11) 28. 5. 1944* *1./Stu. Gesch.Brig. 190*
Sekirka *Jan* *14. 1.1914*	*Hauptmann* *EK II: 3. 6.1940* *EK I: 22. 7. 1941*	*20. 6. 1944* *Commander* *Stu.Gesch.Brig. 301*
Sewera *Axel* *25. 8. 1918*	*Hauptmann* *EK II: 25. 9. 1939* *EK I: 29. 6. 1940*	*22. 9. 1944* *Acting Commander* *Stu.Gesch.Brig. 276*

Sichelschmidt *Herbert* *4. 7. 1909*	*Major* *EK II: 18. 6. 1940* *EK I: 21. 8.1941*	*17. 11. 1943* *Commander* *Stu.Gesch.Abt.210*
Siemers *Fritz* *5.7. 1916*	*Oberwachtmeister* *EK II: 5. 8.1941* *EK I: 5. 8. 1941*	*9.5. 1945* *Gun Commander* *2./Stu.Gesch.Lehr.Brig. 920*
Sing *Kurt* *14. 4.1920*	*Wachtmeister der Reserve* *EK II: 20. 4. 1942* *EK I: 16. 12. 1942*	*24. 7. 1943* *2./Stu.Gesch.Abt.249*
Sitzberger *Michael* *31. 12.1915*	*Wachtmeister* *EK II: 13. 6.1942* *EK I: 22. 10. 1943*	*27. 11. 1944* *Gun Commander* *3./Stu.Gesch.Brig. 202*
Sonnen *Hans* *20. 9. 1919*	*Unteroffizier* *EK II: 13. 10. 1941* *EK I: 8. 8. 1942*	*22.12. 1943* *Stu.Gesch.Abt. 201*
Sparn *Hugo* *21. 3. 1915*	*Leutnant* *EK II: 21. 10.1941* *EK I: 12. 2.1942*	*25. 1.1943* *Section Leader* *3./Stu.Gesch.Abt. 177*
Specht *Heinrich* *7. 12. 1914*	*Leutnant der Reserve* *EK II: 16. 7. 1941* *EK I: 30. 9. 1942*	*8. 11.1943* *Stu.Gesch.Abt. 177*
Spiecker *Karl* *29. 12. 1917*	*Oberwachtmeister* *EK II: 1.10.1941* *EK I: 25. 12.1941*	*23.4. 1944* *Section Leader* *3./Stu.Gesch.Brig. 245*
Spilok *Bernd* *13. 5.1917*	*Oberwachtmeister* *EK II: 9. 8.1940* *EK I: 16. 11.1941*	*16. 6. 1944* *Section Leader* *2./Stu. Gesch. Brig.210*
Sponsel *Heinrich* *24. 5.1914*	*Oberwachtmeister der Reserve* *EK II: 20. 8. 1942* *EK I: 12. 8. 1943*	*27. 7. 1944* *Section Leader* *3./Stu.Gesch.Brig. 202*
Spranz *Bodo* *1.1. 1920*	*Leutnant* *EK II: 26. 6. 1940* *EK I: 2. 7. 1941*	*6. 5. 1942* *Section Leader* *2./Stu.Gesch.Abt.185*
Stahlhacke *Gerhard* *3. 7. 1919*	*Oberleutnant* *EK II: 25. 10. 1943* *EK I: 10. 12. 1943*	*9. 3. 1945* *Battery Commander* *1./Stu.Gesch.Brig. 279*
Stamm *Ernst* *27. 9. 1911*	*Stabswachtmeister* *EK II: 13. 6. 1940* *EK I: 18. 7. 1941*	*10. 8. 1944* *Section Leader* *3./Stu.Gesch.Brig. 277*
Stangasinger *Ludwig* *29. 3.1920*	*Unteroffizier* *EK II: 13. 8.1944* *EK I: 4. 3. 1945*	*8. 5. 1945* *Fahrer* *1./Fallschirm-Stu. Gesch. Brig.12*
Stanneck *Eberhard* *27. 7. 1914*	*Oberleutnant der Reserve* *EK II: 18. 8. 1941* *EK I: 8. 9. 1941*	*7. 10. 1942* *Acting Commander* *2./Stu.Gesch.Abt. 189*

Stegmaier	*SS-Hauptscharführer*	*4. 6. 1944*
Alfons	*EK II: 29. 7.1940*	*Section Leader*
4. 10.1914	*EK I: 23. 2. 1942*	*3. /SS-Stu. Gesch. Abt. „DR"*
Steffen	*Oberwachtmeister*	*10. 5. 1943*
Hans	*EK II: 12. 7. 1941*	*Gun Commander*
13.10.1914	*EK I: 19. 8. 1941*	*3./Stu.Gesch.Abt. 185*
Steiner	*Leutnant*	*5. 11. 1942*
Wilhelm	*EK II: 7. 7. 1941*	*Acting Commander*
6. 5. 1914	*EK I: 30. 8. 1941*	*2./Stu.Gesch.Abt. 201*
Steinwachs	*Hauptmann*	*25. 3. 1942*
Heinz	*EK II: 21. 6. 1940 (Spange)*	*Commander*
5. 10. 1897	*EK I: 21. 4. 1941 (Spange)*	*Stu.Gesch.Abt.197*
Stier	*Hauptmann*	*15. 6. 1944*
Johannes	*EK II: 30. 6. 1940*	*Commander*
10. 7. 1915	*EK I: 30. 6. 1941*	*Stu.Gesch.Brig. 278*
Störmer	*Oberwachtmeister*	*9. 3. 1945*
Kurt	*EK II: 28. 6. 1944*	*Section Leader*
3. 3. 1915	*EK I: 27. 7. 1944*	*2./He.Stu.Gesch.Brig. 912*
Stollmann	*Oberleutnant*	*15. 12. 1944*
Albert	*EK II: 17. 7.1942*	*Battery Commander*
22. 7.1915	*EK I: 25. 2.1943*	*1./Stu.Gesch.Brig. 280*
Stack	*Oberleutnant*	*30. 11. 1944*
Friedrich	*EK II: 20. 7. 1941*	*Battery Commander*
27. 1. 1915	*EK I: 23. 9. 1941*	*3./Stu.Gesch.Brig.276*
Stuiver	*Unteroffizier*	*30.11. 1944*
Johannes	*EK II: 29. 6.1941*	
18. 8. 191	*EK I: 8. 7. 19419*	*2./Stu.Gesch.Brig. 259*
Sturm	*Oberwachtmeister*	*13. 12.1942*
Hermann	*EK II: 1. 5. 1941*	
17. 11. 1914	*EK I: 1. 8. 1941*	*2./Stu.Gesch.Abt. 190*
Susen	*Oberwachtmeister*	*11. 11.1943*
Gerhard	*EK II: 10. 8.1941*	*Section Leader*
30. 6.1913	*EK I: 10. 9. 1941*	*2./Stu.Gesch.Abt.245*
Tadje	*Oberwachtmeister*	*2. 7. 1942*
Fritz	*EK II: 30. 4. 1941*	*Acting Commander*
23.11. 1914	*EK I: 18. 8. 1941*	*1./Stu.Gesch.Abt. 190*
Taschka	*Wachtmeister*	*6. 1.1945*
Emil	*EK II: 13. 10.1943*	*Gun Commander*
22. 5.1916	*EK I: 23. 12.1943*	*3./Stu.Gesch.Brig. 276*
Telkamp	*SS-Obersturmführer*	*28.2. 1942*
Eberhard	*EK II: 6. 6.1940*	*Acting Commander*
8. 5.1914	*EK I: 24. 6. 1940*	*SS-Stu.Gesch.Battr. „Reich"*
Tenner	*Hauptmann*	*16.9. 1943*
Wolfgang	*EK II: 6. 12. 1939*	*Battery Commander*
22. 12.1915	*EK I: ?*	*3./Stu. Gesch.Abt. 191*

Teschke *Kurt* *26. 12. 1913*	*Hauptmann* *EK II: 12. 10. 1939* *EK I: 12. 7. 1941*	*7. 10. 1943* *Battery Commander* *Stu. Gesch. Abt. 189*
Thielert *Willi* *3. 1.1918*	*Oberwachtmeister* *EK II: 9. 9.1941* *EK I: 9. 12. 1943*	*9. 1. 1945* *Section Leader* *He.Stu.Art.Brig. 236*
Thiemann *Willi* *14. 6.1913*	*Oberwachtmeister* *EK II: 30. 6.1941* *EK I: 4. 8. 1941*	*4. 2. 1944* *Section Leader* *3./Stu.Gesch.Abt. 203*
Timpe *Heinz* *12. 10. 1923*	*Leutnant* *EK II: 26. 9. 1942* *EK I: 29. 10. 1943*	*28. 2. 1945* *Acting Commander* *1./He.Stu.Gesch.Brig. 300*
Tittmann *Joachim* *24. 2. 1920*	*Leutnant* *EK II: 1. 6. 1940* *EK I: 20. 8. 1941*	*30. 10. 1941* *Section Leader* *2./Stu.Gesch.Abt.245*
Tornau *Gottfied* *20.12. 1919*	*Oberleutnant* *EK II: 10. 7. 1940* *EK I: 9. 9. 1941*	*28. 5. 1943* *Battery Commander* *3./Stu.Gesch.Abt. 184*
Trispel *Horst* *23. 11.1919*	*Leutnant der Reserve* *EK II: 15. 7.1943* *EK I: 20. 7. 1943*	*3. 10. 1944* *Acting Commander* *2./Pz.-Jäger-Abteilung 69*
Truxa *Rolf* *6. 6. 1921*	*Oberleutnant* *EK II: 27. 8. 1941* *EK I: 18. 7. 1943*	*29. 10. 1943* *Acting Commander* *2./Stu.Gesch.Abt. 190*
Türke *Kurt* *7. 2. 1909*	*Hauptmann* *EK II: 3. 4. 1942* *EK I: 21. 6. 1942*	*20. 9. 1943* *Acting Commander* *Stu.Gesch.Abt. 904*
Twietmeyer *Ernst August* *9. 7. 1914*	*Hauptmann der Reserve* *EK II: 30. 11.1940* *EK I: 29. 7. 1943*	*3. 10. 1944* *Battery Commander* *He. Stu. Gesch. Brig. 185*
Ulbricht *Hellmut* *9. 1.1919*	*Hauptmann* *EK II: 13. 7. 1941* *EK I: 26. 9. 1941*	*3.12. 1944* *Battery Commander* *1. /Pz.-Jäger-Abteilung 653*
Urbanczyk *Rudolf Max* *3. 3. 1915*	*Oberwachtmeister* *EK II: 24. 7. 1941* *EK I: 17. 10. 1942*	*17. 9.1944* *Section Leader* *1./He.Stu.Gesch.Brig. 203*
Vaerst *Georg* *27. 7. 1916*	*Oberleutnant* *EK II: ?* *EK I: ?*	*15. 12. 1941* *Battery Commander* *1./Stu.Gesch.Abt. 191*
Verch *Hans Wilhelm* *19.2.1921*	*Oberleutnant* *EK II: 2. 7.1941* *EK I: 17. 9.1942*	*16. 1.1944* *Battery Commander* *2./Stu.Gesch.Abt. „GD"*
Vincon *Siegfried* *13. 6. 1917*	*Hauptmann der Reserve* *EK II: 25. 6. 1941* *EK I: 5. 11. 1941*	*27. 1.1945* *Battery Commander* *3./Stu.Gesch.Brig. 322*

Wagemann Friedrich 10. 12. 1916	*Oberleutnant der Reserve EK II: 12. 6. 1940 EK I: 6. 12. 1941*	*18. 6.1943 Battery Commander Stu.Gesch.Abt.228*
Wegner Wilhelm 21.10. 1914	*Oberfeldwebel EK II: 7. 7. 1940 EK I: 25. 7. 1940*	*1.4. 1942 Section Leader 16. (Stu.Gesch.)/Inf.-Reg. „GD"*
Wehmeyer August 29. 10. 1915	*Oberleutnant EK II: 30. 6. 1941 EK I: 27. 7. 1941*	*28. 8.1943 Battery Commander 3./Stu.Gesch.Abt. „GD"*
Weil Karl 10. 4.1923	*Leutnant der Reserve EK II: 15. 7. 1943 EK I: 21. 7.1943*	*17. 2. 1944 Stu.Gesch.Abt.244*
Weiß Anton 30.3. 1919	*Wachtmeister EK II: 11. 7.1941 EK I: 7. 3.1942*	*28. 8.1943 Gun Commander 1./Stu.Gesch.Abt. „GD"*
Wersig Heinz 20. 9. 1917	*Oberleutnant EK II: 22. 8. 1940 EK I: 5. 5.1941*	*27. 10.1941 Acting Commander 1./Stu.Gesch.Abt. 190*
Werwick Helmut 3.11.1914	*Wachtmeister EK II: 11. 10.1941 EK I: 19. 8. 1942*	*20. 9.1943 Gun Commander 2./Stu.Gesch.Abt. 236*
Westerkamp Otto 7.1.1920	*Wachtmeister EK II: 8. 2. 1942 EK I: 24. 7. 1943*	*3. 1. 1944 Section Leader 2./Stu.Gesch.Abt. 270*
Wiegels Hans Hennig 7. 7. 1915	*Hauptmann EK II: 30. 5. 1940 EK I: 24. 6. 1941*	*13. 9.1942 Battery Commander 1./Stu.Gesch.Abt.210*
Wieland Helmut 28. 7. 1918	*Unteroffizier EK II: 25. 10. 1941 EK I: 3. 2. 1942*	*27. 2. 1943 Gun Commander 1./Stu.Gesch.Abt. 226*
Wiesemann Emil 11. 9.1914	*SS-Hauptscharführer EK II: 15. 9.1940 EK I: 12. 7. 1941*	*28. 3.1943 Battery Commander 2. /SS-Stu. Gesch. Abt. „LSSAH"*
Willenbacher Rupprecht 3. 1. 1915	*Oberwachtmeister EK II: 20. 7.1941 EK I: 30. 7. 1941*	*16. 1. 1944 Section Leader 2./Stu. Gesch.Abt. 191*
Windmüller Herbert 10. 6.1918	*Wachtmeister EK II: 4. 9.1941 EK I: 30. 1. 1943*	*16. 11. 1943 Section Leader 3./Stu.Gesch.Abt. 190*
Wölfle Maximilian 12.10. 1919	*Oberleutnant der Reserve EK II: 18. 8. 1942 EK I: 30. 8. 1942*	*16. 1.1944 Battery Commander 3./Stu.Gesch.Abt. 667*
Wörner Theo 18.12.1914	*Oberwachtmeister EK II: ? EK I: 17. 7. 1942*	*21. 12. 1942 2./Stu.Gesch.Abt. 189*

Wohlfarth *Werner* *19. 1. 1914*	*Oberleutnant der Reserve* *EK II: 20. 4. 1944* *EK I: 30. 8. 1944*	*15. 4. 1945* *Battery Commander* *1./Stu.Gesch.Brig. 259*
Wolter *Erwin* *2.12.1914*	*Oberleutnant* *EK II: 15. 10. 1941* *EK I: 15. 7. 1941*	*26. 11.1943* *Battery Commander* *3./Stu.Gesch.Abt. 189*
Zahl *Christoph* *1.5.1919*	*Oberleutnant der Reserve* *EK II: 7. 2.1942* *EK I: 22. 10. 1942*	*28. 6. 1944* *Battery Commander* *3./Stu.Gesch.Brig. 286*
Zeidler *Johann* *27. 1. 1922*	*Leutnant der Reserve* *EK II: 8. 2. 1943* *EK I: 22. 7.1944*	*9. 3. 1945* *Section Leader* *He. Stu. Gesch. Brig. 244*
Zettler *Rudolf* *19. 5.1916*	*Hauptmann* *EK II: 10. 10. 1939* *EK I: 10. 5. 1940*	*14. 2.1943* *Acting Commander* *Stu.Gesch.Abtl. 667*
Zillmann *Erich* *10. 1. 1912*	*Stabswachtmeister* *EK II: 30.11. 1941* *EK I: 20. 8. 1942*	*23.2. 1944* *Section Leader* *3./Stu.Gesch.Abt.245*
Zimmer *Fritz* *25. 7. 1916*	*Oberwachtmeister* *EK II: 1. 9. 1942* *EK I: 6. 8. 1943*	*2. 5. 1944* *Section Leader* *2. /Stu. Gesch. Brig. 600*
Zimmermann *Rolf* *26. 6. 1920*	*Leutnant der Reserve* *EK II: 27. 6.1941* *EK I: 21. 3. 1944*	*18. 3. 1945* *Acting Commander* *Stu. Gesch. Brig. 909*
Zimoch *Johannes* *15. 1.1908*	*Oberwachtmeister* *EK II: 3. 7. 1941* *EK I: 24. 12. 1941*	*15.4. 1945* *Section Leader* *3./Stu.Gesch.Brig. 277*
Zollenkopf *Martin* *28.10.1921*	*Hauptmann* *EK II: 17. 9.1941* *EK I: 30. 8. 1942*	*8.2. 1945* *Battery Commander* *3. /He. Stu. Gesch. Brig. 202*

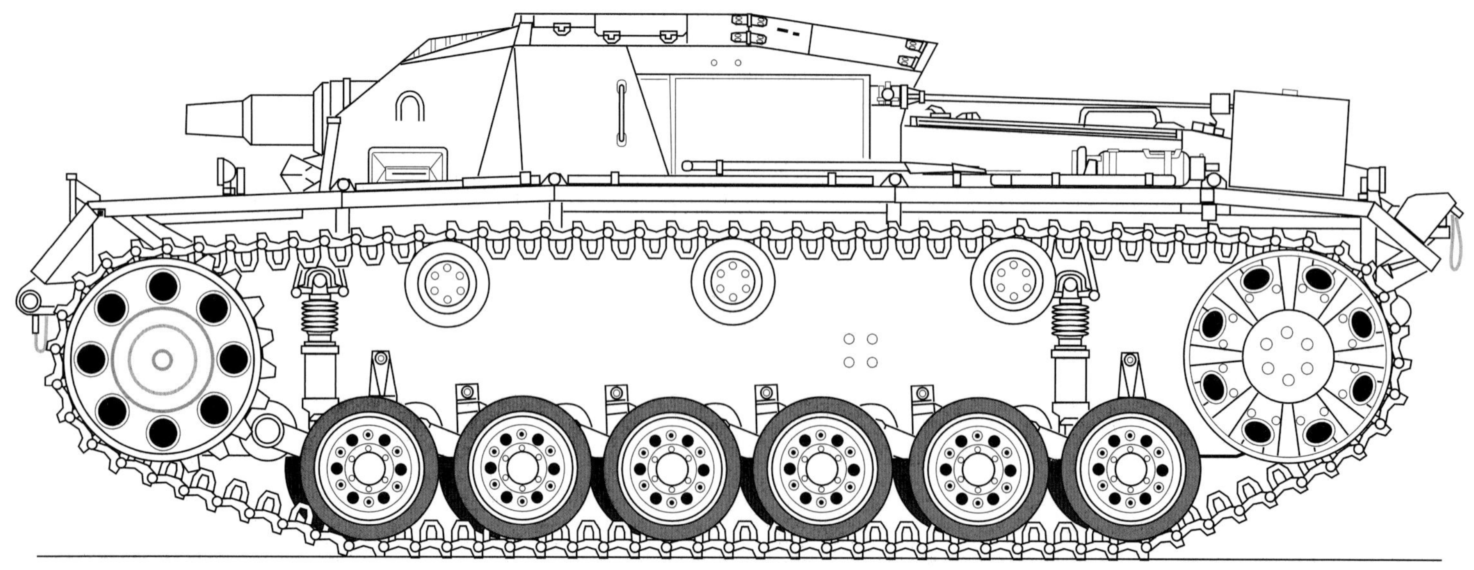

Sturmgeschütz III, Ausführung A

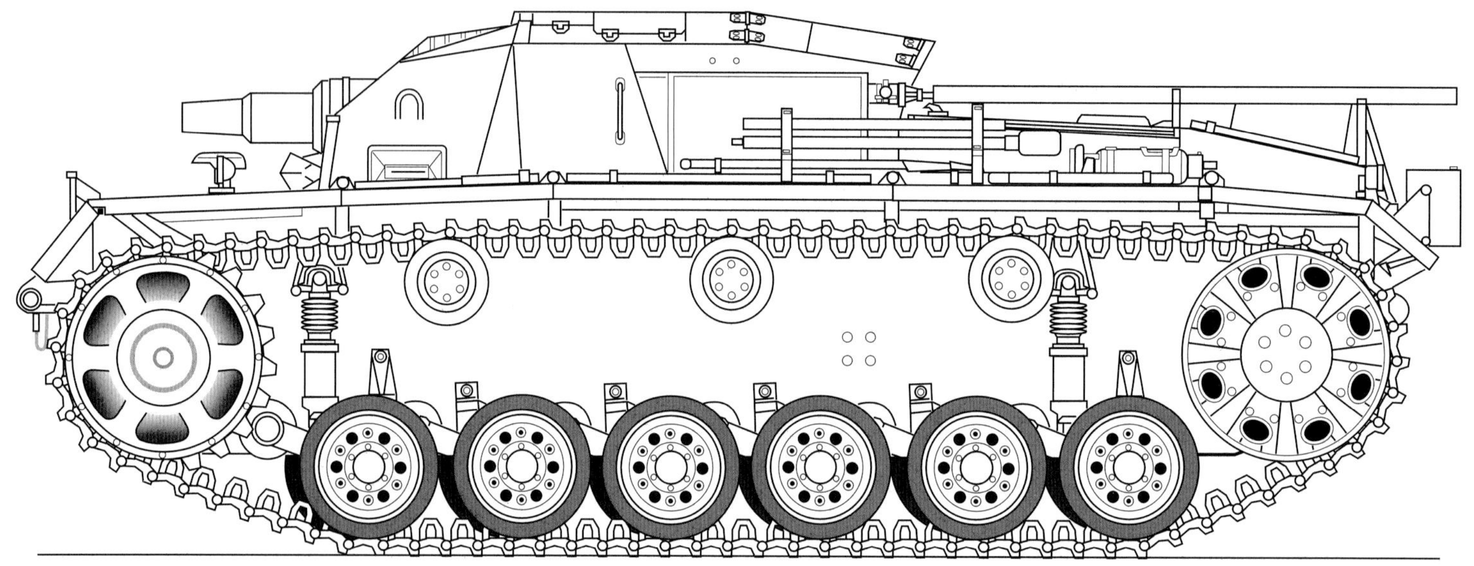

Sturmgeschütz III, Ausführung B

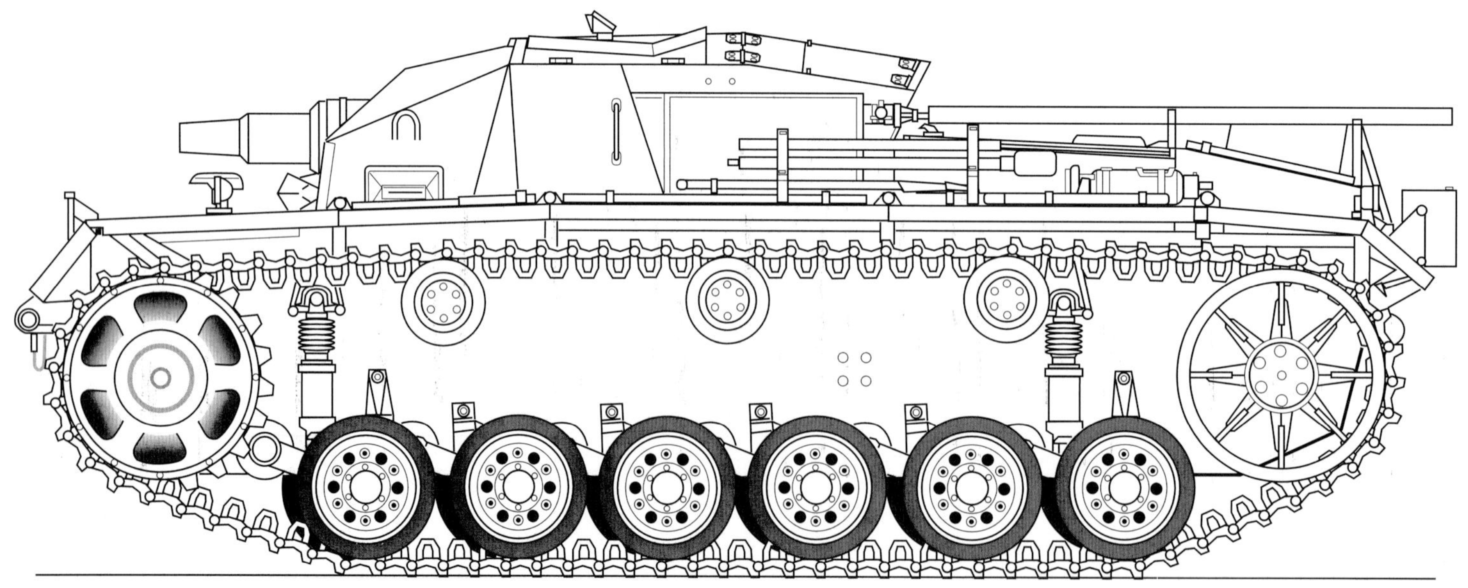

Sturmgeschütz III, Ausführung C

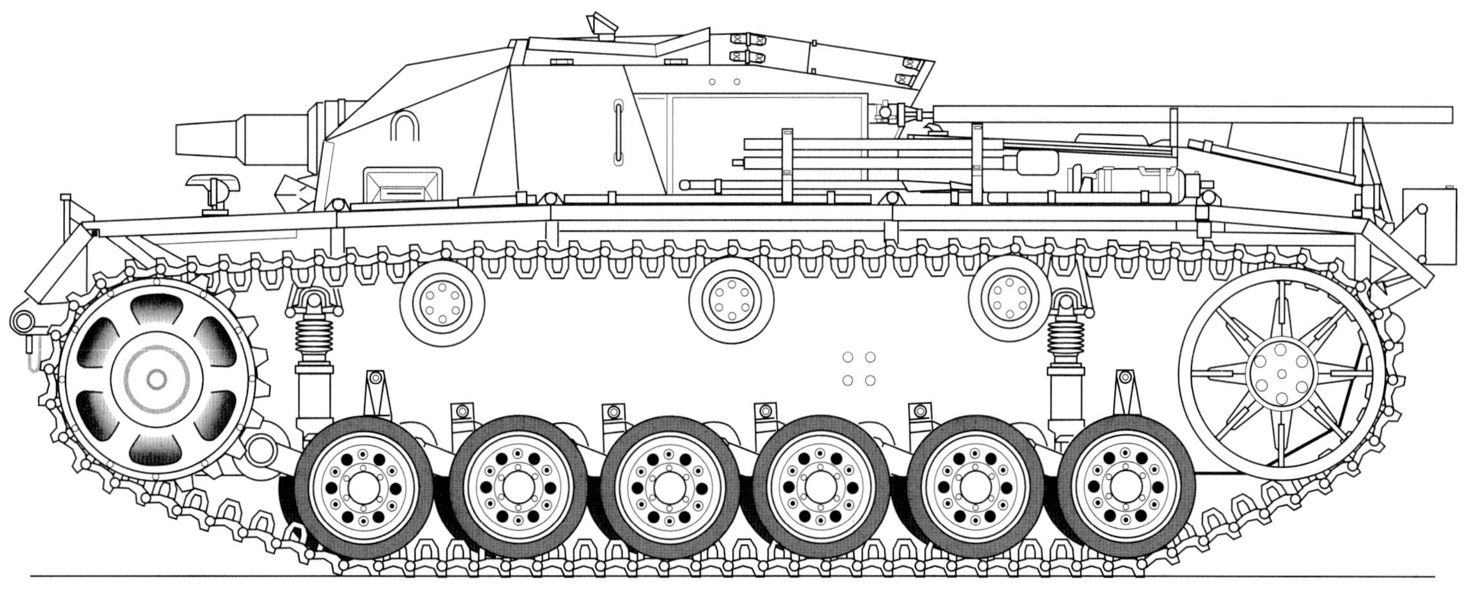

Sturmgeschütz III, Ausführung D

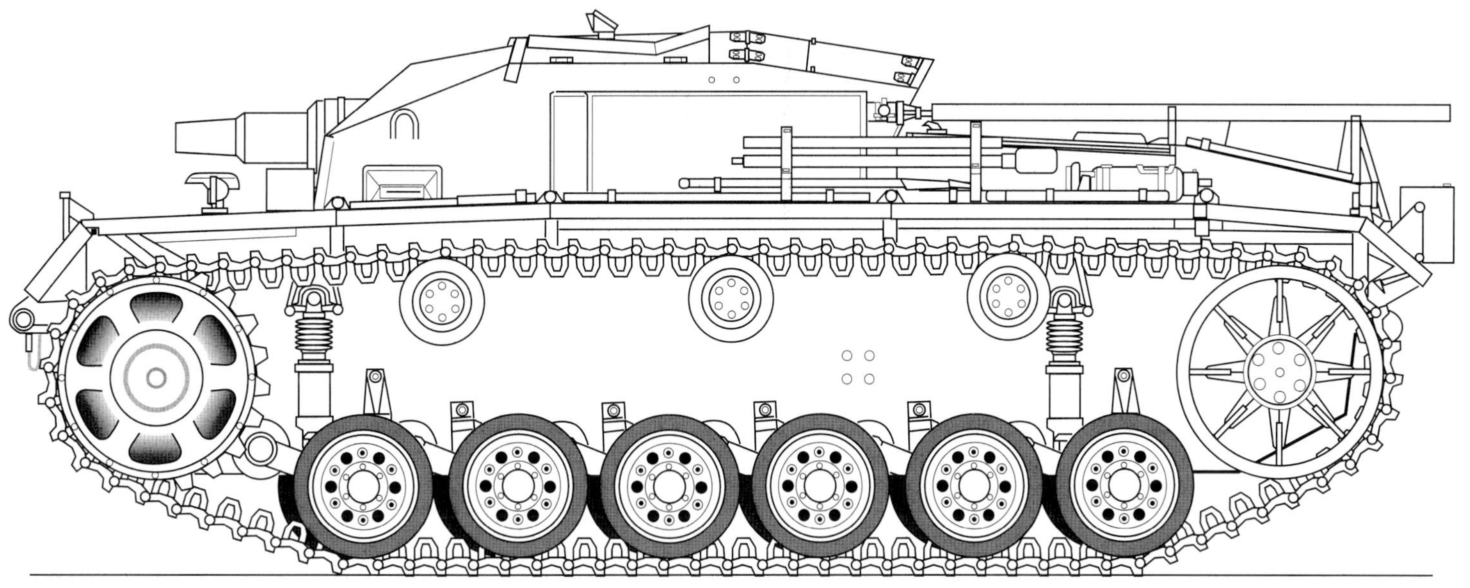

Sturmgeschütz III, Ausführung E

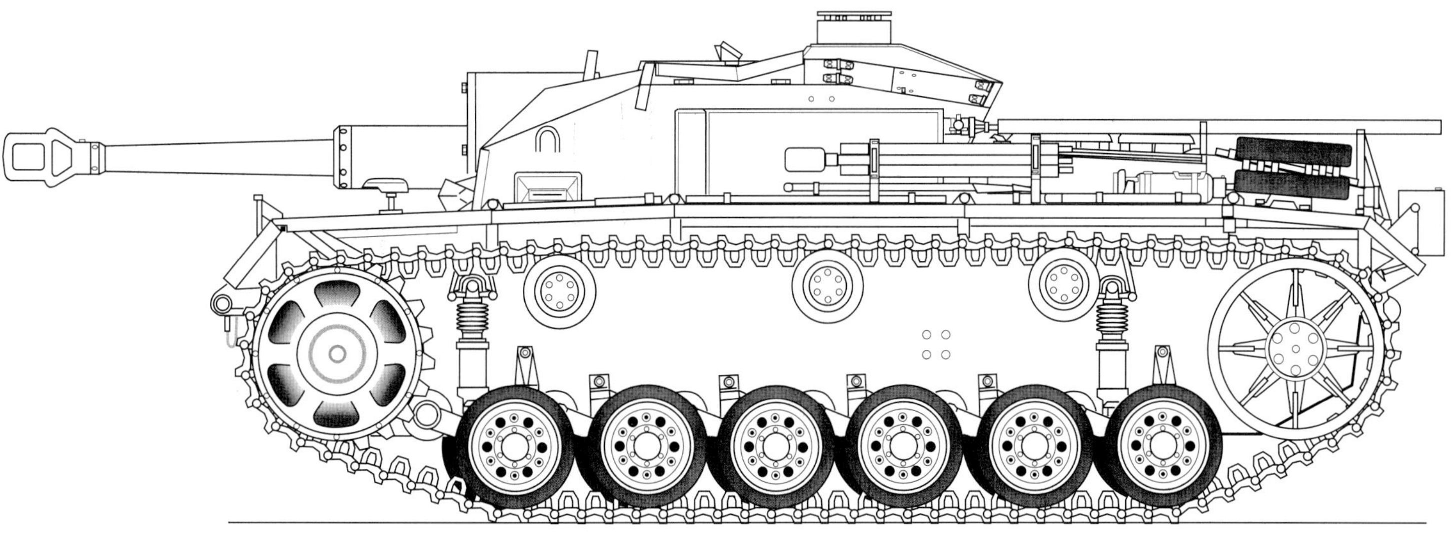

Sturmgeschütz III, Ausführung F8

Sturmgeschütz III, Ausführung G (früh)

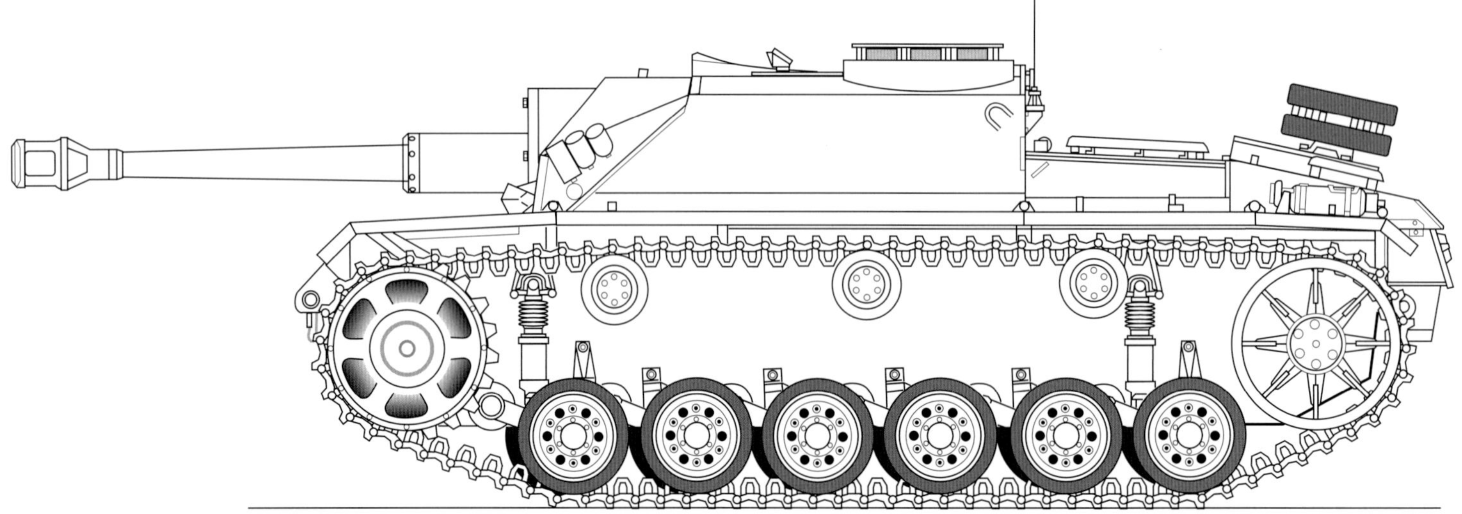

Sturmgeschütz III, Ausführung G (spät)

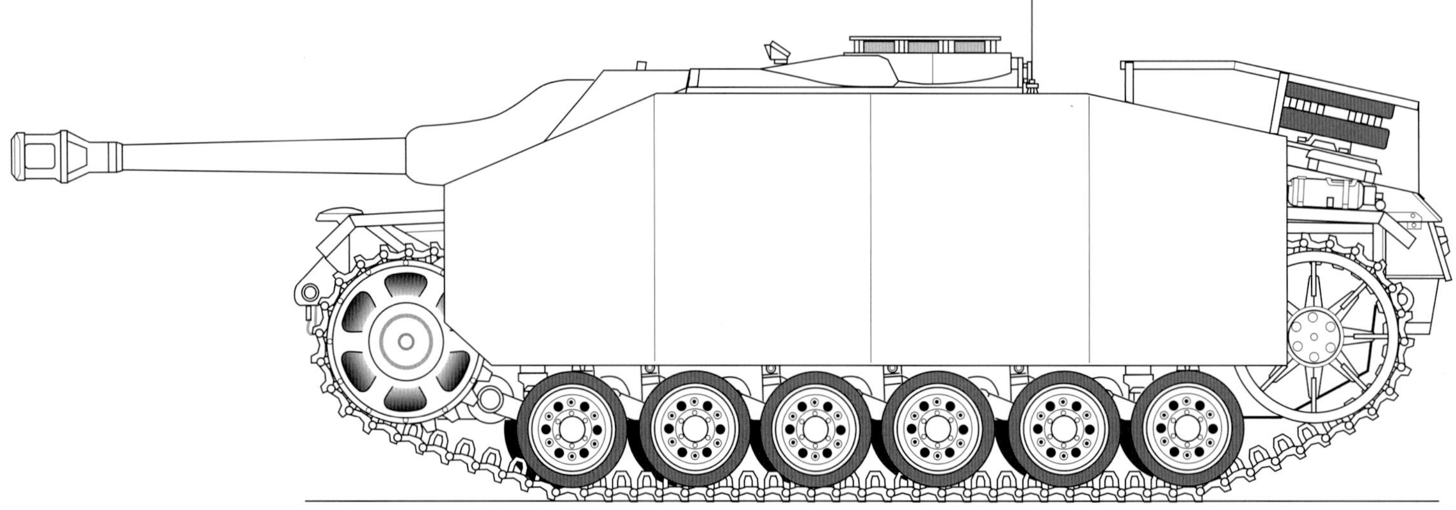

Sturmhaubitze 42

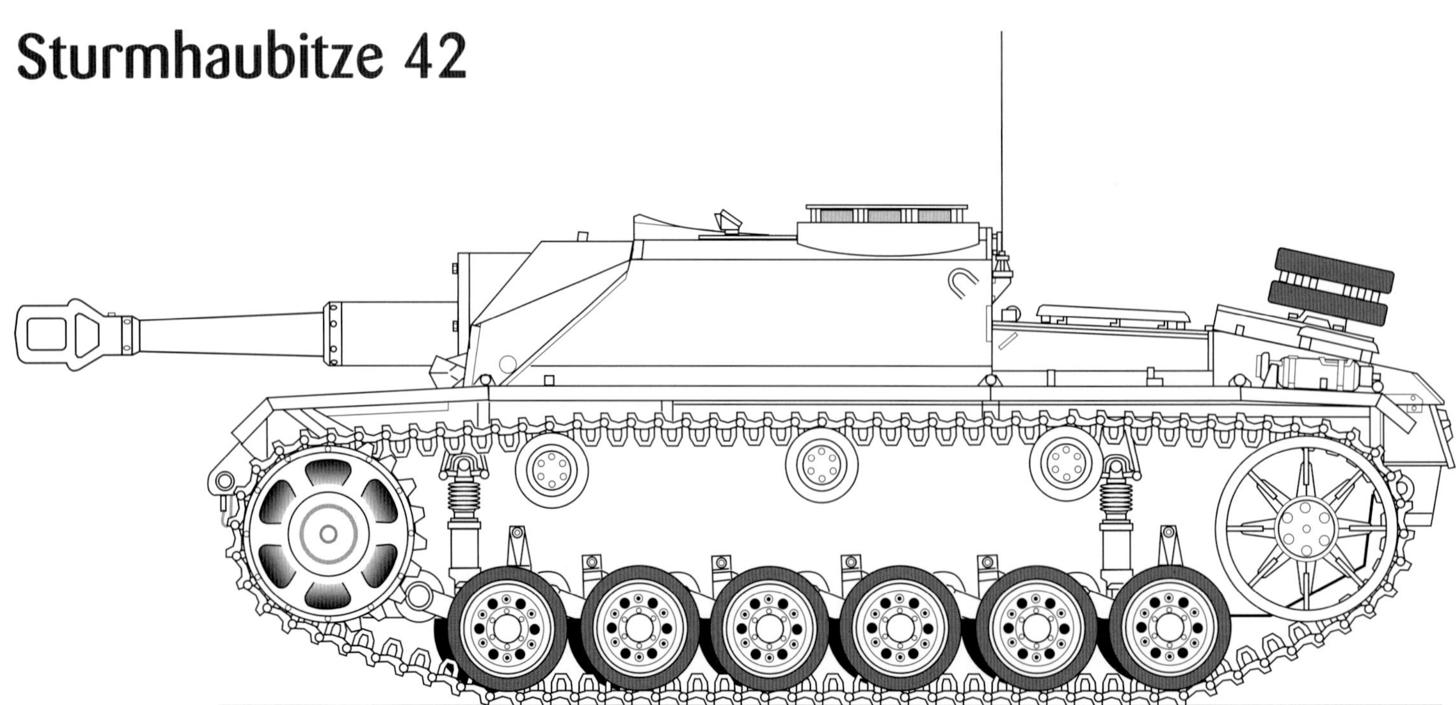